THE
STRANGER
WITHIN YOUR GATES

CHICAGO STUDIES IN THE HISTORY OF JUDAISM

Edited by William Scott Green
and
Calvin Goldscheider

THE
STRANGER
WITHIN YOUR GATES

Converts and Conversion
in Rabbinic Literature

Gary G. Porton

The University of Chicago Press

Chicago and London

Gary G. Porton is professor in the Program for the Study of Religion at the University of Illinois at Urbana-Champaign.

Published with the generous assistance of the John Simon Guggenheim Memorial Foundation.

The University of Chicago Press, Chicago 60637
The University of Chicago Press, Ltd., London

Printed in the United States of America

03 02 01 00 99 98 97 96 95 94 1 2 3 4 5
ISBN: 0-226-67586-6

Library of Congress Cataloging-in-Publication Data

Porton, Gary G.
    The stranger within your gates : converts and conversion in
rabbinic literature / Gary G. Porton.
        p.   cm.—(Chicago studies in the history of Judaism)
    Includes bibliographical references and index.
    1. Proselytes and proselyting, Jewish.   2. Rabbinical literature—
History and criticism.   3. Gentiles in rabbinical literature.
4. Jews—Identity.   I. Title.   II. Series.
BM729.P7P59   1994
296.7′1—dc20   94-1096

For William R. Schoedel

CONTENTS

▓ PREFACE ▓

This study's underlying premise that each rabbinic document should be studied in its own terms derives from the pioneering work of Jacob Neusner, Graduate Research Professor of Religious Studies, University of South Florida. In addition, my skepticism concerning the possibility of writing a conventional history of conversion in rabbinic Judaism, my decision to view conversion to Judaism from the perspectives of religion and ethnicity, and my recourse to the social scientific studies of conversion as a means of understanding the rabbinic texts result from my understanding of Professor Neusner's conclusions concerning the rabbinic corpus and the ways in which it should be interpreted.

Several colleagues at the University of Illinois, Urbana-Champaign, led me to and through the anthropological and sociological works which inform the interpretive scheme of this project. I wish to express my debt to Professor Harvey Choldin, Department of Sociology, Professor Alma Gottleib, Department of Anthropology, and Professor Edward Bruner, Department of Anthropology for their help and advice. Without their guidance I would not have realized what the rabbinic texts were telling me.

This volume owes a great debt to Alan Avery-Peck, the Kraft-Hiatt Professor of Judaica Studies at the College of the Holy Cross, Worcester, Massachusetts, and William Scott Green, Bernstein Professor of Judaic Studies, University of Rochester. Alan read several drafts of the manuscript and made many important corrections concerning content, interpretation, and style. His attention to detail and his uncompromising generosity with his time have made this a much finer study than the one I first produced in manuscript form. Bill spent hours on the phone and in person discussing the issues raised in this study, the interpretation of the rabbinic texts, and the best methods by which to present my conclusions. It was at his encouragement that I submitted the manuscript to the University of Chicago Press.

The volume is the culmination of several years of work. The initial phases of this investigation were accomplished while I was an associate in the Center for Advanced Study at the University of Illinois and the recipient of a John Simon Guggenheim Fellowship. I wish to acknowledge the support of both of these institutions.

The biblical citations are based on the translations in *TANAKH: A New Translation of the Holy Scriptures According to the Traditional Hebrew Text*, published in 1985 by the Jewish Publication Society.

My scholarly work is possible only because of the support and love I receive from my wife, Fraeda, and from our children, Zipporah and Avi. I wish to express my gratitude for their love and faith in me.

This book is dedicated to William R. Schoedel, professor in the Program for the Study of Religion. I was very fortunate to have Bill introduce me to the Church Fathers before he left Brown for the University of Illinois. But I have been even more fortunate to have him as a colleague for twenty years. Bill's high standards of scholarship and teaching have been an example of what we should all strive for in the university. His dedication to his work, his students, and his music provide us all with a model to follow. His breadth of knowledge, his habit of studying topics and languages because they interest him, and his continued pursuit of excellence have inspired all of us in the program. However, I have dedicated this volume to him because of his unflinching support of my work and my career, his faith in my ability to succeed as a scholar-teacher, and his years of sage advice. The successes I have achieved at the University of Illinois are to a good part a result of Bill's support and efforts.

23 Adar 5753
Urbana, Illinois   Gary G. Porton

■ ABBREVIATIONS ■

RABBINIC TEXTS

Arak.	'Arakhim	Mak.	Makkot
A.Z.	'Abodah Zarah	Maksh.	Makshirim
B, b	Babylonian Talmud	Meg.	Megillah
B.B.	Baba Batra	Me.	Me'ilah
B.M.	Baba Mesi'a'	Men.	Menahot
B.Q.	Baba Qama	Mid.	Middot
Bekh.	Bekhorot	Miq.	Miqva'ot
Ber.	Berakhot	Naz.	Nazir
Beṣ	Beṣah	Ned.	Nedarim
Dem.	Demai	Nid.	Niddah
Ed.	'Edduyyot	Ohol.	'Oholot
Erub.	'Erubim	Orl.	'Orlah
Giṭ	Giṭṭin	Par.	Parah
G.R.	Genesis Rabbah	Pe.	Pe'ah
Ḥag	Ḥagigah	Pes.	Pesahim
Ḥal	Ḥallah	Pis.	Pisha'
Hor.	Horayot	Qid.	Qiddushin
Ḥul.	Ḥullin	R.H.	Rosh HaShanah
Kel.	Kelim	Sanh.	Sanhedrin
Ker.	Keritot	Shab.	Shabbat
Kil.	Kila'im	Sheb.	Shebi'it
L.R.	Leviticus Rabbah	Shebu.	Shebu'ot
M, m	Mishnah	Sheq.	Sheqalim
M.Q.	Mo'ed Qatan	Soṭ.	Soṭah
M.S.	Ma'aser Sheni	T, t	Tosefta
Ma.	Ma'aserot	Tan.	Ta'anit
		Tem.	Temurah

Ter.	Terumot	Hag.	Haggai
Ṭoh.	Ṭohorot	Hos.	Hosea
ṬY.	Ṭebul Yom	Isa.	Isaiah
Uqs.	'Uqsin	Jer.	Jeremiah
Y, y	Palestinian Talmud	Josh.	Joshua
Y.T.	Yom Tob	Judg.	Judges
Yad.	Yadaim	IKgs.	I Kings
Yeb.	Yebamot	IIKgs.	II Kings
Zab.	Zabim	Lam.	Lamentations
Zer.	Zera'im	Lev.	Levitcus
		Mal.	Malachi

BIBLICAL BOOKS

Cant.	Canticles (Song of Songs)	Mic.	Micah
		Nah.	Nahum
IChron.	I Chronicles	Neh.	Nehemiah
IIChron.	IIChronicles	Num.	Numbers
Dan.	Daniel	Obad.	Obadiah
Deut.	Deuteronomy	Prov.	Proverbs
Esth.	Esther	Ps.	Psalms
Ex.	Exodus	Qoh.	Qohelet (Ecclesiastes)
Ezek.	Ezekiel	ISam.	I Samuel
Gen.	Genesis	IISam.	II Samuel
Hab.	Habakkuk	Zech.	Zechariah
		Zeph.	Zephaniah

▓ TRANSLITERATIONS ▓

א	= '		מ ם	= M
ב	= B		נ ן	= N
ג	= G		ס	= S
ד	= D		ע	= '
ה	= H		פ ף	= P
ו	= W		צ ץ	= Ṣ
ז	= Z		ק	= Q
ח	= Ḥ		ר	= R
ט	= Ṭ		שׁ	= Š
י	= Y		שׂ	= Ś
כ ך	= K		ת	= T
ל	= L			

▩ ONE ▩

Problem and Method

▩

By examining the references to converts and conversion found in the rabbinic documents from late antiquity, the present volume analyzes the rabbis' ideas about the non-Israelites who joined the Israelite community. Within the study of Judaism in late antiquity, this is an interesting topic because it provides one illustration of the ways in which the rabbis conceived of Israel as both an ethnic group and a religious community.[1] From the perspective of the contemporary study of conversion, this is an engaging issue because the ethnic aspect evidenced in conversion to Judaism is seldom, if ever, discussed in the scholarly literature. Furthermore, most modern studies of conversion approach the subject from the point of view of the converts and not from the perspective of the community into which the converts move.[2] This inquiry, by contrast, concentrates on the rabbis' discussions of the new Israelites, unpacking how the rabbinic views on conversion further our interpretation of the Israelite community in late antiquity. While conversion is an important and interesting phenomenon in its own right, and the data collected and analyzed below broadens our understanding of it, the Israelites of late antiquity, not converts or conversion, are the main topic of study.

Before proceeding to the rabbinic materials, we must first examine the concepts of ethnicity and religion and how these can be applied to the Israelite community of late antiquity. We need to establish what these terms mean for the purposes of this study because they will prove useful in analyzing the rabbinic discussions of conversion. As we shall see, the rabbis viewed conversion both as a change in ethnic groups and as a movement between religious communities, for they perceived of the People Israel as both an ethnic group, united by genealogical ties, and as a religious community, joined together by a covenant with YHWH.

Elsewhere I have argued that the ways in which the rabbis differentiated between gentiles and Israelites in Mishnah and Tosefta can best be understood by recourse to the current scholarship on ethnicity and ethnic groups.[3] Although that body of literature contains a wide divergence of views,[4] there is general agreement that the members of an ethnic group

1

perceive themselves as sharing a common identity. In Barth's words, an ethnic group "has a membership which identifies itself and is identified by others as constituting a category distinguishable from other categories of the same order."[5] Similarly, Bessac argues that an ethnic group is "a group of people who . . . have a sense of common identity."[6] Finally, Enloe states that ethnicity "refers to a peculiar bond among persons that causes them to consider themselves as a group distinguishable from others."[7]

The weight of recent scholarly opinion supports the contention that ethnicity is connected to a perceived common ancestry.[8] Hunt and Walker have written that "an ethnic group is a collection of people whose membership is largely determined by ancestry."[9] Berreman quotes and accepts H. S. Morris's statement that an "ethnic group consists of people who conceive of themselves as being alike by virtue of common ancestry, real or fictitious."[10] Keyes writes that "kin selection provides the underlying motivation that leads human beings to seek solidarity with those whom they recognize 'as being of the same people,' or as 'sharing descent.'"[11] Finally, van den Berghe holds that ethnicity is an extension of the idiom of kinship and that it is in reality an "attenuated form" of kinship selection.[12] We shall argue below that a concern with ancestry is fundamental to the Israelite community's self-definition.[13] Its preferred self-designation in the rabbinic texts, "children of Israel/Jacob," underscores that fact,[14] for it signifies that, from one point of view, Israel's identity is grounded in the belief that all of its members share a common ancestry.[15]

Although it is useful to see the Israelites as an ethnic group which describes itself as forming a descent group, one must also keep in mind the religious aspect of the Israelites' identity. For our purposes, Spiro's definition of religion is pertinent.[16] He sees religion as "an institution consisting of culturally patterned interaction with culturally postulated superhuman beings."[17] This definition is appropriate to Judaism because the People Israel traced their origin back to Jacob, whose name became Israel only after his encounter with the divine (Gen. 32:23–33). In addition, the entire rabbinic system depends on its divine origin. The god who created the world according to a plan, the Torah, revealed that plan to the Israelite people through Moses on Mount Sinai. As the rabbis viewed the event, the totality of Israelite wisdom, contained in the Written and the Oral Torahs, had been transmitted to Moses, and through him to the people. When the rabbis set about their task, they were merely doing what "Moses, our rabbi" had done in YHWH's presence on Mount Sinai. Thus, every aspect of Israelite culture was connected to the divine plan, and it created an environment in which the Israelites concretized that plan in the fullness of their lives. They lived out YHWH's plan because he had commanded them to fulfill his wishes. Of course, they also knew that if they fulfilled his plan, he would reward them by continuing to protect them and allowing them to prosper and that rejecting YHWH's demands led to sure and certain punishment. YHWH's dominion over his creation was recognized in the fields, the towns, the markets, and the individuals' homes, as well as in the Temple. Every aspect of the Israelites' lives as designed by the rabbis was in accord with the Divine Will and was a result of Moses' direct communication with YHWH. So it is clear that the system of culture and society defined by the rabbis was, in essence, religious, depending, in Spiro's terms, upon a "culturally postulated super-human being."

From the point of view derived from the concept of the People Israel, non-Israelites could become Israelites only by demonstrating that they could trace their ancestry back to Jacob. From the perspective of a religious community, by contrast, conversion results from the alteration of one's world-view.[18] The word *conversion* itself is derived from the Latin *convertere*, a "spiritual reorientation."[19] Thus, gentiles who recognized YHWH as their god and accepted the rabbinic myth as their life-organizing principle could become members of the People Israel. After all, it is reported that Yohanan stated that any gentile who rejects idolatry is called a Jew, *yhwdy*.[20] Thus, from the perspective of at least Yohanan's Judaism, by rejecting idolatry and accepting YHWH and his plan for life, gentiles could become Jews. This dual path to becoming a convert explains much of what we shall encounter below. Virtually every rabbinic collection contains the admonition that Israelites should not remind converts of their gentile ancestry. And, we often discover that the converts are responsible for fulfilling YHWH's commands in the same way that Israelites are required to observe the entire Torah. In distinction to these positions, we also find that when converts married or when they were circumcised, for example, one would have to know that they were not native-born Israelites, for in these and other contexts different rules applied to converts from those which were incumbent upon native-born Israelites. Hence we see the tension caused by the two distinct definitional standards at play in the Israelite community: the religious and the ethnic.

In order to understand fully the rabbinic discussions of conversion and converts, we must first briefly review the rabbinic descriptions of gentiles and their relationship to Israelites. As we shall see, the rabbis partially defined the Israelites by contrasting them to non-Israelites, and it was through these contrasts that the sages defined Israelite ethnicity.[21] Furthermore, because the converts' gentile origins are frequently relevant to the rabbis, below we shall often set our analyses of the converts in the context of the requirements incumbent upon gentiles in the various categories of rabbinic concerns. Indeed, we shall discover in chapter 11 that, from the rabbis' perspective, the converts were marginal to both the Israelite and gentile communities.

The religious aspect of the Israelites' culture helps to explain why those whose opinions currently appear in Mishnah and Tosefta, which set the parameters for all subsequent discourses, subsumed their discussions of the gentiles under the standard categories of the documents' symbol system: YHWH, the Land of Israel, the Sacred Periods, the People Israel, the Temple, and Purity, all categories related to YHWH's revelation to the Israelites.[22] The sages did not create any distinct categories through which to analyze the gentiles, nor they did create any unique literary forms or modes of expression in which to cast their opinions concerning the non-Israelites.[23] The sages were not interested in the gentiles *qua* gentiles; rather, they dealt with the non-Israelites in order to sharpen their definition of the Israelites themselves. Drawing distinctions between the two classes of humans[24] in terms of the major symbolates of mishnaic culture served their purposes well. Most often, the differences between Israelites and non-Israelites were that the former did *x*, while the latter did not do *x*, so that, in many instances, the gentiles were pictured as the mirror opposite of Israelites.[25] As several writers have noted, a group creates its own identity only with reference to another aggregate; therefore, the rabbis' activity in this regard is not only expected, but it was also necessary.[26]

While many today envision that clear economic, social, and judicial boundaries existed between Israelites and non-Israelites in late antiquity, closer examination of the relevant *sugyot* in Mishnah and Tosefta demonstrates that the borders were in fact permeable.[27] Although even in the Land of Israel gentiles were not *required* to separate the agricultural gifts which were expected of Israelites, the former could, and perhaps should, separate the heave-offerings and the tithes.[28] The rabbinic Sabbath is a uniquely ethnic holiday, for the sages accepted Deuteronomy's justification for the Sabbath-rest instead of the reason supplied by Genesis and Exodus. Deuteronomy 5:15 explains that Israelites should rest on the Sabbath because they were once slaves in Egypt, while Genesis 2:1–4 and Exodus 20:11 draw parallels between the Israelites' resting and God's ceasing to work at the creation of the world. The latter explanation of the Sabbath should lead to the conclusion that all of creation must celebrate the Sabbath, while the former justification indicates that the Sabbath applies to only Israelites.[29] However, when gentiles came into contact with Israelites, the former, as well as the latter, had to alter their normal activity. For example, if gentiles came to put out a fire in an Israelite's courtyard on the Sabbath, they could not discuss the matter with the Israelite, because the Israelite could not benefit from the gentiles' actions if the former instructed the latter to extinguish the fire.[30] The point of the rabbis' debates on these matters is that the Israelite holidays affected the relationships between gentiles and Israelites, but they did not prevent interactions between the two groups.

Neither do Mishnah and Tosefta draw sharp lines preventing the social interaction among gentiles and Israelites. They lived in close proximity to one another, engaged in commercial activity with one another, shared food with one another, and even jointly owned property.[31] Furthermore, although Israelites could not supply gentiles with any item the latter might use in their "idolatrous" rituals, an Israelite could believe a gentile who said that the articles would not be used for religious purposes. This is the case even though we find expressed the general view that all gentiles are untrustworthy. In light of the fact that the rabbis assumed that all gentiles offered a libation from any wine with which they came in contact, it is noteworthy that Mishnah and Tosefta regularly assume that gentiles purchased wine from Israelite wine-merchants.[32] Important for our purposes is that this rule is in line with the general attitude of the documents, that Israelites and gentiles interact frequently in the social and economic realms.

Even with regard to the Temple, the lines of demarcation between Israelites and gentiles are not unbroken. On the one hand, gentiles were excluded from the Temple precincts; on the other hand, they could bring freewill offerings and vow offerings to the Temple.[33] Also, in the area of purity law the position of the gentiles was ambiguous.[34] Gentiles, as a matter of law, were considered to be similar to Israelites who suffered impurity as a result of their genital emissions.[35] Despite that claim, Mishnah and Tosefta consistently assume that Israelites and non-Israelites interacted socially and professionally without any regard for the gentiles' impurity or without instituting a regular purification rite for those who daily came into direct contact with non-Israelites.

Indeed, from the point of view of the rabbinic texts, it seems clear that Israelites and non-Israelites were in constant contact. While some rabbis held rather negative opinions of the gentiles, others viewed them in a positive light. But, as Goodman writes, "No early source holds gentiles morally guilty for not being full Jews."[36] Along these lines, Goodman cogently argues that the rabbinic discussion of the Noachide Laws reflects the rabbis' attempt to define a righteous gentile.[37] While Josephus and Philo seem to argue that gentiles living outside the Land of Israel could worship idols,[38] the rabbis often claim that "good gentiles who had no desire to convert to Judaism nevertheless had a duty to abstain from idolatry."[39] Thus, taken as a whole, the rabbis were clearly ambiguous concerning the gentiles *qua* gentiles. This is parallel to what we shall see below, that they also were ambiguous concerning the nature of converts.

Most significant, however, is the one matter concerning which there was no ambiguity in the rabbis' minds. While in the majority of social, cultural, and religious realms the rabbis allowed interaction between Israelites and non-Israelites, in the area of sexuality the borders were sharply drawn, and the rabbis attempted to block every crossing point. Israelites and gentiles may not engage in sexual activity with one another, and they may not intermarry.[40] The children of such unions are *mamzerim*, the offsprings of unacceptable sexual unions.[41] This fact should be connected with another datum: The term for members of the People Israel is *bny yśr'l*, Children of Israel/Jacob. The rabbinic texts rarely refer to the people as Jews, a geographical designation derived from the term Judea. Rather, they identify them in terms of their descent; they are all children of the same father, Jacob. Gentiles, on the other hand, may be children of Noah, Esau, Edom, or any other of a number of biblical figures, with the exception of Jacob/Israel.[42] The texts are uniform in their view that Israelites and non-Israelites represent different descent groups.

As noted above, the importance placed on the dissimilarity between Israelite and gentile ancestry is explicable in terms of current scholarly discussions on ethnicity, for, as has recently been argued, an essential element of an ethnic group is its members' perception of their sharing a common ancestry.[43] This lineage need not be biological or genetic, for there can be "culturally determined" genealogical lines through which all the members of an ethnic group trace their ancestry. Thus, the Israelites' claim that they all share a common father, Jacob, need not be biologically correct; it need be only "culturally" recognized.[44] In either case, this "biological unity" would set the Israelites off from other groups of people, to whom they attributed different ancestors. Thus, the prohibition against Jacob's children's marrying anyone else's children is a central element in the way in which the Israelites of late antiquity developed their ethnic self-definition.

As we saw above, the rabbinic prohibition against intermarriage, in conjunction with the Jews' self-designation as the Children of Israel/Jacob, suggests that conversion to Judaism should be a complex matter, for, while we can imagine individuals replacing one system of belief with another or one legal system with another, it clearly is impossible to change one's line of descent. Changing systems of belief is difficult, for it marks a rejection of a former self-definition and the acceptance of a new one. But this can be accomplished. By contrast, changing lines of descent is biologically impossible. The most one can do is to join a socially constructed descent group, which need not be biologically based; but there is no evidence that the rabbis in late antiquity sought to create such a socially constructed descent group, which converts could join.

Unlike late antiquity, today a convert takes on a new name, becoming *x* the son or daughter of Abraham.[45] However, there is no evidence of this practice in the rabbinic texts from the Mishnah to the Babylonian Talmud. As far as can be determined, in late antiquity, the rabbis did not attempt to create this artificial lineage for those who converted. In fact, in liturgical contexts most of the sages stressed that converts *could not claim* Abraham as their father.[46] For this reason, they could not recite the required Avowal when bringing the second tithe or the first fruits, for the Avowal, citing Deut. 6:3–10, referred to the land which YHWH had promised to "Abraham our forefather."[47] Furthermore, according to the Babylonian Talmud, the blessing recited at the circumcision of a native-born Israelite was different from that said at the circumcision of a convert. The benediction for the native-born Israelite refers specifically to the "covenant of Abraham," while the blessing recited for the convert refers to the covenant and to the commandment to circumcise converts, without a specific reference to Abraham.[48] Along these same lines, it is significant that converts are called *gerim*, not Israelites, and that *gerim* are listed as one of *the ten family types* that came up with Ezra from Babylonia to the Land of Israel.[49] Thus, rather than creating a sociological descent group, the rabbis of late antiquity in fact maintained the distinct descent lines of converts and native-born Israelites.

Judaism is distinguishable from Israelite religion by the former's prohibition against intermarriage and by the institution of conversion.[50] Both aspects of Judaism seem to arise and to develop in tandem, and they may serve as correctives to each other. In light of the ethnic definition of the People Israel discussed above, these could be seen as representing the two elements of the Israelites' self-definition, one relating to the maintenance of the ethnicity of the people, the other deriving from YHWH's plan for the whole of creation. But they do represent two opposing forces. If the primary unifying connection among the People Israel was their common descent from Israel/Jacob, as the name by which they called themselves implied, how could they accept converts? How would they treat these people? Could converts ever be integrated fully into Israelite society? On the other hand, if YHWH's message were directed to all humankind, how could the Israelites fail to bring into their fold all those who sought comfort within his domain? These are some of the questions which the present study seeks to answer. To state our fundamental question more succinctly: Insofar as the People Israel understood themselves to share a common ancestry, how did those with a different ancestor fit into the Israelite community?

Starting with the fact that native-born Israelites and converts represent two different genealogies, but that YHWH is the creator of all humankind, the present work examines in detail how the rabbis described the converts in terms of Israelite culture, society, and *halakhah*. It demonstrates how the ethnic definition of the People Israel interacts with the religious definition of the people. The complex picture of the convert vis-à-vis Israelite culture and society in both its ethnic and religious components is fully drawn in this volume.

As we might anticipate from the contrasting underpinnings of Israelite culture, we shall discover that in many respects the converts are equated with native-born Israelites, but that in some cases the two groups are distinct. With regard to the Land of Israel, converts sometimes functioned as native-born Israelites, while at other times they acted differently from them. Like Israelites, converts were required to separate the agricultural gifts, as long as the converts' crops became liable for these gifts after they had joined the People Israel. But there was some question whether or not they could bring the first fruits or the second tithe, because these involved an Avowal which explicitly mentioned the Land which YHWH had given to Israel's ancestors. Although it is frequently assumed that converts could own parcels of the Land of Israel, Sifré Numbers maintains that, like gentiles, they could not. Concerning the Israelite holy days, converts also acted as both native-born Israelites and as a distinct group. Like Israelites, converts were responsible for observing the Israelite sacred days. However, converts could not form their own group for separating the lamb for the Passover sacrifice. The restrictions placed on whom converts could marry also reflect their ambiguous position. While converts could marry unimpaired and impaired Israelites, as well as Levites, many sages held that they could not marry priests. Finally, the fact that converts were different from native-born Israelites also found expression in some of the communal institutions. For example, converts could serve as judges in civil cases, but they could not adjudicate capital cases. These examples underscore the ambiguous place which the converts occupied within Israelite society of late antiquity.

Studying the converts from the perspectives of the ethnicity and religiosity of the Israelite community is a relatively unique approach to the study of conversion to Judaism in late antiquity. Others have recognized the complexity of the converts' relationship to Israelite society,[51] but none have made this relationship the sole focus of their study or seen its complexity as resulting from the ethnic element of Judaism in late antiquity. A major line of analysis from Weil to Braude focused on whether or not the Jews welcomed converts.[52] While this stream of scholarship draws some of its impetus from the diverse manner in which the converts are described in the rabbinic texts, most of it derives from the debate concerning the worthiness of Judaism and its supposed "particularistic" view of the world as compared to Christianity, with its assumed universal message for all humankind.[53] This study does not participate in this debate. The Israelites in late antiquity were like every other people attempting to establish their identity and maintain their existence. Judaism's universal message functions differently at different times in the history of Jewish thought and uniquely for various individuals. As we saw above, some rabbis could claim that YHWH's plan allowed non-Israelites to worship idols outside of the Land of Israel, while other sages argued that YHWH's command was that idolatry be uprooted from the entire earth. While YHWH was the sovereign of the universe, he allowed for diversity, so that for some of the sages, YHWH's and Judaism's universal message mandated and supported diversity among the nations of the world. For many Jewish thinkers, universalism did not mean conformity or sameness. Therefore, disengaged from the theological discussion of Christianity's universal message, focusing on Judaism's universality or particularism does not accomplish much.

A second major line of inquiry concentrates on whether or not Judaism in late antiquity was a missionizing religion. From Bertholet's classic study to McKnight's recent investigation of this issue,[54] scholars have questioned the extent to which there was a concerted effort by Jews to gain converts. Again, this question has been largely framed in terms of the origins of Christianity. Many scholars have sought to explain the rapid spread of Christianity in light of Jewish missionary activity. When one separates the concern for Christianity from an interest in Judaism and focuses exclusively on the Jewish sources, this topic becomes less engaging. A review of the literature on missionizing among the Jews uncovers little evidence which unambiguously answers the question of whether or not there was Jewish missionary activity. Because the present study focuses solely on the rabbinic materials, which do not address this topic, the question is not dealt with here.

A third concern of much of the literature about conversion has been the attempt to establish firm dates for the institution of a fixed rabbinic practice of conversion, for the various rituals, and for rabbinic opinions related to these phenomena.[55] The present investigation does not follow in this tradition of scholarship. Much of the relevant non-rabbinic material cannot be conclusively dated, and the rabbinic sayings and documents permit only vaguely general chronological placement. *Even if* one could establish firm dates for the various works of the apocrypha and pseudepigrapha and could supply convincing interpretations of Josephus and Philo, one would still have to deal with the rabbinic texts. Many accept the attestations of opinions in the rabbinic corpus, date events in terms of the rabbinic masters to whom the comments are assigned, and believe that passages marked as *beraitot* in the two Talmuds are in fact tannaitic creations. The present work questions the accuracy of these views. Much scholarship on the various tannaitic masters has demonstrated the unreliability of attestations, especially in the later documents.[56] Similarly, scholars have long realized that not all passages marked as *beraitot* are tannaitic creations, so that their "historical reliability" is questionable.[57] Given these facts, it is imprudent to follow those scholars who still take the position that unless proven otherwise, all attributions are accurate. The present study accordingly does not concern itself with setting exact dates for the opinions attributed to rabbis throughout the rabbinic corpus. While, for the sake of completeness, I consistently attach the names of authorities to statements attributed to them, this does not imply that I assume their historical accuracy. Furthermore, although I indicate most opinions that occur in *beraitot* as such, this is not meant to suggest any claim on my part for their tannaitic origins. In brief, the present study analyzes the opinions recorded in the rabbinic corpus to present a complete picture of the state of affairs at the close of the talmudic period. It does not seek to construct a history of conversion in the normal sense.

Scholars who have tried to develop a chronology of conversion have amassed evidence from the full range of rabbinic and non-rabbinic literatures: The apocrypha, pseudepigrapha, Philo, Josephus, scattered inscriptions, the scrolls from Qumran, and the New Testament.[58] The present study focuses exclusively on the rabbinic texts: Mishnah, Tosefta, the midrashim, and the two Talmuds. Scholars recently have recognized that Judaism in late antiquity was not a homogeneous phenomenon. Rather, it existed in a number of forms.[59] While the information from these various contexts provides valid evidence concerning what particular Israelites did with regard to proselytes or believed concerning converts, it is impossible to demonstrate that a ritual or opinion in one context was known to or used by those who transmitted information in another environment. While all of the sources of data inform us about the broad range of Israelite practices and beliefs and the various options opened to different types of Israelites, it is unwise to assume that what is stated in one set of data provides information about those who produced any other set of facts. Therefore, this study approaches the problem of conversion from only one corpus of information, that produced by the rabbinic classes of the Land of Israel and Babylonia. Its results, therefore, claim only to describe what the rabbinic collections tell us about converts and conversion to Judaism in late antiquity from the points of view of the sages whose opinions are recorded in the rabbinic collections.

The attempt to write a traditional "history" of conversion also ignores the problem of distinguishing between the "theoretical" discussions by the rabbis and those which actually reflected or affected everyday activity. The rabbinic collections do not distinguish between theory and actual practice. For example, the Mishnah's discussions of Temple ritual are written as if the Temple were a living, active institution. This is despite the fact that it was destroyed over a hundred years before the Mishnah was finally compiled. Similarly, the talmudic sages treat every aspect of conversion as if it were a burning issue in their daily lives. But this clearly was not always the case. Because it is impossible to separate the theoretical from the practical, the present study does not attempt to differentiate between these matters. The present investigation records and analyzes what the texts say, without making any claims about the application of these ideas to the everyday world or to the lives of the Israelites of late antiquity. Because the texts are the only evidence we have about the rabbinic views on converts and conversion, the present study tells us all we can learn about the subject, even though we have no way of determining whether or not all, or any, of the rabbinic opinions contained in these documents were ever translated into actual practice. While we have no means of determining what was actually done in everyday situations, we can discover what the rabbis thought, hoped, or imagined would happen.

We often assume that the rabbis' power assured that what they thought should happen would in fact happen. However, there is little evidence to support this contention. The rabbis were a small, elite class among the Israelite populations of Palestine and Babylonia. For the most part, they had few sources of coercion through which they could put their views and opinions into effect. It is unclear if the rabbis could enforce their points of view among the common people or among any who stood outside of the rabbinic schools and institutions. Therefore, while we know the rabbinic opinions recorded in the various rabbinic texts, we do not know what the common people accepted or did. Therefore, the present study does not claim to describe what actually happened in the everyday live of the Israelite communities. It only claims to record what the rabbis *said* happened or should happen.[60] From the rabbinic collections, we learn how the rabbis viewed the converts, how they constructed their vision of the People Israel, and how they placed the converts into that definition. As a result, we have the *rabbinic* map of the borders of the Jewish People, a map which formed the basis of all subsequent Jewish discussions of the People Israel.

A fourth line of research has focused on the problem of the semi-converts or the "God-fearers." Recently, this topic has received a good deal of scholarly attention.[61] It is well-known that the term "God-fearers" does not appear in the rabbinic collections; the closest rabbinic equivalent is assumed to be "fearers of heaven." In addition, some of the scholarly interest in this idea of the semi-convert stems from an effort to explain passages in Paul and to aid in understanding the rapid spread of Christianity or to explain references in documents outside the rabbinic corpus or inscriptions that come from outside the rabbinic sphere of influence. While this is an interesting and important topic, the present study focuses only on those individuals whom the rabbis classified as full converts, *gerim*.[62] Exactly how gentiles became full converts and exactly what that meant in the various rabbinic collections are the issues addressed below.

Although the material on conversion in the rabbinic texts has been extensively analyzed, the present study approaches these materials from a different point of view. The present work does not assume that the attributions in our documents are reliable or that one can write a conventional history of conversion during the rabbinic period. It maintains that for some unknown reasons some sage or some group(s) of sages transmitted a particular saying or opinion in the name of specific rabbi: Perhaps the transmitter(s) *actually knew* that the sage had uttered the words they recorded, perhaps they *believed* that the sage had said what they attributed to him, perhaps they *felt* that the sage would have said something similar if he had spoken on the topic, or perhaps for some reason unknown to us they *desired* to attach a specific opinion to a specific sage. For this reason, this investigation does not attempt to correlate specific opinions concerning converts and conversion with the names of particular sages.

It is also commonplace for scholars to interrelate statements that appear in one rabbinic document with those which appear in another and to ignore the chronological and geographical differences among the documents. Many writers assume that all one needs to do in order to understand conversion is to interrelate all of the statements on the subject from all of the rabbinic documents. Many authors believe that the totality of the rabbinic collections represent one form of Judaism, rabbinic Judaism, and that, for the most part, the documents generally agree on matters of fact and interpretation. This has led to misreadings of the rabbinic evidence.

For example, we shall see below that many have held that in the first century of the common era there existed in Palestine a conversion ritual that included the extensive interrogation and instruction of the convert recorded in the Babylonian Talmud[63] but unknown in earlier texts. In addition, by interconnecting the various documents and assuming that they speak with one voice, scholars often ignore the contradictions among the texts or the divergence of details which we find in the several parallel accounts of specific *sugyot*. For example, postulating that the circumcision of converts was an essential element of the conversion ritual at all times and in all places, many writers have "explained away" Joshua's rejection of this ritual, recorded in the Babylonian Talmud.[64] Therefore, none have pointed to the fact that there is little consistency among the various rabbinic documents concerning the details of the conversion ritual.

The present study proceeds from a different perspective. In his seminal studies on the development of the rabbinic tradition, Jacob Neusner has firmly established the necessity of approaching each rabbinic text on its own terms. He has shown that neither the specific details nor larger ideology set out in one text can be assumed to have been taken up by another collection. He also has demonstrated that later collectors altered information from earlier documents, either by reworking or significantly expanding earlier versions of stories.[65] Following Neusner's lead, the present work assumes that the information in each rabbinic text should be treated on its own. Therefore, the data from each document are analyzed separately, with chapters two through six setting forth the statements about conversion document by document. Only after that is accomplished, can we undertake synthesizing the details on various topics, the task of chapters 7 through 10. Yet, in light of the concerns just outlined, even in these chapters we move through the documents in roughly chronological order so as to be able to note the points at which the various collections contain similar or different information.[66]

This approach to the sources yields a picture of conversion markedly different from that painted by studies that harmonize the information gleaned from all of the rabbinic documents. For example, although many have claimed that the converts were expected to follow the entire rabbinic torah, this statement appears earliest in Tosefta,[67] not Mishnah, and there it is part of a passage which discusses how one moves from one status to another in various contexts, dealing with the *am ha'ares*, the priest, and the *ḥaber*. Therefore, the claim may be nothing more than the result of the rhetorical requirements of the passage. Similarly, if one reviews the material on the offering converts were expected to bring to the Temple, one is impressed by the inconsistency of information on that rite. One can also see that the contradictions in the Babylonian *sugya*[68] on this rite probably result from its bringing together information which now appears in diverse earlier documents. Therefore, the details surrounding this offering cannot be conclusively determined.

In all, we find that when we take seriously the limitations of our sources it is difficult to ascertain a consistent view of converts and conversion which cuts across the documents. This suggests that, contrary to what prior scholars thought, a standard conversion rite probably was not applied throughout the Israelite communities during late antiquity (see chap. 7 below). In fact, much of the accepted scholarly knowledge about converts and conversion seems much less certain than it did before. In light of the data collected below, even the normal assumption that converts became like "newborn children" needs to be questioned. This is the case especially because that designation occurs first in the Babylonian Talmud. Indeed, as we shall see, all of the documents in fact contain passages which take into account the gentile background of the converts. That is, these people were not treated by most authorities the same as native-born Jews. Perhaps from the point of view of Judaism as a religion, converts were newborn children, whose gentile parentage could be disregarded. However, this view is always mediated by other comments which take seriously the converts' non-Israelite descent.

The inherited scholarly paradigm for the study of conversion derives from the experiences of Paul and Augustine.[69] For this reason, much of the current research on conversion focuses on the proselytes' experiences. However, the rabbinic documents force us to approach the phenomenon of conversion from a different perspective. While there is some discussion of the converts' motives, the main issues which arise in out texts derive from the rabbis' attempt to deal with the new members of the People Israel within the context of an ethnic group whose culture has a major religious component. The rabbinic collections do not allow us to study the converts as individuals or even as religious types. Rather, the rabbinic corpus permits us to study only the sociological aspects of the converts' role in Israelite society as envisioned and described by the rabbis. It allows us to investigate the ways in which one ethnic group dealt with individuals who sought to change their ethnic identity. For that reason, studies on ethnic change have contributed much to the theoretical framework of this study as have the standard studies on converts and conversion.

To summarize: The present study approaches the topic of conversion

to Judaism in late antiquity with a new set of questions and presupposi-
tions. For this reason, it offers new interpretations of an issue which has
received a good deal of scholarly attention for over a hundred years. By
analyzing the rabbinic documents from Palestine and Babylonia, it answers questions concerning how the rabbis envisioned the role the converts played in Israelite society and culture. It does not attempt to construct a history of conversion to Judaism in late antiquity, nor does it
attempt to deal with forms of Judaism or Israelite culture and society not
dealt with by the rabbis in their literary collections. Its problem is generated by the apparent contradiction between the rabbis' acceptance of converts and their contention that Israelites and non-Israelites represent two
different descent groups, a state of affairs that many believed corres-
ponded to a plan devised and executed by YHWH, the Lord of the Universe, from the time that Abraham expelled Hagar and Ishmael from his
household, if not before. Following the rabbis' views, the present volume
views the convert as a marginal being, one who often stands at the edges
of both Israelite and non-Israelite society. By examining this phenomenon,
we shall gain a sharper picture of how the rabbis constructed their definition of the People Israel.

▦ TWO ▦

Converts and Conversion in Mishnah

▦

Mishnah is the foundation document of much of rabbinic literature, for it sets the agenda for Tosefta, the two Talmuds, and much of the early *midrashim*. Edited in Palestine in the first quarter of the second century of the common era, this text eventually came to be considered an authoritative collection of laws and the first codification of the Oral Torah which, like the Written Torah, had been given to Moses at Mount Sinai. Mishnah's relationship to the Hebrew Bible is complex, but one of its outstanding traits is that it only infrequently quotes Scripture. Mishnah's framers apparently wanted to demonstrate that it was possible to express YHWH's will independently of the biblical text. This is important with regard to our subject, for as we noted above, conversion is a postbiblical phenomenon. While undoubtedly Mishnah contains materials which reflect the ideas of several generations of sages and various segments of Israelite society, it is now extremely difficult to move behind the carefully edited text and to place particular teachings in specific historical settings or social contexts.[1] That task does not confront us here.

The convert is a complex phenomenon in the scheme of Mishnah's Israelite community. On the one hand, when gentiles converted and became members of the Israelite community, they were often described as individuals who had severed their ties with their gentile relatives and environment. On the other hand, in several areas under Mishnah's concern, converts are distinguishable from native-born Israelites or, at best, viewed as a subclass of Israelite society. Converts appear as one of the ten distinct family types that emigrated from Babylonia to Palestine in the time of Ezra,[2] thus highlighting their uniqueness within the Israelite community. In Mishnah some uniquely Israelite rituals and practices which, according to Scripture, were not incumbent on gentiles are declared obligatory for converts. For example, the converts are required to give the priests the shoulders, two cheeks, and the maw of their slaughtered animals. But, because they are not native-born Israelites, specific restrictions are maintained with regard to the converts' ability to marry a member of the priestly caste. Underlying this ruling is the recognition that converts were once gentiles and remain inherently different from Israelites.[3]

Many of the sages behind Mishnah believed that Israelites and gentiles represented two subclasses of human beings, and frequently Mishnah divides the world, either explicitly or implicitly, between "us" and "them," between Israelites and gentiles. This difference is often expressed in terms of descent or ancestors. Israelites, the Children of Israel/Jacob, came from a different set of progenitors from non-Israelites, who traced their origins to a variety of biblical personages other than Abraham, Isaac, and Jacob, and who might be referred to, collectively, as the Children of Noah.[4] This has ramifications for which prayers converts could recite.

As we shall see throughout this volume, Mishnah's ambiguity concerning the converts' status is continued in all of the subsequent rabbinic collections. The fact that Mishnah can refer to a convert who has an Israelite mother merely underscores the amorphous nature of the term *gr*. Although Mishnah says little about the rite of conversion, it clearly viewed the act of conversion as effecting a change in the convert. This alteration of the person's status had sociological, as well as religious, implications, and the converts' creating new familial and sociological ties underlies many of Mishnah's discussions of the convert. For the most part, when gentiles became Israelites, they severed all ties with their previous relatives. But even this is mediated by the fact that converts could inherit from their gentile parents.[5] Furthermore, the fact that most Israelite rules, customs, and rites applied only to Israelites is marked by their application to converts only when the situations which caused them to arise occurred *after* the persons had converted.

Thus, the convert occupied the middle ground between Israelites and gentiles. On the one hand, the converts severed all ties with their previous gentile life and were responsible for observing most of the same rituals incumbent upon native-born Israelites. On the other hand, they were treated differently from native-born Israelites, often being listed as a distinct class of persons along with priests, Levites, Israelites, and so forth. They are important for determining Mishnah's conception of the Israelite, because the converts' precarious status within the People Israel underscores the importance of Israel's ethnicity and the fact that the rabbis viewed Israel as both an ethnic group and a religious community.

Ritual of Conversion

Mishnah has little to say about the ritual of conversion. Eliezer b. Jacob mentions a convert's sprinkling the blood of an offering on the altar and implies that a person's conversion is not complete until this rite has been performed.[6] Furthermore, given Eliezer's language, he views the convert as being in need of atonement, *kprh*. Elsewhere, in an indirect manner, the Shammaites and the Hillelites dispute the meaning of the convert's ritual ablution. According to the Shammaites, if a person converts the day before Passover, he may consume the Passover offering immediately after he has performed his ritual ablution. The Hillelites, on the other hand, compare the convert, "one who separates from uncircumcision," to "one who separates himself from the grave," so that he immerses on the third and the seventh days after freeing himself from his impurity.[7] This means that he will not be able to participate in the eating of the Passover sacrifice.[8] It appears that the Hillelites viewed the convert's ablution as a purification ritual,[9] while the Shammaites considered it to be an initiation rite. It is interesting to note that the aside in the Hillelites' comment contains Mishnah's only reference to the converts' being circumcised.

Converts as Subclass of People Israel

Converts were considered a recognizable subclass of Israelites, and they are listed among the ten family types that emigrated from Babylonia to Palestine at the time of Ezra.[10] A hierarchy of these various classes of Israelites was constructed, and one source states that when all else is equal, a priest precedes a Levite, a Levite an Israelite, an Israelite a *mamzer*,[11] a *mamzer* a *natin*,[12] a *natin* a convert, and a convert a freed slave.[13] Apparently the converts continued to be distinguished from Israelites because of their having originally been gentiles.[14]

Differences between Converts and Native-Born Israelites

This division of the Israelite populace into ten family stocks plays a role in some of Mishnah's rulings concerning marriage. Priests, Levites and Israelites could freely intermarry. Converts, on the other hand, could wed only members of the levitical class, impaired priests,[15] freed slaves, *mamzerim, netinim, shetuqim*,[16] and *asufim*.[17] Unlike native-born Israelites whose ancestry was above suspicion, it would appear that converts did not possess a presumed right to marry into the priestly class.[18] However, this issue generated some disagreement among the sages in Mishnah. Eliezer b. Jacob held that as long as *either one* of a converted female child's parents was a native-born Israelite, she could marry into the priesthood. Only if both parents were converts was she forbidden to marry a priest.[19] Yosi disagreed and believed that even the daughter of two converts was qualified for marriage to a priest,[20] while Judah stated that the daughter of a male convert is considered the same as the daughter of a male of impaired priestly stock, a *ḥalal*, married to an Israelite woman.[21] These *sugyot* indicate that converts are seen as a distinct subclass of Israelites and that for some sages the converts' gentile ancestry was important even after they converted. Some rabbis treated the converts as if they were the same as impaired Israelites, for some sages grouped converts together with other types of Israelites whose unblemished Israelite ancestry was uncertain. Because of this, the status of a woman's parents had to be kept in mind, for only in this way could the views of those who objected to a convert's daughter's marrying into the priestly class be put into practice.

Yosi, Judah, and Eliezer speak about the marriage between converts' daughters and members of the priestly class, and their opinions probably reflect differing attitudes concerning the effect that conversion has on a person's gentile nature as well as the need to keep the priestly caste free from non-Israelite members. In addition, they disagree over the necessity of being able to identify converts within the Israelite community. If Judah's view were accepted, a person's status as a convert was relevant for many generations after the conversion, for converts and their daughters could never be elevated into the priestly class, a restriction not placed on native-born Israelites whose Israelite ancestry could be ascertained. At least one of Eliezer's rulings[22] implies that the child of the union of an Israelite parent and a convert could be considered an Israelite for purposes of marriage into the priestly class. In this case, only the conversion of a woman's parents had to be known. After her marriage, the original conversion was no longer relevant. Finally, in Yosi's opinion, a person's status as a convert need not be considered when she sought to marry into the priestly caste.[23]

Also, in selecting judges for capital cases, one had to be able to ascertain whether or not a candidate was a convert. Although anyone may sit as a judge in a noncapital case, only Israelites and members of the levitical and priestly classes may try capital cases. The general principle is that only those who may freely marry into the priestly class were allowed to serve as judges in all types of cases.[24] For this reason, converts, whose marriage into the priestly class was limited, could not serve as judges in the court discussed in tractate *Horayot.*[25] Deciding on whether or not an Israelite should be executed was a serious matter, and our texts insure that such decisions were made only by other Israelites whose ancestry could not be questioned. This ruling speaks both to the esteem in which the priesthood was held and to an ambivalent attitude toward the converts. Because the priests were the only ones who could approach YHWH and the altar, the sages seem to assume that they are beyond reproach. Therefore, anyone worthy to be a priest was also worthy to decide an Israelite's fate. Conversely, those prohibited from becoming priests should also be excluded from deciding whether or not an Israelite should be put to death. Again, it appears that the converts' gentile ancestry, which excluded them from the priesthood, prevented them from serving as judges in capital cases.

Mishnah contains a third case which requires that one be able to identify women who had converted. If an Israelite intended to hit another man but accidentally struck a pregnant woman and the woman miscarried, he had to compensate the fetus's father for its value. If the miscarried fetus's father had died, the money was given to the father's heirs. However, a miscarriage by a freed slave or a converted woman need not be compensated.[26] Although later texts claim that Mishnah speaks of a converted woman married to a converted man, this is not mentioned in Mishnah itself. It is possible that the author(s) of this opinion believed that the fetus of a converted woman was of less value than the fetus of a native-born Israelite, perhaps because whether or not conception occurred after her conversion could not be ascertained with certainty.

The view that converts were not fully Israelites is also illustrated by an opinion attributed to Aqabyya b. Mahaleel. He ruled that the waters of bitterness were not administered to converted women. The implications of Aqabyya's stance are in line with those who believed that the non-Israelite origins of a convert could never be ignored.[27] It is important to note, however, that in this context sages disagree with Aqabyya and hold that the waters of bitterness are administered to converts as well as to native-born Israelites. It should be noted, however, that sages disagree with all of Aqabyya's opinions which appear in this *sugya* which accounts for Aqabyya's excommunication.

Furthermore, one Mishnah states that when converts pray in private, they should refer to YHWH as the god of the ancestors of Israel and not as the deity of their forbearers. When they pray in public in the synagogue, they should refer to YHWH as the god of *your* ancestors. Only if their mother were an Israelite, may they refer to YHWH as the god of *our* ancestors.[28] This same distinction appears in the context of the offering of the first fruits. When Israelites brought their first fruits, they repeated portions of Deut. 26:3–10.[29] However, converts could not recite *which YHWH swore unto our ancestors to assign us*[30] because YHWH had made this promise to the Israelites' ancestors, not to the gentiles' progenitors.[31] However, if the converts' mother were an Israelite, they may recite the words from Deuteronomy.[32] This last opinion also points to the ambiguity of the convert's position, for the term "convert" is applied to one who has an Israelite mother and presumably a father who converted; however, these "converts" are treated as if they were native-born Israelites with respect to the Avowal.

Converts and Their Heirs

Even though converts were not always considered to be the same as native-born Israelites, the fact that converts severed all ties with their gentile relatives had important ramifications for the discussions of the laws of inheritance. If an Israelite male whose wife preceded him in death dies without having produced children, members of his family, such as his parents, nephews, and uncles,[33] may inherit his property. For this reason, few, if any, Israelites, would die without legal heirs. Converts, however, were different. Converts who did not have Israelite spouses, or childless proselytes whose spouses had died before them, could have no one to inherit their estates, for upon their official entrance into the Israelite community, they had severed all ties with their gentile relatives. The property which remained after the death of a convert who had no Israelite relatives was considered to be ownerless. Therefore, if an ox belonging to a convert who died without heirs[34] killed a human being, an anonymous opinion held that the ox is killed. Judah, however, maintained that because such an ox is considered to be ownerless property, it is not killed. This specific discussion appears in Mishnah because the Torah deals only with the case of an ox who has an owner,[35] and here we have, as Judah notes, an ownerless ox.[36]

For similar reasons, Mishnah discusses an Israelite who steals from a convert who dies without heirs before the Israelite can restore the stolen goods. Num. 5:6–8 state that a person who admits to having committed a sin against someone after that person has died must make restitution to the person whom he has wronged. He does this by restoring to the dead person's kinsman, *g'l*, the value plus a fifth. If the person does not have a kinsman, restitution is paid to the priests. Therefore, if an Israelite eventually confesses to having stolen something from a convert who died before restitution of the stolen object could be made, the payment is made to the priests. The converts are treated as having no family. The ties to their biological kin were severed by their conversion.[37]

Mishnah's laws concerning the acquisition of ownerless property are rather complex.[38] Because the property left behind by a convert who died without heirs is considered to be ownerless property, it is an obvious topic to be discussed in this context. We learn that an Israelite may claim possession of the ownerless property of a dead convert through usucaption by shutting in, walling up, or breaking down anything within the property.[39] If an Israelite secured title by usucaption to a field which belonged to a convert who died without heirs, the former secures title to everything that is in it.[40]

The fact that converts could die without leaving legally recognized heirs also affects their relationship to the Temple. If a convert who sent an offering to the Temple died before he or she could include the required drink offerings, the cost of the drink offerings is paid from the communal funds, for the dead convert has no one from whom the drink offerings or their funds may be secured.[41]

Because upon conversion, proselytes severed ties with their gentile relatives, a complex relationship existed between converts and the members of their families, even between parents and children, as well as between spouses. Even if a gentile father and his sons convert at the same time, their familial ties are broken because they were formed while all were non-Israelites. Therefore, if an Israelite borrowed money from a convert whose sons converted with him, after their father has died, the borrower need not repay the loan to the converted children. They are not considered to be the dead man's heirs. However, if the Israelite does repay the loan to the children, the sages support his actions.[42] Bartinoro[43] appears to be correct in his claim that if the loan were not repaid to the sons, they might have regretted their conversion, for the Israelite would have been *obligated* to repay the loan to the children if they and their father had all remained gentiles.

Converts and Their Converted Children and Spouses

Another text[44] deals with the daughter of a female convert. If a woman's daughter converts with her and the latter subsequently played the part of a harlot, she is not treated like the daughter of an Israelite, for she is strangled rather than stoned, and the rules concerning "her father's house"[45] and the payment of a hundred *selas* do not apply to her.[46] The child who was conceived while her mother was a gentile, but born after her mother was converted, falls into a category between a convert and a non-Israelite, so that she is stoned, but the rules concerning "her father's house" or the payment of the hundred *selas* do not apply to her. Only if she were both conceived and born after her mother converted is she treated like an Israelite female. Exactly why this final case is discussed is unclear, for surely a child who was conceived and born after her mother converted should be considered an Israelite. It is possible that this example was included so that all three possible cases were covered in the text: (1) one born before her mother converted, (2) one conceived while her mother was a gentile but born after her mother's conversion, and (3) one conceived and born after her mother's conversion. One could also argue that the third case was included to make it clear that only a girl who has two Israelite parents falls under the stipulations written in the Torah, for an Israelite woman can contract a legal marriage only with another Israelite. Perhaps, however, its inclusion was meant to underscore that a child conceived and born after the conversion of her mother should be considered to be an Israelite and that her mother's former status as a gentile or her present status as a convert are totally irrelevant.[47] However, it is clear that a woman who converted with her mother does not have an Israelite father, having severed all ties with her gentile relatives, so that different rules are applied to her from those relevant to a woman who had an Israelite father. Note, however, that for this rule to be applied, the status of the woman's father would have to be known throughout her life.

Although the relationship between converted parents and their children is affected by conversion, the same need not be true concerning spouses. For example, if a man's wife converts with him, their marriage agreement remains valid, "for on this condition he kept her [as his wife]."[48] This passage does present a problem, however, for it assumes that the gentile contracted a *ketubah*, a decidedly Israelite agreement, with his gentile wife. Although the discussion centers around the validity of a marriage contract after a woman has changed her legal status—either from a minor to an adult or from a gentile to a convert[49]—the rule would discourage males from converting in order to get out of unpleasant marriages.

Converts and Levirate Marriages

The complex rules concerning levirate marriages are also affected by conversion. Because the laws of the levirate marriage apply to only Israelites,[50] converted brothers are not subject to the ceremony of *ḥaliṣah* or to the requirement of engaging in a levirate marriage if one of the brothers died without his wife's bearing children.[51] Because they were born of gentile parents, the sons are not considered Israelite brothers. This parallels the situation described above in which the daughter born before her mother's conversion is not considered a native-born Israelite after her conversion.

Converts as Heirs

Although the above discussions presuppose that converts actually severed all connections to their gentile relatives, from the point of view of the gentiles, this need not have in fact occurred, and rabbinic thought seems to recognize this fact, for Mishnah deals with the possibility of converts' inheriting items from their gentile parents. While this need not present a problem, Mishnah's insistence that Israelites avoid contact with anything associated with idolatry[52] complicates the situation. While it is perhaps possible that "practical considerations" meant that the sages of Mishnah could not rule that converts were prohibited from inheriting from their gentile parents, nor could they state that the converts were ineligible to inherit "forbidden" items from them because this could make conversion unappealing. Such "practical considerations" were possible because of the converts' ambiguous status within the Israelite community.

An anonymous text holds that if a gentile and a convert inherit from their father, the latter may divide the property with his sibling before it comes into his possession, so that the convert receives only those items permissible under Israelite law. The text seems to assume that the convert has no inherent right to his dead father's property,[53] so that the convert may make stipulations concerning what he will choose to take possession of. However, after he has taken formal possession of his inheritance, he may not gain any benefit from those items forbidden to him according to Israelite law.[54]

Converts as Radically New People

For the most part converts are considered to be radically changed from the people they were before their conversions. This altered social status has important implications in many different areas of rabbinic concern. A gentile who converts is compared to a minor who reaches maturity, a deaf mute who gains the ability to speak and to hear, an imbecile who becomes sane, and a blind person who becomes able to see.[55] However, this idea is expressed most often in the distinctions drawn between converts and gentiles with regard to specific rites, rituals, and regulations for which Israelites alone are responsible. Most of the obligations incumbent upon Israelites are not applied to gentiles. If the first-born of a union between Israelites were a male, he had to be redeemed from a priest. Similarly, if the first-born of an Israelite's herd or flock were a male, it had to be dedicated to the priesthood or redeemed.[56] These rules of course did not apply to gentiles or to their animals.[57] The issue is how to handle the convert, who, as before, occupies an ambiguous status. Specifically, if an Israelite male who had had no children married a female convert who had borne children to her former gentile husband, the question arose concerning the first offspring of the new marriage: Was the first child of the union between the Israelite and the converted woman in the status of a first-born or not? Was the fact that she had given birth as a gentile relevant to her situation after she had converted? Or, did her conversion create a new person whose previous child-bearing was irrelevant? From Mishnah's point of view, two different prerogatives fell to a first-born male: (1) He received a double portion of his father's inheritance,[58] and (2) he had to be redeemed from the priest for five *selas*. In the situation under discussion here, Mishnah ruled that the child of the second marriage was entitled to his double portion of his father's inheritance, because he was the Israelite father's first-born; however, he did not have to be redeemed from the priest,[59] because he was not a first-born in all regards, for his mother was not totally transformed into a new person upon her conversion. However, basing himself on the phrase *the issue of every womb among the Israelites*,[60] Yosi the Galilean considers the child to be a first-born because it is the first child of the union of two Israelites, so that the child receives the double portion and must be redeemed from the priests.[61] From Yosi's perspective, the mother's gentile past is totally irrelevant.

The previous discussion focused on the Israelite father who had not produced an offspring. Mishnah also takes up the case of a woman who was pregnant when she converted and rules that the child born after his mother's conversion must be redeemed from the priests. However, he does not receive the double inheritance. The emphasis here is on the fact that the child is the first issue of an Israelite woman's womb. The reason for the son's not receiving the double inheritance is obvious, for he has severed all ties with his gentile father, and, in any case, he has no absolute right to inherit anything from a gentile parent.[62]

Israelites alone had to give the priests the shoulders, the two cheeks, and the maw of slaughtered animals.[63] These gifts supported the ethnic elite of the Israelite people, the priests. Therefore, a convert who slaughtered an animal *before* conversion is exempt from giving portions from the slaughtered animal to the priests. On the other hand, if the animal were slaughtered *after* the conversion, the priestly gifts are due. In cases in which there is a doubt exactly when the animal was slaughtered, the gifts to the priests need not be given. Because the priesthood served the needs only of the Israelites and their deity, YHWH, Israelites alone were required to provide for their maintenance.[64] But it is striking that the rabbis actually wished to ensure that non-Israelites did not contribute to the upkeep of the priestly caste. Accordingly, the priestly gifts were due from converts only when it was certain that the animal was slaughtered *after* the gentile had become a member of the Israelite community.[65] Dough becomes liable for the dough offering, which is given to the priests, only after it has been rolled out. Again, only Israelites are responsible for separating the dough offering from their rolled-out dough.[66] Therefore, if a person rolled out her dough *before* she converted, she need not bring the dough offering. A convert must make this offering only from dough which was rolled out *after* she became an Israelite. However, if it is uncertain whether or not the dough was rolled out before the person converted, the dough offering must be taken.[67]

Along these same lines, only Israelites are responsible for supporting the poor among the Israelite community,[68] so that they alone are *required* to leave the gleanings, the corners, and the forgotten sheaves for the Israelite poor. For this reason, an anonymous passage rules that if gentiles reaped a field and afterward converted, they are exempt from the requirement of leaving the gleanings, the forgotten sheaves, or the corners for the poor among the Israelite community. Judah disagrees with regard to the forgotten sheaves because they become a gift to the poor at the time of their binding, not at the time of the harvest. Therefore, if the gentiles converted between the time of the harvest and the time of the binding of the sheaves, they must leave them for the Israelite poor.[69] Judah agrees with the point that converts, but not gentiles, must give the agricultural gifts to the Israelite poor. He differs only in his emphasizing the point at which the sheaves come under the obligation to be given to the poor.[70]

The Israelites' purity rules also apply only to Israelites, not to gentiles.[71] Mishnah states that converts convey uncleanness through their genital emissions,[72] in which regard the convert is considered to be like an Israelite. If converts suffered an issue of semen before they converted and another emission after they converted, they convey uncleanness only through the second issue, which they experienced as Israelites.[73] Similarly, the laws of skin disease do not apply to gentiles;[74] therefore, if converts had a bright spot on their skin at the time of their conversion, it is considered to be clean.[75]

Finally, one may not remind converts that their parents had not been born as Israelites. This is derived from the phrase, *you shall not wrong a stranger or oppress him*, in Ex. 22:20.[76]

Converts and Their Gentile Past

Some of the sages behind Mishnah considered gentiles to be uncivilized, and this resulted in the view, held by some, that gentiles were sexually uninhibited.[77] This finds expression in the material on the convert in the following way: Some of Mishnah's authors believed that gentiles would have intercourse with any female over the age of three years and one day.[78] Therefore, the *ketubah* of a female who converted before the age of three years and a day is the same as that for an Israelite virgin, 200 *dinars*. Furthermore, a virginity suit may be lodged against her, because one could reasonably assume that she was a virgin.[79] However, if the woman converted after she was three years and one day old, her marriage contract is one *maneh*, and her husband may not lodge a virginity suit against her. She is *assumed* to have had intercourse before her marriage. These rules mean that the age of female converts at the time of their conversion had to be ascertained in order to determine the amount of their marriage contracts.[80] This of course presupposes that one could easily identify converts. The assumed virginity of the woman who converted before the age of three years and one day also stands behind the ruling that a male who has intercourse with such a woman who was betrothed to another is subject to a fine of fifty *sheqalim* prescribed by Scripture.[81] If the woman converted after the age of three years and one day, a male who seduces her is not subject to a fine.[82] In addition, the assumed sexual promiscuity of gentiles stands behind sages' claim that "harlot" in Lev. 21:7 refers to a female convert.[83]

Sexual contact between Israelites and gentiles is strictly forbidden.[84] In fact, if there were rumors that an Israelite had had sexual intercourse with a gentile woman, he should not marry her after she converts, perhaps because, as Rashi states,[85] the union could appear to support the rumors that the Israelite was intimately involved with a gentile. It is also possible, following the *gemara*,[86] that such a marriage was forbidden because it would appear that the woman had converted in order to marry the man, and there were those who did not accept gentiles who joined the Israelite community for the sake of marriage. However, once they are married, the two cannot be forced to divorce each other, for a marriage between a convert and an Israelite is acceptable.[87] Whatever the reason that the marriage should not take place, clearly the text implies that marriages between Israelites and converts should be accepted once they have been undertaken.

The prohibition of sexual activity between Israelites and gentiles was such that an Israelite could not arrange a marriage with a gentile on the condition that the partner convert. If an Israelite male arranges a marriage with a gentile woman on the condition that she convert after the marriage or if a gentile male arranges a marriage with an Israelite woman with the promise that he will convert after the marriage, the marriage agreements are invalid.[88] It would have been obvious that an Israelite could not marry a gentile. Here, the point seems to be that one cannot arrange a marriage with a gentile even if the partner agrees to convert.[89]

Converts from Biblical Nations

When discussing the gentiles, the authors of Mishnah often had recourse to biblical paradigms.[90] Such use of Scripture is evidenced as well in a narrative about Judah, an Ammonite convert, who asks whether or not he is permitted "to enter the congregation," that is, to marry an Israelite woman. The question is based on the statement in Deut. 23:3 which forbids Ammonites and Moabites from "entering the congregation" until the tenth generation. Joshua and Gamaliel dispute the point, for Gamaliel claims that the prohibition is still in force, while Joshua argues that because the foreign tribes mentioned in the Bible are no longer distinct entities, the prohibition is no longer valid. Joshua's position is the one accepted.[91] This narrative underscores the importance of the Bible in setting the rabbis' agenda. The *sugya* projects the nonbiblical idea of the convert onto Scripture's rules concerning the biblical people surrounding ancient Israel. The dispute between Joshua and Gamaliel does not concern the convert; rather, the convert merely provides the peg on which to hang the disagreement over the relevance of the biblical injunction in the social and political world of the first centuries of the common era.

Mishnah's conceptions of the convert are complex and at times contradictory. Converts become Israelites, so that they are responsible for obligations placed on Israelites: for instance, to provide for the poor among the Israelite community and to support the Israelite priesthood. These rulings are important, for gentiles were *obligated* neither to provide the agricultural gifts for the Israelite poor[92] nor to support the priests.[93] Throughout, Mishnah emphasizes that converts are viewed as members of the Israelite community with regard to these gifts *only if* the obligation to make the gifts occurred *after* the gentile had converted. Similarly, when converts become members of the Israelite community, they are often viewed as having severed their ties with their gentile relatives. The opinion that converts were considered to have broken their ties with the gentile relatives led the author(s) of Mishnah to compile several texts which dealt with, from their point of view, the real possibility that a gentile could die without leaving legally acceptable heirs. While a person's conversion could present problems with regard to certain Israelite obligations, such as the laws of firstlings, the ways in which converts may fulfill their duty as Israelites receives much attention.

Although Mishnah contains a good deal of material which treats the converts as if they were native-born Israelites, it also incorporates passages which differentiate converts and native-born Israelites. Some restrictions applied to converts which were not applicable to native-born Israelites. While on the one hand claiming that one should not remind converts of their gentile background, Mishnah also posits many regulations which mandate that converts be recognizable, for some purposes, throughout their lives. Especially with regard to women, the fact that they were converts would be important throughout their lives. In this regard, the Israelites' concern with maintaining the ethnic unity of the priesthood receives a lot of attention.

Because the priests were the ethnic as well as religious leaders of the Israelite people[94] and because they approached YHWH, Israelite tradition carefully regulated whom they might marry. Therefore, the gentile background of the convert could not be forgotten, if one were to uphold the marriage restrictions incumbent upon the priesthood. In fact, the gentile background of a female convert stands behind a number of *sugyot* which deal with sexual activity between Israelite males and female converts. This appears to be the case for two reasons: (1) Mishnah consistently prohibited sexual intercourse between Israelites and gentiles, and this seems to have played a role in the concern for the sexual activity of Israelites and converts.[95] (2) Mishnah considered gentiles to be sexually uninhibited,[96] so that one could not assume that women who converted after they had reached the age of three years and one day had not engaged in sexual intercourse. The result of these concerns was that the fact that a female was a convert could neither be forgotten nor ignored, for at the time of marriage female converts were treated differently from native-born Israelite woman. This underscores Mishnah's conception of Israelites as a descent group,[97] for clearly the converts were different from the native-born Israelites in these contexts because the former had once been gentiles.

Mishnah's description of Israel as a descent group is manifested in other ways. Converts could not claim YHWH, the god of Abraham, Isaac, and Jacob, as their god, unless, according to some, their mothers were native-born Israelites. Furthermore, converts were classified along with other segments of the Israelite community whose legitimate Israelite ancestry was suspect. The result of this concern with lineage meant that according to some sages, in specific contexts converts could not be fully equated with native-born Israelites.

Mishnah juxtaposes the convert and the freed slave in almost 14 percent of the relevant *sugyot*.[98] Mishnah does not explain why this is the case, but it seems to be because both are examples of persons who have undergone a radical change of status.[99] Clearly, one reason for the comparison is that to the authors of Mishnah, the change in status which occurred when a slave was manumitted was comparable to the alteration in status which occurred when a gentile converted.[100] So conversion marked an important change of ethnic and religious status, the same way in which slaves' achieving their freedom marked an important alteration of their status.

Also the sexual purity of a female slave was questionable in the same way that the sexual purity of a female gentile was a matter of doubt. It was assumed that the masters controlled the sexuality of their female slaves and that gentiles were sexually promiscuous.[101]

Above we have reviewed what Mishnah says about converts; however, it is also interesting to note what Mishnah omits. For example, there is no detailed discussion of the rituals connected with conversion; we found only oblique references. Either the rituals were so well known that they did not need to be mentioned or the rituals had not yet come under scrutiny because they were not frequently employed or they did not yield the sort of discussion or debate that interested Mishnah's editors. Furthermore, we do not find any discussions about encouraging or discouraging gentiles from converting, a topic which will be dealt with in later documents. Perhaps the authors of Mishnah took conversion somewhat for granted, so that they did not concern themselves with the rituals involved or with the appropriateness of accepting converted gentiles into the Israelite community. Or, perhaps conversion was not a major issue for the authors of Mishnah because it was not all that common. At this stage, from the point of view of the rabbis, conversion simply is not a topic of much concern. It generates the most interest in matters of damages and inheritance, for the convert alone readily serves as an example of an Israelite who might die without heirs. This could be a theoretical matter, as well as a practical one. However, in these texts the important consideration is the complexity of the laws of inheritance and damages, not the convert. Mishnah also does not discuss the gentiles' motives for converting or the fact that converts must observe the whole Torah.

In Mishnah we see that the act of conversion has important sociological and religious ramifications. Above all we learn that many sages held that conversion marks a radical change in a person's status. However, whether or not this is a good or bad thing is not debated in Mishnah. Mishnah does not evaluate a convert's decision, nor does it discuss how the decision was reached nor the ways in which this decision was put into effect. Mishnah does not seem to be interested in "conversion" as a concept; it focuses on the converts as individuals and their status within the Israelite community. In the opinion of some rabbis, the fact that people were converts clearly distinguished those individuals from native-born Israelites and was important for the individuals throughout their lives. For other sages, a convert was an Israelite who was under certain restrictions which applied only when the converts' or Israelites' ancestry was a significant factor. Taken as a whole document, Mishnah describes the converts as occupying an ambiguous place in the classification of human beings: while the fact that they were once gentiles could not be forgotten, neither could it be thrown in their faces. For the editors of Mishnah, converts were no longer considered to be gentiles; at the same time, however close they came to being full Israelites, in specific contexts the difference between them and the native-born would always remain.

░ THREE ░

Converts and Conversion in Tosefta

░

Tosefta's relationship to Mishnah is rather complex. The two collections probably date from the same general period, the first half of the second century of the common era. It is likely that Mishnah, as a redacted whole, for the most part, antedates Tosefta, so that we can view the former text as primary, both in terms of time and importance. Neusner has noted that passages in Tosefta relate to segments within Mishnah in three ways. (1) In places, Tosefta functions as a commentary on Mishnah, which it quotes verbatim. (2) In some passages Tosefta appears to be autonomous of Mishnah, while actually functioning as a commentary to the earlier collection. (3) In still other sections, Tosefta is totally independent of Mishnah.[1] In the material regarding the convert, we find examples of each of these three relationships.

Tosefta and Mishnah generally agree on the categories through which to discuss the converts. Both documents employ the topic of the convert to refine their laws of usucaption, inheritance, and damage claims. Both texts view the converts as a subclass of the People Israel. Both collections agree that married gentiles do not have to write a new marriage contract upon their conversion. Both texts contain an extensive list of Israelite customs and rituals which are incumbent upon the converts *after* their conversions. However, seldom does Tosefta merely repeat what we now find in Mishnah. Instead, it moves the discussions in its own directions in order to make its own points. As we shall see below, some of these differences have important ramifications for our understanding of the converts and conversion, while others are less significant and offer us little new information.

Tosefta also contains some material which is not in Mishnah. Tosefta presents an extensive discussion of the converts' offering, and it assumes that male converts were circumcised. Tosefta also claims that converts were represented at the revelation on Mount Sinai and therefore must follow the totality of rabbinic *halakhah*. If one suspects that gentiles will be unable to follow both the Written and the Oral Torahs, Tosefta holds that they should not be admitted into the Israelite community. Finally, some of Tosefta's sages assume that gentiles prepared themselves for their conversion by observing rabbinic practices even while they were gentiles. Taken as a whole, this unique material in Tosefta suggests that Tosefta's editors had views of converts and conversion different from those we now find in Mishnah.

Ritual of Conversion

Tosefta states that converts may not eat parts of sacrificial animals[2] until the bird offering has been brought. However, even if they brought one pigeon, they may eat the consecrated meat in the evening.[3] The proselytes may bring cattle instead of birds, for the birds were specified only to make it easier for converts to provide their offerings, birds being less expensive than cattle.[4] At any rate, they must offer an animal, for merely presenting a meal offering or a drink offering does not suffice in this case. Normally when the Torah instructs one to bring two bird offerings, one of them is counted as a sin offering, and the other is considered to be a whole burnt offering.[5] This is not the case with the two birds offered by converts, for both of these were considered to be whole burnt offerings. If converts brought an offering at the end of a bout with a skin disease or at the end of a Nazirite period, they must bring another offering as the atonement offering for their conversion.[6] After the Temple was destroyed, this rite was suspended, according to R. Simeon. But an anonymous opinion held that the converts had to set apart two birds, although they did not have to kill them, even after the Temple was destroyed.[7] According to this anonymous opinion, the separation of the birds was so important that it had to be done symbolically even after the Temple no longer existed.

We have before us a rather detailed analysis of the converts' offering. Several points of Tosefta's discussion are striking. (1) Even though a bird offering is not mentioned in Mishnah, Tosefta treats the ritual as if it were a well-known activity. (2) Although it is called a bird offering, *qyn*, cattle are also permitted. Meal offerings and libations are unacceptable. This would parallel Eliezer b. Jacob's oblique reference in Mishnah to the blood of the offering.[8] (3) Although it requires two birds, one is sufficient to allow the convert to eat the offerings in the evening. (4) Similar to Eliezer b. Jacob's reference in Mishnah to the converts' sacrifice, there is a concept of atonement connected to this ritual. Eliezer stated that the converts' atonement is not complete until the offering's blood was tossed on the altar. Tosefta claims that the converts may bring cattle "for atonement" and that one who has brought an offering after a bout with a skin disease or after the Nazirite period must bring another offering "for atonement."[9] (5) The two birds which the converts brought were classified differently from all of the other offerings which required two birds. (6) There was a disagreement concerning the fate of the offering after the Temple had been destroyed. (7) Eliezer's statement in Mishnah does not appear in Tosefta *Sheqalim*, but it does occur in Tosefta *Keritot*.

It is impossible to know if Eliezer b. Jacob in Mishnah and the passages in Tosefta refer to the same offering. Tosefta does not specifically mention that the blood had to be tossed against the altar; however, this is probably implied by the fact that libations and meal offerings are not acceptable. Furthermore, while both Eliezer and Tosefta refer to the converts' need for "atonement," the concept functions differently in the two texts. Tosefta states that the convert must bring the birds in order to eat from the other sacrifices and does not refer to the matter of atonement until it discusses the cattle and the offerings required of the converts after their bout with skin diseases or after their completion of a term as a Nazirite. Elsewhere in Tosefta,[10] Eliezer's comment in Mishnah is juxtaposed to Tosefta's references to "atonement," so that it appears that the compilers of Tosefta's version of *Keritot* believed that Eliezer and Tosefta were discussing the same ritual. However, that is not obvious in Tosefta's version of the passage in *Sheqalim*. It may be that Eliezer appears in Tosefta's *Keritot* because he also appeared in mKer. 2:1, while his absence from tSheq. 3:21–22 reflects the fact that he does not appear in Mishnah at this point.[11] Therefore, it is possible that the connection between the offering in Tosefta and Eliezer in Mishnah is the result of editorial activity.

Simeon b. Eleazar reports that the Hillelites and the Shammaites assume that converts must be circumcised. However, they differed concerning the necessity of performing the ritual for a gentile who was already circumcised at the time of his conversion. The House of Shammai held that such a person should undergo a symbolic circumcision, while the House of Hillel ruled that he need not undergo even a symbolic rite, for the requirement was merely that all Israelites were circumcised. Exactly when the circumcision was performed and who performed it were unimportant.[12] As Neusner notes,[13] the original Houses dispute, which does not appear elsewhere independent of Simeon's interpretation, must have concerned an Israelite who was born circumcised. Simeon, who flourished three generations after the Houses, juxtaposes the Houses' opinions with the converts. In another passage, an anonymous opinion states that one who was circumcised before he converted can be circumcised symbolically only during the day. Eleazar b. Simeon responds that if the circumcision takes place on the proper, that is the eighth, day, he is circumcised only during the day; however, if he is circumcised after the eighth day, the ritual is performed during the day or night.[14]

Leazar b. Sadoq states that the Hillelites and the Shammaites agreed concerning an uncircumcised male who is sprinkled and then permitted to eat the Passover sacrifice. He suggests that they disagreed concerning a circumcised gentile, and it is to this case that he attaches the dispute found in Mishnah.[15]

Converts as Subclass of People Israel

According to Yosi, a male convert may marry a female *mamzer*, but the child of such of union is considered a *mamzer*. Judah rules that a convert may not marry a *mamzer*.[16] This seems to relate to the discussion of whether or not the converts were a distinct "community" which came up from Babylonia to Israel at the time of Ezra. According to mQid. 4:1, the converts were a separate community, and they could marry Levites, impaired priests, freed slaves, *mamzerim*, *netinim*, and *shetuqim*. In tQid. 5:1 Judah holds that there are four separate castes—priests, Levites, Israelites, and converts[17]—and implies that only these may intermarry. Judah's discussion of "communities," *qhl*, parallels Meir's treatment of "nations," *'wmwt*.[18] According to Judah, the converts are equated with native-born Israelites whose ancestry can be definitely ascertained, so that converts can freely intermarry with priests, Levites, and Israelites, and they should not marry those members of the Israelite community whose ancestry is uncertain. This stands in marked contrast to the statement in mQid. 4:1 which holds that converts may *not* marry priests, but that they are permitted to marry Levites, Israelites, and all those, such as *mamzerim*, whose ancestry cannot be firmly established.

Differences between Converts and Native-Born Israelites

Tosefta also takes up the issue of whether or not converts, like native-born Israelites, can marry into the priestly clan. Above we saw that Judah taught that converts were the same as Israelites, Levites, and priests, so that they all could intermarry. However, elsewhere opinions are attributed to Judah which correspond to his teaching in Mishnah. In fact, a more "complete" version of Judah's comment in mQid. 4:6 also appears in Tosefta,[19] for in the latter text Judah specifically states that the daughter of a male convert "is like the daughter of a male impaired priest, and she is unfit for the priesthood." Tosefta also contains an anonymous statement which holds that a male convert can marry a female from the priestly class.[20]

The major question is whether or not consistent views are attributed to Judah. It should be noted at the outset that Judah's two comments appear in different contexts: The context of one is a discussion of whether or not converts are a separate "community"; the other appears in a discussion of the daughter of an impaired priest. MQid. 4:6 and tQid. 5:3 seem to be related, and the latter text is more explicit than the former. The problem is the relationship of this teaching to Judah's claim that converts could intermarry with priests because they represent distinct "communities," tQid. 5:1. Of course it depends on what Judah means here by the term "convert." If tQid 5:1 refers to converts themselves, not to the children of converts, one could argue that he is talking about two different cases. In tQid. 5:1 Judah maintains that converts themselves, but not their children, may marry into the priesthood, while in tQid. 5:3 he teaches that the children, specifically daughters, of converts may not marry priests. This does not make much sense, given that in the latter text Judah holds that marriages between converts and Israelite women do not produce daughters who can marry into the priesthood. If converted males and Israelite women cannot produce children fit to marry priests, how could converted males married to priestly women produce children who could marry priests, for the daughter of an impaired priest cannot marry a priest? One could maintain that in tQid. 5:1 Judah permits the marriage between converted women and priests, while in tQid. 5:3 he prohibits the daughters of converts to marry priests; again, this does not make logical sense. It appears that Tosefta contains contradictory opinions attributed to Judah. This points to the complexity of the issue and to our impossibility of determining exactly what particular sages had to say on this or on any other topic.

Statements in both Mishnah and Tosefta agree that the children of a convert kept the status of their converted parent. In most cases, children's status follows that of their mother. However, if an Israelite woman who comes from a priestly, Levitical, or Israelite clan marries a convert, the children follow their father's status, for they are considered to be converts. Thus, the marriage between an Israelite woman and a convert produces a *gr*, not a *bn/bt yśr'l*.[21] Because the marriage is legally valid, the child is not a *mamzer*, which is the case when an Israelite marries a gentile. This reflects the idea that Israelites should marry Israelites, for the ethnic nature of the Israelite group mandates endogamous marriages. It also points to the ambiguous status of converts, for they are neither gentiles nor native-born Israelites.[22]

Converts and Their Heirs

Tosefta, like Mishnah, employs discussions of converts who died without heirs in order to underscore the fact that converts had severed all ties with their gentile relatives; therefore, it was conceivable that the converts' property would become ownerless upon their death.[23] Israelites may lay claim to the ownerless property of a dead convert through usucaption;[24] however, if it were discovered that the convert had dedicated the property to the Temple before his death, his wishes must be carried out.[25] If one Israelite locked up the property but another Israelite walled it up, they may not take possession of the property, for the first has negated the second's act. But, if two Israelites perform the same act of usucaption, they acquire the field.[26] Eliezer holds that if one traverses the dead convert's property, either lengthwise or breadthwise, or two traverse the property, one lengthwise and one breadthwise, the person acquires what he trespassed, while sages state that the property may not be claimed in this manner.[27] The convert who died without heirs and left behind ownerless property provided the sages with the occasion to refine their laws of usucaption. The major issue in these discussions are the methods by which one acquires ownerless property.

If an Israelite lays claim to one of a dead convert's ten fields, he has secured title to all ten fields because they are considered to be one block of land. However, laying claim to one of the convert's ten slaves does not allow the Israelite to take possession of the other nine slaves, for each slave is a separate individual; therefore, each must be acquired on its own. If one lays claim to the dead convert's chattels and slaves, he may not claim the slaves, for the chattels and slaves represent different categories of items. If he claims the slaves and the chattels, he may possess only the slaves. Similarly, if the Israelite claims chattels and real estate, he may take possession only of the chattels, for the chattels and the real estate are considered to be different categories of items. In these two cases, a different claim of possession must be made for each item, for acquisition of one item does not entail acquisition of the other made at the same time in one act of acquisition. If he claims land and chattels, he may possess only the land. If he wishes to claim the slaves and the real estate, separate claims must be made for each set of items. Similarly, if he claimed real estate and slaves, he may possess only the former. The major concern here is whether or not chattels, slaves, and land are the same or different categories with regard to matters of acquisition. Again, the *sugya* focuses on the complex laws of acquisition but provides no information of interest about the convert.[28]

If Israelites took possession of a convert's property after the latter's death on the assumption that he had no heirs, but later it was discovered that his Israelite wife was pregnant or that he had legitimate Israelite children, the property must be returned to the legitimate heirs. However, if the wife miscarried or the sons died, the property may be taken over by other Israelites, for it now falls into the category of ownerless property. But a new situation was created when the property was returned to the convert's heirs, so that a new set of Israelites can now take possession of the ownerless property.[29]

The fact that converts sever ties with their gentile family also had ramifications with regard to damage claims. If an ox which was deemed harmless killed a convert, it is stoned, but its owner need not pay the ransom payment so long as the convert had no legitimate Israelite heirs. Judah holds that the ox of a convert who died without heirs that later gored is exempt from the death penalty because it had no legitimate owner who could be warned about the ox's dangerous nature in the same way that an Israelite would be.[30] Because the rules of damages apply only to Israelites, warning the deceased convert's gentile heirs would not fulfill the biblical injunctions.[31]

If two men are fighting and they strike a pregnant woman, causing her to miscarry, compensation is paid to her husband.[32] Tosefta implies that if the husband died, the compensation is paid to his legal heirs. Therefore, if a convert impregnated the woman and he died, the Israelite who caused the miscarriage does not have to pay damages. It is assumed that the convert had no legal heirs to whom the compensation could be paid.[33]

If one steals from an Israelite who has no heirs, when he admits his sin, if the Israelite has died, the stolen money plus an added fifth goes to the priests, and a guilt offering is made.[34] Tosefta[35] builds on Mishnah's[36] discussion of an Israelite who robs a gentile, but Tosefta changes the case. Now, the convert encounters the Israelite thief while the latter is going up to Jerusalem, and the former loans the stolen money to the thief. What now happens if the convert dies? Must the thief make restitution to the Temple? According to Yosi the Galilean,[37] the thief must still bring a guilt offering if he had not done so before the convert died; however, the coins are now his as a result of the loan which the convert made to him. Sages respond that unless the thief has returned the money to the convert and the convert has lent the returned money back to him, no loan has taken place.[38] In what appears to be another version of this pericope, Aqiba states[39] that if the robber died on his way to Jerusalem, the money is given to his sons, and the guilt offering from the robber is put out to pasture until it suffers a blemish. At that point it is sold, and the money earned from the sale is used for a freewill offering. Aqiba's teaching is based on an interpretation of Num. 5:8,[40] which is read to mean that only the thief himself may bring a guilt offering. As before, these passages are not primarily concerned with the convert. The dispute between Yosi and sages, tB.Q. 10:16, sharpens the definition of a loan. Aqiba's ruling expounds the verse from Numbers and makes clear who is responsible for bringing the guilt offering. The fact that the convert does not have any heirs to whom the restitution can be paid merely provides the context in which the nature of a loan is refined and the ruling on who must bring the guilt offering is made.[41]

Converts and Their Converted Children and Spouses

Although much in Mishnah and Tosefta emphasizes the fact that upon conversion gentiles sever all ties with their gentile relatives, the discussion of a married couple who converted stands against this. Tosefta repeats Mishnah's ruling[42] that if a man and wife convert together, the marriage agreement they executed before their conversion holds. However, Tosefta adds that if the husband writes a new agreement after they became Israelites, the latter accord goes into force.[43] If a convert died and his property were taken over by Israelites, his wife has the right to collect according to the terms of her marriage contract, and all debtors also have the right to collect on their legitimate claims.[44] While Mishnah and Tosefta assume that gentiles wrote acceptable marriage contracts for their wives, Tosefta allows the converts to execute a new marriage contract. This latter notion probably results from the view that the converts have undergone a change of status, so that a new marriage contract may be executed. Tosefta's other opinion, which agrees with Mishnah, ignores the converts' change of status. This teaching would have the effect of discouraging a person from converting in order to alter a marriage agreement, while the other ruling would have the opposite effect. The underlying issue is whether or not the converts' change of status allows the husband to execute a new marriage contract, suggesting that the marriage undertaken while the partners were gentiles is no longer valid when they became Israelites.

Converts and Levirate Marriages

The fact that converts change status but that their relatives do not has important implication for some Israelite practices. For example, a woman who is married to a convert does not cause the rite of *halisah* to be performed, nor does she enter into a levirate marriage if her husband dies before she bears his children.[45] Neither do converts engage in these activities.[46] The reason is that the convert's brothers are not necessarily Israelites; therefore, they cannot contract a valid marriage with the women, nor would they be keeping their brother's name alive *in Israel*[47] through the offspring which might result from such a marriage. If a convert's brother does perform the rite of *haliṣah*, it is meaningless. If he engages in sexual relations with the woman, she cannot marry into the priestly clan.[48] If a woman is a convert, only her sons who were conceived and born after her conversion are considered at all, because only in that case are they Israelites.[49] If the sons were conceived and born before she converted and they converted with her, they do not perform the rite of *haliṣah*, they do not engage in levirate marriages, but they are not prohibited from marrying their brother's wife. If they were conceived before their mother converted, but were born after she converted, they are prohibited from marrying their brother's wife, but they still may not perform the rite of *haliṣah* or engage in a levirate marriage.[50]

Converts as Heirs

Despite the fact that upon conversion a gentile severs all ties with his previous family, he may still inherit from his father. However, he may take possession of only those items which he may own under Israelite law. Mishnah teaches that a convert and his brother may inherit from their gentile father as long as the convert and the gentile divide the property before it comes into their possession, so that the convert will not have any items forbidden to him under Israelite custom.[51] Tosefta repeats Mishnah's *sugya* and adds a story about one specific convert, Onqelos,[52] and another illustration concerning a bathhouse which was jointly inherited.[53] We are told that Onqelos was so righteous that he threw his portion of the inheritance into the Dead Sea. This act symbolizes Onqelos's total rejection of his former family and their way of life. The other text informs us that if the gentile and a convert jointly inherited a bathhouse, the convert may take the profits earned during the week and allow his gentile brother to take the profits earned on the Sabbath. In this way, the convert does not profit from work done on the Sabbath, so that he follows Israelite law. These pericopae illustrate two very different views regarding the convert's appropriate behavior.

Converts as Radically New People

We saw in Mishnah that conversion marked a major transformation of the individual, and Tosefta expresses this by stating that converts embarked on totally new lives and could not return to their previous status. Accordingly, after conversion, the proselytes who were suspected of transgressing one item of the rabbinic Torah, or even the whole Torah, retained their Israelite status, for they were classified as apostate *Israelites*.[54] But they could not become gentiles again. In light of the finality and significance of conversion, if, prior to conversion, there were reason to believe that the potential converts would violate the Torah, they could be refused admission.[55] According to Yosi b. Judah, converts are not accepted even if they refuse to follow only a relatively minor injunction enacted by the scribes. The point is that the converts' change of status must be total; they must accept the entirety of Israelite culture.[56] However, it is interesting to note that Tosefta, but not Mishnah, emphasizes that the converts must follow the Oral as well as the Written Torah, and that the former text alone states that not all who express a desire to convert should be accepted into the Israelite community.[57] Thus the redactors of Tosefta explicitly state a much more rigorous standard for conversion than that found in Mishnah.

The fact that the act of conversion effects an important change in the gentiles' status can be illustrated in other ways. If a convert's ox committed manslaughter but the case did not come before the court until after the convert had died, the ox is not stoned, because the requirement that its owner guard it[58] could not have been fulfilled. The problem is that the ox's owner had to be in the same status when the case comes before the court as he or she had been when the ox killed the person. Because the convert has died, presumably leaving no legitimate Israelite heirs, the status of the ox's owner has changed, because the new owner is presumably a native-born Israelite who took possession of the ownerless ox.[59] The underlying point is that the convert and the Israelite were different subclasses of the Israelite people.

Gentiles may not give valid testimony concerning an Israelite's status, and even after they converted, their testimony concerning events they may have witnessed as gentiles is not accepted. Yohanan b. Beroqa seems to hold that their testimony is valid.[60] Although the *gemara*[61] states that the gentile is not believed because he did not pay attention to details of importance to Israelites while he was a gentile, Tosefta's view is that gentiles are not accepted as valid witnesses on Israelite matters because they were not part of the People Israel.[62] Even though they converted and joined the People Israel, this does not negate their gentile past, a time when they were not fully aware of the subtleties of Israelite law and custom. The governing principle is that "any evidence for which one is at the outset invalid, but at the end is valid, the evidence is invalid."[63] However, the general principle which ends the *sugya* states that the reason the converts' testimony is invalid is because they became radically new people. Had they remained gentiles, there would have been no question that their testimony was invalid. The issue is raised only because their status had changed from gentiles to converts, and converts' testimony was valid in Israelite courts, but only testimony to events which transpired after they converted.

Although in some texts the converts are considered to be a subclass of Israelites and therefore not fully equal to native-born Israelites, the convert often is described as obligated to fulfill the same ritual and liturgical obligations as a native-born member of the Israelite community. Like Israelite women, converted women suspected of adultery must survive the ordeal of the bitter waters[64] if, upon divorce, they are to receive the amount stipulated in their marriage contract if their husband divorces them.[65] According to Tosefta, converts are included along with the unimpaired and impaired Israelites who are required to recite the grace after a meal, so that converts must perform the same ritual after eating a meal as native-born Israelites, even though they are specifically mentioned apart from Israelites.[66] In a similar way, all Israelite males, including converts and those of questionable lineage, are permitted to lay their hands on sacrifices[67] and to wave offerings before YHWH.[68] Also, they are obligated to hear the sounding of the *shofar* on Rosh HaShanah[69] and the reading of the *megillah* on Purim.[70] In brief, with regard to these rituals, converts are equated with native-born Israelites. It must be stressed, however, that they are listed separately from the native-born Israelites. This not only underscores the fact that converts and Israelites are required to do the same things, but it also suggests that the term Israelites did not automatically incorporate those who had converted. However, the fact that converts stand on an equal footing with native-born Israelites is stressed by the fact that they too are understood to have witnessed YHWH's revelation at Sinai.[71] A further example of the converts' being equated with native-born Israelites is the fact that the reference to the converts has been assimilated into the Israelite community in the daily prayers in a benediction which also mentions the righteous, the pious ones, the elders, the remnant of the scribes, and "us." [72]

Although gentiles are not *required* to separate the tithes from their crops grown in the Land of Israel, they may do so if they wish. Converts, on the other hand, are required to make these offerings.[73] Also, Israelites and converts, unlike gentiles, are obligated to separate the dough offering.[74] Therefore, if a gentile who had prepared dough converted before the dough had reached the stage where the dough offering had to be separated, she is obligated to make the offering. However, if the conversion occurred when the dough was not subject to the offering, the convert need not separate the offering. The point is that converts are obligated to make the dough offering in the same way that Israelites are required to do so, and this differentiates them from gentiles, who are not required to separate this offering.[75] Tosefta[76] contains a statement attributed to Judah which agrees with the anonymous comment in Mishnah that converts bring the first fruits but do not recite the Avowal.

The Torah[77] states that if an Israelite is unable to offer the Passover sacrifice at its proper time because he is on a long journey or has been rendered ritually unfit by corpse, he should bring the Passover sacrifice and eat it together with the bitter herbs and the unleavened bread at twilight on the fourteenth day of the second month. Rabbi states that if a gentile converted between the end of the regular Passover but before the alternate Passover, he should observe the second Passover because he was an Israelite at that time. Nathan responds that because the person was a gentile at the time of the regular Passover, and therefore not obligated to observe it, he need not observe the second Passover.[78] Both agree, however, that converts, like Israelites, must observe Passover. Eleazar b. Jacob reports that guards[79] and "watchers of hinges"[80] in Jerusalem were immersed and ate the Passover sacrifice on that very evening.[81] The general assumption is that these were Roman soldiers who converted to Judaism.[82]

If one who lives among gentiles converts and inadvertently violates the Sabbath, Aqiba states he is liable for punishment, while Monobases declares him exempt. For Aqiba, the convert is responsible for violating the Sabbath just like any other Israelite, even though he may not have the benefit of an Israelite environment. Monobases, on the other hand, believes that a convert who does not have the benefit of an Israelite environment is not liable. We know that this is the issue because, as the passage develops, it focuses on whether or not the convert had enough information to know that he was violating Israelite custom, and Monobases explicitly raises the possibility that the convert lacked adequate information. The example of the convert who lives among gentiles is used because such a person could be one who does not have adequate information at the time of his action, and this leads Aqiba and Monobases to discuss the liability of anyone who does not have sufficient information about proper Sabbath observance.[83] The passage, however, points to the fact that after conversion, converts had to learn the Israelite way of life, that this process could take some time, and that the environment in which one lived could affect the process.

Although the purity rules do not apply to gentiles,[84] they do apply to converts.[85] If an Israelite takes a vow not to benefit from Israelites, he may also not benefit from converts. But if he takes a vow not to benefit from converts, he may benefit from Israelites.[86] Similarly, with regard to kidnapping, the converts are equated with the native Israelites, for the phrase "one who steals a person from among his among his brothers, from the children of Israel" is taken to include converts.[87]

Some texts indicate that the rabbis assumed that gentiles who were planning to convert were extremely careful about their activities, so that they might be easily accepted into the Israelite community. Given the choice between marriage to a freed slave woman and marriage to a female convert, Israelites prefer the latter because it is assumed that the convert has guarded her chastity in preparing to convert. The slave woman, however, has been readily available to all who desired her because she did not have the power to protect herself even if she wished.[88] In fact, we assume that slaves are generally guilty of bad conduct, while converts are not. The basis of this assumption is an exegesis of Ps. 135:19–20 which mentions that Israelites, priests, Levites, and *you who fear YHWH*, converts, bless YHWH.[89] However, Judah required converted women to wait three months before they married.[90]

In some cases, converts are described as being stricter in their interpretation of Israelite law than were native-born Israelites. As we saw above, this was the case especially with Onqelos and the property he inherited from his gentile father. According to one tradition, Gamaliel and Onqelos were in Ashqelon, a gentile town,[91] when they both needed to undergo a ritual purification through immersion. Gamaliel immerses himself in an immersion pool, while Onqelos uses the sea. Kanter suggests that the difference in action reflects Gamaliel's lenient stand with regard to the permissibility of the gentiles' immersion pools, so that Onqelos appears to be the more restrictive, accepting the validity of only the Israelites' immersion pools. Joshua b. Qibusai states that he was with Gamaliel and Onqelos and that he saw that Gamaliel in fact immersed himself in the sea, so that Onqelos does not appear to apply a stricter standard to himself than does the Patriarch.[92] Onqelos's strictness is again illustrated by the fact that he ate all of his food in a state of purity required of the priests who would eat holy things, an extremely high degree of ritual cleanness.[93]

We also learn that both Israelites and converts may have gentile-sounding names.[94] Recognizing the fact that Israelites who live abroad may have gentile names, Tosefta states that writs of divorce which were executed outside of the Land of Israel are valid even if they contain gentile names. Similarly, we learn that converts may change their names to gentile-sounding names.[95] This points to the fact that people's names should not be an important factor in determining their status within the Israelite community. Thus, the converts are symbolically assimilated to native-born segments of the Israelite community.

Finally, if an Israelite observes a convert who wishes to study Torah, he may not remind him that his parents were not Israelites, but were among those who ate forbidden foods.[96]

Converts and Their Gentile Past

Some rabbis believed that gentiles were sexually promiscuous and un-inhibited,[97] and this played a role in some of the sages' teachings concerning converted women. For example, Ishmael b. Yohanan b. Beroqa reports a tradition[98] that a divorcee or widow must wait three months before she may be betrothed or remarried. Judah applies the rule to a convert, a captive, or a freed slave and specifies that this rule is employed in order to ascertain whether or not the woman was already pregnant. Yosi allows all women, except widows, to be betrothed immediately; however, they must wait three months before marriage.[99] The convert is included with the freed slave and redeemed captive because even though all three women have drastically changed their status, their previous sexual activity is undetermined, but still relevant. This implies that one cannot be certain about the sexual activity of gentile women,[100] even those who plan to convert.

Sexual intercourse between a gentile and an Israelite does not effect a marriage. Even if the gentile converted after the sexual encounter, the marriage is not valid. To validate the marriage, the two must execute a marriage contract after the gentile's conversion; however, the woman is treated as a nonvirgin.[101] This means that one would have to be able to distinguish between native-born Israelite women and converted women at the time of their marriage, so that the proper marriage contract could be executed. A gentile cannot contract a marriage with the stipulation that after he marries, he will convert, nor may an Israelite contract a marriage on the condition that after the marriage the woman will convert.[102] Thus the importance of conversion as a distinct act is maintained, and this view would discourage those who wished to convert only in order to marry.

Wine with which gentiles came into contact is forbidden to Israelites.[103] However, because some of the rabbis seemed to believe that under certain circumstances a prospective convert would take precautions concerning Israelite custom, there were those who permitted wine which converts brought with them upon their conversion. For example, if a convert brings wine with him when he converts and claims that the wine is fit for use, the anonymous ruling is that he alone may use it as long as he was the only one who had come into contact with it. However, if other gentiles had handled the wine, no one, not even the convert, may use it.[104] Aqiba demurs and states that if the wine is permitted to the convert, it should be permitted to any Israelite. The assumption of the anonymous opinion is that the convert was careful about the wine because he knew he was going to convert. Aqiba accepts this and reasons that the convert is a full Israelite; if he may use the wine, any other Israelite should also be able to make use of it.[105] Aqiba and the anonymous opinion also exhibit different views concerning the converts' place within the Israelite community. According to Aqiba, if the wine is considered fit for the convert, any Israelite should be able to use the wine because the same rules apply to the convert and to all other Israelites. The anonymous opinion, on the other hand, believes that in this instance the converts are a special case. The converts alone may use the wine, perhaps because there is some suspicion that as gentiles, they did not take sufficient care with the wine. Their assurances concerning the purity of the wine, therefore, should not be fully accepted. Although the converts are confident that the wine meets the Israelites' standards of purity, we should not expect other Israelites to take their word for it.[106]

In one *sugya*, the converts' gentile past is ignored. Yosi holds that if an Israelite borrowed money from a gentile who converted, the Israelite must pay interest on the loan if he were liable for it before the gentile's conversion.[107] In this case, the person's gentile background is ignored, but still the convert is treated differently from native-born Israelites, to whom interest would not have been paid.[108]

Converts from Biblical Nations

While some debated whether or not the converts were a specific clan, Judah reports that Aqiba rejected the whole concept. When Benjamin, an Egyptian convert who was married to an Egyptian convert, told Aqiba that he was marrying his son to an Egyptian convert so that his grandson could enter the Congregation of Israel according to the ruling in Deut. 23:7–8,[109] Aqiba responded that since the time of Sennacherib the peoples had intermarried, so that there were no longer any pure Egyptians, Moabites, or Ammonites. Therefore, the ruling in Deuteronomy no longer applied.[110] This parallels the dispute between Joshua and Gamaliel in Mishnah[111] concerning the Ammonites' and Moabites' ability "to enter the congregation."

Tosefta says a good deal about the bird offerings which converts were to bring upon their entrance into the Israelite community, while Mishnah says virtually nothing at all about this rite or the rest of the conversion ritual. Clearly Tosefta *presumes* that birds were offered, for it engages in at least a "second level" discussion of the category of sacrifices into which the birds fell, the reason for the use of birds, and the permissibility of using other animals. Similarly, Tosefta's discussion of the proselyte who was circumcised before his conversion points to the assumption that converts should be circumcised, a point not stressed in Mishnah. Both Tosefta and Mishnah refer to immersion; however, both texts connect it only with Passover, so that its importance with regard to conversion is open to some question. Should we argue that one or all of three elements were so well established that neither document had to discuss the need for their being performed? Or should we state that the ritual was still inchoate, so that those behind both texts did not yet view them as three elements of one ritual act? At this point, it seems that either is a possibility.

Tosefta states that a convert must follow the totality of the rabbinic Torah. However, failure to do so does not exclude one from the Israelite community. Tosefta also expresses concern for the quality of those who wish to join the People Israel. If there is reason to believe that prospective proselytes will not follow the Torah, they should not be admitted into the Israelite community. Clearly this presupposes some analysis of the future converts' personality; however, we are a long way from the rather detailed examination of the convert which will appear later in the Babylonian *gemara*. Perhaps related to this issue is the dispute between Aqiba and Monobases concerning the importance of the environment in which the convert lived, for it was from the surrounding Israelites that a convert would learn about Israelite customs and practices. This seems to assume that after conversion, the new member of the Israelite community had a good deal to learn. These issues are not covered in Mishnah, which contains no demand that the converts follow the whole Torah and does not suggest that some should be prohibited from entering the Israelite community.

Tosefta does not present a consistent view concerning what we may suppose about the character of those gentiles who might wish to convert. There were those who assumed that gentile women were sexually active, so that one had to be sure that they were not pregnant when they sought to convert. Elsewhere, however, we are told that those women who were planning to convert would guard their chastity, so that it was "safer" to marry a convert than to marry a freed slave woman. There were those who assumed that prospective converts would prepare their wines according to Israelite custom, so that it was permitted to them, and, in Aqiba's opinion even to other Israelites, after they entered into the Israelite community.

Although we cannot probe the sages' minds to discover exactly why they expounded their rulings, there are several *sugyot* whose purpose seems to be to prevent the converts from suffering any hardships after they became Israelites. Marriage agreements entered into when the persons were still gentiles remained in force if the husband and wife converted together. If a convert died, his wife still was entitled to everything permitted to her by her marriage agreement. Yosi holds that if an Israelite borrowed money from a gentile who converted, the former still had to pay the interest on the loan. Finally, wine which converts prepared while they were gentiles could be used after their conversion, at least by them, if they could guarantee that they were the only ones who had come into contact with it.

Like Mishnah, Tosefta views conversion as effecting a change in a person's status. This change is evidenced by the fact that the converts had severed all ties with their gentile relatives. This finds expression in several areas, the most common of which is in matters of inherited property. Because converts could have no relatives other than their Israelite spouses and offspring, it was quite possible that upon their death their property would become ownerless and available to anyone in the Israelite community. Thus, in both documents the dead convert's property forms the basis for discussions of the rules for acquiring ownerless property. Along these same lines, the laws of damages which require that a sum be paid to an injured party's heirs or spouse are also discussed with reference to the convert. Tosefta's discussion of *halisah* and the levirate marriage are also related to the fact that a convert's legitimate children are those conceived and born after the conversion.

Tosefta contains a much fuller discussion than Mishnah concerning those rituals a convert must follow. We saw above that the convert was responsible for fulfilling the entire rabbinic Torah. Tosefta specifically mentions that the converts must recite the grace after meals, must lay their hands on and wave sacrifices, must hear the *shofar* on Rosh HaShanah, and must listen to the reading of the *megillah* on Purim. Similarly, converts are obligated to observe Passover, although there is a dispute concerning their observance of the Second Passover. The different opinions depend upon the time of their conversion. We further learn that converts must separate the tithes from their crops and the dough offering from their rolled-out dough.

Finally, we are told that some converts were overly punctilious in their observance of Israelite ritual. Onqelos threw into the sea everything he inherited from his gentile father, even those items permitted to him under Israelite law. Additionally, he engaged in ritual baths in the sea, for he would not accept the validity of the gentiles' immersion pools, something which some claimed the Patriarch Gamaliel was willing to do.

In brief, Tosefta contains a much fuller exposition on the convert's ritual life than does Mishnah. The former text has a good deal to say about the conversion ritual, offering a detailed discussion of the converts' sacrifices as well as a statement concerning their need to be circumcised, along with those rituals for which the convert could be held responsible. Furthermore, some passages in Tosefta assume that the converts prepared themselves for conversion, and some pericopae suggest that perhaps the Israelites had to ensure the converts that they would not suffer a loss by entering the Israelite community. On the other hand, those who were suspected of being unable to follow the rigors of the Israelite way of life should be prohibited from entering the community in the first place. Also, while some passages in both Tosefta and Mishnah considered the convert not to be a full Israelite, that view is more strongly expressed in Mishnah, which has a good deal to say about the permissibility of a converted woman's marrying into the priestly caste. Tosefta knows this issue and also claims that the converts formed a separate "nation" or "community"; however, it does not focus on this issue as much as does Mishnah. Thus, it seems that Tosefta is much more willing to accept converts as full members of the Israelite community. Perhaps, this is because it believes that only those who have prepared themselves and were fully cognizant of the rigors of the Israelite way of life would seek to become members of the People Israel. This is strikingly different from Mishnah's discussions.

Because the Amoraim used the Mishnah as the basis for their discussions, they may have considered the Mishnah to be the "official" document of Judah the Patriarch's bureaucracy and Tosefta as an "unofficial" collection. If we accept this implied claim, we discover a marked difference between the "official" and the "unofficial" view of the convert. The "official view" does not consider the conversion ritual, the converts' adherence to the two Torahs, or the converts' preparing themselves for entrance into the Israelite community as worthy of discussion. Exactly why this is the case is unclear. It may result from the fact that conversion was not a common phenomenon, so that it commanded little attention. Or, it may reflect a situation in which conversion was so common that the Jewish "government" considered all of the questions to be settled. Because the later documents exhibit a good deal of disagreement concerning these matters, I suspect that conversion was not a common phenomenon. It appears that Mishnah's lack of concern with the conversion ritual and with the insistence that converts accept the Oral as well as the Written Torah results from the fact that the rituals connected with conversion and the practices of the converts were simply not a burning issue to Mishnah's authors. It may be that conversion was a rather ad hoc phenomenon which was not all that common, and Mishnah's authors were willing to accept a good deal of flexibility in the matters related to conversion. Mishnah's uncertainty concerning whether or not converts were equal to native-born Israelites may result from the fact that the sages simply had not worked this out yet. Mishnah's inconsistencies remain in the subsequent documents partially because their authors also were unsure about the converts' status and partially because Mishnah sets the agenda for the ensuing treatment of the converts.

The "unofficial" view, however, is much more concerned with presenting specifics concerning the conversion ritual and with providing the theoretical basis for exactly what was expected from converts: Like Israelites, converts had to accept both Torahs. And, if the prospective converts could not be trusted to adhere to the totality of rabbinic *halakhah*, they should not be allowed to enter the Israelite community. Also, for many of Tosefta's sages, conversion was not an ad hoc decision, but one for which the gentiles had prepared themselves for some period of time. Therefore, the gentile past of the converts could at times be ignored, a view not found in Mishnah. Also, because converts were expected to adhere to the entirety of rabbinic practice, conversion should be uniform and the treatment of the convert should be consistent. Thus, Mishnah and Tosefta appear to reflect two different conceptions of the converts.

▨ FOUR ▨

Converts and Conversion in the Early Midrashic Texts

▨

Although drawing on biblical ideas and concepts, Mishnah and Tosefta essentially present their teachings independent of Scripture. In these collections, we encounter relatively few citations of biblical texts, and their principles of organization differ from the sequence of topics as they appear in the Torah. Furthermore, the agenda of Mishnah and Tosefta are their own; they do not merely repeat the Bible's itinerary. Speaking of Mishnah, Neusner writes:

> framers of ideas ultimately to be located in the Mishnaic system drew heavily and informedly upon what they found in the Scriptures. But they drew upon materials they found relevant to concerns already defined, framed essentially independent of issues and themes paramount in Scripture itself. . . . [O]nce people had chosen a subject, they knew full well how to develop their ideas about that subject by examining and reflecting upon relevant verses of Scripture. But what dictated the choice of subject awaiting amplification and expansion was hardly a necessary or ineluctable demand of Scripture. . . . Thus, a relationship of ambiguity—freedom of choice of topic, on the one hand, disciplined liberalism in working out what is to be said about a stated topic, on the other—characterizes the final product of the long period of interplay between Scripture and the philosophers of the Mishnah. . . . What the philosophers of the Mishnah's ultimate system will say about any topic is, if not predictable, at least highly probable, upon the basis of what Scripture says about that same topic. But what topics the philosophers of the end product will choose for their reflection is not to be foretold on the basis of a mere reading of Scripture."[1]

Neusner's description of the relationship between Mishnah and the Bible can be applied equally well to the association of Tosefta's teaching to Scripture's content.

The *midrashim* are essentially different from Mishnah and Tosefta in

51

this regard.[2] Sifra, Mekhilta, Sifré Numbers and Sifré Deuteronomy are
running commentaries on Leviticus, Exodus, Numbers, and Deuteronomy, respectively.[3] While these documents often contain teachings parallel
to those in Mishnah and Tosefta, at times taking *sugyot* from those documents and juxtaposing them with appropriate biblical passages, they are
organized according to the Bible's sequence of verses, and the items covered in each midrashic collection are closely related to the content of the
biblical book which it interprets. For this reason, the *midrashim* do not all
contain the same material even when treating a common general subject
or presenting the words of the same sage.[4] When the several midrashic
collections contain the same teachings, often they juxtapose them to different biblical texts because each document seeks to formulate its pericopae around the book of the Torah it is exegeting. For these reasons, each
midrashic collection stands as an autonomous document, exhibiting its
own characteristics.[5] Therefore, below we shall treat each midrashic collection separately.

It is difficult to assign exact dates to the early *midrashim*—Sifra,
Mekhilta, Sifré Numbers, and Sifré Deuteronomy.[6] However, it is generally believed that they come from the second half of the third century of
the common era. Much of Sifra's style and content reflect material we now
find in Mishnah. Neusner has argued that "Sifra . . . [is] a massive, integrated, and coherent critique of *Mishnah*, insisting that *Mishnah*'s laws are
true only because *Mishnah*'s laws derive from the written Torah."[7] This
suggests that Sifra was edited shortly after Mishnah or coterminus with
Mishnah's compilation. In terms of style and agenda, Sifré Numbers
seems to date perhaps a little later than Mishnah, and Stemberger would
place it after the middle of the third century.[8] The exact date of Mekhilta
Ishmael is a matter of debate and some uncertainty;[9] however, a date in
the second half of the third century seems plausible.[10] Sifré Deuteronomy
is a complex document; it is not a homogeneous work. However, a date in
the late third century seems appropriate for this text.[11]

In general, the discussions of the convert found in these documents
are connected to the appearance of a form of the Hebrew root *gwr* in the
Torah. Morton Smith argued that *ger* originally meant "resident alien, a
meaning it never lost [in the Bible]." The aliens were an important segment of the poor with whom the deuteronomic code is concerned; however, the authors of the code "did not . . . subject them to the laws it made
for Israelites." It was not until the later period, in which the holiness code
was created, that the concern was to "protect the people from contact with
unclean things," so that the *ger* was made subject to the same civil laws as
Israelites and that the latter were urged to treat the former as if they were

native-born. However, the *ger* was not granted the "religious privileges of the law," or considered a "fellow Israelite." Neither Ezra nor Nehemiah believed that non-Israelites, even those married to Israelites, could become proselytes. However, on the basis of selected passages from Numbers—such as 19:10 and 35:15—along with Joshua 20:9 and Deut. 29, "the *gerim* are included as part of 'the people,' in Israel's covenant with Yahweh." Smith sees this as a result of the "assimilationist priesthood['s] attempt to settle by compromise the problem of mixed marriages: the separatists' concern for purity and observance of the law would be satisfied, but the marriages could be tolerated."[12] In virtually all instances found in the *midrashim* and the other rabbinic documents, the biblical *ger* has been transformed into the rabbinic convert.

SIFRA

Converts as Radically New People

Sifra is an early collection of exegetical comments on Leviticus, so that its discussions of the convert are largely determined by Leviticus' agenda. One of the major topics of the third book of the Torah is the sacrificial cult, and a large part of Sifra's treatment of the converts centers around the sacrificial ritual. In general terms, the sacrificial cult provided a visible means of separating gentiles from Israelites. According to Mishnah and Tosefta, gentiles could bring only free will offerings and vow offerings to the Temple in Jerusalem. And when gentiles presented offerings to YHWH, they did so in ways different from Israelites. They could not wave offerings before YHWH, nor could they lay their hands on their offerings. Furthermore, they occupied their own space in relation to the altar.[13] Converts, on the other hand, participated in the cult, for the most part, like native-born Israelites.

Converts may bring burnt offerings to YHWH, and like Israelites, they bring them only to the Temple. Similarly, like Israelites, converts are prohibited from eating the blood of the sacrificial animals or from animals captured in a hunt.[14] Furthermore, the rulings with which Leviticus opens are applicable to converts as well as to native-born Israelites.[15] Converts may bring offerings of well-being, *zbḥ šlmym*,[16] and they are included in the Torah's discussion of the vow offering.[17] In Tosefta we saw that a convert may lay his hands on his offerings, and Sifra implies that each person must lay hands on only his own offering.[18] Although gentiles do not bring sin offerings,[19] converts and slaves may make them if they commit an unintentional sin.[20] Additionally, the rules concerning the slaughtering of the guilt offering apply to Israelites, converts, women, and slaves.[21]

In a passage which discusses the theoretical issue of what happened on the high places, we learn that converts, women, and slaves may sprinkle the blood of their offerings at such sites, in agreement with Tosefta.[22] Furthermore, converts, along with Israelites, women, slaves, and converts' wives are warned that they should bring their burnt offerings only to the entrance of the Tent of Meeting.[23] These matters, which had no relevance at the time that the rabbis discussed them, appear because they are dealt with in Leviticus. These rulings fine tune the laws of the converts' relationship to the sacrificial ritual. By the time Sifra was edited, the Temple had lain in ruins for almost two hundred years, so that these are probably theoretical discussions meant to demonstrate that converts were not exactly equal to native-born Israelites. While in the main converts and Israelites were treated the same with regard to the Temple's sacrifices, as we shall see below, an examination of the details of the ritual indicates they were not always fully the same.

Within the Temple's precincts, converts were treated for the most part as if they were native-born Israelites. They could bring the full range of offerings and could place their hands on their offerings. This was not the case with gentiles whose activity around the Temple was severely limited. Similarly, the gentiles could not pay the half-*sheqel* tax to support the Temple,[24] and the rules concerning a gentile's ability to dedicate his valuation to the Temple were different from those which applied to Israelites.[25] However, Sifra maintains that the process of valuation for converts is the same as that for native-born Israelites, so that converts are similar to Israelites and different from gentiles.[26]

Purity is also a major concern for the authors of Leviticus, as it is for the rabbis.[27] In general, the non-Israelites stand outside the rabbis' system of purities.[28] The signs which the rabbis considered as signifying impurity do not render gentiles unclean, and gentiles do not transmit uncleanness in the same ways that Israelites do. The converts, however, are affected by the rabbis' system, for here they are closer to Israelites than to gentiles. Non-Israelites do not render unclean by means of genital emission; however, they are treated as if they do.[29] On the other hand, Israelites, along with converts and slaves, do render unclean by a genital emission.[30] A female convert, a handmaiden, a freed slave, and an Israelite woman are rendered unclean by a flow of vaginal blood.[31] A female convert, like a native-born Israelite woman, experiences a prescribed period of uncleanness after giving birth.[32]

Gentiles are not responsible for observing the Israelite periods of sacred time. The holiness of these periods requires only that Israelites alter their activity. Gentiles are not expected to alter their normal activity unless they come into contact with Israelites whose actions force the non-Israelites to change their usual practices.[33] Israelites, converts, and slaves, but not gentiles, observe "the sacred occasion," Rosh HaShanah, on the first day of the seventh month.[34] Similarly, converts are required to practice self-denial, interpreted to mean fasting, and abstain from work on the Day of Atonement.[35] While gentiles would not have to dwell in booths during Sukkot, male converts and freed slaves are obligated to dwell in them.[36] Thus, with regard to the Israelite holidays, converts are considered to be like Israelites, not like gentiles.

We have noted above that in general gentiles do not have to separate the agricultural gifts which are given to the Israelite poor, for these gifts were seen as a means of building group solidarity among the Israelites.[37] Gentiles are not obligated to leave the gleanings, the corners, or the forgotten sheaves when they harvest their crops in the Land of Israel. If a gentile farmer converted after he harvested his field, he is still not obligated for these offerings, because he was not an Israelite when they would have been separated. Judah, however, claims that because an Israelite becomes liable for giving the forgotten sheaf to the poor when he binds the sheaves, not when he harvests the grain, the convert is liable for this gift if he converted after the harvest, but before he bound the sheaves. This parallels the discussion in Mishnah.[38] A portion of the Israelite agricultural laws deals with leaving produce for the poor, and the grapes which are left in the vineyard after harvest are to be given to the poor Israelite and the poor among the converts.[39]

As we saw in Mishnah and Tosefta, when converts enter the Israelite community, they achieve a new status. Tosefta expressed the expectation that converts should adhere to the full range of Israelite customs, laws, and practices. Sifra cites Tosefta and agrees with the view that converts must accept the whole Torah or they should not be accepted into the Israelite community.[40] Like native-born Israelites, converts who blaspheme YHWH's name should be executed.[41] Converts, like Israelites, are prohibited from offering their children to Molech.[42] Furthermore, the sexual prohibitions found in Lev. 18 apply to converts as well as to native-born Israelites.[43] Finally, Aaron's or the priest's sprinkling the blood of the sacrifice on the altar brings atonement for the guilt incurred by men, women, converts, and slaves.[44]

Israelites are liable for supporting fellow Israelites, even four or five different times, as long as their aid does not lead the needy to become overly dependent, so that they are discouraged from developing the skills needed to support themselves. However, one cannot make any profit from this help, for one cannot charge interest on a loan, or benefit from a gift one gives to another Israelite.[45] This applies also to the converts whom one is obligated to support. The biblical verse mentions the *gr twšb*, and the midrash exegetes both elements of the term: The *gr* is the righteous convert, *gr ṣdq*, and the *twšb* is the *gr twšb* who eats unfit meat, *nbylh*.[46]

Because converts are to be viewed as totally new human beings, Israelites are admonished not to remind the proselytes that their parents were once idolaters.[47] Also, Israelites are commanded to love the converts as they love one another.[48] This is a new point, hardly mentioned in Mishnah or Tosefta.

We learn that the rules concerning the purity of the skin which has been burned[49] apply to gentiles after they convert and even before they convert. This last ruling is curious, for the Israelite purity rules normally do not apply to gentiles. In fact, the inclusion of the gentiles before they convert may be a result of the style of the *sugya*, which deals with the application of the rules of the biblical passages to opposing cases: Before and after revelation, before and after conversion, and a child before and after it is born.[50] Because the Israelite purity laws do not apply to gentiles, spots on gentiles are clean, even after they have converted,[51] and a boil which appears on gentiles before they converted is clean after they converted.[52] The point of both rulings is that the laws of purity do not apply to gentiles, so that if they had the signs of impurity when they converted, they are considered clean. If they are examined anew after they have achieved the status of an Israelite and then are declared unclean, they are unclean. If converts or native-born Israelites eat an animal which has died or been torn apart by another animal, they must wash their clothes, bathe, and wait for sundown in order to be considered clean.[53]

Yosi the Galilean claims that converts are culpable for death only if they curse their mother, but not if they curse their father. Aqiba responds that those who are culpable for cursing their father are also culpable for cursing their mother, so that converts, like Israelites, must not curse either parent.[54]

Differences between Converts and Native-Born Israelites

In Mishnah we saw that one indication of the difference between the converts and the native-born Israelites was centered around the permissibility of marrying into the priestly caste. This issue also appears in Sifra. On the basis of Lev. 21:15,[55] Sifra prohibits a priest from marrying the daughter of an impaired priest (*hll*), and it quotes Judah's statement from Mishnah[56] which states that the daughter of a male convert is the same as the daughter of an impaired priest. Thus, at least in Judah's opinion, a convert's daughter is not equal to the children of the union of two native-born Israelites.[57] Elsewhere Sifra makes the point that converts cannot be priests.[58] Even though Sifra draws several parallels between the offerings brought by native-born Israelites and those brought by converts, the text does recognize some differences between the two groups. The skin of an Israelite's offering is given to the priests, and some held that this was also true of a skin of a convert's offering. However, Yosi b. Judah believed that a priest could not receive the skin of a convert's offering. Although the reason behind Yosi's teaching is unclear, he seems to base it on the repetition of *burnt offering* in Lev. 7:8.[59] Similarly, while Aaron and his sons may eat the residue of the Israelites' meal offerings, they may not consume the residue of a meal offering brought by converts, women, or slaves. This teaching is derived from juxtaposing Lev. 2:3 with Num. 15:13. The latter verse specifically refers to the native-born, *'zrḥ*.[60]

One accepts a person's claim that he or she is a convert only if he or she is well known to the Israelite. If the Israelite is unfamiliar with the person, the latter is required to bring witnesses who can testify to the fact that the person was properly converted.[61]

Converts as a subclass of People Israel

Converts, like *mamzerim* and *netinim* cannot serve in the court system.[62] Also, sages interpret the reference to prostitute in Lev. 21:7 as referring to a converted woman or a freed slave, so that this is used to explain why priests cannot marry women who are converts.[63] This points to the gentile background of the converts, for many sages considered the gentiles to be sexually uninhibited.[64]

MEKHILTA DERABBI ISHMAEL

Converts as Radically New People

Mekhilta deRabbi Ishmael is organized around the biblical book of Exodus, specifically, Ex. 12–23:19, 31:12–17, and 35:1–3, so that its agenda is shaped primarily by the contents of the Torah's second book. Mekhilta opens with the discussion of Passover, and the midrash seeks to explain how converts and Israelites are equal with regard to this holiday.[65] For example, converts, like native-born Israelites, celebrate Passover on the fourteenth of Nisan, and not immediately after their conversion.[66] Simeon b. Eleazar teaches that if a person converted after the twenty-first of

Nisan, the first month, but before the fourteen of Iyyar, the second month, he is not obligated to keep the alternate Passover.[67] Simeon basis his argument on the fact that the convert and the native-born Israelite should be treated in the same way: Only those who were obligated to observe Passover in the first month but failed to do so are obligated to observe it in the second month.[68] The Torah states that the stranger who wishes to observe Passover must be circumcised,[69] and Mekhilta argues that not only must converts be circumcised before they may eat the Passover sacrifice, but also, they are like Israelites with regard to all of the commandments in the Torah.[70] Mekhilta establishes the fact that converts who become slaves are freed after six years of service, the same as Israelites who are slaves.[71] Furthermore, converts are equated with Israelites concerning the damages they may claim if they are injured by an ox.[72]

Once people have converted, Israelites must not throw up their past in their faces. Israelites are not to remind converts that they used to worship idols or to eat prohibited foods. One should not say to converts that yesterday they were idolaters but today they are worshipers of YHWH.[73] An anonymous comment employs Ex. 23:9,[74] 22:20, and Deut. 10:19[75] as proof that God loves converts, for in these three verses he admonishes the Israelites to love and respect them. Simeon b. Yohai argues that the converts are more precious to YHWH than are Israelites, for those whom the king loves are greater than those who love the king. Furthermore, we learn that converts are beloved by YHWH because the Bible often applies the same terms to them as to Israelites: Israelites[76] and converts[77] are called servants, ministers,[78] and friends.[79] Also, a covenant is connected to both the converts and Israel,[80] acceptance is used with regard to both groups,[81] and guarding is used with reference to Israelites and converts.[82] In addition Abraham[83] and David called themselves converts.[84] Furthermore, we learn how important conversion is from the fact that Abraham was not circumcised until he was ninety-nine, so that people could convert and be circumcised until the age of ninety-nine. Moreover, the reference to those who *shall use the name of Jacob* in Isa. 44:5 refers to the converts.[85] We see here that converts are an important segment of the People Israel, hardly distinguishable from the native-born members of the community.

Differences between Converts and Native-Born Israelites

While the convert and the Israelite are treated as equals in many instances, in some cases the difference between the two groups is still maintained. Mekhilta first argues that the convert is not required to bring the *choice fruits of your soil* to the Temple. The converts are exclude because, in line with Mishnah's ruling, they may not recite the required biblical verse when they offer the fruit. The passage ends, however, by stating that they may bring the fruits without reciting the verse.[86] The converts are distinguished from the native-born Israelites, for only the latter may claim that YHWH was the deity of their ancestors.

Although we have seen that some believed converts were an honored segment of the People Israel, others expressed negative views about them. Eliezer stated that the reason the Torah contains so many admonitions to love the converts is because converts have a bad streak in them, implying that they are difficult to love.[87] Eliezer's less than enthusiastic opinion of converts is also evident in his interpretation of Ex. 23:4 which instructs an Israelite to return the ox of his enemy which he might find wandering on the road. Eliezer claims that "enemy" refers to a convert who returned to his gentile background.[88] In contrast, Isaac suggests that the term refers to an apostate Israelite.

Converts from Biblical Nations

Theoretically, all who wish to enter the Israelite community should be allowed to do so, and one passage explains that the Torah was given in the desert, and not within the borders of a particular land, so that anyone who wished to accept it might do so.[89] However, Eliezer teaches that God swore, "by his holy throne," that the Amalekites could not convert. In support of his position, Eliezer recounts a story of David's encountering one who was a descendant of Amalek the *gr.*[90] David remembered Moses' injunction that no Amalekite should be allowed to convert, and he placed a curse upon the young man.[91] Above we saw that Mishnah[92] and Tosefta[93] discussed the possibility of the Egyptians', Ammonites', and Edomites' entrance into the Israelite community. In those collections some of the sages claimed that because the biblical peoples had intermarried, there were no longer Egyptians, Ammonites, or Edomites to whom the biblical injunctions could be applied. We do not find a similar statement in this context, because the Amalekites had come to represent all of Israel's enemies.[94]

Discussions of Specific Converts

Mekhilta has a good deal to say about Jethro, whom it takes as a paradigmatic convert,[95] and Rahab the harlot, who is also believed to have converted. Eliezer teaches that YHWH told Moses that when a prospective convert approaches and wishes to convert for the sake of Heaven, Moses, and by implication all rabbis, should encourage the person, just as YHWH encouraged Jethro.[96] Jethro's conversion to Judaism was so complete that he was willing to bring others to his new faith. After advising

Moses to establish an advisory counsel, Jethro indicated that he would do more good if he left Moses and the Israelites and returned to his own people and proselytized among them, "leading them to the study of Torah and bringing them under the wings of the *shekhinah.*" The interesting point about this story is that it is Jethro, not a native-born Israelite, who undertakes the conversion of a large number of people.[97] Furthermore, the various names by which Jethro is known are interpreted in terms of his relationship to YHWH and also point to his noble character as a convert.[98] Similarly, Mekhilta claims that Rahab, the harlot who helped the spies whom Joshua sent to Jericho, eventually converted.[99] According to Mekhilta, Rahab was ten years old at the time of the Exodus. During the forty years that the Israelites wandered between Egypt and the Land of Israel, Rahab was a harlot. At the end of her fiftieth year, she converted to Judaism.[100] Rahab's conversion points to the fact that all people, even harlots, may enter the Israelite community at any stage during their lives.

These passages from Mekhilta point to the wide divergence of opinions attributed to the rabbis concerning the converts. On the one hand, some of the sages considered the converts to be as precious to YHWH as the native-born Israelites. On the other hand, some sages believed that the converts were essentially inferior to the native-born members of the community. From the point of view of the entire rabbinic tradition, this diversity points to the ambiguous role which the converts played in the mythic structure of the People Israel. The converts' precarious position within the Israelite community is typical of marginal people, as we shall see below.[101]

SIFRÉ NUMBERS

Ritual of Conversion

Sifré Numbers is the first text we have examined in which the three standard elements of the conversion ritual are unambiguously mentioned. They appear in the context of a discussion of the sacrifices' blood which was sprinkled on the altar. One opinion holds that both Israelites and converts make offerings involving the blood rite. However, this is challenged on the basis of the phrase *for you* in Num. 15:14, which is interpreted to mean that Israelites, but not converts, perform sacrifices with animals which include the sprinkling of the blood.[102] Rabbi states that the phrase *for you* should be taken in another sense: Just as the Israelites entered the covenant through circumcision,[103] immersion, and an offering,[104] so too converts should enter into the obligations of the covenant in the same way. Rabbi's statement is the only one we have seen so far which indicates that the converts should undergo rituals of circumcision and immersion and that they should bring an offering.[105]

Motives for Conversion

In a story which makes the point that anyone may become a worthy convert to Judaism, we also see some discussion of why a gentile decided to convert. Num. 15:37–41 deal with the commandment that Israelites must wear fringes on the corner of their garments to remind them of all the commandments which they are supposed to do to fulfill their obligation to be holy as YHWH is holy. The midrash contains an elaborate story in which a student refuses to have sex with the most desirable prostitute in the world because when the two prepared for sex, the man's fringes "fell out and appeared to him like four witnesses." The whore was so impressed by the man's actions, that she gave away one-third of her wealth to the government and one-third to the poor. She took the remaining third with her and stood before the school of R. Hiyya, the man's teacher. After talking with the woman, Hiyya commented that the woman would now use the possessions she had employed for prohibited sexual activity for permitted sexual acts with her husband. The story makes many important points, which are irrelevant to our study. However, the woman's activities are important for us. The story implies that the woman converted because she realized the power of the man's convictions. He had given up having sex with the most desirable woman in the world because of his belief in the fact that YHWH rewards those who obeyed him and punished those who defied him. Furthermore, Hiyya implies that conversion for the purpose of marriage was not unheard of in his day; however, he seems to disapprove of the act. Presumably, Hiyya believed that the woman wished to marry the man because of his righteousness and his principles, and this is acceptable to Hiyya. Furthermore, the woman has established her own righteousness by distributing two-thirds of her money. She has kept one-third for herself only as a means of rewarding her future husband. The final point of the story is that any person, from any station, may become worthy enough to convert to Judaism.[106]

Converts as Radically New People

In several places, Sifré Numbers points to the fact that converts and native-born Israelites have the same obligations with regard to the sacrificial cult; however, the Torah must specifically mention the converts, the implication being that one would not automatically include them among the Israelites. Converts and Israelites perform the same rites with regard to an offering by fire. In fact, Sifré Numbers makes the point that proselytes and native-born Israelites are equal with regard to all the laws which are mentioned in the Torah.[107] Furthermore, because one law applies to both groups, they bring exactly the same number of drink offerings for each sacrifice.[108] Similarly, converts may participate in the community offering which was brought if the community committed an unwitting sin.[109] If a convert offers the Passover sacrifice, he should follow the same laws as the native-born Israelite.[110] And, the rules applicable to the one who gathered the heifer's ashes are followed by a convert as well as by a native-born Israelite.[111]

The equality of the Israelites and the converts is also seen in the fact that Aaron recited the priestly blessing over the converts as well as over the native-born Israelites.[112] Similarly, the pure gold frontlet which the High Priest wears makes the converts acceptable to YHWH in the same way that it makes the native-born Israelites acceptable to him.[113]

Differences between Converts and Native-Born Israelites

As part of its discussion of the conversion ritual, the midrash asks if converts are subject to the rite of the blood offering and the peace offering in the same way as Israelites.[114] The midrash argues that the offering by fire to which Num. 15:14 refers must be an offering which is totally consumed by fire, so that none of it may be used by the individual making the offering. The text concludes that only bird offerings meet this requirement, for the whole bird, not just some of its parts, must be sacrificed to YHWH. Therefore, while the converts and Israelites both must bring offerings, they bring different offerings. The Israelites may offer cattle or oxen, but the converts bring birds, and their bird offerings are classified differently from those which native-born Israelites bring.[115] Furthermore, only the Israelite may participate in the blood rite. However, although Israelites and converts bring different offerings, they bring the same drink offerings with their sacrifices.[116] Thus, Israelites and converts are similar, but not exactly the same, with regard to the sacrificial cult, at least with regard to the blood rite and with regard to the manner in which their bird offerings are classified.

Although with regard to the sacrificial rituals converts and Israelites are sometimes similar and at other times dissimilar, their differences are clear-cut with respect to the Land of Israel. The Land was promised to the Israelites, so that the converts may not receive a portion of it.[117] When Ezekiel stated that the land should be allotted to the *strangers who reside among you*,[118] he meant that although the converts could not possess a por-

tion of the Land of Israel, they could receive atonement through it. Therefore, a convert who resides among the tribe of Judah in their portion of
the Land receives atonement when the members of the tribe receive
atonement. Some disagreed with this interpretation and suggested that
Ezekiel believed that the converts may be buried in a parcel of the Land
of Israel, even though they could not possess a portion of the Land as an
inheritance.[119] Elsewhere, Sifré Numbers states that it might be possible
to conclude that converts, along with priests, Levites, Israelites, women,
slaves, those of doubtful gender, and androgynous beings could be included among those who were assigned a portion in the Land of Israel.
However, others hold that converts are excluded by the phrase *according
to the names of the tribes of their father they shall inherit.*[120] Because the parents
of the converts were not Israelites, they cannot be included among those
to whom the land was apportioned according to the ancestral tribes.[121]
In this regard converts are more similar to gentiles than they are to Israelites.[122]

The fact that Israelites and converts were different also appears in the
context of Sifré Numbers' treatment of the cities of refuge, Num. 35:9ff.
Num. 35:10 commands Moses to speak to the children of Israel, and the
reference to the *gr* in Num. 35:15 means that he spoke also to the converts.
One could reason that just as a convert is banished for killing an Israelite,
so also an Israelite is banished for killing a convert. But, the ruling is that
when an Israelite kills a convert he is exempt from banishment. This becomes an *a fortiori* argument, for they are not banished unless they kill an
Israelite. The text is awkward, and later commentators have "corrected"
it to refer to a resident alien, who did not convert to Judaism, so that there
would be no distinction between the Israelite and the convert.[123] Num.
35:22–24 detail the case of one who inadvertently kills another and is
therefore qualified to be sent to one of the cities of refuge. The midrash
states that the phrase *in accordance to these ordinances* indicates that the converts are included in these rules.[124] There seems to have been those who
believed that Israelites and converts were so different that the rules applied when one killed an Israelite did not necessarily apply when one
killed a convert. Another indication of the difference between Israelites
and converts is the appearance of Aqabyya's claim that the waters of bitterness are not given to a convert's wife.[125]

Converts and Their Heirs

Upon their entrance into the Israelite community, the converts severed all ties with their gentile relatives. An anonymous passage in Mishnah[126] indicated that if an Israelite steals from a convert and swears falsely

to him, and the latter dies, the thief must make restitution to the priest, for the convert is the only member of the People Israel who does not have a kinsman.[127] In one passage in Sifré Numbers the statement is attributed to Ishmael.[128] The phrase *and that person is guilty* in Num. 5:6 teaches that if the person who stole the object had a change of heart but died before he could return the value of what he had stolen or could bring the guilt offering, his heirs do not need to bring it, for he alone is described as the guilty party. However, the heirs do have to make restitution for what was stolen, for the verse ends *and giving it to him whom he wronged.*[129] This discussion of the one who stole from a convert is also related to Num. 18:9, *which they shall return to me.*[130]

Discussions of Specific Converts

Sifré Numbers' ambivalent attitude toward the convert is seen in its discussion of Jethro, whom it sees as a paradigmatic convert, viewing him both in a negative and a positive manner. This corresponds to the ambiguous view our sources hold with regard to converts. The fact that converts do not receive a portion of the Land of Israel is dealt with in the context of Jethro's actions. Moses' attempt to keep Jethro with him and the Israelites[131] is explained as being important for those who might wish to convert to Judaism. If Jethro were to leave the Israelites, the latter would claim that he wished to join the People Israel only in order to receive part of the Land of Israel. They would claim that when he realized that this were not the case, he decided to leave, so that his conversion was not out of love of YHWH, but for material gain. Furthermore, his leaving would decrease YHWH's glory because in reality, he would not be able to convert many people in his own land, given the fact that he deserted Moses and the Israelites. Furthermore, if he were to leave, future generations would state that if Moses could not convert Jethro, why would anyone else wish to join Moses' people? Still another explanation is that Jethro had decided to convert to Judaism because he believed that he would receive many gifts as a consequence of this act. However, when he realized that he would receive only a few gifts, he decided to leave the Israelites and to return to his own land.[132] At this point, the midrash paints a rather unflattering picture of Jethro and imputes to him base motives for seeking to join the People Israel.

On the other hand, Jethro is also viewed in a positive light. The reference to Jethro's becoming "the people's eyes" means the he is as precious to the Israelites as their eyes. For this reason, the Israelites are commanded to love the converts[133] and not to oppress[134] nor wrong them.[135]

Sifré Numbers also contains the discussion of Jethro's various biblical names, and these statements testify to the positive nature of Jethro's character.[136] The midrash further claims that Jethro's descendants are the same as the descendants of Jonadab the son of Rechab, for IChron. 2:55 states that the Kenites, from whom Jethro had come, were connected by marriage to the ancestors of the Rechabites. A problem arises from the fact that Jeremiah reports that YHWH told the Rechabites that because Jonadab had done everything that YHWH had asked of him, he would always have a descendant who would stand before YHWH, which is taken to mean that a descendent of a convert would be able to enter the Holy of Holies, for only there could one actually stand before the presence of YHWH. Joshua objects: If normal Israelites cannot enter the Holy of Holies, how can one claim that converts can enter into the most holy place in the Temple? Joshua concludes that the text means that Jonadab's descendants would become members of the Sanhedrin who would teach Torah and thus symbolically sit in the presence of YHWH. The important point here is that Joshua was willing to let converts become members of the Sanhedrin. Others interpret the verse to mean that Jonadab's female descendants would marry into the priestly clan.[137] Similarly, as Mekhilta had described Rahab as a convert, so Sifré Numbers contains a statement by Eliezer who claims that eight priests and eight prophets descended from Rahab the whore.[138] These passages make no distinction between the rewards and privileges granted to Rahab and Jethro and to native-born Israelites.

The ambiguous picture of the convert, which is reflected in the complex discussions of Jethro, appears elsewhere in this midrashic collection. One tradition places the converts in the outlying parts of the Israelite camp during the exodus from Egypt.[139] And another passage explains that *the rabble* (*h'spsp*) who caused Israel to sin were the converts who were gathered (*hm'wspyn*) from every place.[140] On the other hand, Simeon b. Yohai held that a female convert who converted at an age of less than three years one day is considered to be sexually pure, so that she may marry into the priestly clan.[141]

Sifré Numbers has brought before us some interesting new information. It is the earliest text which contains the three elements of the conversion ritual which are going to be seen as standard in latter documents, and it is also the first text which contains clear speculations concerning the possible motives behind a gentile's decision to join the People Israel. Finally, it contains the clearest picture we have seen so far of the ambiguous place the convert occupied in the minds of the rabbinic class.

▨

SIFRÉ DEUTERONOMY

Motives for Conversion

Sifré Deuteronomy is generally favorably disposed toward converts and encourages Israelites to follow Abraham's lead in making converts. Abraham sought out converts because he loved YHWH; therefore, all Israelites should seek converts, for this demonstrates their love for YHWH.[142] Seeking converts is not difficult, for when the gentiles come to do business in the Land of Israel, they will become so impressed with the ways the Israelites worship their god and their distinctive rituals that they will want to join in the worship of YHWH.[143] Also, Israelites are admonished to treat converts fairly and justly.[144]

A story is told that the Roman government[145] sent two soldiers with instructions to become Jews[146] and investigate the nature of Jewish law.[147] They studied Bible, Mishnah, Midrash Halakhah, and Midrash Aggadah with Gamaliel at Usha. After completing their study, they informed Gamaliel that the only thing they found objectionable in the whole of Jewish law was the opinion that something stolen from a gentile is permitted to Israelites, but something stolen from another Israelite is prohibited. However, they promised Gamaliel that they would not inform the government about this ruling.[148] The story implies that non-Israelites who studied the Israelite's holy books would be impressed by their contents. They would discover that in general they showed respect for all people. Even though they might find minor elements within these corpora which were incomprehensible or even slightly offensive, they would still respect Israelite culture and religion.

Converts as Radically New People

The Israelite community is responsible for supporting the poor among the converts, and they are included among those who should receive the tithe for the poor.[149] The forgotten sheaf could be given to the convert,[150] as well as the doubtful forgotten sheaf, the doubtful corner, and the doubtful gleaning.[151] One also leaves for the poor, including the convert, the grapes and olives left after the pickers have initially passed through the orchard or vineyard.[152] Eleazar b. Azariah indicates that if one dropped a coin from his hand and a poor person found it, even if that poor person is a convert, an orphan, or a widow, Scripture credits the person with contributing to the support of the poor.[153] One gives to each of the needy according to his or her portion, whether the person is a convert, an orphan, or a widow.[154] Although converts are important, and one should strive to aid them, when one sets priorities concerning to whom charity should be given, they come after Israelites have fulfilled their obligations to their children, their servants, the orphan, and the widow.[155]

Israelites, including converts, who worship a deity other than YHWH are to be stoned.[156] Furthermore, if converts entice an Israelite to worship other gods, they are to be executed.[157]

Differences between Converts and Native-Born Israelites

Even though the converts are equated with the Israelites in the matter of the gifts to the poor, Sifré Deuteronomy[158] specifically excludes the convert from those required to bring the second tithe and to recite the Avowal because they were not among those to whom Joshua gave a portion of the Land of Israel.

We have seen above that converts change their status upon entrance into the Israelite community. One sign of this altered state is the fact that previous family relationships are invalidated. Thus, if a female was conceived before her parents converted, but was born after they converted, if she both converts and marries, her father is not entitled to 100 *sheqelim* of silver paid to the father of a woman whose husband falsely charged her with not being a virgin on her wedding day. This is because the paternal relationship between the gentile father and the converted daughter is not considered legitimate by Israelite law.[159]

Converts and Levirate Marriages

The problem of levirate marriages is addressed in this midrash. Two brothers who were conceived before their mother converted, but born after she was convert are exempt from the laws of *haliṣah* and the levirate marriage.[160] Furthermore, the rites cannot be performed before a court composed of converts.[161]

The most important element in Sifré Deuteronomy's discussions of the convert is that the poor among the converts receive the same agricultural gifts that one gives to the poor among the Israelites. This is significant because Mishnah and Tosefta indicate that these gifts were used to maintain the solidarity of the People Israel. For this reason, Israelites could give money to the poor among the gentiles, but they could not leave for them the agricultural gifts.

Although the midrashic collections share many of their conceptions of the convert with one another and with Mishnah and with Tosefta, the agenda of the exegetical collections are set by the individual biblical books around which they are organized and which they purport to interpret. Therefore, it is best to conclude as we began, by dealing with each collection in its own terms before making any general observations.

Sifra, like Tosefta, states that only those gentiles who are able to follow the entire Torah should be accepted as converts, and once they join the community, the Israelites must not remind them of their past deeds. Their circumcision indicates that the converts have accepted the whole Torah. However, those who were not known to the rabbis had to bring proof that they had been properly converted. This implies that there was a formal act of conversion and that converts were different from gentiles and native-born Israelites. However, the majority of the *sugyot* in Sifra indicate that converts and native-born Israelites were equal. While the gentiles stood outside of the rabbinic purity system, Sifra consistently applies the purity rules in the same way to converts and to native-born Israelites. Similarly, for the most part, Sifra equates the converts and the Israelites with regard to the sacrificial cult, for it points to only two relatively minor differences between the two groups: (1) The priests did not consume the residue of the converts' meal offerings, and (2) Yosi b. Judah held that skins of the converts' offerings were not given to the priests. With regard to the Israelite periods of sacred times, Sifra pictures the converts and the native-born Israelites on equal terms. Furthermore, it is clear from its discussion of the agricultural gifts that the rabbis of Sifra considered the converts to be full members of the Israelite community.

When Sifra draws distinctions between the converts and the native-born Israelites, it does so in terms of the priesthood and the judicial system. Converts cannot be priests, and many sages held that their daughters could not marry into the priestly clan. Furthermore, converts could not become judges, a position open to all Israelites whose untainted ancestry could be ascertained. It is significant that in those areas which most clearly distinguished the Israelites from the gentiles—the Temple and its cult, the purity laws, the periods of sacred times, and the agricultural rules— Sifra equates the converts and the native-born Israelites. Clearly, given the contents of Leviticus, if the authors of Sifra wished to distinguish between the converts and the Israelites, they could have found many occasions to do so.

Mekhilta exhibits a positive view toward the convert; all but Amalek's descendants could enter the Israelite community, gentiles may convert at any age, and converts were not to be reminded of their pasts. It pictures Jethro as the ideal convert and contains a long passage which is totally favorable to him. This stands in sharp contrast to Sifré Numbers' parallel passage in which Jethro is painted in both positive and negative terms. Similarly, Mekhilta contains a long *sugya* which points out that YHWH had described the converts and some of the folk heroes of the Israelites in the same glowing terms. Furthermore, the converts and the Israelites are totally equated in terms of Passover. This is significant because Passover was considered by the rabbis to be the festival which celebrated the creation of the People Israel.[162] In addition, the converts who become slaves are treated the same as native-born Israelites who were forced to sell themselves into slavery, and the laws of damages apply the same to both groups.

Although Mekhilta equates the convert with the native-born Israelite in many areas, most significantly in terms of Passover, it does note that the two are not entirely the same. Therefore, some held the converts could not bring the first fruits to the Temple because they could not recite the verse which mentions that YHWH was the deity of their ancestors. Mekhilta also contains two comments attributed to Eliezer which are highly critical of the converts' character.

On the basis of several biblical passages, Sifré Numbers claims that the converts, just like native-born Israelites, are responsible for all the laws in the Torah. However, the Torah specifically had to mention this fact by referring to the *gr*, for without these clear references, one would not automatically assume that the two groups had to relate to the Torah in the same ways. In fact, the equality of the two groups is seen most clearly in the fact that the priestly benediction was recited over converts as well as over Israelites.

On the other hand, the two groups are not considered to be entirely the same. Although both groups entered the covenant through circumcision, a sacrifice, and ritual immersion, each group offered different sacrifices. The Land of Israel was given only to the Israelites, so that the converts, like gentiles, could not own parcels of the Holy Land. Also, some held that a severer penalty applied to an Israelite who killed another Israelite than to one who murdered a convert. Furthermore, upon conversion, gentiles severed their ties with their non-Israelite families, so that it was possible for a convert to die without legal heirs, a presumed rarity among native-born Israelites. The clearest indication of Sifré Numbers' ambivalent attitude toward the convert is found in its discussion of Jethro, which is much more negative than the parallel found in Mekhilta. Finally, Sifré Numbers claims that the *rabble* which joined the Israelites in their departure from Egypt was composed of converts and that the converts occupied the outskirts of the Israelite camp as they traveled from Egypt to the Land of Israel.

Sifré Deuteronomy encourages Israelites to seek converts and suggests that the gentiles will be so impressed by the Israelite way of life that they will ask to become members of the community. Even if they find some things in the Israelite way of life which do not please them, they will overlook them. Israelites are responsible for supporting the needy convert in the same way that they are responsible for supporting the needy native-born Israelites. This indicates that the converts were viewed as an integral part of the People Israel. However, converts and Israelites are not totally the same, for the laws of the levirate marriage and the *ḥaliṣah* ceremony apply only to brothers who were conceived and born after their parents converted.

In general, the midrashic collections are favorably disposed toward the convert, and in most instances they claim that converts and native-born Israelites are equal. Most significantly, taken together the texts equate the two groups in terms of the sacrificial cult, the purity laws, the periods of sacred time, the agricultural gifts to the poor, and the laws of damages. Furthermore, many biblical verses are brought to demonstrate the equality of the two groups and the fact that YHWH considered the converts to be precious and praiseworthy, as long as they accept the whole Torah. However, the two groups are not entirely equal. The converts cannot own a parcel of the Land of Israel, for they cannot claim that YHWH was the deity of their ancestors. Thus, even though the midrashic collections contain a large number of *sugyot* which are favorable to the converts and which equate the converts with the native-born Israelite, they still do not totally merge the two groups. In fact, many *sugyot* make it clear that it would be natural to think of the two groups as distinct had not the Torah *specifically* equated them in so many places. Thus, the *midrashim* distinguish between native-born Israelites and converts because the Bible itself had often referred to the *gr*, along with the native-born, *'zrḥ*, and the children of Israel, *bny yśr'l*. Because the Torah did not fully equate the *grym* with the Israelites, the *midrashim* hold that they should not be automatically equated. It is clear, however, that whatever the term *gr* meant to the various biblical writers, the rabbis believed that it referred to converts. Therefore, the rabbis are merely following the Bible's lead when they draw distinctions between converts and native-born Israelites in some areas, while equating them in others.

FIVE

Converts and Conversion in the Palestinian Talmud

The Palestinian Talmud reached its final form in the fifth century of the common era.[1] It contains a *gemara* to thirty-nine of the sixty-three mishnaic tractates, occurring in four of the Mishnah's six major Orders; it does not cover *Qodashim* or *Ṭohorot*, with the exception of the first three chapters of *Niddah* in the last Order. In addition, there is no *gemara* to the third chapter of *Makkot*, to the twenty-first through the twenty-fourth chapter of *Shabbat*, or to the fourth through the tenth chapter of *Niddah*.[2] It is often claimed that when compared with the Babylonian Talmud, the *sugyot* in the Palestinian *gemara* are frequently shorter, less clear, and more elliptical,[3] but this has not really been demonstrated. The Palestinian pericopae frequently lack the editorial introductions and connections often found in the Babylonian Talmud. A passage in the former document may consist of nothing more than the juxtaposition of a tannaitic text which seems to be at variance with the relevant section of Mishnah and a reconciliation of the two. Many other *sugyot* in the Palestinian Talmud open by quoting an amoraic statement to which tannaitic sources or other amoraic statements are brought to support or contradict it. If the quoted statements disagree, the amoraim frequently seek to smooth out the differences.[4] Neusner writes that the Palestinian *gemara* "appears in the main to provide mere commentary and amplification for the Mishnah," by doing one of four things to it: "(1) text criticism; (2) exegesis of the meaning of the Mishnah, including glosses and amplifications; (3) addition of scriptural proof texts of the Mishnah's central propositions; and (4) harmonization of one Mishnah passage with another such passage or with a statement of Tosefta."[5] Neusner estimates that 90 percent of the Palestinian *gemara* focuses on Mishnah. The other 10 percent of the Palestinian Talmud contains (1) theoretical questions of law not associated with a particular passage of the Mishnah, (2) exegesis of Scripture separate from Mishnah, (3) historical statements—stories about things which happened, and (4) stories about and rules for sages and disciples, separate from discussions of a passage of the Mishnah.[6]

The Palestinian Talmud contains Palestinian amoraic discussions of the convert dating from the third through part of the fifth century of the common era. Some of the *gemara's* discussions merely bring new examples to illustrate points made in the tannaitic texts. Other *sugyot* build on earlier pericopae and interpret them in unexpected ways. Some of the Talmud's passages bring forward completely new material. While in some of the tannaitic texts we have seen discussions of the converts' need to be circumcised and immersed, the Palestinian Talmud contains several *sugyot* that treat the relative importance of these two rituals as conversion mechanisms. Although we have encountered several discussions which illustrate that converts form a distinct segment of the People Israel, the Palestinian *gemara* is the first to use the problem of the apostate town to make that point. The notion that converts die without heirs, a much discussed topic in all strata of the rabbinic texts, is used to illustrate the difference between acquring adult and minor slaves. The *gemara* employs the collapse of an idol's shrine to discuss what converts may inherit from their gentile parents, a much debated topic in the earlier documents. While we have encountered references to Rahab, Jethro, and Onqelos as converts, the Palestinian Talmud expands the list of converts, including Roman nobility. Finally, similiar to the earlier texts, the Palestinian *gemara* contains debates concerning when Ammonites, Amorites, Edomites, and Egyptians can enter the People Israel; however, it is the first document to discuss the Palmyrans and the Libyans.

Ritual of Conversion

The Palestinian *gemara* addresses the question of the rituals gentiles must perform upon their conversion. From Tosefta we find Simeon b. Eleazar's report of the Houses dispute concerning the need to circumcise a male convert who had already been circumcised while he was a gentile,[7] and a development on the Houses dispute concerning one who converts immediately before Passover.[8] Elsewhere we discover that the date on which the newborn son of a convert should be circumcised depends upon the relationship of his birth to his mother's conversion. If the child were born shortly before her conversion, he is considered a gentile, and he must be circumcised immediately after his mother completes her conversion. However, if the child were born right after his mother converts, he is circumcised eight days after his birth, just like any other Israelite baby.[9] One must be circumcised as an Israelite in order to eat the heave offering. For this reason, one whose foreskin is drawn forward in order to disguise his circumcision, one who was born circumcised, and one who was circumcised before he converted may not eat the food in the status of heave offering.[10] Because under normal circumstances converts could not be priests, it is possible that the reference was included here merely to complete the list of those who were circumcised but who were not able to eat food in the status of heave offering.[11] Finally, the circumcision of a convert on Purim is assumed to be acceptable.[12]

In one place we are informed that female proselytes are immersed only during the day,[13] but most of the discussions of immersion deal with the immersion of males and the relative importance of circumcision and immersion as elements of the conversion ritual. It may be that because most often one was circumcised only once during his lifetime, while one could immerse himself frequently in order to be cleansed from a variety of impurities, circumcision was viewed by some as a more accurate sign of conversion than immersion.

We saw in Sifré Numbers[14] that a convert required circumcision, immersion, and a sacrifice. However, the Palestinian *gemara* contains a discussion on the need for a convert to undergo *both* immersion and circumcision. Eliezer rules that a convert must have only been circumcised, so that a proselyte who has been circumcised but not immersed is still a valid convert, while one who has been immersed but not circumcised is not a valid convert. Joshua states that both rituals are required. However, the *gemara* concludes that while a convert must be both circumcised and immersed, any immersion for any reason is accepted as valid with regard to conversion.[15] Because any immersion after circumcision is acceptable, a converted male who immersed after a nocturnal emission is considered to have performed the ablution required for a proselyte.[16] Bar Qappara claimed that the immersion of the converts was intended to cleanse them of the impurity of being a non-Israelite. The necessary immersion could take place on the Sabbath, although this generates some discussion because some held that conversion "improved the person," something which was prohibited on the Sabbath.[17] Thus, the difference of opinion which is expressed throughout the Palestinian *gemara* concerns the requirement that a gentile undergo a ritual immersion *at the time* of his conversion. Some taught that *at the time* of his conversion, a gentile only needed to be circumcised, while others taught that the converted needed to be both circumcised and immersed. Furthermore, it seems that the sages whose opinions have been recorded in the Palestinian *gemara* considered the converts' immersion to be a method by which they were cleansed from ritual impurity.

When the Temple stood, the convert brought a bird offering as part of the conversion ritual. Now, with the Temple in ruins, in place of their bird sacrifice the proselytes should bring a quarter-weight of silver.[18] If, while the Temple is in ruins, converts separated a bird for an offering and the Temple is rebuilt in the future, they would not need to separate a new bird for an offering. Therefore, while converts at the present time are not encouraged to separate birds for an offering because the Temple is no longer standing, if they do separate a bird, it is considered to be an acceptable act.[19]

Motives for Conversion

The Palestinian *gemara* takes up the converts' motives for joining the People Israel. Gentiles should join the Israelite community only "for the sake of Heaven"; that is, they should have no ulterior motives for becoming Israelites. They should convert only out of desire to serve YHWH. If a woman converted for improper reasons, that is not "for the sake of Heaven," and married into the priestly caste, she may not eat even the lesser holy things, which were consumed outside of the Temple's precincts. In contrast, women who converted for proper reasons and were married to priests, could eat even the most holy things, edibles which had to be consumed within the precincts of the Temple and which were permitted to only the priests and their households.[20] Entering the Israelite community in order to marry one of its members was not considered by some to be valid reason for conversion. An anonymous opinion[21] states that if a gentile converts because he or she loves an Israelite, the proselyte should not be accepted into the community.[22] Rav demurs and teaches that in contrast to the case of normal converts, who are discouraged at first, these others should be encouraged to enter the community, for it is possible that they actually will come to the true worship of YHWH. In fact, they should be given a cordial reception, *qyrwb pnym*.[23] This aside by Rav is our first reference to the practice of *discouraging* those who wish to enter the Israelite community, a practice ritualized in the Babylonian *gemara*.[24] Some also believed that female children who converted might not realize the significance of their actions, so that they might need to undergo ritual immersion for a second time when they are older.[25] In response to the question about why Samaritans are unfit to serve as witnesses for a divorce document, Yohanan responds that this is because they are "lion converts"; that is, they did not convert for the sake of Heaven but out of fear of being harmed by the lions.[26] This opinion is challenged by the claim that if someone converted for an illegitimate reason,[27] but converted again for the proper reason, that person would be accepted into the community as a proper convert.[28] This means that as Yohanan stated, people who converted for an improper reason should be accepted into the community if they undergo a second conversion "for the sake of Heaven."[29] Also, Bar Qappara teaches that one should be careful to treat converts fairly, for if they perceive that they might suffer a disadvantage after their conversion, they will return to their former lives.[30] Finally, we are told that during David's reign many converted because they were impressed by the care that YHWH took in protecting those who converted to his worship.[31] The rabbis also realized that some might not convert because they feared the Israelites and had misapprehensions about them.[32]

Converts as subclass of People Israel

The issue of a female convert's right to marry a priest is dealt with from the view of the claim that converts form a distinct segment of society which may not intermarry with all of the other units within the community.[33] For example, Judah held that the priests, Levites, Israelites, and converts each constituted a separate class within the Israelite community, while the rabbis did not count the converts as a unique and distinct entity and held that there were only three segments of the society.[34] Meir's statement that it is possible for a man and a woman to produce five castes is taken from Tosefta and appears in the Palestinian *gemara*.[35] The assumption is that converts form a distinct element of Israelite society. The distinction between Israelites and converts is maintained even in Heaven.[36]

In addition to the discussions of the permissibility of a converted female's marrying into the priestly caste, we also encounter in the Palestinian *gemara* some concern about exactly whom a convert could marry. It is reported that a convert asked Yosa if he could marry a female *mamzer,* and Yosa responded that the marriage was permitted. The convert then asked Judah the same question, and the latter responded that although the marriage was permitted, the children would be considered *mamzerim.* The issue relates to the intermarriage of the various "classes" of Israelites, as well as to the matter of from which parent the child inherits its status.[37]

Mishnah[38] contains a ranked list of the various elements within Israelite society. In the Palestinian Talmud the list ends with Abun's claim that apostate Israelites are more important than converts, for the community should seek the readmittance of an apostate Israelite before it seeks to admit a convert.[39]

With regard to an apostate town, the issue is raised whether or not the converts are counted as part of the population to make up the majority of those who have been misled, so that it is considered an apostate town. The assumption behind the question is that the converts are not necessarily considered to be the same as native-born Israelites.[40] This question stands unanswered, as do the other questions in this section of the *gemara*.[41] It

was also decided that converts could not form an independent unit for
the Passover sacrifice, for they might perform the sacrifice incorrectly;[42]
however, it is assumed that they may join in the celebration of Passover,
the event which marked the creation of the People Israel.[43]

All of these pericopae assume that converts compose a distinct class
within the People Israel. These *sugyot* presuppose that one could easily
distinguish between converts and native-born Israelites. For some of these
rulings to be effective, one would have to know a woman's status at the
time of her marriage. In addition, the ruling concerning the Passover sacrifice assumes that converts could be identified. While these may well be
theoretical discussions, since the Passover sacrifice was not offered during
the talmudic period and the apostate towns were also no longer dealt with,
they still point to the fact that in theory converts remained classified as
converts throughout their lives, so that they formed a distinct segment of
the Israelite community.

Differences between Converts and Native-Born Israelites

Above we saw that the marriages between converts and members of
the priestly caste were dealt with in terms of the converts as a subclass of
the people Israel. The question of these marriages is also discussed from
other points of view, which emphasize the differences between converts
and native-born Israelites. While Yosi b. Bun in the name of Rav taught
that a convert[44] may marry a woman of the priestly caste,[45] the topic of
whether or not converted women may marry a male of a priestly family
receives a good deal of attention.

The sages also discussed whether or not the daughter of a convert
may marry into the priesthood. Judah's comment in Mishnah[46] that the
daughter of a male convert is like the daughter of a male *halal* forms part
of the discussion of Liezer b. Jacob's claim that a woman who is the daughter of a convert cannot marry into the priesthood unless her mother is an
Israelite.[47] Elsewhere it was assumed that the priests customarily guarded
their family purity by overseeing their own marriages. Eleazar b. Jacob
reports that one priest married the daughter of a convert and that the case
came before Abbahu, who prepared to flog the priest. Bibi intervened and
reminded Abbahu that the law followed Yosi, who had ruled that if the
daughter were born after her parents had entered into a marriage legally
acceptable to Israelites, that is, after they had both converted, their child
may marry into the priesthood. Eleazar assumed that the priests carefully
regulate the marriages within the priestly class; therefore, it was not clear

why Abbahu was preparing to flog the priest. Abbahu relented and did not flog the priest.[48]

It seems to have been generally agreed upon that converts, along with *netinin, mamzerim,* and slaves, could not serve in the Sanhedrin.[49] And there is a general assumption that converts may serve as judges in civil cases, but not in capital trials. However, the *gemara* notes that there is a disagreement about whether or not converts may serve as judges for the *halisah* ceremony. At least part of the *gemara's* discussion centers on the problem of whether or not converts are considered to be the same as native-born Israelites. One tannaitic statement allows them to serve as judges for this ceremony, while another tannaitic tradition prohibits their adjudicating these cases. The anonymous text suggests that the different traditions are based on different interpretations of *in Israel* in Deut. 25:10. One teaching argues that the phrase includes converts, while another holds that it excludes them. The *gemara* draws attention to the discussion of the *sukkah* in Lev. 23:42. There we find *all citizens [in Israel shall dwell in booths].* The text notes that both *citizens* and *in Israel* exclude the convert. However, when a limiting term follows a limiting term, it serves to expand the meaning of the verse, so that the converts are included in the verse's injunction and are obligated to dwell in a *sukkah.* However, with regard to the *halisah* ceremony, we find only one limiting term, so that the convert may not serve as a judge.[50] The point is that converts are not completely equal to native-born Israelites.

The Palestinian *gemara* takes up the dispute between Aqabyya b. Mahaleel and sages about whether or not the bitter waters are administered to a converted woman whom her husband has accused of adultery.[51] It concludes that the dispute concerns the marriage of two converts to each other, for the case of an Israelite married to a convert could be deduced from the biblical text.[52] Similarly, Mishnah states[53] that converts are among those who bring the first fruits but who do not recite *which YHWH swore unto our fathers to give us.*[54] However, if their mothers were Israelites, they do recite the verse. This implies that the offsprings of converted males and native-born Israelite females are considered to be like native-born Israelites. But the offsprings of two converts are different from native-born Israelites. The Palestinian *gemara* creates an extensive *sugya* on this passage which discusses Moses' father-in-law and the Kenites, gentiles who have illicit intercourse with Israelite females, and those who are the children of converts.[55] The Talmud's final answer is that Mishnah's teaching should be rejected, for converts do bring the first fruits and do recite the Avowal.[56] In Sifra, Yosi the Galilean and Aqiba dispute the issue of whether a convert is liable for cursing his mother or his father, and the *gemara* expands on the dispute.[57] Part of the *sugya* focuses on when the mother gave birth to the child, and this relates to the problem of proselytes' severing ties with their parents upon their conversion.

Converts and Their Heirs

The problem of a convert's dying without leaving heirs occupied the tannaim, and it also was an important issue for the amoraim. However, it was often meaningful only because it allowed the rabbis to discuss a number of issues related to inheritance and to acquiring property, not because they were overly concerned with converts. For example, the difference between acquiring adult or minor slaves is discussed in the context of a convert's dying without leaving heirs.[58] Furthermore, the case of acquiring from one owner two fields separated by a narrow pathway is fine-tuned through the discussion of a convert's dying without heirs.[59] And this is set in the context of extended discussions on the rules of acquiring fields through various means. Similarly, in a *sugya* which deals with one's acquiring an animal by drawing it by its reins, the case of a convert who died without heirs is mentioned.[60] The *gemara* reports a dispute between Samuel and Leazer over whether or not a fetus counts as a viable heir, and the discussion from Tosefta[61] of a convert about whom it was believed that he died without heirs but about whom it was learned that his wife was pregnant or that he had a son who lived outside of the Land of Israel is brought to settle the matter.[62] The reliability of a claim made by adults that a child found in the market is their son is also refined through reference to a convert who died without heirs.[63] Also, the problem of using leaven after Passover is discussed in terms of a proselyte who died without heirs.[64] Furthermore, the issue of whether daughters as well as sons inherit from their father is rarefied with regard to the convert who died without heirs.[65]

Converts and Their Converted Children and Spouses

At least one relationship remains intact throughout the conversion process. A marriage contract an adult male convert executed before his conversion is valid after his conversion, even if it contains conditions. One anonymous amora held that only the marriage contract is valid but not the stipulations it might contain.[66] Thus, if a husband and wife convert, their marriage agreement need not necessarily be renegotiated. This carries on the discussion in Mishnah[67] and Tosefta.[68] Mishnah had stated that the marriage contract between married gentiles remained valid if they converted at the same time, and Tosefta added that if a new marriage contract were executed after the conversion, the latter document takes precedence. The discussion of stipulations is an amoraic expansion on these two tannaitic teachings. The amoraic disagreement centers on whether the conditions are considered to be an essential part of the marriage contract or additions to the marriage agreement. If they are viewed in the former way, they must be maintained; if they are additions, they may be ignored. Thus, for the amoraic discussion, the converts serve as a peg on which to hang the treatments of the essential or nonessential nature of the conditions contained in the marriage contract. Again, this passage, like the ones in Mishnah and Tosefta, assumes that gentiles executed marriage agreements considered valid by rabbinic authorities, a curious assumption.

Converts and Levirate Marriages

The issue of levirate marriages receives some attention in the Palestinian Talmud. The problem is complex because, upon conversion, the new Israelites sever all ties with their previous relatives, so that exactly whom one may count as a brother, father, or mother is open to some interpretation. Yasa raised the issue of converted brothers entering into a levirate marriage. Yohanan rules that these brothers are forbidden from entering into a levirate marriage. However, the text interprets Yohanan's objection and discusses a woman who has children, or two men who are not brothers according to rabbinic law. However, Jacob b. Aha in the name of Isaac b. Nahman argues that the law of the levirate marriage applies to only Israelites; therefore, Yohanan's original objection stands. The question arises only if the brother-in-law approaches his brother's wife after she has converted.[69]

Converts as Heirs

MA.Z. 3:6 states that if an Israelite's house adjoined an idol's shrine, and the house collapses, the Israelite could not rebuild unless he moves four cubits away from the shrine into his own property, and Yohanan explains that this can apply to only a house a gentile and a convert inherited from their gentile father. It appears that here the convert is used to refine a rabbinic teaching, in this case the rule about the use of materials from an idol's shrine.[70] The major issue is the original use intended for the building material, and a convert is the only Israelite whom the rabbis could conceive of who could have a house close to a shrine originally built for an idol, for they assume that no native-born Israelite would build a house which shared a common wall with an idol's temple. However, the *sugya* does deal with the issue of converts' inheriting from their gentile parents, a topic that also appeared in Mishnah and Tosefta.[71]

The tannaitic materials[72] discuss the Israelite who steals from a convert and lies about the theft, and the *gemara* adds that the offering the Israelite brings after the theft may be consumed outside of the Temple precincts and even outside of Jerusalem.[73]

Converts as Radically New People

Conversion effects an essential change in a person's status. Haninah stated that if gentiles cursed YHWH and converted, they are exempt from punishment because their status changed so that they are no longer liable for previous transgressions.[74] Zeira also knew a teaching which suggested that proselytes were forgiven for their previous sins when they converted.[75] These passages point to the fact that the convert is a new person. But this point is hardly striking. Gentiles were not responsible for observing Israelite law, so that even converts could not be held responsible for violating Israelite customs while they were gentiles. Rather, indicating that the converts' previous sins are forgiven appears to be a way by which the sages indicated that the converts' lives began anew when they became part of the People Israel. The fact that the converts' gentile ancestry, but not their actions as gentiles, remained important to the rabbis points to the ethnic nature of conversion. While the new Israelites were not held responsible for their actions as gentiles, their gentile ancestry could not be completely discounted; the reason was that some aspects of Israelite identity depended on the fact that all Israelites shared a common ancestry with Jacob, an ancestry in which converts did not participate.

A convert's change of status is comparable to that of a person who reaches puberty,[76] one who was appointed an anointed priest,[77] or a slave who was freed.[78] The fact that upon conversion the proselytes cut all ties with their former relatives led some tannaim to conclude that the Torah's reference to an Israelite who had no kinsmen must refer to a convert, and this is accepted by the amoraim in the Palestinian *gemara*.[79] The fact that converts sever all ties with their previous family probably explains why converts and orphans are equated at certain places within the Torah.[80]

The Palestinian *gemara* also notes that even if a gentile converted and then left his new community and returned to his old way of life, he is not to be rejected by the Israelite community. This parallels Tosefta's teaching, which is repeated in the Babylonian Talmud, that such a person is classified as an apostate *Israelite*.[81] In this instance the converts are equated with the native-born Israelites, for neither lose their Israelite identity if they becomes apostates.[82] In fact, the converts' presumed knowledge of the Israelite community means that Israelites may continue to purchase certain ritual objects from them.[83]

The converts should accept the totality of their new way of life. Huna reports that there once was a convert who was an astrologer. One time before he went out, he studied all of his signs which proved to be unfavorable. Whereupon he realized that he had joined himself to Israel in everything except for his reliance on his astrological signs. Therefore, he declared his attachment to YHWH, renounced his dependence on his astrological knowledge, and proceeded to leave his house. He encountered a wild animal which sought to devour him; however, he saved himself by giving his pack animal to the wild animal.[84] The story points to the fact that the convert was protected only when he put his full faith in YHWH and totally rejected his previous ways. It also suggests that conversion could be a process, and not a one-time event, for clearly the astrologer was already a member of the Israelite community when he realized that he had not totally given himself over to YHWH. As we shall see in chapter 11, it is not unusual for proselytes to strengthen their ties to their new community's beliefs over a period of time after they have converted.

We find several other instances in which the converts' change of status is discussed in order to refine points of rabbinic law. The relationship between the first and last days of Sukkot and Passover is framed with reference to the convert. Those who hold that the two days are intimately related, so that one must be an Israelite on the first day in order to celebrate the last day, would exempt one who converted during the festival week from observing the last day of the festival.[85] It is difficult to know if the sages envisioned the conversion of gentiles during the festival week, so that this was a real issue, or if the discussions of the convert were used as pegs on which to hang the disagreements concerning the relationship of the first and last days of the festivals. In a *sugya* which deals with one's making sure that he recognizes the Sabbath, so that he does not perform any work on it, the rule that an Israelite may marry a converted woman decides the case.[86] Along these same lines, the Palestinian *gemara* cites mHul. 10:4, which states that if a convert possessed a heifer which was slaughtered before he converted, he is exempt from offering the shoulder, cheeks, and maw.[87] If it is uncertain whether the animal was slaughtered before or after he converted, he is exempt from bringing the offerings, for the one who requires the offering must bring proof that it is required. This counters the teaching in mHal. 3:6, which deals with a person who had dough in her possession when she converted, for this mishnah states that if it is uncertain whether or not the dough was rolled out, thus requiring the removal of the dough offering, before or after the conversion, she must separate the dough offering.[88] Thus, the passage refines the issue of cases in which there is doubt concerning exactly when a person became liable for making an offering. The fact that the convert changes status and becomes a "new" person serves as a convenient way to deal with the issue of doubt. The matter of whether or not a convert may marry a *mamzer* and the definition of those whose status is transmitted through the mother or the father are also partially dealt with by reference to the marriages of converts.[89] The *gemara* also discusses the penalties incurred by a man who falsely charges that his wife was not a virgin at the time of their marriage in terms of an Israelite's marriage to a convert.[90] The woman's change of status upon her conversion and her severed relationship with her father both play into the discussion and refinement of the rabbinic laws. The converted woman who committed adultery is the only woman who could be subject to death by stoning if the charge proved true, but who did not have a father to whom the penalty could be paid if the charge proved false.

The converts' change of status also finds expression in discussions of Israelite customs. For example, only Israelites are obligated to observe Passover. Therefore, according to Yohanan, if a gentile separated the Passover sacrifice before he converted, it is invalid, and he must separate another offering after his conversion.[91] After converts undergo ritual immersion, they are considered to be members of the Israelite community and subject to its laws. Hence, if converts are immersed on the Sabbath after the beginning of sunrise, the place where they were immersed counts as their primary residence for purposes of movement on the Sabbath.[92] Nahman b. Jacob's opinion is cited with reference to Purim, so that if a gentile is circumcised "after the East became light" on Purim, he is required to hear the *megillah* read, an obligation which falls only upon Israelites.[93] Similarly, because the requirement to leave a portion of the crop for the poor falls only upon Israelites,[94] following earlier tannaitic texts, the amoraim state that only if a person converts *before* he harvests his field is he liable for providing for the poor Israelites.[95] Furthermore, in line with Tosefta, if a gentile from whom an Israelite leased a field converted,[96] the Israelite had to remove the tithe before he paid his rent, for the converted gentile is treated the same as any other Israelite.[97]

The manner in which the prohibited sexual relationships among Israelites apply to converts is also discussed in ways which emphasize that the convert is a new individual.[98] If a gentile married to both a woman and her daughter or to both a woman and her sister converted, he must send one of them away after his conversion, because Israelite law forbids a male to marry a woman and her sister or mother. However, the choice is entirely his as to which one he keeps as his wife. However, if he had designated one as his wife before he converted, by having intercourse with her,[99] he cannot change his mind after his conversion. Meir states that if a gentile were married to his sister, whether by his father or his mother, upon his conversion, he must send her away. Judah disagrees and holds that he may stay married to the sister by the same father; he must only send away a sister by the same mother. Similarly, Meir holds that upon conversion the convert must send away his mother's sister and his father's sister if he had married one of them while he was still a non-Israelite. Judah holds that he may stay married to his mother's sister from the same father. He may not remain married to his mother's sister from the same mother or to his father's sister in either case. If he were married to any other woman who is one of the forbidden relationships to Israelites and had brought her into his home, he need not send her away after his conversion. This latter rule applies if it had already happened; however, after he converted these are all forbidden to him. This discussion revolves around Lev. 18:9, which prohibits an Israelite from marrying his sister. Pinhas said that Yosi said in Yosi's name that a slave who has intercourse with his mother[100] is liable for a sin offering. He argues that *and you shall say to them* includes slaves, and the *gemara* proceeds to draw an analogy between converts and slaves.[101] These pericopae indicate that while gentiles may marry relatives in violation of the laws stated in Lev. 18, once they convert, they must adhere to at least some of the Israelite interpretations of the Torah, even if they have to divorce some of the women to whom they are married.

Converts and Their Gentile Past

One set of passages centers around the sexual purity of women who converted. Some held that with respect to marrying a priest, a female convert is the same as a prostitute.[102] A tradition which is claimed to be tannaitic and which is very similar to a *sugya* in Mishnah states that the prostitute mentioned in Lev. 21:7[103] refers to a converted female or to a freed slave.[104] And Lev. 21:14 is taken to mean that at least the High Priest cannot marry a convert.[105] Simeon taught that if a female converted at an age of less then three years and one day, she is fit for marrying into the priesthood, for she is assumed not to have engaged in any sexual activity.[106] Jacob b. Idi in the name of Joshua b. Levi reports the case of a family in the south against whom a charge of impurity had been lodged. Rabbi sent Rominos to examine the family. When he discovered that the grandmother was younger than three years and one day when she converted, he ruled that the family was qualified to marry into the priestly class.[107] Along these same lines, Zeira states that a freed handmaiden or a girl who converted after the age of three years and one day is assumed to have engaged in sexual activity before she converted or was freed. However, a woman who converted before she was three years old and one day and a handmaiden who was freed before the age of three years and one day is considered to be like an Israelite woman, so that she does not need to bring proof to establish her virginity before the marriage.[108]

Similarly, it appears that Hoshiya does not consider the change of status brought about by conversion to be significant in all cases, for if a woman gave birth and then immediately converted, her flow of blood is considered to be unclean, because she had just given birth.[109]

The passage from Tosefta in which Aqiba deals with the case of the convert who brought wine with him when he converted is brought to explain one of Yohanan's teaching.[110] The disagreement between Aqiba and the anonymous opinion centers around the equating of converts with Israelites, for the anonymous opinion suggests that converts should not be trusted by Israelites on the matter of wine offered to idols.

Converts from Biblical Nations

As we have seen, on the basis of the Torah, not all non-Israelites were accepted equally as converts. For example, Deut. 23:4–8 contain restrictions concerning the ability of Ammonites, Moabites, Edomites, and Egyptians to join the community of Israel.[111] Thus, similar to what we have found in the tannaitic materials, we find in the Palestinian Talmud discussions which center around the entrance of these peoples and their descendants into the People Israel and whether or not their females who convert may marry into the priestly caste.[112] Yosi b. Bun states that the rabbis do not consider converts to be a separate congregation. Judah believes that converts are part of the congregation of YHWH, so that they may not marry a *mamzer.* Abbahu taught before Yohanan that Judah reported the story about Benjamin, the Egyptian convert who was one of Aqiba's students. Benjamin stated that he, an Egyptian convert, was married to an Egyptian convert and was arranging a marriage between his son, an Egyptian convert, and a female Egyptian convert. He was doing this so that his grandson would be eligible to enter the congregation of Israel, for then he would be a third-generation Egyptian convert.[113] Aqiba responds that this will not work unless Benjamin marries his son to the daughter of an Egyptian convert, so that each partner in the marriage is a third-generation Egyptian convert.[114] Here, Aqiba and Benjamin accept the biblical injunction concerning when Egyptian converts may be fully accepted into the congregation of Israel.[115]

If an Ammonite, Moabite, Edomite, or Egyptian convert—also a gentile, a slave, a Samaritan, a *ḥalal,* a *mamzer,* or a *natin*—has intercourse with a woman of the priestly, Levitical, or Israelite class, she is prohibited from marriage into the priestly caste. This means that the priestly woman may not eat the heave offering and that the Israelite or Levitical women may not marry priests. Yosi states that if the male's child ($zr'w$) is prohibited, an Israelite woman may not have intercourse with him; but if his seed is not prohibited, intercourse with him is not prohibited. Therefore, the Israelite woman could not have intercourse with a male Ammonite, Moabite, Edomite, or Egyptian convert. Simeon b. Gamaliel states that if an Israelite can marry the convert's daughter, he may marry his widow. But if he may not marry the convert's daughter, the Israelite may not marry his widow.[116]

In yYeb. 7:5 Yohanan states that Yosi and Simeon differed concerning the Ammonite and Moabite convert, for although the males are prohibited for all times, the women are not. According to Yohanan, Yosi rules that because the Ammonite and Moabite males are always prohibited, intercourse with them is prohibited, so that the women who have intercourse with them may not marry priests, and their women may not marry into the priestly caste. Simeon, on the other hand, would allow marriages with their women; thus he would permit the High Priest to marry their daughters and their widows. Jeremiah in the name of Ba[117] stated that both Yosi and the opening anonymous opinion would prohibit the widow of an Ammonite and Moabite convert or a second-generation Egyptian convert from entering the congregation of Israel or marrying into the priestly class. The point seems to be that unless all of the offsprings, both male and female, are permitted, the marriages cannot take place. However, according to Yosi, the High Priest cannot marry a widow; therefore, the seed of the convert is also prohibited. This opinion is repeated when Zakkai and Alexandria posed a question to Yosa, who then quotes Jeremiah in "our rabbis' name" along with Ba. Next, Jacob b. Aha reports a dispute between Yohanan and Simeon b. Laqish in which Yohanan states that the daughter of an Ammonite convert and the daughter of a second-generation Egyptian convert are fit to marry into the congregation, while Simeon rules they are unfit.

We also learn that Zakkai taught before R. Yohanan that the daughter of a male Ammonite convert is fit, while the daughter of a female Ammonite convert is unfit, to marry into the priestly class. Yohanan responded that there is no difference between the daughter of a male Ammonite convert and the daughter of a female Ammonite convert, for both are fit to marry into the priestly class. Yosa cites Yohanan's opinion that the only reason one needs to mention the daughter of a male Ammonite convert is so that the daughter of the marriage of an Israelite woman and an Ammonite male is not considered disqualified to marry into the priestly class. Abbahu cites another opinion attributed to Yohanan in which he claims that the daughter may even marry the High Priest. This view is connected to an interpretation of the phrase *among his people* in Lev. 21:15. If the widow comes from two nations, which means in this context that her parents are an Ammonite and an Israelite, the High Priest may marry her, for in this case the males are prohibited, but the females are permitted. Haggai in the name of Pedat and Simeon b. Laqish object and state that the daughter of a male Ammonite convert is unfit. Yohanan responds that if two gentiles were married to each other before they converted, the male's offsprings can never enter the Israelite community, but the females are permitted to enter the congregation immediately. After they converted, the males are prohibited forever, but the daughters are permitted after the third generation.[118] We are also told that if a converted Ammonite slave married a converted Egyptian handmaiden, their descendants must be converted after three generations.[119]

There are a number of different issues which stand behind these extended discussions. Primarily, these *sugyot* result from the sages' perceived need to deal with the biblical references concerning the ability of the various biblical peoples to marry Israelites. However, the extensive debates concerning marriage into the priesthood point to other matters. These disagreements indicate a deep concern with the priestly lineage and the possibility that the converts' non-Israelite origins can never be ignored in the context of the priestly class. From this point of view, the discussion of the converts merely serves as a means of underscoring the need to keep the priestly class's lineage intact. On the other hand, these pericopae also indicate that the converts' gentile background remained relevant throughout their lives.

There is also a debate over whether or not the citizens of Palmyra and Kardunia may be accepted as converts[120] as well as over the status of those who live in Libya.[121] With reference to Libya, the issue is whether or not it is considered to be the same as Egypt. Although these people are not mentioned in the Bible, some of the discussions concerning them are framed in terms of a biblical people, the Egyptians. It is likely that these discussions of various "peoples" derive from the fact that the Ammonites, Edomites, and Egyptians were treated as units on the basis of the biblical texts.

Discussions of Specific Converts

Tosefta[122] had referred to the convert Onqelos, and the Palestinian *gemara* also contains stories about him. He is credited with translating the Torah,[123] with defending Judaism before Adrianos,[124] and, as earlier, with applying strict rules to himself when dividing his father's estate with his gentile brother.[125] Rahab is also viewed as a convert in the Palestinian Talmud.[126] The Palestinian *gemara* states that some held that the emperor Antoninus, who often was in conversation with Rabbi, converted, while others did not believe this claim.[127] Others claimed that Domitian's daughter also converted to Judaism.[128] Finally, Amasa's father, a person mentioned in the Bible, is named as a convert.[129]

There are a few miscellaneous topics covered throughout the Palestinian Talmud. We also learn that the word *man*, '*dm*, in Lev. 1:2 means that the converts are included in the rules stated there.[130] Furthermore, a tannaitic teaching appears in a debate between Leazar b. Yosi and Yosi in which we are told that the blessing for the elders and the converts is included in the *amidah* in the blessing "for the righteous,"[131] and a statement is attributed to Yohanan to the effect that when dealing with a convert, one follows a strict interpretation of the law.[132] In one text it appears that the converts' joining Israel reflects YHWH's happiness with them, for when they do his will "he traverses the earth, and whenever he finds a righteous person he attaches him to Israel."[133] Solomon's propensity for marrying foreign women is sanitized, for Yosi explains that Solomon married these non-Israelite women in order to bring them to the words of Torah and under the protection of the *Shekhinah*.[134] From Job 31:32, *the convert did not lodge in the street; my doors I opened to the roadside*, Yohanan concludes that one should bring the convert near with the right hand, while repelling him with the left.[135] Eliezer b. Jacob reports the story from Tosefta that two soldiers and "guards of the hinges" in Jerusalem were immersed and ate the Passover sacrifice on that very day.[136]

We have seen that the Palestinian *gemara* contains discussions about the required elements of the conversion ritual. There seems to be general agreement that male converts needed to be circumcised. The disagreement centered around the importance of the ritual immersion. There were those who believed that while circumcision was a necessary act for one who wished to convert, ritual immersion was not a requirement because all gentiles had been immersed because of their nocturnal emissions, while others held that a convert needed to undergo both rituals at the time of his conversion. The disagreement appears to center on the necessity of a ritual immersion *specifically* for conversion. Also, some held that although one did not need to separate a bird for an offering because the Temple was no longer standing, those who wanted to could do so. It is clear that the exact nature of the conversion procedure was still under discussion among the Palestinian rabbis, especially with regard to the importance of ritual immersion at the time of conversion.

The Palestinian Talmud also discusses the motives of the gentiles who wished to convert to Judaism. Ideally, conversion should be "for the sake of Heaven." Some held that gentiles should not be accepted as converts merely because they wish to marry an Israelite; however, Rav believed that these persons should not be discouraged from entering the community, for they might eventually come to worship YHWH for the proper reasons. Some even held that those who converted as children should undergo a second conversion as adults when they would fully understand the significance of their actions. We are also told that YHWH searches the earth for the righteous ones whom he brings into the Israelite community.

The Palestinian *gemara* also stresses the fact that conversion effects a major change in a person's status which is equal to the changes effected by puberty or by slaves' acquiring their freedom. The point of the parallels is that gentiles, minors, and slaves were not obligated to fulfill the totality of the rabbinic *halakhah*. However, converts, adults, and freed slaves were responsible for observing the rabbinic Torah. Therefore, these three changes of status were somewhat similar.

Converts sever all ties with their gentile families and their previous way of life, and once they become members of the Israelite community, they are expected to participate fully in their new community's ritual and communal activities. However, the Palestinian sages realized that converts might still hold on to their old customs and previous beliefs, so that the complete acceptance of the Israelite life-style might occur some time after the conversion. For that reason, Israelites had to take care to treat converts fairly and to aid them in their new life-style.

It is clear that although one should not disparage the convert, the fact that a woman was a convert or that her parents were converts would have to be kept in mind, for there was a good deal of discussion concerning a converted woman's ability to marry into the priestly class. Also, because there were limits placed on the converts' participation in the Israelite judicial system, at least in theory, one would have to be able to distinguish between native-born Israelites and converts. Furthermore, the issue of a convert's dying without leaving heirs occupies the minds of the Palestinian amoraim. However, the issue is important because it allows the sages to discuss problems of ownerless property, and not necessarily because they were interested in the converts' problems. In fact, the amoraic discussions of the convert often provide a means of refining rabbinic legal principles, so that the converts are discussed not for their own sake but because they allow other issues to be brought forward.

Although the converts were expected to participate fully in Israelite rituals, they were not fully equated with native-born Israelites. There was a good deal of discussion about the ability of converted women and their daughters to marry into the priestly caste. Furthermore, the problem with the convert's reciting the Avowal at the time of bringing the first fruits, which was raised in the tannaitic materials, is also discussed here. The issue of the levirate marriages receives a good deal of attention, because the convert has severed all ties with his gentile brothers, even should they convert with him. Moreover, restrictions are placed on the converts' participation in the legal institutions of the Israelite community.

In brief, many of the same points made in the earlier materials appear here. Although in many cases converts are equated with native-born Israelites, in other instances they are not the same, for their gentile background was relevant for their relationship to the priesthood and their appointment as judges. Although the issue of the Avowals recited with the offerings was not relevant during this period, at least in theory the Palestinian amoraim used this case to stress again the difference between native-born Israelites and converts. It is also interesting that some sages could fantasize that some members of the Roman nobility converted to Judaism, a point which will be expanded in the Babylonian Talmud. Finally, the Palestinian *gemara* contains a good deal of material concerning the gentiles' motives for conversion. While we have encountered this issue in the tannaitic stratum, it receives more attention here than it did in the earlier texts.

It is impossible to ascertain whether conversion was a more pressing "real life" issue for the amoraim of the Palestinian Talmud than it was for the tannaim. The problem arises because many of the amoraic passages seem to focus on theoretical issues, and often references to converts appear only to refine specific categories of rabbinic law. Furthermore, because the Palestinian *gemara* is the most extensive document we have examined so far, we would expect it to contain more discussions of the converts than the previously examined texts. All that can be demonstrated conclusively is that the amoraim saw the converts as a specific subclass of the People Israel which could serve as a topic of concern in many different contexts. Certainly because they were a topic of discussion in Mishnah and Tosefta, the two "foundation" texts of the Palestinian Talmud, it would be surprising if they were not dealt with in the Palestinian *gemara*. Thus, even if conversion was not a common phenomenon in Palestine during the amoraic period, the Palestinian Talmud would still have dealt with the topic because it appeared in Mishnah and Tosefta.

▓ SIX ▓

Converts and Conversion in the Babylonian Talmud

▓

The Babylonian Talmud, apparently reaching closure by the beginning of the eighth century,[1] is the most recent rabbinic text we shall consider.[2] Our conceptions of rabbinic Judaism tend to be either drawn from this text or are filtered through the views it contains. This means that we should expect to find here more familiar conceptions of the convert than we have encountered in the earlier materials. For example, this document contains the most developed conversion ritual, it employs the term "new-born child" for the convert, and it includes the famous Hillel-Shammai disagreements concerning converts. Scholars maintain that the Babylonian Talmud contains more angelology, demonology, sorcery, magic, astrology, and other folk beliefs than does the Palestinian *gemara*.[3] For Neusner, however, the major difference between the two Talmuds is in their use of the Hebrew Bible. He estimates that the Babylonian *gemara* contains four to five times more Scriptural units than the Palestinian Talmud.[4] Further, only the Babylonian Talmud uses Scriptural units independently of its interpretation of Mishnah, for the framers of the Babylonian Talmud "were prepared to organize their larger compositions around more than the single focus of a context of discourse dictated by the Mishnah or by points of law or theology deemed pertinent to the Mishnah."[5]

The material in the Babylonian Talmud clearly reflects the rabbinic ambivalence toward converts. A number of passages indicate that there were sages who believed that encouraging converts to join the Israelite community was a central part of YHWH's universal plan. For instance, Eleazar said that YHWH exiled Israel throughout the world only so that converts might join them. He based his comment on Hos. 2:25, *I will sow her in the land as my own,* which Eleazar takes to mean that the converts will be counted as YHWH's own people. He argues that one engages in the effort of planting only if one expects to have a successful harvest, as the proverb states: "Surely one plants a *se'ah* only if he intends to harvest many *kors.*" Yohanan agrees with Eleazar's opinion, and he bases his ideas on the latter part of Hos. 2:25.[6] In another passage,[7] Eliezer assumed that in the future gentiles would naturally join the Israelite community.[8] Another *sugya*[9] records that YHWH told Abraham that in the future Ruth and Naamah[10] would convert. We also discover[11] that YHWH reckoned the eras of the world from the time that Abraham and Sarah "made souls in Haran,"[12] which the sages understand to mean their making converts. Still another pericope[13] implies that in the future all people will convert to Judaism. The *gemara* cites a tannaitic tradition[14] which states that if Israelites see a statute of Mercury, they bless YHWH for being long-suffering. If they observe a place within the Land of Israel from which an idol has been removed, they state, "Blessed be he who uprooted idolatry from our land; and as it has been uprooted from this place, so may it be uprooted from all places belonging to Israel; and turn the heart of those who serve them to serve you." The *gemara* then asserts that outside of the Land of Israel one does not need to say "turn the heart of those who serve them to serve you" because most of these people are idolaters. However, Simeon b. Eleazar responds that the phrase also should be recited outside of the Land of Israel "because in the future they will become converts." In support of his claim, Simeon cites Zeph. 3:9: *For then I will make the peoples of pure speech, [so that they will invoke YHWH by name and serve him with one accord].*[15]

In contrast to these opinions, there were some who believed that converts were by their nature unsavory and brought evil upon the Israelite community, so that one should not encourage them to join the Israelite people. The *gemara* asks why the converts are addressed before their conversion and informed about some of the minor and major commandments. The anonymous response is that in this way they are given the opportunity to change their minds if they desire. Helbo goes so far as to state that converts are like sores, *spḥt*; therefore, he implies, Israel should not be overly anxious to have them join the community. In support of his claim, he cites Isa. 14:1, *And converts (gr) shall join them and shall cleave (nspḥw) to the House of Jacob.*[16] Elsewhere,[17] Isaac states that "evil after evil comes to those who receive converts," and the *gemara* states that this agrees with Helbo's statement, which it quotes. Helbo's statement is brought to support the teaching in a *beraita* that "converts and those who play with children delay the coming of the Messiah."[18]

Some carefully examined the converts' motives for joining the community, while others did not. Although some equated the converts with native-born Israelites, others carefully pointed out the differences between the two groups. Hama b. Hanina said that the *Shekhinah* will rest only upon families of pure birth, *mšpḥwt mywḥswt*, in Israel, and he cites Jer. 31:1 in support of his assertion: *At that time—declares YHWH—I will be God to all the families of Israel, and they shall be my people.* Hama points to the fact that *families of Israel* is specifically mentioned. Rabbah b. Huna said that Hama's teaching points to an advantage which the Israelites have over the converts. Rabbah applies Ezek. 37:27 to Israel, *[My presence shall rest over them;] I will be their God and they shall be my people.* However, Jer. 30:21 applies to the converts: *For who shall otherwise dare approach me? You shall be my people, and I will be your God.* The difference is that with regard to Israel, YHWH promises to be their god before they promise to be his people. This implies that YHWH will protect them even if they are not worthy to be called his people. However, with reference to the converts, as seen from Jer. 30:21, they must first declare their allegiance to YHWH and demonstrate that they are worthy of his support, before he will be their god.[19] In fact, as we have seen above, among some there was a tendency to classify the converts as a subset of the Israelite people,[20] so that the former never achieve full identification with the latter.

As we would expect, the Babylonian Talmud contains much fuller discussions of many of the points raised in the earlier rabbinic collections. It has the most extensive treatments of the conversion ritual, and it is the only text that outlines the detailed procedure of examining the converts upon their entrance into the community. It also seems to interpret the Palestinian *gemara*'s debate about the importance of ritual immersion as a dispute concerning the need for the converts to be *both* circumcised and immersed. Also, in contrast to the earlier documents, the Babylonian Talmud informs us that some of Israel's worst enemies had converted to Judaism, and it identifies Onqelos the convert as the nephew of the Roman Emperor.

As we shall see below, it appears that the authors of these pericopae wished to make some specific points which were not important to the editors of the earlier documents we have reviewed. At least some of the sages behind the *gemara*'s material assumed that conversion was the culmination of a process and not the result of sudden enlightenment. The Babylonian *gemara* also contains the view that gentiles might become familiar with Judaism before their conversion, so that they would act in ways which would be acceptable within the context of the People Israel. Below we shall discover several passages which discuss the converts' motives, and we shall also learn that when they achieve adulthood, child converts may reject their conversion.

Although the Babylonian *gemara* discusses some new motifs, it also takes up many familiar topics. It is concerned with marriage between priests and converts, it treats the problem of the converts who die without heirs, it deals with converts' inheriting from their gentile parents, it details Israelite rituals which the converts must observe and those in which they cannot participate, and the like. At times the discussions in Babylonian Talmud appear to rework material we have seen elsewhere, and on other occasions it handles familiar subjects in new ways by bringing information we have not encountered before. In brief, the Babylonian material offers us a good deal of new information about conversion even when it deals with familiar topics, and it is an error to read the Babylonian Talmud's views of the convert and conversion back into the earlier materials.

The *sugyot* in the Babylonian *gemara* present a diverse picture on virtually every issue dealing with converts and conversion. This is exactly what one would expect because of the massive amount of material in the Talmud and because it is the product of numerous generations of sages who lived during a period of several hundred years. It does seem clear that the Talmud's final editors did not feel it was necessary to present one picture of the converts and conversion. From our perspective, the material in the Babylonian Talmud indicates that throughout the whole amoraic period much remained unsettled with regard to conversion.

Ritual of Conversion

In the documents we examined above, the conversion ritual had three main components—circumcision, immersion, and a bird offering—to which a fourth, an interview together with some instruction, is added in the Babylonian Talmud. This latter rite finds theoretical expression in the fact that converts, like slaves purchased from gentiles, are required upon their ritual ablution to make a declaration concerning their agreement to observe the commandments.[21] There is also some evidence that there were amoraim who accepted Eliezer b. Jacob's comment in Mishnah that the conversion ritual purified the converts.[22]

The Palestinian Talmud contains discussions of the need for converts to be ritually immersed at the time of their conversion,[23] and this issue also becomes a point of dispute in the Babylonian *gemara*. Hiyya bar Abba quoted Yohanan's opinion that a male is not accepted as a convert until he has been circumcised *and* immersed.[24] However, if a male appeared before the rabbis and stated that he had been circumcised but had not been immersed, Judah would permit him to be immersed and would accept him as a convert on the basis of his immersion alone, without any regard to the reason for his circumcision, for Judah is willing to accept a person as a convert who has been *either* circumcised *or* ritually immersed. Yosi, on the other hand, would not allow the male to be immersed, for Yosi requires both circumcision *and* immersion for conversion, and he has no way of ascertaining the validity of the man's circumcision.[25] Rabbah[26] reported that one convert who had been circumcised but had not undergone the ritual ablution came before Hiyya b. Rabbi's court and requested immersion, whereupon Hiyya told him to wait until the next morning. The *gemara* deduces three rules from this incident: (1) Conversion must be performed before a court of three sages,[27] (2) conversion requires both circumcision and immersion,[28] and (3) ritual immersion for a convert cannot take place at night. Clearly in this passage conversion is a *legal* procedure which must be performed before a rabbinic court, and the male converts must be both circumcised and immersed at the time of their conversion.[29]

There were those, however, who disagreed with these requirements and held that converts did not require both circumcision and immersion. Eliezer held that if a gentile male had been circumcised but had not been ritually immersed, he was accepted as a convert, for "our forefathers were circumcised but did not perform the ritual immersion." Joshua, on the other hand, ruled that if a male had been immersed but not circumcised, he was accepted as a convert, for "[our] foremothers had performed only ritual immersion, but had not been circumcised."[30] Sages, however, required both circumcision and ritual immersion.[31]

The dispute between Joshua and Eliezer has elicited a good deal of scholarly discussion. These interpretations fall into two groups. One collection of scholars rejects the plain meaning of the dispute. They base their comments on the assumption that a noted rabbi could not claim that male converts did not have to be circumcised. Braude ignores Joshua's opinion and states that whatever Joshua's statement signifies, "it is safe to say that it does not mean that R. Joshua held that immersion without circumcision was sufficient to qualify a gentile as a convert to Judaism."[32] Bamberger rejects the Babylonian *gemara*'s version of the dispute between Joshua and Eliezer and favors the account in the Palestinian Talmud.[33] Although Bamberger gives many reasons for his rejection of the claim that Joshua would not require circumcision of a convert, his basic reason is that he cannot conceive of an important sage's not requiring a male convert to be circumcised. Bamberger concludes that the point of debate is the exact time at which the gentile becomes a convert. Following the Palestinian *gemara*, he argues that Eliezer held that one was considered a convert from the time of his circumcision, while Joshua held that one was not considered a convert until he had been immersed.[34] While this may be an appropriate explanation of the *sugya* in the Palestinian *gemara*, it does not reflect the text in the Babylonian Talmud. McKnight also states that "it is very possible that these disputes arose not from the issue of whether circumcision was required but from the issue of at what point a Gentile became a convert. In other words, the issue may have been one of social and religious status not legal requirement."[35] McKnight holds this opinion even though he had previously pointed to the ambiguous evidence concerning the necessity of the circumcision of converts.[36] Weil ignores this passage and merely assumes that every convert was always circumcised and that the threefold conversion ritual always applied.[37] Hoenig also ignores this passage and writes that "circumcision was a *sine qua non*."[38] Bialoblocki follows the Talmud's explanation of the dispute that Eliezer and Joshua debated about only one who was already circumcised when he wished to convert, and he then argues that this is really a discussion of the importance of the converts' ritual immersion. The question then revolves around the importance of a symbolic circumcision, and Bialoblocki connects this issue with the Hillel-Shammai dispute on bShab. 135a.[39] While accepting the text as it appears, Nolland writes that "there would appear to be a number of indications that R. Joshua's hypothetical uncircumcised proselyte is just that—a theoretical construct to make a point without the slightest intention of abandoning circumcision."[40] He asserts that "since the ablution of proselytes always followed the circumcision, generally after some days, the situation of circumcision without ablution was always a real one. . . . The converse situation, however, did not arise naturally and would have to be deliberately created by innovation."[41] Nolland concludes[42] that "R. Joshua was all for circumcision but located the sacramental efficacy in the ablution, but even if he did consider that circumcision could be dispensed with, the idea certainly never got any further than pure theory." Thus, Nolland accepts the text but relegates it to an intellectual dispute with no actual importance. Why this dispute is only "theoretically" important while others are not is totally unclear.

Neusner, by contrast, accepts the possibility that this disagreement between Eliezer and Joshua should be taken seriously. On the basis of this passage Neusner writes that "the rules of admitting a proselyte evidently were not settled by early Yavnean times."[43] Rowley,[44] Finkelstein,[45] and McEleney[46] also seem to accept the positions of Joshua and Eliezer at face value. Smith writes that "it was possible for a group of Jews to define themselves as Jews without circumcision."[47] Collins takes a middle ground. He notes that Philo's position is similar to that attributed to Joshua and states that "both discussions are theoretical, and do not prove the actual existence of uncircumcised proselytes, but they have at least potential significance nevertheless."[48]

If we take the text in the Babylonian *gemara* at face value, it appears that someone in the amoraic period was willing to include or to create a tannaitic disagreement concerning the necessity for converts to undergo circumcision upon their entrance into the Israelite community. This point is made even clearer when the Babylonian version is compared with the pericope in the Palestinian Talmud, for the latter *sugya* seems to be a debate about the importance of immersion as a conversion ritual. Even if we reject Joshua's position, as clearly the sages and later rabbinic tradition did, it is striking that it was included in the Babylonian Talmud, for this implies that someone wanted to indicate that there was some disagreement concerning the circumcision of converts.

According to Rabbi, the phrase *you and the convert shall be alike, (kkm),*[49] indicates that just as the Israelites' forefathers had entered into the Covenant through circumcision, immersion, and the sprinkling of the blood of their animal sacrifices, so should all others express their commitment to YHWH with these three ritual acts.[50] Furthermore, the *gemara* contains Simeon b. Eleazar's explanation of the Houses dispute over whether or not a circumcised gentile who converted to Judaism must undergo a symbolic circumcision. In the larger context of the totality of the discussions in the Babylonian *gemara*, this *sugya* becomes part of the debate over whether or not a convert must undergo a specific circumcision upon his entrance into the Israelite community.[51]

The *gemara*[52] contains the benediction recited upon the circumcision of a convert. The one who performs the circumcision recites the same blessing as the one who circumcises a native-born Israelite.[53] While in the case of a native-born Israelite the father recites a blessing which specifically refers to the "covenant of Abraham,"[54] at the circumcision of a convert, he who pronounces the benediction recites: "Blessed are you, YHWH, our God, king of the universe who has sanctified us with your commandments and has commanded us to circumcise converts and to cause the drops of the blood of the covenant to flow from them, because if it were not for the blood of the covenant heaven and earth would not endure, as it is said, *if not my covenant by day and by night, I would not have appointed ordinances of heaven and earth.*[55] Blessed are you, YHWH, who makes the covenant." It is important to note that the convert is circumcised *without* a specific reference to the covenant of Abraham,[56] so that a liturgical distinction is clearly made between the circumcision of a native-born Israelite and the circumcision of a convert. A *beraita*[57] teaches that an Israelite should not receive compensation for circumcising a gentile for the purposes of the latter's conversion because this is not considered to be a medical procedure.[58]

The immersion required of a convert is parallel to the immersion required for anyone who needs a ritual ablution, so that the rules of interposing apply with regard to both. The issue of something's interposing between an embryo and the waters of ablution in which its mother immerses herself is discussed in the *gemara*. In that context Rabba stated that if a pregnant gentile woman converted, her newborn child does not need to undergo ritual immersion. In this case the *gemara* concludes that the mother did not "interpose" between the waters and the embryo, because the embryo is like a natural growth, *rbytyh*.[59]

The discussion of the bird offering in the Babylonian Talmud,[60] which is marked as a *beraita*,[61] seems to contain elements from Tosefta[62] and Sifré Numbers.[63] Like Tosefta, the *gemara* states that converts cannot eat the holy things until they bring their bird offering. However, if they brought one pigeon in the morning, they may eat the holy things in the evening, although they still must bring the second bird.[64] Normally, when one brings two bird offerings, one bird offering is considered a sin offering, and the other is classified as a whole burnt offering, *'wlh*. In the case of the convert, both birds are considered whole burnt offerings. Birds are specifically mentioned with respect to the convert because they are less expensive than animal offerings, but converts may bring a cow, or other animal, if they can afford it. The offering of one cow can take the place of two birds, following the usual rule. Also, if converts offer one burnt offering and one peace offering, they have fulfilled their obligations. However, they may not bring one meal offering and one peace offering. The *gemara* indicates that these are not sufficient because Num. 15:14 states that *as you do, so shall he do*.[65] This is taken to mean that just as Israelites bring a burnt offering and a peace offering, so converts may bring a burnt offering and a peace offering, similar to the conclusion in Sifré Numbers. Ex. 24:5 records that the Israelites offered burnt offerings and peace offerings at the altar which Moses erected at the foot of Mount Sinai. Furthermore, the *gemara* concludes that the word *as*, *k'šr*, specifically excludes the meal offering, for the word indicates that the converts should do exactly as the Israelites had done. While the *gemara* reaches the same conclusion as Sifré Numbers, it does so by using different biblical texts. In addition, just as the Israelites brought blood sacrifices, so also the converts should bring blood sacrifices; therefore, the meal offering is unacceptable. Curiously, to further establish this point, the *gemara* concludes on the basis of *you and the convert shall be alike before YHWH*, Num. 15:15, that the converts do not act completely like Israelites with regard to the offerings; therefore, they do not fulfill their duty upon conversion by bringing a meal offering.[66] This is a curious statement, for the entire previous discussion was based on the fact that the convert does act the same as the Israelites. Clearly, this artificial interpretation was meant to justify an already accepted practice: The meal offering was not acceptable. We learn about the permissibility of the bird offering from Num. 15:14, *And when, throughout the ages, the convert who has taken up residence with you . . . would present an offering by fire of pleasing odor to YHWH . . .* , for the bird used as a burnt offering is the only offering which is totally offered up to YHWH,[67] a point also made in Sifré Numbers. The skin of cattle is not burnt; it is given to the priests. In addition, the *gemara* offers a rather labored argument to prove that the converts must bring *two* birds. Because the offering of one bird is not mentioned in the Torah, it is not sufficient to offer only one pigeon. The *gemara* responds, however, that with reference to the freewill offering Lev. 1:15 states that *the priest shall bring it. . . .* The singular objective pronoun indicates that there was only one bird. The text responds that no *obligatory* offering which consists of only one bird is found in the Bible, a point also made in Sifré Numbers. To this the text responds that when the period of confinement for the woman who has borne a child is over, she brings one pigeon or turtledove as a sin offering. However, an anonymous sage responds that in addition, she brings a lamb for a burnt offering, based on Lev. 12:6. Therefore, the one bird does not suffice as her offering.[68]

The *gemara* asks if converts can be accepted at the present time, for the Israelites no longer offer sacrifices, so that the two birds can no longer be brought to the Temple. A *beraita* states that although the converts cannot now bring a bird offering, they should put aside one-quarter of a *dinar*, the minimum one could spend on the bird offering. However, Simeon claims that Yohanan b. Zakkai held a vote on this rule and abolished it, and Idi b. Gershom taught in Adda b. Ahaba's name that Simeon's teaching is accepted, so that the money is not put aside.[69] At one point, Aha b. Jacob responds that converts are always accepted, no matter the historical situation;[70] however, as we shall see, this view was not universally accepted. While Tosefta had connected only Simeon with this issue, the Palestinian Talmud[71] had already linked Yohanan's name to it. Although Tosefta and the Palestinian Talmud noted that converts do not bring bird offerings with the Temple in ruins, no earlier text had asked if this meant that gentiles could no longer convert; the Babylonian Talmud is the only text to raise this possibility. By asking the question in this way, the *gemara* demonstrates that the bird offering was no longer an essential feature of the conversion ritual. It also suggests that some may have thought that conversion may be inappropriate after the destruction of Temple.

The new element in the conversion ritual is found in a *beraita*[72] that details the procedure for the questioning and instructing of the prospective converts.[73] When gentiles desire to convert, they are asked why they wish to change communities, given the fact that "at the present time" Israel is oppressed, persecuted, and suffering. If they reply that they realize that even though Israel is suffering they are still unworthy to join the community, but that they still desire to convert, they are immediately accepted. At that time they are told about some of the commandments and informed about the punishments due to those who violate them. They are informed about the importance of supporting the Israelite poor through the gleanings, the forgotten sheaves, the corners, and the poor man's tithe.[74] They are reminded that as gentiles they would not have been punished for eating animal fats or for working on the Sabbath. But now, if they eat fat or profane the Sabbath, they will be punished by "cutting off" for the former and by stoning for the latter. In addition, they are acquainted with the reward of the world-to-come, which is given "only to the righteous." In the *sugya* the sages are warned that the prospective converts should not be encouraged or dissuaded inordinately by the sages' going into excessive details.[75] If after this instruction the gentiles still wish to convert, the males are immediately circumcised. If any shreds of the foreskin remain, they must be circumcised again. As soon as the male has recovered from the circumcision, he is ritually immersed. At that time, two sages stand by his side and further instruct him in some of the minor and major commandments. When he finishes his immersion, he is considered an Israelite "in all respects."[76] For the immersion of a woman, the sages have her sit in water up to her neck, while two learned men instruct her in the commandments.

Of interest is the fact that the converts are taught about the agricultural gifts given to the poor, which were incumbent only upon Israelites in the Land of Israel and served as a means of strengthening group cohesion and solidarity. This symbolism is underscored by the fact that this discussion occurs in a Babylonian text, edited in a country in which the agricultural gifts were not applicable or observed.[77] Furthermore, they are warned about the restrictions placed on their eating habits and on their activity on the Sabbath, two facets of Judaism that fascinated the gentiles and most obviously distinguished Israelites from non-Israelites in the ancient world.[78] Also, while this whole *sugya* assumes that male converts are circumcised *and* immersed, it makes no reference to the bird offering. Finally, the instruction takes place at the time of the conversion, not before.

In a set of stories meant to illustrate the contrasting characters of Shammai and Hillel, we also see paradigms of two rabbinic types: One which tried to accommodate those who wished to convert, and one which did not. The passages imply that those sages who were kind and considerate would also strive to aid those who wished to join the Israelite community. The first story is based on the assumption that the convert had to learn the totality of Israelite tradition,[79] both the Written and the Oral Torah. Once, a gentile approached Shammai to inquire about conversion. When the former discovered that he would have to learn two torahs, he stated that he would convert on the condition that Shammai teach him only the Written Torah. Shammai became angry and sent the gentile away. Hillel, however, accepted him as a convert, presumably accepting his condition. On the first day, Hillel taught him the first three letters of the alphabet. On the second day, he reversed the order of the letters. When the student objected, Hillel replied that the student had to trust him concerning the Oral Torah. Although the story is primarily intended to contrast the personalities of Hillel and Shammai,[80] it does make the point that the converts were responsible for learning the totality of Israelite culture, the Written *and* the Oral Torah, so that they had to have a rabbinic mentor.

In the second account, a gentile approaches Shammai and states that he will convert if the latter would teach him the Torah while he stands on one foot. Shammai becomes angry and drives him away with a builder's cubit. Hillel, on the other hand, summarizes the Torah by stating, "What is hateful to you, do not to your neighbor. That is the whole Torah, while the rest is a commentary on it. Go and learn." Again, the story's purpose is to contrast Hillel and Shammai, but it also makes the point that there were some who favored encouraging converts and would do whatever they could to help them join the community, while there were others who were not so accommodating.[81]

In the third story, through the use of his own reasoning the gentile is led by Hillel to the understanding that neither converts nor King David could be high priests.[82] The point of the passage is that while the converts are not equal to high priests, in this regard they have the same standing as one of Israel's greatest kings. After hearing the portion of the Torah that lists the spectacular garments the high priest wore, Ex. 28:4, a gentile approached Shammai and said that he would convert on the condition that he be made a high priest. Shammai became angry and drove the gentile away with a builder's cubit. When the gentile approached Hillel, the latter accepted him as a convert. Hillel then instructed the gentile to study the Torah, so that he would become familiar with the rites and rituals incumbent upon Israel and the priesthood. When the convert read Num. 1:51, *when the Tabernacle is to set out, the Levites shall take it down, and when the Tabernacle is to be pitched, the Levites shall set it up; any outsider who encroaches shall be put to death,* and discussed it with Hillel, he realized that even King David would be put to death if he attempted to serve as high priest. He reasoned that if King David would be put to death, surely a convert "who comes with his staff and his wallet" will be executed if he encroaches upon the spaces reserved for the Levites and priests. Thus, the convert is led by his own reasoning to understand that he could not become a high priest, and he is led to understand Shammai's harsh rejection. He approached Shammai and indirectly criticized him for not explaining the matter to him. He then went to Hillel and blessed him for allowing him to enjoy the benefits of Judaism, even though he could not be a high priest. Eventually, the three converts met and praised Hillel, for it was his patience which allowed them to benefit from Judaism.[83]

Normally, conversion is a public matter which is performed in the presence of a rabbinic court. However, if people claim that they are converts, they are believed if they are well-known to the person to whom they make the claim.[84] One time a male convert appeared before Judah and claimed that he had converted in a private ritual and that he did not have any witnesses to the ceremony; however, he did have children. Judah rejected the person's claim, because through it he had made his children acceptable within the Israelite community, so that he might have had an ulterior motive in claiming that he was a convert.[85]

Motives for Conversion

Like earlier documents, the Babylonian Talmud is concerned about a person's motives for converting. It argues that those who convert only in order to benefit from the advantages which Israelites enjoy should not be accepted into the community. A *beraita*[86] states that converts will not be accepted in the days of the Messiah,[87] just as they were not accepted during the days of David and Solomon.[88] The reason for this is that during these times one could not be sure that the converts had joined the Israelites for reasons other than their hoping to share in the Israelites' material rewards.[89] Yosi says that in the messianic future[90] idol worshipers will come to convert. The *gemara* then raises an objection, based on the statement that converts will not be accepted during the messianic age, just as they were not accepted at the time of David and Solomon. The *gemara* responds that they will be *grym grwrym*,[91] who will place *tefilin* on their arms and foreheads, fringes on their garments, and *mezuzot* on their doorposts. However, when the battle between Gog and Magog rages, they will throw away these religious objects and return to their gentile communities. In response to their actions, YHWH will laugh at them.[92] Thus, by their actions these *grym grwrym* illustrate the sages' point that those who would seek to convert at the time of the Messiah were doing so for illegitimate reasons. On the other hand, the phrase *in your land*[93] teaches that converts within the Land of Israel are accepted even though it is possible that the

only reason they have become converts "at the present time" is so that
they might benefit from the gifts given to the Israelite poor, such as the
gleanings, the forgotten sheaf, the poor man's tithes, and the grain left in
the corner of the fields.[94] Finally, the Samaritans presented a problem to
some of the sages because the latter questioned the sincerity of the former's original conversion.[95]

Of interest is the fact that if gentiles convert as children, they may
rescind their actions as adults. Huna states that a gentile minor[96] who
wishes to convert is immersed upon the order of the court. Because it is
to the person's advantage to be converted, the court may do so for a minor.
However, an anonymous opinion argues that minors are converted by their
parents without the participation of the court because they willingly accept what their parents do. In response to this discussion, Joseph stated
that proselytes who were converted as minors may, as adults, reject their
conversion and return to their status as gentiles without any court-imposed
punishment.[97] The *gemara* also states that when a female convert reaches
adulthood, she has one hour during which she may decide to leave the
Israelite community.[98] Clearly, the rabbis wanted to emphasize that conversion is a gentile's free choice.[99]

Some passages in the Babylonian Talmud imply that conversion does
not necessarily improve the converts' lot. In a *beraita*[100] Hanania b. Simeon
b. Gamaliel stated that converts "at the present time" are oppressed
because while they were still gentiles they had not observed the seven
Noachide commandments incumbent upon all human beings, and, by implication, they have yet to atone for their misdeeds as gentiles. Yosi responds that because converts are considered to be newborn children, they
cannot now be held accountable for previous deeds. Therefore, they are
suffering now because they are not as well versed in the commandments
as the native-born Israelite, so that they cannot yet fully observe them.
Abba Hanan said in Eleazar's name that converts suffer because they perform the commandments out of fear of being punished by god; they do
not perform them out of love for god. "Others" say that they are punished
because they delayed in converting. Abbahu[101] cites Ruth 2:12 in support
of the opinion attributed to "others": *May YHWH reward your deeds. May
you have a full recompense from YHWH, the God of Israel, under whose wings you
have sought refuge!*[102] In general, these passages do not place the converts in
a favorable light.

Converts as a Subclass of People Israel

Meir's claim that converts, gentiles, slaves, and *mamzerim* constitute
different classes of society and that one couple may produce five such

castes derives from his claim that converts represent a distinct class within the People Israel.[103] However, there were those who did not accept Meir's claim that the converts constituted a separate assembly within the Israelite people. Aqiba[104] held that those who are subject to the penalty of negative precepts, such as a man-made eunuch, with whom marriage is forbidden by a negative precept,[105] are equal to those who are punished by "cutting off." But those who are not subject to the penalty of "cutting off" may not perform the *halisah* ceremony or engage in a levirate marriage. Therefore, how could Aqiba state in mYeb. 8:4 that a man-made eunuch engages in the *halisah* ceremony? Ammi replied that we are dealing with the case where the eunuch's deceased brother had married a convert. In this case Aqiba agrees with Yosi that the assembly of converts is not considered an assembly, so that the converted woman may marry the eunuch and the *halisah* ceremony applies.

Elsewhere, a *beraita*[106] records that Yosi held that a convert may marry a female *mamzer*, while Judah taught that a convert may not marry a female *mamzer*. An anonymous ruling states that a convert, along with a freed slave and a *halal*, may marry a priest's daughter. The *gemara* claims that because Yosi does not consider the converts to constitute one of the assemblies mentioned in Deut. 23:3–4 and 23:9, he allows a convert to marry a female *mamzer*. However, because Judah does consider the converts to constitute one of the assemblies—he counts the priests and Levites as *one* of the five assemblies—he prohibits the marriage between a convert and a female *mamzer*. Another view is that Judah bases his opinion on Num. 15:15: *the rest of the congregation. There shall be one law for you and for the convert who dwells with you.* Because the word "congregation" seems to be superfluous, Judah deduces that convert is included in the term wherever it occurs. Yosi, on the other hand, focuses on the requirement that converts and Israelites be treated the same.

Also, Yohanan said that had not R. Judah declared that with regard to the children of Egyptians who could enter the congregation Scripture made the ruling dependent on birth, so that the females are also forbidden until the third generation, his teaching would not have been accepted, for it was taught that converts constitute a separate assembly.[107]

The fact that converts are considered to be a distinct class within Israelite society produces an interesting interpretation of Mishnah's[108] discussion of the relationship among these various classes. With regard to the saving of lives, Mishnah states that a *natin* takes precedence over a convert and that the convert takes precedence over the freed slave. The anonymous *gemara* states that the *natin* takes precedence over the convert because the former was raised in holiness—that is in the Israelite community—while the latter was not. Similarly, the convert takes precedence over the freed slave because the latter was included in Noah's curse,[109] while the former was not. The *gemara* also contains a *beraita*[110] in which Simeon b. Yohai says that it is logical that an emancipated slave should take precedence over a convert, for the former was raised in holiness, while the latter was not. However, the former was cursed, while the latter was not; therefore, a convert takes precedence over the freed slave, just as we find in Mishnah.[111] Eleazar b. Zadoq's disciples asked him why people are willing to marry a convert, but not a freed slave. He responded that this was because the slave was included in the curse, while the convert was not. Another answer states that the convert is considered to have protected her chastity, while the freed slave is not. One assumption here is that the woman who planned to convert would take pains to maintain her sexual purity.[112]

Differences between Converts and Native-Born Israelites

A lengthy discussion attempts to explain Judah's teaching that the daughter of a male convert is like the daughter of a male *halal*.[113] Here we discover that to some authorities converts are not like the majority of the congregation.[114] Additional evidence of the fact that converts did not achieve the same status as native-born Israelites can be found in the treatment of their role in the Israelite judicial system. For example, as we have seen before, the *halisah* ceremony could be performed only before a court composed of Israelites, not converts.[115] Rav Judah once asked Samuel b. Judah to officiate at a *halisah* ceremony. However, Samuel responded that on the basis of the phrase *in Israel* in Deut. 25:7 we know that the ceremony must be performed before Israelites, not converts. Samuel therefore excuses himself because he is a convert.[116] Rabba holds that according to the Bible, a convert may adjudicate capital cases involving only converts.[117] Similarly, Ashi explains that the converts brought the first fruits to the altar, but could not recite Deut. 26:3,[118] because the Land of Israel was not given to their ancestors. For this reason, Yosi could not make the recitation of the verse an essential feature of the ritual involved with the first fruits.[119] Finally, we learn that converts are eligible to try only civil cases.[120] And, even though in theory converts could be civil administrators in Israelite towns, this was not often put into practice according to the *gemara*.[121]

Another difference between converts and native-born Israelites regards their ability to purchase a Hebrew slave or to fall under the rules concerning Hebrew slaves. Some held that a convert could not be acquired as a Hebrew slave and that a convert (or a woman) may not acquire a Hebrew slave. The former rule derives from Lev. 25:10, which teaches that the slaves should be redeemed by their *nearest redeemer;* that is, they must be returned to their families, which is impossible for converts, who had severed all ties with their families. And because it is a general rule that only one who can be acquired as a Hebrew slave may acquire a Hebrew slave, converts cannot acquire Hebrew slaves. Nahman b. Isaac claims, however, that the convert can acquire a Hebrew slave under the same terms that a gentile acquires a slave. In this case, upon their master's death, the slaves are freed, for the gentile's—or convert's—children cannot inherit the slaves.[122]

One of the major topics of discussion was the converts' ability to marry into the priestly caste,[123] a priest,[124] or a priest's daughter.[125] This concern derived from the rabbinic view of the sanctity of the priesthood,[126] and from the uniquely ethnic nature of the priestly class which was related to the view that the Temple was an ethnic shrine of the People Israel.[127] Judah rules that a woman may marry a priest only if both of her parents were Israelites. Eliezer b. Jacob argues that a woman may marry into the priestly caste even if only one of her parents was a native-born Israelite, a view attributed to him in Mishnah.[128] Commenting upon Yosi's statement in Mishnah[129] that the daughter of two converted parents may marry into the priestly caste, Hamnuna in the name of Ulla and Rabbah b. Bar Hana agree that the *halakhah* follows Yosi. However, Rabbah states that since the destruction of the Temple, the priests have guarded their dignity by abstaining from marrying the daughter of two converts, thus following Eliezer b. Jacob's opinion in Mishnah.[130] Nahman stated that Huna said that if a priest came for advice, he was given Eliezer b. Jacob's teaching. However, if he came for approval after he had married, he was told about Yosi's view.[131] This discussion again points to the fact that during the amoraic period in Babylonia there were those who held contradictory opinions concerning the converts' place within the People Israel. Here, Rabbah holds that priests did not marry the daughter of two converts, while Yosi permitted such marriages. Nahman offers a compromise position: Priests should not marry the daughters of two converts; however, such marriages, if they did occur, were not dissolved after the fact.

On the basis of Lev. 21:14,[132] Zakkai taught in Yohanan's presence that the High Priest may marry a woman whose parents were from the same gentile nation, but who was born after her parents converted.[133] Yohanan responded that *of his own kin* in the verse means that the High Priest may marry a virgin descended from two nations; that is, the priest may marry the daughter of an Ammonite convert who is married to an Israelite woman.[134] Another version is reported in which Yohanan states the same ruling, only here deriving it from an inference instead of a biblical verse.[135]

Converts and Their Heirs

Converts were considered to be newborn children without any legal ties to their gentile relatives and so could die without any legally recognized relatives.[136] Again in the Babylonian Talmud, therefore, discussions of gentiles who died serve as a means of refining the rules for acquiring ownerless property.[137] Helbo teaches in Huna's name that an Israelite cannot acquire the animal which belonged to a convert who died without heirs by seizing its reins. The *gemara* supports this ruling by connecting the word *mwsyrh*, reins, with *msr*, to hand over. Because the property belonging to a convert who died without heirs is considered to be ownerless property, there was no one who could "hand it over."[138]

Joseph and Abayye deal with one who acquires a dead convert's field and digs in it. According to Joseph, if an Israelite digs in a field he believes is his property but later discovers that the field belonged to a convert who died without heirs, the Israelite has not acquired the field. Even though the field could have been acquired by any Israelite and digging constitutes an accepted form of "acquiring," the Israelite did not take possession of the field because he did not intend to acquire it, for he believed that it already was his. However, as Abayye notes, if an Israelite digs in a field which he believes belongs to one convert who had recently died without leaving heirs, but later discovered that it actually was the possession of another convert who had recently died without leaving heirs, he has still acquired the field. Because he intended to acquire the field, it is his. His error concerning who owned the field does not matter. The discussion of the Israelites' needing to intend to acquire a field which belonged to a convert who died without leaving heirs is brought to explain why betrothal for a levirate union is regarded as invalid, even though ordinary betrothal with the same woman would have been acceptable.[139]

Elsewhere we find a discussion of whether or not by erecting a wall on it one may acquire the property of a convert who died without heirs. If one partition was put up upon another, Hisda ruled that it may establish a Sabbath limit, but it may not be used to take possession of the property of a convert who died without leaving heirs. Sheshet ruled that a partition on top of another partition does not even establish a valid *'erub*. Even if the bottom fence were sunk into the ground, the second fence does not effect possession of the dead convert's property. In Judah's name, Jeremiah Bira'ah ruled that if an Israelite threw vegetable seeds into a crevice which he had not dug himself on a dead convert's land and another Israelite came and hoed a little, the second Israelite acquires the land, for the first Israelite did not effect any improvement on the property, while the second Israelite did improve it. This is used to illustrate the fact that even if a second fence were placed on a fence which was sunk into the ground, the second fence does not constitute an improvement on the property which could lead to one's acquiring the dead convert's estate. This ruling is then illustrated by the following story: A certain woman put up a fence on top of another fence in a dead convert's estate. A man came and hoed the ground a little. When the latter appeared before Nahman, he granted the estate to the man who had hoed on the property. When the women objected, Nahman told her that she had not acquired the land in an acceptable manner.[140]

In fact, the issue of improving the property one has acquired is dealt with in several different pericopae. MB.B. 3:3 states that usucaption for a period of three years without providing proof that the person has a right to the property does not constitute acquisition. However, if one received the property as a gift, shared it with his brothers, or claimed title to the property of a convert who died without heirs, one may acquire the property by shutting it in, walling it up, or breaking down something in it. The *gemara* states that the three-year term does not apply to the property taken from a convert who died without heirs, the property received as a gift, or that owned by brothers because all one needs to do in these cases is to establish ownership of the property; no money needs to change hands. Therefore, if the new owner does anything at all to establish his ownership—such as setting up a door, making a fence, or building an opening— he has acquired the land.[141]

Ulla held that any act which confers legal ownership of the property of a deceased convert on the person who seizes it first also confers legal ownership of a fellow Israelite's property. Similarly, any act which does not confer legal ownership of the property of a deceased convert does not confer legal ownership of the property of a fellow Israelite. Sheshet objected to this general principle, for although one may gain possession of a dead convert's plowed field by holding it for three years, one may not acquire an Israelite's property in this way. Similarly, one may acquire an Israelite's property by gathering the field's crops, but one may not acquire a dead convert's property in this manner. In order to acquire a deceased convert's property, one must improve it, which is not necessary for the acquisition of an Israelite's property.[142]

In Yohanan's name, Assi states that if an Israelite establishes some advantage to himself by placing or removing a pebble on the estate of a convert who died without leaving heirs, he acquires title to the land. However, this is acceptable only if by placing the pebble, the Israelite causes the water to flow to the place it is required in the field, or if by removing the pebble he makes a passage, so that the water can run onto the field where it is needed. If his action causes water to render the field useless, he does not acquire the field. If he allows the water to flow from a flooded field, he also does not acquire the field, because his actions are those of any good neighbor, not those of one who has improved the field for his own use.[143]

Nahman teaches in the name of Rabbah b. Abbuha that if an Israelite builds a large villa on the estate of a deceased convert who left no heirs, and another man comes and fixes the doors, the latter becomes the owner. In this case, because the first Israelite did not complete the building, it is considered to be like a pile of bricks, so that he is not considered to have improved the property.[144] As noted above, these rules primarily detail procedures for acquiring ownerless property. They tell us nothing about attitudes toward the convert.

Dimi b. Joseph said in the name of Eleazar that if an Israelite finds a villa already erected on the estate of a convert who died without leaving heirs, he may acquire ownership of the property by adding one coat of whitewash or by painting a mural decoration on the building, because he has improved the building. Joseph said that he must whitewash a cubit of the building, and Hisda added that this must be done by the door. If it is done elsewhere, he must whitewash more than a cubit.[145] Rav said that if an Israelite draws a figure of an animal or a bird on a villa which belonged to a convert who died without heirs, even if it covers an area less then a cubit or is not near the door,[146] he has acquired the property. In fact, we are told that Rav acquired the garden adjoining his school only by drawing a figure on it.[147] These passages, by the way, should end all discussion of the rabbis' application of the second commandment.

Amram claimed that Sheshet taught the following: If an Israelite spreads mattresses on the floor of the estate of a convert who died without heirs and sleeps on them, he acquires ownership to the estate because he has derived benefit from it. According to the *gemara*, Sheshet based this teaching on a *beraita* which deals with taking possession of a slave who ties or unties his master's shoes, carries his clothes for him to the bath, undresses him, washes him, anoints him, scrapes him, dresses him, puts his shoes on him, or lifts him up. The analogy is that just as the master acquires the slave from whom he has derived benefit, so also one acquires property from which he has derived benefit.[148]

The Palestinian Talmud[149] contained a discussion of acquiring the fields separated by a path which had belonged to a convert who died without heirs, and this is also taken up in the Babylonian *gemara*. Assi taught in Yohanan's name that if the convert who died without heirs owned two adjacent fields with a boundary between them, and the Israelite takes possession of one of the fields with the intention of acquiring it, he acquires ownership of only that one field. If he takes possession of one field with the intention of acquiring both fields, he becomes the owner of only the field he acquires, for the boundary makes them two separate pieces of property. If he takes possession of one field, but intends to acquire the other, he may not acquire either, because he has not intended to acquire the field he possesses, and he cannot acquire the other field only by intention. Zera asks what happens if the Israelite takes possession of one of the fields with the intention of acquiring that field, the boundary, and the other field. Zera's case is left unresolved. Eleazar asks what happens if the Israelite takes possession of the boundary with the idea of acquiring both fields. This is also left unresolved.[150] Assi said in Yohanan's name that a narrow path and a cistus hedge serve as a partition in a convert's estate, so that separate acts are required for acquiring fields on either side of the hedge or the narrow path.[151] Elsewhere[152] we are told that when Aha b. Awia was sitting in front of Assi b. Hanina, he stated in the name of Assi b. Hanina that a cistus hedge forms a partition in a dead convert's estate.[153]

A discussion about the ways in which slaves acquire their freedom is phrased in terms of whether or not one acquires slaves when taking possession of a dead person's property, and this is also dealt with in terms of a convert who died without heirs. A *beraita*[154] contains an anonymous opinion which states that if a convert dies without heirs and Israelites take possession of his property, which includes slaves, all the slaves gain their freedom. Abba Saul disagrees and rules that the adult slaves acquire their freedom, but the minor slaves become the property of whomever acquires the dead convert's estate. The issue is a discussion of the manner in which a slave is freed.[155] Our *sugya* follows a story about the convert Judah the Indian. He became ill and was visited by Mar Zutra. Seeing that Judah was about to die, Mar Zutra acquired Judah's slave by means of *hazaqah*, for he had the slave serve him by removing his shoes and taking them to his house. The *gemara* then raises the point that some thought the slave was a minor, so that according to Abba Saul, he should have gone to whomever acquired Judah's property.[156]

The means by which one can acquire Hebrew slaves also is discussed in the context of how one acquires items from a dead convert's estate. MQid. 1:2 states that a Hebrew slave is acquired by money or a deed (*štr*). The *gemara* discusses the possibility of *hazaqah* as a valid means of acquir-

ing a Hebrew slave. As part of this discussion, the *sugya* states that because
a dead convert's property can be acquired by *ḥazaqah*, one should conclude
that a Hebrew slave can also be acquired by the same means.[157]

In support of his claim that an embryo can acquire ownership of property upon the death of its father, Sheshet cites a *beraita*[158] which deals with
the death of a convert who had no heirs. If a convert died without leaving
heirs and Israelites seized his estate, but subsequently it was discovered
that the dead convert had a son or that his wife was pregnant, the property
must be returned to the legal heir. If, however, the son dies or the wife
miscarries, a second Israelite may acquire the estate. Sheshet's point is
that the embryo must have acquired the property. If not, why did the
Israelites have to acquire it again if the woman suffered a miscarriage?[159]

Similarly, the rules concerning the payment due as a result of injury
to a pregnant woman are dealt with in the context of a convert who died
without heirs. MB.Q. 5:4 states that if a man intended to strike another
man but accidentally struck a pregnant woman and caused her to miscarry,
compensation is paid for the value of the embryo. Simeon b. Gamaliel
states that the embryo's value is paid to the husband or to his heirs. If the
woman was a convert who was married to a convert who had died without
heirs,[160] no compensation is paid because there are no heirs. The same
rule applies if the woman was a freed slave married to a freed slave.[161]
Rabba taught that this rule applied only if the woman was struck while
her husband was alive, for in that case, the husband would have been
entitled to compensation as would his heirs. However, because he subsequently died without leaving heirs, no compensation need be paid. However, if the woman was struck after her husband had died, she would have
been entitled to compensation, so that the one who struck her would have
to pay her, even though her husband had died. Hisda objects and states
that only when the husband is alive is compensation an issue, for the
mother does not have a claim.[162] On bB.Q. 49b an attempt is made to
show that the difference between Hisda and Rabbah relates to an earlier
disagreement between tannaitic teachings: If the blow were delivered
after the death of the converted husband, one tannaitic teaching holds that
the one who delivered the blow is liable for paying compensation, while
another tannaitic tradition teaches that he does not have to pay compensation. While Rabbah would hold that two tannaitic teachings disagreed
about liability, Hisda could maintain that the two tannaitic teachings
taught about different things. One taught about the compensation due to
the husband, while the other dealt with the decrease in the woman's value
as a result of the miscarriage. One tannaitic statement followed the opinion of the rabbis that the decrease in the woman's value must be compen-

sated for by payment to her husband, while Simeon b. Gamaliel in mB.Q. 5:4 holds that the loss of value is shared by the husband and wife, so that even if the husband dies, compensation must still be paid to the woman. In fact, the *gemara* suggests, while her husband is alive she receives half of the compensation, but after his death, she is entitled to the total amount of the compensation. The *gemara* then suggests that we could read one tannaitic statement as dealing with the increase in the woman's value due to the embryo, while the other discusses the loss of the value of the embryo itself. This possibility, however, is rejected, for with regard to the increase of her value due to the embryo, she can acquire all of it upon her converted husband's death. However, she cannot acquire any compensation for the death of the embryo.

Another *beraita*[163] states that if a man injures a woman and causes a miscarriage, he pays to the woman compensation for depreciation and pain and to her husband compensation for the embyro's value. If either the man or the woman is not alive, the compensation is paid to the heirs. If the woman and her husband were converts, no compensation is paid if they died, for they have no legal heirs.

The punishment meted out to an ox which caused injury is also discussed in terms of a convert who died without heirs.[164] A *beraita*[165] states that the word ox, *šwr*, appears seven times in Exodus 21:28–32[166] in order to teach us that the ox of a woman, of an orphan who is a minor, of a guardian, of the wilderness, of the Sanctuary, of a convert who died without heirs, as well as a man's ox, are included in the section. Judah states that one does not stone the ox of the wilderness, of the Sanctuary, or of a convert who died without heirs, because they do not have private owners. Huna says that Judah would also exempt from stoning the ox which gored a person and then was consecrated to the Temple and the ox which was abandoned after it gored a person. This is derived from the fact that Judah specifically mentioned the ox of the wilderness and the ox of a convert who died without heirs. Because it is obvious that in both of these cases the ox is ownerless, Judah did not need to mention both cases specifically. He specified them, therefore, only to teach us that an ox which gored a person and then was abandoned or dedicated to the Sanctuary was also exempt from stoning.

Financial transactions too could become complicated when dealing with a convert who died without heirs. Rabbah stated that if a convert who held an Israelite's pledge died without leaving an heir, another Israelite may not take possession of the pledge, because the lien on the pledge became null when the convert died. On the other hand, if an Israelite held the pledge of a convert who died, another Israelite may take possession of it. In that case, the creditor may collect what is due him, and the one who took possession of the pledge is entitled to the balance.[167]

Similarly, the biblical discussion of one who has no kinsman to whom restitution can be made is dealt with in terms of a convert who died without heirs.[168] In an attempt to define a person *who has no kinsman*, Num. 5:8, the *gemara* cites the dispute between Yosi the Galilean and Aqiba from tB.Q. 10:16, concerning an Israelite who robs a convert who he thought died afterwards. However, the two met near Jerusalem, and the convert granted the Israelite a loan for the amount he had stolen. Yosi teaches that the Israelite acquires title to the loan, while Aqiba states that the Israelite may not acquire the money, but must divest himself of it. The *gemara* states that according to Yosi, the plaintiff frees him of his liability in any case, while Aqiba believes that the plaintiff may not free one of his liability. The *sugya* also claims that in Yosi's opinion, the law would apply whether or not the convert turned the money into a loan, while Aqiba goes so far as to claim that even if the stolen money is made into a loan the robber cannot acquire the funds, but he must divest himself of the money.[169]

The *gemara* then asks if it is possible that if one steals from a convert he will ever need to make restitution to the priest, for when the convert dies, does not the thief acquire title to the money? Rabba concludes that if an Israelite robbed a convert and falsely denied that he had stolen from him, but after the convert died, he admitted that he had stolen from the convert, God acquires the title to the money, and it is granted to the priest. This, in effect, is the teaching of mB.Q. 9:11, so that the *gemara* ends by accepting Mishnah's teaching over that found in Tosefta. If the robber were a priest, the money is taken from him and restitution is made to another priest.[170]

Rabina then asks about the case of a converted woman who has been robbed, for Num. 5:8 specifically mentions *a man*.[171] Aaron responds that in fact *a man* refers only to men. However, we learn about the woman from the phrase, *[the amount] repaid* (*hmwšb*), in the same verse which refers to two cases, the man and the woman.[172] A *beraita*[173] argues that *šm* in Num. 5:8 refers to the principal, and the root *šwb* refers to the added fifth. If we claim that *šm* refers to the ram, then we would have to reject Rabba's teaching that restitution cannot be made at night for a theft committed against a convert.[174] Because sacrifices cannot be made at night, if one made restitution with a ram, we would have to reject Rabba's ruling. Rabba also stated that if there was not enough money for each priest of the division to receive a *perutah*, the thief's obligation would not be fulfilled.[175] A *beraita*[176] teaches that *the trespass*, Num. 5:8, refers to the principal, and *be restored* refers to the added fifth, for the verse deals with one who steals from a convert. It is possible, however, that *be restored* refers to a doubling of payment, and the reference is to the theft from a convert which is the subject of Ex. 22:3. On the basis of the full reading of Num. 5:7, the *sugya* concludes that in fact it refers to the principal and not a double payment. Rabba also asked if the priests could set one payment for a robbery committed upon a convert against another payment for a robbery committed upon another convert? Aha b. Raba stated that Rabba taught on the basis of the word *'m* that in fact one payment would have to be shared by each priest of the division, so that the different priests could not take payment from the robbery of different converts.[177] It is assumed that the recompense from one who robbed a convert is given to the priests of a specific division and not to any priest he wishes. Rabba next asks if the priests who receive the compensation were considered heirs or the recipients of an endowment, and the *gemara* concludes that they are considered to be the recipients of an endowment. This is based on the fact that receiving the payment from one who steals from a convert is mentioned among the twenty-four gifts given to the priests.[178]

Even the laws concerning the Sabbath limit are refined by reference to the convert who died without leaving heirs. If an Israelite and a convert shared a dwelling which opened out onto a courtyard, and the convert died during the day on Friday without leaving heirs, even though another Israelite took possession of the dead convert's estate, he imposes restrictions on the other Israelites because the former did not join the 'erub, so that those who possessed the house had not joined with the others around the courtyard. If the convert died after dusk on Friday, no restrictions are imposed, even if no one took possession of his estate because a valid 'erub had been established.[179]

Some of the rules concerning security for loans also relate to converts who died without heirs. If a creditor unlawfully seized and destroyed a pledge belonging to a convert, he is flogged because he is liable to pay compensation but cannot pay it, for there are no legitimate heirs to whom compensation can be made. Zera poses the case of the convert which is explained by the anonymous *gemara*.[180]

In addition, we have a discussion about acquiring land of a convert after he has died through a document which also serves to refine the matter of the value of the document. Yeba the Elder asked Nahman about the legal position of an Israelite who takes possession of documents which were executed by another Israelite for a convert's property. The question revolves around the fact that if the Israelite intends to acquire the land specified in the document by taking possession of the document, he has not actually taken possession of the land, and it is possible that he has not acquired the value of the document because he intended to acquire the land, not the document. However, Nahman suggests that he in fact intended to acquire the document itself, for he could have made practical use of the document by employing it to cover the mouth of a flask.[181]

In a *beraita*[182] we find an exegetical dispute between Judah and Yosi b. Judah on the meaning of Lev. 7:8: *[The priest who offers] a man's burnt offering [shall keep the skin of the burnt offering that he offered]*. Judah states that this excludes the *heqdesh*,[183] and Yosi b. Judah states that it excludes the converts' burnt offerings. Simlai b. Hilkai asked Rabina if Yosi's interpretation means that we do not consider a convert to be a man. Rabina responds that it refers to a convert who died without heirs, so that it does not belong to *a man* when it is offered.[184]

Converts and Their Converted Children and Spouses

Daughters who were conceived before their parents were converted but who were born after they converted also receive attention in the *gemara*. Mishnah[185] states that the daughter of a convert who was conceived before her mother converted[186] but who was born after her mother converted,[187] is to be stoned if she engaged in sexual acts with a man other than her husband or other than the man to whom she was engaged. However, the woman's husband does not need to pay the 100 *sela* fine if he wrongfully accuses her of harlotry, because she is treated only in some respects as an Israelite. Resh Laqish explains that the clause *that she die*, Deut. 22:21, supports the inclusion of the described woman in Mishnah, for this appears to be superfluous because it seems to be an obvious result of the clause *shall stone her with stone*. Her husband need not pay the fine if he falsely accuses her because the clause *that she die* includes the daughter of the convert only with regard to her punishment; it does not include such a woman among those whose husbands are required to pay the fine. Because the proselyte's daughter who was both conceived and born after her mother's conversion is considered to be a full Israelite, she is not mentioned in Mishnah. And, the phrase *in Israel* excludes the convert's daughter who was conceived and born before her mother converted. In this way the sages of the Babylonian *gemara* explain why Mishnah dealt with only the woman who was conceived before her mother's conversion, but born after her mother's conversion.[188]

If before he converted a man had married a woman and her daughter and they converted, he may remain married to one of them after they converted. He must divorce one of them, so that he does not assume that an Israelite may marry a woman and her daughter. If his wife died, some held that he could marry his mother-in-law, while others claimed that such a marriage was prohibited.[189] The Babylonian Talmud deals with the converts who had executed a marriage contract while they were gentiles, an issue raised in earlier documents. If before their conversion two gentiles had executed a *ketubah* upon their marriage, it remains valid after their conversion.[190] However, the *gemara* concludes that the woman is entitled only to the basic value of the marriage agreement and not to anything that might have been added to it after the conversion.[191]

Converts and Levirate Marriages

The complexity concerning the relationship of the converts to their siblings finds further concrete expression in the rabbis' discussions of the *haliṣah* ceremony and levirate marriages. Mishnah[192] states that the sons of a female convert who converted with her neither perform the *haliṣah* ceremony nor engage in levirate marriages. The *gemara* suggests that the reason behind Mishnah's opinion is that the brothers are forbidden to marry each other's wife. The text answers that this is incorrect; rather, the reason for the ruling is that the widow is not subject to the ceremonies, so that the brothers are not obligated to perform them. However, she may marry anyone she wishes, including her brother-in-law.[193]

The *gemara* then takes up the next clause in Mishnah,[194] "even if the one was not conceived in holiness, but was born in holiness, and the other was both conceived and born in holiness," and it focuses on the word "even." If one assumes that the converts who are brothers cannot marry each other's wife, then the "even" makes sense, for they might be regarded as the sons of two different mothers who might be permitted to marry each other's wife, and the "even" signals that this is not the case. However, if one suggests that converts who are brothers can marry each other's wife, what does the "even" clause signify? If both of the brothers were born after their mother converted, so that people might mistake them for Israelites, the widow may still marry anyone she wishes. However, the obligation for levirate marriage and *haliṣah* falls on paternal brothers, which is not applicable if they had a gentile father. Therefore, even if they were both born in holiness, they could not marry each other's widow, so that Aha ruled that they were permitted to marry her only if they both converted with their mother.[195] Another analysis of the text follows which reverses these arguments.

Twin brothers who were converts may not perform the *haliṣah* ceremony or contract a levirate marriage. Referring to the brothers as twins is important for that indicates that they were born at the same time in relationship to their parents' conversion. However, they are not subject to

punishment if they marry each other's wife. If, however, they were conceived before their mother converted but were born after she converted,
they still may not participate in the *halisah* ceremony or contract a levirate
marriage. But they are subject to punishment for marrying each other's
wife, like Israelites. If they were conceived and born after their mother
converted, they are treated like Israelites in all respects. The *gemara* now
deals with the statement in the first case that the brothers are not subject
to punishment if they marry each other's wife. The *gemara* states that even
though they were not guilty of committing a punishable offense, the
rabbis forbid such marriages, so that Israelites would not take this as a
precedent, thinking that the converts were native-born Israelites and that
Israelites could marry each other's wife. The *gemara* concludes, however,
that there was no rabbinical decree on this matter. The clause appears in
the first case only in order to contrast it with the necessary clause in the
second case. In brief, the literary style of the rabbinic text mandated the
appearance of the clause in the first case; it has no logical or legal significance.[196]

Converts as Radically New People

When gentiles joined the Israelite community, some considered them
to be completely new people, like newborn children. In the Babylonian
Talmud, as in the previous rabbinic collections, this change of status is
reflected in several ways. Hanina states that a gentile who blasphemed
YHWH cannot be punished after he converted because different judicial
procedures are applied to an Israelite from those utilized for a gentile.
Therefore, the punishment that applied when the person committed the
crime was no longer applicable when he was to be punished, after he converted, because he was not the same person.[197] Similarly, if a gentile
killed[198] another gentile or had intercourse with another gentile's wife and
converted, he is exempt from punishment.[199]

Along these same lines, the *gemara* cites a tannaitic tradition which
emphasizes the change of status effected by conversion. Israelites may not
marry gentiles, but they may marry converts. If a man betroths a woman
on the condition that she convert, the betrothal is invalid because the condition represents a radical change from what is now reality;[200] that is, the
woman in the future would be qualitatively different from the woman who
now exists. Meir accepts the betrothal, following the principle that one
may take possession of something which does not yet exist, so that he
agrees that the convert is qualitatively different from the gentile.[201] On
the other hand, as we have seen above, if before their conversion two
gentiles had executed a *ketubah*, it remains valid after their conversion.[202]

However, the *gemara* concludes that the woman is entitled only to the basic value of the marriage agreement and not to anything that might have been added to it after the conversion.[203]

If an Israelite loans money to or borrows money from another Israelite, no interest may be charged on the loan. However, interest may be charged on loans made between Israelites and non-Israelites. Therefore, the issue of what one does with regard to loans made to or by converts presents some problems. According to a *beraita*,[204] if an Israelite borrowed money on interest from a gentile and then recorded the principal and interest as a loan, so that the principal and the interest were combined and recorded only as the principal of the loan, and the creditor later converted, the Israelite may exact both the principal and the interest; if the recording of the loan followed his conversion, he may collect the principal, but not the interest. Similarly, if a gentile borrowed money on interest from an Israelite, recorded the principal and the interest as the loan, and then converted, the Israelite may exact both the principal and the interest; if the recording of the loan followed his conversion, he may exact the principal but not the interest. Yosi ruled that the former gentile may collect both the principal and the interest no matter when he converted. Rabba taught in Hisda's name who taught it in Huna's name that the law follows Yosi. Rabba said that Yosi taught what he did so that the person should not convert in order to gain a monetary advantage.[205]

Many sages believed that upon conversion, the new Israelites severed all ties with their non-Israelite relatives. However, not all held this view in all cases. For example, Yohanan taught that if a gentile male had children *before* he converted, his first-born *after* his conversion did not enjoy the privileges of inheritance which the first-born of an Israelite father enjoyed.[206] One might argue that because the son was born while his father was a gentile, he naturally would not receive the privileges accorded to the first-born of an Israelite father. However, Yohanan also taught that if a gentile had children before he converted, he had already fulfilled his obligation to produce children.[207] Therefore, Yohanan does not hold that the converted male is a totally new person, for the children he fathered before his conversion are considered to be his children even after he joined the People Israel. On the other hand, Resh Laqish ruled that because a convert is like a newborn child, the first-born after his father's conversion does receive the special inheritance reserved for the first-born male of an Israelite male. Rabina[208] essentially holds the same opinion as Resh Laqish.[209] If a gentile woman were pregnant for the first time when she converted and she gave birth to a son, he must be redeemed from the priest.[210] The child cannot claim that he is the son of a gentile who is not subject to the

Israelite laws of the first-born because upon conversion, all relationship with gentile relatives are severed.[211] We thus have two different conceptions of the relationship between a converted male and the children he fathered before his conversion.

Although the converts break all ties with their gentile relatives, the *gemara* still distinguishes between a converted woman and an orphan.[212]

As newborn children, the converts severed all ties with their gentile relatives. The fact that their legal relationship to their relatives might not be accurately discerned by members of the Israelite community stands behind some rabbinic discussions. For example, if a convert lives with his sister, Israelites might assume that they too might live with their sisters because they would not realize that the convert, being considered a newborn child, has no legal relationship to his siblings. However, in matters which come before the court, Israelites would know that the convert is like a newborn child. Therefore, two paternal brothers who are converts may testify against each other in court because the Israelites would realize that they were converts, so that they would know that native-born Israelite brothers cannot testify against each other.[213] The rules concerning court testimony could be rather complicated when dealing with converts and their relatives.[214] The *gemara* also contains an extended discussion between Aha b. Jacob and Sheshet concerning whether paternal or maternal brothers who are the children of converts can marry each other's wife.[215]

Rabba makes use of Judah's story about Benjamin,[216] the Egyptian convert who was one of Aqiba's disciples,[217] in a dispute concerning whether one's status passes through the mother or the father. Rabina taught in Yohanan's name that if a person's parents were converts from different nations, the child's status follows that of the parent with the lesser status.[218] In response to Mishnah's[219] statement that a male child's status within the Israelite community follows that of his father if the betrothal is valid and permitted, Simeon brings before Yohanan the case of a male convert who married a female *mamzer.* In this instance, even though the betrothal is valid and no sin was involved in the marriage, the child is considered to be a *mamzer,* for his status follows that of his parent with the lesser status. In support of his position, Simeon quotes Yosi's statement that if a convert marries a *mamzer,* the child is a *mamzer.* Yohanan responds that Mishnah follows Judah who held that a convert could not marry a *mamzer;* therefore, the betrothal in Simeon's example is valid, but the marriage is invalid.[220]

As members of the Israelite community, the converts are responsible for observing the Israelite periods of sacred time. Above we saw that part of the discussion with the prospective convert centers around the Sabbath.[221] The *gemara* contains the earlier discussion about one who converts between the regular Passover and the second Passover.[222] Although only circumcised converts can celebrate Passover, a convert who has been circumcised but who has not undergone the ritual immersion cannot participate in the rituals associated with the Passover sacrifice.[223] On the other hand, similar to a passage in the Palestinian Talmud, Jacob taught in Yohanan's name that for the purposes of selecting, slaughtering, and eating the Passover sacrifice, one may not form a company entirely of converts because they may be too strict about the rules and incorrectly reject an acceptable animal for the ritual.[224] The *sugya* implies that some rabbis believed that converts often did not comprehend the subtleties of Israelite law. The *gemara* agrees with an opinion in Sifra that converts are obligated to observe Sukkot by dwelling in the *sukkah* for seven days.[225] According to Eliezer, gentiles who converted during the week of Sukkot[226] are required to construct a *sukkah* and to dwell in it from the time of their conversion until the end of the holiday.[227] Furthermore, a *beraita*[228] teaches that all males are required to blow the *shofar*, even converted males, which is similar to the view in Tosefta and Sifra that converts must hear the *shofar* when it is blown on Rosh Hashanah.[229]

The converts are also required to fulfill the other religious obligations of the Israelite community. The *gemara* accepts Mishnah's teaching that if a convert died without heirs and left an animal sacrifice, the community pays for the accompanying drink offering if one was not left because the sacrifice is acceptable.[230] According to Hisda and Hiyya[231] there are eight paradigmatic cases of doubt involving a convert.[232] In four of these cases the convert must assume that he is required to fulfill the obligations like any other Israelite because they are considered religious obligations: (1) His wife's sacrifice,[233] (2) the dough offering,[234] (3) the first-born of an unclean animal,[235] (4) the first-born of a clean animal.[236] With regard to the other four cases, which involve monetary issues, the convert is not obligated to fulfill the duty unless the priest can present proof that the convert became liable for these obligations after he or she had converted: (1) The first fleece, (2) the priestly dues, (3) the redemption of his first-born son, and (4) the redemption of the firstling of an ass.[237] In addition, converts may bring the wave offering,[238] must wear fringes,[239] must undergo the rite of the bitter waters,[240] and may be the objects of the priestly benediction.[241] Only the matter of the fringes had not appeared in an earlier document. Some held that if a gentile woman discovered she was in the process of menstruating at the time of conversion, she was to be treated like any other Israelite woman.[242] Also, the rules concerning the firstlings of animals applied to converts and Israelites alike.[243]

If an Israelite woman gives birth, because of her impurity she must undergo prescribed periods of separation from the community, and, at the end of her confinement, she must bring an offering. These rules also apply to converts.[244] However, if the forehead of the baby emerged from a gentile woman's womb, and then she converted, the woman is not required to undergo the period of separation, nor must she bring an offering, for the emergence of the forehead is considered to be a birth, so that the child was born while the woman was still a gentile.[245] The *gemara* brings this highly improbable situation to underscore the difference between converts and gentiles: Converted women follow Israelite purity rules; gentile women do not. According to Jeremiah, if a woman bears a child while she is a gentile, but delivers a sandal-shaped abortion after she converted, she must bring a sacrifice for the sandal-shaped abortion because it is counted as a birth, and it occurred after she became an Israelite who is liable for the offerings after childbirth. She, however, does not need to bring an offering for the child who was born while she was still a gentile.[246]

Converts and native-born Israelites are similar in other ways, for they are both punished in a similar fashion if they blaspheme YHWH.[247] Along these same lines, a convert is considered equal to a native-born Israelite with regard to the laws of kidnapping.[248] Ashi indicated that the converts' "guiding star" was present at Sinai when the Israelites received the Revelation, so that they shared the experience with the native-born Israelites who were there.[249] Elsewhere we discover that at Sinai future generations of both native-born Israelites and converts became obligated to follow YHWH's will as revealed to Moses, an idea which also appears in Tosefta.[250]

Above we saw that converts are on a par with Israelites with regard to their obligation to perform many religious obligations and commandments. In addition, one *sugya* informs us that everyone considers a convert to be an Israelite's brother.[251] The Torah states that Israelites may sell themselves to their brothers in order to pay a debt, and Rabbi tells us that under these rules a native-born Israelite may sell himself to a convert.[252] This, of course, contradicts those who taught that converts could not acquire Hebrew slaves. This contradiction points to the fact that there were competing and contradictory views on the converts and their place within the Israelite community. Some of the material in the Babylonian Talmud suggests that the ideas concerning the converts were being refined throughout the amoraic period. Clearly, not all of the amoraim agreed on exactly how the converts fit into the People Israel.

Related to the converts' change of status are the discussions which center on the converts' inheriting from their gentile parents.[253] The *gemara* concludes that the laws governing what converts may inherit from their gentile parents derive from the scribes, not from the Torah. However, the rules concerning a convert's inheriting from another convert are neither from the scribes nor from the Torah. The *gemara* first states that the converts' inheriting from their gentile father is in accordance with scribal law, not biblical law. The reason for this is that mDem. 6:10 states that a convert and his gentile brother may divide their father's property before they take possession of it, so that the convert will not come into possession of the idols or the libation wine. The *gemara* claims that according to biblical law, even when he takes the money, the convert takes something in exchange for his father's idols. However, the rules governing a gentile's inheriting from a convert or a convert's inheriting from another convert are not covered by the scribes or the Torah, and in support of this claim, the *gemara* cites mSheb. 10:9.[254] These statements may be a reflection of the realization that conversion was not really a biblical phenomenon; therefore, the Torah did not deal with the legal issues involved with the converts' inheritances. However, given the fact that as early as Mishnah we find discussions of what converts may inherit from their gentile parents, the sages had to find an early source for these laws; therefore, they attributed them to the scribes. Because there are no early rabbinic discussions of converts' inheriting from one another and this issue is not covered in the Torah, there was no need for the amoraim to posit an early source for these laws. In fact, the issue is not discussed in the rabbinic texts, for it was assumed that a convert's legally recognized heirs were treated the same as Israelite heirs. As we have seen, the only issues that concern the rabbis center around converts who died without legally acceptable heirs. Of course, the assumption that the Torah did not deal with conversion or converts stands in opposition to the claim that certain biblical figures had converted to Judaism and to the midrashic interpretations of the biblical references to forms of the Hebrew root *gwr*. Again, this points to the fact that there is no single Babylonian amoraic view of the converts or conversion.

When some gentiles appeared before Rabbah b. Abbahu in order to convert, he told them that they should sell all of their possessions before they converted, because after they became Israelites, their forbidden items, such as articles used in the worship of foreign deities, could not be freed of their taint, and as Israelites they could not enjoy any benefit from their possessions or the money gained through their sale. However, in the case of an inheritance, the rabbis took a lenient view, for they were afraid that the converts would return to their gentile life if they thought they would lose their inheritances.[255] Therefore, if a convert inherits dogs and pigs, he may sell them one at a time; he need not dispose of them all at once.[256]

There was also the question concerning whether or not those who sought to convert to Judaism would prepare themselves before their conversions. One *sugya* states[257] that a gentile boy who converted is not believed when he offers testimony about a family based on his observations while he was a gentile. Yohanan b. Beroqa, however, claims that the boy is believed. The reason for the difference between the anonymous opinion and Yohanan's view is that the anonymous sage holds that a gentile would not pay careful attention to what occurred, so that his testimony would be invalid in an Israelite context. Yohanan, on the other hand, believed that because the child intended to convert, he would have known about the matters relevant in an Israelite context, so that his testimony would have been appropriately informed. In Yohanan's view, from the time that people decide to convert to Judaism, they would seek to become familiar with Israelite traditions, so that they would be concerned with matters important to other Israelites.[258] Similarly, Rabbah explains that Yosi permitted a convert to marry immediately upon her conversion because the latter believed that women who were considering conversion would use a contraceptive when they engaged in sexual activity, so that they would not be pregnant upon their conversion.[259] Again, it is difficult to know if any of these discussions deal with real life situations. Nevertheless, they do assume a particular view of conversion. These *sugyot* assume that at least some conversions were not the result of "sudden enlightment," for the converts had time to prepare for their entrance into the Israelite community. In fact, they presuppose that the gentiles had some familiarity with Israelite law and custom, so that they knew what to do in relationship to rabbinic *halakhah* while they were still gentiles. Thus, in the opinion of the sages behind these pericopae, converts were gentiles who had some of knowledge of Judaism and who prepared themselves for entrance into the People Israel before the actual conversion ritual.

The marriage laws concerning converts were extremely complex because (1) children could be conceived while their parents were gentiles but born after their parents' conversion,[260] and (2) converts severed all legal relationships with their gentile relatives upon their conversion. If a convert were conceived before his mother converted but born afterwards, he must follow the marriage taboos with regard to his mother's relatives but not with regard to his father's relatives.[261] Yosi reports the incident of the convert Niphates, who married the wife of his deceased maternal brother, who was also a convert. The *gemara* takes this occasion to debate whether or not Israelites will get the impression that Israelites are allowed to marry the wives of their deceased maternal brothers.[262] Ben Yasyan reported that while in a coastal town he encountered a convert who had married the wife of his deceased maternal brother. Upon questioning, the convert told Ben Yasyan[263] that Aqiba had permitted the woman and her children to contract such marriages. In fact, he reported that Aqiba had specifically stated that a convert may marry the wife of his maternal brother.[264] The pericope presupposes that native-born Israelites would follow the practices of converts because they will not perceive any differences between themselves and the converts.

Converts and Their Gentile Past

According to Mishnah,[265] if an Israelite is suspected of having intercourse with a gentile who eventually converted, he may not marry her. However, if he had already married her, the marriage is accepted. Ashi explains that the reason Mishnah prohibited the marriage between the convert and the Israelite was to prevent the spreading of rumors that the Israelites had engaged in sexual activities with gentiles.[266] Elsewhere we are told that people cannot contract a marriage on the condition that their intended spouse will convert after the marriage,[267] because people's ability to convert is not in their own power, for conversion must have the approval of a rabbinic court.[268] Finally, there were even those who totally opposed marriage between native-born Israelites and converts. Rabba had told his children that they should not sit on the bed of an Aramean woman, and some interpreted this to mean that one should not marry a convert.[269] Both of these notions result from a concern with the reality that the converts were once gentiles. As in the earlier texts, the Babylonian Talmud notes that there were those who claimed that a converted woman had to wait for three months after her conversion before she could marry an Israelite in order to ensure that she was not pregnant. Some claimed that Samuel ruled that converts who were minors, along with emancipated slaves, need not wait three months after ending one marriage before they enter into another marriage. Israelite minors, however, must wait three months. With regard to this ruling, the *gemara* explains that the rabbis required a minor to wait three months between marriages as a precaution against those who were not minors. Others claim that Samuel said that neither mature converts nor Israelite minors need to wait the three months between marriages. The *gemara* explains that here he was concerned with harlotry, and harlotry with a minor was such a rare occurrence that he did not require the Israelite minor to wait the three months.[270]

Converts from Biblical Nations

The Torah had laid down some restrictions concerning the permissibility of Moabites', Ammonites', Edomites', and Egyptians' joining the Israelite community,[271] and this is discussed in the Babylonian Talmud as it was in earlier documents.[272] We even find a passage which explains how one should count the generations so as to fulfill the Torah's injunctions.[273] The dispute between Joshua and Gamaliel concerning Judah, an Ammonite convert, also appears in our document.[274] Furthermore, the *gemara* contains an interesting *sugya* which discusses Solomon's marriage to Pharaoh's daughter in terms of the biblical injunction against marrying Egyptians, the rabbinic concern with the converts' motives for joining the Israelite community, and the rabbis' attempt to place Solomon's activities in the best possible light.[275]

One of the major problems the rabbis discussed was the permissibility of a marriage between a converted woman and a priest. This is also framed in terms of the Ammonites and the Egyptians. Ulla said that Yohanan permitted the daughter of a male Ammonite convert to marry a priest. Rabin reported that Yohanan permitted the daughter of an Ammonite convert who had entered into an invalid marriage with an Israelite and the daughter of an Egyptian of the second generation who had also entered into an invalid marriage with an Israelite to marry a priest, while Simeon b. Laqish would not allow these marriages.[276] Along these same lines, a *beraita*[277] states that if an Ammonite, Moabite, Egyptian, or Idumean convert[278] who is older than nine years and one day has intercourse with the daughter of a priest, she cannot eat the heave offering. If the intercourse is with the daughter of a Levite or an Israelite, she cannot marry into the priesthood.[279] In order for these rules to be followed, the Israelites would have to be able to identify converts, their original communities, and the time of their conversion.

Other issues also arise based on the biblical rules concerning these nations. Mishnah[280] states that "all who are forbidden to enter into the congregation may intermarry with one another," and that "Judah 'forbids.'" The *gemara*[281] suggests that Judah would have forbidden the marriage of a convert with a female *mamzer,* but this is rejected. Rav Judah suggests that "all who are forbidden to enter into the congregation" refers to a female convert who is less than three years and one day old who cannot marry into the priestly caste, which would then mean that the interpretation of Judah's statement is correct, for in this case a convert could marry a female *mamzer.* The *sugya* also suggests that the Mishnah refers to the daughter of a convert who is married to a convert, for that one may not marry a priest, but she may intermarry with the others who may not enter the congregation. The *sugya* concludes that the Mishnah refers to the Ammonite and Moabite convert who may not enter the assembly, and Judah would forbid a convert who is permitted to enter the assembly from marrying a *mamzer*. However, he would permit an Ammonite and Moabite convert to marry a *mamzer* because they cannot enter the congregation.

Simeon b. Gamaliel said[282] that if one can marry a man's daughter, he can marry that man's widow. The *gemara* seeks to discover the practical difference between Yosi's[283] and Simeon's views. Ullah explains that they differ in their treatment of the case of an Ammonite and a Moabite convert, for according to Yosi, marriage to a convert causes the woman to be disqualified, while according to Simeon b. Gamaliel, it does not cause the woman to be disqualified. The reason for Simeon's opinion is that, because the daughter of Ammonites and Moabites may marry into the congregation, the males do not disqualify the women with whom they have intercourse. Yosi, however, claims that if the convert's seed disqualifies, as in the case of the male descendants of the Moabites and Ammonites, the convert himself disqualifies the woman with whom he has intercourse.

There is some question concerning whether or not the Cordenians and the Tardomites should be allowed to join the Israelite community. Dosa b. Harkinas[284] taught that the prophet Haggai had ruled that converts could be accepted from the Cordenians[285] and the Tarmodites. However, Rami b. Ezekiel knew a tradition which stated that converts were not accepted from the Cordenians. Ashi claimed that Rami had misunderstood, for the prohibition applied to the Kartuenians, not the Cordenians. Another tradition held that Rami prohibited converts from the Kartuenians and that Ashi distinguished between the Kartuenians and the Cordenians. A further teaching claims that Yohanan and Sabya maintained that converts were not accepted from the Tardomites. A dispute between Judah and Yohanan concerning blood stains of uncertain origin found on linens in Rekem is brought to counter this claim. Yohanan held that bloodstains from Rekem were clean, because the people from Rekem were not Israelites, while Judah held that they were unclean because the people from Rekem were converts, although no longer observant. After a discussion, the *gemara* concludes that it is impossible to discover what Yohanan actually taught concerning the Tarmodites.[286]

Opinions about Converts

Some looked down their noses at converts. We have a *sugya* in which one insults his companion by calling him "convert, son of a convert." The latter retorts that unlike the one who jeered at him, he has not eaten the fruits of the Sabbatical year. The point is that converts are more observant of Israelite law than are native-born Israelites.[287] Thus, this story opens by suggesting that some employed the term convert as an insult, but ends with the lesson that converts could be more observant than native-born Israelites. And Rav quoted the following proverb: "Do not insult an Aramean, i. e., a gentile, before a convert, even unto the tenth generation." The implication of the proverb is that converts, even until the tenth generation, still have feelings for gentiles.[288] Furthermore, there is the curious passage which claims that slaves, converts, and ravens love only one another.[289] Above we saw that Helbo considered converts to be as troublesome to Israelites as sores on the skin.

In contrast to this negative view of the converts, a *beraita*[290] concludes that even though it is taught that one who wounds the feelings of a convert transgresses three negative commandments and one who oppresses a convert transgresses two negative commandments, in fact, one who does either of these violates three negative commandments.[291] Another *beraita*[292] reports in response to a question, raised by Eliezer the Great, that the Torah contains thirty-six, or forty-six, warnings against wronging converts because their original nature is evil.[293] Also, a *beraita*[294] reports Nathan's interpretation of Ex. 22:20:[295] "Do not taunt your fellow with the blemish you have,"[296] so that he draws a clear parallel between native-born Israelites who were "strangers" in Egypt and converts who are "strangers" in Israel.[297] Furthermore, one may not remind the children of a convert about the deeds of their gentile ancestors, and one may not reject a convert who wishes to study Torah with the words, "shall the mouth of one who ate unclean and forbidden food, abominable and creeping things, come to study Torah which was uttered by the mouth of the Omnipresent?"[298] Resh Laqish taught that if one treated a convert unjustly it is considered as if one treated YHWH unjustly.[299] In fact, some believed that converts retained their special status even if they returned to their original gentile community.[300] Given the variety of places in which Israelites are warned not to insult converts, one is tempted to suggest that in fact some of them were guilty of not treating converts with "familial love."

Evidence suggests that the rabbis considered some areas to be overly populated by converts and that in these locations the rabbis had to take care concerning what they taught. When Zera lectured in Mahuza that a convert could marry a female *mamzer*, he was pelted with stones. Rabba stated that he was a fool to make such a statement in a place "where converts abound." When Rabba lectured in Mahuza he stated that a convert may marry a priest's daughter, and his audience rewarded him with a large quantity of silk. When Rabba continued and taught that a convert could marry a female *mamzer*, his audience complained that he had "destroyed his first teaching." Rabba responded that he had really taught to the converts' advantage. If a convert wishes, he may marry a female *mamzer,* and if he wishes, he may marry a priest's daughter; thus, both women are available to him. He is permitted a priest's daughter because they were not prohibited from marrying the unfit, and he may marry a female *mamzer* in accordance with Yosi's view.[301]

Discussions of Specific Converts

In earlier documents we saw that Jethro and Rahab are considered to be paradigmatic converts from the biblical period, and these traditions appear also in the Babylonian *gemara.* Joshua, Eleazar of Modim, and Rav assume that Jethro converted, but they disagree over whether he converted as a result of the dividing of the Reed Sea, the events at Mount Sinai, or the Israelites' victory over the Amalekites.[302]

Rahab, who converted when she was fifty years old, was impressed when she heard about the dividing of the Sea of Reeds.[303] Ena Saba[304] maintained that eight prophets[305] who were also priests were descended from Rahab—Neriah, Baruch, Serayah, Mahseya, Jeremiah, Hilkiah, Hanamel, and Shallum. The *gemara* also states that Rahab must have married Joshua upon her conversion.[306] Ephraim Makshah quoted his teacher Meir, who stated that another prominent biblical personality, the prophet Obadiah, was an Edomite convert,[307] and Tamar was said to have been a convert.[308] Thus, not only did people convert during the biblical period, but these converts could be the progenitors of priests, prophets, and even Israelite kings, as in the case of Ruth.[309] Furthermore, the *gemara* notes that Abraham was the first convert.[310] The Babylonian *gemara* expands the earlier discussions of the biblical converts. It seems important to some of the editors of the Babylonian *gemara* to stress the fact that biblical personalities had converted, so that conversion does not appear to be a comparatively recent phenomenon.

Prominent Romans also converted,[311] even though this did not always please the Roman authorities. When Onqelos the son of Kalonymus, who is also identified as the son of Titus' sister,[312] converted, the emperor had to send several contingents of Roman soldiers to bring him back to Rome, because Onqelos kept convincing those whom the emperor sent after him to convert to Judaism.[313] The passage explains that the soldiers converted because they were impressed by YHWH's concern for the well-being of his people.[314] Another set of stories relates that when he decided to convert, Onqelos raised Titus, Balaam, and the "sinners of Israel"[315] from the dead in order to question them about Israel's worth. Even though they discouraged Onqelos from joining the Israelite community, because it would be difficult for him to follow their rules, he still joined the community.[316] The latter passage demonstrates that Israel was YHWH's favorite people and that those who sought to destroy her would suffer severe punishments in the other world. The author(s) of this passage believed that gentiles thought that it was difficult to follow the Israelites' customs, a view which many Israelites probably also held. Although here Onqelos's role is secondary,[317] he is important because he serves as a symbol for Rome, identified as the emperor's nephew, who is advised not to harm Israel, but rather, to accept her ways even though that might be difficult. It is curious that the Babylonian Talmud did not take up the traditions found in the Palestinian Talmud that the emperor Antoninus had converted to Judaism. Exactly why the Babylonian *gemara* chooses to include accounts of an emperor's nephew instead of an emperor himself is unclear. It seems that the sages behind the Babylonian Talmud were content with the existence of powerful gentile rulers who were friends with some of the sages without claiming that they eventually converted to Judaism. Instead, the Babylonian Talmud maintains that those non-Israelite rulers who caused Israel to suffer eventually saw the error of their ways and joined the People Israel.

The Babylonian Talmud tells us that Nero, who is pictured as an ancestor of Meir,[318] and Nebuzaradan,[319] who is described as a righteous convert,[320] also became members of the Israelite community. Sennacherib and Sisera also are pictured as having converted to Judaism. In fact, Shemaya and Abtalion are said to be descended from Sennacherib.[321] Furthermore, we are told that Naaman[322] was a *ger twšb*, that Haman's descendants learned Torah in Benai Berak, and that Sisera's descendants taught children in Jerusalem.[323] In addition, we find that Aqiba married the wife of the wicked Tineius Rufus,[324] who would eventually convert.[325] In brief, many of Israel's major enemies either converted to Judaism or produced descendants who became proselytes. These stories mediate the wickedness of Israel's enemies. They imply that no one is totally wicked and that some of the most ardent opponents of Judaism ultimately accepted YHWH as their deity. This underscores the truth of Judaism, the transitory nature of its being oppressed, and the fact that it eventually will win over the totality of humankind.

The Babylonian *gemara* also contains the story of the harlot who was so impressed by an Israelite's refusal to have sex with her that she gave up her old way of life, distributed her money, and sought to convert in order to marry the Israelite who preferred to follow YHWH's commandments rather than to engage in sex with her.[326] The *gemara* contains the story of Valeria, clearly meant to be a Roman, who asked Gamaliel to explain an apparent contradiction in the Hebrew Bible,[327] and we also find a reference to her having her slaves ritually immersed.[328] Issur the convert reports to Rabba that when he was a gentile they used to joke about the Israelite's laxity in their observance of the Sabbath,[329] and Rabba is said to have adjudicated a case concerning Issur's son, Mari, who became a rabbi.[330] Finally, we find a story in which Mar Zutra attempts to take control of the slaves who belonged to the convert Judah the Indian upon the latter's death.[331] On the other hand, the *gemara* does know of groups who "never saw the light" and refused to convert.[332]

The Babylonian Talmud is the most extensive document of rabbinic Judaism, and it was composed from a number of different sources over a period of at least four hundred years. For this reason the fact that the Babylonia *gemara* contains an abundance of material on the convert, some of it contradictory, is not unexpected. Furthermore, it is completely natural that the Babylonian Talmud should contain material drawn from earlier sources and pericopae which parallel *sugyot* from earlier documents, even though the various versions of the passages are not completely identical. Finally, the repetition of material in the Babylonian *gemara* is exactly what we would expect. Therefore, the Babylonian Talmud contains a variety of sometimes contradictory information about the convert.

On the one hand, some of the passages in the Talmud tell us that the converts' entrance into the Israelite community was part of YHWH's master plan for the universe. We are told that the Israelites were forced to leave the Land of Israel and settle throughout the world, so that converts would join the community. On the other hand, several pericopae emphasize that conversion is a free choice by the gentiles and that it is not inevitable. While the birth and death of human beings are inevitable parts of world history, the conversion of gentiles is not. In line with this idea, we have seen that some sages believed that children could renounce their conversions when they reach adulthood. We are also told that some gentiles who planned to convert became familiar with Israelite law, so that they could act in ways acceptable to the Israelites.

In many instances the converts are equated with native-born Israelites. We discovered a long list of ritual obligations incumbent on both populations. Furthermore, Israelites are warned not to oppress converts or to remind them of their gentile past. Much of this material is paralleled in earlier documents. However, in contradiction to this view, there are some areas of Israelite culture in which converts and Israelites are clearly distinct. There are those who maintained, as in earlier collections, that the converts were a distinct segment of the Israelite community from the time of Ezra onward. And one of the curious aspects of the rabbinic discussions of the converts is that they seem to apply the term "convert" to people throughout their lives. Given the fact that there were severe restrictions on which converts could marry into the priestly caste, it would have been important to remember who the converts were, the age at which they converted, and nations from which they converted. Additionally, it was clear that converts were different from the native-born descendants of Abraham, Isaac, and Jacob. When the former were circumcised, they were not circumcised according to the commandment given to Abraham, a point made only in the Babylonian Talmud. Furthermore, converts could not recite the Avowal when offering their first fruits because the Land of Israel had not been given to *their* ancestors, an idea which was expressed in earlier documents. Finally, there were those who claimed that the *Shekhinah* did not rest on the converts and the native-born Israelites in the same way.

It is difficult to know how common conversion was. It is clear, however, that even by the time of the Babylonian amoraim the conversion ritual had not achieved a set pattern. There is a good deal of discussion over whether or not a male convert needed to be both circumcised and immersed. Furthermore, the extensive question-and-answer segment of the conversion ritual is found only in the Babylonian Talmud. Thus, it is not at all clear that by the end of the rabbinic period there was a formalized and universally accepted means of converting a gentile. Also, the reason for the various rituals is unspecified; however, at least one source suggests that the converts have to be purified from their sins as gentiles. In addition, some raised questions about the propriety of the conversion of children, and some held that adults could renounce their childhood conversion, if they did so immediately upon reaching the age of majority.

While the conversion process may have been rather inchoate, the effect of conversion on the former gentile was clear. Upon conversion, the former gentile had to observe the totality of Israelite law and custom. Furthermore, converts severed all ties with their gentile relatives, and many considered them to be like newborn children. This had ramifications in sexual relationships, court testimony, bequests and inheritances, transfers of property, recouping damages, collecting debts, and the like. In fact, the convert who died without heirs or the one who was like a newborn child become almost stereotypes in the Babylonian Talmud.

Although Israelites and converts are often equated and the entrance of converts into the Israelite community is part of YHWH's plan, there were those who were less than enthusiastic about converts. One could argue that the reason that the Israelites are warned against insulting or oppressing converts is that some of the native-born Israelites engaged in these practices. Furthermore, we find one passage which attempts to explain why converts suffer, perhaps along with Israelites, "at the present time": They are evil, they are not well versed in Israelite laws so that they make mistakes, or they serve YHWH out of fear instead of out of love. Also, the rabbis are warned to take care when they teach in areas heavily populated by converts, for teaching things which might cause offense to the converts could lead to trouble.

The ambiguity we find in the discussions about the converts probably results from the ethnicity of the People Israel. When gentiles entered the community, they had to enter into a community which saw itself as a descent group. Therefore, the converts had to graft themselves onto the branches which had sprouted from the family tree of Abraham, Isaac, and Jacob. Thus, while they could become a part of the tree, they never really achieved the same status as the natural limbs which the tree normally produced. They were hybrids, and this stands behind much of the complexity of the Talmud's discussions.

SEVEN

The Conversion Ritual

The preceding five chapters reviewed the materials on the convert and conversion as they appear in each individual document. This approach was adopted for two reasons. First, each rabbinic text is an independent collection, edited at a particular time and in a specific location. Because each exhibits its own agenda and deals with its unique concerns, it is important that we begin by treating each document separately. Second, in light of these distinct agendas, a good deal of confusion concerning conversion in the rabbinic period arises from the inappropriate confluence of information from different rabbinic documents. That is, when material from amoraic documents is sometimes read into the tannaitic texts or contradictions among the various rabbinic collections are ignored, we create a supposed system that never exited. In order to overcome this problem, we must delineate the relationship between the data and the texts from which they come.

Having completed this initial process, in this and the following three chapters, we are able to turn from the documents to specific topics: the conversion ritual, marriage between converts and Israelites, converts as newborn children, and converts and the Israelite way of life. The final chapter then interprets the rabbinic sayings about the convert and conversion in terms of the religious and ethnic natures of the People Israel. These chapters seek to uncover how various issues concerning the convert are treated in each rabbinic collection in order to reveal the continuities and discontinuities among the several rabbinic texts. Our goal is to develop a theory which explains how the disparate rabbinic statements about the convert and conversion contribute to the rabbis' understanding of the People Israel.

In Sifré Numbers, Rabbi claimed that native-born Israelites and converts entered into the covenant with YHWH through the same three rituals: Circumcision, immersion, and sacrifice,[1] and many scholars have generally agreed that this is how conversion was carried out. For example, under a section entitled "The Three Indispensable Requirements,"[2] Bamberger first quotes Rabbi's statement from Sifré Numbers. He then reviews the material we shall examine below and concludes that circumcision and immersion were both required. After discussing the disagreement between Joshua and Eliezer on the matter of circumcision which appears on bYeb. 46a–b, he states, "whatever the present controversy may involve, it does *not* mean that R. Joshua . . . allowed the candidates [for conversion] who came to him to omit circumcision altogether."[3] Braude writes, "I am quite convinced that these three rites [listed by Rabbi] were required by the rabbis throughout the so-called Talmudic period, except of course that the Sacrifice had been abolished after the Destruction of the Temple."[4] Moore states that "the initiatory rite by which a man was made a proselyte comprised three parts: Circumcision, immersion in water (baptism), and the presentation of an offering in the temple."[5] Schiffman comments that "since Second Temple times, there have been four basic requirements for conversion to Judaism: (1) acceptance of the Torah, (2) circumcision for males, (3) immersion, and (4) sacrifice (no longer required after the destruction)."[6] Bialoblocki concludes that both circumcision and immersion were a prerequisite (*Voraussetzung*) for conversion.[7] Rowley writes, "There is general agreement that the tradition that the male proselyte was required to undergo circumcision and baptism, and to offer a sacrifice is trustworthy. The tradition clearly refers to the time prior to the destruction of the Temple."[8] Collins notes that "in the Talmud, there are three requirements for a proselyte: circumcision, baptism, and sacrifice," although he also maintains that "the requirements of baptism and sacrifice are not attested before the end of the first century."[9] Jeremias defined "full proselytes" as "gentiles converted to Judaism who had been circumcised, baptized and had offered sacrifice."[10] Schürer claims that "for the acceptance of real proselytes into the Jewish community during the existence of the Temple three demands were to be made according to the rabbis: (1) . . . circumcision; (2) . . . baptism, i. e., a purificatory immersion; (3) . . . an offering to the Sanctuary."[11]

As we shall see, these scholarly claims obscure the fact that there is wide-ranging controversy recorded in the rabbinic documents concerning the necessity of these three rites. We shall discover a good deal of inconsistency concerning the details of the converts' sacrifice, and we shall ascertain that some rabbinic traditions are preserved which challenge the necessity of the converts' being circumcised or of their being immersed. After reading the following material, one could easily conclude that the conversion ritual had not yet been established at the close of the talmudic period. With the exception of Rabbi's statement and a similar comment attributed to sages, no one unambiguously requires all three rites. The evidence suggests much diversity and flexibility with regard to the conversion ritual, at least as it is recorded in the rabbinic documents from Mishnah through the Babylonian Talmud.[12]

Sacrifice

Mishnah, Tosefta, Sifré Numbers, and both Talmuds agree that while the Temple existed, converts were required to bring an offering to the altar before they could participate fully in the life of the People Israel. However, as we clearly shall see below, these five rabbinic texts contain diverse, and sometimes contradictory, information. When one juxtaposes the contents of the relevant *sugyot*, one discovers a good deal of uncertainty about the nature of the offering, why it was required, or whether or not one had to make the offering symbolically after the Temple was destroyed.

Although Mishnah and Tosefta were edited almost a century after the Temple was destroyed, for one reason or another they maintain that while the Temple was standing, those entering the People Israel needed to bring sacrifices to the altar.[13] Eliezer b. Jacob states that converts "lack atonement (*mḥwsr kprh*)" until the blood of an offering has been sprinkled for them on the altar.[14] In addition to the converts mentioned by Eliezer, the anonymous text notes that those who "lack atonement" are males and females who experience a genital emission, women who have given birth, and lepers.[15] At the Temple, one who "lacks atonement" may not enter the court of the Israelites, the holiness of which is surpassed only by the court of the Priests.[16] Furthermore, those who "lack atonement" cannot eat the holy things, unless they undergo a ritual immersion,[17] but they may eat the heave offering and the second-tithe produce.[18] A priest who immersed "that selfsame day" in order to purify himself from an uncleanness may not eat the holy things in the evening if he "lacks atonement."[19] Also, virtually anything which has been dedicated to the Temple or which will serve as an offering can be rendered invalid by the touch of one who "lacks atonement."[20] Thus, the converts' classification as one "who lacks atonement" probably is a reflection on their supposed state of ritual purity. Eliezer's comment most likely means that until the blood of the converts' offering has been sprinkled on the altar, they are in a state of second-degree "uncleanness"; therefore, they cannot approach the altar, nor may they eat from items which have been placed on the altar.[21]

It is important to note that Eliezer does not specify anything about the type of sacrifice the converts were to bring, nor does he specifically mention either ritual immersion or circumcision.[22]

The version of Eliezer's comment in Tosefta is rather different from what we find in Mishnah, for the former does not mention the need for sprinkling the blood on the altar. Instead of explaining how the converts' state of uncleanness is eliminated, the text in Tosefta details the effects of the state of uncleanness: "R. Eliezer b. Jacob says: 'A convert lacks atonement for eating [from] offerings (*zbḥym*).'"[23] This makes explicit what was only implied in Mishnah: While converts "lack atonement" they may not eat foods which derive from items placed on the altar.

Tosefta also contains an anonymous comment which parallels Eliezer's two statements: "A convert is prevented from eating offerings (*zbḥym*) until he brings his bird offering (*qynw*). [If] he brings one pigeon, he may eat offerings in the evening."[24] Although this text does not mention one who "lacks atonement," a key term in both of Eliezer's comments, it does refer to the converts' need to bring an offering before they can partake of foods derived from items placed on the altar. The reference to the converts' eating of the offerings "in the evening" probably relates to their uncleanness, for there were certain types of uncleanness from which a person could not be made clean until the evening.[25]

Tosefta's anonymous *lemma* details the converts' need to bring a bird offering, and the *sugya* that immediately follows the *lemma* provides information about the converts' bird offering.[26] Usually, when one is required to bring two birds, one of them counts as a sin offering, and the other is classified as a whole offering. However, in the case of the converts' bird offering, both of them are considered to be whole offerings. The reasons one brought a sin offering and a whole offering were different.[27] But, the major dissimilarity for our purposes probably is the fact that the priests received a major portion of the sin offerings, while the whole offerings were virtually totally consumed on the altar.[28] At the least, the passage indicates that the two birds which the convert brought were considered to be different from the two birds which Israelites might bring to the altar during the course of the year. If the converts wished to offer a cow instead of the birds, they were permitted to do so, for the birds were specified only because they were less expensive than cattle. However, the converts could not effect their "atonement" by means of meal offerings or drink offerings. These were not animals, so that no blood was placed on the altar, and Eliezer's statement in Mishnah indicates that the blood was an important aspect of the rite. Furthermore, the animal which the converts offered had to have been sacrificed only for the express purpose of effecting their conversion.[29] Even though the Temple no longer functioned, an anonymous opinion holds that the converts still had to bring their offering. Simeon disagrees, for if one brings it now, it would be showing disrespect (*tqlh*) for the holy things. Thus, there was some disagreement during the tannaitic period over whether or not the converts had to re-enact symbolically the sacrificial ritual which was practiced while the Temple stood, and a definitive resolution of this issue appears only in the Babylonian Talmud, which states that one should not set aside money which would have been used for the offering if the Temple were still standing.

Based on an interpretation of Num. 15:14–16, Sifré Numbers contains a rather full discussion of the converts' sacrificial ritual.[30] Sifré Numbers claims that the converts' sacrifices must involve a blood rite, in line with Eliezer's comment in Mishnah. While Tosefta implies that one may perform the blood rite with any animal appropriate for the altar, Sifré Numbers specifically excludes any animal except for birds. At this point in the passage Sifré Numbers implies, but does not specifically state, that the converts must bring birds. Later in the *sugya*, however, Sifré Numbers specifically states that the converts must bring the whole offering of birds because they are the only offerings which are totally consumed by fire on the altar.[31] Although Israelites achieve atonement through the blood of whole offerings and peace offerings, converts achieve atonement only through bird offerings.

The Palestinian *gemara* deals only with the need to make the offering symbolically, even though the Temple is no longer standing.[32] The *gemara* states the following on tannaitic authority, *tny:* "At this time the convert needs to bring [in place of] his bird offering a quarter [*denar*] of silver. Said R. Simeon: 'Rabban Yohanan b. Zakkai annulled [this ruling] because of the possible offense it would cause (*htqlh*).'" However, a following comment concludes that converts may set aside the money for their offering, and if the Temple is rebuilt, they may use that money with which to purchase the birds for their offering. In what appears to be a variation on the tradition recorded in Tosefta, the Palestinian *gemara* states that after the Temple was destroyed the converts set aside a small amount of money to represent their bird offering; however, Yohanan b. Zakkai annulled that practice for the same reason attributed to Simeon in Tosefta. Even though according to tradition Yohanan annulled the symbolic sacrifice, the *sugya*'s final point seems to be that although one need not make the symbolic sacrifice, if one has done it, it is acceptable. By the time this discussion appears in the Palestinian Talmud a specific amount of money is mentioned which was to represent the value of the birds used for the converts'

offerings, and Yohanan b. Zakkai replaced Simeon as the sage who rejected the need for the symbolic sacrifice.[33] However, the *gemara* deems
the symbolic sacrifice valid post facto.

The discussion of the bird offering in the Babylonian Talmud appears
to be a combination and reworking of elements drawn from Tosefta, Sifré
Numbers, and the Palestinian *gemara*.[34] This suggests that rather than de-
scribing an actual practice, it is an attempt theoretically to systematize the
diverse inherited views. Following Tosefta, one *beraita* states that until
they have brought the bird offering, the converts cannot eat from the holy
things (*qdšym*). Converts who bring one pigeon in the morning may eat in
the evening.[35] Unlike the other offerings of birds referred to in the Torah,
both of the converts' birds are whole offerings. Furthermore, the converts
may bring their offering from the cattle; however, later in the passage, the
gemara cites another *beraita*, possibly derived from Sifré Numbers, which
concludes that the offering must be a bird. While Sifré Numbers stated
that the offering could not be a peace offering, the *beraita* states that the
converts may bring a whole offering and a peace offering. However, they
may not bring a meal offering and a peace offering. Sifré Numbers also
disallowed a meal offering. A final *beraita* seems to be derived from the
Palestinian Talmud. It states that at the present time the converts put
aside a quarter of a *denar* for the sacrifice of their birds. Again Simeon[36]
reports that Yohanan b. Zakkai annulled this practice "after a vote." Unlike the passage in the Palestinian Talmud which seems to approve of the
converts' setting aside their money post facto, in the Babylonian passage
Idi b. Gershom in the name of Ada bar Ahaba specifically states that the
law follows Simeon.[37]

To summarize: Eliezer's statement in Mishnah suggests that the converts were considered to be unclean—they lacked atonement—until
blood was sprinkled on the altar on their behalf. A statement attributed to
him in Tosefta makes it clear that they needed to be purified from this
state of uncleanness in order to eat from those items which were placed
on the altar, and this is paralleled by an anonymous opinion. Furthermore,
although Tosefta allows the offering to be taken from the cattle, it clearly
prefers a bird offering. But one bird is allowed, for if the converts bring
one pigeon, they may eat of the offerings that evening. Tosefta establishes
that unlike the other bird offerings, the converts' offerings are whole offerings, so that they are completely burned on the altar, unlike the sin offering. While the converts could bring cattle or birds, they could not bring a
drink offering or a meal offering. These are excluded because they did
not provide any blood for the altar. Tosefta also records the difference of

opinion between Simeon and an anonymous comment over whether or not the converts had to set aside something, even though the Temple was no longer standing.

Sifré Numbers focuses on the importance of the blood, so that it specifically excludes a meal offering, agreeing with the anonymous statement in Tosefta. Also, Sifré Numbers permits the use only of birds; it specifically disagrees with Tosefta and one of the *beraitot* in the Babylonian Talmud, which allowed the converts to bring cattle.

The Palestinian Talmud contains the disagreement over whether or not the converts should set something aside for their offering, even though the Temple had been destroyed. At this point, Yohanan b. Zakkai has replaced Simeon as the authority who claims that the converts do *not* have to set something aside, for the money might be used improperly. Exactly when Yohanan and this position were conjoined is unclear. Whatever the reason, the same tradition appears twice in the Babylonian Talmud. Despite the opinion attributed to Yohanan, a tradition in the Palestinian *gemara* accepts post facto the converts' setting aside funds to provide for their offering in the hope that the Temple will be rebuilt.

The discussion in the Babylonian *gemara* contains some inconsistencies, primarily because it appears to have drawn elements from the three previous documents. At one point the converts may bring their offerings from the cattle, like Tosefta, while at another point they may offer only birds, like Sifré Numbers. It also appears that one bird suffices. Against Sifré Numbers, the *gemara* states that peace offerings are permitted if conjoined with a whole offering, while in agreement with Sifré Numbers and Tosefta, the Babylonian Talmud excludes meal offerings. An Amora of unknown date, Idi b. Gershom,[38] clearly states that the converts are not to set aside a quarter-*denar* for their bird offering, for the law follows Simeon who reported Yohanan's ruling.

The sources agree that while the Temple stood the gentiles brought sacrifices upon their conversion, and it appears that the ritual originated because some felt that the gentiles "lacked atonement," which seems to mean they suffered from a state of uncleanness.[39] Also, at the earliest stage, the sprinkling of the blood of the offering marked the removal of the converts' uncleanness, so that they could eat from items placed on the altar. These reasons for the sacrifice appear *only* in Mishnah and Tosefta. As we move through the documents, little about the offering becomes certain besides the fact that the offering was a whole offering. While a bird offering seems to be preferred, was it one or two birds? Could an offering be brought from cattle in place of the bird(s)? Was a peace offering permitted? Finally, were the converts permitted to set aside funds while the

Temple was in ruins as a symbolic enactment of the sacrifice which was brought to the Temple while it functioned as the cultic center of the People Israel?

Circumcision

We saw above that many scholars stress the fact that male proselytes were circumcised upon their conversion. However, Collins pointed to Philo as evidence for the existence of some Alexandrian Jews who were probably uncircumcised,[40] and Smith writes that "it is possible for a group of Jews to define themselves as Jews without circumcision."[41] The matter of circumcision does present some problems. As we shall see in this section of the present chapter, when our sources discuss circumcision alone, they seem to agree that converts had to be circumcised. However, in an oft repeated Houses debate, it appears that the Hillelites did not required a *specific* circumcision for *the purpose* of conversion. Further, when circumcision and ritual immersion are treated in the same context, the need for the converts to be circumcised is less clear.

In Tosefta,[42] Sifra,[43] the Palestinian *gemara*,[44] and the Babylonian Talmud[45] Simeon b. Eleazar reports that the Houses disagreed concerning whether or not upon his conversion a circumcised gentile needed to undergo a symbolic circumcision. The Shammaites held that such a person needed to have three drops of blood drawn from his penis, while the Hillelites taught that he did not have to have this done. For the Shammaites, the male's circumcision had to be for the expressed purpose of entering the Israelite community. The Hillelites, on the other hand, required only that the male be circumcised; they did not require that it be done in any particular way, at any special time, or for any specified reason.[46] But even that oft stated perspective does not stand alone, for an anonymous comment in Tosefta,[47] repeated in the Babylonian Talmud,[48] agrees with the Shammaites and assumes that circumcised gentiles are symbolically circumcised upon their conversion. It further states that the rite is performed only during the daytime.

In explaining how precious converts are, Mekhilta Ishmael[49] states that Abraham was circumcised at the age of ninety-nine so that gentiles would know that they had their whole lives to convert. Clearly, Abraham's circumcision symbolically represents his conversion in the same way that the gentiles' circumcision marks their entrance into the People Israel.[50]

The Palestinian *gemara* contains several references to the circumcision of converts. The date on which the newborn son of a convert should be circumcised depends upon the relationship of his birth to his mother's conversion. If the child were born shortly before her conversion, he is considered a gentile, and he must be circumcised *immediately* after his mother completes her conversion, a rather obvious conclusion. However, if the child were born right after his mother converts, he is circumcised eight days after his birth, just like any other Israelite baby.[51] In order to eat the heave offering, one must have undergone a ritualized circumcision upon his birth or at his conversion. For this reason, one whose foreskin is drawn forward in order to disguise his circumcision, one who was born circumcised, and one who was circumcised before he converted may not automatically eat the heave offering.[52] Finally, the circumcision of a convert on Purim is assumed to be acceptable.[53] All of these texts assume that male converts should be circumcised, and at least one of them requires the circumcision be done for the expressed purpose of conversion.

The Babylonian *gemara*[54] contains the benediction recited upon the circumcision of a convert. The one who performs the circumcision recites the same blessing as the one who circumcises a native-born Israelite.[55] While in the case of a native-born Israelite the father recites a blessing which specifically refers to the "covenant of Abraham,"[56] at the circumcision of a convert, "he who pronounces the benediction"[57] recites the following: "Blessed are you, YHWH, our God, king of the universe, who has sanctified us with your commandments and has commanded us to circumcise converts and to cause the drops of the blood of the covenant to flow from them, because if it were not for the blood of the covenant heaven and earth would not endure, as it is said, *if not my covenant by day and by night, I would not have appointed ordinances of heaven and earth.*[58] Blessed are you, YHWH, who makes the covenant." The convert is circumcised *without* a specific reference to the covenant of Abraham,[59] so that a liturgical distinction is clearly made between the circumcision of a native-born Israelite and the circumcision of a convert. Finally, the *gemara* implies that an Israelite may circumcise a gentile for the purpose of the latter's conversion without receiving monetary compensation, for it is not considered to be a medical procedure for which the Israelite physician should be compensated.[60]

From these passages, it seems clear that male converts had to be circumcised. The only disagreement encountered so far is in the Houses dispute. There, it appears that the Shammaites required the gentile to be circumcised for the expressed purpose of his conversion, and this position is supported by the discussion of the heave offering in the Palestinian Talmud. On the other hand, the Hillelites held that while converts, like all other Israelites, needed to be circumcised, they did not have to be circumcised upon their conversion. If they had been circumcised before they decided to convert, that circumcision was valid. From the Hillelites' point of view circumcision was not necessarily a part of the conversion ritual, it was merely the physical mark of the covenant between YHWH and the Israelites. For the Shammaites, on the other hand, circumcision was a ritual which had to be performed specifically for the purpose of joining the People Israel; therefore, a circumcised gentile had to undergo a symbolic circumcision at the time he became an Israelite. Thus, while both the Shammaites and the Hillelites require converts to be circumcised, they do so for different reasons because they seem to have different views concerning the significance of the act. For the Shammaites, circumcision appears to be an entrance requirement into the People Israel: Native-born Israelite babies and converts must be circumcised as a sign that they have *entered* the Israelite community. According to the Hillelites, males are circumcised as a sign that they *belong* to YHWH's people, so that gentiles do not need to undergo a symbolic circumcision if they were already circumcised at the time of their conversion.

We have also seen that an anonymous teaching in the Babylonian Talmud makes a clear liturgical distinction between the circumcision of converts and that of native-born Israelites. The latter were circumcised because of YHWH's command to Abraham; the former were circumcised because YHWH considered circumcision to be part of his universal plan of creation. This liturgical distinction points to the ethnicity of the People Israel: Native-born Israelites are Abraham's progeny, and they are circumcised because of that fact. Converts may join YHWH's People as part of the deity's universal plan of creation, but they are still somewhat distinct from those who were descended from the patriarchs.

Immersion

The ritual immersion of converts receives a good deal of attention in our sources. On the one hand, the materials discussed below debate the reasons for the immersion and the meaning of the ritual. On the other hand, some of the pericopae raise the possibility that gentiles do not need to undergo *both* immersion and circumcision upon their conversion, while others clearly state that both acts are required of those who wish to become part of the People Israel.

Mishnah contains a Houses dispute on the meaning of the converts' ritual immersion. The Shammaites hold that immersion is a conversion ritual, while the Hillelites maintain that it is part of an extended purification rite. The *sugya* states: "If a man converts on the eve of Passover—the House of Shammai say: 'He immerses and eats the Passover sacrifice in the evening.' But the House of Hillel say: 'One who separates himself from uncircumcision is like one who separates himself from the grave.'"[61]

As Neusner notes, the Houses' comments are not well matched, and it appears that the House of Hillel do not respond to the issue at hand, the eating of the Passover sacrifice.[62] More important for our purposes, the dispute seems to be over the significance of ritual immersion as a conversion ritual. It appears that the Shammaites believed that immersion was a conversion ritual, so that when the gentiles were immersed they became part of the People Israel and were therefore permitted to eat the Passover lamb. The Hillelites, on the other hand, considered the immersion to be part of an extended purification ritual, so that the converts could not eat the lamb because they were not in a state of ritual purity.

Given the fact that the Torah permits only those who are circumcised to eat the Passover offering,[63] we might *assume* that the convert was circumcised. The Hillelites seem to make this explicit, for they refer to one "who separates himself from uncircumcision." The Hillelites differ from the Shammaites concerning whether or not the convert may eat the Passover sacrifice *immediately after* he has been immersed. The Shammaites permit this. However, because the Hillelites compare one "who separates himself from uncircumcision" to one "who separates himself from the grave," they would not allow those who converted on the eve of Passover to eat the offering, because they were in a state of ritual impurity. According to the Torah, individuals must wait seven days after they have touched a corpse before they are considered to be clean,[64] so that the Hillelites imply that the converts must wait seven days after their conversion before they are clean for the purpose of eating the Passover sacrifice. It is also possible that the Hillelites would have required an immersion seven days after the gentile converted. The Hillelites consider all gentiles to suffer from corpse uncleanness, so that they must undergo a seven-day period of cleansing upon their entrance into the Israelite community. The Shammaites, on the other hand, do not believe that gentiles suffer from any uncleanness. Furthermore, it is possible that the Hillelites required the convert to undergo several ritual immersions: perhaps one upon their conversion, one on the third day after their conversion, and one on the seventh day. If this is the case, whether or not one immersion effects conversion is open to question.[65]

In Tosefta,[66] Eleazar b. Zadoq offers an interpretation of the Houses dispute. Eleazar claims that the Shammaites and Hillelites agreed that an uncircumcised Israelite male was sprinkled with water and then allowed to eat the Passover sacrifice at once. However, they disagreed about an uncircumcised gentile. The Shammaites allowed him to eat the Passover sacrifice in the evening after his immersion, while the Hillelites did not. While Mishnah specifically refers to a convert (*gr šntgryr*), Eleazar refers to an uncircumcised gentile ('*rl gwy*); however, this probably amounts to the same thing.[67] Thus, Eleazar changes the dispute from a disagreement about the convert's purity to one focusing on the fact that the convert was uncircumcised. It is interesting that there is no mention of the fact that the convert was circumcised, only that he was immersed. Does the lack of a reference to circumcision and the emphasis on immersion relate to the later discussions in the two Talmuds concerning the importance of the converts' undergoing both rituals, or is it merely assumed that the individual was circumcised upon his conversion?

The Palestinian *gemara*[68] provides alternative reasons for the Houses' statements. The Talmud explains that both Houses derive their rulings from an interpretation of the phrase *you and your captive* in Num. 31:19.[69] The Shammaites supposedly interpreted the verse to mean that just as the Israelites were not considered to be unclean until they sought to enter into the covenantal relationship with YHWH, so too their gentile captives were not considered to be unclean until they sought to enter into the convenantal relationship with YHWH. The Hillelites, on the other hand, interpreted the verse to mean that just as the Israelites required the sprinkling of water on the third and the seventh days, so too the gentile captives had to be sprinkled on the third and seventh days. This interpretation of Num. 31:19 attributed to the Shammaites is insightful, for below we shall argue that gentiles were not considered to be unclean unless they sought to become converts. According to this view, the issue concerns the applicability of the Israelite purity rules to gentiles.

In the Babylonian Talmud[70] Rabbah b. Bar Hanah in Yohanan's name offers still another interpretation of the Houses dispute, and he agrees with the *sugya* in Tosefta that the dispute concerned an uncircumcised gentile. But Rabbah argues that the difference between the Houses centered on the converts' understanding of the reason for their immersion. The Hillelites enacted a preventative measure, so that if in the future the convert becomes defiled by a corpse near Passover, he will not reason that because he ate the Passover sacrifice in the past immediately after he immersed, he may do so now. The Hillelites are afraid that the convert will not understand that "previously he was a gentile and not susceptible to uncleanness, whereas now he is an Israelite and susceptible to uncleanness." The Shammaites, on the other hand, do not enact preventative measures.[71]

The various interpretations of the original Houses dispute offer an example of how later authorities reread earlier materials. Each discussion of Mishnah's dispute changes the issues under discussion and the thrust of the Houses' positions. While the original disagreement seems to have been about immersion as a conversion ritual, as we move through the later materials that issue is pushed further and further into the background. We also saw that Tosefta's *sugya* is problematic, for its emphasis on the *uncircumcised* gentile seems to raise an issue unknown in Mishnah. The Palestinian Talmud argues that the disputed topic was whether or not the Israelite purity rules applied to gentiles or to only Israelites, an important point but one which is unknown in either Mishnah or Tosefta. In the Babylonian *gemara* a new issue is raised: Whether or not one enacts measures which will inform future actions. Thus, in the subsequent rabbinic documents, Mishnah's Houses dispute is constantly reinterpreted, and in each text it is used to raise new issues.

Both the Shammaites and the Hillelites require a convert to undergo a ritual immersion before he may eat the Passover sacrifice. This probably means that they did not consider a person to be an Israelite until he had been immersed. However, apparently the Shammaites believed that a person was considered a convert free from all previous impurities, if any existed, immediately after his immersion as part of a conversion ritual. The Hillelites may have also considered the person to be a convert, but they may have required immersion on the third and seventh day after the person began the conversion ritual because they required gentiles who wished to become converts to be purified in the same way that Israelites had to be purified.[72]

Somewhat related to the issue of the Houses dispute is the report in Tosefta and the Palestinian *gemara* by Eliezer b. Jacob about two Roman[73] guards in Jerusalem who immersed and ate the Passover sacrifice on the evening of the same day.[74] However, the import of this account is unclear. McKnight notes that this may refer to a pre-Passover "lustration for the sake of ritual purification and thus have nothing to do whatsoever with proselyte baptism."[75] Beasley-Murray accepts the historical accuracy of this passage, Graetz's date of 67 C.E., and accepts the story as good evidence for the existence of proselyte immersion in the first century.[76] Given the nature of the *sugyot*, it is impossible to determine their point. Also, their value as a historical source is uncertain.

While the so-called tannaitic midrashim do not contain discussions of the ritual immersion of the converts, the matter is discussed in both Talmuds. There is no doubt that female converts had to be immersed, and the following story maintains that they are immersed only during the day. One time Isaac b. Nahman, Joshua b. Levi, and Yudan the Patriarch were in Laodicea. Yudan wished to leave the city, but Joshua asked him to postpone his trip until the next morning, for he needed a court of three rabbis to witness the immersion of a female convert, which would take place at that time. Isaac responded to Zeira that they needed to wait until the morning because a female convert is not immersed at night.[77] Furthermore, the same rules applied to the immersion for converts as applied to the immersion of Israelites who sought to be cleansed from their ritual uncleanness.[78] Also, the story about Valeria and her handmaidens points to the ritual immersion of female converts.[79]

While it is fairly clear that female converts *required* immersion,[80] the issue is more complicated when dealing with male converts. Both Talmuds contain a good deal of discussion about the relative importance of circumcision and immersion with regard to male gentiles who wished to join the Israelite community. The issue is whether the male convert requires *both* circumcision *and* immersion. We encounter sages in both Talmuds who expressly state that male converts must be both circumcised and immersed. However, in some pericopae in the Palestinian Talmud some rabbis opine that circumcision alone effects conversion and that ritual immersion does not actually alter the males' status, even though they should undergo the ritual. Finally, we shall encounter a different set of opinions in the Babylonian *gemara*, for there Eliezer requires only circumcision, while Joshua demands only immersion. Taken together, these *sugyot* suggest that the precise nature of the conversion ritual for males was far from uniform throughout the rabbinic period.

In the Palestinian *gemara* Eliezer teaches that in the case of a convert who was circumcised but not immersed or immersed but not circumcised, everything depends on the circumcision. Joshua, however, states that "even [the absence of] immersion prevents" the person from being regarded as a member of the Israelite community. Thus, it appears that Eliezer does not require *both* circumcision *and* immersion, while Joshua requires both rites. Joshua b. Levi agrees with Bar Qappara, who taught that a convert who was circumcised but not immersed is "fit," *kšr*. However, the *gemara* continues and states that in reality no gentiles ever became converts who were not immersed, because all of them had been immersed in order to be cleansed from their nocturnal emissions.[81] From this it appears that the *gemara* wants to explain why some of the sages did not require immersion *as part of* the conversion ritual. It states that immersion was not part of the conversion because all converts had undergone ritual immersion sometime during their lives. This view reflects the author(s)'s common, but odd, perception that even on occasion gentiles behaved like native-born Israelites who would immerse themselves after experiencing a wet dream. It also becomes clear that the point of the immersion was to purify the converts from some uncleanness. Because they had all undergone this rite during their lives, they were considered to be

"fit" members of the People Israel. However, at this point we cannot conclude that all agreed that immersion *was a necessary part of a conversion
ritual.*[82]

Others cited in the Palestinian Talmud also seem to hold that a convert who was circumcised but not immersed is accepted into the People
Israel. A tannaitic tradition is cited which states that if a convert who was
circumcised but not immersed and who had children came and said that
he was circumcised but not yet immersed, he is believed, and they immerse him on the Sabbath. The *gemara* explains that he was immersed in
order to be purified, which means that his immersion did not effect his
conversion. In fact the *gemara* claims that Abbahu would have allowed the
immersion on the Sabbath because it made no difference concerning the
person's conversion whether he was immersed on the Sabbath or not, for,
as a ritual of conversion, Abbahu required only circumcision.[83] Elsewhere,
the immersion of a convert on the Sabbath is taken for granted, for the
sugya focuses on the issue of whether or not the place where the person
was immersed serves as his "residence" for the purpose of traveling on
the Sabbath.[84] Thus, some of the sages whose opinions are recorded in the
Palestinian *gemara* believed that a male gentile had only to be circumcised
as part of his conversion ritual. While immersion was important, it was
needed only to purify the male, not to make him a member of the People
Israel. Only Eliezer requires both immersion and circumcision as part of
the conversion ritual.

While the majority of opinions recorded in the Palestinian Talmud
require only circumcision as part of the conversion ritual, passages in the
Babylonian Talmud take a rather different position. In its discussion of
why the gentile is excluded from those who are counted to recite the grace
after a meal,[85] the Babylonian *gemara* contains Zera's citation of Yohanan's
opinion that converts must be *both* circumcised *and* immersed, for "so long
as he has not performed the ritual immersion, the male is still a gentile."[86]
Hiyya b. Abbah also cited this opinion in Yohanan's name in a rather different context.[87] Similarly, the *gemara* deduces that Hiyya b. Rabbi believed
that a convert must be both circumcised and immersed.[88]

Yosi and Judah disagree concerning the importance of immersion and
circumcision with regard to the conversion of a male gentile. This *sugya*
has some affinities with similar discussions in the Palestinian Talmud. Judah requires *either* circumcision *or* immersion, so that if a gentile informed
the rabbis that he had been circumcised but not immersed, Judah allows
the person to be immersed without determining the validity of the person's circumcision. But also, Judah would allow a gentile who had been

properly circumcised to be immersed on the Sabbath because the immersion would not "improve" the person by completing his conversion. Yosi, on the other hand, requires *both* circumcision *and* immersion. Therefore, if he could not establish the validity of the gentile's circumcision, he would not permit the person to be immersed. Also, he would not allow a circumcised convert to be immersed on the Sabbath because that would "improve" him by completing his conversion.

Finally, a *beraita*[89] holds that Eliezer taught that a person is accepted as a convert if he has been circumcised but has not been immersed, while Joshua maintained that a person who was immersed but who was not circumcised was a valid convert. Only sages teach that a person must be both immersed and circumcised. According to the text, Eliezer based himself on the fact that the patriarchs had been circumcised but not immersed, while Joshua drew an analogy with the matriarchs who had been immersed but not circumcised. Following this *beraita*, the *gemara* states that all agree that immersion without circumcision effects conversion, presumably on the basis of the parallel with the matriarchs. The status of one who has been circumcised but not immersed, however, is open to question. Basing himself on the patriarchs, Eliezer concludes that circumcision without immersion is valid. The *gemara* then attempts to explain how Joshua can assume that the patriarchs were immersed as well as circumcised. First the text claims that from Ex. 19:10[90] and Lev. 15:16[91] Joshua could reason that the patriarchs were immersed as well as circumcised. If in the case of an emission of semen, Lev. 15:16, a person must immerse but does not need to wash his clothes, is it not logical to assume that when he is required to wash his clothes, Ex. 19:10, he must also immerse his body? This, however, is rejected because one could state that the washing of the garments in Ex. 19:10 was done only to clean the garments and that it had nothing to do with the males' suffering from a ritual impurity. The *gemara* then suggests that Joshua could prove his point from Ex. 24:8, *Moses took the blood and dashed it on the people,* for elsewhere[92] it is stated that the blood can be sprinkled only after there has been a ritual immersion. The *gemara* finally asks how Joshua knows that the matriarchs underwent ritual immersion. It responds that the matriarchs could not have "entered under the wings of the *Shekhinah*" without any ritual. Because they could not possibly have been circumcised, Joshua concluded that they must have been immersed. The *gemara* goes out of its way to explain how Joshua could maintain that immersion without circumcision effects conversion. This suggests that some sages wished to support this position even though it went against what others had taught.[93]

With regard to the importance of circumcision and immersion, the texts we have reviewed contain every possible opinion. In the Babylonian Talmud, Yohanan, sages, and Yosi, among others, held that the male gentile had to be both immersed and circumcised upon his entrance into the Israelite community. This is contradicted by those, such as Joshua in the Babylonian *gemara*,[94] who taught that the male needed only to undergo a ritual immersion, and by those who maintained that he needed only be circumcised.[95] Judah stated the curious view that either ritual—circumcision *or* immersion—was acceptable. In the Palestinian Talmud, Eliezer, Joshua b. Levi, and Abbahu require only circumcision. The documents, especially the two Talmuds, suggest that there was a good deal of disagreement concerning the requirement of gentile males to be *both* circumcised *and* immersed.

Taken together, it is impossible to determine what the general or majority opinion was on this matter in any given period. Thus, it is difficult to agree with Cohen's claim that "the only ritual that, as far as is known, was demanded of all male converts by all non-Christian Jewish communities" was circumcision.[96] This would mean that we would have to ascribe Joshua's view in the Babylonian Talmud to a source in a Christian Jewish community, clearly an absurd possibility. Furthermore, as we noted above, Smith[97] allows that some Jews could have conceived of themselves as being Jewish even though they were not circumcised, and Collins posits the existence of noncircumcised Israelites, at least in Alexandria.[98] Even if all Israelite males had to be circumcised, this does not demonstrate that every sage viewed circumcision as part of a conversion ritual.[99]

Similarly, from the Houses dispute in Mishnah onward, the exact meaning of the converts' immersion is open to question. Did their immersion effect their change of status from gentiles to Israelites, so that they could eat the Passover offering, or was it merely one stage in an elaborate purification ritual required of all who had touched a corpse? Should we accept the opinions of those who claimed that circumcised male converts could be immersed on the Sabbath because their "improvement" had been effected by their circumcision, or should we follow those who claimed that only after a male gentile had been both circumcised and immersed did he become an Israelite? While Judaism eventually concluded that male converts required both circumcision and immersion, exactly when that occurred is open to question. At the very least, Judah's statement in Sifré Numbers that conversion required circumcision, immersion, and sacrifice was not accepted by all the sages whose opinions are recorded in the rabbinic collections.

Examination of the Convert

A *beraita*[100] in the Babylonian Talmud is the only source which details the procedure for the questioning and instructing of the prospective converts.[101] When gentiles desire to convert, they are asked why they wish to change communities, given the fact that "at the present time" Israel is oppressed, persecuted, and suffering. Perhaps this should be related to the aside comment attributed to Rav in the Palestinian Talmud. Rav teaches that in contrast to the case of normal converts who are discouraged at first, those who seek to enter the People Israel not "for the sake of heaven," but for marriage, should be encouraged to enter the community, for it is possible that they actually will come to the true worship of YHWH. In fact, they should be given a cordial reception, *qyrwb pnym*.[102]

If they reply that they realize that even though Israel is suffering they are still unworthy to join the community, they are immediately accepted. At that time they are told about some of the commandments and informed about the punishments due to those who violate them. They are informed about the importance of supporting the Israelite poor through the gleanings, the forgotten sheaves, the corners, and the poorman's tithe.[103] They are reminded that as gentiles they would not have been punished for eating animal fats or for working on the Sabbath. But, now if they eat fat or profane the Sabbath, they will be punished by "cutting off" for the former, and by stoning for the latter. In addition, they are acquainted with the reward of the world to come, which is given "to only the righteous." Within the *sugya* the sages are warned that the prospective converts should not be overburdened with details about Israelite practice.[104] If after this instruction the gentiles still wish to convert, the males are immediately circumcised. If any shreds of the foreskin remain, they must be circumcised again. As soon as the male has recovered from the circumcision, he is ritually immersed. At that time, two sages stand by his side and further instruct him in some of the minor and major commandments. When he finishes his immersion, he is considered an Israelite "in all respects."[105] For the immersion of a woman, the sages have her sit in the water up to her neck, while two learned men instruct her in the commandments.

Of interest is the fact that the converts are taught about the agricultural gifts given to the poor, which were incumbent only upon Israelites in the Land of Israel and which served as a means of strengthening group cohesion and solidarity. Gentiles were not required to separate these gifts, nor were they given to non-Israelites. The ethnic nature of supporting the poor with the agricultural offerings is underscored by the fact that Israelites were encouraged to support the gentile poor by giving them money, not by allowing them to enjoy the agricultural gifts. This symbolism is highlighted by the fact that this discussion occurs in a Babylonian text, edited in a country in which the agricultural gifts were neither applicable nor observed.[106] Furthermore, they are warned about the restrictions placed on their eating habits and on their activity on the Sabbath, two facets of Judaism which in the ancient world fascinated the gentiles and which most obviously distinguished Israelites from non-Israelites.[107]

Two other points are important. First, this *sugya* assumes that male converts are circumcised *and* immersed, and there is no reference to the bird offering. Second, the instruction takes place at the time of the immersion, not as preparation for the conversion ritual occurs. This last point argues against those who claim that converts had to undergo an extensive period of training before they joined the People Israel.

This passage in the Babylonian Talmud describes a rather extensive conversion ritual: (1) a question about motives; (2) a reminder about the position of Israel in the world; (3) instruction about specific Israelite obligations; (4) information about the punishments which are incurred if the obligations are ignored; (5) circumcision for males; (6) immersion; (7) more instruction. It is striking that no other source clearly refers to the examination of converts. It is clearly missing from the tannaitic stratum, and Rav's admonition that converts should not be overly discouraged from converting is at best a vague reference to something like this ritual.[108] Although Cohen favors "a mid-second-century C.E. date,"[109] his two major supporting arguments are not strong. While the Talmud does mention that *two* sages administered the rite and that Yohanan required *three* rabbis for conversion, this does not necessarily mean that our passage predates Yohanan. How do we know that all of the sages who lived after Yohanan accepted his opinion on this matter? Because we have encountered virtually nothing upon which all the rabbis agreed with regard to the conversion ritual, this seems to be a dangerous assumption. Second, even though the *beraita's* language exhibits "linguistic parallels with Mishnah, the Tosephta, and other putative *baraitot*," this does not preclude the possibility that an Amora wrote it. In fact, it would be curious to find a *beraita* which did not employ "linguistic parallels" with the tannaitic collections. Lacking any indication that this ritual was known by any text earlier than the Babylonian Talmud, it seems best to accept Cohen's caveat that "[a] firm terminus ante quem for the text (with all its additions and interpolations, if indeed there be any) is provided by its inclusion in the Babylonian Talmud (edited in the sixth to eighth century C.E.) and by its service as a source for [a parallel passage in tractate] Gerim (sixth to eighth century C.E.)."[110]

The Converts' Motives

The *sugya* which details the examination of the converts as a prelude to their conversion may well relate to a concern with the converts' motives for joining the People Israel which appears elsewhere. Converts should join the Israelite community only "for the sake of Heaven." [111] According to a *sugya* in the Palestinian Talmud, if a woman converted to Judaism for improper reasons, that is, not "for the sake of Heaven," and married into the priestly caste, she may not eat even the lesser holy things, which were consumed outside of the Temple's precincts. In contrast, women who converted for proper reasons and were married to priests could eat even the most holy things, edibles which had to be consumed within the precincts of the Temple and which were permitted to only the priests and their households. [112] Entering the Israelite community in order to marry one of its members was not considered by some to be a valid reason for conversion. An anonymous opinion [113] states that if a man converts because he loves an Israelite woman or a woman converts because she loves an Israelite man, the proselyte should not be accepted into the community. [114] Rav demurs and teaches that in contrast to the case of normal converts who are discouraged at first, these others should be encouraged to enter the community, for it is possible that they actually will come to the true worship of YHWH. In fact, they should be given a cordial reception, *qyrwb pnym*. [115] Some also believed that female children who converted might not realize the significance of their actions, so that they might need to undergo ritual immersion for a second time when they are older. [116] In response to the question about why Samaritans are unfit to serve as witnesses for a divorce document, Yohanan responds that this is because they are "lion converts"; that is, they did not convert for the sake of Heaven, but converted out of fear of being harmed by the lions. [117] However, his opinion is challenged by the claim that if someone converted to Judaism for an illegitimate reason, [118] but converted again for the proper reason, that person would be accepted into the community as a proper convert. [119] This means that as Yohanan stated, people who converted for an improper reason should be accepted into the community if they undergo a second conversion "for the sake of Heaven." [120] Also, Bar Qappara teaches that one should be careful to treat converts fairly, for if they perceive that they might suffer a disadvantage after their conversion, they will return to their former lives. [121] Finally, we are told that during David's reign many converted to Judaism because they were impressed by the care that YHWH took in protecting those who converted to his worship. [122] There were also those who claimed that converts would not be accepted during the times of David, Solomon, Esther, and the Messiah, because they probably wanted to convert only in order to share in the benefits which the Israelites experienced at those times.[123]

We have encountered a few *sugyot* which state that upon their conversion gentile males must be circumcised, immersed, and, at least at one time, must have brought an offering to the Temple, while gentile females needed to be immersed and to make an offering. However, at least with regard to the ritual requirements for a male convert, throughout the rabbinic period there was a wide variety of opinions about the nature, importance, and necessity of these requirements. Furthermore, the exact nature of the converts' offering and the need symbolically to make the offering after the Temple was destroyed are also a matter of dispute. The only things which consistently appear in our documents are that females underwent immersion and that while the Temple stood an offering was presented to YHWH. Furthermore, it seems clear that, while the immersion of a convert followed the same procedures and requirements as any other immersion, whether or not it effected the conversion of a male was open to question. We have seen that several sages cited throughout the Talmuds raise serious questions about the requirement that males be circumcised.[124] And, only in the Babylonian Talmud do we find the requirement to examine/instruct the gentiles who seek to convert; this procedure is not even alluded to elsewhere in the entirety of the rabbinic texts.[125] Even the importance of the converts' exhibiting the "correct" motives for their conversion is not fully accepted, for Rav maintains that even if gentiles enter the community not "for the sake of Heaven," that is acceptable, because eventually they may come to the true worship of YHWH.

It does appear clear, however, that at least at some stages during the rabbinic period both immersion and the sacrifice were required as a result of the belief that gentiles suffered from an impurity which had to be removed upon their entrance into the Israelite community.[126] As early as Mishnah, the Hillelites suggested that this was corpse uncleanness, a result of the fact that in rabbinic belief, gentiles did not clearly mark their graves, so that they would regularly be defiled by corpses.[127] On the other hand, the Palestinian Talmud refers to nocturnal emissions as the type of impurity from which gentile males are regularly purified. Elsewhere I have argued that the rabbinic system of purity did not apply to gentiles,[128] and this still seems to be correct. As long as gentiles remained gentiles, their purity or impurity was not an issue. And at least Mishnah and Tosefta presume regular interaction between Israelites and non-Israelites without any concern for the ritual purity of the latter. Only when the gentiles sought to enter the People Israel did their ritual impurity become important, for now they were required to live their lives according to Israelite standards. This position is clearly stated in both Talmuds in their attempts to explain why the Hillelites did not permit converts to eat the Passover sacrifice immediately after they had been immersed.[129]

Exactly why some held that converts need not be circumcised is unclear.[130] On the one hand, it could be argued that YHWH commanded only that Abraham, his offspring, and those purchased for money should be circumcised,[131] so that one could maintain that gentiles who converted freely did not need to undergo this rite.[132] It is also possible that the Babylonian *gemara* implies that because women could not be circumcised, immersion was the only rite for conversion applicable to all converts. Of course, it was just as easy for others to hold that all males who wished to be part of the Israelite community had to be circumcised, especially if they wished to participate in the Passover ritual, which marked the creation of the People Israel. Whatever the reason, it seems clear that as late as the amoraic period arguments could be mustered for those who did not require all converts to be circumcised.[133]

There were also those who dismissed the importance of ritual immersion as a means for effecting conversion. Some sages held that the circumcision of a gentile was sufficient for his entrance into the Israelite community. There were also those who maintained that *either* circumcision *or* immersion effected conversion, while there were those who required both rites. Of course, one could argue that the sages who asserted that immersion alone was sufficient were expressing only a theoretical view, or one could dismiss their views as being the position of the minority, which was not followed. Further, one could simply dismiss those statements as being the result of textual problems. Or, one could take the material at face value and admit that from the mass of contradictory statements in the rabbinic documents we have no way of determining what exactly effected conversion. And this seems to be the most obvious solution to the problem before us. If one takes into account the totality of the information in the rabbinic collections and does not attempt to dismiss or to alter some of them according to a preconceived notion of what *should have been* the case, it is impossible to demonstrate from the rabbinic documents exactly what *was* the case, which ritual acts a gentile had to undergo in order to become a member of the People Israel.[134] Attempts to prove from the rabbinic sources exactly what ritual acts effected conversion are doomed to failure.[135]

The significance and meaning of the inconsistency concerning the ritual requirements for conversion are difficult to ascertain. It is conceivable that the rabbis did not feel a need to develop a set conversion ritual because in fact there were few gentiles who sought to become full members of the Israelite community.[136] The rabbis did not devote an inordinate amount of attention to converts, and many of their treatments of the phenomenon were designed to refine details of rabbinic law and not to further develop their ideas about converts or conversion. If conversion was a relatively infrequent occurrence, the discrepancies among the documents may reflect genuine disagreements among the sages from different locations and generations over exactly what one had to require of those who wished to become members of the People Israel. Of course, this could have been true even if there were many converts to Judaism during late antiquity. The first generations of Christians could not agree on the requirements for all those who wished to become members of their community,[137] and it is possible that the Jews also could not reach agreement on the conversion rituals. In any event, taken as a whole, the rabbinic sources do not present us with a set ritual required of all those who wished to become members of the People Israel, nor do they evidence a deep concern that a uniform ritual be created.

▨ EIGHT ▨

Marriages between Converts and Israelites

▨

Two seemingly contradictory positions arise at about the same time in the postbiblical Israelite community. On the one hand, Israelites are forbidden from marrying non-Israelites. On the other hand, Israelites begin to accept gentiles as converts. As Cohen writes, "One of the central characteristics of postbiblical Judaism is its prohibition of intermarriage. . . . Of the numerous differences between Judaism and Israelite religion, two are important here: (1) Judaism prohibited intermarriage with all outsiders but (2) permitted gentiles to convert and become (almost) equal to the native born."[1] The former underscores the separation of Israelites from other people, while the latter provides a mechanism for almost erasing the distinctions between gentiles and Israelites. Both stances assume that Israelites are in contact with their non-Israelite neighbors and that there were opportunities for the two groups to join together, either through the matrimonial bond or through the act of conversion.

For the most part, the Israelite materials assume that Israelites came into constant contact with non-Israelites and that the two groups interacted in a variety of social, economic, and political arenas. Given the fact that the rabbinic texts permit gentiles to bring a limited number of offerings to the Temple, the authors of these documents even assumed some intermingling in the religious sphere as well, at least on the part of the gentiles.[2] The only area in which the sages of Mishnah and Tosefta consistently prohibited interaction between Israelites and non-Israelites was in matters of marriage and sexual intercourse.[3] Even if intermarriages were not common in the Talmudic period, as Cohen argues,[4] the rabbinic sources are consistent in their rejection of such unions. Although many reasons have been put forth to justify this position,[5] the stance is most comprehensible if we understand the rabbis to have viewed the Israelite people as an ethnic group, for endogamy is a central characteristic of ethnicity.[6]

Given the rabbinic stand against intermarriage, the discussions of marriages between Israelites and converts should serve as a means of assessing whether or not converts were viewed the same as native-born Israelites.

If converts are the same as Israelites, then the two groups should freely intermarry, or the restrictions placed on the converts should be similar to those placed on Israelites and should be justified in the same terms. If, on the other hand, converts are not equal to native-born members of the People Israel, we should discover some restrictions concerning the marriages between converts and Israelites.

Most of the discussions on this topic concern the marriage between converts and members of the priesthood. However, the documents do deal with connubial relationships between converts and other elements of the Israelite community. In general, the segments of the Israelite community available for marriage to converts were different from the sectors permitted to native-born, unimpaired Israelites. For example, many held that converts could not marry unimpaired priests, but they could wed priests who were unable to serve at the altar. Furthermore, while priests, Levites, and Israelites could *not* engage in an acceptable sexual relationship with Israelites of questionable ancestry, such as *mamzerim*, converts could wed them. Finally, when we compare the Torah's discussions with those in the rabbinic documents, we shall notice a subtle shift in emphasis concerning the reasons that particular women are forbidden from marrying into the priestly caste. The Torah emphasizes the women's sexual activity, while several of the rabbinic documents focus on the women's ancestry.

Rabbinic literature divides the Israelite community into three major classes: Priests, Levites, and Israelites. It further separates the priestly class into unimpaired priests, *khnym*, and impaired priests, *hllym*. The latter are those who have engaged in a sexual relationship forbidden to priests or who are the offsprings of such liaisons.[7] The priesthood is also divided into those who are fit to serve at the altar, *kšr*, and those who become disqualified as a result of a physical defect, *pswl*, from actually participating in the sacrificial service.[8]

Although the Levitical class does not appear to have been subdivided, the Israelites were separated into various divisions. *Mamzer* referred to a person who was the offspring of a union not accepted by the rabbis as a legal marriage.[9] A *natin* was the descendant of the Gibeonites whom Joshua made into Temple slaves.[10] The *shetuqi* is defined as a child whose mother is known, but whose father is unknown,[11] while an *asufi* is a child whose parents cannot be identified.

A *sugya* in Mishnah[12] places converts somewhere between Israelites of questionable ancestry and Israelites who are the offspring of acceptable marriages. Priests, Levites, and Israelites may intermarry. Converts may not marry unimpaired priests; but, they, along with Levites, Israelites, and freed slaves, may wed impaired priests. Unlike Levites, Israelites, or priests, however, converts may also marry *mamzerim, netinim, shetuqim,* and *asufim.* The focus of attention is on family lineage. This is made clear by the fact that converts, but not priests, Levites, or Israelites, may wed members of the community whose Israelite family lineage cannot be firmly established.

According to Tosefta, if a woman from a priestly, Levitical, or Israelite clan marries a convert, the children follow their father's status, so that they are classified as converts. Even though the marriage is legally acceptable, the union produces children with a defective lineage, which would mean that a female child of such a union could not marry into the priestly class.[13] Similarly, Yosah states that the children of the union of a male convert and a female *mamzer* are classified as *mamzerim.* However, Judah prohibits marriages between *mamzerim* and converts.[14] For Yosah and the anonymous ruling, ideal marriages occur among the three native-born segments of the People Israel. When a member from one of these groups marries a convert, the children take on the status of the parent with the most defective lineage. Judah, however, equates the converts with the Israelites, priests, and Levites, and he considers the family lineage of all four groups to be equal. Therefore, because Israelites, Levites, and priests cannot marry *mamzerim,* neither can converts.[15]

Although there is some discussion concerning the marriage of converts to Israelites and *mamzerim,* most of the discourse concerns marriages between members of the priestly class and converts. The priests occupied a special place within the People Israel. They were the only ones who actually approached YHWH's altar, so that they were the members of the People Israel who could physically approach the closest to Israel's deity. For this reason, they had to maintain their separateness from the rest of humankind. One way in which their distinctiveness was maintained was through the restrictions placed on whom they could marry.[16] As we shall see below, the Torah laid down certain restrictions concerning whom the regular priests and the High Priest could marry. It is significant that the reasons behind the prohibited marriages in the rabbinic texts do not totally agree with the justifications for the restrictions found in the Torah.

The Torah laid down constraints concerning whom male members of the priestly caste might marry. Common priests were forbidden from wedding harlots or divorced women. Levine contends that in biblical times "it is likely that divorce always involved a charge of infidelity by the husband,"[17] so that both of these classes of females were considered to be sexually promiscuous. Their unbridled sexual activity made them unfit for marriage to priests. High Priests could marry only virgins from the priestly clan. If they married outside the priestly caste their children would be defiled.[18] These marriage rules are related to the sanctity of the priesthood, to their being separated for service to YHWH, and to their being distinct from the other members of the Israelite community.[19] Thus, improper marriages could negate the priests' sanctity. Although the Torah focuses exclusively on the sexual activity of the prohibited women, we shall see that the rabbinic texts often raise another concern with regard to the converts.[20]

We saw above that while converts, like Israelites and Levites, could marry impaired priests, converts alone could marry those members of the Israelite community whose ancestry could not be firmly established. The importance of the converts' ancestry finds expression in Mishnah's other passage which treats our subject.[21] Judah excludes the daughter of a male convert from marrying into the priestly class by equating her with the daughter of an impaired priest, *ḥalal*.[22] Yosi, on the other hand, states that the daughter of two converts may marry a priest. Although Eliezer b. Jacob expressly prohibits the daughter of two converts from marrying a priest, his other opinion is less clear. At one point he states that the daughter of any Israelite married to any convert is eligible for the priestly class. At another point he seems to state that only if the convert's mother is an Israelite may she marry a priest.[23]

Clearly, the important matter is not the sexual activity of the woman who wishes to marry a priest; rather, the status of her family line is under dispute. The issue seems to be whether or not converts can produce children who are considered to be unimpaired Israelites. Yosi considers converts to be equal to native-born Israelites with regard to their family lineage. Therefore, the daughter of two converts may marry into the priestly class just like any other unimpaired Israelite. Eliezer does not view converts and Israelites as equal. Although it is impossible to ascertain exactly what he taught, both statements agree that if she wishes to marry a priest, the woman must have one Israelite parent, for two converts cannot produce unimpaired Israelite children. Judah does not equate converts with Israelites. Rather, he correlates the daughter of converts with the daughter of an impaired priest. While Judah would agree that the convert was now an Israelite, just as the impaired priest was a member of the priestly class, he believed that converts suffered some limitations which native-born Israelites did not share, so that the former did not produce unimpaired Israelite offspring.[24]

These rulings have a second implication. Several *sugyot* throughout the rabbinic collections state that one should not remind converts that they or their ancestors were once gentiles, and this implies that one should ignore the fact that converts are not native-born Israelites.[25] However, in order to follow the rulings in Mishnah, one would have to be able to distinguish between converts and native-born Israelites. Thus, at least for purposes of marriage, the person's status as a convert had to be discernible throughout her lifetime. When a priest sought to marry a woman, he would have to ascertain the status of his perspective spouse's parents.

The few passages in Tosefta which deal with the marriage between a convert and a priest also focus on the problem of family lineage. We learn that a male convert may marry a female from the priestly clan.[26] Tosefta also contains a fuller version of Judah's statement in Mishnah.[27] Further, it excludes a converted woman, like an impaired priestly female, *ḥllḥ*, from marrying into the priestly class.[28] Finally, if a woman of priestly, Levitical, or Israelite parents marries a converted male, her children take on the status of converts. While their ability to marry into the priestly class is not dealt with in the passage, the point at issue is the child's family status which depends on the parents, not on the child,[29] and, given the fact that the children are classified as converts, this would affect their ability to marry into the priestly class.

We have seen that Mishnah and Tosefta deal with the issue of the converts' marrying into the priestly caste from the perspective of family lineage, not from a concern with the women's sexual activity. Because the women's sexual activity is the Torah's concern, it is not surprising that this issue is raised in Sifra and Sifré Numbers. Sifra presents Judah's statement from Mishnah and Mishnah's prohibition against a priest's marrying the daughter of an impaired male priest,[30] and here the midrash focuses on the women's ancestry. But, Sifra concentrates on the converted woman's sexuality when it interprets the reference to harlotry in Lev. 21:7 as referring to a converted woman or a freed slave.[31] Exactly why the converted women were equated with prostitutes is not stated, but it is probably the result of the rabbis' belief that gentiles were sexually promiscuous and uninhibited.[32] In Sifré Numbers,[33] Simeon b. Yohai is explicit on this point, for he teaches that only women who converted before the age of three years and one day are fit, *kšrh*, for the priestly caste.[34] The assumption is that a woman under the age of three years and one day would not have engaged in any sexual activity. Thus, the two exegetical texts follow the Torah's reasons for limiting the women with whom a priest might marry.

The Palestinian *gemara* contains a number of *sugyot* which discuss our issue, and here both perspectives are represented. The Palestinian Talmud contains Sifra's equation of the prostitute in Lev. 21:7 with the converted woman[35] and Sifré Number's interpretation of Num. 31:18.[36] And, the Palestinian Talmud deals with converted men marrying women of the priestly class as well as converted women marrying male priests. Yosi b. Bun in the name of Rav taught that a converted male could marry a woman of priestly descent. However, the *gemara's* discussion of Yosi's statement is phrased in terms of "fit" versus "unfit," *kšr* versus *psl*, individuals, so that the Talmud clearly views the converts and the members of the priestly caste as different. Although the difference is never made clear, it may relate to their ability to partake of the food placed on the altar. It need not revolve around family lineage or sexuality.[37] Women who were members of the priestly caste were allowed to eat some of the foodstuffs which had been offered to YHWH. If they engaged in unacceptable sexual relationships, they lost this privilege.[38]

The question of whether or not a priest may marry a converted woman receives a variety of answers in the Palestinian Talmud. In its discussion of mBik. 1:5, the Palestinian *gemara* offers an extended treatment of this issue.[39] In response to Eliezer b. Jacob's view recorded in Mishnah, that a converted woman whose mother was an Israelite may marry into the priestly caste, the Talmud cites Judah's opinion that the daughter of a male convert is the same as the daughter of a defective priest, another opinion attributed to Judah, which follows an exegesis of Ezek. 44:22,[40] which states that a convert may marry into the priestly caste if his mother is an Israelite, Eliezer's ruling that one parent must be an Israelite, Yosi's ruling that both parents may be converts if the woman were born after her parents converted,[41] and Simeon's view that she must be a virgin born after her parents converted.[42] The interpretation of Num. 31:18 which appeared in Sifré Numbers is now cited.[43] Because Pinhas was among those at the conquered city mentioned in Numbers, Simeon's view that the woman who converted before the age of three years and one day may marry a priest seems acceptable. However, the rabbis offer a different exegesis of the verse and maintain that the women are allowed to live so that they may become slaves and handmaidens, which implies a rejection of Simeon's view. Yosa quotes Yohanan who concludes that the law follows Yosi, so that women who were born after their parents converted may marry priests. Thus, Simeon's concern with the woman's sexual purity is unimportant; the issue is her family lineage. This section of the *gemara* is a virtual litany of the various rabbinic views concerning the permissibility of the daughter of a convert marrying into the priestly caste. The Talmud reaches the conclusion that only a woman of unquestioned lineage, in this case one who was born *after* her parents became Israelites, may marry into the priestly caste, for in effect, she is an Israelite even though her parents were converts.

Two narratives follow the above discussion which suggest that not all sages happily accepted Yosi's view. Abbahu sets out to punish a priest who married a woman whose parents were both converts, thus rejecting Yosi's opinion.[44] When Bibi reminded Abbahu that the law followed Yosi's view, the latter begrudgingly relents and does not punish the priest.[45] Jacob b. Idi b. Oshiah reports that Rabbi sent Rominos to investigate a woman in the South whose fitness was being questioned.[46] When it was discovered that her grandmother had converted at an age of less than three years and one day, she was declared fit to marry into the priestly caste.[47] However, the passage ends with the statement that *a virgin from among his kin* means that at least the High Priest cannot marry a converted woman.[48]

The permissibility of converts marrying into the priestly caste is also discussed with reference to Ammonite, Edomite, and Egyptian converts. The Torah prohibits Ammonites and Moabites from entering the congregation of YHWH, but it allows third generation Egyptians and Edomites to join YHWH's congregation.[49] If an Ammonite, Moabite, Edomite, or Egyptian convert[50] has intercourse with a woman of the priestly, Levitical, or Israelite classes, she may not eat the heave offering. Thus male converts from these nations may not marry into the priestly caste.[51] The *gemara* then presents a long and complex pericope in which several sages debate whether or not Ammonite and Moabite women may marry priests. In the course of the discussion we learn that according to Yosi, women who have intercourse with Ammonite or Moabite males may not marry priests. Simeon, on the other hand, allows even the High Priest to marry their daughters and widows. According to Yohanan, Yosi held that because Ammonite and Moabite males are always prohibited from joining the People Israel, any woman who has intercourse with them cannot marry priests, and their women cannot marry priests. Simeon, on the other hand, allows their women to convert and to marry priests. Jeremiah in Ba's name[52] states that Yosi would not allow the widow of an Ammonite or Moabite convert or a second generation Egyptian convert to marry a priest.[53] Jacob b. Aha reports a dispute between Yohanan and Simeon b. Laqish in which Yohanan states that the daughter of an Ammonite convert and the daughter of a second generation Egyptian convert are fit, *kšr*, while Simeon rules them unfit, *psl*. We also learn that Zakki taught before Yohanan that the daughter of a male Ammonite is fit to marry into the priestly caste, while the daughter of a female Ammonite convert is unfit for such a marriage. Yohanan disagrees and holds that the daughter of a

male or female Ammonite may marry a priest. Yosa interprets Yohanan's
opinion to mean that the daughter of a male Ammonite convert and a
female Israelite may marry a priest, and Abbahu cites another opinion attributed to Yohanan which holds that the daughter of such a union may
marry even a High Priest.[54] Haggai, in the name of Pedat, and Simeon b.
Laqish object and state that the daughter of a male Ammonite convert is
unfit. Yohanan responds that if two gentiles were married to each other
before they converted, the male offsprings can never enter the Israelite
community, but the females are permitted to enter the community as soon
as they are born. After they converted, their daughters are permitted to
marry anyone after the third generation.[55] This complex discussion, which
is less than fully comprehensible, clearly is based on the issue of the woman's lineage, and not on her sexual activity. The major point of dispute is
whether or not Ammonite and Moabite women can become valid converts.
If they may become converts, several sages held that they could marry
priests, even, perhaps, the High Priest.

The Babylonian Talmud contains little that is new. Simeon b. Yohai's
interpretation of Num. 31:18 finds its way into the Babylonian *gemara*.[56]
Joshua b. Levi relates the story about Romanos's investigation of the inhabitants of a town whose legitimacy was being questioned.[57] We also find
the discussion of a priest who married a woman who had converted before
the age of three years and one day. When Nahman b. Isaac inquired on
whose permission the marriage had been contracted, the priest responded
that Jacob b. Idi stated in the name of Joshua b. Levi that the *halakhah*
followed Simeon b. Yohai's teaching that a priest could marry a woman
converted before the age of three years and one day. Nahman responded
that if the priest did not divorce his wife, he would place him under a
ban.[58] It is possible that Nahman rejects Simeon's view because the former
is concerned only with the woman's lineage, and not with her sexual activity. However, the equation of the harlot with the female convert also appears in the *gemara*.[59] Samuel, on the other hand, stated that in no case
may a priest marry a convert, and specifically, he may not marry a convert
who has been held captive by gentiles. Rav ruled that if it were the priest's
first sexual activity, he may marry a convert who was a captive because
"the Torah takes account of a man's passions." Samuel, however, rejected
this view.[60]

Elsewhere,[61] Ezek. 44:22[62] is used as the basis for the rulings of Judah,
Eliezer b. Jacob, and Simeon b. Yohai. Judah interprets the verse to mean
that both of the women's parents must be Israelites, so that he would not
allow the daughter of converts to marry priests. Eliezer b. Jacob interprets
the phrase *from the stock, mzr'*, to mean that even if a portion of their seed,

mqsṭ zr', is from an Israelite, the women may marry priests. Yosi states that anyone who was conceived by an Israelite could marry a priest, and this means that even if both of her parents were converts, she could marry a priest if she were conceived after her parents converted. Simeon b. Yohai interprets the verse to refer to one "whose virginity was sown in Israel"; that is, a woman who converted before the age of three years and one day. In another *sugya*,[63] Judah interprets the verse to mean that the priest may marry the widow of those whose daughters may marry into the priesthood, which excludes the widow of a convert. Still elsewhere,[64] Judah rejects Simeon b. Yohai's view, and the former teaches that a female convert of less than three years and one day may not marry a priest.

The Torah disqualifies women from marrying into the priestly class on the basis of the former's sexual activity, and this view also finds expression in the rabbinic texts. However, by far the major concern of the rabbinic documents is the women's family lineage. The basis for most of the sages' disagreements seems to be whether or not one considers converts to be the same as Israelites whose family lineage can be firmly ascertained. Those who held that converts were the same as native-born Israelites allowed priests to marry converted women. On the other hand, several sages believed that converts could not be equated with native-born Israelites, so that they placed restrictions on the marriage between priests and converts. Even the discussions of the Ammonite and Moabite women seem to relate to family lineage and not to sexual matters. Clearly, the issue had not been resolved, for there were sages who believed that converts were not the same as native-born Israelites, while there were others who totally equated the two groups.

The fact that the marriage between priests and converts affects the former's sanctity becomes clear in the discussions of marriages between priests who suffer from a physical blemish and converts. Sheshet states that a priest whose testicles have been harmed may marry a convert because the priest's sanctity has been diminished. Sheshet based his ruling on the fact that an Israelite with crushed testicles could marry a *netinah*. The point is that in neither case can the marriages produce children, so that the question of family lineage is irrelevant. Rabba responds, however, that in the case of the marriage between the *netinah* and the Israelite the issue is not the family lineage of the children, for the adults cannot procreate. However, in the instance of the marriage between any priest and a convert, the issue is the priest's sanctity. Therefore, for Rabba, converts are not the same as native-born Israelites, and a priest's marriage to them affects his ability to carry out the priestly rites because somehow his sanctity has been diminished.[65]

Elsewhere Yohanan asked Oshaiah if the converted wife of a priest whose testicles were crushed could eat heave offering. Oshaiah could not answer the question. In seeking the answer to Yohanan's question, the *gemara* attempts to discover the reason he asked it. It concludes that Yohanan must be asking about Eliezer b. Jacob's ruling that a convert whose mother is an Israelite may marry a priest.[66] Elsewhere,[67] Aha b. Hinea cited Lev. 22:11[68] as proof that the converted wife of a priest whose testicles were crushed could eat the heave offering. The point of the passage is that Eliezer b. Jacob's opinion means that the Israelite mother of a converted woman increases the latter's status, so that she may eat the heave offering even if her husband is a defective priest.

When the corpus is viewed as a whole, we see that the rabbis focus most often on the family lineage of the convert. Their major concern is that the priests not marry those whose family lineage is not equated with unimpaired members of the Israelite community. The disagreement centers around whether or not converts fall into this category. Many sages believed that converts are not just like native-born Israelites. While converts were members of the Israelite community, they were not unimpaired Israelites. For this reason, many held that the converted women could not marry priests. Yosi holds the most liberal position, maintaining that the daughter of two converts could marry a priest. However, the amoraim in both Talmuds believed that Yosi held this view *only if* the woman was conceived *after* her parents had converted, a position not specifically stated in the Mishnah. Thus, according to the amoraic interpretation of Yosi's statement, the female child of converts was held to have an unimpaired Israelite lineage only if she were conceived and born after her parents became Israelites, so that the children of converts would not be the same as unimpaired Israelites if they were conceived before their parents converted. It is striking that the rabbis deemphasized the Torah's concern for the sexual purity of the priests' spouse and focused on the issue of her family lineage. From this point of view, the amoraim held that the family lineage of converts was not the same as the family lineage of native-born Israelites. But the interesting point is the concern with the status of the converts' children. The material suggests that conversion, while not changing people's own lineage, does affect the lineage of their children. So, in this context, conversion means more than merely accepting a set of beliefs, a religious system, or a new culture. Conversion, in the view of some sages, changes a couple's biological essence, so that they produce children whose lineage is different from that of their parents. This explains the view held by some that converts were essentially dissimilar to native-born Israelites and that that difference resulted from their having diverse ancestries. In the opinion of many of the sages, only those who could definitely trace their lineage to Jacob/Israel were full-fledged members of the People Israel and could freely intermarry with all of the unimpaired segments of the People Israel. However, Yosi, at least, would disagree, holding that this statement applies to only first-generation converts. This concern with lineage is a common trait of ethnic groups, which are usually defined by contemporary scholars in terms of a shared lineage. And it underscores the fact that many of the rabbis viewed the People Israel as an ethnic group a well as a religious community.

NINE

Converts as Newborn Children

The rabbinic texts take account of the fact that conversion involves a transformation of the proselytes' sociological status. In the amoraic documents this is expressed by the comparison of the convert to "a newborn child,"[1] which has implications for several areas of rabbinic concern.[2] First, the converts were considered to have severed all ties with their gentile family. Second, misdeeds which the converts performed while they were gentiles do not have any importance after they become members of the Israelite community. Third, the converts, unlike gentiles, are required to follow Israelite custom and law to the same, or almost the same, degree as any native-born Israelite.

The converts' breaking the ties with their gentile relatives has consequences in several areas of rabbinic law and practice. For example, the laws concerning whom one can marry are derived from the forbidden family relationships recorded in Leviticus 18.[3] But, because the converts have severed all ties with their gentile relatives, it becomes unclear exactly to which relationships these marriage restrictions apply. This also finds expression in the discussions of the laws of levirate marriages and similar matters of family law. Also, the laws of inheritance become complicated after conversion, for some believed that converts did not have a natural right to inherit from their gentile parents. And, because it is conceivable that converts who have severed all family ties with their gentile relatives could die without leaving acceptable heirs according to Israelite law, several problems arise in the areas of the transfer of property, the concept of ownerless property, and the responsibilities concerning the dead converts' financial and ritual obligations. Furthermore, the laws concerning the prohibition against testifying in court against one's relatives are also affected by the converts' change of status and severing ties with their gentile relatives.[4] In addition, some monetary situations become complicated when dealing with converts.[5] Let us now turn to some of these issues.

The fact that converts become new people is reflected in several ways in our texts. For example, in Mishnah and Tosefta a gentile who converts is compared to a minor who reaches maturity, a deaf-mute who gains the ability to speak and to hear, an imbecile who becomes mentally competent, and a blind person who becomes able to see. These comparisons illustrate that conversion effected the gentiles' moving from one halakhic category into a totally new bracket within the Israelite legal framework.[6] The *sugyot* in the Palestinian[7] and Babylonian Talmuds[8] which equate gentiles who converted with slaves who were emancipated[9] also point to the converts' altering their legal and social status. These comparisons also imply that the converts occupy an "improved" status from when they were gentiles.

The former gentiles are now Israelites, and this change in identity is expressed by the fact that while non-Israelites need not follow Israelite laws and customs, converts are obligated to observe them. While this should be obvious, it takes on added importance when we remember that from the perspective of the Israelites as a religious community, the major difference between Israelites and gentiles is that the two groups act differently with respect to the major symbolates of Judaism.[10] Thus, the actions incumbent upon converts clearly marked them as members of the Israelite *religious community*. In the next chapter, we shall see that with regard to the conception of Israel as an ethnic group, the equating of converts and native-born Israelites is less complete.

A most important example in this regard concerns the agricultural gifts. Gentiles are not required to separate the agricultural gifts incumbent upon Israelites. This is because those gifts served as a means of promoting group cohesion among YHWH's people.[11] While the Israelites could support the poor among the gentiles by providing them with money, they could not aid them by providing them with the agricultural gifts left for the poor. Therefore, it is particularly significant that our texts draw a distinction between something done by gentiles before and after they converted in terms of the dough offering,[12] the forgotten sheaves,[13] the tithes,[14] the grapes left on the vine after the vineyard had been harvested, and the olives left on the trees after the orchard had been picked.[15] Furthermore, converts are specifically included among those who may receive the tithe separated for the poor.[16] When the Babylonian *gemara* details its elaborate conversion ritual, it specifically states that the converts should be instructed about the gleanings, forgotten sheaves, corners, and poor man's tithes.[17] Also, the suggestion is made that gentiles might convert only to receive the agricultural gifts which are given to the poor.[18] Finally, the Babylonian Talmud includes the dough offering among those Israelite obligations the converts should assume that they must fulfill.[19]

The gifts were left to demonstrate that the Land of Israel originally belonged to YHWH who had given it as a gift to only the Israelites. Therefore, leaving the agricultural gifts for the poor is an *Israelite* obligation. This is underscored by the fact that only *after* the gentiles have converted are they liable for these gifts, for only then are they recognized as members of the People Israel. Thus, setting aside these gifts serves to identify people as Israelites. These offerings functioned as a clear marker to distinguish between Israelites and gentiles and to indicate that the former gentiles were now to be considered as Israelites. Given the importance of agriculture in the lives of the Palestinians and the role that the Land of Israel played in the rabbis' mythological system, it was important to distinguish between Israelites and non-Israelites in this realm, and with regard to these gifts to the poor, the converts were clearly Israelites.[20]

Similarly, the converts' new status is expressed in the earlier texts in terms of Israel's purity laws. Differences surrounding purity concerns were important to the various segments of the Israelite community in late antiquity. They served as a means of separating various groupings within the Israelite community from one another as well as distinguishing the Israelites from the other peoples of their environment.[21] The Israelite laws of purity do not apply to gentiles,[22] but they are relevant to converts.[23]

Although the two Talmuds do not explicitly refer to the radical change of status converts undergo in terms of purity and the agricultural gifts, they do express this phenomenon in their own terms. In the Palestinian[24] and Babylonian[25] Talmuds, Haninah taught that if a gentile cursed YHWH, he was not liable for punishment after he converted. The Palestinian *gemara* contains Zeira's report of a teaching which states that upon conversion the proselytes are forgiven for the sins they committed as gentiles.[26] In the Babylonian *gemara*, Yosi holds that because converts are like newborn children, they are not held accountable for the misdeeds they performed as gentiles.[27] Even if a gentile killed another gentile or had intercourse with another gentile's wife, after he converted he is not punished for these acts.[28] The point of these amoraic pericopae is that after conversion the individual is not the same person who existed before conversion; therefore, the punishment would not be administered to the party who had violated the law. This is made explicit in a passage which states that a man may not betroth a woman on condition that she convert. Upon conversion, she will be a totally different person.[29]

Perhaps the most radical expression of the change which occurs upon conversion is that the former gentiles sever all ties with their non-Israelite relatives. One of the primary results of this situation was that converts could die without leaving legitimate heirs. This was much less frequent among native-born Israelites, for if a native-born male Israelite had not produced offspring, his father, his nephews on his father's side, and his paternal uncles could inherit his property or take on any obligations incumbent upon his heirs.[30] While there probably were cases in which a convert's death without heirs produced real problems for those who administered the Israelite legal system, it seems that often the situation of a convert's dying without heirs was used for the purposes of developing legal theory or advancing a number of concepts important in the *halakhah*. Many of these *sugyot* are not interested in the converts or the problems of conversion; rather they use the phenomenon of the convert as a peg on which to hang the development of legal issues. This means that often discussions of the converts need not have been engendered by the presence of converts within the People Israel or by the rabbis' interest in these new Israelites or former gentiles; rather, they may reflect the internal halakhic concerns of the rabbinic system. Unfortunately, it is virtually impossible for us today to distinguish between these discussions of the convert and those which arose from actual situations or from a pressing interest in actual converts.

For example, Ex. 21:28–30 deal with the punishment meted out to an ox which gores a person to death and to its owner. Taking the biblical text literally and assuming that it deals *only* with an ox which has an owner, the rabbinic sources discuss an ox which does not have an owner according to the Israelite legal system, such as a wild ox, an ox belonging to a woman, an orphan's ox, a guardian's ox, an ox belonging to the Temple, or an ox possessed by a convert who died without heirs.[31] Most likely the ox of the convert who died without heirs is mentioned here only because it provides a classic example of an ownerless ox. The convert *qua* convert is of no interest to the creator(s) of these passages.[32]

Similarly, a set of *sugyot* deals with Num. 5:6–8. The basic topics of the discussion are found in Mishnah, Tosefta, and Sifré Numbers.[33] The Torah states that if a person wrongs another individual, the former must confess and make restitution to the injured party. If the latter has died and does not have a kinsman to whom restitution can be made, the amount due is given to the priests.[34] The rabbinic sources focus on the phrase *if the man has no kinsman*, and from Mishnah onward this is taken to refer to a convert who had died without leaving heirs; the assumption is that every Israelite has some kinsman to whom restitution could be made.[35] In Sifré Numbers, this point is attributed explicitly to Ishmael.[36] In Tosefta, the

theft from a convert who died without heirs is used as the point of departure for dealing with other halakhic issues. In Tosefta's version, the convert meets the thief on the way to Jerusalem, and the former loans the
stolen money to the latter. The issues in which the text is interested are
whether or not the money the thief has is a loan, whether or not he needs
to make restitution to the priests if the convert dies, and whether or not
he must bring a guilt offering.[37]

The exposition of the laws of usucaption of a field includes[38] the
methods of usucaption of the field of a dead convert who died without
heirs.[39] Similarly, within its treatment of the relationship between the primary and the associated secondary items of a sale or purchase,[40] Mishnah
states that an Israelite who acquires the field of a dead convert acquires
everything within the field.[41] In both instances the property belonging to
a convert who died without heirs is comparable to property given as gift
and to property which brothers jointly inherited. In both of these *sugyot*
the main topic of interest is how one acquires a field and/or its contents;
Mishnah is not primarily interested in the convert, dead or alive, with or
without heirs. Although Tosefta has a different version of Mishnah's discussions, its pericope also comes as part of its section on usucaption, which
is its main concern.[42] Elsewhere, Tosefta deals with the case in which one
believed that the convert died without heirs but discovered after the property had been acquired that the convert did have legitimate heirs.[43] This
sugya occurs as part of a longer section which deals with one's transfer
of property based on a wrong assumption concerning his children,[44] and
our pericopae merely provide one more example of this issue. In both
Mishnah and Tosefta the convert who died without heirs appears in order
to refine the laws of usucaption and the rules concerning the transfer of
property. The *sugyot* tell us nothing about converts other than the fact that
the Israelite halakhic system considered it possible for them to die without
heirs. Given the view attributed to Ishmael in Sifré Numbers, at least
some believed that the converts were the *only* segment of the Israelite
people who could possibly not leave heirs upon their death. Thus, these
discussions also indicate that for some of the sages the converts were not
exactly similar to native-born Israelites.

While the *midrashim* do not deal with the dead convert's property, the
matter is taken up in both Talmuds. The Palestinian Talmud discusses
the acquisition of the dead convert's slaves,[45] whether or not usucaption
effects possession of a field and its contents,[46] and the correct procedure
for acquiring a dead convert's domesticated animal which is ownerless.[47]
It devotes most of its attention, however, to what happens if one takes
possession of one of the two fields which had belonged to a dead convert

and which were separated by a narrow path.[48] The concern here is with
the acquisition of ownerless property, for if the two fields had been owned
by an Israelite, the acquisition of one would have effected the acquisition
of the other. Although the Babylonian *gemara* also deals with the transfer
of a dead convert's domesticated animal,[49] the problem of acquiring two
fields with a path between them which had belonged to a dead convert,[50]
and the acquisition of a dead convert's slaves,[51] it devotes most of its attention to how one acquires ownerless property, such as that which belonged
to a convert who died without heirs. The amount of detail involved in
these *sugyot* is striking, and it is unlike anything which we have seen in
the other texts. Throughout these discussions the *gemara* frequently draws
a contrast between the manner in which one acquires the property which
belongs to Israelites and the ways in which one acquires ownerless property, such as that which belonged to a convert who died without heirs.[52]
While the use of the dead convert's property as an example of ownerless
property stands behind all of these discussions, the issue is most clearly
articulated in the extended pericopae of the two Talmuds. This is an example of the *gemarot* focusing on the actual or assumed theoretical issue
which stood behind the pericope in Mishnah and Tosefta.

The converts' creating new family relationships upon their entrance
into the Israelite community had ramifications in all areas of family law, so
that levirate marriages become a thorny issue when dealing with converts.
Deut. 25:5–10 provide the biblical warrant for this practice.[53] These verses
have received a variety of interpretations; however, deVaux seems correct
when he claims that this "is an expression of the importance attached to
blood-ties. A secondary, but similar, purpose was to prevent the alienation
of family property."[54] For the purposes of our discussion, the most important aspect of the levirate relationship is that it applies to only brothers
who are Israelites. Although Mishnah does not explicitly indicate that to
be subject to levirate marriages, the brothers must have the same father,
Tosefta states that "the brother[s] from the [same] mother do not engage
in the levirate relationship,"[55] and Rabbah's ruling to this effect in the
Babylonian Talmud[56] becomes normative.

Mishnah states that if two brothers convert along with their gentile
mother and one of them leaves a childless widow, they are not required
to engage in a levirate relationship. Nor do they engage in the ritual of
haliṣah, normally performed by the brother who did not wish to enter into
a levirate marriage with his sister-in-law. Even if their mother were pregnant with the first brother before she converted but bore him after she
converted, and the second brother was conceived and born after their
mother joined the Israelite community, the brothers do not engage in the

levirate relationship.[57] The text implies that the status of the parents at the moment of the males' conception was the crucial factor in determining the Israelite status of the children for the purposes of the levirate relationships. In the first case, the male children were conceived by two gentile parents, and the conversion of the mother does not change that fact. Even though the males have converted, they are not considered Israelites for the purposes of the levirate relationship. Nor are they viewed as newborn children who are now Israelite brothers. The second case is easier to explain, for here the males do not have the same parents at the time of conception. The first was conceived by a gentile mother, while the second was conceived by an Israelite parent. One was conceived by two gentile parents, and the other was conceived by two Israelite parents, one native-born and the other a convert. Even if the woman's husband had converted with her, he would be considered a different person after his conversion from whom he was while he was a gentile, so that the son conceived before his conversion would not have the same father as the one conceived after his father joined the Israelite community.

Although the issue of the levirate relationship is only briefly mentioned in Mishnah, it receives considerable attention in Tosefta. According to Tosefta, the wife of a convert does not enter into the levirate relationship with her brothers-in-law.[58] TYeb. 12:2 parallels mYeb. 11:2. The former opens by citing the latter and then expands upon it.[59] Tosefta adds a discussion of a male's being prohibited from marrying his brother's wife,[60] an issue not addressed in Mishnah. Commenting on the phrase *in Israel* in Deut. 25:6, Sifré Deuteronomy states that the levirate relationship does not apply to converts. It claims that this text was the basis for the statement[61] that "two converted brothers who were conceived not in a state of sanctity but were born in a state of sanctity are exempt from the obligation of *ḥaliṣah* and the levirate relationship." Sifré Deuteronomy seems to support the contention that Mishnah's concern is the parents' status when the brothers were conceived.[62]

The discussion in the Palestinian *gemara*[63] deals with the problem of a convert's engaging in a levirate relationship from a different perspective.[64] While Yasa was in Hamas, members[65] of the house of Bar Ashtin who were converts asked him whether they could engage in levirate marriages. Yasa responded that according to Yohanan, converts were forbidden from engaging in levirate marriages.[66] Someone[67] "sought to reason"[68] that Yohanan's opinion applied to a woman who had children; but concerning a woman who had not had children, Yohanan's ruling would not hold. If she were the wife of his real brother, the convert could engage in a levirate marriage with her. If she were not his brother's wife, the convert could marry her just like he could marry any other woman. However, Jacob bar Aha in the name of Isaac bar Nahman stated that even if the woman did not have any children, the convert could not engage in a levirate marriage, so that "they" would not mistakenly reason that the laws of the levirate marriage applied to converts. The whole discussion supports the claim that converts may not engage in levirate relationships, but the reason is that Israelites may not realize that the rules of the levirate relationship are incumbent only upon those who have native-born Israelite parents.

The *gemara* now refines the case further and states that the above discussion concerns a situation in which the dead brother had intercourse with the woman after he converted. In that case, the surviving brother who is also a convert cannot engage in a levirate marriage with the woman. However, if the dead brother did not have intercourse with the woman after he converted, the surviving brother may marry the woman, because she is not considered to be the wife of the dead brother. She is classified as "like a woman from the marketplace." Again, the laws of levirate relationships do not apply to converts. In this case no marital relationship was established between the dead brother and the woman because they had not consummated the marriage after the dead brother had become an Israelite.[69]

The Babylonian *gemara* includes Tosefta's discussion of the two brothers who converted with their mother. However, the Talmud explains that the two brothers who converted with their mother were twins. This addition makes it clear that they shared the same father, a point not made explicit in the earlier versions of the *sugya*.[70] This is important, for by this time it was clear that only native-born Israelites with the same father were required to engage in the levirate relationship. The Babylonian Talmud further claims that Aha and Sheshet disagreed concerning the prohibition of converts' engaging in levirate marriages and that the disagreement centered around whether or not the brothers were considered to be newborn children upon their conversion.[71] This is not the place to explicate the Talmud's complicated discussion. We need only realize that the issue of whether or not converts became newborn children was not as simple an issue as one might assume,[72] for not everyone held this view.

The ambiguity of the converts' relationship to their gentile parents also finds expression in the discussion concerning their right to inherit from their parents. Israelites must not worship idols, nor may they engage in any activity which could be construed as supporting idolatry.[73] For this reason, converts may divide their father's estate with their gentile siblings *before* the former take possession of those items which their parents bequeathed to them.[74] In the Babylonian Talmud, Rabbah states that the right of gentiles to inherit from their parents is derived from the Torah, specifically, Lev. 25:50.[75] On the other hand, the right of converts to inherit from their gentile parents is derived from "the words of the scribes." This implies that the latter practice is not as ancient as the former and that it has less authority behind it, for it was not part of YHWH's original revelation to Moses.[76] An anonymous statement claims that the right of converts to inherit from their gentile parents is a rabbinic decree[77] which the rabbis enacted so that the converts would not leave the Israelite community and return to their former people.[78] Thus, while the right of gentiles to inherit from their parents is part of the initial revelation, the right of converts to inherit from their gentile parents had to be established by the rabbis, because in the rabbinic mind, the familial relationship between the converts and their gentile parents did not exist. The *gemara* continues that converts have no right to inherit from converts, either according to the Bible or to the rabbis. This is derived from mSheb. 10:9, which states that if an Israelite borrows from a convert whose sons have converted with him, he need not repay the debt to the sons. The Israelite does not need to repay the loan because the loan is not transferred to the converts' heirs.

The legal transformation of the converts is relevant too with regard to their firstborn. A male who was the firstborn of two Israelite parents had to be redeemed from the priest,[79] and he inherited a double portion from his father.[80] Mishnah discusses these matters with regard to converts. Suppose that an Israelite male who had no children married a convert who had children while she was a gentile. If she bore a male offspring after she converted, an anonymous opinion states that the son receives the double portion because he is his father's firstborn; however, he does not need to be redeemed from the priest because he is not his mother's firstborn. For the authority behind this ruling, the woman was not totally transformed into a new person upon her conversion. According to Yosi the Galilean, however, the woman was totally transformed, and the son needs to be redeemed from the priest.[81] Similarly, if an Israelite male who had fathered children married a convert who was pregnant, if the child were the woman's firstborn, he must be redeemed from the priest. According to this opinion, the mother's status at the time of the child's birth is the crucial factor. Because the woman is an Israelite and he is her first child as an Israelite, his parents must redeem him from the priests.[82] In this case, the woman is a totally new person upon her conversion.

Although these matters are not discussed in the relevant sections of either Mekhilta or Sifré Deuteronomy,[83] they are naturally dealt with in the Babylonian *gemara* to our Mishnah.[84] Yohanan holds that if a male fathered children while he was a gentile, a son born to him after he converted does not receive a double inheritance, while Simeon b. Laqish rules that the first son born after his father's conversion does receive a double inheritance. Simeon based his opinion on the fact that the convert was a newborn child; Yohanan based his argument on the phrase *the first fruit of his vigor*,[85] which does not refer to the Israelite nature of the father. Following this same reasoning, Yohanan holds that a convert who fathered children while he was a gentile has fulfilled his obligation to procreate,[86] while Simeon states that he has not fulfilled this obligation; he is now a new person, and as a new person he must produce additional children. In this context Yohanan and Simeon disagree about the "newborn" status of male converts.

The changed status of the convert has an impact in other halakhic situations. According to Tosefta, if a woman who was impregnated by a convert who had died suffered a miscarriage as a result of being injured during a fight between two Israelites, compensation need not be paid after he died because it is assumed that the convert died without heirs.[87] If the woman had been married to a native-born Israelite, compensation was paid to either her husband or to his heirs.[88] Although the version of this *sugya* which appears in Mishnah mentions only that the woman was a convert, the Babylonian *gemara* assumes that she was married to a male convert. Rabbah states that if the woman were injured while her converted husband were alive, then compensation need not be paid because he was the one who was entitled to the payment. However, if the injury occurred after her husband died, the *gemara* states that compensation is paid to the woman. Hisda disagrees with this anonymous ruling, for he claims that only males are entitled to compensation.[89]

The rabbinic texts hold that gentiles who convert radically change their status. This is most clearly expressed in the idea that converts become like newborn children.[90] The outward expression of the converts' altered state is their severing their original familial relationships. Family relationships were important in matters of inheritance, the transfer of property, collecting debts, compensation for damages, court testimony, and whom one could and could not marry. This means that converts presented unique problems in several different areas of the halakhic system. In addition, the converts also provided a convenient point from which to develop certain matters of theoretical as well as practical law. It also becomes clear, however, that not all sages at all times believed that the converts' change of status should be taken into account. Thus, not all of the rabbis agreed that upon their conversion converts became like newborn children. In fact, the idea that converts were like newborn children is first expressed in the amoraic texts. Furthermore, the converts' relationship to their relatives could be complicated by taking into consideration the status of the converts' parents when the former were conceived and/or born.

The above discussions reflect the ambiguity with which the sages viewed the converts. Some thought that converts become radically new people when they entered the Israelite community. Others were not convinced that conversion produced a totally new individual, or at least an individual who was totally the same as a native-born Israelite.[91] In the next chapter we shall see that the converts' ambiguous status is also expressed by some vis-à-vis those rituals, customs, and laws which are incumbent upon native-born Israelites.

■ TEN ■

Converts and the Israelite Way of Life

■

Many of the rituals, customs, and ceremonies developed by the sages served to separate the Israelites from the peoples among whom they lived. Frequently, the rabbinic texts distinguish between Israelites and gentiles with reference to the different ways in which the two groups related to the social, judicial, and ritual conventions of the People Israel and to their major symbolates: The Land, the Sacred Periods, the People Israel, the Temple and YHWH, and purity.[1] Converts seem to fall conceptually somewhere between Israelites and gentiles, so that it is important to examine exactly how the converts functioned within these same realms: How did converts treat the soil and crops of the Land of Israel? How did converts act during the Israelite sacred seasons? How did converts interact with native-born members of the People Israel? How did converts fit into the Israelite judicial system? How did converts worship YHWH within the Temple precincts? How did the purity rules apply to converts? Basically, we want to delineate the extent to which our sources draw distinctions between the native-born Israelites and the converts.

In a passage quoted by Sifra[2] and the Babylonian Talmud,[3] Tosefta states that only gentiles who agree to follow the whole Torah (including, according to Yosi b. Judah, even the relatively minor scribal teachings) should be accepted as converts.[4] But, once gentiles have become Israelites, even if they are suspected of violating all of the Torah's requirements, they still are classified as Israelites, albeit apostate Israelites.[5] This passage points to the fact that some sages believed that converts underwent a radical transformation, for once the adult gentiles freely became Israelites, they were Israelites for life. Another *sugya* in Tosefta, echoed in the Babylonian Talmud,[6] underscores the converts' obligation to follow the Torah by stating that at Sinai, Moses abjured all those Israelites present with him, all future generations of native-born Israelites, and all who in the future would convert to follow the whole Torah,[7] and elsewhere the Babylonian *gemara* informs us that the converts' "guiding star" was present at Sinai when the Israelites received the Revelation.[8]

Although from Tosefta onward some rabbis claimed that converts were required to follow the entire rabbinic Torah,[9] just like native-born Israelites, a passage in the Palestinian *gemara* suggests that a convert's adopting the complete Israelite system could take some time. The story tells of a convert who retained his belief in astrology even after he declared his attachment to YHWH. Eventually, however, he realized that he had to reject astrology totally and to put his trust solely in YHWH.[10] In the view of this pericope, converting and accepting the entire Torah could be two distinct actions, which occurred at different times. Contrary to the above views, accepting the entire Torah need not be complete at the time that the gentile became an Israelite. And, at least according to this passage, conversion was not the result of a sudden one-time "enlightenment."

Agricultural Laws

Mishnah and Tosefta indicate that Israelites and gentiles treated the crops which grew in the Land of Israel differently. Non-Israelites were not required to separate those agricultural gifts which were designated for the Israelite poor—such as the corners, the forgotten sheaves, the gleanings, and the like[11]—nor were they responsible for separating the dough offering,[12] for observing the restrictions surrounding "mixed kinds" of produce,[13] or for the constraints related to the sabbatical years.[14] Some sages held that gentiles could separate the tithes and the heave offering and give gifts as freewill offerings because non-Israelites, like Israelites, had to acknowledge YHWH's claim to the Land of Israel. However, the rituals which the gentiles performed were different from those practiced by Israelites.[15] Others seem to hold that gentiles could not own a parcel of the Land of Israel.[16]

Mishnah,[17] followed by Sifra,[18] Sifré Deuteronomy,[19] and the Palestinian Talmud,[20] take up the gifts for the poor, and Mishnah,[21] Tosefta,[22] and the Babylonian *gemara*[23] deal with the converts' responsibilities with regard to the dough offering. Only a person who converted *before* he reaped his field is required to leave the gifts for the poor, and only a woman who converted *before* she rolled out her dough must remove the dough offering. Because these practices are followed at specific times during the harvest or the preparation of dough, the texts emphasize that the gentiles must have joined the Israelite community *before* the time at which these gifts were due in order to be obligated to separate them. Furthermore, Sifra[24] and Sifré Deuteronomy[25] remark that converts as well as native-born Israelites can be among the recipients of the gifts which Israelites are respon-

sible for giving to the poor members of their community. Sifré Deuteronomy, however, qualifies this by teaching that Israelites should take care
of their children, their servants, orphans, and widows before turning to
aid converts.[26]

Gentiles were not required to separate the agricultural gifts for the
poor, because those gifts acknowledged YHWH's gift of the Land of Israel
to the Israelite People. The people's participation in this acknowledgment
had the effect of enhancing group solidarity.[27] Therefore, it is significant
that the converts are included among those who are allowed to receive
them,[28] as well as among those who are required to separate them. The
importance of the agricultural gifts in this context is underscored by the
fact that a *sugya* in Tosefta states that Israelites may collect charity funds
from both Israelites and gentiles and that they may distribute these funds
to the needy in both communities.[29] Thus, while Tosefta expressly states
that *money* may be given to the poor among the gentile community, it does
not allow the *agricultural gifts* to be given to them. The symbolic importance of the agricultural gifts designated for the poor Israelites helps to
explain why the Babylonian *gemara* suggests that even when the Israelites
experience hard economic times, gentiles might still wish to join the Israelite community because of the gleanings, the forgotten sheaves, the corners, and the poor people's tithes,[30] and why these Israelite obligations are
specified by the Babylonian Talmud to be mentioned during the instruction of gentiles upon their conversion.[31]

The unique nature of the gifts to the poor is further illustrated by the
fact that there are other agricultural gifts which are not related to the poor
among the People Israel and about which there is some disagreement concerning the converts' responsibility. The Torah instructs the Israelites to
bring their first fruits to YHWH's house,[32] and it specifies[33] that when the
person brings the first fruits to the priest he should say, "*I acknowledge this
day before YHWH, your God, that I have entered the land that YHWH swore to
our ancestors to assign to us.*" The question arises whether or not the converts can bring this offering and/or recite the Avowal. Mishnah[34] allows the
converts to bring the offering, but prohibits them from reciting the
Avowal, for YHWH had not promised to give the Land of Israel to their
ancestors, a view attributed to Judah in Tosefta.[35] According to Mishnah,
only if the converts had Israelite mothers could they recite the Avowal.
Although Mekhilta's *sugya* is somewhat ambiguous, it seems to agree with
Mishnah's ruling, without mentioning the stipulation that converts with
Israelite mothers are permitted to recite the Avowal.[36] The Palestinian Tal-
mud[37] contains a dissenting view, recorded in a *beraita* "in the name of R.
Judah," which claims that converts should bring the first fruits and recite

the Avowal because Genesis records that Abraham was the father of a multitude of nations,[38] which means that the converts could maintain that YHWH had promised to give the Land of Israel to their ancestors, for in fact Abraham was their progenitor as well as Israel's Patriarch.

Mishnah,[39] followed by Sifré Deuteronomy,[40] also holds that converts may not recite the Avowal which accompanied the second tithe,[41] because they do not inherit a portion of the Land of Israel. In this instance, converts are similar to freed slaves, priests, and Levites, who also were not among those to whom Joshua allotted the Land.[42]

The converts' inability to recite the Avowal which accompanied the first fruits was related to their non-Israelite ancestry, for having an Israelite mother, according to Mishnah, enables the convert to recite that Avowal, and the phrase quoted in Mishnah refers to that which *YHWH swore to our ancestors*. However, in the case of the Avowal related to second tithe, the converts are excluded because they did not receive a portion of the Land of Israel at the time of the Conquest, even though in this instance they are similar to freed slaves, priests, and Levites. Therefore, we would expect some ambiguity concerning the converts' right to own real estate within the Land of Israel. For the most part, as we have seen above, it is assumed that converts could own real estate and bequeath it to their descendants.[43] However, Sifré Numbers contains passages which argue that converts were not assigned a portion of the Land at the time of the Conquest. And one could derive from these *sugyot* that their title to any real estate was less secure than that held by native-born Israelites. The *sugya* notes, on the basis of Num. 10:29,[44] that the Land of Israel was not divided among the converts. Even though Ezek. 47:23 states that *you shall give the convert (gr) an allotment within the tribe where he resides*, some held that this does not indicate that they received a portion of the Land. Rather, it means either that converts experience atonement for their sins along with the tribe among whom they dwelt or that they could be buried alongside the members of the tribe to whom that portion of the Land had been given.[45] Even if these texts were eventually read as referring to only the original division of the Land, they still imply that some sages believed that converts were not equal to native-born Israelites with regard to the former's *inherent right* to own a parcel of the Land of Israel.

There are no discussions concerning the converts and the majority of the agricultural rules, and we must assume that they were obligated to follow those rules along with the native-born Israelites. Converts are mentioned in only two contexts—the agricultural gifts to the poor and the Avowals connected with the first fruits and the second tithe. Only Israelites could separate and receive the agricultural gifts set aside for the poor, so that it is significant that converts are specifically obligated to set aside these gifts and that they are included among those who may receive them. This demonstrates that some sages considered the converts to be full members of the People Israel. On the other hand, the discussions of the first fruits and the second tithe imply a difference between converts and native-born Israelites. In all but one relatively late collection, converts *could not claim* that YHWH had promised to give the Land of Israel to their ancestors; therefore, although they brought the first fruits like native-born Israelites, they could not recite the Avowal which the native-born members of the Israelite community were required to recite. Similarly, most texts record that converts could not recite the required Avowal when they brought their second tithe to Jerusalem, for they were not included among those to whom a portion of the Land was given at the time of the Conquest. At least in the minds of those who formulated the discussions concerning the second tithe, converts were not equal to native-born Israelites with regard to their right to own a parcel of the Holy Land.[46]

Holiday and Ritual Laws

The Israelite periods of sacred time were another means of marking the difference between the People Israel and the gentiles. Only Israelites had to follow the regulations connected to the holidays; if gentiles were affected, it was an indirect result of the fact that the Israelites had to alter *their* normal activity, even when coming into contact with non-Israelites.[47] There are a relatively small number of pericopae which discuss the converts vis-à-vis the Sabbath, and the accepted opinion is that converts are considered to be equal to native-born Israelites with regard to their obligation to observe the Sabbath. This is important, for from the point of view of the rabbinic texts, the Sabbath is a decidedly ethnic holiday. Rejecting the view of Genesis[48] and Exodus[49] that the observance of the Sabbath was related to YHWH's resting upon his completion of the creation of all of humanity, the rabbis accepted Deuteronomy's claim that only Israelites needed to rest on the Sabbath because only they acted in commemoration of the Exodus.[50] The Sabbath becomes a uniquely Israelite phenomenon,[51] and converts, like native-born Israelites, must observe it completely.[52] Because converts are expected to observe the Sabbath, they cannot profit from a bathhouse which they inherited from their gentile father and which operated on the Sabbath.[53] The Palestinian *gemara* notes that converts must follow the travel restrictions placed upon native-born Israelites during the Sabbath. If converts are immersed on the Sabbath after sunrise, the place where they were immersed counts as their primary residence, so that they cannot move more than 2,000 cubits in any direction from that spot.[54]

On the other hand, some questioned the converts' ability to "keep the Sabbath" fully. Tosefta,[55] quoted by the Babylonian Talmud,[56] records that Aqiba and Monobases disagreed over whether or not converts who live in a gentile environment are liable for punishment if they inadvertently violate the Sabbath. If Israelites who are ignorant of the restrictions placed on their activity on the Sabbath commit several misdeeds on one Sabbath, they are liable for one sin offering.[57] By declaring the converts exempt, Monobases draws a distinction between the converts and native-born Israelites. Aqiba, on the other hand, treats converts and Israelites the same; both are liable for a sin offering. Monobases reasons that converts who were raised and lived among gentiles might not have had accurate knowledge about all the details of Sabbath law and could inadvertently err. Aqiba argues that there were no inadvertent errors.

Passover plays a unique role within Israelite culture, for it recalls the creation of the People Israel.[58] Our sources emphasize that once gentiles become Israelites, they are obligated to celebrate Passover.[59] The Palestinian *gemara* quotes Yohanan's teaching that if a gentile separated the Passover offering before he converted, he must offer another one after he joined the People Israel because only Israelites can bring this offering.[60] Because converts, but not gentiles, are required to keep Passover and to bring the Passover offering, the celebration of this holiday is used as a peg on which to hang several discussions of the importance of immersion as a conversion ritual. In these *sugyot*, which appear in virtually every collection, the celebration of Passover is equated with being an Israelite. A Houses' dispute concerning the efficacy of immersion as a conversion ritual is related to Passover.[61] We also have the account of the guards and "watchers of hinges" in Jerusalem who were immersed and who ate the Passover sacrifice that same evening.[62] We are told too that a convert who has been circumcised but who has not undergone ritual immersion may not offer the Passover sacrifice.[63] The several *sugyot* which discuss the converts' obligation to observe the second Passover[64] all assume that converts must commemorate Passover. The disagreements in these pericopae cover whether or not gentiles who converted between the first and second Passovers are obligated to observe the second one even though they were not obligated to observe the first Passover.[65] A *sugya* in the Palestinian Talmud asks if a gentile who converts during the Passover week is required to celebrate the last day of Passover by appearing before YHWH.[66] Although converts are required to keep Passover, both Talmuds contain a pericope which notes that they cannot form their own group for selecting and slaughtering the Passover sacrifice because they might not sufficiently know the details of the laws concerned with this ritual.[67]

There are miscellaneous remarks concerning other holy periods and sacred rituals. Converts are obligated to hear the *shofar* on Rosh HaShanah[68] and the *megillah* on Purim,[69] to dwell in booths during Sukkot,[70] and to abstain from food on the Day of Atonement.[71] With regard to the ritual of the priestly benediction, we are told that the priests recited it over the converts as well as over the native-born Israelites.[72] Furthermore, Aqabyya b. Mahaleel ruled that converted women were not subjected to the rite of the bitter waters because they were not included among *the children of Israel*. Even though sages disagree with this ruling, the discussion does point to the ambiguous status of the converts.[73] Finally, according to Tosefta,[74] converts are counted among those who must recite the grace after a meal.

The Sabbath and Passover received the most attention in the rabbinic texts, for the sages viewed them as the most important sacred seasons of the People Israel. Thus, it is significant that the converts are most often equated with the native-born Israelites with regard to these two periods of sacred time. However, the dispute between Aqiba and Monobases concerning the punishment meted out to a convert who lived among gentiles points to the recognition by some that converts are not completely like native-born Israelites, for they were raised and now live in different environments. A similar picture is drawn with regard to Passover. The celebration of Passover is used as a marker for members of the People Israel; therefore, converts are required to observe this festival. However, the ambiguous relationship of the converts to Passover finds expression in both Talmuds, for they each contain the opinion that a group composed exclusively of converts cannot be formed to select and to offer the Passover sacrifice because they may not fully understand the complicated rituals connected with these practices. To ensure that the rites are properly followed, the group must contain at least one native-born Israelite.[75] Thus, converts are required to follow all the details of the Israelites' sacred period. However, unlike native-born Israelites who were raised from birth in an Israelite environment, converts, who were nurtured in a gentile environment, might not know exactly how to observe these sacred seasons. This is a subtle way of denoting an important difference between native-born Israelites and converts.

Social Interactions

The complex status of converts within the People Israel is evidenced in a broad range of social interactions and institutions, as well as in the areas of the Israelite agricultural and holiday legislation. As early as Mishnah,[76] a *sugya* instructs native-born Israelites not to remind converts that their parents were not Israelites, and Tosefta admonishes Israelites not to insult converts by bringing up their former lives as gentiles.[77] This view is repeated in Sifra,[78] which also admonishes native-born Israelites to love the converts as they love one another.[79] Mekhilta Ishmael[80] follows Mishnah's use of Ex. 22:20[81] to support its opinion on this issue. Also in Mekhilta Ishmael, Simeon b. Yohai argues that converts are more precious to YHWH than are native-born Israelites,[82] and this view also appears in the Babylonian Talmud.[83] Resh Laqesh is reported to have said that one who treats converts unjustly is considered to be the same as one who treated YHWH in an unjust fashion.[84]

While many of the rabbinic texts contain passages which admonish the Israelites not to insult converts by reminding them of their non-Israelite origins, these same texts make it clear that converts were not fully assimilated into the Israelite community, for many pericopae picture converts as a distinct element of Israelite society. Mishnah lists the converts as one of the ten family types which migrated from Babylonia to Jerusalem with Ezra,[85] and this division within the People Israel is expressed in Tosefta[86] and the Babylonian Talmud.[87] Converts are also listed as one of the major subclasses of the People Israel.[88] The distinctive nature of converts is expressed throughout; at best they were a distinct subgroup of the People Israel.

Marriages between Converts and Israelites

From the perspective of rabbinic law, converts have complex familial ties which are reflected in the discussions concerning the marriages of converts. The intricate laws and discussions concerning the converts' ability to marry into the priestly clan or with other types of native-born Israelites demonstrate the difference between these groups of the People Israel with regard to the Israelite marriage taboos.[89] This is also expressed in controversies about levirate marriages. If a female convert's sons convert with her, they are not subject to the ceremony of *haliṣah*, and they do not engage in levirate marriages. A woman who is married to a convert also does not engage in levirate marriages.[90]

The validity of a marriage agreement executed between two gentiles who converted is also discussed in our texts. It is doubtful that gentiles wrote marriage contracts which the rabbis would have accepted, so that this theoretical discussion reflects the ethnocentric nature of rabbinic law. However, it also points to the sociological implications of conversion and the ways in which it could affect marriage relationships.[91] If a convert dies, his wife has full rights to the property agreed upon in the *ketubah*.[92] The fact that this had to be stated perhaps indicates that some believed that one might question the validity of a convert's previously executed marriage agreement with his wife.

There is even some discussion concerning the applicability to converts of the laws concerning the forbidden marriage relationships listed in Lev. 18.[93] Sifra holds that the forbidden relationships listed in Leviticus apply to converts,[94] and the Babylonian *gemara* contains a discussion between Aha b. Jacob and Sheshet concerning whether paternal or maternal brothers who are the children of converts can marry each other's wife, an unambiguous issue with regard to native-born Israelites.[95] Also, the Palestinian Talmud deals with a gentile who was married to a woman and her mother or to a woman and her sister when he converted.[96] No question was raised about these matters in the case of native-born Israelites; discussions arose only with regard to those who were once gentiles, but were now converts. Also, Mishnah[97] discusses a woman who converted with her mother and then is accused of engaging in illicit sexual activity. Because she is not considered to be an Israelite, if found guilty, she is strangled, not stoned, and she does not have to be brought before her father's house. If she is found innocent, her father does not receive the 100 *sheqalim* due to the father of a daughter who upon her marriage was unjustly accused of not being a virgin. Sifré Deuteronomy repeats this last comment.[98] The important point derived from these pericopae is that at the time of the marriage or the death of a childless husband, one had to know who was and who was not a convert. This stands in sharp contrast to the claim that one does not remind converts that they were not native-born Israelites.

Even the belief that converts severed their ties with their gentile relatives was not fully accepted, and this resulted in some complex familial situations which were regulated by Israelite law and custom. For example, it is clear that the rabbis believed that converts could inherit their gentile parents' property; they only stipulated that converts could not take possession of any item which violated Israelite law, custom, or practice. But with regard to some forbidden items, the Babylonian *gemara* stipulates that converts may dispose of things forbidden to Israelites a little at a time.[99]

The complex and intricate discussions related to the converts' marriages to Israelites again point to the ambiguous status of the converts within the Israelite community. Furthermore, the sages' exchanges concerning the converts' inheriting from their gentile parents also suggest that they were different from native-born Israelites. These issues derive from the ethnic nature of the Israelites, for only those who were considered to be descendants of Jacob/Israel were free from the concerns raised in these *sugyot.* Native-born Israelites were subject to the laws of levirate marriage, had valid marriage contracts, and were clearly prohibited from marrying those relatives enumerated in Lev. 18. While converts were Israelites, their presence within the community and the applicability of Israelite law to them was a matter of intense discussion throughout the rabbinic texts with regard to their familiar and marital relationships. This also means that one's status as a convert was important throughout one's life. Converts had to be recognized and known, at least to the sages and to those administering their teachings.

Converts and Their Heirs

As we have seen above, one of the major issues connected with the converts is the possibility that they could die without leaving Israelite heirs. Because an Israelite's parents, nephews, and uncles could inherit his property upon his death, it was unlikely that a native-born Israelite would die without heirs.[100] But, converts who had severed all ties with their gentile parents, uncles, and nephews could die without heirs if they had not produced any Israelite children. Thus, it was possible that converts' property could become ownerless upon their death. This had ramifications in especially two areas of Israelite jurisprudence—the areas of damages and the acquisition of property.

Mishnah,[101] followed by Tosefta[102] and the Palestinian *gemara*,[103] records that if an ox belonging to a convert who died without heirs killed a human being, Judah maintained that the ox was not killed, because it was an ownerless ox. Tosefta[104] maintains that if two men were fighting and they caused a woman who had been impregnated by a convert who died without heirs to miscarry, those who caused the miscarriage do not have to pay compensation, because the fetus' father had no legal heirs to accept the payment. Mishnah[105] had described the case differently and had indicated that the woman, who was a convert, could not receive compensation. Tosefta also teaches that if a convert's ox killed someone but the case did not come before the court until after the convert had died without leaving heirs, the ox is not stoned because its new owner, presumably an Israelite, occupied a different status from its owner at the time that the ox had killed the individual.[106]

On the other hand, Mekhilta Ishmael[107] states that a convert who is injured by an ox should receive the same compensation as a native-born Israelite who had been so injured. Sifré Numbers[108] contains a difficult *sugya* which appears to state that an Israelite who kills a convert is not subject to the penalty of banishment to a city of refuge. On the other hand, if a convert inadvertently kills an Israelite, the former is treated the same as a native-born Israelite.[109]

Our texts focus a good deal of attention on the ways in which Israelites can acquire the property that had belonged to a convert who died without heirs. Mishnah contains only two discussions of the issue and makes the point that in gaining possession of a dead convert's property, Israelites should follow the same rules which apply to a field received as a gift or to one which is jointly owned by two brothers.[110] Tosefta deals with a more complex set of issues. It speaks of a dead convert's property which he dedicated to the Temple before his death,[111] it deals with two Israelites' acquiring the same field,[112] it addresses the problem of acquiring secondary items along with the primary item to which the Israelite laid claim,[113] and it brings up the case in which an Israelite acquires a dead convert's property on the assumption that the latter had not left any heirs, but subsequently discovers that in fact he did have heirs.[114] While the Palestinian *gemara* takes up Tosefta's discussion of an Israelite who acquires a dead convert's property on the basis of the incorrect assumption that he had not left any heirs,[115] it also deals with a number of new topics. The different means of acquiring adult or minor slaves,[116] the acquisition of two fields which are separated by a narrow pathway between them,[117] and the method by which one acquires an animal[118] are all dealt with in the context of a converts' dying without leaving heirs.[119] The Babylonian *gemara* includes discussions of the issue of acquiring an animal which belonged to a dead convert,[120] deals with an Israelite who digs in a field which he believed was his but which turned out to belong to a convert who died without heirs,[121] treats one who set up a wall in the estate of a dead convert,[122] as well as other instances in which an Israelite improves a field which he has acquired.[123] A discussion about the ways in which slaves' acquire their freedom is phrased in terms of whether or not one acquires slaves when taking possession of a dead person's property, and this is also dealt with in terms of a convert who died without heirs.[124] The means by which one can acquire Hebrew slaves is discussed in the context of how one acquires items from a dead convert's estate.[125] In support of his claim that an embryo can acquire ownership of property upon the death of his father, Sheshet cites a *beraita*[126] which deals with the death of a convert who had no heirs.[127]

The possibility of converts' dying without heirs was intriguing to the sages, and in later texts culminating with the Babylonian Talmud, they created more and more complex cases related to acquiring the dead converts' movable and immovable property. It is difficult to determine whether or not these are theoretical discussions or *sugyot* which had practical import. What they do point to, however, is the rabbis' belief that the converts were inherently different from native-born Israelites. Because it was difficult for the rabbis to conceive of the possibility that Israelites who had died could not have heirs or relatives who could be responsible for them and their property,[128] the sages turned to the converts when refining the rules concerning the acquisition of ownerless property. Converts offered the sages the paradigmatic case of people who left ownerless property upon their death, and the ownerless property left behind by converts who died without heirs seems to have become a specific category of ownerless property.[129]

The converts' breaking their ties with their gentile relatives and dying without heirs also had implications for financial transactions. Mishnah[130] holds that if an Israelite borrowed money from a convert whose sons converted with him, the former does not have to repay the loan to the man's children after he died, for their familial ties had been broken upon their conversion. However, sages praise the Israelite who repays such a loan. In the Babylonian *gemara*, Rabbah deals with a convert who held an Israelite's pledge but died without leaving heirs.[131] Another *sugya* in the Babylonian Talmud discusses the case in which a creditor unlawfully seized and destroyed a pledge belonging to a convert who died without heirs.[132]

All of these *sugyot* point to a major difference between converts and Israelites; the former severed familial ties with their gentile relatives and could die without leaving legitimate heirs. For some sages, this was an essential, if not the most essential, characteristic of being a convert. So central was this trait that it even produced a specific category of ownerless property. It also served to distinguish theoretically the converts from native-born Israelites. When native-born Israelites died, their heirs could take over their property, collect their debts, and be responsible for claims made by and against their parents and their parents' estates. When converts died, the sages believed that more often than not no one remained who could inherit their estate or be responsible for it. Converts and native-born Israelites were essentially and existentially different in this regard. Again, this means that sages would have to be able to distinguish between converts and native-born Israelites at the time of the latter's death.

Converts and the Temple Cult

The Temple,[133] its cult, and its priesthood were major symbolates in rabbinic thought and culture. Gentiles could not bring the majority of Israelite offerings to the altar; they could sacrifice only freewill offerings and vow offerings. The complex rules which applied to Israelite sacrifices did not apply to those of gentiles, and gentiles could not occupy the same space on the Temple Mount as could native-born Israelites.[134] We have already seen that the problem of a convert's marriage to a member of the priestly caste generated a good deal of discussion among the sages, and this clearly points to a difference between native-born members of the People Israel and converts. On the other hand, the priestly benediction was recited upon native-born Israelites and converts. We now turn to the details of the Temple cult in order to ascertain how converts interacted in this sphere of Israelite activity.

With regard to the details of the Temple cult, the beginning of Sifra[135] implies that the converts are equated with Israelites, and this is the general thrust of the *sugyot* concerned with this topic. Mishnah notes that if a convert sent an offering to the Temple but died before he or she could include the drink offering, the community pays for the drink offering on the assumption that the converts did not have any legal heirs who could take on the responsibility of the offering.[136] Israelites, but not gentiles, supported the priests by supplying them with the shoulders, the two cheeks, and the maws of slaughtered animals. Therefore, Mishnah[137] and Sifré Deuteronomy,[138] followed by the Palestinian Talmud,[139] teach that if the gentiles converted before they slaughtered an animal, they are required to give these portions to the priests. Tosefta[140] states that all Israelite males, including converts and those of questionable lineage, lay their hands on their sacrifices and make the wave offerings before YHWH; the former view is also found in Sifra,[141] and the latter appears in the Babylonian Talmud.[142] Sifra states that converts, like Israelites, may not ingest the blood of the sacrifices,[143] may bring the offerings of well-being,[144] and may sacrifice vow offerings,[145] guilt offerings,[146] and sin offerings.[147] Sifré Numbers adds that the converts follow the same laws as Israelites with regard to offerings which are burned on the altar,[148] that both groups bring the same number of drink offerings with their sacrifices,[149] and that both sectors of the People Israel participate in the community offering.[150]

Even though converts seem to act much like Israelites in the context of the Temple cult, there were some differences. Yosi b. Judah believed that a priest could not receive the skin of a convert's offering.[151] And the priests may not consume that residue of a convert's meal offering.[152] In this case, converts are the same as women and slaves. Furthermore, Tosefta[153] and Sifra[154] note that converts, women, and slaves formerly were allowed to sprinkle the blood of their sacrifices on the High Places. Thus, converts are not fully equated with male Israelites, the paradigmatic native-born member of the People Israel.

With regard to the Temple, converts are most often equated with native-born Israelites. Although these discussions of the Temple cult took place long after the Temple had been destroyed, the Temple's symbolic importance as an ethnic shrine makes these pericopae valuable for assessing the sages' view of the converts as members of the People Israel. However, even this context, albeit in minor ways, the converts were pictured differently from native-born Israelite males. In the mind of the rabbinic masters who created our documents, converts were not quite the same as the paradigmatic Israelites, native-born males, but they clearly were not similar to gentiles, who had many more restrictions placed on their relationship to the Temple and its cult.

Converts and Purity

Purity was a major category of rabbinic thought, and it served as a means of separating Israelites from non-Israelites. Although the gentiles were considered to be like Israelites who suffered from a genital emission,[155] none of the purity laws actually applied to them.[156] Converts, unlike gentiles, do convey uncleanness through their genital emissions.[157] Thus, they are like Israelites. If a gentile had an emission of semen before and after he converted, he conveys uncleanness only through the second one, for then he was an Israelite, and the laws of uncleanness would apply to him. If a convert had a bright spot on his skin when he converted, he is considered clean, for the spot arose while he was a gentile, and it is compared to a bright spot on one before the Torah was revealed.[158] In Tosefta, Yosi and Judah dispute the period of time for which a convert is unclean the first time she emits vaginal blood after her conversion.[159] As an exposition of Leviticus, Sifra focuses a good deal on the issue of purity. Sifra notes that converts, along with slaves, are rendered unclean by a genital emission.[160] A female convert, a handmaiden, a freed slave, and an Israelite woman are rendered unclean by a flow of vaginal blood.[161] A female convert, like a native-born Israelite woman, experiences a prescribed period of uncleanness after giving birth.[162] Rules concerning the purity of the skin which has been burned[163] apply to gentiles after they convert.[164] Because the Israelite purity laws do not apply to gentiles, spots on gentiles are clean, even after they have converted,[165] and a boil which appears on a gentile before he or she converted is clean after he or she converted.[166] The point of both rulings is that the laws of purity do not apply to gentiles, so that if they had the signs of impurity when they converted, they are considered clean. If they are examined anew after they have converted and achieved the status of an Israelite and then are declared unclean, they are unclean. If a convert or a native-born Israelite eats an animal which has died or been torn apart by another animal, that person must wash his clothes, bathe, and wait for sundown in order to be considered clean.[167] The only purity issue which the Babylonian Talmud takes up is that concerned with a woman who has given birth. The discussions are rather complex and continually stress that only females who are part of the People Israel when they gave birth are required to separate themselves from the community.[168]

Few discussions concern converts vis-à-vis the Israelite purity laws, partially because the two Talmuds contain only tractate *Niddah* from the order *Tohorot*. And all of the discussions we do have equate the converts with Israelites. Thus, in this category alone it is clear that once gentiles become members of the People Israel they are obligated to follow the community's purity rules and taboos. This is important because the purity rules served to demarcate clearly between the Israelites and the non-Israelites.

For the most part, converts are classified as Israelites, and they seem to be required to fulfill the same obligations as the native-born members of the People Israel. While the Israelite purity laws do not apply to gentiles, all of them apply to converts. The Babylonian Talmud's complex discussions of a converted woman's need to separate herself after she has given birth stress this fact, for she needs to undergo a period of separation only if it is clear that she bore the child *after* she converted. Because purity laws most clearly distinguish between the Israelites and the non-Israelites, the lack of ambiguity concerning these matters is significant. Converts are Israelites, and as Israelites, the purity laws apply to them in the same way that they apply to native-born Israelites.

While the position of converts as Israelites with regard to the purity laws is unambiguous, the same is not the case in the other major categories of rabbinic law. We have seen that although converts are counted among the Israelites with regard to the agricultural gifts given to the poor, most pericopae claim that they cannot declare that YHWH gave the Land of Israel to their ancestors. In fact, Sifré Numbers implies that converts did not have a sound claim to real estate within ancient Palestine. With regard to the laws of the Sabbath and of Passover, the converts are differentiated from native-born Israelites because the former were not raised in an Israelite environment. For this reason they may not know the details of how to keep the Sabbath or of how to offer the Passover sacrifice. Thus, although one should not remind converts of their non-Israelite origins, that background meant that they suffered some disadvantages. Native-born Israelites had been schooled in the Torah from birth; converts had not.

Another essential difference between converts and Israelites was their relationship to their families. The rabbis believed that it was virtually impossible for Israelites to die without leaving heirs who could inherit their property or who would be responsible for their debts and loans. Converts, on the other hand, most likely would not have legitimate heirs or relatives who could see to matters after the former's death. In these instances, which the rabbis viewed as normal and frequent, the stress is on the fact that the convert alone established a relationship with the People Israel. And, unless the converts produced offspring with Israelites or other converts, that relationship was not necessarily continued by the convert's family after her or his death. The converts were not members of the People Israel at their birth, and upon their death, their families could have no ties to the Israelite community.

Converts were members of the People Israel; however, they were different from native-born Israelites. Despite the fact that the sages from Mishnah on warned Israelites about insulting converts by referring to their past, that past was always important. One had to know who the converts were, for they had certain marriage restrictions which did not apply to native-born Israelites. Also, upon a person's death, the converts' estates were treated differently from those of native-born Israelites. Even if the discussions of the Temple offerings and the Passover offerings were theoretical and did not apply at the time that the rabbis dealt with them, the differences between the converts and the native-born Israelites expressed in those contexts point to the fact that converts were essentially and existentially different from native-born Israelites. Both the Temple and Passover were important ethnic symbolates, and it is significant that the converts *are not* fully equated with native-born Israelites with regard to them. Converts formed a distinct subgroup of the People Israel, and it was important that those who administered the Israelite legal and religious systems could distinguish the converts from the native-born.

The complex position of the converts within the People Israel is a result of the dual nature of the Israelite community: It was both a religious community, in which the converts could become full members, and an ethnic group, to which the former gentiles could not be assimilated fully. We shall now turn to an analysis of this situation and of the complexities surrounding the concepts of conversion and converts within the rabbinic collections of late antiquity.

ELEVEN

The Stranger within Your Gates

Judaism in late antiquity was a diversified phenomenon. The Israelite communities described in Mishnah, Tosefta, the early midrashim, the Palestinian Talmud, and the Babylonian *gemara* differed from one another. Indeed, even within each of these documents, various strands of Jewish thought and life, representing disparate locations, periods of time, populations, cultural views, and intellectual environments, have been joined together.[1] As Segal writes, "different Jews . . . reached different opinions about proselytism and behaved accordingly."[2] This suggests that the divergent views we have encountered *may* represent varying sectors within the Israelite community. This fact is significant because as McKnight states, "conversion is a local factor. One does not . . . convert to Judaism so much as one converts to a local display of Judaism."[3] Therefore, not every gentile necessarily entered exactly the same Israelite community, and not every Israelite community or every member of a particular Israelite population automatically viewed the convert in the same way.

Even though the documents we have reviewed were constructed by the rabbis, the intellectual elite of the People Israel, they still present a variety of views, for "the rabbis" were not a homogeneous group. While the rabbis formed a distinct class within the People Israel, with its own distinctive features,[4] our documents picture the individual sages as differing among themselves on almost every topic.[5] In fact, one of the striking characteristics of the rabbinic collections is the diversity of opinions they record. Thus, it is virtually impossible to determine the "rabbinic view" on any topic. Rather, we can recount the *opinions* of the rabbis, either as anonymous figures or named authorities, on any topic covered in our documents, including the converts and conversion. Therefore, it is most correct to speak of the rabbinic *views* on conversion.

Because we do not know the scope of rabbinic authority or the esteem in which the various sages were held by other Israelites,[6] it is impossible to move from the rabbinic opinions to the practices of the ordinary Israelites, who lived in various locations in the Land of Israel and ancient Babylonia throughout late antiquity. We simply do not know which rab-

binic opinions, if any, were put into practice by the sages themselves or
by the general population in any community during a particular period
of time. Furthermore, given the impossibility of distinguishing between
pseudepigraphic and nonpseudepigraphic rabbinic sayings, we cannot
even achieve certainty concerning the views of specific sages to whom
opinions are attributed on individual topics. All we know is what our texts
have transmitted to us. We do not know for certain whether they have
reported the views of the various sages accurately. We cannot determine
what percentage of a given sage's opinions have been passed on to us,
whether the views handed down are a particular rabbi's "final word" on a
subject, or whether they are what he would have chosen to have recorded
in his name.[7] In general, the rabbinic teachings, sayings, and stories we
now possess have been disengaged from the worlds in which they originated.

Even if we could accurately determine the authenticity of the various
rabbinic statements and place them in their correct contexts, we still
would not have the converts' views of themselves. Thus, for the case of
antique Judaism, what we can know is far different from what the contemporary analyses of conversion in virtually all other cultures seeks to discover: the attitudes of the converts themselves. Modern social scientists
have devoted a good deal of effort to interviewing converts, assessing the
reasons for their conversions, and analyzing the phenomenon of conversion from the converts' point of view.[8] In contrast, we do not have "first
person" testimony by converts to Judaism in late antiquity. All we possess
are the *rabbinic* discussions of what *they* thought the converts felt and believed.[9] While this may provide us with insight into the rabbis' minds, it
tells us nothing about the views, motives, and ideas of the converts themselves. We learn only about the rabbis' image of the People Israel and
what it meant to the sages for a gentile to join that community. While we
gain a better impression of the *rabbis'* understanding of Israel as an ethnic
entity and a religious system, from the passages we have analyzed above
we learn nothing about the *converts'* conception of the People Israel, its
culture, its religion, or its deity. We do not know how individual native-
born Israelites interacted with converts, nor can we ascertain how these
two groups viewed each other. All we have is the world as the rabbis described it.

However, we do have a unique set of data for the study of conversion
and the converts. I refer to the perspectives of a segment of the community into which the converts moved. From the material available to us, we
discover that many of the rabbinic discussions are in line with the current

scholarly ideas concerning conversion. But at the same time, we find views that are not paralleled in the scholarly literature. For example, it is clear that the rabbis distinguished between native-born Israelites and converts. As far as can be determined, the term *gr* was applied to people throughout their lives. Given the ethnic nature of the People Israel, the two groups could never be fully equated, for it is virtually impossible to change ethnic affiliation.[10] Converts and native-born Israelites were similar in a number of ways, but they were also different, and these differences were maintained and regulated, according to the rabbis, throughout the lives of the people. Therefore, when a person married, it had to be determined whether the bride or groom was a native-born Israelite or a convert. Similarly, upon a person's death, the heirs had to be sought out, so that the deceased's status as a convert or native-born Israelite was relevant. There were also certain rituals which served to differentiate, at least in theory, the convert from the native-born Israelite. These instances, which seem most often to center around the Temple, while not practiced during the periods in which our documents were compiled, did serve in the minds of the rabbis to distinguish symbolically native-born Israelites from converts.

As we have seen above, ethnic descent lines are culturally determined; they do not necessarily reflect biological reality. Therefore, theoretically it would have been possible for the rabbis in late antiquity to assimilate the converts completely into the People Israel, to treat them as people born into the community. It is important that they chose not to do so. Conversion to a religious system which contained a number of different ethnic groups of equal status would not parallel the rabbinic conception of the People Israel. On the one hand, Israelite culture was a religious system to which anyone who accepted YHWH and the Israelite system derived from his revelation could adhere. On the other hand, Israelites were Jacob's children, who enjoyed a special relationship to YHWH, and that designation was limited to those who could trace their genealogy back to the last Patriarch.[11]

This dual nature of Israelite society has a major impact on the rabbis' discussions of the convert and conversion, and it may limit the applicability of the findings in this study to other groups to which one might convert. Much of what we find applies to only those communities in which there exists a sense that some members are "native-born" members of the group while others join from the outside. If the entire community views itself as "converts" or if the culture's ethnic descent lines are flexible so that anyone can be assimilated into them, the rabbis' points of view would be irrelevant. However, approaching conversion from the point of view of the converts' new community instead of from their perspective does offer some interesting insights and does point to some significant problems that have been ignored by previous scholars.

◼

Scholars have noted that conversion and commitment are two different acts, which may occur at different times. One may convert to a new religion or movement before one has fully committed to the groups' doctrines and beliefs.[12] The rabbis clearly viewed conversion as necessitating a complete reorientation of the gentiles' belief system and way of life. But some of them realized that this complete acceptance of the Israelite way of life could come only after a period of time.

To be an Israelite meant to accept YHWH as the sole deity of the People Israel and as the sole object of worship.[13] From Tosefta onward our sources demand that the convert accept the whole Torah, even the comparatively minor teachings of the scribes. In fact, unless it was certain that the gentiles could accept the entire Torah, they were not admitted into the People Israel.[14] Once accepted as a member of the People Israel, however, Tosefta claims that the converts never lost their status as Israelites, for if they left the community, they were classified as apostate *Israelites*. Although nowhere else are converts who withdrew from the People Israel identified as apostates,[15] it is clear that some later sages believed that "once an Israelite, always an Israelite." Rabbah b. Samuel stated that Simeon b. Gamaliel permitted Israelites to use the torah scrolls produced by a gentile in Sidon because the latter was a convert who had returned to his non-Israelite community. The mere fact that the gentile had once been an Israelite meant to Rabbah that even after the convert abandoned the Israelite community he still produced ritual objects which were fit for use by native-born Israelites.[16]

The view that conversion necessitated a total acceptance of Judaism has been recognized by previous scholars. Moore's view of Judaism as "a religion of authority; a revealed religion, which . . . demanded obedience to the whole and every part" meshes completely with the idea that converts had to accept the totality of the Torah.[17] Braude composed an entire chapter around the converts' obligations with regard to rabbinic *halakhah*,[18] and Bamberger opened his chapter entitled "Requirements for Admission" by quoting the above passage from Tosefta.[19] Finally, Nock wrote that "Judaism . . . demanded renunciation and a new start. . . . [N]ot merely acceptance of a rite, but the adhesion of the will to a theology, in a word faith, a new life in a new people."[20]

Accepting the whole Torah meant much more than merely following the commandments, for the Torah's demands make sense only if one accepts the ideas that YHWH created the universe according to a plan, the Torah, revealed that plan to Moses on Mount Sinai, and would reward or punish the Israelites according to their adherence to that revealed plan. Schiffman is correct when he writes that "the Torah which the convert had to accept is to be understood in its widest sense. The proselyte must identify fully with the past, present, and future of the Jewish people and live in accord with *halakhah*, the Jewish way of life. The Tannaim expected the convert to become part of the nation of Israel and to suffer its collective destiny."[21] Schiffman's last point finds early expression in Tosefta's claim that the souls of all those who would convert to Judaism stood with the souls of all the native-born Israelites—past, present, and future—at the foot of Mount Sinai at the time of the revelation to Moses,[22] for this symbolically places the converts alongside the native-born Israelites among those who were freed from Egypt and who experienced and accepted the revelation at Sinai that bound the Israelites and YHWH one to the other. The implication is that the converts always were, and always would be, a part of the People Israel. This also finds symbolic expression in Mekhilta Ishmael's note that Abraham and David called themselves converts[23] and in Rabba's claim, found in the Babylonian Talmud, that Abraham was the first convert.[24]

Many of our *sugyot* have indicated that converts become new people when they enter the Israelite community, and we have encountered several metaphors which point to the radical change of status gentiles undergo when they become converts. Converts are compared to minors who become adults, to slaves who gain their freedom, and to physically disabled individuals who overcome their disabilities. Furthermore, the fact that converts sever their ties with their gentile relatives also symbolizes their radically altered state of being. This change of status which is signaled by these comparisons resulted from the converts' accepting a new way of life guided by the Torah. The view that converts undertake a "new life" is standard among contemporary scholars of conversion. Snow and Machalek have stated that conversion "entails the displacement of one universe of discourse by another,"[25] and this is in line with the rabbis' insistence that the converts adhere to the rabbinic Torah, which placed the totality of existence within the framework of YHWH's cosmic plan. Segal writes that "the central aspect of the conversion is a decision to reconstruct reality,"[26] and this clearly is what the rabbis had in mind when they insisted that the converts subscribe to the totality of the Torah. The claim by C. L. Staples and A. L. Mauss that conversion is essentially a process of "self-transformation"[27] also fits the rabbis' ideas, for the rabbis believed that everything hinged on each convert's acceptance of the Torah. This is expressed in the Palestinian Talmud's claim that a female child should reconvert as an adult when she fully realizes the implications of her actions.[28] This might also relate to the fact that children, especially female children, do not act on their own accord, so that conversion only counts when it is done by independent, consenting adults. Similarly, McKnight holds that conversion involves, among other things, "cognitive agreement with the religion to which one is turning,"[29] and this accurately reflects the rabbis' ideas.

Even the Palestinian Talmud's story of the astrologer whose total rejection of astrology and complete acceptance of YHWH comes only after he has joined the People Israel is in line with much current thought on the conversion process. Converts do not enter their new communities as a *tabula rasa*. They bring with them their previous ideas, beliefs, symbols, and the like.[30] Following Snow and Machalek, these previously held items must be reconfigured in light of the new "universe of discourse" to which the convert adheres.[31] In the astrologer's case, his new "universe of discourse" demanded that he reject his ties to astrology and put his complete trust in YHWH. In addition, many have realized that conversion may be an extended process. William James early on recognized that conversion could be "gradual or sudden,"[32] and, as we have noted, contemporary scholars have pointed out that, as Segal writes, "conversion most often precedes commitment, so that the phenomenon of commitment includes more aspects than merely conversion. Conversion merely begins a process of commitment to the group."[33] Thus, the astrologer's entering the Israelite community *before* he completely committed himself to YHWH is not unusual among converts. Again, this story suggests that at least some of the later sages understood the difference between conversion and commitment.

In fact, the rabbis in general seem to have realized that under normal circumstances, developing commitment to the Israelite community's values was a rather slow process. Only infrequently do they refer to sudden conversions resulting from witnessing miracles or miraculous events occurring during their time.[34] While the rabbis in the Talmuds point to instances of sudden conversions, most of these date back to the biblical period. For example, although the conversions of Rahab and Jethro are first mentioned in Mekhilta Ishmael, only in the Babylonian *gemara* do we encounter rabbinic speculations on the *single event* which caused each of them to move into the Israelite community, implying that they suddenly changed communities in response to YHWH's miraculous deeds.[35] Also, both Talmuds contain the story of the sudden conversion of 150,000 individuals who saw Saul's sons and grandsons impaled on a tree for seven months.[36] Along these same lines, the Babylonian Talmud records that Nero converted when a young child expounded a verse from Ezekiel.[37]

More often the rabbis view conversion and commitment as the result of a longer process, and, as the stories of Hillel and the converts illustrate, commitment to Judaism usually develops over a period of time.[38] When one convert rejected Hillel's demand that the former learn both the Oral and the Written Torah, Hillel began an extended period of instruction to demonstrate the need to study with a sage in order to learn the totality of YHWH's revelation. Although Hillel taught another gentile "the entire Torah" while the latter stood on one foot, he was immediately instructed to continue his education. Thus, even though conversion might occur as a one-time event, commitment to the values and teachings of the Israelite community developed over time. Finally, only after a period of study with Hillel did a new convert understand that he could not be a High Priest. The realization that a full grasp of the Israelite traditions necessitated an extended period of study may also stand behind the Talmuds' teaching that converts could not form an association by themselves for securing a lamb for the Passover sacrifice. They might not fully understand the teachings on this matter and might inadvertently defile the sacrifice.[39]

One needed a good deal of time to learn the Torah, but as we have seen, some held that one had to know the Torah to be accepted as a convert. This apparent contradiction might explain some of the rabbis' ambivalence toward the converts. On the one hand, it took a lifetime of study to become a fully practicing member of the Israelite community, and it was virtually impossible to expect that a convert could acquire sufficient knowledge of Israelite traditions, customs, and practices without participating in the full life of the community. On the other hand, there was a long-standing tradition that converts must accept the whole Torah upon their entrance into the Israelite community. But how could the converts accept both the Written and the Oral Torah if they did not know what they contained? For this reason, there probably were rabbis and other Israelites who suspected that the converts joined the community without fully realizing the implications of their decisions. Therefore, was it unreasonable to assume that at least some converts were not as deeply committed to the People Israel as were native-born members of the community?

The rabbinic texts describe the difference between conversion and commitment in terms readily understandable to the contemporary students of conversion. The rabbinic materials maintain that commitment to the Israelite community and its religious system must be complete, but also that it may come only after an extended period of attachment and study, for the sages also seem to comprehend that people could first "convert" and then become committed only after they had joined the Israelite community. The rabbis also realized that people could change their minds or fail to become committed to the new system, so that they might return to their former way of life. This concern with commitment raises the question of the motives the rabbis attributed to persons who wished to join the Israelite community, the topic before us now.

A good deal of recent study concerns what motivates a person to convert. The rabbis were also concerned with this issue, and they attributed a variety of reasons to those gentiles who wished to join the People Israel. As we examine these motives, we must remember that they were attributed to the converts by the rabbis; they do not derive from the converts themselves. Thus, they tell us a good deal about the rabbis' views of themselves, their community, and the converts, but, to the best of our knowledge, they do not provide us with reliable information about what the converts themselves were thinking when they changed communities.

The rabbinic ideal was that gentiles would join the Israelite community "for the sake of Heaven," a view which first appears in Mekhilta Ishmael.[40] There we are told that if gentiles seek to convert "for the sake of Heaven," they should be encouraged to do so. They should be accepted immediately and not turned away. Whatever else may be implied in the phrase "for the sake of Heaven," in this context it seems to mean "without any ulterior motives." The Palestinian Talmud states that if a woman converted "for the sake of Heaven" and married a priest, she was permitted to eat *even* the most holy things; however, if she did not convert "for the sake of Heaven," she was not allowed to consume even the lesser holy things.[41] In line with the idea that commitment and conversion were two separate acts, the Palestinian *gemara* holds that a person who converted "not for the sake of Heaven" was allowed to convert a second time "for the sake of Heaven."[42]

The earliest rabbis accepted the possibility that a gentile would join the Israelite community in order to marry an Israelite. Mishnah[43] and Tosefta[44] both assume that gentiles may wish to convert in order to marry an Israelite, and both disallow such conversions: An Israelite may not betroth a gentile on the condition that the latter convert, nor may a gentile betroth an Israelite on the promise that the Israelite will convert. Interestingly, this is the only motive for conversion mentioned in these two documents. The Palestinian Talmud takes up this idea and also rejects gentiles who seek to enter the Israelite community because they love an Israelite. Rav, however, disagrees and argues that these people should be accepted, for perhaps later they will convert again "for the sake of Heaven."[45]

The rabbis also believed that some gentiles would become members of the Israelite community because the former sought some material advantage by their conversion. Sifré Numbers suggests that Jethro sought to follow Moses because the former hoped to receive a material reward for his adherence to YHWH.[46] The Babylonian *gemara* opines that some gentiles may seek entrance into the Israelite community so that they can receive the agricultural gifts which were given to the poor.[47] Similarly, passages in both of the Talmuds argue that those who wished to convert during the reigns of David and Solomon were rejected because they desired only to benefit from the "king's table," and those who would seek to become Israelites in order to benefit from the Messiah's actions toward the People Israel should also be rejected.[48] Finally, one *sugya* in the Palestinian Talmud claims that Antoninus converted so that he could eat the Passover offering.[49] And Keti'ah b. Shalom seems to have converted in order to achieve eternal life.[50] Keti'ah is described as a prominent Roman who defended the Jews against the Emperor and who was martyred. The pericope implies that he circumcised himself before his death. Thus, he surely was seen as a unique case.

The rabbis also speculated that some gentiles might wish to become Israelites in order to avoid being punished by YHWH. Both Talmuds contain the story of the 150,000 gentiles who joined the Israelite community because they saw how YHWH had punished those who harmed the Israelites.[51] When Nero realized that YHWH sought to destroy Jerusalem and place the blame on him, he converted.[52] Nebuzaradan converted in order to avoid punishment for having killed a large number of Israelites.[53] In one set of stories, Onqelos, the son of Titus's sister, converted because he learned from Titus, Balaam, and "the sinners of Israel" that Israel was the nation held in highest repute by YHWH. However, given the fact that all of those Onqelos consulted were suffering hideous punishments in the afterlife, the story also implies that Onqelos converted to avoid being punished for his/Rome's treatment of the Israelites.[54]

Some rabbis also argued that there were those who joined the Israelite community because they were impressed by the ways in which YHWH acted. Some later sages claimed that Rahab and Jethro converted as a result of the miraculous deeds YHWH performed for the Israelites at the time of the Exodus. Similarly, the 150,000 converts at the time of David were impressed by YHWH's care for his people. Finally, in one set of stories, Onqelos, Titus's nephew, convinces the Roman soldiers who had been sent to bring him back to Rome that they too should convert by demonstrating to them that, unlike earthly kings, YHWH places the honor and welfare of the Israelites before his own honor.[55]

Others converted, according to some of the sages, because they were impressed by the Israelites' actions. Sifré Numbers and the Babylonian *gemara* contain the story of a prostitute who was so astounded that an Israelite had refused to have sex with her that she mended her ways and converted.[56] Sifré Deuteronomy tells us that when gentiles engage in business in the Land of Israel they will be so astonished with the ways in which the Israelites worship YHWH that they will convert.[57]

Finally, some rabbis believed that gentiles joined the People Israel after conversations with Israelites who convinced them of the soundness of the Torah and of the Israelite teachings about YHWH and the universe. Valeria converted after Gamaliel was able to explain an apparent contradiction in the Hebrew Bible.[58] Antoninus converted after extended conversations with Rabbi,[59] and in the Palestinian Talmud, Judah b. Pazzi in the name of Yosi b. Judah reports that Adrianos converted after Onqelos demonstrated the truth of the Israelite claim that the world was suspended in air.[60]

The above examples illustrate the argument made by Lofland and Stark that, before they changed communities, the prospective converts had to experience "acutely felt tension." They also had to operate normally "within a religious problem-solving perspective," which means that they sought out the religious dimension of everyday events. Furthermore, they needed to be "religious seekers," who were open to alternative explanations of the religious aspects of the events they experienced. Additionally, they had to come into contact with the "new" religious system at a turning point in their lives. This meant that they could become free of their previous relationships with those not in the "new" religious system and establish "an effective bond" with some adherents of the "new" system of belief. Finally, they must be subject to "extensive interaction" with other adherents of the "new" system.[61]

Greil places most of his emphasis on the importance of personal relationships as the factor effecting conversion. He claims that "what seems to an individual to be true is determined essentially by the situation in which the individual finds himself and by the sedimentation of past experiences that bear on his current situation." People will adhere to a set of solutions to everyday problems and a "stock of knowledge" as long as it works in both the normal and the new situations in which individuals find themselves. If their "stock of knowledge" ceases to be useful, they will "'learn something new' or 'work out the answer' or 'realize that what [they] thought was true has been wrong all along.'" Because people's beliefs are at least in part a function of their reference group, "conversion from one perspective to another can be expected to occur in those cases where an individual orients himself to a new reference group. . . . When an individual's social relationships change, his perspectives are likely to change as well." [62] This means that "the conversion process then becomes a process of coming to accept the opinions of one's significant others." [63] If people's significant others are members of the "new" group, then they are likely to convert. Similarly, if individuals' significant others have converted, the individuals are likely to follow those others into the new movement. [64]

Not all people convert to a new movement as a result of close personal contacts with those in the new system, and Greil explores why only some people seek out new "sets of knowledge" in order to deal with the realities of their lives. He posits several reasons that cause peoples' perspectives to become discredited, so that they search for new "stocks of knowledge." Individuals look for new perspectives when those "significant others" upon whom the individuals depend for the maintenance of their perspective become unavailable, or when the perspective does not appear to deal with the problems the individuals encounter in their everyday lives. Also, "periods of rapid social change" or the increasing heterogeneity of a social setting can lead to the discrediting of an individual's perspective. [65] Finally, Greil argues that a key factor in determining which new perspective individuals choose and whom one will select as a "significant other" is their previous "cognitive style and stock of knowledge." [66]

Heirich has challenged many of the assumptions about the causes of religious conversion. For example, he has shown that the social networks affect conversion only *"for those already oriented toward a religious quest."* While "conversion occurs through use of available social networks . . . [i]f one is not already a religious seeker, such contact is insufficient in most cases to produce a 'change of heart.'" [67] Thus, Greil's stress on "significant others" seems not to serve as a viable explanation *unless* the converts have already found something in their accepted "set of knowledge" which no longer sufficiently explains "reality." Heirich provides three possible causes of the destructions of people's "clarity about root reality." People will reject their "explanatory schemes" if (1) "experiences or encounters take place that cannot be encompassed within current explanatory schemes yet cannot be ignored"; (2) current understandings of root reality are correct but "quite unacceptable outcomes appear imminent and inevitable"; or (3) "respected leaders publicly abandon some part of past grounding assumptions."[68] People convert, according to this scheme, if "the new 'reality'. . . speak[s] directly to the problem . . . and . . . explain[s] it more successfully than its earlier competitor."[69] In brief, Heirich focuses on the *content* of the new system as the reason for conversion.[70]

The world of late antiquity was a world in flux. The social, economic, political, and intellectual systems of the Roman Empire were changing,[71] and the Persian Empire was also experiencing new forces and influences.[72] Thus, various competing systems sought to explain a person's "reality" and those who were unsatisfied with their system's explanations could easily encounter an alternative set of theories. If one were a religious seeker, there were numerous phenomena for one to explore. The conditions were ripe for those who sought to change their religious outlook.

If Heirich is correct, we must *assume* that the converts discussed in our texts were already religious seekers. Clearly, the rabbis assume that the true converts were those who sought out YHWH's revelation as the correct explanation for the events they encountered in their lives. To convert "for the sake of Heaven" could easily mean to accept YHWH's Truth as the exclusive explanation for the events in one's life. At least the rabbis envisioned YHWH's plan as adequate to explain any set of circumstances.

The rabbis understood the concept of "religious seekers," and they present us with a few examples. Antoninus engaged in extended conversations with Rabbi, presumably to discover why Rabbi accepted YHWH's revelation. And in the view of some, the Emperor converted. Similarly, Valeria challenged Gamaliel with contradictions in the Torah, which presumably she had studied. She also found the answers she was seeking and converted. Along these same lines, Adrianos knew enough to ask Onqelos a rather sophisticated question challenging what he perceived to be a basic assumption of the Torah. Also, the gentiles who approached Hillel and Shammai can be classified as "religious seekers." Finally, Sifré Deuteronomy tells us that the Roman government sent two soldiers to become Jews and to investigate the entirety of the Torah. After studying Bible, Mishnah, Midrash Halakhah, and Midrash Aggadah with Gamaliel, they discovered only one thing which was objectionable.[73] Clearly, the rabbis believed that everyone who investigated their traditions would find nothing significantly objectionable and would be able to use YHWH's revelation as a guide for their lives. The Israelite traditions were open and available to all who wished to adopt them; all one had to do was to examine them. And, with the help of a rabbi, this could be done by anyone. The interaction between the rabbis and the prospective converts also fits with those who claim that converts establish social bonds with members of their new community. Relationships established between the rabbis and the converts would surely have facilitated the latter's entrance into the Israelite community, according to the sages.

While we learn nothing about those whom the rabbis described as converting out of love or in order to marry an Israelite, they may well fit into Greil's category of those who convert because of "significant others." It seems that some rabbis understood that one could convert because of significant others. However, with the exception of Rav, these converts were rejected. The rabbis wish to separate the formation of social networks from the conversion process. With the exception of Rav, the rabbis reject those who convert in order to marry an Israelite, because they did not join the People Israel "for the sake of Heaven." For the rabbis, a true religious seeker formed new social networks independently of discovering the truth of YHWH's revelation. In fact, the only social relationship the rabbis wholeheartedly accepted with regard to the converts was that which existed between the rabbis and the prospective new member of the Israelite community. One converted first and then later sought out a spouse among the People Israel.

It also seems likely that the rabbis understood that some people converted because their previous "stock of knowledge" did not fit their needs in everyday life or did not explain "reality." This, after all, is why there are religious seekers. It does not stretch the imagination too much to view the prostitute who converted as an example of someone whose "stock of knowledge" failed to explain her everyday situation. The story goes out of its way to explain that the woman was the most sought after prostitute in the realm. Clearly, her expectation was that no male could resist her, and when she was rejected by the rabbinical student, her entire frame of reference was destroyed. Here was a male whose "stock of knowledge" caused him, and him alone, to reject her sexual favors. Clearly his "stock of knowledge" had to be investigated, for it made him a most unusual person. Finally, she rejects her old way of life, seeks him out, accepts YHWH and his revelation, and marries the student. Her old system had caused severe cognitive dissonance, so that she had to find a new system, one which explained the young man's actions.

The rabbis' view that YHWH's revelation offered an explanation for reality also plays into their description of those who were impressed by YHWH's care for the Israelites. The sages offer several examples of converts who were impressed by the punishments YHWH meted out to those who caused Israel to suffer. The 150,000 converts at the time of David, Onqelos's questioning of Titus and Balaam, and Nebuzaradan's experience all testify to the rabbis' belief that there were those who converted upon realizing that YHWH was above all a protector of his people. This served to explain why Israel existed and prospered, even against the might of Rome and Persia during their period and against Assyria, Egypt, and Babylonia in the past. If the gentiles' religious and political theories did not explain the existence of Israel, the rabbis' understanding of YHWH's relationship to his people provided a rationale for present and past reality, and this perspective could be accepted by converts who were looking for an explanation of Israel's existence and prosperity.

For those who were dissatisfied with the ways in which the rulers of the ancient world treated their subjects, the rabbis offered the paradigm of YHWH's relationship to his people, Israel. Onqelos explains to the Roman soldiers sent to fetch him back to Rome that unlike earthly kings, YHWH places the honor of his people before his own. Again, to those who could not understand the Israelites' loyalty to YHWH, the rabbis furnished a simple answer: The Israelites were loyal to YHWH because YHWH was loyal to them. In the rabbis' mind the relationship YHWH established with Israel was sufficient to impress gentiles and to encourage them to join the People Israel. Similarly, in the rabbis' mind, the Israelites' loyalty to YHWH was also impressive from the gentiles' point of view.

The current scholarly literature on conversion focuses on social and psychological "rewards" that converts achieve but does not deal with the material gifts they might be seeking. The rabbis, however, believed that gentiles would seek to join the People Israel for purely material gain. They envisioned converts during the reigns of David and Solomon who sought to benefit from Israel's prosperity, and they believed that at the time of the Messiah gentiles would seek to be included among Israel, so that they would receive the special benefits YHWH reserved for his people. Although this testifies to the rabbis' belief that YHWH had caused his people to prosper in the past and would again bring them rewards in the future, they also thought that Israel's lot was better than most others' in the present. The Babylonian *gemara's* suggestion that gentiles would join the Israelite community in order to benefit from the agricultural gifts to the poor evidences the sages' presupposition that the People Israel fared better than their gentile counterparts.

While much contemporary scholarship points to the converts' predisposition to conversion and some psychological factors which lead them to change communities,[74] none of this finds expression in the rabbinic discussions. The rabbis tell us nothing about the lives of the individuals before they converted. We do not learn if the converts approached the Israelite community at a point of crisis or stress in their lives. While we might surmise that some of them were "religious seekers" and that others had experienced severe cognitive dissonance between reality and their "stock of knowledge," we have no way of knowing if the average converts were experiencing any psychological stress, a breakdown in their previous social networks, or the like. It is clear, however, that the rabbis conceived of the possibility that people might consider conversion before they actually joined the community, so that they would prepare themselves for that event.[75] In this view, conversion was a conscious act performed after a period of careful consideration and personal assessment.

The rabbis believed that YHWH's system presented a comprehensive explanation of reality which explained the situation of the Israelites and the gentiles in the world. They believed that their religious system could serve anyone who sought a better or more exhaustive explanation of reality in the rapidly changing environment in which they lived. They held that the way in which YHWH treated his people and the manner in which the Israelites worshiped YHWH and maintained their relationship to him would impress those who were seeking a better way of life. For them, people converted to the worship of YHWH because it was a better way of life and offered the best set of knowledge by which to deal with the realities of everyday life. In brief, the rabbis believed that people converted to the worship of YHWH for many of the same reasons that contemporary scholars explain conversion in the present world. Even if converts were seeking to improve their material existence or wished to establish a new set of social networks because of contact with a new "significant other," the rabbis' ideal was that these people would convert "for the sake of Heaven"; that is, they would become members of YHWH's people because they realized that this offered the best life on earth and the best interpretation of that life.

Conversion is not only an intellectual event; it is also a sociological transformation. As we saw above, Lofland and Stark pointed to the importance of establishing "effective bonds" with those in the new community, and Greil focused most of his attention on the role "significant others" play in shaping one's frame of reference and in causing one to change communities. Segal draws an analogy between the "socialization of children" and the "way in which conversion works in developing commitment." He argues that "conversion resembles a new and conscious choice to socialize to a particular group—resocialization."[76] McKnight argues that one aspect of conversion is the socialization into the new group.[77] He also describes conversion as resocialization or nationalization.[78] He writes, "to convert was essentially (for most converts) to switch nations and sociological groups."[79] Nock claimed that converts became "naturalized members" of the Jewish people,[80] and, as we saw above, Schiffman argues that the convert becomes identified with "the destiny" of the Jewish people. Collins writes that "quite apart from the legal ramifications . . . conversion to Judaism involved a major social transition."[81] Gaventa points to the importance of the converts' establishing "a relationship of interdependence with other believers"[82] and of their moving into "a community of mutual responsibility and commitment."[83]

While contemporary scholars stress the new bonds the converts form, the rabbis stressed the breaking of the converts' previous relationships, focusing on familial ties.[84] Beginning in Mishnah, the abrogation of existing familial ties is expressed throughout our texts in terms of the converts' dying without heirs. Unlike native-born Israelites, converts who had not produced children with an Israelite spouse could conceivably die without leaving heirs. Parents, nephews, or uncles could inherit a dead Israelite's estate or take on the estate's obligations;[85] however, in the case of converts who had severed ties with their gentile relatives upon entrance into the Israelite community, this was not the case. We have seen that the image of the converts' dying without heirs became so much a part of the rabbinic picture of the convert that it produced a specific category of "ownerless property." The convert who died without heirs also became a paradigm for dealing with cases of damages, inheritance, debt, and the like. In the minds of the rabbis, the breaking of previous familial ties was an essential feature of the converts' nature. It almost became a caricature of the convert in the rabbinic texts.

There are two obvious reasons for the rabbis' emphasizing the converts' breaking from their gentile families. First, if an essential part of the conversion process was the total acceptance of YHWH and his revelation, breaking relationships with "significant others" who were idolaters and not worshipers of YHWH was important for ensuring that the converts would develop the needed commitment to YHWH and to their new community. This method of isolating the converts from their families is a familiar technique of the "New Religions." What is interesting, however, is that the rabbis do not detail the relationships the converts are to form in the Israelite community, which would aid them in developing their commitment to the new group. Scholars claim that the formation of these new relationships and the process of encapsulation of the new convert are important features of conversion in the contemporary world.[86] We saw above that the rabbis pictured themselves as the "guides" for the new converts, so that the only new relationships they considered to be valid were those established between the rabbis and the converts. We also saw that they discouraged conversion for marriage or "out of love," so that they could have been suspicious of converts' developing close ties with members of the Israelite community before the former had demonstrated their commitment to the People Israel. Also, given McKnight's arguments that Judaism was not a missionary religion,[87] the various modern techniques of encapsulation—that is, enclosing the prospective converts within a tightly controlled environment designed to make them members of the new group,[88] which are detailed in Richardson's collection[89]—would not have been used by the rabbis, who were not actively seeking to bring outsiders into their group.

The second reason for stressing that the converts had to sever ties with their gentile relatives probably relates to the rabbis' concern with the transferring of property upon the death of the converts. Acceptance of the legitimacy of the converts' familial ties with their gentile relatives would lead to the movement of the converts' property out of the Israelite community. The rabbinic ideal was that the Land of Israel belonged only to the Israelites, as expressed in Sifré Number's contention that converts did not receive a portion of the Land of Israel at the time of the Conquest,[90] and this could well have served as a paradigm for all Israelite possessions. In order to ensure that Israelite belongings remained within the People Israel, the rabbis had to prevent the converts from bequeathing their property to gentiles. One concern is that property that converts purchased from Israelites had to remain within the Israelite community. Recall that converts could inherit from their gentile parents anything that did not violate Israelite law. The issue thus was clearly the movement of property out of, but not into, the community.[91]

Although the severing of familial ties with gentile relatives is an essential feature of conversion and it marked the converts' sociological transformation, there were other ways in which the rabbis indicated that converts were new persons who experienced an altered sociological status. Mishnah compares the converts' radical transformation to that of minors who reach maturity, deaf-mutes who gain the ability to speak and to hear, imbeciles who become sane, and blind persons who regain their sight.[92] The two Talmuds add that the conversion of gentiles is similar to the emancipation of slaves.[93]

These comparisons point in at least two directions. First, mature adults, normal sighted people, sane individuals, and freed slaves have a different relationship to the Israelite community from minors, physically or mentally impaired people, or slaves. The former enjoy unrestricted social and religious interaction with the other members of the community. The minor, the slave, or the physically and mentally impaired individual, in contrast, is not held responsible for a myriad of social and religious obligations. Mishnah's analogy points to the fact that while the gentile could not freely participate in a wide range of Israelite activities, the convert could be, in fact was obligated to be, involved in these events. The converts, like the mature Israelites, took upon themselves the obligation of actualizing YHWH's demands in their daily lives in the social context of the People Israel. Although some limits were placed on the converts' activities within the Israelite community, these were few in number. For the most part, the convert, like the free, unimpaired adult Israelite, was obligated to participate fully in the life of the Israelite community. Mishnah specifically states that the converts are required to separate the agricultural gifts for the poor, the dough offering, and the priestly gifts only if the time of their separation occurred *after* the gentiles had joined the Israelite community.[94] Thus, from the earliest rabbinic collection onward, the converts were clearly distinguished from gentiles, because the former were responsible for the full range of social obligations incumbent upon Israelites, while the latter were not.[95]

Second, these analogies indicate that, from the rabbinic point of view, conversion improved the person. Just as it is better to be sighted than to be blind, sane rather than mentally disturbed, an adult instead of a minor, free and not enslaved, it is better to be a convert than a gentile. This idea finds clear expression in the talmudic discussions of whether or not conversion can take place on the Sabbath, for conversion improves the person.[96]

Another set of sayings points to this change of status. While the phrase "newborn child" occurs first in the Babylonian Talmud, other texts seem to reflect this idea. For example, some passages claim that a convert is not responsible for misdeeds performed as a gentile. Haninah stated that if gentiles cursed YHWH and then converted, they were not punished, because they were not the same person.[97] It was even maintained that if a gentile killed another gentile or had intercourse with another man's wife, he was not to be punished after his conversion.[98] Similarly, Zeria knew a teaching which suggested that upon their conversion, converts were forgiven for all their previous sins.[99] Yosi maintained that converts could not be held accountable for their previous deeds because they were "newborn children."[100]

Thus, the rabbis were fully cognizant of the sociological implications of conversion. However, while modern scholars point to the breaking of familial bonds and the establishing of new sociological networks, the rabbis focused only on the former. For the sages, the paradigmatic relationships the converts experienced were those between themselves and the rabbis. The rabbis seem not to have favored the creation of effective relationships between converts and lay Israelites until after the former had evidenced their commitment to YHWH and to the People Israel. This was one means of ensuring that conversion was "for the sake of Heaven" and not the result of a personal relationship between two human beings. This commitment to YHWH and this conversion "for the sake of Heaven" were evidenced by the converts' severing ties with their gentile relatives and by their fulfilling the many obligations which were incumbent upon native-born Israelites.

To this point we have been able to deal with the rabbinic views on conversion in terms of modern scholarly discussions of this topic. We have also seen, however, that the correspondence is not exact. While many of the rabbinic statements about converts and conversion are comprehensible in terms of current scholarly thought on these topics, the rabbis stress certain aspects and deemphasize or ignore others. We now turn to the one facet of the rabbinic discussions that is not paralleled in contemporary discussions of the converts, the rabbinic descriptions of the differences between converts and native-born Israelites. This is unique because virtually no previous research has attempted to delineate the host community's opinions about the converts.

One can imagine the reluctance of investigators to probe into the community's views on its new members or the reticence of the group's members to express their opinions of the recent converts freely. This may partially explain why little has been written on this topic. However, the fundamental difference between the rabbinic view of the Israelite community and the believers' conception of the religions that have been studied recently may also explain why this topic has not been covered more thoroughly in the current literature on conversion.

The rabbinic conception of the Israelite community has both a religious and an ethnic element.[101] While one statement in a late collection claims that Abraham was the first convert, ultimately one is a member of the People Israel by virtue of being born into the community. An Israelite mother produces a native-born Israelite, and these native-born Israelites cannot engage in sexual relationships with different ethnic groups. Israelites cannot legally marry non-Israelites. The contradiction between the ethnicity of the People Israel and the nonethnicity of YHWH's universal plan for humankind, as indicated by the inclusion of the first eleven chapters of Genesis before YHWH's call to Abraham, runs throughout the rabbinic discussions of the convert. On the one hand, converts are like new-born children who are expected to cut their ties with their gentile past and to take upon themselves the obligations incumbent upon the People Israel. On the other hand, because they are not native-born Israelites, converts remain under some limitations with regard to their position within the People Israel. Simply stated, converts were once gentiles by birth, and they cannot change that fact.

While we can never distinguish between the "practical" and "theoretical" nature of the rabbinic discussions, we can agree that rabbinic discourses about the Temple and its rituals are most likely theoretical in nature. Because the Temple was destroyed in 70 C.E. and our earliest rabbinic document was edited in the first part of the third century of the common era, the Temple was not a viable institution during the rabbinic period. Furthermore, there is no evidence that even the earliest rabbinic discussions about the Temple are based on what really happened while the Temple and its cult functioned. Most likely, the rabbis present us with their idealized view of what should have happened within the Temple's precincts, or they offer us their opinion of what will occur when the Temple is rebuilt in the distant future. For this reason, it is important to note that various distinctions are drawn between the converts and the Israelites with regard to the Temple. At best this means that in the ideal situation, when the Temple and its cult are viable institutions within the Israelite community, there will be a clear differentiation between the converts and the native-born Israelites. Whether or not the differences between the converts and the native-born Israelites were manifest during the rabbinic period in any meaningful way, it is significant that *ideally and theoretically* converts were different from native-born Israelites.

In Mishnah, Aqabyya b. Mahaleel argued that converts were not included in the phrase *children of Israel* in Num. 5:21ff, so that converted women did not undergo the rite of the bitter waters. Even though Aqiba and the sages reject Aqabyya's claim, his view points to his belief that converts were different from native-born Israelites.[102] Also, as early as Mishnah we are told that converts who bring their first fruits to the Temple cannot recite the Avowal which describes the Land of Israel as that *which YHWH swore to our ancestors to assign to us*.[103] According to some views, only if the converts had an Israelite mother could they claim the right to recite the Avowal.[104] The opinion that converts cannot recite the Avowal with regard to first fruits appears throughout our texts, and some add the prohibition against the recitation of a similar Avowal with regard to the second tithe.[105] The Palestinian *gemara* alone rejects the earlier position and claims that converts do recite the Avowal.[106]

In Sifra, Yosi b. Judah disagrees with those who believed that the skins of the converts' sacrifices were given to the priests and holds that in fact the priests do not receive these gifts,[107] a view which is also recorded in the Babylonian Talmud.[108] Sifra also equates converts with women and slaves, thus separating them from the adult Israelite males. Although the priests consume the residue of the male Israelites' meal offerings, they may not eat the residue of the converts' meal offerings, nor those brought by women and slaves.[109] Also, converts, women, and slaves may sprinkle blood on the high places, a view which first appeared in Tosefta.[110] Sifré Numbers makes the point that although converts perform the same sacrificial rituals as Israelites, we would not have known that fact if the Torah had not specifically referred to the converts' obligations. The implication of this passage is that one would not naturally conclude that converts and native-born Israelites have the same responsibilities with regard to the Temple cult.[111] Both Talmuds also claim that converts cannot form a separate association for procuring the Passover sacrifice. While this may relate to the fact that it takes a good deal of time to learn the complex laws related to this offering, it may also imply that converts are not on an equal footing with native-born Israelites.[112]

It seems clear that a few sages believed that with regard to the Temple, converts were not equal to native-born Israelites. The Temple was not a viable institution during the rabbinic period, so that this way of distinguishing between the native-born Israelites and the converts did not affect actual converts at the time that the comments were collected or even created. However, this theoretical distinction between converts and Israelites should not be ignored. The Temple was a central mythic institution during the rabbinic period, and differentiating between native-born Israelites and converts in the context of Temple worship points to a fundamental difference between these two groups within the People Israel.

We saw above that at least Sifré Numbers differentiated between converts and native-born Israelites with regard to the original distribution of the Land of Israel at the time of the conquest.[113] Also, Sifré Numbers records that some held that native-born Israelites were banished to the cities of refuge if they inadvertently killed a native-born Israelite, but not if they killed a convert.[114] Furthermore, although the Palestinian *gemara* does not resolve the matter, it raises the issue of whether or not the converts are included along with the native-born Israelites in the population which makes up those who live in an apostate town.[115] While the "practical" implications of these discussions are unclear, these pericopae do underscore at least the "theoretical" distinction between the native-born Israelites and the converts.

There are many other *sugyot* in our sources which point to the difference between native-born Israelites and converts. It is important that converts are designated as *grym* throughout our texts and that they are a specific subclass of the People Israel. For some, converts were inherently different from native-born Israelites. Mishnah claims that among those who returned from Babylonia with Ezra converts constituted a distinct group,[116] and this concept or its implications are stated in several of our documents.[117] In Tosefta,[118] Judah holds that there are four classes of Israelites: Priests, Levites, Israelites, and converts, and Meir holds that converts, gentiles, slaves, and *mamzerim* are distinct segments of society.[119]

Without making any assumptions about the practical implications of the rabbis' statements, we have seen above that there was a good deal of discussion concerning whom converts could marry.[120] Unlike native-born Israelites, converts could marry impaired Israelites, while many held that they could not marry priests. At least this places converts among the impaired Israelites and distinguishes them from the unimpaired native-born Israelites. We saw that in the minds of many sages the converts were excluded from marrying the priests because of the former's genealogy, while the Torah excluded the priests from marrying women only for the reason of the latter's presumed or known sexual activity. Furthermore, because converts were not native-born members of the Israelite community, there was a good deal of discussion concerning the applicability of the laws of levirate marriage and the *haliṣah* ceremony to them.[121]

It is unclear which courts functioned during the rabbinic period. But whatever they may have been, the converts are described as somewhat restricted concerning their participation in the judicial institutions of the Israelite community. The Palestinian *gemara* maintains that converts could not serve in the Sanhedrin,[122] although against this view Joshua had maintained in Sifré Numbers that Jonadab's descendants would become members of the Sanhedrin.[123] Joshua alone seems to imply that at least with regard to the Sanhedrin there should be no distinctions between native-born Israelites and the descendants of converts. Mishnah holds that converts cannot be judges[124] because they, along with *mamzerim*, *netinim*, the aged, and those who did not have children, are not included in the term *congregation*, Lev. 4:13 and Num. 35:24. And this position is repeated in Sifra[125] and the Palestinian Talmud.[126] The Babylonian *gemara* states that converts can serve as judges only in civil, not capital, cases.[127] Thus, at least in theory and perhaps in practice, converts were distinguished from native-born Israelites with respect to the Israelites' court system. Finally, a late text maintains that converts could not own Israelite slaves. This theoretically could have important economic consequences.[128]

There is a consistent stream of thought in our texts that distinguishes between native-born Israelites and converts. While these differences are most often stated in the context of the Temple, others are related to marriage or to the judicial institutions. At the least the converts were considered to be a subclass of the People Israel, a subclass that maintained its distinctive nature throughout time. At the most, the converts represented a different ethnic group that could never be assimilated *fully* into the People Israel. We have seen over and over again that while in most cases converts are equated with Israelites, there are important instances in which the two populations are clearly distinguished from each other. Even at the time of their circumcision, the prayers differentiated between native-born Israelite males and converts, for the former were led into "the covenant of Abraham" while the latter were attached to "the covenant of circumcision."[129]

The rabbinic texts present the converts as marginal beings,[130] occupying the liminal space between the Israelite and the gentile communities. From the point of view of the totality of the rabbinic tradition, converts were marginal, "quite literally on the margins of society, indeed of all societies. . . ."[131] They had severed their ties with their gentile community, but in some sense they remained on the outer edges of their new community. They were not gentiles, although their gentile past seems to have been important in certain contexts. And they were not fully equated with native-born Israelites, although they had many traits in common. They were alien and familiar at the same time. The converts never totally lost their "otherness." They never seem to have discarded their strangeness completely.

All social groups distinguish themselves from other social entities, and often the ethnocentrism of one group is phrased in terms of the deprecation of other units.[132] As Rodney Needham states:

It is a frequent report from different parts of the world that tribes call themselves alone by the arrogant title "man," and that they refer to neighboring peoples as monkeys or crocodiles or malign spirits. When European voyagers explored the world, they often enough had a clear eye for physique, dress, and habitations, but they more often had a distorted or derogatory view of the moral aspects of exotic peoples. Typically, these strange societies had

no religion, or no law, or no idea of the family or not even a true
form of languages to qualify them as truly human.[133]

Similarly, Barbara Babcock has collected a number of essays which demonstrate the different ways in which a particular community applies "nor-
malcy" to itself while classifying other human groupings as "abnormal."[134]
Finally, Simmel writes that "stranger . . . has no positive meaning; the relation to him is a nonrelation."[135] Elsewhere, I have demonstrated that in
Mishnah and Tosefta the Israelites classified gentiles as entirely "other":

> In Mishnah-Tosefta, the gentile is primarily the "other." At times
> the term *goy* symbolizes that part of humanity not represented by
> the term *benai yisrael*. In other places, the gentile is merely one of
> the several groups who occupies the Land of Israel, but who does
> not adhere to the rabbinic practices, such as tithing. As the
> "other," the gentiles may be characterized as dangerous and sex-
> ually deviant. In a word, they are "uncivilized."[136]

This essential difference between gentiles and Israelites meant that converts had to leave their original group before they could join the Israelites.
This is symbolized in the Babylonian Talmud by the expression that converts are like a "newborn child." This concept is expressed in the rabbinic
view that although converts may inherit from their gentile parents, they
have no intrinsic right to this inheritance because they have no legal connections to their former relatives. This does not mean, however, that the
converts necessarily create ties with native-born Israelites, for, as we have
seen, an *essential* feature of the converts in many rabbinic *sugyot* is that they
do not have any legally recognized Israelite heirs. In brief, unlike normal
Israelites, the converts *do not necessarily have* any family ties, and this makes
them marginal to the Israelite society.

An important element of the Israelite mythology is the relationship
between the People Israel and the Land of Israel. As early as the Patriar-
chal narratives of Genesis, the Land is promised to Abraham's descendants,[137] and this promise revolves around the tribal portions of the Land
as well. Each tribe was to apportion its segment of the Land of Israel only
among its members.[138] Additionally, a major line of thought within the
rabbinic system prohibits the sale of portions of the Land of Israel to gentiles. Although the rabbis could not prevent such sales, they consistently
disapproved of them.[139] There is a clear tendency in the rabbinic texts to
argue that gentiles should not, and perhaps could not, own a parcel of the
Land of Israel. Therefore, it is significant that passages in Sifré Numbers
prohibit the converts from owning a parcel of real estate within the Land

of Israel. While this is the only text which contains such statements, it is made clear throughout the rabbinic corpus that unless converts have legally recognized *Israelite* heirs, they cannot bequeath their property to their children. Thus, while it is assumed that Israelites may own and bequeath portions of the Land of Israel and that gentiles may not do either, converts are placed in an intermediate position.

The debate concerning whether or not converts bring their first fruits and recite the Avowal referring to the land *which YHWH swore unto our ancestors to assign us*, Mishnah's rule that when converts pray in public they should refer to YHWH as the God of *your* ancestors, Aqabyya's view that the ritual of the bitter waters did not apply to converts, and the complex discussions over the permissibility of converts or their children marrying into the priestly caste also point to the converts' marginality. At best, some believed that this marginality could be ignored if the converts had *Israelite* mothers. However, note that even if they have Israelite mothers, they are stilled referred to as *converts*.

The rabbinic texts fully accept the principle that gentiles will seek to convert and to join the People Israel, and many statements seek to negate the converts' marginality by making them an integral part of the People Israel from its inception. The claims that Abraham was the first convert, that David and Abraham called themselves converts, and that the souls of the converts or their "guiding star" was present at the revelation on Mount Sinai suggest that some rabbis believed that converts had always been and would always be a legitimate element within the Israelite community. This is underscored by Mishnah's claim that the converts were a recognized segment of the Israelite community that accompanied Ezra from Babylonia to the Land of Israel. In fact, a *sugya* in the Palestinian Talmud claims that YHWH "traverses the earth, and whenever he finds a righteous person he attaches him to Israel."[140] Similarly, in Mekhilta Ishmael, Simeon b. Yohai claims that the converts are more precious to YHWH than the native-born Israelites, "for those whom the king loves are greater than those who love the king."[141] Furthermore, Mekhilta Ishmael asserts that YHWH revealed himself in the desert and not within a specific country, so that any who wished to convert could do so.[142] And the same text tells us that Abraham was not circumcised until the age of ninety-nine, so that gentiles would realize that they could convert at any time during their life.[143] In the Babylonian Talmud, Eleazar claimed that YHWH had exiled Israel throughout the world so that they might make converts,[144] and another passage implies that in the future all people will convert.[145]

Along these same lines, the Babylonian Talmud maintains that noted rabbis were the descendants of converts: Meir was related to Nero,[146] and

Shemaia and Abtalion were descended from Sennacherib. Haman's descendants learned Torah in Benai Berak, and Sisera's descendants taught children in Jerusalem.[147] These imagined genealogies negate the hostility of many of Israel's foes, but they also serve to blur any lines between converts and rabbis. We must also remember that Ruth was David's ancestor and that the rabbinic texts claim that Rahab married Joshua and that her descendants included priests and prophets. In these instances, the marginality of converts as a segment of Israelite society is vitiated by the fact that some produced descendants who were among the cultural heroes of the People Israel. But the rabbis' need to create these imagined relationships reflects the concerted effort of some to bring the converts in from the edges of Israelite society. These fanciful stories about the conversion of Israel's archenemies and the prominence of those who had converts as ancestors testify to the reality of the converts' marginality.

This marginality shows through other passages as well. The earliest sages distinguished between Israelites and gentiles, for they each represented different ethnic groups. The former were Jacob's/Israel's descendants, while the latter had any number of progenitors. This genealogical distinction between Israelites and gentiles was not totally negated when the latter converted and joined the People Israel. A passage in the Palestinian Talmud states that the distinction between Israelites and converts is even maintained in Heaven.[148] Furthermore, Hama b. Hanina argues that the *Shekhinah* rests only upon the native-born Israelites, and Rabbah argues that God's special relationship to Israel is different from the relationship he has with converts.[149] While we cannot ascertain the "practical" consequences of this distinction, we can see that it was expressed in virtually every document we have analyzed and that it served to maintain, at least mythologically, the converts' marginality.

The smattering of negative comments about converts also speaks to their marginality. Eliezer referred to the converts' inherent "bad streak,"[150] and he claimed that the "enemy" in Ex. 23:4 is a convert.[151] Sifré Numbers tells us that the converts occupied the actual fringes of the Israelite camp during their travels through the desert,[152] clearly a spacial indication of their communal marginality. Identifying as converts the rabble who accompanied the Israelites out of Egypt and who caused them to sin also points to their marginality within the context of Israelite society.[153] Yohanan's advice that one should bring converts near with the right hand while repelling them with the left[154] is also a metaphor for the converts' marginality.

Helbo's famous statement that converts are like sores on Israel,[155] Isaac's comment that "evil upon evil comes to those who receive converts,"[156] and the anonymous observation that converts are among those "who delay the coming of the Messiah"[157] all point to the abnormal qualities of the converts within the context of the Israelite community. But these traits are balanced by the frequent admonition that Israelites are not to insult converts but are to love them as they love one another.[158] While these *sugyot* envision the possibility, if not the reality, that Israelites would look down their noses at converts, they also point to the ambiguous way in which the Israelites viewed the converts. Although some held that they might be the reason that the Messiah has not yet come, others reproached those Israelites who insulted the converts. Again we see the liminal position the converts occupied within the context of rabbinic thought. While an Israelite might insult someone by calling him "a convert, the son of a convert,"[159] this was clearly unacceptable to at least some sages.

The converts posed a problem for the rabbis. On the one hand, because they had once been gentiles, they were essentially different from Israelites. On the other hand, because they had left their native society and entered the People Israel by accepting its religious/cultural system, they were essentially different from gentiles. The rabbis thus had to include the converts without at the same time negating the uniqueness of the People Israel. All of the material we have reviewed in this study is a result of their efforts. We have seen that the rabbis' major task was to integrate the converts into Israelite culture and society. For the most part, converts acted like Israelites in virtually every aspect of life. In fact, it is striking that many of the differences between the two groups were phrased in terms of symbols and institutions which did not function during the rabbinic period: the Temple and the sacrificial cult, the Land of Israel fully controlled by Israelites, the legal institutions which decided capital cases, the *sotah* ritual. The rabbis seemed to have solved their problem by integrating the converts into the realities of daily life, while at the same time excluding them symbolically from some important institutions of the past. On the level of cultural symbols, the converts could not be assimilated fully; they had to live on the margins of the society.

Kopytoff and Miers argue that there are three dimensions to the reduction of the strangers' marginality: formal status, informal affect, worldly achievement and success.[160] With regard to the first and the last dimensions, the converts achieved mobility. They were formally accepted into Israelite society, and they functioned within it with few restrictions. One suspects that this was slow to develop, and that is why the elaborate conversion ritual does not appear until the Babylonian *gemara*. Furthermore, nothing we have discovered indicates that the converts could not enjoy the same "worldly achievement and success" as native-born Israelites.

Only a limited number of cultural institutions and positions were closed to them, such as the priesthood and service within some courts, but these were not important in the daily lives of the Israelites in late antiquity. However, within the dimension of "informal affect," in the area of "the esteem and affection in which [they are] held"[161] the converts achieved less mobility, at least in the minds of some sages.

The rabbinic views on converts and conversion illustrate the dual focus of rabbinic Judaism. On the one hand, it was an ethnic system designed for native-born Israelites. On the other hand, it was a religious system open to all who accepted its beliefs and practices. Israelites were included in both; gentiles were excluded from either. Converts occupied a middle ground. While they could never fully become part of the ethnic People Israel, they could almost fully participate in the religious Congregation of Israel, as a distinct segment of that Congregation.

▥ NOTES ▥

Chapter 1

1. Shaye Cohen has stated that "a convert is not an Israelite, but he is a Jew"; Shaye J. D. Cohen, "Conversion to Judaism in Historical Perspective: From Biblical Israel to Postbiblical Judaism," *Conservative Judaism* 36, no. 4 (Summer 1983): 33.

2. The bibliography on conversion grows daily. The most recent bibliography, which is now woefully out of date, is Lewis R. Rambo, "Current Research on Religious Conversion," *Religious Study Review* 8 (April 1982): 146–59.

3. Gary G. Porton, *Goyim: Gentiles and Israelites in Mishnah-Tosefta* (Atlanta, 1988).

4. Ibid., 288–93.

5. Fredrik Barth, *Ethnic Groups and Boundaries: The Social Organization of Cultural Difference* (Bergen-Oslo, 1969), 11.

6. Frank D. Bessac, "Comments," *Current Anthropology* 5, no. 4 (October 1964): 293.

7. Cynthia H. Enloe, *Ethnic Conflict and Political Development* (Boston, 1973), 15.

8. While scholars easily may agree that an ethnic group perceives itself and is perceived by others as an identifiable aggregate of individuals, there is a lack of consensus concerning exactly what unites these individuals into a recognizable assemblage. Several writers have suggested that the members of an ethnic group form a unity because of the culture they share, but others have offered cogent arguments against this position; see those cited in Porton, *Goyim*, 292–93. Barth seems correct when he writes that a shared culture is a *result*, rather than a "definitional characteristic" of an ethnic group's organization; Barth, *Ethnic Groups*, 1.

9. Chester L. Hunt and Lewis Walker, *Ethnic Dynamics: Patterns of Intergroup Relations in Various Societies* (Homewood, 1974), 3.

10. Gerald D. Berreman, "Race, Caste, and Other Invidious Distinctions in Social Stratification," in Norman R. Yetman, *Majority and Minority: The Dynamics of Race and Ethnicity in American Life*, 4th ed. (Boston, 1985), 23.

11. Charles F. Keyes, *Ethnic Change* (Seattle and London, 1981), 5.

12. Pierre L. van den Berghe, "Race and Ethnicity: A Sociological Perspective," in Yetman, 56.

13. This concern with ancestry begins in the biblical period. Meyers writes: "It should be noted that . . . 'Israelites' is literally 'sons/children of Israel' in Hebrew. As such it is an expression of a family term. Its usage as a term for all Israel

indicates the conceptual importance of biological relationship as a meaningful indicator of common destiny" (125). She also writes that "Israel conceived of itself genealogically, via a family tree" (127); Carol Meyers, *Discovering Eve: Ancient Israelite Women in Context* (New York and Oxford, 1988).

14. It is significant, that of the three "Patriarchs," Jacob is the only one who produces only followers of YHWH. Abraham sired Ishmael, as well as Isaac, and Isaac fathered Esau along with Jacob.

15. This point has been fully developed in Porton, *Goyim,* esp. 221–29, 285–307.

16. On the problem of defining religion, see Jonathan Z. Smith, *Imagining Religion* (Chicago and London, 1982); Jonathan Z. Smith, *Map Is Not Territory* (Leiden, 1978); John H. Morgan, *Understanding Religion and Culture: Anthropological and Theological Perspectives* (Washington, 1979); Porton, *Goyim,* 295.

17. Melford E. Spiro, "Religion: Problems of Definition and Explanation," in Benjamin Kilborne and L. L. Langness, eds., *Cultural and Human Nature: Theoretical Papers of Melford E. Spiro* (Chicago, 1987), 197.

18. Arthur L. Greil, "Previous Dispositions and Conversion to Perspectives of Social and Religious Movements," *Sociological Analysis* 38, no. 2 (1977): 115–25.

19. Cohen, "Conversion to Judaism," 31.

20. BMeg. 13a. It is interesting that Yohanan does not call this person one of Jacob's children.

21. For the rabbinic views on gentiles, see Porton, *Goyim.* See also Martin Goodman, "Proselytising in Rabbinic Judaism," *Journal of Jewish Studies* 40, no. 3 (Autumn 1989): 175–85. Although it deals with much more than Judaism in late antiquity, see also David Novak, *The Image of the Non-Jew in Judaism: An Historical and Constructive Study of the Noachide Laws* (New York, 1983).

22. This is fully delineated in Porton, *Goyim,* 171–283.

23. Ibid., 113–44.

24. It is important to note that while the rabbis distinguished among several different categories of Israelites, all non-Israelites were called *goyim,* no matter what their ethnic origins, their religious preferences, or their cultural background. On the rabbinic differentiation of Israelites, see William S. Green, "Otherness Within: Toward a Theory of Difference in Rabbinic Judaism," in Jacob Neusner and Ernest S. Frerichs, eds., *"To See Ourselves as Others See Us": Christians, Jews, "Others" in Late Antiquity* (Chico, 1985), 57–59.

25. This is most clearly seen in the extended essay on leaven in tPis. 2:5–10; Porton, *Goyim,* 205–20, esp., 219–20.

26. See the authors cited in Porton, *Goyim,* 288–90.

27. For those like Schürer who concentrate only on selected comments from the Israelite documents or related texts and who wish to draw sharp distinctions between Israelites and non-Israelites, these porous boundaries and conflicting views about the righteousness of gentiles are disconcerting. See Emil Schürer, *A History of the Jewish People in the Time of Jesus Christ,* trans. Sophia Taylor and Peter Christie (New York, 1891), 2.i, 51–56. Cf. Emil Schürer, *The History of the Jewish People in the Age of Jesus Christ (175 B.C.–A.D. 135),* rev. and ed. Geza Vermes, Fergus

Millar, and Matthew Black (Edinburgh, 1979), 2:81–84; see also 3.i (Edinburgh, 1986), 150–86. And see Joachim Jeremias, *Jerusalem in the Time of Jesus: An Investigation into Economic and Social Conditions during the New Testament Period*, trans. F. H. and C. H. Cave (Philadelphia, 1977), 271–344. However, as we know from studies of the formation of ethnic groups, the broken borderlines are expected. Ethnic groups more often than not find ways to interact, and the evidence adduced from Mishnah and Tosefta merely confirms that point.

28. Porton, *Goyim*, 173–203.

29. Ibid., 206–12.

30. MShab. 16:6. For a fuller discussion of the interactions of the gentiles and Israelites on the Sabbath, see Porton, *Goyim*, 206–11, 216–18.

31. Porton, *Goyim*, 221–39.

32. Ibid., 241–58, esp. 251–53.

33. Ibid., 259–68.

34. Technically, the purity rules concerning mildew, skin disease, genital emissions, and the like do not apply to non-Israelites.

35. Porton, *Goyim*, 269–83.

36. Goodman, "Proselytising in Rabbinic Judaism," 175.

37. Ibid., 176–77.

38. Ibid., 176.

39. Ibid., 177.

40. Cohen writes: "One of the central characteristics of post-biblical Judaism is its prohibition of intermarriage. A Jew may not marry a non-Jew. . . . The prohibition of intermarriage with all gentiles is not biblical. . . . Of the numerous differences between Judaism and Israelite religion, two are important here: (1) Judaism prohibited intermarriage with all outsiders but (2) permitted gentiles to convert and become (almost) equal to the native-born. The process which yielded these innovations had already begun by the time of Ezra and Nehemiah, was well under way by the time of the Maccabees, and was substantially completed by the time of the Talmud"; Shaye J. D. Cohen, "From the Bible to the Talmud: The Prohibition of Intermarriage," in Reuben Ahroni, ed., *Hebrew Annual Review Biblical and Other Studies in Honor of Robert Gordis* 7 (1983): 23–39. Quotations are found on p. 23.

41. On the *mamzer*, see Lawrence H. Schiffman, *Who Was a Jew? Rabbinic and Halakhic Perspectives on the Jewish-Christian Schism* (Hoboken, 1985), 10–11.

42. It is interesting that non-Israelites may be called the Children of Noah, while Israelites are designated the Children of Israel/Jacob. Clearly, the relationship to Noah was common to all human beings, but it was not significant in differentiating among peoples after the Flood. It is also significant that Rome/Christians are designated in later texts as Esau or Edom, again pointing to a common ancestry in Abraham, but noting that the split occurred in later generations. Thus, while all peoples are somehow related, the important genealogical distinctions came about with Jacob's progeny. On Esau/Edom as a designation for Christians, see Jacob Neusner, *Judaism and Its Social Metaphors: Israel in the History of Jewish Thought* (Cambridge, 1989), esp. 112–44.

43. See the works cited in Porton, *Goyim*, 291–92.

44. Keyes writes: "While . . . ethnicity is a form of kinship reckoning, it is one in which the connections with forebearers or with those with whom one believes one shares descent are not traced along precisely genealogical lines. Americans, for example, predicate their national identity upon connections with the 'Pilgrim Fathers' and with the forefathers 'who brought forth upon this continent a new nation' even though few Americans could actually trace genealogical connections with members of the Plymouth community or with those who wrote the Constitution or fought in the Revolutionary War." In his note to this passage Keyes states: "In fact, those who have been able to trace actual genealogical connections to ancestors who fought (on the American side) in the Revolutionary War have sometimes attempted to set themselves apart from other Americans, as in organizations like the Daughters of the American Revolution"; Keyes, *Ethnic Change*, 6.

45. Hayim H. Donin, *To Be a Jew: A Guide to Jewish Observance in Contemporary Life* (New York, 1972), 284. Klein writes that "Since Abraham is considered to be the father of all proselytes . . . , it is customary for proselytes to be called son, or daughter, of our father Abraham. In most cases, a male convert is given the Hebrew name Avraham ben Avraham Avinu, and a female convert, the name Sarah bat Avraham Avinu. A convert need not necessarily be given the Hebrew first name Avraham or Sarah . . . , but the patronymic 'ben' or 'bat Avraham Avinu' is insisted upon for purposes of identification"; Isaac Klein, *A Guide to Jewish Religious Practice* (New York, 1979), 445. It is interesting that while Israelites are called "the Children of Israel/Jacob," converts are called "the Children of Abraham." This corresponds to the fact that Christians were often connected to Esau. Those related to Israelites, Christians and converts, might trace their descent back to Abraham, but only native-born Israelites could claim Jacob as their ancestor. On the creation of different subgenealogies of the Israelites in the Bible, see Howard Eilberg-Schwartz, *The Savage in Judaism: An Anthropology of Israelite Religion and Ancient Judaism* (Bloomington and Indianapolis, 1990), 167–68.

46. YBik. 1:4, Venice 64a does contain a *beraita* in the name of Judah which states that converts could claim Abraham as their father because Gen. 17:5 states that he was the father "of a multitude of nations"; however, Judah does not rename the converts as Abraham's children.

47. See mBik. 1:4; tBik. 1:2; Mekhilta Ishmael Mishpatim 20, Horovitz and Rabin 335; Sifré Deuteronomy Ki Tabo 299, Horovitz 299; yBik. 1:4, Venice 64a; bMak. 19a.

48. BShab. 137b.

49. MQid. 4:1, mHor. 3:8, bYeb. 85a, bYeb. 37a, bQid. 75a.

50. See note 40 above.

51. For example, Cohen states: Judaism "permitted gentiles to convert and become (*almost*) equal to the native-born"; Cohen, "From the Bible," 23, italics mine. Elsewhere, Cohen writes, "The ambiguity of the convert's status is clear in rabbinic legislation. The rabbis declare that a proselyte is a Jew (*yisrael*) in all respects, but this ideology cannot mask the fact that the proselyte remains, in some matters at least, a non-Israelite"; Cohen "Conversion," 33. Moore wrote: "Equality

in law and religion does not necessarily carry with it complete social equality, and the Jews would have been singularly unlike the rest of mankind if they had felt no superiority to their heathen converts"; George F. Moore, *Judaism in the First Centuries of the Christian Era: The Age of the Tannaim* (Cambridge, reprint 1966), 1:335.

52. Isaac Weil, *Le Prosélytisme chez les juifs selon la bible et le talmud* (Strasbourg, 1880); William G. Braude, *Jewish Proselyting in the First Five Centuries of the Common Era: The Age of the Tannaim and Amoraim* (Providence, 1940). For a brief review of the literature on conversion until his time from this perspective, see Bernard J. Bamberger, *Proselytism in the Talmudic Period* (New York, 1968), 5–9.

53. Bamberger writes: "Our subject has engaged the attention of many previous writers. . . . Many of them have misrepresented it. This is especially, though not exclusively, true of Christian writers. Starting with a false picture of the Pharisees as narrow, exclusive and misanthropic and of Rabbinic Judaism as antithetical to Christianity in every way, they have concluded that the Rabbis must have been hostile to proselytes and proselytizing, and have adjusted the facts to fit their theories"; Bamberger, 5. On the view of Christian scholarship toward rabbinic Judaism, see E. P. Sanders, *Paul and Palestinian Judaism: A Comparison of Patterns of Religion* (Philadelphia, 1977), 1–12, 33–59.

54. Alfred Bertholet, *Die Stellung der Israeliten und der Juden zu dem Fremden* (Freiburg i. B./Leipzig, 1896); Scot McKnight, *A Light among the Gentiles: Jewish Missionary Activity in the Second Temple Period* (Minneapolis, 1991). See now Louis Feldman, *Jew and Gentile in the Ancient World* (Princeton, 1993), 290–304.

55. Schiffman's chapter on conversion is the latest attempt to date the rabbinic views on conversion. Zeitlin and Finkelstein engaged in a fruitless discussion on the exact year in which ritual immersion became a requirement for conversion. In addition, Simon unsuccessfully attempted to date the origins of conversion to Judaism. Schiffman, *Who Was a Jew?* 19–39; Solomon Zeitlin, "A Note on Baptism for Proselytes," *Journal of Biblical Literature* 52 (1933): 78–79; Solomon Zeitlin, "The Halaka in the Gospels and Its Relation to the Jewish Law in the Time of Jesus," *Hebrew Union College Annual* 1 (1924): 357–63; Louis Finkelstein, "The Institution of Baptism for Proselytes," *Journal of Biblical Literature* 52 (1933): 203–11; Marcel Simon, "Sur les débuts du prosélytisme juif," in A. Coquot and M. Philonenko, eds., *Hommages a André Dupont-Summer* (Paris, 1971), 509–20. I understand that Professor Shaye J. D. Cohen is now working on a history of conversion to Judaism.

56. The most important essay concerning the historical accuracy of attributions of opinions to rabbinic masters is by William S. Green, "What's in a Name?—The Problematic of Rabbinic 'Biography,'" in William S. Green, ed., *Approaches to Ancient Judaism: Theory and Practice* (Missoula, 1978), 77–96. See also Gary G. Porton, *The Traditions of Rabbi Ishmael*, 4 vols. (Leiden, 1976–82); Gary G. Porton, "The Artificial Dispute: Ishmael and Aqiba," in Jacob Neusner, ed., *Christianity, Judaism, and Other Greco-Roman Cults: Studies for Morton Smith at Sixty* (Leiden, 1975), 4:18–29; Jacob Neusner, *The Rabbinic Traditions about the Pharisees before 70*, 3 vols. (Leiden, 1973); Jacob Neusner, *Development of a Legend: Studies in the Traditions concerning Yohanan ben Zakkai* (Leiden, 1970); Jacob Neusner, *Eliezer ben Hyrcanus:*

The Traditions and the Man, 2 vols. (Leiden, 1973); Joel D. Gereboff, *Rabbi Tarfon: The Tradition, the Man, and Early Rabbinic Judaism* (Missoula, 1979); Robert Goldenberg, *The Sabbath Law of Rabbi Meir* (Missoula, 1979); William S. Green, *The Traditions of Joshua Ben Hananiah, Part I: The Early Traditions* (Leiden, 1981); Shamai Kanter, *Rabban Gamaliel II: The Legal Traditions* (Chico, 1980); Jack N. Lightstone, "Yose the Galilean in Mishnah-Tosefta and the History of Early Rabbinic Judaism," *Journal of Jewish Studies* 30, no. 1 (Spring 1980): 37–45; Jack N. Lightstone, "R. Sadoq," in William S. Green, ed., *Persons and Institutions in Early Rabbinic Judaism* (Missoula, 1977), 49–148; Jack N. Lightstone, *Yose the Galilean I: Traditions in Mishnah-Tosefta* (Leiden, 1979); Charles Primus, *Aqiva's Contribution to the Law of Zera'im* (Leiden, 1977); Tzvee Zahavy, *The Traditions of Eleazar ben Azariah* (Missoula, 1978).

57. David Goodblatt, "The Babylonian Talmud" in Hildegard Temporini and Wolfgang Haase, eds., *Aufstieg und Niegergang der römischen Welt* (Berlin and New York, 1979), II.19.2, 285–88.

58. The most recent scholar to point out the importance of employing the New Testament as an historical source for determining the origin of specific rabbinic practices and opinions is Alan F. Segal, *Paul the Convert: The Apostolate and Apostasy of Saul the Pharisee* (New Haven and London, 1990).

59. See, for example, Robert A. Kraft and George W. E. Nickelsburg, eds., *Early Judaism and Its Modern Interpreters* (Atlanta, 1986). They write: "early Judaism appears to encompass almost unlimited diversity and variety—indeed, it might be more appropriate to speak of early Judaisms"; p. 2.

60. This work is shaped by Jacob Neusner's view of the rabbis and their power. See Neusner, *A History of the Jews in Babylonia*, 5 vols. (Leiden, 1965–70). The information concerning the power and mythology of the rabbis has been conveniently summarized by Neusner in *There We Sat Down: Talmudic Judaism in the Making* (Nashville, 1972).

61. McKnight, Schiffman, and Simon are among the most recent scholars to approach this topic within the context of larger studies on conversion. Most recently see also A. Thomas Kraabel, "The Disappearance of the God-fearers," *Numen* 28 (1981): 113–26; R. S. MacLennan and A. T. Kraabel, "The God-Fearers: A Literary and Theological Invention," *Biblical Archaeologist Review* 12 (1986): 46–53; R. F. Tannenbaum, "Jews and God-Fearers in the Holy City of Aphrodite," *Biblical Archaeologist Review* 12 (1986): 54–57; Thomas M. Finn, "The God-Fearers Reconsidered," *Catholic Biblical Quarterly* 47 (1985): 75–84; J. A. Overman, "The God-Fearers: Some Neglected Features," *Journal for the Study of the New Testament* 32 (1988): 17–26; J. Reynolds and R. F. Tannenbaum, *Jews and Godfearers at Aphrodisias: Greek Inscriptions with Commentary* (Cambridge, 1987); Feldman, *Jew and Gentile*, 342–82.

62. The present work does not address in any detail the problem of the *gr twšb*, the "resident alien." Most often, this term appears in the rabbinic corpus because it occurred in the biblical text.

63. BYeb. 47a–b.

64. Ibid., 46a–b.

65. Jacob Neusner, *Development of a Legend: Studies in the Traditions concerning Yohanan ben Zakkai* (Leiden, 1970); Jacob Neusner, *The Rabbinic Traditions about the Pharisees before 70;* Jacob Neusner, *Eliezer ben Hyrcanus: The Traditions and the Man,* 2 vols. (Leiden, 1973). In my investigation of the traditions attributed to Ishmael, I showed that the agenda assigned to that sage differed from document to document; Gary G. Porton, *The Traditions of Rabbi Ishmael Part Four: The Materials as a Whole* (Leiden, 1982), 94–159. Even the picture of Ishmael as a biblical exegete differed from document to document, pp. 160–211.

66. This approach does not assume that the redacted rabbinic collections are seamless wholes. I recognize that each collection is a combination of sources and traditions from various sages or schools of sages and from several different time periods, but I have not sought to disengage the various sources from their present contexts. While that is an important enterprise, it does not always yield useful results. There is still a good deal of scholarly debate on how sources are to be identified and dated. For example, there is no way to determine when a group of *sugyot* was combined in the editorial process. Were they combined by the ultimate, penultimate, or antepenultimate editor(s)? Therefore, identifying the sources and making claims about the editorial process and stages do not provide much certain information, and as yet these procedures do not allow us to create a clear history of the creation of the various pericopae or the ideas which they contain.

67. TDem. 2:4–5. This requirement does appear in other documents, but its absence from Mishnah is striking.

68. BKer. 8b–9a.

69. Segal argues time and again that Paul has been viewed as the paradigmatic case of the convert. Furthermore, it is not accidental that Nock ended his classic study of conversion in the ancient world with Augustine; Arthur D. Nock, *Conversion: The Old and the New in Religion from Alexander the Great to Augustin of Hippo* (London, 1933). Also note that Rambo's section "Psychoanalytic Perspectives" has a separate section on Augustine, and his section "Theological Perspectives" has a separate section on Paul.

CHAPTER 2

1. My views of Mishnah, in fact of the totality of rabbinic literature, are shaped by the work of Jacob Neusner: *Judaism: The Evidence of the Mishnah* (Chicago and London, 1981); *The Modern Study of the Mishnah* (Leiden, 1973); *A History of the Mishnaic Law of Damages,* 5 vols. (Leiden, 1982); *A History of the Mishnaic Law of Holy Things,* 6 vols. (Leiden, 1978–79); *A History of the Mishnaic Law of Purities,* 20 vols. (Leiden, 1974–77); *A History of the Mishnaic Law of Women,* 5 vols. (Leiden, 1979–80); *A History of the Mishnaic Law of Appointed Times,* 5 vols. (Leiden, 1981–82).

2. Ten family stocks are listed as coming up from Babylon: The priestly, levitical, Israelite, impaired priestly, convert, freedman, *mamzer, natin, shetuqi,* and *asufi* stocks; mQid. 4:1. On this mishnah and the related discussions in the Talmuds,

see Bernard J. Bamberger, *Proselytism in the Talmudic Period* (New York, 1968), 81–84. Cf. bYeb. 85a, bYeb. 37a, bQid. 75a, mHor. 3:8.

3. See Gary G. Porton, *Goyim: Gentiles and Israelites in Mishnah-Tosefta* (Atlanta, 1988), esp. 285–307.

4. Ibid., 221–39.

5. MDem. 6:10. Cf. tDem. 6:12, bQid. 17b, bA.Z. 64a.

6. MKer. 2:1. Cf. tKer. 1:11. In Mishnah, Eliezer states that the convert's "atonement" is not complete until the blood has been tossed against the altar. The commentators argue that this refers to the convert who has been circumcised and undergone his ritual ablution; Bartinoro, *loc. cit.* Hanokh Albeck, *The Six Orders of the Mishnah: Order Qodashim* (Tel Aviv, 1958), 251. In Tosefta, Eliezer states only that the convert lacks atonement to eat sacrifices, *zbhym*. The *gemara*, bHor. 8b, argues that the convert may eat holy things even if he has not brought his offering. On the basis of this passage Moore argued that "the offering of a sacrifice is not one of the conditions of becoming a proselyte, but only a condition precedent to the exercise of one of the rights which belong to him as a proselyte, namely, participation in a sacrificial meal"; George F. Moore, *Judaism in the First Centuries of the Christian Era: The Age of the Tannaim* (Cambridge, reprint, 1966), 1:332. However, see Bamberger's refutation of Moore, Bamberger, *Proselytism*, 45. Schiffman argues that the anonymous statement in the text indicates that "the sacrifice is part of the initiatory conversion rites"; Lawrence H. Schiffman, *Who Was a Jew? Rabbinic and Halakhic Perspectives on the Jewish-Christian Schism* (Hoboken, 1985), 30.

7. Num. 19:18–19.

8. MPes. 8:8, mEd. 5:2. Cf. tPis. 7:14; yPes. 8:8, Venice 36b; bPes. 92a; Jacob Neusner, *The Rabbinic Traditions about the Pharisees before 70* (Leiden, 1971), 2:141–42; and Bamberger, *Proselytism*, 69–71.

9. McKnight states that it is unclear whether this is "an initiation baptism as a rite for inclusion or a simple purification"; Scot McKnight, *A Light among the Gentiles: Jewish Missionary Activity in the Second Temple Period* (Minneapolis, 1991), 84.

10. Ten family stocks came up from Babylon: The priests, Levites, Israelites, the impaired priests, the converts, the freedmen, the *mamzerim*, the *natin*, the *shetuqi* and the *asufi;* mQid. 4:1.

11. *Mamzerim* are the offspring of marriages which are not recognized by Israelite law.

12. According to Danby, who follows the *gemara*, "These are the descendants of the Gibeonites whom Joshua made into Temple slaves (Josh. 9:27)"; Herbert Danby, *The Mishnah, Translated from the Hebrew with Introduction and Brief Explanatory Notes* (Oxford, reprint, 1964), 795.

13. MHor. 3:8, tHor. 2:10. On bYeb. 37a Samuel reports that according to Hillel the ten classes who came up from Babylonia were priests, Levites, Israelites, impaired priests, converts, emancipated slaves, *mamzerim, netinim, shetuqim, asufim;* that is, the list as it appears in mQid. 4:1. Many previous scholars have made a good deal over the fact that the convert appears in a different place in each list. For example, Bamberger refuted Ginzberg's suggestions that the tradition in mQid. 4:1 is the older version of the list and that the order in mHor. 3:8 reflects the situation

after the rise of Christianity when Judaism became less friendly toward converts; Bamberger, *Proselytism*, 64–65. There is no reason for claiming that the different sequence of the classes of people in the list has any underlying meaning. We may simply have several versions of the same list. For our purposes the only significant point is that the convert is consistently marked as a distinct subclass of Israelites. Cf. bYeb. 85a, bYeb. 37a, bQid. 75a.

14. Bartinoro, *loc. cit.*, states that the *natin* grew up "with us in holiness," while the gentile did not. A convert precedes a slave because the slave was included in Noah's curse pronounced against Canaan, Gen. 9:25. This follows the *gemara*, bHor. 13a; cf. Rashi, *loc. cit.* This is not explicitly stated in Mishnah. It does point to the fact, however, that the later sages considered the non-Israelite origin of the converts to be the source of their impairment.

15. This means that converted women were not accorded the same status as a native-born Israelite female. While a physically impaired priest, Deut. 23:1, could not marry an Israelite woman, he may marry a female convert; mYeb. 8:2 and mQid. 4:1. Cf. bYeb. 76a–b; bYeb. 57a; yYeb. 8:2, Venice 9b; yQid. 4:6, Venice 66a.

16. Danby states that the *shetuqi* "is 'silent' when reproached with his origin"; Danby, *The Mishnah*, 327, n. 5. MQid. 4:1 defines a *shetuqi* as "one who knows his mother, but not his father."

17. Danby suggests that *asufi* has "the sense of 'foundling'"; Danby, *The Mishnah*, 327, n. 6. MQid. 4:2 defines an *asufi* as one "who is gathered in from the streets and does not know either his father or his mother."

18. MQid. 4:1.

19. In mBik. 1:5 Eliezer states that "a woman who is the daughter of converts may not marry into the priesthood *unless her mother is an Israelite.*" This does not make any sense unless one takes *grym* in the first clause as a collective noun and not a plural noun referring to both of her parents. This is the way in which it is interpreted on bYeb. 57a, which refers to Eliezer's opinion in mBik. 1:5, but ignores his opinion in mQid. 4:7 even though the two are contradictory. While such a contradiction is not uncommon in Mishnah, it is possible that the phrase *unless her mother is an Israelite* has been placed here incorrectly because it occurs later in this passage as well as in the second part of mQid. 4:7. Given the change of gender in the second part of both texts in which the slave and the convert are equated (*unless his* [mQid. 4:7] or *their* [mBik. 1:5] *mother is an Israelite*), it is possible that this does not have anything to do with the ability of a convert's daughter to marry into the priesthood. However, it is normally interpreted to mean that the daughter of a slave or a convert cannot marry into the priesthood unless she is ten generations removed from her freed or converted parent. See Hanokh Albeck, *The Six Orders of the Mishnah: Order Zera'im* (Jerusalem and Tel Aviv, 1959), 327. Danby, *The Mishnah*, 328, merely translates the sentence without attempting to explain it: "A proselyte is regarded as of like standing to freed slaves even to ten generations, until such time as his mother is of Israelitish stock." Neusner ignores the possessive pronoun of the mother and renders the passage: "All the same are proselytes and freed slaves, even down to ten generations—[the daughters cannot marry into the priesthood] unless the mother is an Israelite," but this contradicts the opening

part of Eliezer's comment; Jacob Neusner, *The Mishnah: A New Translation* (New Haven and London, 1988), 497. Freedman's translation reads "[The same law applies to] a proselyte as to freed slaves, even unto ten generations, [his daughter is unfit] unless his mother is of Israelite stock." This would seem to mean that the male convert had to have an Israelite mother in order for his daughter to be allowed to marry into the priesthood before ten generations. This could be seen as a qualification of Eliezer's earlier reference to the converted male who married an Israelite woman, but that would not make any sense, for the girl's mother would have been an Israelite all along; H. Freedman, *Kiddushin: Translated into English with Notes, Glossary, and Indices* (London, 1936), 393–94. This last part of the text does not make sense in relationship to Eliezer's earlier comments. If we claim that it is not part of Eliezer's comment, as well may be the case, then the change of the gender of the possessive pronoun makes the subject under discussion totally obscure.

20. MQid. 4:7.

21. MQid. 4:6. Cf. tQid. 5:3, bYeb. 57a, and Sifra Emor Pereq 2:9, Weiss 95a where mQid. 4:6 is presented as an interpretation of Lev. 21:15. The main topic of the text is the daughter of a impaired priest. Judah's comparison of the daughter of a male convert to the daughter of a male impaired priest comes at the end. Bamberger, *Proselytism*, 84–85, concludes the prohibition against marrying into the priestly class does not reflect a negative attitude toward the converts; rather, it relates to the stress that the priestly class laid on an "unblemished family tree," so that they "married only with families whose origins were known to be of the finest. No matter how friendly one might be toward the convert, one could not regard him as of the aristocracy of Israel"; Bamberger, *Proselytism*, 85. One might add that the convert's status was viewed by many as considerably lower than that.

22. MQid. 4:7.

23. These three opinions represent the three possibilities: The daughters of converts cannot marry into the priesthood (Judah); the daughters of converts can marry into the priesthood (Yosi); the daughters of converts can marry into the priesthood only if they have an Israelite mother (Eliezer). Yosi's comment is in dispute with Eliezer's remark, while Judah's statement appears in the context of a discussion of the *halal*. On these passages, see Jacob Neusner, *A History of the Mishnaic Law of Women Part Four Sotah, Gittin, Qiddushin: Translation and Explanation* (Leiden, 1980), 255–56.

24. MSanh. 4:2.

25. MHor. 1:4; similarly, neither a *mamzer* nor a *natin* could serve as a judge in all cases. Cf. Sifra WaYiqra (Hobah) Parashah 4:3; Weiss 19a where those listed in mHor. 1:4 are exempted from the requirement of making a public offering under the terms of Lev. 4:14, for they are not suitable to serve as judges.

26. MB.Q. 5:4. The *gemara*, bB.Q. 49a, assumes that the converted woman is married to a converted man who died without heirs. However, nothing in Mishnah's text requires this reading. It could simply be the case that the author of this mishnah assumed that converted women were different from native-born Israelite women. It is also possible that the author of this passage in Mishnah assumed that

the child's father was not an Israelite, in which case, he would not be entitled to compensation. It is likely that the authors of the argument in the *gemara* have read a different case into Mishnah from what its original author had designed. Bartinoro, *loc. cit.*, follows the interpretation given in the *gemara*. Cf. E. W. Kirzner, *Baba Kamma: Translated into English with Notes, Glossary, and Indices* (London, 1935), 277. Neusner, *The Mishnah*, 514, and Danby, *The Mishnah*, 338, do *not* interpolate any reference to the converted woman's marriage to a converted man.

27. MEd. 5:6. Cf. Sifré Numbers Naśo 7, Horovitz, 11, which presents an abbreviated form of Aqabyya's comment in Mishnah and states that he referred to *the convert's wife*, while in mEd. 5:6 he referred to a *converted woman*, two very different people. Also see ySot. 2:5, Venice 18b and bBer. 19a.

28. MBik. 1:4. Cf. Sifré Deuteronomy Ki Tabo 299; Finkelstein 318, where Deut. 26:3, *When I came to the Land which YHWH swore to our fathers*, is interpreted so as to exclude the convert, and the phrase *to give to us* excludes the slaves. Basing himself on Bartinoro(!) and the discussion in the Palestinian Talmud, yBik. 1:4, Venice 64a(!), Bamberger chastises Schürer for claiming that this passage proves that the rabbis were unfriendly toward converts; Bamberger, *Proselytism*, 65–67. Bialoblocki argues that this rule reflects a time after the Hadrianic period when a distinction was drawn between the nation and religion of Israel. At that time, one could convert to the religion of Israel without joining the nation; S. Bialoblocki, *Die Beziehungen des Judentums zu Proselyten und Proselytentum* (Berlin, 1930), 21–22. Moore, however, writes that the word *ger* refers to "a convert to Judaism who had been received by circumcision and baptism not only into the religion but into the Jewish people"; George F. Moore, *Judaism* 1:338. See also tBik. 1:2 and Mekhilta Ishmael Mishpatim 20, Horovitz and Rabin 335.

29. *I acknowledge this day before YHWH your God that I have entered the land that YHWH swore to our ancestors to assign us. . . . My ancestor was a fugitive Aramean. He went down to Egypt with meager numbers and sojourned there; but there we became a great and very populous nation. The Egyptians dealt harshly with us and oppressed us; they imposed heavy labor upon us. We cried to YHWH, the God of our ancestors, and YHWH heard our plea and saw our plight, our misery, and our oppression. YHWH freed us from Egypt by a mighty hand, by an outstretched arm and awesome power, and by signs and portents. He brought us to this place and gave us this land, a land flowing with milk and honey. Wherefore I now bring the first fruits of the soul which you, O YHWH, have given us.*

30. Deut. 26:3.

31. Mishnah also prohibits the converts from reciting the Avowal related to the second tithe; mM.S. 5:14; cf. Sifré Deuteronomy Ki Tabo 301; Finkelstein 320.

32. MBik. 1:4. The reason for this statement is unclear, for the person with an Israelite mother is still classified as a convert. It may be based on a literal interpretation of *'bwtykm* in Deut. 26:3. Or it may imply that the child of an Israelite woman and a gentile father had to convert, so that the child would not be counted as a *mamzer*, which is the status of a child one of whose parents is a non-Israelite. I suppose that it could mean that the child of a male convert is considered to be a convert, even if his mother is a native Israelite. The writer in Sifré Deuteronomy Ki Tabo 301; Finkelstein, 320 ignores the fact that Deut. 26:11 specifically men-

tions the *gr*, a term which the *midrashim* usually take as a reference to converts, and states that because the converts do not have a portion in the land, they may not thank YHWH for the crops he has given them.

33. MB.B. 8:1–2.

34. Or a woman's ox, an orphan's ox, a guardian's ox, the Temple's ox, or a wild ox.

35. Ex. 21:28–30: *When an ox gores a man or a woman to death, the ox shall be stoned and its flesh shall not be eaten, but the owner of the ox is not to be punished. If, however, that ox has been in the habit of goring, and its owner, though warned, has failed to guard it, and it kills a man or a woman—the ox shall be stoned and its owner, too, shall be put to death. If ransom is laid upon him, he must pay whatever is laid upon him to redeem his life.*

36. MB.Q. 4:7. In mB.Q. 4:7 we read "R. Judah says: 'A wild ox, an ox belonging to the Temple, and the ox of a convert who died are exempt from death, because they do not have owners.'" In tB.Q. 4:6 we find the following: "R. Judah says: 'A wild ox, an ox belonging to the Temple, and an ox belonging to a convert who died without heirs is exempt, for it is said, *and its owner, though warned, has failed to guard it* . . . because these do not have owners.'" The version in Tosefta has cited the biblical text upon which Judah based his opinion and made it clear that he was speaking of the ox belonging to a convert who died without heirs. Tosefta does not contain the anonymous comment in Mishnah with which Judah disagrees. We find the quotation in Tosefta brought to justify Judah's statement in Mishnah in yB.Q. 4:8, Venice 4c.

37. MB.Q. 9:11; Sifré Numbers Naśo 2, Horovitz 4–5 and Naśo 4, Horovitz 7. In the latter text, the passage is attributed to Ishmael. Cf. tB.Q. 10:16; bB.Q. 109a; yB.Q. 9:15, Venice 7a.

38. See mB.B. 3.

39. MB.B. 3:3, tB.B. 2:11. As we shall see in the next chapter, tB.B. 2:11 contains a good deal of additional material.

40. MB.B. 4:9, tB.B. 2:11. The text mentions only a convert; however, it must refer to a convert who died without heirs or the Israelite would have no right to claim possession of the property. See Tiferet Yisrael, *loc. cit.;* Albeck, *Zera'im,* 133.

41. MSheq. 7:6. This may be attributable to Simeon, as in Neusner, 263. The problem is that Simeon seems to say that he is going to state one rule which the court ordained; however, three different rulings appear. In mMen. 4:5 we find only the last of these three. All three are listed on bMen. 51b and attributed by implication to Simeon. Yom Tov Lipmann Heller notes that if a dead Israelite forgot to provide the drink offerings, they may be secured from his heirs; however, in the case of a convert, this may not be possible; Tosefot Yom Tov, *loc. cit.*

42. MSheb. 10:9. Cf. bQid. 17b which contains two traditions concerning the sages' view of one who repays the debt to the children. In one version they disapprove of the repayment, and in the other they approve of his actions, as it appears in mSheb. 10:9. Newman argues that Mishnah's point is that "responsible people repay their debts, even if they have no legal duty to do so"; Louis E. Newman, *The Sanctity of the Seventh Year: A Study of Mishnah Tractate Shebiit* (Chico, 1983), 213.

43. *Loc. cit.*

44. MKet. 4:3.

45. Deut. 22:21 states that when a man charges that his wife was not a virgin at the time of their marriage and his accusations are justified, *then the girl is brought to the entrance of her father's house, and the men of her town shall stone her to death.*

46. If an Israelite claims that his wife was not a virgin and the charges are disproved, *they shall fine him a hundred [sheqels] of silver and give it to the girl's father;* Deut. 22:17–18.

47. This would seem to parallel the view attributed above to Eliezer b. Jacob that if a convert's mother were an Israelite the woman could marry into the priesthood. In both cases, the issue is the Israelite status of the mother, not the father. However, if the daughter wished to marry into the priestly caste, some problems could occur.

48. MKet. 9:9. The woman who converts is equated with a mature woman who received a marriage contract while she was a minor. This parallel underscores the fact that the woman has changed her legal status. Cf. tKet. 9:7; bKet. 90a; yKet. 9:13, Venice 33c. Tosefta adds that if the husband executed a new marriage contract after the conversion in order to confirm the marriage, the wife collects according to the terms of the new marriage contract. Both *gemarot* take up Tosefta's addition, which is cited only in the Babylonian Talmud.

49. This would explain the assumption that gentiles issue *ketubot* to their gentile wives, for it is merely a theoretical assumption used to illustrate the text's concern with the validity of a *ketubah* issued to a woman who has changed her legal status.

50. Porton, *Goyim,* 68.

51. MYeb. 11:2. Because both brothers must be Israelites, this ruling holds even if one of the brothers was conceived and born after the woman converted, and the other was conceived while his mother was a gentile, but born after she converted. Again the parallel is drawn between a woman who converts and a handmaiden who is freed. Cf. tYeb. 12:2. BYeb. 97b–98a, deals with the case of twin brothers; a different situation from that presented in Mishnah or Tosefta. Sifré Deuteronomy Ki Taṣa 289; Finkelstein 308 deals with two brothers who were conceived before their mother converted, but born after she converted, a case not covered in Mishnah. The comment is connected to the phrase *in Israel* in Deut. 25:7. The Palestinian *gemara* takes the discussion in an entirely different direction; yYeb. 11:2, Venice 11d.

52. Porton, *Goyim,* 242–68.

53. On bQid. 17b this law is said to be from the Scribes, not from the Torah, for according to the Torah converts cannot inherit from their gentile parents.

54. MDem. 6:10, tDem. 6:12, bQid. 17b, bA.Z. 64a. See Richard S. Sarason, *A History of the Mishnaic Law of Agriculture, Section Three: A Study of Tractate Demai* (Leiden, 1979), 229.

55. MGiṭ. 2:6. The pericope concerns the transmittal of a divorce document from a husband to his wife.

56. Ex. 13:2, 13:13, 22:28, 34:20, Num. 3:13, 18:15–18.

57. Porton, *Goyim,* firstlings, *passim.*

58. Deut. 21:17.

59. The same rule applies to the following case: If a man who had no children by a previous marriage marries a second wife who was a freed slave and who had borne a child while she was a slave.

60. Ex. 13:2.

61. MBekh. 8:1.

62. Ibid.

63. Deut. 18:3. The issue is covered in mḤul. 10.

64. Porton, *Goyim*, priestly gifts, *passim*.

65. MḤul. 10:4. Cf. Sifré Deuteronomy Shoftim 175; Finkelstein 214, where it is a comment on Deut. 18:3, *This then shall be the priests' due from the people: Everyone who offers a sacrifice* . . . .

66. Porton, *Goyim*, 182, 185, 186.

67. MḤal. 3:6. Cf. tḤal. 1:12. However, if the offering were not taken from the dough about which it is uncertain exactly when it was rolled out, a nonpriest who might eat this dough does not become liable for the added fifth mentioned in Lev. 22:14 and detailed in mḤal. 1:9. The apparent contradiction between the rule concerning the doubtful dough offering, for which the convert is liable, and the doubtful slaughtered animal, for which the convert is not liable, is discussed on bḤul. 134a.

68. Porton, *Goyim*, 180–84.

69. MPe. 4:6. Cf. Sifré Deuteronomy Ki Taṣa 282, Finkelstein 298, where Mishnah's pericopae is attached to *your harvest* in Deut. 24:19. On Sifra Weiss Qedoshim 87b, Pereq 1:6 this mishnah is connected with Lev. 19:9.

70. MPe. 5:8.

71. Porton, *Goyim*, 269–83.

72. MZab. 2:1. TZab. 2:1, on the other hand, seems to state that converts do not convey uncleanness through their genital emissions, even though they are treated as if they do. The problem with the text is that it contains a reference to both the *gr* and the *twšb*. It is possible that it should refer to only the *gr twšb*, which is usually distinct from the *gr*. On the *gr twšb*, see Moore, *Judaism* 1:338–41; Bialoblocki, 4–11.

73. MZab. 2:3. If an Israelite had an emission of semen and then had a second emission, the second one does not convey uncleanness. Cf. Bartinoro, *loc. cit.*; Hanokh Albeck, *The Six Orders of the Mishnah: Order Tohorot* (Tel Aviv, 1957), 443; S. M. Lehrman, *Zabim: Translated into English with Notes* (London, 1948), 509, n. 3. Cf. TZab. 2:7.

74. Porton, *Goyim*, 272.

75. MNeg. 7:1. The spot on the convert is equated with the spot on a person before the Torah was revealed, the spot on a child when it was born, and the spot in a crease which was later laid bare. Eliezer b. Jacob and sages disagree concerning the appearance of the spots on certain parts of the head and the beard under specific circumstances. While in some cases, Eliezer declares the spots to be unclean, the sages declare all of them to be clean; however, only by appearing in this context could one claim that Eliezer and sages are discussing the case of converts. Cf.

tNeg. 2:14–15. TNeg. 2:15 discusses the instance in which the gentile had a bright spot before he converted to which was joined another bright spot after he converted, an issue not covered in Mishnah. In Sifra Negaim Pereq 1:1; Weiss 59d–60a we read that Eleazer b. Azariah declares clean a gentile who exhibits signs of skin disease upon his conversion. Eleazar b. Hisma states that if one wishes to be lenient, they are clean; if one wishes to be strict, the signs should be examined again. Aqiba states that in any case the signs must be examined afresh upon the person's conversion. This is attached to Lev. 13:2.

76. MB.M. 4:10. TB.M. 3:25 is considerably different and cites different biblical texts. Sifra Behar Pereq 4:2, Weiss 107d follows Mishnah. Note the parallels cited by Bamberger, *Proselytism*, 158–59. BB.M. 58b contains the opening section from Tosefta's pericope.

77. Porton, *Goyim*, uncivilized, *passim*.

78. Wegner points out that even if the gentile women had been sexually abused before the age of three years and one day, the women would still be considered virgins after they converted because the sages assumed that a hymen ruptured before the age of three would spontaneously regenerate. Judith Romney Wegner, *Chattel or Person? The Status of Women in the Mishnah* (New York and Oxford, 1988), 21–22.

79. MKet. 1:2.

80. MKet. 1:4.

81. MKet. 3:1. The fine is derived from Deut. 22:9 and Ex. 22:16. The fine should be paid to the woman's father; however, in the case of the convert this would be impossible. It is interesting that this problem does not occur to those who stand behind this text. The converted woman is listed along with the *mamzerah*, the *netinah*, the Samaritan, the captive, the handmaiden, the man's sister, his father's sister, his mother's sister, his wife's sister, his brother's sister, the wife of his father's brother, and the menstruant woman. On the *netinah*, see Bamberger, *Proselytism*, 80–81.

82. MKet. 3:2.

83. MYeb. 6:5. Sages also classify as a harlot a freed bondwoman and a woman who has intercourse with a man who is forbidden to her. Cf. Sifra Emor Pereq 1:7; Weiss 94b. Although Judah's comment is different in Sifra from that in Mishnah, sages' teaching is virtually the same in both versions. Sages' comment also appears on bYeb. 61b. For another discussion, although unrelated to our present text, of the conditions under which a converted woman is considered a harlot, see yQid. 4:1, Venice 65b.

84. Porton, *Goyim*, 222–23.

85. Rashi, bYeb. 24b.

86. BYeb. 24b.

87. MYeb. 2:8. Cf. tYeb. 4:6. Tosefta opens with the case of a male slave or gentile who had intercourse with a female Israelite. Although they should not marry after the male converts, they are not forced to obtain a divorce if they do marry. Tosefta discusses the case of a male Israelite who has intercourse with a female gentile or slave. The difference between Mishnah and Tosefta is that the

former discusses an Israelite male who is *suspected* of having intercourse, *hnt'n*, while Tosefta treats a male who *engaged in intercourse, hb' 'l;* see Saul Lieberman, *Tosefta Ki-fshutah: A Comprehensive Commentary on the Tosefta, Part VI: Order Nashim* (New York, 1967), 30–31.

88. MQid. 3:5; tQid. 4:9. Cf. bQid. 63a where we are told that because a person may convert only in the presence of three judges, conversion is not in the person's power, so that he cannot make a promise concerning his conversion.

89. The *gemara* claims that these marriages are invalid because the person making the contracts does not have the power himself to ensure that the stipulations are carried out. The male does not have control over the woman's converting, nor does he have full control over his own conversion, for an Israelite court must agree to accept him into the Israelite community, bQid. 63a–b. However, Mishnah's ruling need not be read in this way.

90. Porton, *Goyim*, 285–86.

91. MYad. 4:4, tYad. 2:17. William S. Green, *The Traditions of Joshua Ben Hananiah, Part One: The Early Legal Traditions* (Leiden, 1981), 309–10. In tYad. 2:18 the anonymous statement rules according to Joshua, for it states that Judah may enter the congregation. Gamaliel then rules that if they allow the Ammonite to enter the congregation, they must also allow the Egyptian; however, the anonymous response rejects Gamaliel's extension of the ruling. Cf. Shamai Kanter, *Rabban Gamaliel II: The Legal Traditions* (Chico, 1980), 213–15. Bamberger notes that the biblical law referring to "entering the congregation" does not refer to conversion; rather, the issue is marriage to an Israelite; Bamberger, *Proselytism*, 76–81.

92. Porton, *Goyim*, 173–203.

93. Ibid., priest, *passim*.

94. Ibid.

95. Ibid., 223, 248, 305.

96. Ibid., 236, 286.

97. Ibid., 221–22, 287–307.

98. This juxtaposition appears in five of the thirty-seven passages from Mishnah: MYeb. 8:1, 2:8, mKet. 1:4, 1:2, mHor. 3:8.

99. Unfortunately, our texts do not tell us whether reference is to gentile slaves or Israelite slaves. Urbach suggests that like converts, foreign slaves were circumcised and immersed upon their entering the service of an Israelite, and he claims that this is why the two classes are comparable; Ephraim E. Urbach, "The Laws Regarding Slavery as a Source for Social History of the Period of the Second Temple, the Mishnah and Talmud," in J. G. Weiss, ed., *Papers of the Institute of Jewish Studies London* (Jerusalem, 1964), 1:40–41.

100. Urbach also notes that gentile slaves, upon gaining their freedom, were recognized as full members of the Israelite community; Urbach, "Laws," 45–49. Unfortunately Urbach supports his claim by citing passages from the *talmudim*, as well as Mishnah and Tosefta; therefore, it is difficult to know the views of those who produced Mishnah.

101. Wegner, *Chattel or Person?* 21–22.

CHAPTER 3

1. Jacob Neusner, *The Tosefta: Its Structure and Its Sources* (Atlanta, 1986), ix.

2. *Zbḥym.*

3. TSheq. 3:20. Cf. bKer. 8b. In mKer. 2:1 Eliezer b. Jacob holds that "antonement" is not complete until the blood has been sprinkled on the altar for the convert, without referring to a bird. Lieberman concludes that the opinion in tSheq. 3:20 should be attributed to Eliezer b. Jacob; Saul Lieberman, *Tosefta Ki-fshutah: A Comprehensive Commentary on the Tosefta Part IV Order Mo'ed* (New York, 1962), 710–11.

4. TSheq. 3:21. Cf. bKer. 8b.

5. *'wlh.*

6. TSheq. 3:21 and tKer. 1:12. Cf. Sifré Numbers Shelaḥ 107, Horovitz, 112 which states that the convert's bird offerings are burnt offerings, *'šym,* while tSheq. 3:21 terms them whole burnt offerings, *'wlwt.*

7. TSheq. 3:22. Cf. ySheq. 8:4, Venice ySheq. 8:6, 51b; bR.H. 31b, bKer. 9a. Allon concludes, on the basis of the passages cited here and in tractate *Gerim* 2:4, that the convert had to offer a bird sacrifice, and not a burnt offering from the cattle. However, Allon uncritically brings all of the sources together and into conversation with one another, thus ignoring the ambiguity of the situation. He also accepts the later tradition of Yohanan's role, reported in the two *gemarot,* in suspending the ritual after the Temple was destroyed; Gedalyahu Allon, *Jews, Judaism and the Classical World: Studies in Jewish History in the Times of the Second Temple and Talmud,* trans. Israel Abrahams (Jerusalem, 1977), 176–79.

8. MKer. 2:1.

9. This matter will be discussed below, in chap. 7.

10. TKer. 1:11–12.

11. Lieberman claims that the discussion of the converts' sacrifices in tSheq. was included because it was one of the offerings which was brought only while the Temple was standing and that this relates to mSheq. 8:8; Lieberman, *Tosefta Ki-fshutah: A Comprehensive Commentary on the Tosefta Part IV Order Mo'ed,* 710.

12. TShab. 15:9. Cf. Sifra Tazri'a Pereq 1:6, Weiss 58c; yShab. 19:4, Venice 17a; yYeb. 8:1, Venice 9a; bShab. 135a. In other versions of this pericope, the dispute concerns an Israelite who is born circumcised and whose day of circumcision falls on the Sabbath; Saul Lieberman, *Tosefta Ki-fshutah: A Comprehensive Commentary on the Tosefta Part III Order Mo'ed* (New York, 1962), 252–53; Jacob Neusner, *The Rabbinic Traditions about the Pharisees before 70,* Part 2: *The Houses* (Leiden, 1971), 132–33. In Sifra and on bShab. 135a this pericope follows a discussion of whether or not one who was born circumcised may be circumcised on the Sabbath, so that in those two texts the Houses dispute could be read as focusing on the Sabbath and not on the requirement of symbolically circumcising a gentile who was circumcised when he converted. Immediately following our passage in Tosefta, tShab. 15:10, Simeon reports a dispute between Liezer and Joshua concerning the circumcision of a child on the Sabbath; however, in Tosefta, the Houses dispute is

clearly unrelated to issues of the Sabbath. The text in Genesis Rabbah 46:12 appears to be a confused combination of Tosefta's text and the later versions, for if we eliminate the square brackets supplied by Theodor and Albeck, we have a pericope that opens like the passage in Tosefta, but ends with a discussion of the issue of the Sabbath; J. Theodor and Ch. Albeck, *Midrash Bereshit Rabba: Critical Edition with Notes and Commentary* (Jerusalem, 1965), 469. Braude calls this "a casuistic problem"; William G. Braude, *Jewish Proselyting in the First Five Centuries of the Common Era: The Age of the Tannaim and Amoraim* (Providence, 1940), 76. Cf. Bernard J. Bamberger, *Proselytism in the Talmudic Period* (New York, 1968), 42–43.

13. Neusner, *Rabbinic Traditions*, 2:133.

14. TShab. 15:9. Cf. bYeb. 72a–b. The passage also discusses one who was born circumcised, a baby whose time for circumcision has passed, and all those who were circumcised.

15. TPis. 7:14. Cf. mPes. 8:8; mEd. 5:2; yPes. 8:8, Venice 36b; bPes. 92a.

16. TQid. 5:2. This is the reading which Lieberman prefers; Saul Lieberman, *The Tosefta According to Codex Vienna, with Variants from Codices Erfurt, Genizah Mss. and Editio Princeps (Venice 1521), Order Nashim: Sotah, Gittin, Kiddushin* (New York, 1973), 293, note on line 2, and Saul Lieberman, *Tosefta Ki-fshutah: A Comprehensive Commentary on the Tosefta, Part VIII Order Nashim* (New York, 1973), 966. Cf. bQid. 72b.

17. Cf. Sifré Deuteronomy Ki Taṣa 247; Finkelstein 276, where Judah's comment is connected with Deut. 23:2.

18. TQid. 5:11. Cf. yQid. 3:15, Venice 64d and bYeb. 99a.

19. TQid. 5:3. See Lieberman, *Part VIII Order Nashim*, 970. Cf. mQid. 4:6–7, bYeb. 57a, bQid. 74b.

20. TQid. 5:2.

21. This parallels MBik. 1:4 which speaks of converts with Israelite mothers who are able to refer to YHWH as the god of *our* ancestors.

22. TQid. 4:15. See Gary G. Porton, *Goyim: Gentiles and Israelites in Mishnah-Tosefta* (Atlanta, 1988), marriage, *passim*. According to Lieberman this would mean that a female child of such a union could not marry into the priestly class, as Judah rules in mQid. 4:6; see Lieberman, *The Tosefta: The Order of Nashim: Sotah, Gittin Kiddushin*, 292, note to lines 45–46 and Lieberman, *Tosefta Ki-fshutah Part VIII Order Nashim*, 962.

23. MB.B. 8:1 states that if an Israelite dies childless, he may bequeath his property to a variety of relatives, such as his brothers or uncles. However, because by definition a convert's gentile brothers and uncles are no longer his relatives, they may not inherit his property, so that the property of a convert who died without producing children by an Israelite woman after his conversion is considered to be ownerless property. Even if a gentile had intercourse with an Israelite woman and then converted, upon his death his estate is considered to be like that belonging to a convert. This means that the property is considered to be ownerless property unless the convert had children by his Israelite wife who were conceived and

born after his conversion. If this were not the case, whichever Israelite first took possession of the ownerless property gains possession of it; tB.B. 7:1.

24. TB.B. 2:11, Cf. mB.B. 3:3.

25. TSheq. 3:11. The point seems to be that a convert's wishes are carried out after his death, just as one would do with regard to an Israelite's desires. The lack of legitimate heirs does not free those who take over the property from following the convert's wishes. Lieberman and Neusner connect this text to mSheq. 7:6; Lieberman, *Tosefta Ki-fshutah Part IV Order Mo'ed*, 703–4. Jacob Neusner, *A History of the Mishnaic Law of Appointed Times Part Three. Sheqalim, Yoma, Sukkah: Translation and Explanation* (Leiden, 1982), 51–52.

26. TB.B. 2:11. See Saul Lieberman, *Tosefta Ki-fshutah: A Comprehensive Commentary on the Tosefta Part X Order Nezikin* (New York, 1988), 351. Neusner has a different reading for the text, for he states that "[If] one party has locked up, and another party has walled in, lo, this constitutes securing a claim through usucaption"; Jacob Neusner, *The Tosefta: Translated from the Hebrew. Fourth Division Neziqin (The Order of Damages)* (New York, 1981), 153.

27. TB.B. 2:11. Cf. yQid. 1:3; Venice 59d where the same issues are discussed without specific reference to taking possession of a dead convert's property.

28. TB.B. 2:11. See Lieberman, *Tosefta Ki-fshutah Part X Order Nezikin*, 352–53. Cf. bB.Q. 12a which talks about the same problems of acquisition without referring to ownerless property or to converts.

29. TKet. 4:16.

30. TB.Q. 4:6; Cf. mB.Q. 4:7 where Judah's ruling is based on the fact that the ox does not have an owner. The citation of the biblical text, Ex. 21:29, appears only in Tosefta. Cf. yB.Q. 4:8; Venice 4c.

31. On the rules of damages as applied to gentiles, see Porton, *Goyim*, 225.

32. Ex. 21:22.

33. TB.Q. 9:20. This also carries forth the idea that the laws of damages as set forth in the Bible apply only to Israelites. This *sugya* is considerably different from mB.Q. 5:4, which states that if the woman were a convert compensation would not be paid. However, the commentators to Mishnah's text assume that the converted woman was married to a convert; Saul Lieberman, *Tosefta Ki-fshutah A Comprehensive Commentary on the Tosefta Part IX Nezikin* (New York, 1988), 104.

34. Num. 5:6–8 state that if one wrongs an Israelite who dies, restitution is made to the Israelite's kinsman.

35. TB.Q. 10:16.

36. MB.Q. 9:11.

37. Who expounds, *drš*.

38. TB.Q. 10:16. Cf. bB.Q. 109a. The case is slightly different in the *gemara*, and the pericope appears as a words-of dispute between Yosi the Galilean and Aqiba. Lieberman notes the differences between the way the pericope in the Tosefta views the issue as compared to the way it appears in the Babylonian Talmud; Lieberman, *Tosefta Ki-fshutah Part IX Nezikin*, 122. The *sugya* in yB.Q. 9:9; Venice 9:15, 7a relates Yosi's comment to the issue of whether or not the thief

needs to pay the principal and the added fifth after the convert has died. In brief, it frames the issues in terms of Mishnah's discussion and ignores the passage in Tosefta. It does connect it to Num. 5:8. See Jack Lightstone, *Yosi the Galilean: I. Traditions in Mishnah-Tosefta* (Leiden, 1979), 62–67.

39. Actually he expounded, *drš*, on his way from Ziprin.

40. *If a man has no kinsman to whom restitution can be made, the amount shall go to YHWH for the priest.*

41. TB.Q. 10:17. Cf. mB.Q. 9:11; bB.Q. 109a; and yB.Q. 9:15, Venice 7a. On Sifré Numbers Naśo 4, Horovitz 7, Ishmael, Nathan, and Eliezer offer several interpretations of Num. 5:8, and Ishmael connects the verse to a convert from whom something was stolen before he died. Cf. Gary G. Porton, *The Traditions of Rabbi Ishmael Part Two: Exegetical Comments in Tannaitic Collections* (Leiden, 1977), 143–44. Aqiba's comment is not related to this comment in Tosefta, but rather discusses the men who served in the priestly watch; cf. tB.Q. 10:18 where it is unclear that this discussion should be attributed to Aqiba. If a priest is blemished, he may not receive the restitution made by one who stole from a convert and confessed, but the restitution is given to any priest whom the blemished priest chooses; tMen. 13:17. That which is given to the priests may "be eaten in the provinces," for it is less holy than other items which had to be consumed near or in the precincts of the Temple; tHal. 2:9. Cf. Sifré Numbers Qoraḥ 119, Horovitz 142; yHal. 4:11, Venice 60b; bB.Q. 110b; bHul. 133b.

42. MKet. 9:9.

43. TKet. 9:7. Cf. bKet. 90a; yKet. 9:13, Venice 33c.

44. TKet. 10:4. Later authorities favor the view that this refers to movable property and that the wife's claim to her deceased husband's property applies only to that which was specified in the marriage contract. The importance of their right to collect is emphasized by the fact that the debtor and the wife may collect from anyone who has the funds; Lieberman, *Tosefta Ki-fshutah. Part VI Order Nashim*, 350–53.

45. TYeb. 2:5.

46. TYeb. 2:6; cf. tYeb. 11:2.

47. Deut. 25:5–10.

48. TYeb. 11:2.

49. These rules apply only if the brothers have the same father.

50. TYeb. 12:2, which opens by quoting the opening statement of mYeb. 11:2. Cf. bYeb. 97b. See Saul Lieberman, *The Tosefta According to Codex Vienna, with Variants from Codices Erfurt, Genizah Mss. and Editio Princeps (Venice 1521), Together with References to Parallel Passages in Talmudic Literature and a Brief Commentary. The Order of Nashim Yebamoth, Kethuboth, Nedarim, Nazir* (New York, 1967), 40, note to lines 6–7 and Lieberman, *Tosefta Ki-fshutah Part VI Order Nashim*, 122–23. On the other hand, if a person's relatives convert along with him, their relationships may still be valid according to Israelite custom; tKet. 4:16.

51. MDem. 6:10.

52. TDem. 6:12. Cf. bQid. 17b and bA.Z. 64a which quotes the passage from Mishnah.

53. TDem. 6:13.

54. TDem. 2:4. Cf. bBekh. 30b. Erfurt reads gentile, *gwy,* for convert, *gr;* Saul Lieberman, *Tosefta Ki-fshutah: A Comprehensive Commentary on the Tosefta. Order Zera'im, Part I* (New York, 1955), 212.

55. TDem. 2:5; cf. Sifra Qedoshim Pereq 8:3, Weiss 91a and bBekh. 30b. Bamberger suggests that the rise of Christianity forced the rabbis to stress the halakhic elements of Judaism, and this led to this ruling; Bamberger, *Proselytism,* 31–32. Tosefta's comments are set in a unit which discusses various types of individuals who fulfill all but one of the obligations of their class. Thus, we find more or less parallel passages which discuss the *am ha'ares,* the convert, the priest, and the Levite. With regard to the *am ha'areş* and the convert, we have two discussions of each, for both of them are pictured as *joining* a specific group, so that the problem arises both before and after they achieve their new status. This is not true with regard to the priest or the Levite, for both were members of their group by reason of birth. Therefore, the parallel is drawn between an *am ha'areş* who joins a *haburah* and a convert who joins the Israelite people.

56. For a discussion of these passages, see Richard S. Sarason, *A History of the Mishnaic Law of Agriculture Section Three: A Study of Tractate Demai* (Leiden, 1979), 80–84. Sarason notes that the text draws a distinction between the convert and the *am ha'areş* for whom the violation of one commandment is significant, 83. Sarason suggests that the various units within the larger section were originally autonomous, so that we have a redactional unit, 83. On the basis of *[I make this covenant, with its sanctions, not with you alone, but both with those who are standing here with us this day before YHWH, our God,] and with those who are not with us here this day,* Deut. 29:13–14, tSoṭ. 7:5 concludes that Moses abjured even the gentiles who would later be converted to keep the commandments given at Sinai and all those which would be given at later times. The point is that the converts, just like the native-born Israelites, are obligated to follow the totality of Israelite law.

57. Several scholars have made a good deal out of the requirement that converts accept the whole Torah; therefore, it is curious that this appears in Tosefta first and not in Mishnah. For example, see Lawrence H. Schiffman, *Who Was a Jew? Rabbinic and Halakhic Perspectives on the Jewish-Christian Schism* (Hoboken, 1985), 38; Marcel Simon, "Sur les débuts du prosélytisme juif," in A. Caquot and M. Philonenko, eds., *Hommages a André Dupont-Sommer* (Paris, 1971), 509; George F. Moore, *Judaism in the First Centuries of the Christian Era: The Age of the Tannaim* (reprint; Cambridge, 1966), 1:331.

58. Ex. 21:29.

59. TB.Q. 4:6.

60. TKet. 3:3. There is some question concerning Yohanan b. Beroqa's statement that "they" are believed. The *gemara,* bKet. 28b, claims that he stated that the gentile who converts is believed because he intended to convert, so that he paid special attention to the events which occurred while he was a gentile. However, there are some who question this interpretation of Yohanan's comment; Lieberman, *Tosefta Ki-fshutah Part VI Nashim,* 222.

61. BKet. 28b.

62. Porton, *Goyim*, 226.

63. TSanh. 5:4.

64. Num. 5:11–31.

65. TSoṭ. 5:4. This follows sages' opinion in mEd. 5:6. There, Aqabyya b. Mahalaleel states that converts do not drink the waters of bitterness. Cf. bSoṭ. 26a. The issues is discussed in ySoṭ. 2:4, Venice 18b; however, it does not follow Tosefta's text. The dispute in mEd. 5:6 is taken up in Sifré Numbers Naśo 7, Horovitz, 11. The passage in tSoṭ. 5:4 includes the suspected descent groups, such as the *mamzer* and the *natin*, and this is probably why the convert is included in the text. If she does not undergo the rite, she cannot collect on her marriage contract. However, the rule points to the fact that the wife of a convert is treated the same as one married to a native-born Israelite.

66. TBer. 5:14. In mBer. 7:1 the list is considerably different, for it centers on the amount or type of food which one eats and not on the person's status. The only persons specifically mentioned are the Samaritan who is included and the gentile who is excluded. In Tosefta's list, the convert is placed after the Israelite and before the freed slaves: Priests, Levites, Israelites, converts, freed slaves, *halalim*, *netinim*, *mamzerim*, eunuchs castrated by a human, eunuchs born that way, one with crushed testicles, and one whose penis has been cut off.

67. TMen. 10:13. Neither women nor gentiles are permitted to lay their hands on sacrifices; see Porton, *Goyim*, 264–65.

68. TMen. 10:17. Women and gentiles are also excluded from this rite; Porton, *Goyim*, 264–65.

69. TR.H. 2:5.

70. TMeg. 2:7.

71. TSoṭ. 7:5. Citing and commenting on Deut. 29:13–14, *I make this covenant, with its sanctions, not with you alone, but both with those who are standing here with us this day before YHWH our God and with those who are not with us here this day,* Tosefta tells us that the revelation at Sinai was given to all Israel, including those who would convert in the future. Cf. bShebu. 39a.

72. TBer. 3:25. Tosefta implies that at one time there was a special benediction in the *amidah* which dealt with the converts; however, that blessing has been merged with the blessing of the elders, which now appears in the blessing for the righteous; see Lieberman, *Tosefta Ki-fshutah Zera'im, Part I*, 54.

73. TDem. 6:2. If Israelites, or converts, desire to use their grain for food, they must separate the tithe from the produce; Porton, *Goyim*, 189–91. For this reason, an ambiguous situation arises with respect to crops in a field which is jointly owned by an Israelite and a gentile. An anonymous opinion holds that the Israelite separates the tithe before the produce is divided between its owners, while Simeon states that the Israelite separates only the heave-offering. However, if the gentile converted, he must tithe his portion, for he is now obligated to fulfill the Israelite agricultural rules, just like native-born Israelites. The anonymous opinion is that the Israelite separates the tithe from the crop before it is divided between the Israelite and the gentile, because the owners cannot designate their portions of the crop before it has been harvested. Simeon's opinion differs from the anony-

mous text, although the reason behind his ruling is unclear; Sarason, *A History*, 207–10. What is clear is that Simeon considers the converted gentile to be responsible for the Israelite agricultural rules.

74. On the gentiles' obligations concerning the agricultural gifts, see Porton, *Goyim*, 173–203.

75. THal. 1:12. The major discussion in the pericope focuses on when the dough is liable for the offering. All the discussants agree that converts, but not gentiles, are liable for the dough offering. Cf. mHal. 3:6.

76. TBik. 1:2

77. Num. 9:1–14.

78. TPis. 8:4. Moore uses this passage along with Sifré Numbers Beha'alotekha 71; bQid. 70a; and yPes. 8:8, Venice 36b to argue that "the criterion" which defined a convert was his or her ability to celebrate Passover; Moore, *Judaism*, 1:330, n. 4. For Rabbi, the paramount issue is that each Israelite should observe Passover. Because the convert is now an Israelite, he is obligated to observe Passover, even if it is the second one. Thus, he considers the two holidays to be equal. Nathan, on the other hand, holds that the Passover in the second month is secondary, and its observance is limited to those *Israelites who were unable to observe Passover at its regular time*, just as the Torah states. Lieberman discusses the text in Tosefta in light of the later versions in the Babylonian and Palestinian Talmuds and comes to the same conclusion that the issue is whether the second Passover is secondary or a completion of the first; Lieberman, *Tosefta Ki-fshutah Part IV Mo'ed*, 620–21. Thus, because the person was a gentile, and not obligated to observe this central Israelite ritual, during the first month, he is not obligated to observe it during the second month. For the importance of Passover, see Baruch M. Bokser, *The Origins of the Seder: The Passover Rite and Early Rabbinic Judaism* (Berkeley and Los Angeles, 1984). For the importance of Passover as a means of distinguishing between Israelites and non-Israelites, see Porton, *Goyim*, 211–13, 219–20.

79. *'stdrywṭwt*.

80. *Ṣyryn*.

81. TPis. 7:14.

82. Cf. yPes. 8:8, Venice 36b and yNaz. 8:1, Venice 57a. Bamberger claims that "here [is] an ancient report that some of the Roman soldiers stationed around the Temple to preserve order during the holiday period . . . themselves converted to the Jewish faith"; Bamberger, *Proselytism*, 232. He claims that the fact that the conversion is mentioned only "incidentally" and the fact that Dio Cassius reports "the great impression made on the Roman soldiery by Judaism in general and the Temple in particular" support the historicity of this report; Bamberger, *Proselytism*, 232–33. Lieberman holds the same opinion; Lieberman, *Tosefta Ki-fshutah Part IV Mo'ed*, 614–15. McKnight raises the possibility that the immersion was merely a ritual cleansing before the soldiers sought to offer the sacrifice; Scot McKnight, *A Light among the Gentiles: Jewish Missionary Activity in the Second Temple Period* (Minneapolis, 1991), 83. McKnight may well be correct, for neither Mishnah nor Tosefta indicate that immersion is a conversion ritual. Both texts associate the rite only with Passover.

83. TShab. 8:5. Cf. bShab. 68a–b.

84. Porton, *Goyim*, 269–83.

85. See the dispute between Yosi and Judah concerning a converted woman with a flow of blood; tNid. 1:3.

86. TNed. 2:4. Lieberman explains that Israelites is a more general term than converts, so that if one makes a vow concerning the general term all the subsets are included. However, if one makes a vow concerning one of the subsets, the more general category is not included. Lieberman, *The Tosefta Order Nashim: Yebamoth, Ketuboth, Nedarim, Nazir,* 104, note to line 9. Lieberman also makes the point that many claim that mNed. 3:11, [If he said] *"qonam* if I have any benefit from the seed of Abraham"* implies what is specifically stated in tNed. 2:4; Saul Lieberman, *Tosefta Ki-fshutah Part VII Nashim,* 421–22. Cf. Braude, *Jewish Proselyting,* 92.

87. TB.Q. 8:1. Cf. bSanh. 85b. The convert is not mentioned in the parallel discussion in Mekhilta Ishmael Neziqin 5, Horovitz and Rabin, 266.

88. THor. 2:11.

89. THor. 2:13. See Lieberman's discussion, which is based on bHor. 13a and yHor. 3:7, Venice 48b along with variant readings; Saul Lieberman, *Tosefeth Rishonim: A Commentary Based on Manuscripts of the Tosefta and Works of the Rishonim and Midrashim in Manuscripts and rare Editions Part II Seder Nashim Nezikin Kadashim* (Jerusalem, 1939), 202–3. In his translation of this passage, Neusner follows Lieberman's interpretation; Jacob Neusner, *The Tosefta,* 353.

90. TYeb. 6:6.

91. Emil Schürer, *The History of the Jewish People in the Age of Jesus Christ (175 B.C.–A.D. 135),* rev., ed. Geza Vermes, Fergus Millar, Matthew Black (Edinburgh, 1979), 2:105–8.

92. TMiq. 6:3; Lieberman, *Tosefeth Rishonim* IV, 30. Kanter suggests that the two men had to immerse themselves because they experienced genital emissions. Furthermore, he sees this as an anti-Gamaliel tradition, which is revised by Joshua; Shamai Kanter, *Rabban Gamaliel II: The Legal Traditions* (Chico, 1980), 177–78.

93. THag. 3:3; Kanter, 125–26.

94. TGit. 6:4.

95. Ibid.

96. TB.M. 3:25. Cf. mB.M. 4:10, bB.M. 58b, Sifra Behar Pereq 4:2, Weiss, 107d and parallels. Tosefta's comment is based on ISam. 10:12: *But another person there spoke up and said, "And who are their fathers?"*

97. Porton, *Goyim,* 236.

98. Which he had heard in the "vineyard at Yavneh."

99. TYeb. 6:6. Cf. yYeb. 4:11, Venice 6a; yNid. 4:5, Venice 49b; bYeb. 35a. On bKet. 37a, Judah states that only if the woman is more than three years and one day old must she wait the three months. Lieberman suggests that Judah's comment has been contaminated by the mishnah to which it is attached; Lieberman, *Tosefta Ki-fshutah Part VI Order Nashim,* 53.

100. Porton, *Goyim,* sexual matters, *passim.*

101. TKet. 1:3; Porton, *Goyim,* 221–23.

102. TQid. 4:9; Cf. mQid 3:5. On bQid. 62a we are told that because conver-

sion is not totally under the individuals' power, they must have the approval of a rabbinic court, they cannot make conversion a stipulation of marriage. However, this may not be the issue in our text.

103. Porton, *Goyim*, 251–55.

104. This follows the version of tṬoh. 9:7 in the Vienna Manuscript, which must be the correct reading of the passage, as against Zuckermandel's text. See Saul Lieberman, *Tosefeth Rishonim: A Commentary based on Manuscripts of the Tosefta and Works of the Rishonim and Midrashim in Manuscripts and Rare Editions Part IV Mikwaoth—Uktzin* (Jerusalem, 1939), 90.

105. TṬoh. 9:7. Cf. yErub. 9:4; Venice 25d. See Saul Lieberman, *Yerushalmi Ki-fshuto: A Commentary Based on the Manuscripts of the Yerushalmi and the Books of Our Rabbis, the Rishonim, and Midrashim in Manuscripts and Ancient Manuscripts Part I Shabbat, Erubim, Peshim* (Jerusalem, 1934), 353.

106. Bamberger explains the converts' ability to use wine which they had prepared before their conversion as an attempt by the rabbis to ensure that the proselytes would not suffer a loss upon their entrance into the Israelite community; Bamberger, *Proselytism*, 75.

107. Israelites may charge interest only on a loan made to a gentile, and the former may pay interest on a loan made only by the latter. In brief, an Israelite may neither collect nor pay interest on a loan to another Israelite; Lev. 25:35–37, Ex. 22:24, Deut. 23:20–21; Porton, *Goyim*, 229–30. According to Meir, if an Israelite borrowed money from a gentile or if a gentile borrowed money from an Israelite and the gentile converted, no interest may be paid on the loans, regardless if they were made before or after the gentile converted. For Meir, the status of the person when payment is made is the important factor. Yosi holds that if a gentile borrowed money from an Israelite and then converted, he must repay the principal, but he does not need to pay the interest. If an Israelite borrowed money from a gentile who converted, the Israelite must pay interest on the loan if he were liable for it before the gentile converted. Yosi seems to believe that if the gentile knew he would not collect interest after he converted, he would not convert. For Yosi, the convert occupies a special status with regard to loans and the interest he may charge; tB.M. 5:21. The importance of gaining gentile converts seems more important to Yosi than the gentile's adhering to the Torah's law as a native Israelite must. On bB.M. 72a Yosi holds that if a gentile borrowed money from an Israelite, he must pay interest on the loan whether it occurred before or after he converted. This again underscores Yosi's point that converts are not treated like native-born Israelites; however, here Yosi does not deal with the Israelite who borrowed money from a gentile. Yosi's comment may be directed against those who might convert in order not to have to pay the interest on money borrowed from Israelites. Meir does not appear in the Babylonian *gemara*. See Lieberman, *Tosefta Ki-fshutah Part IX Neziqin*, 228–29. On yB.M. 5:7; Venice 10c Yosi states that an Israelite who borrows from a gentile who converted does not have to pay interest on the loan, no matter when it was assumed. A gentile who borrowed money from an Israelite must pay the interest if the loan was made before he converted; if it were made after he converted, he does not need to pay the interest. Although the opinions

attributed to Yosi in the various versions of this passage are not consistent, the view attributed to him in Tosefta makes a clear point, a point not made in the later versions.

108. Cf. Bamberger, *Proselytism*, 105–7. Bamberger's failure to separate the discussions in the amoraic documents from those in the tannaitic collections makes his comments useless for our purposes.

109. The text states that the third generation of Egyptians may enter the congregation of YHWH.

110. TQid. 5:4. Cf. Sifré Deuteronomy Ki Taṣa 253; Finkelstein 279–80.

111. MYad. 4:4.

CHAPTER 4

1. Jacob Neusner, *Judaism: The Evidence of the Mishnah* (Chicago and London, 1981), 168–69.

2. The following is my working definition of midrash: A type of literature, oral or written, which stands in direct relationship to a fixed, canonical text, considered to be authoritative and the revealed word of God by the midrashist and his audience, and in which this canonical text is explicitly cited or clearly alluded to. See Gary G. Porton, "Midrash: Palestinian Jews and the Hebrew Bible in the Greco-Roman Period," in Hildegard Temporini and Wolfgang Haase, eds., *Aufstieg und Niedergang der römischen Welt* (Berlin and New York, 1979), II.19.2, 103–38; Gary G. Porton, "Defining Midrash," in Jacob Neusner, ed., *The Study of Ancient Judaism I: Mishnah, Midrash, Siddur* (New York, 1981), 55–92. Cf. Daniel Boyarin, *Intertexuality and the Reading of Midrash* (Bloomington and Indianapolis, 1990).

3. The midrashic collections do not cover the entire biblical books. Mekhilta is a commentary on Ex. 12:1–23:19, 31:12–17, 35:1–3. Sifra in its present form comments on all of Leviticus. Sifré Numbers begins with Num. 5:1 and omits Num. 13–14 and 16–17. Sifré Deuteronomy is a midrash on Deut. 1:1–30, 3:23–29, 6:4–9, 11:10–26:15, 31:14–32:34.

4. The fact that each midrashic collection exhibits its own agenda which is largely determined by the biblical book around which it is organized is illustrated by studying the sayings attributed to the same sage in each collection. In my investigation of the traditions attributed to Ishmael, I was able to show that each midrash contained its own collection of Ishmael's sayings. See Gary G. Porton, *The Traditions of Rabbi Ishmael Part Two: Exegetical Comments in Tannaitic Collections* (Leiden, 1977); Gary G. Porton, *The Traditions of Rabbi Ishmael Part Four: The Materials as a Whole* (Leiden, 1982), 95–211.

5. For examples from each collection which illustrate their uniqueness, see Gary G. Porton, *Understanding Rabbinic Midrash: Texts and Commentary* (Hoboken, 1985). This work also contains brief discussions on the dates of each collection.

6. See David Hoffmann, *Zur Einleitung in die halachischen Midraschim* (Berlin, 1886–87); Moshe D. Herr, "Sifra," *Encyclopedia Judaica* (Jerusalem, 1972), 14: 1518–19; M. Friedman, *Mekhilta deRabbi Ishmael* (Vienna, 1870), xvii–xix; J. N. Ep-

stein, *Prolegomena ad Litteras Tannaiticas*, ed. E. Z. Melamed (Jerusalem, 1958), 495–747; M. Loeb, *Sifra debe Rav* (Bucharest, 1860), introduction; C.M.H. "Sifra," *Jewish Encyclopedia* (New York, Reprint, n.d.), 2:30; Herman L. Strack, *Introduction to the Talmud and Midrash* (New York, reprint 1965), 201–9; Jacob Z. Lauterbach, "The Two Mekhiltas," *Proceedings of the American Academy of Jewish Research* 4 (1932–33): 113–29; Louis Finkelstein, "The Mekhilta and Its Text," *Proceedings of the American Academy of Jewish Research* 5 (1933–34): 3–54; Hanokh Albeck, *Untersuchungen über die halakhischen Midraschim* (Berlin, 1927); Jacob Z. Lauterbach, *Mekhilta deRabbi Ishmael* (Philadelphia, Reprint 1976); Ben Zion Wacholder, "The Date of the Mekilta de-Rabbi Ishmael," *Hebrew Union College Annual* 39 (1968): 117–44; Moshe D. Herr, "Sifrei," *Encyclopedia Judaica* 14: 605–8; Jacob Neusner, *Sifra in Perspective: The Documentary Comparison of the Midrashim of Ancient Judaism* (Atlanta, 1988); Jacob Neusner, *Sifré to Deuteronomy: An Introduction to the Rhetorical, Logical, and Topical Program* (Atlanta, 1987); H. L. Strack and G. Stemberger, *Introduction to the Talmud and Midrash*, trans. Markus Bockmuehl (Edinburgh, 1991), 254–341.

7. Quoted in Strack and Stemberger, *Introduction*, 287.

8. Ibid., 292.

9. See the comments of Jacob Neusner, *Midrash in Context: Exegesis in Formative Judaism* (Philadelphia, 1983), 108; Strack and Stemberger, *Introduction*, 277–79.

10. Strack and Stemberger, *Introduction*, 279.

11. Ibid., 296–97. Fraade offers the provisional date of the mid third century; Steven D. Fraade, *From Tradition to Commentary: Torah and Its Interpretation in the Midrash Sifre To Deuteronomy* (Albany, 1991), 17, 185–86, n. 56. Hammer states that "the basic work" was edited in the third century; Reuven Hammer, *Sifre: A Tannaitic Commentary on the Book of Deuteronomy* (New Haven and London, 1986), 8.

12. Morton Smith, *Palestinian Parties and Politics That Shaped the Old Testament* (New York and London, 1971), 176–82.

13. Gary G. Porton, *Goyim: Gentiles and Israelites in Mishnah-Tosefta* (Atlanta, 1988), 259–68.

14. Sifra Aḥarei Mot Pereq 10:1; Weiss 84a. The passage is an exegesis of Lev. 17:8–9: *If anyone of the house of Israel or a stranger (gr) who resides (ygwr) among them offers a burnt offering or a sacrifice. . . . The stranger* refers to the converts, and *who resides* refers to the wives of the converts. As the section in Sifra develops, we discover that the obligation to bring offerings to the Temple applies to all offerings and sacrifices, not just to burnt offerings. The same exegetical pattern appears with the exegesis of Lev. 17:11 in Sifra Aḥarei Mot Parashah 8:1; Weiss 84c, and with the exegesis of Lev. 17:13 in Sifra Aḥarei Mot Pereq 11:1; Weiss 84c. The former passage discusses the prohibition against eating blood, and the latter deals with the consumption of the blood of hunted animals.

15. Sifra VaYiqra Parashah 2:3; Weiss 4c. Cf. ySheq. 1:5, Venice 46b, which includes the opening of the passage in Sifra and bḤul. 5a which deals with the apostate, but not with the convert. Lev. 1:21 states that YHWH's commandment was given through Moses to *a man from among you who offers. . . .* Sifra suggests that this parallels the *children of Israel* who also appear in the verse; therefore, *a man*

refers to the convert, for he, like the Israelites, accepts the covenant. *From among you* excludes the apostate. The seemingly repetitious nature of the verse is explained as necessary in order to exclude the Israelite apostates, for they did not accept the covenant, but rejected it. The text goes through a rather long exercise arguing that perhaps the Torah wishes to exclude the convert, for the apostate and the Israelite share the trait that their parents had accepted the covenant, while the convert does not share this with the Israelite. However, this argument is rejected, for both the Israelites and the converts willingly accept the covenant upon themselves.

16. Sifra Ṣaw Parashah 11:3; Weiss 39b. Lev. 7:28–34 deal with the offering of well-being. Again, YHWH instructs Moses to *speak to the children of Israel*. In this case converts and slaves are included by the phrase *who offers* in Lev. 7:29.

17. Sifra Emor Parashah 7:1; Weiss 98a. Lev. 22:17f state: *Any man of the house of Israel or from among the stranger (hgr) in Israel. . . .* The exegesis follows the pattern that we saw above in note 4; however, it does not follow the reading of the biblical text as we have it. The midrash reads: "*Israel*, these are the Israelite[s], *stranger*, these are the converts, *who dwell*, to include the convert's wives; *in Israel* to include women and slaves." In fact, the phrase *who dwell* does not appear in the verse. The exegetical formula has become standard, so that it is employed even when it does not correspond to the biblical text. The Wilna Gaon has corrected the text to read that *Israel* refers to Israelites and *from among the house* refers to the women. Simeon of Shantz, *loc. cit.*, seems to recognize the problem that the midrash does not actually follow the text of the Torah. Cf. Qorban Aaron, *loc. cit.*, who also sees a problem.

18. Sifra VaYiqra Pereq 17:3; Weiss 13c. Lev. 3:7 states that when a person presents a sheep as an offering of well-being to YHWH, he should lay his hand on his offering. Sifra takes this to mean that a person lays his hand only on his offering, but not on his father's offering, another's offering or a convert's offering. The parallel passage on bMen. 93a reads gentile, *gwy*, for convert, *gr*. The appearance of the phrase *the stranger who dwells (hgr hgr) among you* in Lev. 17:8 with reference to the bringing of a burnt offering is taken to refer to the convert and the converts' wives, as is the same phrase in Lev. 17:10 with reference to the prohibition against eating blood. In the latter case, Eleazer b. Simeon takes the word *man* in the verse to refer to the Israelite child of a convert or a slave; Sifra Aḥarei Mot Parashah 8:2; Weiss 84c.

19. On exactly which offerings gentiles could bring to the Temple, see Porton, *Goyim*, 259–68. For the most part, the complex rules concerning sacrifices apply only to Israelites. Gentiles could bring only a few offerings to the Temple, and even then they did not follow the same ritual procedures as the Israelites.

20. Sifra Ḥobah Parashah 1:1; Weiss 15b. This is derived from Lev. 4:1–2. In Lev. 4:1 YHWH commands Moses to speak the following words to the *children of Israel: When a person (npš) unwittingly incurs guilt in regard to any of YHWH's commandments. . . .* The reference to the children of Israel indicates the applicability of this to Israelites, while the reference to a person (*npš*) includes the converts and slaves.

21. Sifra Ṣaw Parashah 4:3; Weiss 33c. The inclusion of the groups other than Israelites probably results from the repetition of *they shall slaughter* in Lev. 7:2: *In the place where they shall slaughter the burnt offering they shall slaughter the guilt offering.*

22. Sifra Aharei Mot Pereq 9:7; Weiss 84a. According to Lev. 17:6, the priest sprinkles the blood for YHWH on the altar. The midrash states that while, following this verse, only the priest may sprinkle the blood on the altar, anyone, including converts, women, or slaves, may sprinkle an offering's blood on a high place. This is part of the highly theoretical discussion of the offerings which can be made on the high places, such as peace offerings and burnt offerings. Cf. mZeb. 14:4–10 and tZeb. 13:1–13:19. In a parallel passage in tZeb. 13:11 we read that women, converts, and freed slaves could make offerings on the high places. Cf. Sifra Aharei Mot Parashah 6:1; Weiss 83c. Here we are told that gentiles may create high places and present offerings there, but converts may not do this. The inclusion of the converts and slaves, along with the Israelites, is based on *and say to them* in Lev. 17:1–2, *YHWH spoke to Moses, saying, speak to Aaron, his sons, and to all the children of Israel and say to them.* Cf. bZeb. 116b where the discussion of the gentile occurs, but not the treatment of the convert and slaves.

23. Sifra Aharei Mot Pereq 10:1; Weiss 84a. In its warning not to bring offerings to a place other than to the entrance of the Tent of Meeting, Lev. 17:8 refers to *any man of the house of Israel or of the strangers who reside among you (wmn hgr hgr btwkm).* Following the pattern common in Sifra, the midrash states that *any man of the house of Israel* refers to the Israelites, *the strangers,* refers to the converts, *who reside,* includes the convert's wives, and *among you,* includes the women and slaves.

24. Porton, *Goyim,* 266.

25. Ibid., 228–29.

26. Sifra Bahuqotai Parashah 3:3; Weiss 112d. Lev. 27:2ff discuss the procedure for collecting for the Temple from one who dedicates a person's worth. The section opens with YHWH instructing Moses to *speak to the children of Israel and say to them.* Although the reference to the Israelites might lead one to think that converts and slaves may not be included in the procedures discussed in this section of the Torah, the phrase *to them,* which appears to be repetitious, includes the converts and the slaves.

27. Jacob Neusner, *The Idea of Purity in Ancient Judaism. The Haskell Lectures, 1972–73* (Leiden, 1973).

28. Porton, *Goyim,* 269–84.

29. Ibid., 282–83.

30. Sifra Zabim Parashah 1:1; Weiss 74d. We learn about Israelites from Lev. 15:1 where YHWH commands Moses and Aaron *speak to the children of Israel;* we learn that converts and slaves are included from the continuation of the verse, *and say to them.* Cf. bShab. 83a, bNid. 24b, mZab. 2:1, and tZab. 2:1.

31. Sifra Maṣorah Parashah 5:1; Weiss 78d. Lev. 15:25f deal with a woman who discharges vaginal blood other than during her period, and the midrash states that these rules apply to any woman, whether a convert, a handmaiden, a freed slave, or an Israelite. Exactly how the midrash reads the text so that it applies to all these

women is unclear; however, it may be based on the particle, *w*, which some took as an inclusive term. On the other hand, the Qorban Aaron, *loc. cit.*, states that the noun *woman* covers all of the females listed in the midrash.

32. Sifra Tazri'a Parashah 1:1; Weiss 57c. Lev. 12:2f deal with the state of impurity a woman experiences after she has borne a child. The midrash includes the converts on the basis of *when a woman (w'šh)*. It appears that the *w* serves as an inclusive particle. The Qorban Aaron, *loc. cit.*, claims that the word *l'mr* refers to Israelites, so that the phrase *children of Israel* is superfluous.

33. Porton, *Goyim*, 205–20.

34. Sifra Emor Parashah 11:1; Weiss 101c. We learn that converts and slaves, along with Israelites, observe the holy convocation from the phrase *you shall observe* in Lev. 23:24: *Speak to the children of Israel thus: In the seventh month, on the first day of the month, you shall observe complete rest, a sacred occasion commemorated with loud blasts.* TR.H. 2:5 states that the converts must hear the *shofar* on Rosh HaShanah.

35. Sifra Aḥarei Mot Pereq 7:9; Weiss 83a. Lev. 16:29 states that on the tenth day of the seventh month Israelites shall practice self-denial and *shall do no manner of work, neither the native-born, nor the stranger who dwells among you (h'zrh whgr hgr btwkkm)*. The midrash explains that *native-born* refers to the native-born, and the definite article includes their wives. Similarly, *stranger* refers to the converts, and the definite article includes their wives. *Among you* refers to the women and slaves. The exegesis follows a familiar pattern. However, it also follows an internal pattern which causes it to be slightly awkward. Because it has included the reference to the wives of the native-born in the definite article, it also includes the convert's wives in the definite article. However, because *hgr* is repeated, the second appearance of the radical *gr* could have referred to the wives. They were connected with the definite article to parallel the previous reference to wives in the *sugya*.

36. Sifra Emor Pereq 15:9; Weiss 103a. Lev. 23:42 states, *You shall live in booths seven days; all the native-born in Israel shall live in booths.* Apparently the midrashist considered this verse to be unnecessarily repetitive, for he taught that *native-born*, referred to the native-born; the definite article excluded the women from being included in the commandment, *all* included the minor children—however, see mSuk. 2:8 which excludes minors from the obligation of residing in the *sukkah*— and *in Israel* included the converts and the freed slaves; cf. bSuk. 27b. On bSuk. 28a the discussion of the convert does not appear.

37. Porton, *Goyim*, 173–203.

38. Sifra Qedoshim Pereq 1:6; Weiss 87b; Sifré Deuteronomy Ki Taṣa 282; Finkelstein, 298. Cf. MPe. 4:6. In fact, Sifra appears to quote Mishnah. The passage cites *when you harvest*, Lev. 19:9, and states "from here they said," which introduces the quotation from Mishnah.

39. Sifra Qedoshim Pereq 3:4; Weiss 88b on Lev. 19:10: *You shall not pick your vineyard bare, or gather the fallen fruit of your vineyard; you shall leave them for the poor and the stranger (gr): I YHWH, am your God.* While it is clear that Lev. 19:10 refers to the convert, for *gr* appears in the text, the text distinguishes between the *gr* and the *gr twšb*. Lev. 19:10 refers to the former on the basis of a quotation from Deut. 26:12–13 which mention the Levite. The argument is that just as the Levite fully

accepts the covenant through circumcision, also the *gr* to which the verse refers fully accepts the covenant through circumcision. The problem with the argument is that Deut. 26:12–13 do not specifically mention the gleaning from the grapes; rather, they mention the tithes. The Qorban Aaron, *loc. cit.*, mentions this fact, but still accepts the midrash's argument. Clearly we have a standard argument, for above we also saw that the text wanted to read *gr* in the Torah as referring to the *gr*, and not to the *gr twšb*. In Sifra Qedoshim Pereq 3:5; Weiss 88b, the Levite, who receives the gifts for the poor, is described as poor and a "son of the covenant," and this is equated with a poor convert who is also "a son of the covenant."

40. Sifra Qedoshim Pereq 8:3; Weiss 91a. Lev. 19:34 states that *the stranger who resides with you shall be to you as one of your native-born,* and this is interpreted to mean that "just as a native-born has accepted all of the words of the Torah, so also a convert is one who has accepted all of the words of the Torah." To this is added a citation of tDem. 2:5 which states that if a convert rejects even one item of the Torah, he is not accepted into the community. Cf. bBekh. 30b which contains the reference to the convert who does not accept even just one word of the Torah. Bamberger claims that this statement is a result of the rise of Christianity which forced the rabbis to stress the halakhic requirements of Judaism; Bernard J. Bamberger, *Proselytism in the Talmudic Period* (New York, 1939), 31–32.

41. Sifra Emor Pereq 19:7; Weiss 104d on Lev. 24:16: *A stranger (gr) or native-born ('zrh), if he has thus pronounced the Name, he shall be put to death.* Cf. Sifra Emor Parashah 14:1; Weiss 104c. Lev. 24:10–13 is the story of a young man with an Israelite mother and an Egyptian father who fights with an Israelite. During the fight, the young man *pronounced the Name in blasphemy.* Eventually he was stoned. The story opens as follows: *There came out among the Israelites one whose mother was an Israelite. . . .* The midrash argues that man was a convert on the basis of *among the Israelites.* However, the text also states that even though there were not *mamzerim* at that time, the child was like a *mamzer.* See Bamberger, *Proselytism,* 192–93.

42. Sifra Qedoshim Parashah 4:1; Weiss 91b. On Molech see Porton, *Goyim,* 248–49, n. 16. Lev. 20:1–6 deal with those who might offer their children to Molech. YHWH commands Moses to tell the Israelites that the laws apply to *any man among the Israelites or among the strangers residing in Israel (wmn hgr hgr byśr'l).* Yosi teaches that *Israel* refers to the Israelites, *stranger* refers to converts, *residing* refers to the converts' wives, and *in Israel* was said to include women and slaves. My edition of Weiss incorrectly marks this as Parashah 10.

43. Sifra Aḥarei Mot Pereq 13:18; Weiss 86c. Lev. 18:26 states *you must keep my laws and my rules, and you must not do any of these abhorrent things, neither the native-born, nor the stranger who resides among you (h'zrh whgr hgr btwkkm).* Following the style that we have seen above, Sifra states that *native-born, 'zrh,* refers to the native-born, *the, h, 'zrh* includes their wives, *stranger, gr,* includes the convert, *the, h, gr* includes their wives, and *among you* includes the women and the slaves among those who must not do the abhorrent things.

44. Sifra VaYiqra Nedabah Pereq 4:10; Weiss 6a. This is connected with Lev. 1:1. The ruling is based on an exegesis of *any sin arising from the holy things* (Ex. 28:38) which is taken to be an inclusive statement; that is, it includes the

holy things of the various classes of Israelite society: Men, women, converts, and slaves.

45. One may charge interest only on a loan given to a gentile; Porton, *Goyim*, 229–30.

46. Sifra BeHar Parashah 5:1; Weiss 109b. This is based on an interpretation of Lev. 25:35–38: *If your kinsman, being in straits, comes under your authority, and you hold him as though a resident alien (gr twšb), let him live by your side: do not exact from him advance or accrued interest, but fear your God. Let him live by your side as your kinsman. Do not lend him money at advance interest, or give him your food at accrued interest. I, YHWH, am your God, who brought you out of the land of Egypt, to give you the land of Canaan, to be your God.* According to the midrash, *gr* refers to a righteous convert, *gr sdq*, and *twšb* refers to a convert, *gr*, who eats impure meat, *nbylh*. The latter is one of the definitions for a *gr twšb;* however, the term is not used here. See note 53 below.

47. Sifra BeHar Pereq 4:2; Weiss 107d. The admonition not to *wrong one another,* Lev. 25:17, is taken to mean that one should not remind converts that their parents were idolaters. See also Sifra Qedoshim Pereq 8:2; Weiss 91a where the same ruling is connected to *you shall not wrong him* in Lev. 19:33. Cf. bB.M. 58b; Mekhilta Ishmael Mishpatim 18 on Ex. 22:20, Horovitz and Rabin 311, l. 11–312, l. 18; mB.M. 4:10, tB.M. 3:25.

48. Sifra Qedoshim Pereq 8:4; Weiss 91a. The command to *love the stranger (gr) as yourself,* Lev. 19:34, is taken as a parallel to Lev. 19:18, *you shall love your neighbor as yourself,* and the former statement is connected to the fact that the Israelites were strangers in the land of Egypt. Because the Israelites were strangers (*gerim*) in Egypt, they should know the soul of one who is a convert. Cf. Bamberger, *Proselytism*, 158–59.

49. Lev. 13:24.

50. Sifra Tazri'a Pereq 7:4, Weiss 65a. MNeg. 9:1 parallels the part of the text which discusses a burn caused by any type of fire; cf. bPes. 75a–b and bHul. 8a. The latter does not exegete Lev. 13:24, and neither passage in the Talmud specifically mentions the convert.

51. Sifra Tazri'a Nega'im Pereq 1:1, Weiss 59d–60a. Cf. mNeg. 7:1 and tNeg. 2:14–15. The ruling is based on juxtaposing Lev. 13:1–2 with Lev. 13:38.

52. Sifra Tazri'a Pereq 6:6, Weiss 64c; cf. mNeg. 9:1.

53. Sifra Aharei Mot Pereq 12:1; Weiss 84d on Lev. 17:15: *Any person, whether a citizen ('zrh) or a stranger (gr), who eats what has died or has been torn by beasts, shall wash his clothes, bathe in water, and remain unclean until evening; then he shall be clean.* The midrash differentiates between the full convert, *gr,* and the resident alien, the *gr twšb.* Scholars claim that the full convert is distinguished from the resident alien, the *gr twšb,* by the fact that the former has accepted the full obligations of the Israelite community and has undergone the rituals involved with a formal conversion. Because the text also mentions the native, the midrashist states that just as the native has fully accepted the covenant so also the *gr* to whom the text refers is the convert who has also accepted the covenant. On the *gr twšb,* see George

F. Moore, *Judaism in the First Centuries of the Christian Era: The Age of the Tannaim* (Cambridge, Reprint 1966), 1:338–41; S. Bialoblocki, *Die Beziehungen des Judentums zu Proselyten und Proselytentum* (Berlin, 1930), 4–11; Emil Schürer, *The History of the Jewish People in the Age of Jesus Christ (175 B.C.–A.D. 135)*, rev. and ed. Geza Vermes, Fergus Millar, Martin Goodman (Edinburgh, 1973–87), III, 1, 171–72.

54. Sifra Qedoshim Pereq 9:9; Weiss 92a. Aqiba's response is based on Lev. 20:9: *If any man repudiates his father or his mother, he shall be put to death.* His argument is that if one is liable for cursing his father, he is culpable for cursing his mother. On the other hand, if one is not liable for cursing his father, he is not liable for cursing his mother. However, the *sugya* ends by stating that Aqiba agreed that a *shetuqi* is liable for cursing his mother even though he is not liable for cursing his father. In brief, the last line of the passage points to Aqiba's inconsistency, and perhaps suggests that his refutation of Yosi's opinion should be rejected. Cf. yYeb. 11:2; Venice 11d.

55. *[Only a virgin of his own kin may he* [the priest] *take to wife]—that he may not profane his offspring among his kin, for I, YHWH, have sanctified him.*

56. MQid. 4:6.

57. Sifra Emor Pereq 2:9; Weiss 95a. Sifra quotes the end of Lev. 21:15, *For I, YHWH, have sanctified him*, in support of Judah's comment. Cf. tQid. 5:3, mBik. 1:5, bQid. 74b, bYeb. 57a.

58. Sifra Aharei Mot Pereq 12:11; Weiss 85b. A question arose concerning whether or not a bird which was killed by pinching its neck in the Temple should render unclean any clothing in its gullet. The text argues that because Lev. 17:15–16 deal with animals which have died a natural death or been torn apart by a beast, this excludes the bird whose neck was pinched within the Temple's precincts. "Others" respond that because Lev. 17:15–16 speak of things with regard to which the native-born and the convert are equal, the bird pinched at the neck is excluded, for such a bird is permitted only to priests, and converts cannot be priests. Therefore, the bird is a matter about which the convert and the native are not equal, as Lev. 17:15–16 specifically state they should be.

59. Sifra Saw Pereq 9:1; Weiss 33d on Lev. 7:8: *The priest who offers a man's burnt offering shall keep the skin of the burnt offering that he offered.* Cf. bZeb. 103a. Judah teaches that this excludes the skin of an offering which was dedicated to the sanctuary, and Yosi b. Judah states that it excludes a convert's offering. An anonymous opinion rejects Yosi's reasoning and claims that the phrase *skin of the burnt offering* refers to the convert, while the phrase *a man's burnt offering* refers to an offering which was not slaughtered in the proper place. Exactly why the skin from a convert's sacrifice is prohibited to the priest is unclear. Simai b. Hilkai states, bZeb. 103a, that this refers to a proselyte who died without heirs, but again whether this is the case or not in the disagreement is not clear. There is no hint of this issue in Sifra.

60. Sifra VaYiqra Nedabah Pereq 11:2; Weiss 10c. This is based on interpreting Lev. 2:3, *And the remainder of the meal offering shall be for Aaron and his sons, a most holy portion from YHWH's offerings by fire*, in terms of Num. 15:13, *Every native-born*

(kl h'zrh), when presenting an offering by fire of pleasing odor to YHWH. . . . The "native-born" in the latter verse is read into the former one. The verses are joined by the phrase "offerings of fire."

61. Sifra Qedoshim Pereq 8:1; Weiss 91a. Neusner suggests that this becomes an important issue when the person claiming to be a convert wishes to marry an Israelite; Jacob Neusner, *Sifra: An Analytical Translation* (Atlanta, 1988), 3:128. This discussion is based on Lev. 19:33: *When a stranger resides with you in your land you shall not wrong him.* The comment on this verse begins with accepting a person's statement that he or she is a convert. However, the text continues that one should not accept a person as a convert unless he or she is well-known in the area. This is derived from the phrase *with you.* If he or she is not well-known, he or she should bring witnesses to testify to his or her conversion, and this is derived from *when a stranger resides.* One might conclude from the phrase *in your land* that the rule to bring witnesses applies only to events which occur in the Land of Israel; however, the phrase *with you* means that this applies anywhere that Israelites reside. The phrase *in your land* is also taken to mean that within the Land of Israel one must bring proof of conversion, while outside of the Land one need not bring proof. Cf. bYeb. 46b–47a where part of the *sugya* is attributed to Judah.

62. Sifra VaYiqra Parashah 4:2–3; Weiss 19a; cf. mHor 1:4 and yHor 1:4; Venice 46a. The actual reason that the midrash gives for their not being able to administrate in the judicial system is that they are not considered fit as authorized teachers, *lhwryh.*

63. Sifra Emor Pereq 1:7; Weiss 94b. Cf. mYeb. 6:5; bYeb. 61b; yQid. 4:1, Venice 65b; Bamberger, *Proselytism,* 83–84.

64. Porton, *Goyim,* 236.

65. This is based on Ex. 12:49: *There shall be one law for the citizen and for the stranger (gr) who dwells (ygwr) among you.*

66. Mekhilta Ishmael Bo, 15; Horovitz and Rabin, 56, ll. 8–9. Cf. Sifré Numbers Beha'alotekha 71, Horovitz, 67, ll. 6–7.

67. Num. 9:1–14.

68. Mekhilta Ishmael Bo, 15; Horovitz and Rabin 56, ll. 9–11. Cf. Sifré Numbers Beha'alotekha 71, Horovitz, 67, ll. 7–9. This corresponds to Nathan's opinion in tPis. 8:4. On bPes. 93a Rabbi holds that converts should observe the second Passover, while Nathan holds that they should not. In several comments on Ex. 12:49, Mekhilta repeats the point that the convert and the native-born Israelite are equal; cf. Mekhilta Ishmael Bo 15 on Ex. 12:49; Horovitz and Rabin 57, ll. 6–9 which is paralleled in Sifré Numbers Beha'alotekha 71, Horovitz, 67, ll. 10–12. The midrash asks why Ex. 12:49 states that there should be one law for the native and the convert, given that Ex. 12:48 noted that the convert *shall be like the native-born.* The conclusion is that Ex. 12:48 equates the convert and the native with regard to Passover, while Ex. 12:49 equates the two with reference to all of the laws in the Torah. Despite this fact, the midrash also notes that in Ex. 12:19 the convert is specifically mentioned with regard to the prohibition against possessing leaven during Passover, and there the text states that the Torah specifically mentions the convert whenever it discusses something which is obligatory for Isra-

elites; Mekhilta Ishmael Bo 10 on Ex. 12:19; Horovitz and Rabin, 35, ll. 3–4. Cf. Sifré Numbers Shelaḥ 111 on Num. 15:29, Horovitz, 118, ll. 5–7. This seeming contradiction is a result of the language of the Hebrew Bible. The midrashists had to deal with the biblical text they had before them, so that they had to explain why the convert is specifically mentioned in Ex. 12:19. This verse is taken to mean that the convert and the native-born Israelite are equal with regard to all of the laws in the Torah.

69. Ex. 12:48: *If a stranger who dwells with you (wky ygwr 'tk gr) would offer the Passover to YHWH, all his males must be circumcised; then he shall be admitted to offer it; he shall then be as a citizen ('zrḥ) of the country. But no uncircumcised person may eat of it. There shall be one law for the citizen ('zrḥ) and for the stranger who dwells among you (wlgr hgr btwkkm).*

70. Mekhilta Ishmael Bo 15, Horovitz and Rabin, 57, ll. 6–10.

71. Mekhilta Ishmael Mishpatim 1 on Ex. 21:2; Horovitz and Rabin 248, ll. 1–4. Ex. 21:2 states that a Hebrew slave may serve an Israelite for only six years. Ishmael argues that from this verse we learn that converts who become slaves are treated like Hebrew slaves. Eliezer responds that we do not need to learn that converts who are slaves are equal to Hebrew slaves from a specific verse because we can derive this rule by the use of human reason. It appears that the creator of this pericope wishes to demonstrate that the rule stipulating that a convert may be a slave for only six years is actually a biblical precept, and not one derived merely by reason. There is some confusion in later versions concerning which statement should be attributed to Ishmael, see Me'ir 'Ayin, *loc. cit.*, but these appear to be later corruptions of this text. Cf. bB.M. 71a where some hold that a convert may not sell himself as a Hebrew slave.

72. Mekhilta Ishmael Mishpatim 11; Horovitz and Rabin, 287, ll. 1–2. Ex. 21:28–32 discuss the penalty applied to an ox which gores a person, and its owner. Among the ox's victims the text specifically mentions a man, a woman, a male minor, and a female minor. The midrash states that the text refers to Israelite victims, and it asks the basis for applying the rules if the victim were a convert. The phrase *shall be dealt with according to this law* (Ex. 21:31) is taken to include the convert. By doing this, the text makes it clear that the convert is a full Israelite, for the Israelite laws of damages apply differently to gentiles and to Israelites, so that the application of the same rules to converts and Israelites disconnects the converts from their gentile background; see Porton, *Goyim,* 225.

73. Mekhilta Ishmael Mishpatim 18 on Ex. 22:20; Horovitz and Rabin 311, ll. 3–5. The verse reads: *You shall not wrong a convert (gr) or oppress him, for you were strangers (grym) in the land of Egypt.* Nathan states that this verse teaches the general lesson that one should not charge a person with the failings that one has himself or herself. The implication of the verse is that the Israelites' experience in Egypt parallels the converts' experience when they enter into the Israelite community. For similar ideas see Sifra BeHar Pereq 4:2, Weiss 107d; Sifra Qedoshim Pereq 8:2, Weiss 91a; bB.M. 58b; mB.M. 4:10; tB.M. 3:25.

74. *You shall not oppress a convert (gr), for you know the feelings of the convert (npš hgr), having yourselves been strangers (grym) in the land of Egypt.*

75. *You too must befriend the convert (hgr), for you were strangers (grym) in the land of Egypt.*

76. Lev. 25:55: *For it is to me that the Israelites are servants; they are my servants whom I freed from the Land of Egypt, I, YHWH, your God.*

77. Isa. 56:6: *As for the foreigners who attach themselves to YHWH to minister to him, and to love the name of YHWH to be his servants. . . .*

78. Isa. 61:6: *While you shall be called "Priests of YHWH," and termed "Servants of our God"* . . . and Isa. 56:6.

79. Isa. 41:8: *But you, Israel, my servant, Jacob, whom I have chosen, seed of Abraham my friend* and Deut. 10:18: *[For YHWH, your God,] . . . upholds the cause of the fatherless and the widow, and befriends the convert (gr). . . .*

80. Gen. 17:13: *Thus my covenant will be marked in your flesh as an everlasting pact* and Isa. 56:4: *As for the eunuchs who keep my sabbaths . . . and hold fast to my covenant. . . .*

81. Ex. 28:38: *[And it shall be on Aaron's forehead] . . . to win acceptance for them before YHWH* and Isa. 56:7: *Their burnt offerings and sacrifices shall be acceptable on my altar. . . .*

82. Ps. 121:4: *See: the guardian of Israel neither slumbers nor sleeps!* and Ps. 146:9: *YHWH guards the converts (grym).*

83. Gen. 23:4: *"I am a resident alien (gr twšb) among you . . . .*

84. Ps. 119:19: *I am only a sojourner (gr) in the land . . .*, IChron. 29:15: *For we are sojourners (grym) with you*, and Ps. 39:13: *I am an alien (gr), resident with you.*

85. Mekhilta Ishmael Mishpatim 18 on Ex. 22:20; Horovitz and Rabin 311, l. 11–312, l. 18. The midrash claims that if Abraham would have been circumcised earlier in his life, converts could have been circumcised only at a younger age, so that there would have been a shorter time for the converts to join the Israelites. Because YHWH wanted to give gentiles every possibility to become Israelites, he allowed them to convert as late in life as possible. For a collection of similar discussions in later material, see Bamberger, *Proselytism*, 154–56.

86. Mekhilta Ishmael Mishpatim 20 on Ex. 23:19; Horovitz and Rabin, 335, ll. 9–11 and notes. Ex. 23:19 states that *the choice fruits of your soil you shall bring to the house of YHWH* your *God*. According to the midrash, this excludes the converts and slaves, for *your* God refers only to Israelites. The relationship of the gentiles to the Israelite agricultural rules was rather complex, for they were obligated to fulfill some of them, but not others. The requirement to bring the first fruits seems not to have been mandatory for gentiles; see Porton, *Goyim*, 173–203. According to mBik. 1:4, converts may bring the first fruits; however, they may not recite the avowal, *which YHWH swore to our fathers to give us*, Deut. 26:3, unless their mother were an Israelite. The final opinion in Mekhilta agrees with Mishnah, but the former does not contain the requirement about the convert's mother. In Mishnah, the issue is that the Patriarchs are called *our father*, while in Mekhilta, the key factor is that YHWH is identified as *your* God. Given the opening of the passage in Mekhilta, there may have been some ambiguity concerning the right of a convert to bring the first fruits. In Sifré Deuteronomy Ki Tabo 299, Finkelstein, 318,

ll. 3–4, we find that the converts are excluded from the rite of the first fruit. The comment is on Deut. 26:3.

87. Mekhilta Ishmael Mishpatim 18 on Ex. 22:20; Horovitz and Rabin 311, ll. 8–9. On this passage and a collection of sayings attributed to Simeon b. Yohai, see Ephraim E. Urbach, *The Sages: Their Concepts and Beliefs*, trans. by Israel Abrahams (Cambridge and London, 1987), 549–50. Cf. bB.M. 59b.

88. Mekhilta Ishmael Mishpatim 20 on Ex. 23:4; Horovitz and Rabin, 324, ll. 5–6. Braude suggests that Eliezer is not really negative toward the converts. Rather, "he believes that the proselyte is equal but not superior to the born Jew"; William G. Braude, *Jewish Proselyting in the First Five Centuries of the Common Era: The Age of the Tannaim and Amoraim* (Providence, 1940), 39.

89. Mekhilta Ishmael BaHodesh/Yitro, 1; Horovitz and Rabin, 205, ll. 16–19.

90. IISam. 1:13.

91. IISam. 1:16. Eliezer sees this as related to the statement in Ex. 17:16: *YHWH will be at war with Amalek throughout the generations.* Mekhilta Ishmael Amalek/BeShalah 5:2 on Ex. 17:16; Horovitz and Rabin, 186, l. 17–187, l. 5. McKnight suggests that this text is one which reflects "social dissonance: some Jews were prone to accept proselytes while others were not"; Scot McKnight, *A Light among the Gentiles: Jewish Missionary Activity in the Second Temple Period* (Minneapolis, 1991), 42.

92. MYad. 4:4.

93. TQid. 5:4.

94. Elimelech Epstein Halevy, "Amalekites in the Aggadah," Cecil Roth and Geoffrey Wigoder, eds., *Encyclopaedia Judaica* (Jerusalem, 1972), 2:791.

95. On Jethro as a convert, see Bamberger, *Proselytism*, 182–91. Weil accepts the fact that Jethro was a convert; Isaac Weil, *Le Prosélytisme chez les juifs selon la bible et le talmud* (Strasbourg, 1880), 15.

96. Mekhilta Ishmael Amalek/Yitro 1:1 on Ex. 18:7; Horovitz and Rabin 193, ll. 5–6. Eliezer's comment is based on Ex. 18:7: *And he said to Moses, I.* In the Torah this is attributed to Jethro; however, the midrashist attributes these words to God and joins it to Jer. 23:23, *"Am I only a God near at hand,"—says YHWH,* on the basis of the pronoun I. This forced exegesis suggests that the midrashist wanted to make the point that converts should be welcomed into the Israelite community and merely sought to find a way to support his argument. The attempts that some medieval collections made to solve this problem by connecting the exegetical comment to another verse do not suffice; see notes on Horovitz and Rabin 193, l. 5. Braude takes this passage as proof that despite his comments elsewhere, Eliezer supported the conversion of gentiles *as long as* they converted for the proper reason, so that the motives of the converts had to be carefully examined; Braude, *Jewish Proselyting*, 39–41, especially 41.

97. Mekhilta Ishmael Amalek/Yitro 2 on Ex. 18:25 Horovitz and Rabin 199, l. 16–200, l. 4. Moses comments to Jethro on the good advice the latter has given and on the fact that YHWH agreed with the advice. Moses asks Jethro to stay, but Jethro responds that he is a mere candle in the presence of the sun and the moon;

therefore, he can spread his light only among his own people, for they do not have the benefit of Moses and Aaron to lead them to YHWH.

98. Mekhilta Ishmael Amalek/Yitro 1; Horovitz and Rabin, 189, ll., 7–10. Jether (*ytr*) means that he caused a chapter to be added (*hwtyr*) to the Torah. He was called Jethro (*ytrw*) because he abounded (*šyytyr*) in good deeds. Hobab (*ḥwbb*) marks the fact that he was one of God's loved ones (*ḥbyb*). Reuel (*r'w'l*) signifies that he was like God's friend (*kry'*). Heber (*ḥbr*) signifies that he was like God's companion (*kḥbr*). He was called Putiel (*pwty'l*) because he freed himself (*nptr*) from idolatry. The name Keni (*qny*) signifies the fact that Jethro was zealous (*qn'*) for God and the Torah. Cf. Sifré Numbers Beha'alotekha 78, Horovitz 72, ll. 5ff., where this idea is greatly expanded and the comments are attributed to a variety of sages.

99. Josh. 2:1–24. On Rahab see Bamberger, *Proselytism*, 193–95. See also the extensive discussion by Judith Baskin, "The Rabbinic Transformations of Rahab the Harlot," *Notre Dame English Journal* 11, no. 2 (1978–79), 141–57 and the literature cited there. Baskin suggests that "perhaps, her chief attractions [for being described as a convert] were the possibilities she offered the rabbis as a model of the repentant fallen woman who finds the true God and emerges as a mother of Israel. In a Jewish setting apparently anxious for female figures of conversion and repentance, Rahab assumed a special importance which justified a broad reading of the biblical evidence," 143.

100. Mekhilta Ishmael Amalek/Yitro 1, Horovitz and Rabin, 188, l. 12–189, l. 6 on Ex. 18:1 and notes. Mekhilta attributes the following to Rahab: "Lord of the World, by three things I sinned, by three things forgive me, the cord, the window, the wall, for it is said: *She let them down by a rope through the window—for her dwelling was at the outer side of the city wall and she lived in the actual wall* (Josh. 2:15). Some versions state that she sinned with regard to the menstrual laws, the dough offering, and the lighting of the Sabbath candles, while other versions suggest that these were things through which she was to be forgiven. In any event, these are listed only in the first printed edition of the Mekhilta, not in the manuscripts. It is possible, however, that they were in the text used by Rashi. It seems that the cord, window, and wall should be the things that earned her forgiveness, not caused her sin. On Rahab see Sifré Numbers Beha'alotekha 78, Horovitz, 73, l. 19–74, l. 8

101. See chap. 11.

102. Sifré Numbers Shelaḥ 108; Horovitz 112, ll. 2–4. Cf. tSheq. 3:21 which states that converts can bring offerings from cattle and that the only reason that birds were specified was because they were relatively inexpensive. Cf. bKer. 8b–9a. On bKer. 9a the text revolves around *as you do, so shall he do* instead of *for you*.

103. Gen. 17.

104. The references to immersion and an offering are indirect. Ex. 24:8 states that *Moses took the blood and dashed it on the people and said, "This is the blood of the covenant that YHWH now makes with you concerning all these commandments."* The commentators, Rabbenu Hillel, *loc. cit.*, and Toledot Adam, *loc. cit.*, state

that immersion and an offering must accompany the sprinkling of the blood on the people.

105. Sifré Numbers Shelaḥ 108; Horovitz 112, ll. 5–6. Cf. bKer. 9a, mKer. 2:1, tKer. 1:12 and its parallel in tSheq. 3:21.

106. Sifré Numbers Shelaḥ 115; Horovitz 128, l. 16–129, l. 11. Cf. bMen. 44a. See Baskin's point that the discussion of Rahab was designed to demonstrate that prostitutes could become worthy converts. Baskin writes, "That a proselyte and former prostitute could achieve such a name for herself in the annals of Jewish history is proof to all that a sincere return to God will work salvation, no matter how great previous sins"; 144. The same could be said about the current story.

107. Sifré Numbers Shelaḥ 109, Horovitz 112, ll. 15–16. Num. 15:14–16 state that with regard to an offering by fire, the same law applies to Israelites and strangers who dwell with them, *wlgr hgr*. The midrash takes this as a references to converts. However, it also states that the reference to the convert was needed, for when the Bible states a law which is incumbent upon Israelites, it must also explicitly refer to the converts. The implication is that unless the converts are specifically mentioned, the laws in the Torah need not necessarily apply to them. However, another passages takes the repetition of the reference to the *gr* in Num. 15:15—the Hebrew root *gr* appears seven times in Num. 15:14–16—to mean that the convert and the native-born Israelite, *'zrḥ*, are equal with regard to every commandment which is stated in the Torah; Sifré Numbers Shelaḥ 109; Horovitz 113, ll. 2–3. The comment occurs several times in this section. The phrase *just as you shall do, thus he shall do* in Num. 15:14 confirms the fact that the convert and the Israelites are to do exactly the same thing with regard to the offerings which are mentioned.

108. Sifré Numbers Shelaḥ 108; Horovitz 112, ll. 11–14.

109. Sifré Numbers Shelaḥ 111; Horovitz 118, ll. 5–13. Num. 15:24–26 discuss the community offering which must be brought if the whole community commits an unwitting sin, and Num. 15:26 specifically notes that *the whole congregation of Israel and the stranger who dwells (wlgr hgr) in your midst* are forgiven. The midrash again notes that the converts had to be specifically mentioned, for unless they are specifically mentioned, the rules in the Torah do not apply to them. However, the anointed priest, not the convert, is the major topic of this passage.

110. Sifré Numbers Beha'alotekha 71; Horovitz, 67, ll. 10–12. The exact same wording appears in Sifré Numbers Shelaḥ 109; Horovitz 113, ll. 2–3 without reference to Passover. The former passage is preceded by a *sugya* which is paralleled in Mekhilta Ishmael Bo, 15; Horovitz and Rabin 56, ll. 9–11. The passage notes that converts may not offer the Passover sacrifice immediately upon their conversion, but must wait until the 14th of Nisan. In addition, it contains Simeon b. Eleazar's statement that only one who was permitted to celebrate the first Passover may celebrate the second Passover. Moore, *Judaism*, 1:330, n. 4, uses this passage along with tPis. 8:4; yPes. 8:8, Venice 36b; and bQid. 70a to argue that "the criterion" that defined a convert was his or her ability to celebrate Passover.

111. Sifré Numbers Shelaḥ 124; Horovitz, 159, ll. 15–16. Num. 19:1–20 state

that the person must wash his clothes and be considered unclean until evening; Num. 19:10 refers to the *children of Israel and the convert who dwells (lgr hgr) among you.*

112. Sifré Numbers Naśo 39; Horovitz, 43, ll. 10–11 on Num. 6:22; however, the reference to the convert is based on Num. 6:27. See Sifré Numbers Naśo 43; Horovitz, 49, ll. 1–3 on Num. 6:27. Cf. bSoṭ. 38a. Num. 6:22–27 contain the priestly benediction, the blessing with which Aaron and his sons were to bless the children of Israel. The midrash explains that the converts, women, and slaves are included in the blessing because Num. 6:27 contains the phrase *I will bless them,* and *them* includes the converts, women, and slaves.

113. Sifré Numbers Shelaḥ 109; Horovitz 112, l. 16–113, l. 2. Num. 15:15 ends with the phrase *you and the convert (hgr) shall be alike before YHWH.* The midrash draws attention to Ex. 38:38 which mentions the *frontlet of pure gold* which the high priest wore on his forehead in order *to win acceptance for them before YHWH.* Unless Num. 15:15 told us that the converts and the Israelites were to be the same before YHWH, we would not know it. In another place, the midrash claims that when something is said to Israelites concerning a commandment which everyone is required to perform, the converts are included among the Israelites to whom Moses is commanded to speak; Sifré Numbers Naśo 39; Horovitz, 42, ll. 9–12.

114. The implication of the wording of the Midrash's question is that converts are not subject to these offerings.

115. Cf. tSheq. 3:21 and tKer. 1:12.

116. Sifré Numbers Shelaḥ 108; Horovitz 112, ll. 6–11. Cf. bKer. 8b–9a.

117. In its context, Num. 10:29 is taken to mean that the Israelites were traveling to the Land which YHWH had promised to them alone. This is made clear by the fact that Moses invites his father-in-law to join the Israelites and that he promises him that the Israelites will treat him well.

118. Ezek. 47:21–23 state: *[This land you shall divide for yourselves among the tribes of Israel. You shall allot it as a heritage for yourselves and for the strangers who reside among you (wlhgrym hgrym btwkkm), who have begotten children among you. You shall treat them as Israelite citizens; they shall receive allotments along with you among the tribes of Israel.] You shall give the stranger (gr) an allotment within the tribe where he resides— declares YHWH, God.*

119. Sifré Numbers Beha'alotekha 78; Horovitz, 75, ll. 20–24. Bamberger, *Proselytism,* 65, claims that this is a "purely theoretical discussion," as if much of the other material is not!

120. Num. 26:55.

121. Sifré Numbers Qoraḥ 119; Horovitz, 142, ll. 8–13. Cf. Sifré Numbers Pinḥas 132; Horovitz, 174, ll. 1–5.

122. On the problem of gentiles owning portions of the Land of Israel, see Daniel Sperber, *Roman Palestine, 200–400: The Land* (Ramat-Gan, 1978), 160–76.

123. Sifré Numbers Masei 160; Horovitz 216, ll. 15–18. The meaning of the text is uncertain. The Wilna Gaon moves the discussion to a comparison between an Israelite and a resident alien, thus eliminating the problem of the convert, for

the resident alien was one who did not fully accept Judaism. This would follow the discussion in mMak. 2:3 and bMak. 9a. See the notes in Horovitz, 216, l. 17.

124. Sifré Numbers Masei 160, Horovitz, 219, ll. 18–19. The Wilna Gaon prefers *the convert shall be as the native-born* or *there shall be one law for you*. See Horovitz's note, p. 219, l. 19.

125. Sifré Numbers Naśo 7; Horovitz, 11, ll. 2–4. Cf. mEd. 5:6; ySot. 2:5, Venice 18b; bBer. 19a.

126. MB.Q. 9:11.

127. Num. 5:8.

128. Sifré Numbers Naśo 4; Horovitz 7, ll. 1–3. Cf. Sifré Numbers Naśo 2; Horovitz, 4, ll. 24–29 where Ishmael does not appear. The latter *sugya* is an interpretation of Num. 5:5, *And YHWH spoke to Moses saying, speak to the children of Israel, a man or a woman who commits any of the sins of humans . . .*, and Lev. 5:20–25, *When a person sins and commits a trespass against YHWH by dealing deceitfully with his fellow in the matter of a deposit or an investment, or through robbery; or if he has intimidated his fellow or if he has found something lost and lied about it and sworn falsely—any one of the various things one may do and sin thereby—when one has thus sinned and, realizing his guilt, would restore that which he got through robbery or intimidation, or the deposit that was entrusted to him, or the lost thing that he found, or anything about which he swore falsely, he shall repay the principal amount and add a fifth part to it. He shall pay it to its owner when he realizes his guilt. Then he shall bring to the priest, as his penalty to YHWH a ram without blemish from the flock, or the equivalent, as a guilt offering.* Even though Lev. 5:20ff. set forth the rules concerning what one who has stolen something and lied about must do, it does not specifically mention stealing from a convert. Therefore, we needed Num. 5:5f. to prohibit stealing from a convert. Interestingly, at this point we do not find a reference to Num. 5:6–8 which mention what one does if he steals from one who does not have a valid kinsman, the verse which elsewhere is cited as the basis for the matters spoken of here. Cf. bB.Q. 109a; mB.Q. 9:11; tB.Q. 10:16; yB.Q. 9:15, Venice 7a.

129. Sifré Numbers Naśo 2; Horovitz, 5, ll. 21–24.

130. Sifré Numbers Shelaḥ 117; Horovitz 135, ll. 15–16.

131. Num. 10:31. In the Torah Jethro is named as Hobab the son of Reuel the Midianite, Moses' father-in-law. The midrash refers to him as Jethro.

132. Sifré Numbers Beha'alotekha 80; Horovitz, 76, ll. 11–19.

133. Deut. 10:19.

134. Ex. 23:9.

135. Ex. 22:20. Sifré Numbers Beha'alotekha 80; Horovitz, 77, ll. 7–8. Num. 10:29 notes that YHWH spoke good things to Israel. However, because YHWH had spoken other good things to Israel, the midrash asks the meaning of this verse. It concludes that here YHWH commanded the Israelites to be good to the converts and to treat them kindly; Sifré Numbers Beha'alotekha 78; Horovitz, 76, ll. 4–6.

136. Sifré Numbers Beha'alotekha 78; Horovitz 72, ll. 5–14. Cf. Mekhilta Ishmael Amalek/Yitro 1; Horovitz and Rabin, 189; ll. 7–10.

137. Sifré Numbers Beha'alotekha 78, Horovitz 73, ll. 5–18.

138. Sifré Numbers Beha'alotekha 78; Horovitz, 73, l. 19–74, l. 8. See also Baskin's discussion of Rahab.

139. Sifré Numbers Beha'alotekha 85; Horovitz, 85, ll. 9–10.

140. There were others who identified the rabble as the elders. Sifré Numbers Beha'alotekha 86; Horovitz, 86, ll. 6–7. Cf. Leviticus Rabbah 27:8, Margulies, 641, where we are told that the converts who came out of Egypt with the Israelites were the ones who made the golden calf. There the converts are identified with the mixed multitude, 'rb rb, mentioned in Ex. 12:38.

141. Sifré Numbers Maṭot 157; Horovitz 212, ll. 8–10. He based himself on Num. 31:18 where the Israelites are told that they may spare any of the young Midianite girls who have not engaged in sexual activity. Cf. bQid. 74b, 78a, bYeb. 60b.

142. Sifré Deuteronomy Ve'etḥanan 32; Finkelstein, 54, ll. 13–16. Gen. 12:5 has the curious phrase that Abraham *made* souls in Haran. The midrash notes that even if all humankind joined together they could not create a mosquito. For this reason, the verse is read to mean that Abraham made converts to Judaism in Haran, and this is seen as a result of his love of YHWH. Therefore, Deut. 6:5, *you shall love YHWH your God*, is taken to mean that Israelites should seek converts as an expression of their love of YHWH. Cf. Genesis Rabbah Lekh Lekha 39:14; Theodor and Albeck, *Midrash Bereshit Rabba*, 378–79 and Genesis Rabbah VaYeshev 84:5; Theodor and Albeck, 1004, where this is attributed to Eleazar in the name of Yosi b. Zimra. For other parallel passages, see Finkelstein, 54–55, note to l. 14.

143. Sifré Deuteronomy VeZot 354; Finkelstein, 416, ll. 3–9. This account is connected to Deut. 33:19, *they shall call peoples to their mountain, there they shall offer sacrifices of righteousness*. Cf. Genesis Rabbah VaYehi 98:12; Theodor and Albeck 1263. Braude, *Jewish Proselyting*, 35; Bamberger, *Proselytism*, 157–58.

144. Sifré Deuteronomy Ki Taṣa 281; Finkelstein, 297, l. 16–298, l. 3. If an Israelite does not treat a convert justly in legal matters, the former transgresses two negative commandments, one stated in Deut. 24:17, *You shall not pervert the justice due to a convert (gr)*, and one found in Deut. 16:19, *You shall not pervert justice, nor shall you show favoritism*. If the converts were orphans, and an Israelite did not deal with them properly in legal matters, the latter transgresses a third negative commandment, for Deut. 24:17 also states that one should not pervert justice concerning an orphan. Similarly, see Sifré Deuteronomy Ki Taṣa 278; Finkelstein, 296, ll. 6–8 where the wording of Deut. 24:14 leads the midrash to conclude that one who abuses a needy or destitute laborer who is a righteous convert violates two negative commandments. It is unclear exactly which two negative commandments are violated. Yosi b. Judah responds that this falls under the class of "not abusing"; however, it is unsure if he disagrees with the claim that one violates two negative commandments or not. Rebbenu Hillel, *loc. cit.*, suggests that the person violates the rules that he must give the pay on that day, and he must not withhold the payment for work (Lev. 19:13). This part of the *pisqa* has several problems; see Finkelstein, 296, note to l. 7. Cf. bB.M. 111b.

145. *Mlkwt*.

146. *W'św 'ṣmkm yhwdym*.

147. *Twrtm my tybh.*

148. Sifré Deuteronomy VeZot 344; Finkelstein, 401, ll. 2–6. Cf. yB.Q. 4:3, Venice 4b; bB.Q. 38a, Gamaliel is not mentioned here.

149. Sifré Deuteronomy Re'ah 110; Finkelstein, 171, ll. 3–6. According to Deut. 14:27–29, every third year the tithe was to be given directly to Levite, the stranger, the orphan, and the widow who lived within the gates of the individual cities; they were not to be taken to Jerusalem and given to the priests. This is taken to mean that all of the poor who have accepted the covenant are to be supported by this tithe, and this includes the poor convert. The Israelites were commanded to give the agricultural gifts only to the poor among their own people, for these served as a way to maintain group solidarity; Porton, *Goyim*, 173–203. Therefore, the present passage indicates that the converts were viewed as an integral part of the Israelite community.

150. Sifré Deuteronomy Ki Taṣa 283; Finkelstein, 299, ll. 6–7, which merely cites Deut. 24:19.

151. Sifré Deuteronomy Ki Taṣa 283; Finkelstein, 300, ll. 10–11. Again the midrash merely quotes Deut. 24:19 and by implication indicates that the converts, like the native-born Israelites, receive these agricultural gifts to the poor.

152. Sifré Deuteronomy Ki Taṣa 284; Finkelstein, 301, ll. 10–11 and Sifré Deuteronomy Ki Taṣa 285; Finkelstein, 302, ll. 7–8. In both cases the midrash merely quotes the biblical text which refers to the *gr*. Deut. 24:20 instructs the Israelites as follows: *When you beat down the fruit of your olive trees, do not go over them again; that shall go to the convert (gr), the orphan and the widow.* Similarly, Deut. 24:21 informs the Israelites that *when you gather the grapes of your vineyard, do not pick it over again; that shall go to the convert (gr), the orphan, and the widow.* Cf. Jacob Neusner, *Sifré to Deuteronomy: An Analytical Translation* (Atlanta, 1987), 2:236 and 238; Hammer, *Sifre*, 275 and 276.

153. Sifré Deuteronomy Ki Taṣa 283; Finkelstein, 300, ll. 12–13, which merely quotes Deut. 24:19. Deut. 26:13 is interpreted also as referring to the poorman's tithe; here we are told that even if the farmer has not given them, he may still recite the confession concerning the tithes with which this section of Sifré Deuteronomy opens; Sifré Deuteronomy Ki Tabo 303; Finkelstein, 321, ll. 13–14.

154. Sifré Deuteronomy Ki Taṣa 303; Finkelstein, 321, l. 5.

155. Sifré Deuteronomy Re'ah 138; Finkelstein, 193, ll. 3–4. Deut. 16:11 is taken as a list of the members of the community in the order of their importance: *[You shall rejoice before YHWH, your God with your son, your daughter, your slave, your handmaiden, the Levite, the convert, the orphan, and the widow.* See the parallel passage Sifré Deuteronomy Re'ah 69; Finkelstein 133, ll. 10–11 where the convert does not appear.

156. Sifré Deuteronomy Shoftim 149; Finkelstein, 204, ll. 6–7. Although Deut. 17:4 mentions those among Israel (*byśr'l*) who are guilty of the transgressions, converts, women, and slaves are included under the reference to *that particular man or that particular woman* (Deut. 17:5).

157. Sifré Deuteronomy Re'ah 87; Finkelstein, 151, ll. 14–15. The reference to the convert is derived from the phrase *your neighbor* in Deut. 13:7. Cf. Sifré

Deuteronomy Re'ah 93; Finkelstein, 154, ll. 13–14, where the biblical phrase *that abhorrent thing was perpetrated in your midst* is used to include the convert and the freed slave among those who can cause a city to be condemned. See, however, Finkelstein, 154–55, note to l. 13 which gives those sources where this issue is debated. See also Hammer, *Sifre*, 430, n. 7. Cf. tSanh. 14:2 in some versions; ySanh. 10:7, Venice 20c.

158. Sifré Deuteronomy Ki Tabo 299, Finkelstein, 318. Cf. mBik. 1:4, tBik. 1:2.

159. Sifré Deuteronomy Ki Taṣa 238; Finkelstein, 270, ll. 6–8. Cf. mKet. 4:3, which deals with a female convert who had illicit sexual relations after she was betrothed. Cf. yKet. 4:4, Venice 28b; bKet. 44b.

160. Sifré Deuteronomy Ki Taṣa 289; Finkelstein, 308, ll. 16–18. This is based on the phrase *in Israel* in Deut. 25:6. Cf. mYeb. 11:2, tYeb. 12:2, bYeb. 97b–98a, and yYeb. 11:2, Venice 11d, all of which give different situations in which the brothers are not subject to these Israelite rituals. Bamberger, *Proselytism*, 86–87.

161. Sifré Deuteronomy Ki Taṣa 291; Finkelstein, 310, ll. 13–15. Cf. bYeb. 101b; bQid. 14a; yYeb. 12:1, Venice 12a.

162. Porton, *Goyim*, 211–13, 219–20; Baruch M. Bokser, *The Origins of the Seder* (Berkeley and Los Angeles, 1984).

CHAPTER 5

1. Baruch Bokser, "An Annotated Bibliographical Guide to the Study of the Palestinian Talmud," in Hildegard Temporini and Wolfgang Haase, eds., *Aufstieg und Niedergang der römischen Welt* (Berlin and New York, 1979), II.19.2, 192–99; L. I. Rabinowitz, "Talmud, Jerusalem," in Cecil Roth and Geoffrey Wigoder, eds., *Encyclopedia Judaica* (Jerusalem, 1973), 15: 772; Abraham Goldberg, "The Palestinian Talmud," in Shmuel Safrai, ed., *The Literature of the Sages First Part: Oral Tora, Halakha, Mishna, Tosefta, Talmud, External Tractates. Compendia Rerum Iudaicarum ad Novum Testamentum* (Assen-Maastricht and Philadelphia, 1987), 312–14; H. L. Strack and G. Stemberger, *Introduction to the Talmud and Midrash*, trans. Markus Bockmuehl (Edinburgh, 1991), 182–207.

2. There is a Palestinian *gemara* to all of the tractates of *Zera'im* and to *Sheqalim*. A version of the missing chapter of *Makkot* has been found in the Cairo *geniza*. Although some medieval authorities refer to the existence of a Palestinian *gemara* to *Qodashim* and *Tohorot*, most scholars agree that none actually existed, and no fragments of a *gemara* to these Orders have yet been discovered. See Bokser, "Annotated Bibliographical Guide," 167–68; Rabinowitz, "Talmud, Jerusalem," cols. 772–74.

3. Bokser, "Annotated Bibliographical Guide," 170.

4. Goldberg, "The Palestinian Talmud," 307.

5. Jacob Neusner, *Judaism: The Classical Statement: The Evidence of the Bavli* (Chicago, 1986), 18.

6. Ibid., 19–21. Avery-Peck comes to the same conclusions with regard to tractate *Terumot;* Alan J. Avery-Peck, *The Talmud of the Land of Israel: A Preliminary Translation and Explanation,* Volume 6, *Terumot* (Chicago and London, 1988), 16–37, esp. 37.

7. YYeb. 8:1, Venice 9a. Cf. yShab. 19:4, Venice 17a; tShab. 15:9; bShab. 135a. The Shammaites rule that the convert must undergo a symbolic circumcision, while the Hillelites do not require this act. Immediately following this discussion, we find a report of a case which focuses on the issue of circumcision on the Sabbath, and a good deal of the context, especially in yYeb. 8:1, focuses on the Sabbath, so that the relationship of this dispute and the Sabbath remains complex.

8. YPes. 8:8, Venice 36b. Here we read that the Hillelites and the Shammaites based their statements on Num. 31:19: *Everyone among you or among your captives [who has slain a person or touched a corpse shall cleanse himself on the third and seventh days].* According to the *gemara,* the Shammaites reasoned that just as Israelites do not become unclean until they have entered the covenant, so also the captives (gentiles) do not become unclean until they have entered the covenant. The Hillelites reason that just as the Israelites must be sprinkled on the third and seventh days, so also the captives (gentiles) must be sprinkled on the third and seventh days. Cf. mPes. 8:8, tPis. 7:14, bPes. 92a.

9. YShab. 19:5; Venice 17b.

10. YYeb. 8:1; Venice 8d.

11. In dealing with this passage, the *gemara* focuses on the one whose circumcision was covered up. Zeriqan and Yannai b. Ishmael in Yohanan's name claim that he cannot eat the food in the status of heave offering as a penalty for covering up his circumcision. Jeremiah and Samuel b. Isaac in Rav's name teach that this is merely "a decree they have issued," so that it will not appear that an uncircumcised male is eating the food in the status of heave offering. The latter explanation is the one accepted. However, neither reason makes sense when applied to one who is born circumcised or to the one who was circumcised before his conversion, for both are circumcised, and it is not clear why either should be penalized. Therefore, I assume that David Fränkel and Moses Margolioth are correct when they claim that these males may not eat the food in the status of heave offering unless they have been symbolically circumcised by having blood taken from their penises. See the comments of David Fränkel and Moses Margolioth, *loc. cit.* Shortly after our *sugya,* we find the statement that in fact these males must be symbolically circumcised, and we also find Simeon b. Eleazar's interpretation of the Houses dispute on this issue.

12. YMeg. 2:3; Venice 73b. Nahman bar Jacob implies that if a convert were circumcised after the East became light on the day the *megillah* is to be read, he is still required to hear it read. Moses Margolioth spends a good deal of time indicating that the circumcision occurred very early in the day; see comments of David Fränkel and Moses Margolioth, *loc. cit.*

13. YYeb. 8:1; Venice 8d. Isaac bar Nahman and Joshua b. Levi were with Yudan the Patriarch in Laodicea. Yudan wanted to leave the city to start a journey,

but Joshua b. Levi asked him to wait until the next morning when they would immerse a new female convert. Zeira asked Isaac if they were waiting until the morning out of respect for Yudan or because female converts are not immersed at night. Isaac responded that it was for the latter reason. Reference is then made to an instance in which they brought a female convert to Yosi to be immersed at night. He refused to do so because he did not want to set a precedent by his actions.

14. Sifré Numbers Shelaḥ 108, Horovitz 112.

15. YQid. 3:12; Venice yQid. 3:14, 64d. Bar Qappara agrees with Eliezer; however, the *gemara* comments that because we assume that all converts have undergone ritual immersion because of a nocturnal emission, they have been both circumcised and immersed. Thus, according to the *gemara*, any ritual immersion at any time suffices for the convert who in fact must be both circumcised and immersed before he may enter into a valid marriage with a female Israelite. Yosi b. Bun states that as long as the immersion is "for the sake of the holiness of Israel" it is accepted. Cf. bYeb. 46a, where Eliezer requires only circumcision and Joshua requires only immersion. In yQid. 4:7, Venice 66a, Abbahu seems to hold that a convert needs only to be circumcised. A tannaitic tradition is cited which notes that if a convert states that he was circumcised but not immersed, he is believed, and they immerse him on the Sabbath. However, this cannot be an immersion related to conversion because one cannot "be improved" on the Sabbath; therefore, it is an immersion for uncleanness. Abbahu accepts this immersion on the Sabbath because he does not believe that it effects conversion, for conversion is a result of circumcision only. Segal writes that "the frequently cited controversy between Rabbi Eliezer and Rabbi Joshua (j. Yeb. 16a) [*sic*] does not imply that some rabbis accepted converts without circumcision; rather, it underlines a legal question of some importance for the convert—namely, at what moment does a conversion actually take place and thus when does a convert take on all the responsibilities of a Jew?" Alan F. Segal, *Paul the Convert: The Apostolate and Apostasy of Saul the Pharisee* (New Haven and London, 1990), 103.

16. YQid. 3:12; Venice yQid. 3:14, 64d. Zakkai taught before R. Yohanan that Hiyya asked Yohanan about the status of a child born from the union of a convert who had been circumcised but had not yet immersed and an Israelite woman. Yohanan responded that Hiyya should have ruled on his own. Hiyya responded that Joshua b. Levi had been lenient in the matter and left the child alone. The *gemara* notes that the opinion attributed to Joshua b. Levi here contradicts his statement elsewhere. In another place Jacob b. Aha, Simeon b. Ba, and Joshua b. Levi taught in the name of Gamaliel b. Rabbi that the child was neither fit, *kšr;* nor unfit, *pswl;* rather, he was rejected, *mwzhm.* The text next brings a dispute between Eliezer and Joshua over the importance of circumcision and immersion. Eliezer rules that circumcision is the crucial factor; it does not matter whether the convert was immersed or not. Joshua, however, rules that immersion is *also* required, for the omission of immersion prevents the convert from being considered a member of the Israelite community. However, Bar Qappara taught that if a convert who was circumcised but who had not undergone immersion had intercourse

with an Israelite woman, the child is fit, *kšr,* for every male convert has immersed himself as a result of his nocturnal emissions. Thus, Bar Qappara counts any immersion as valid for meeting the requirement that a convert undergo ritual immersion. The *gemara* then asks if the two types of immersion are equal, since the one for a nocturnal emission cleanses a minor impurity, while the one for conversion cleanses the person from the major impurity of being a gentile. Yosi b. Bun responds that because both immersions were for the sake of the holiness of Israel, either one will suffice. Bamberger supports the claim that converts were immersed because of their gentile impurity; Bernard J. Bamberger, *Proselytism in the Talmudic Period* (New York, 1968), 44. Moore, however, rejects this idea. He states: "[M]odern writers have frequently satisfied themselves with the explanation that proselytes were required to bathe in order to purify themselves, really or symbolically, from the uncleanness in which the whole life of the heathen was passed. This explanation seems to be nowhere explicitly propounded by Jewish teachers in the early centuries. The rite itself differs fundamentally from such baths of purification in that the presence of official witnesses is required"; George F. Moore, *Judaism in the First Centuries of the Christian Era: The Age of the Tannaim* (Cambridge, reprint, 1966), 1:332–33. He concludes that "it is essentially an initiatory rite, with a forward and not a backward look"; Moore, 1:334. However, it is clear that at least in the Palestinian *gemara* some drew close parallels between the women's purification-immersions and those of converts.

17. In yErub. 4:5; Venice 22a, the immersion of a convert on the Sabbath is taken for granted, and no questions about its legitimacy are raised. Huna reported that Nahman b. Jacob raised a question concerning a convert who immersed on the Sabbath after the beginning of the sunrise, *l'ḥr šh'yr hmzrḥ.* Because the convert was awake at that time, was the place where he was immersed counted as his primary location for the Sabbath, so that he could move 2,000 cubits from there? The *gemara* concludes that such a person follows Yohanan b. Nuri's position in mErub. 4:5, so that the place of his immersion counts as his primary residence, and he can move 2,000 cubits in any direction. Thus, the convert is considered the same as an Israelite who fell asleep and did not know when night had fallen, and the accepted opinion is that of Yohanan b. Nuri. In his comment on mErub. 4:5, Bartinoro notes that the law follows Yohanan's opinion. However, the passage in yQid. 4:7; Venice 66a, raises the issue of the permissibility of "improving a person" on the Sabbath through conversion. An anonymous teaching states that if a convert who was circumcised but had not yet immersed had children and said, "I have been circumcised but not yet immersed," he is believed, and they immerse him on the Sabbath for reasons of cleanliness, not for reasons of conversion because the latter immersion would cause an improvement in the person, and this is prohibited on the Sabbath. Abbahu responds that because a convert needs only to be circumcised, not immersed, it makes no difference whether he is immersed on the Sabbath or not, for the immersion does not affect the convert's status.

18. YSheq. 8:4; Venice ySheq. 8:6, 51b. Cf. tSheq. 3:22 and bKer. 9a. Simeon reports that Yohanan b. Zakkai suspended the rite. Neusner suggests that the

Simeon here is Simeon b. Yohai. He further states that this may well be an amoraic creation, which seems likely given the fact that Yohanan does not appear in Tosefta; Jacob Neusner, *Development of a Legend: Studies on the Traditions concerning Yohanan ben Zakkai* (Leiden, 1970), 135–36. On bR.H. 31b Simeon b. Eleazar reports that Rabban Yohanan took a vote and suspended the rite. On bKer. 9a Simeon reports that Yohanan b. Zakkai held a vote and suspended the ritual. With regard to the passage on bKer. 9a, Neusner suggests that it may be tannaitic; however, he is unsure; Neusner, 109. Cf. Jacob Neusner, *A Life of Yohanan Ben Zakkai, Ca. 1–80 C.E.*, 2d ed. (Leiden, 1970), 210, where he places it among Yohanan's decisions at Yavneh.

19. YSheq. 8:4; Venice ySheq. 8:6, 51b.

20. YQid. 4:1; Venice 65b. The *gemara* raises this issue in an exegesis of Ezra 2:61–62. The Bible states: *Of the sons of the priests, the sons of Habaiah, the sons of Kakkoz, the sons of Barzillai who had married a daughter of Barzillai and had taken his name—these searched for their genealogical records, but they could not be found, so they were disqualified for the priesthood.* The text notes that if Barzillai's daughters converted to Judaism for proper motives, literally, "for the sake of Heaven," they should be allowed to eat the most holy things. However, if they converted for improper reasons, they may not eat even the lesser holy things which may be consumed throughout the provinces outside the Temple-precincts. The *gemara* then moves onto the topic of the sexual purity of a woman who converts; however, we shall discuss this below.

21. YQid. 4:1; Venice 65b.

22. The passage also mentions those who converted at the time of Solomon in order to enjoy the benefits of serving the Israelite king, following the interpretation of David Fränkel, *loc. cit.*, those who were converted because of the fear of lions, that is, the Samaritans, IIKgs. 17:25, and those who converted at the time of Mordecai and Esther.

23. YQid. 4:1; Venice 65b. Those who convert for the proper reasons are mentioned in Ezra 6:21 as those *who joined them* [the children of Israel in observing the Passover and] *in separating themselves from the uncleanliness of the nations of the lands.* Bamberger states that "Rab's statement is the accepted law—necessarily, since motives cannot be accurately determined. . . . In sum, the law is willing to accept any convert without too searching a scrutiny of his motives"; Bamberger, *Proselytism in the Talmudic Period*, 32–33.

24. BYeb. 47a b.

25. YQid. 4:1; Venice 65b.

26. IIKgs. 17:25.

27. Lit., "not for the sake of Heaven."

28. David Fränkel, *loc. cit.*, notes that IIKgs. 17:32 reads *they feared YHWH.*

29. YGiṭ. 1:4. The notation 4 is missing in the Venice edition, so that this is improperly marked as Venice yGiṭ. 1:5; 43c.

30. YB.M. 5:5; Venice yB.M. 5:7, 10c. If an Israelite borrowed money from a gentile or a gentile borrowed money from an Israelite and the gentile converted,

whether the lender had written a document in which he combined the interest and the principal together as the loan—this seems to be the meaning of *zqpn;* see Penei Moshe, *loc. cit.*, and Marcus Jastrow, *A Dictionary of the Targumim, the Talmud Babli and Yerushalmi, and the Midrashic Literature* (New York, reprint, 1971), 409—before or after the gentile converted, the borrower pays the principal, but not the interest. This does not make sense, given the end of the *sugya,* for the end of the passage deals with a gentile who borrowed money from an Israelite. Moses Margolioth states that the opening of the passage should be attributed to Meir, while the end of the passage is attributed to Yosi. This would follow the reading in tB.M. 5:21, and it would allow the passage to make sense. Cf. bB.M. 72a. If we accept Margolioth's view that this is really the Yosi-Meir dispute in tB.M. 5:21, then the difference between the sages centers on when one considers the statuses of the borrower and the lender, and in the situation presented above, one focuses on the status of the people when the loan is paid. If a gentile borrowed money from an Israelite and converted, if the Israelite had written a document in which he combined the interest and the principal together as the loan before the gentile converted, the convert pays the principal and the interest. If the Israelite had written a document in which he combined the interest and the principal together as the loan after the conversion, he pays the principal, but not the interest. According to this opinion, the status of the persons when the loan was made is the crucial factor. If the agreement was executed between a gentile and an Israelite, interest must be paid. However, if the loan was executed between a convert and an Israelite, no interest is paid. Bar Qappara rules that the Israelite should pay both the principal and the interest, because, according to Jacob b. Aha, Bar Qappara believed that if the convert realized that he would now suffer a financial loss because he could not collect the interest, he would leave the Jewish community.

31. YQid. 4:1; Venice 65c. The relevant part of the *sugya* appears in ySanh. 6:7; Venice ySanh. 13:9, 23d. IISam. 21:7–11 report that David handed over to the Gibeonites Saul's sons by Rizpah, Armoni and Mephibosheth, and Saul's grandsons who were born from the marriage of his daughter Merab to Adriel, the son of Barzillai the Meholathite. The Bible reports that the Gibeonites impaled them on a mountain and that *they were put to death in the first days of the harvest.* The Bible also records that Rizpah stayed with the bodies *from the beginning of the harvest until rain from the sky fell on them* in order to protect them from the birds and animals which might harm their corpses. The *gemara* explains that the bodies were exposed for a full seven months, from the sixteenth of Nisan until seventeenth of Merheshvan. Those who saw the bodies explained that they had received this severe punishment because they had persecuted those who had become *grym grwrym.* Deut. 21:22–23 state that *you must not let his corpse remain on the stake overnight, but must bury him the same day. For an impaled body is an affront to God: you shall not defile the land that YHWH your God is giving you to possess.* Given these verses, the fact that God allowed these bodies to hang on the stake for seven months demonstrates his anger with them. The *gemara* concludes that many of those who saw how harshly YHWH treated these people converted to Judaism on the assumption that if

YHWH exhibited so much concern for those who had not converted to Judaism
for the correct reason and thus were not even accepted as converts by the Israelite
community, how much more concern would he have for those who were true converts to Judaism. The text refers to these as those who converted to Judaism "for
the sake of Heaven." Proof for the fact that many converted to Judaism at that
time is found in IIChron. 2:16: *Solomon took a census of all the converts (hgrym) who
were in the Land of Israel* . . . . On the Gibeonites see Bamberger, *Proselytism in the
Talmudic Period,* 199–203. Weil clearly would like to accept this tradition; in fact, he
suggests that the large number of converts, 150,000 according to some traditions, is
entirely possible when we consider the number of Solomon's wives and the number of those who worked on the Temple's construction for Solomon; Isaac Weil, *Le
Prosélytisme chez les juifs selon la bible et le talmud* (Strasbourg, 1880), 20–23. On these
passages see Ernst Bammel, "Gerim Gerurim," *Annual of the Swedish Theological
Institute* 7 (1968–69): 129–30. Cf. bYeb. 79a.

32. YA.Z. 2:2; Venice 41a. Once there was a gentile barber who was also an
astrologer, and he was planning to convert to Judaism. He consulted his astrological
signs and saw that the Jews would shed his blood upon his conversion, probably
misinterpreting the blood which would result from circumcision. Therefore, when
Israelites came to him for a haircut, he would kill them. Leazar b. Yosi claimed
that he had killed eighty Israelites, while Yosi b. Bun claimed that he had killed
six hundred Israelites before the Israelites prayed for him, and he returned to
his senses.

33. YQid. 4:3; Venice 65d. In the passage, this ruling parallels the position that
an Israelite may not marry a *mamzer.* Cf. mQid. 4:1.

34. YYeb. 8:2; Venice 9b. Cf. yQid. 4:2; Venice 65c. In its explanation of mQid.
4:1, the Palestinian *gemara* explains that Ezra 6:21, *[The children of Israel who had
returned from the exile,] together with all who joined them in separating themselves from the
uncleanliness of the nations of the lands to worship YHWH, the God of Israel, ate of it [the
Passover sacrifice],* demonstrates that the converts were a distinct group among the
different classes of Israelites who came up to Israel from Babylonia with Ezra. It is
easy to see how this could be taken to refer to the converts, for the ones mentioned
separated themselves from the deities (uncleanliness) of the other nations of the
world in order to worship YHWH and to eat the Passover sacrifice, which was
available to those "strangers" who underwent circumcision, Ex. 12:48–49; yQid.
4:1, Venice 65b.

35. YQid. 3:13; Venice yQid. 3:15, 64d. This is yQid. 3:12 in David Fränkel's
commentary. Cf. tQid. 5:11. If a gentile man has a slave boy and a slave girl who
have two children, and one of them converted, one is a convert and one is a gentile.
If their master and the slaves converted and then produced a son, the offsprings
are slaves.

36. YHag. 1:1; Venice 66a. In response to Samuel bar Abba's question concerning a minor who is a deaf-mute, Zeira notes that a person on earth has the same
status when he is in heaven. He asks, "Do we have a native-born [Israelite] on

earth and a convert in the height of the heavens?!" The answer is, of course, no. A person has the same status in this world and the next. For our purposes the point of the parable is that native-born Israelites and converts are not quite the same.

37. YQid. 3:12; Venice yQid. 3:14, 64c. After hearing Judah's response, the convert returned to Yosa—the text has Yosi at this point—and asked him why he had not told him what Judah had told him. Yosa responded that he answered the question he was asked, for the marriage is permitted. The following proverb is then attributed to Yosa—the text has Yosah at this point: "A convert is comparable to cotton. If you want to weave it together with wool, it is permitted, or with flax, it is permitted." The point is that just as the laws of "mixed-kinds" do not apply in Yosa's proverb, so that convert is allowed to marry a *mamzer*, without violating any Israelite laws, as long as he is willing to accept the fact that his children will be considered *mamzerim* before Heaven.

38. MHor. 3:8.

39. YHor. 3:5; Venice yHor. 3:7, 48b. When all else is equal, the sage precedes the king, the king precedes the high priest, the high priest precedes the prophet, the prophet precedes the priest anointed for war, the priest anointed for war precedes the priest who is the head of the watch, the priest who is the head of the watch precedes the priest of the house of the father, the priest of the house of the father precedes the supervisor of the temple cashiers (*mrkl*), the supervisor of the temple cashiers precedes the treasurer (*gyzbr*), the treasurer precedes the common priest, the common priest precedes the Levite, the Levite precedes the Israelite, the Israelite precedes the *mamzer*, the *mamzer* precedes the *natin*, the *natin* precedes the convert, and the convert precedes the freed slave. Abun states that in the case of a convert and an apostate Israelite—Venice reads *mwmd*, and the printed text reads *mwmr*—who seeks to return to the Israelite people, the apostate Israelite takes precedence. The text makes it clear that the Israelites and the converts were not considered fully equal. The native-born Israelite had an advantage over the convert. In fact, an apostate Israelite who wished to return to the community was dealt with before one accepted a convert.

40. It is difficult to know exactly what this text implies. In a private communication Professor Alan Avery-Peck raised several points which might be behind this question: Is there a question of whether or not they had converted by the time the rest of the community was misled? Or that converts could be misled? Or that we expect them to be misled? The biblical context, Deut. 13, suggests that the town is populated by Israelites: *If you hear it said, of one of the towns that* YHWH, *your God, is giving you to dwell in* .... This would imply that the question might be whether or not the converts, who some believed were incapable of inheriting portions of the Land of Israel, were legitimate inhabitants of the town. However, Avery-Peck raises some interesting questions which simply cannot be answered given the talmudic *sugya*.

41. YSanh. 10:6; Venice ySanh. 17:7, 29c.

42. YPes. 8:7; Venice 36a. Jacob bar Aha in the name of Aisi rules that a group

of converts may not join together to offer the Passover sacrifice because they will defile it. Cf. bPes. 91b and Bamberger, *Proselytism in the Talmudic Period*, 71.

43. See Baruch M. Bokser, *The Origins of the Seder: The Passover Rite and Early Rabbinic Judaism* (Berkeley and Los Angeles, 1984).

44. Along with a defective priest and a freed slave.

45. YQid. 3:12; Venice yQid. 3:14, 64c and comment of David Fränkel, *loc. cit.* See also yYeb. 9:1; Venice 10a. Yosi b. Bun quotes Rav's statement that a convert, a freed slave and an impaired priest (*ḥalal*) are permitted to a woman of the priestly caste. The *gemara* explains that fit men are warned against marrying unfit women, and unfit women are warned against marrying fit men. However, fit women are not warned against marrying unfit men, nor are unfit men warned against marrying fit women. An objection is raised based on the repetition of *they shall not marry* in Lev. 21:7: *They shall not marry a woman defiled by harlotry, and they shall not marry one divorced from her husband.* The verse is interpreted to mean that invalid women are warned against marrying valid men. Therefore, Yosi's position is accepted.

46. MBik. 1:5.

47. YBik. 1:5; Venice 64a. The *gemara* argues that all of these laws concerning the daughter of converts, including the statement by Liezer b. Jacob, are derived from Ezek. 44:22, *They [priests] shall not marry widows or divorced women; they may marry only virgins of the stock of the house of Israel, or widows who are widows of priests.* In a discussion between Joshua the Great and Yudan the Patriarch the issue of the acceptability of the marriage to a converted woman by a priest whose penis has been damaged is raised. A secondary matter is whether or not the woman is allowed to eat the heave offering; see David Fränkel and Moses Margolioth, *loc. cit.* There is no question about a convert, for with regard to marriage to a priest she is considered to be comparable to a prostitute. Similarly, there is no question about an Israelite woman, for she is considered to be unfit through her intercourse with the damaged priest. Therefore, the question must concern the daughter of a convert. To this the final reply is that according to Judah, the daughter of a male convert is like the daughter of a male damaged priest; yYeb. 8:2; Venice 9b. Cf. yQid. 4:6, Venice 66a; mYeb. 8:2; bYeb. 76a–b; bYeb. 57a.

48. YBik. 1:5; Venice 64a; Cf. yQid. 4:6; Venice 66a. The story ends with someone saying to Abbahu that he too should be able to marry such a woman, and I assume that Bibi is the speaker. However, the text is totally unclear as to the speaker.

49. YHor. 1:4; Venice 46a. This view is based on an exegesis of Num. 11:16, *[Then YHWH said to Moses, "Gather for me seventy of Israel's elders of whom you have experience as elders and officers of the people, and bring them to the Tent of Meeting] and let them take their place there with you."* Moses Margolioth, *loc. cit.*, notes that although converts cannot adjudicate capital cases, they can be judges in cases of torts. Cf. Sifra VaYiqra Parashah 4:2–3.

50. YYeb. 12:1; Venice 12b–c. The *sugya* next deals with another set of contradictory tannaitic teachings: One teaching declares that the *ḥaliṣah* ceremony is invalid if it is performed before two judges, for mYeb. 12:1 states there must be three

judges. However, another tradition states that it is valid if it is performed before two judges. The text then equates the ruling prohibiting two judges with the ruling excluding converts, and the ruling permitting converts is equated with the teaching allowing two judges. Here, David Fränkel and Moses Margolioth, *loc. cit.*, suggest that the issue is whether or not the *halisah* ceremony is considered a court procedure. If it is considered a court procedure, there must be three judges, and they must all be Israelites. The text next states that even the one who ruled that the ceremony may include converted judges would agree that there must be three judges, for in civil cases, the judges may be converts; however, there still must be three of them. A third set of tannaitic statements is now brought forward. Those who claim that the *halisah* ceremony may be performed at night are like those who accept converts as judges, and those who do not allow the ceremony to occur at night are like those who do not allow converts to serve as judges. The text concludes that the one who accepts converts as judges would also agree that the ceremony cannot be performed at night, for civil cases may be tried before judges who are converts, and such trials must occur during the day.

51. MEd. 5:6.

52. YSoṭ. 2:5; Venice 18b. The anonymous text argues that the case of an Israelite male married to a converted female is covered by the phrase *children of Israel* in Num. 5:12, which indicates that a converted female does not undergo the rite. Similarly, Num. 5:15, *then you shall bring his wife to the priest*, demonstrates that the Israelite wife of a converted male does not drink the water. Moses Margolioth and David Fränkel, *loc. cit.*, state that she does not drink the water because the verse implies that both the wife and the husband should occupy the same status. The latter commentator argues that because we assume that gentile women had been sexually active before their conversion, the Israelite male married the convert knowing that she probably had engaged in sexual activity. Therefore, the rite is not appropriate in this case. For this reason, the dispute in mEd. 5:6 can only be about the case of a male convert married to a female convert. Aqabyya follows Num. 5:12, so that he believed that the rite applied only to Israelites. Sages, on the other hand, rely on Num. 5:13, which teaches that the rite applies to a woman with whom a man has had sexual relations after the marriage, so that her husband becomes jealous of her *after* their marriage. This could apply to the two converts. Cf. Sifré Numbers Naśo 7; Horovitz, 11, ll. 2–4; bBer. 19a.

53. MBik. 1:4

54. Deut. 26:3.

55. Jethro's name is not mentioned.

56. YBik. 1:4; Venice 64a. Yonah and Yasa in the name of Samuel bar Isaac state that the mishnah applies to the Kenites, the people of Moses' father-in-law, for the Kenites eventually married Israelite women. An anonymous opinion states that the Kenites do recite the verse from Deuteronomy because Num. 10:29 reads *come with us, and we will do you good.* Hezekiah in the name of Leazar supplies another reason for the rule, for the converts are mentioned in the section which discusses the first fruits. Deut. 26:11, which occurs at the end of the section that

discusses the first fruit, states *And you shall enjoy, together with the Levite and the convert (hgr) in your midst, all the bounty that YHWH your God has bestowed upon you and your household.* Samuel bar Isaac states that the Kenites bring the first fruit but do not recite the Avowal. Yosi stated that Benjamin bar Eshtor established before Hiyya bar Ba that the mishnah deals with a gentile who had prohibited intercourse with an Israelite woman. Yonah reports that Rabbi learned from the school of Bar Eshtor that converts who are the children of converts say, "the God of our fathers." However, because the mishnah states that only those who have Israelite mothers recite this phrase, how do we accept Yonah's teaching? Yosi states that Benjamin bar Eshtor established before Hiyya b. Ba, Hezekiah and in the name of Hiyya b. Ba who reported that Bar Eshtor taught that the mishnah speaks of a gentile who has illicit intercourse with an Israelite woman. Zeriqa said that Zeira noted that all of them are meant, for if the intention were to deal only with those to whom God swore, we would have to limit ourselves to the males, for YHWH spoke only to Abraham, Isaac, and Jacob. However, Judah taught that a convert himself brings the first fruit and makes the Avowal, for it says, *I will make you the father of a multitude of nations,* Gen. 17:5. Joshua b. Levi concludes that the law follows Judah.

57. YYeb. 11:2; Venice 11d. According to Yosi the Galilean, a convert is liable for cursing his mother, but not for cursing his father. Aqiba states, however, that the convert is liable for cursing either parent. He interprets Lev. 20:9 to mean that those who are liable for cursing their father are also liable for cursing their mother, while those who are not liable for cursing their father are also not liable for cursing their mother. Jacob bar Aha and Yasa in the name of Yohanan suggest that Yosi and Aqiba disagreed about the case of a convert who was made pregnant without the benefit of a marriage accepted by Israelite law, that is before her conversion, but who gave birth after she had entered into an acceptable marriage, that is, after her conversion. If the convert had become pregnant and gave birth after entering into an acceptable marriage, Yosi agrees with Aqiba that the children are guilty for cursing either one of their parents. David Fränkel, *loc. cit.,* prefers the reading that Yosi agrees with Aqiba in the case where the convert became pregnant and gave birth both without engaging in a legally acceptable marriage. Cf. Sifra Qedoshim Pereq 9:9, Weiss 92a.

58. YGiṭ. 4:4; Venice 45d. If a convert died without legal heirs and his property was acquired by Israelites, the slaves are freed. Abba Saul states that the adult slaves may go free, but the minor slaves may be acquired by Israelites. Ba explains that the adults have the ability to acquire their own freedom, while the minors do not; therefore, only the latter may be acquired by other Israelites. The point of the passage is that a convert may die without heirs, so that Israelites may validly acquire his property after his death. The disagreement has nothing to do with the dead man's status as a convert. According to Joshua b. Levi, the law follows Abba Saul.

59. YQid. 1:5; Venice 60d. If a convert died without heirs and left two fields, if an Israelite takes possession of one field, he does not acquire the other field, even if there is only a small boundary path between them. Hisda states that if an Israelite took possession of the dead convert's northern field on condition that he

would acquire the southern field, or the southern field on condition that he acquire the northern field, but he did not intend to acquire what is between the two fields, he has not effected any acquisition until he intends to acquire also what is between the two fields. Hisda's opinion is challenged by the citation of tPe. 2:10: If Israelites took over the property of a convert who died without heirs, the former are liable for all the tithes due from the crops if they acquired the land. However, if they acquired the standing crop (*qmh*), but not the land, they are liable for only the gleaning, the forgotten sheaf, and the corners, but they are exempt from the tithes. This stands against Hisda's ruling because there is airspace between the standing crops, so that each would have to be acquired separately according to Hisda's ruling, for the land which would have connected them into one field was not acquired. In support of this interpretation, a teaching by Samuel is cited, and it is claimed that with regard to a convert's property Samuel and Hisda would argue that if one takes possession of the crops, he also takes possession of each item in the field separately. The *gemara* implies that this is the case only with property taken over from a convert who has died without leaving heirs. This stands in opposition to the case of two fields owned by an Israelite. For example, if an Israelite had a field in Judah and one in the Galilee, if another Israelite takes possession of one with the intention of acquiring the other, he has acquired ownership of both fields. Cf. yB.B. 3:1; Venice 13d, where the text is slightly different. It opens with Yasa in Yohanan's name discussing two fields with a narrow path between them which belonged to a convert who died without leaving heirs. If an Israelite uproots the trees and grass from one field with the intention of buying both fields but not the narrow pathway between them, the field from which he uprooted the trees and grass has been acquired, but he has not acquired the other field. Zeira asks Yasa about the instance in which the Israelite intended to acquire the narrow pathway and what is below it. Hisda responds that if he uproots from the north of the field with the intention of purchasing the northern and southern parts of the field but not the middle, he has acquired rights to only the northern part of the field. Then Samuel's comment follows with the response by Abduma. We find elsewhere that if one takes possession of the field of a convert who died without leaving heirs by means of usucaption, he acquires everything in or on that field; yB.B. 4:8; Venice 4:11, 14d. Venice incorrectly marks this as page 18.

60. YQid. 1:4; Venice 60a. Huna states that one may not acquire the animal of a convert who has died without heirs by accepting delivery of the animal's reins. This is the reading of the text on bB.M. 8b where Helbo quotes Huna. This reading is accepted by David Fränkel and Moses Margolioth, *loc. cit.* Venice reads that it is an acceptable way to acquire the dead convert's property. Neusner also accepts this reading; Jacob Neusner, *The Talmud of the Land of Israel: A Preliminary Translation and Explanation*, Volume 26: *Qiddushin* (Chicago and London, 1984), 67.

61. TKet. 4:16.

62. YB.B. 9:1; Venice 16d. If a convert died without heirs and Israelites divided his property, and afterwards it became known that he had a son or that his wife was pregnant, they must return the property. However, if the son died or the wife miscarried after they returned the property, the one who acquired the prop-

erty after the death or miscarriage may keep it. However, Leazar's statement is brought for purposes of the text, so that the discussion of the convert is important only for the flow of the text and as a possible example for dealing with Samuel's position. The discussion of the convert is cited as a tannaitic teaching on yYeb. 4:1; Venice 5a.

63. YB.B. 3:1; Venice 13d. If a baby is found in the marketplace, Simeon the brother of Judah b. Zabdi in the name of Rav says that his parents are considered valid witnesses concerning the baby's status. Abbahu responds that we should be concerned that a couple could lie about the baby and claim that the child is theirs even if it is not. The anonymous *gemara* suggests that Abbahu said this only with reference to a convert who had no heirs, for it is possible that such a person would find a child in the market and claim it as his heir. This interpretation follows Moses Margolioth, *loc. cit.* The Gilyon Ephraim, *loc. cit.*, suggests that the problem arises that a convert may testify that the child was born after the parent converted, when in fact the baby was born while the parent was still a gentile. The interpretations of Jacob David ben Ze'ev Willowski and the Mareh HaPanim, *loc. cit.*, seem to go far astray from the text.

64. YPes. 2:2; Venice 29a. If a convert who had no heirs died before Passover and when the Israelites divided his property among them after Passover they found leaven, all agree that the leaven is permitted for use by Israelites. The argument is that the leaven was part of ownerless property; therefore it was not possessed by an Israelite during Passover. The *gemara* at this point discusses the issue of whether or not one has attempted to evade the requirement not to possess leaven during Passover. The issues discussed are matters of evading the law concerning the removal of leaven by a ruse or by transmitting it to another. No matter which issue one is concerned with, the leaven found in the convert's estate is not disqualified for use for either of these two reasons.

65. YSheb. 10:4; Venice ySheb. 10:9, 39d. Moses Margolioth cites the text as ySheb. 10:9. MSheb. 10:9 states that if a man borrows from a convert whose sons have converted with him, he need not repay the debt to his sons. But, if he repays it to them, sages are pleased with him. Liezer states that if he wishes, he may repay the debt, but *only* to the lender's sons. Yosi rules that if he has sons, the debtor repays the loan to them. However, if he has only daughters, they also may collect the debt, for you may not say that since the inheritance from a convert is not mentioned in the Torah, only sons may inherit. However, the sages are pleased with him only if he repays the sons, and not the daughters.

66. YKet. 9:10; Venice 9:13, 33c. This is yKet. 9:11 in David Fränkel's commentary. Cf. tQid. 4:9, mQid 3:5, bQid. 62a.

67. MKet. 9:9.

68. TKet. 9:7.

69. YYeb. 11:2; Venice 11d–12a. Cf. mYeb. 11:2; bYeb. 97b–98a; Sifré Deuteronomy Ki Taṣa 289, Finkelstein, 308, ll. 16–18.

70. YA.Z. 3:6; Venice yA.Z. 3:8, 43b. Yohanan explains that mA.Z. 3:6 speaks to the situation where a convert and a gentile inherited two houses with a common wall from their gentile father. The convert took the house which did not contain

the idol, while his gentile brother took possession of the house in which the idol resided. The *gemara* explains that Yohanan connected the mishnah to this case because if a temple containing an idol were built next to an Israelite's house and the temple were moved after the wall collapsed, the Israelite may use the materials from the wall because the material returns to its former state and is not connected with the idol. However, if a convert and a gentile inherited an estate from their gentile father, the convert is forbidden from using the materials from the collapsed wall because the materials were always intended to be used for the idol's temple. Therefore, in Yohanan's opinion, mA.Z. 3:6 must be dealing with the case he described. This follows the explanation of David Fränkel, *loc. cit.*

71. MDem. 6:10, tDem. 6:12.

72. MB.Q. 9:11; Sifré Numbers Naśo 2, Horovitz 4–5 and Naśo 4, Horovitz 7; tB.Q. 10:16. Cf. bB.Q. 109a.

73. YḤal. 4:4; Venice 4:11, 60b. The heave offering, the heave offering of the tithe, the dough offering, the shoulder, the cheeks, the fat, the first fleece, that brought for the redemption of the first-born son, for the first-born of an ass, for dedicated property, or for an inherited field are in the same class as the guilt offering for one who stole from a convert.

74. YQid. 1:1; Venice 58c. Cf. bSanh. 56a. The symbol of the change in the person's status is that different types of penalties apply to the Israelite from those which apply to the gentile. The former were stoned, while the latter were executed by the sword. The passage also deals with a person who agreed to follow gentile law, but then converted to Judaism. If the parties agree that a gentile should be tried according to Israelite law, he is still liable after he converts. However, if it were agreed that he should be tried under gentile law, after he converts, he is no longer liable, for gentile law does not apply to Israelites.

75. YBik. 3:3; Venice 65c. Zeira was reluctant to be ordained until he heard an interpretation of Lev. 19:32–33, *You shall rise before the aged and show deference to the old; you shall fear your God: I am YHWH. When a convert (gr) resides with you in your land, you shall not wrong him.* This was interpreted to mean that just as they forgive all of a convert's sins, so also they forgive all the sins of an ordained sage. For our purposes it is important that upon his conversion, the person is forgiven for all of the sins he or she committed as a gentile. The change of status marks a major change in the person and the Israelites' perception of him or her. Braude wishes to limit the application of this principle, for he requires that the convert seek forgiveness for his "moral sins" from God; William G. Braude, *Jewish Proselyting in the First Five Centuries of the Common Era: The Age of the Tannaim and Amoraim* (Providence, 1940), 99.

76. YShebu. 2:1; Venice 33d. In a discussion concerning matters of doubt, Yohanan teaches that in some cases of doubt the doubt is ignored, and one is assumed to have certain knowledge. For example, if a person is made unclean, but it is uncertain whether the source of the uncleanness was a dead creeping thing or a corpse, the uncertainty is unimportant. Similarly, if one ate an olive's bulk of fat but it is uncertain if he did it before or after he converted or before or after he had grown two pubic hairs, the uncertainty is ignored. The point for our pur-

poses is that the act of conversion parallels puberty, for both represent important changes of status. This reading and interpretation follow Moses Margolioth, *loc. cit.*

77. YHor. 3:2; Venice 3:3, 47b. If one ate an olive's bulk of an edible item which was prohibited to Israelites, but it was uncertain if it was before he was designated or after he was designated as an anointed priest, before he converted or after he converted, before he brought forth two pubic hairs or after he brought forth two pubic hairs, he must bring a special guilt offering, an *'šm tlwy*. Cf. mKer. 3:1. Lev. 5:17ff.

78. YNid. 1:4, Venice 1:5, 49b; YYeb. 4:11, Venice 6a. Cf. bKet. 37a, bYeb. 35a. According to Judah, a gentile who converted must wait three months before she may marry to ensure that she was not pregnant upon her conversion. Yosi, however, states that she does not need to wait for any length of time. Similarly, a captive who was freed or a slave who was emancipated must wait three months. Although the *sugya* focuses on the sexual practices of the gentiles and slaves, it does indicate that an important change of status has occurred when the woman converted or when she was emancipated.

79. YB.Q. 9:9; Venice yB.Q. 9:15, 7a. A truncated version of tB.Q. 10:16 appears in the text.

80. At least, this is how David Fränkel explains the fact that the *gemara* equates the convert and the orphan in Deut. 24:17. However, the verse mentions both an orphan and a *gr*, so that it is unclear if Fränkel's opinion can be attributed to the amoraim. On the equation of the convert and the orphan, see yYoma 6:1, Venice 43a; ySanh. 3:9, Venice ySanh. 10:10, 21c; and yShebu. 4:1, Venice 35b. See Fränkel's comments on yYoma 6:1 and ySanh. 3:9.

81. TDem. 2:4. Cf. bBekh. 30b.

82. "Apostasy in Jewish Law," *Encyclopaedia Judaica*, 3: 211–12.

83. YA.Z. 2:2; Venice 41a. The *gemara* quotes mGiṭ. 4:6's ruling that Israelites should not buy torah scrolls, *tefillin*, or *mezzuzot* from a gentile. However, the Talmud also refers to a tannaitic tradition which records that the sages permitted the purchase of these items from a certain gentile in Sidon. Samuel b. Nathan in the name of Hama bar Hanina taught that the gentile in the latter story was a gentile who converted to Judaism but then returned to his gentile ways. The story indicates that the Jews realized that some people who joined the Israelite community could also leave it. However, the further implication is that even after they left, their former status still might be considered by the Israelites. Moses Margolioth, *loc. cit.*, states that because the convert left Judaism because he was afraid the gentiles would kill him, he still honored his Israelite ways and continued to prepare the ritual objects correctly.

84. YShab. 6:1; Venice 8d. On astrology in Judaism during late antiquity, see James H. Charlesworth, "Jewish Astrology in the Talmud, Pseudepigrapha, the Dead Sea Scrolls and the Early Palestinian Synagogue," *Harvard Theological Review* 70 (1970): 183–200.

85. YHag. 1:1; Venice 76a. Illa argues that if a gentile converted to Judaism during the week of Passover or Sukkot, Hezekiah would exempt him from appearing before YHWH on the last day of the festival because he was not an Isra-

elite on the first day of the festival. However, Yohanan and Hoshiya would require him to appear on the last day, because he was an Israelite on that day.

86. YShab. 7:1; Venice 9a. The *sugya* centers on the Sabbath. However, Jacob bar Aha reports a dispute between Yohanan and Simeon b. Laqish in which Yohanan taught that one should be concerned about every woman he seeks to marry, while Simeon states that one need not worry about every possible spouse. One may follow Simeon's position because there was a rabbinic ordinance which permitted marriage with a converted woman and a freed handmaiden. The dispute fits into the context because if one follows Yohanan's ruling, he would constantly be worried that he were working on a Sabbath, because he had to worry about each day. If one follows Simeon, however, one need not be concerned. The anonymous text responds, however, that Simeon's position was special because there was an ordinance which permitted certain marriages, so that there was less reason for one to be concerned about every woman, because so many of them were permitted to Israelites to marry.

87. This follows Moses Margolioth, *loc. cit.* Naturally, if it were slaughtered after his conversion, he is liable for these offerings.

88. YHal. 3:4; Venice yHal. 3:5, 59b. Moses Margolioth cites this as yHal. 3:5. In the case of the dough offering, some held that the priest had to reimburse the woman for the dough's value. Cf. Bamberger, *Proselytism in the Talmudic Period,* 72–73.

89. YQid. 3:12; Venice yQid. 3:14, 64c. MQid. 3:12 states that if two people are engaged in a valid betrothal and their marriage does not violate any Israelite laws, the child's status follows that of the father. In commenting upon this text, Simeon b. Laqish presented the following case to Yohanan: If a convert marries a female *mamzer,* even though the betrothal is valid and the marriage is acceptable, the child's status follows that of the impaired parent. Yohanan responded that the mishnah's teaching applies only to the specific examples it contains; that is, the rule applies when the daughter of a priest, a Levite, or an Israelite marries a priest, a Levite, or an Israelite. The *gemara* then notes that Abin heard the same case applied to the end of the mishnah: In any situation in which there is a valid betrothal but there is also the commission of a transgression, the offspring follows the status of the impaired party. The *gemara* responds in the same way to Simeon's point, only here it quotes the end of the mQid. 3:12: A valid betrothal but a legally unacceptable marriage occurs when a widow marries a high priest, when a divorced woman or one who has undergone the *halisah* ritual marries a common priest, when a female *mamzer* or a female *natin* marries an Israelite, or when a female Israelite marries a male *mamzer* or a male *natin.* The point of the passage seems to be that although a convert may marry a *mamzer,* the child is considered to be a *mamzer.*

90. YKet. 4:4; Venice 28b. Cf. bKet. 44b; Sifré Deuteronomy Ki Tasa 238; Finkelstein, 270, ll. 6–8. If an Israelite charges that his wife was not a virgin when he married her, but her virginity can be demonstrated, the man is flogged and fined one hundred *sheqels, for the man has defamed a virgin in Israel* (Deut. 22:13–19). The *gemara* claims that this should exclude the daughter of a convert, for she is not counted as a virgin *in Israel.* However, if the woman was conceived before her

father converted, literally, "not in a state of sanctity," but was born after he converted, literally, "in a state of sanctity," she is included among the virgins *in Israel*, so that she may be stoned under the stipulations of Deut. 22. However, her father does not receive the monetary penalty, for in this case the relationship between the father and his daughter does not hold. Hezekiah offers an exegesis of Deut. 22:21, which states that if the husband's charges can be substantiated, *the men of her town shall stone her to death*. Hezekiah asks why the seemingly unnecessary *to death* occurs in the verse, for it should be obvious that the result of stoning is death. He responds that this teaches that there was a woman who is subject to stoning if the charges prove true, but whose father does not receive the monetary fine if they prove false: The converted woman who was conceived while her father was still a gentile, but who was born after he converted.

91. YPes. 8:2; Venice 35d. The issue involves changes of status, for Yohanan also mentions that a slave who separated the Passover offering before he was free, must separate a new one after he is freed and that a minor who separated the Passover sacrifice must separate a new one after he has sprouted two pubic hairs. Again this points to the fact that converts achieve an entirely new legal status upon conversion.

92. YErub. 4:5; Venice 22a. Huna reported that Nahman b. Jacob raised the question concerning a convert who was immersed on the Sabbath after the beginning of the sunrise, *'ḥr šh'yr hmzrḥ*. Because the convert was awake at that time, was the place where he was immersed counted as his primary location for the Sabbath, so that he could move 2,000 cubits? The *gemara* concludes that such a person follows Yohanan b. Nuri's position in mErub. 4:5, so that the place of his immersion counts as his primary residence, and he can move 2,000 cubits in any direction. Thus, the convert is considered the same as an Israelite who fell asleep and did not know when night had fallen, and the accepted opinion is that of Yohanan b. Nuri. In his comment on mErub. 4:5, Bartinoro notes that the law follows Yohanan's opinion.

93. YMeg. 2:3; Venice 73b. Nahman asks a rhetorical question in order to object to a previous opinion in the *gemara*. The rule to be derived, however, is that the convert must still hear the *megillah* read even if he were circumcised after sunrise on Purim itself.

94. Gary G. Porton, *Goyim: Gentiles and Israelites in Mishnah-Tosefta* (Atlanta, 1988), 182–84.

95. YPe. 4:7; Venice 4:8, 18c. Yohanan—Venice reads Judah—taught that Judah b. Hagra had taught that a convert who possessed standing corn that was harvested before he converted is exempt from the requirement of leaving in his field the grain which fell from the sickle or the back of the hand for the poor. This grain was classified as the gleaning, *lqṭ*. If the corn were harvested after he converted, he is liable for leaving what fell for the poor. And if there were doubt whether the corn was harvested before or after the conversion, the anonymous opinion is that the convert is exempt from leaving the fallen grain. However, Judah b. Hagra declares him liable in cases of doubt for leaving the fallen grain for the poor.

96. Or sold the field to an Israelite.

97. YDem. 6:1; Venice yDem. 6:2, 25b. Moses Margolioth cites the text as yDem. 6:2. I have followed the reading suggested by Margolioth, and Jacob David ben Ze'ev Willowski, *loc. cit.* Cf. tDem. 6:2, which forms the basis of their interpretations of the text.

98. YYeb. 11:2; Venice 12a.

99. David Fränkel, *loc. cit.*

100. The printed edition and Moses Margolioth, *loc. cit.*, read *'mw;* Venice reads *'mh.*

101. YYeb. 11:2; Venice 12a. Torah Or, *loc. cit.*, Moses Margolioth, *loc. cit.*, and Schwab cite Lev. 1:2; see Moise Schwab, *Le Talmud de Jerusalem: Traduit pour la Premiere Fois. Tome Septeieme: Traites Yebamoth et Sota* (Paris, 1885), 161. However, David Fränkel, *loc. cit.*, cites Lev. 18:1, which opens the section on the forbidden relationships. Given the fact that the slave's intercourse with his mother is the topic under discussion, the latter seems to be the better reading. However, reference to "fats" suggests that the former reading might also be correct. The *gemara* then raises the possibility that this verse refers to the offering of fats and has nothing to do with the forbidden sexual relationships. At this point, the *gemara* draws an analogy between converts and handmaidens: Just as a convert cannot marry his mother before or after his conversion, so also a handmaiden is the same whether or not she has been freed. Exactly what this text means is unclear, for both the convert and the handmaiden are female, and the initial question dealt with a male having intercourse with his mother. The point seems to be that certain rules applied to converts before and after they converted and to slaves before and after they were freed. But exactly what this analogy means is open to interpretation. David Fränkel raises the issue of whether the convert and slave are culpable for the death penalty or for bringing an offering. He concludes that they are liable for the latter, but not for the former. He also believes that the handmaiden is one who is half-free and half-slave who is engaged to an Israelite and with whom another Israelite has intercourse. Moses Margolioth ignores the fact that females are mentioned in the text. Thus the passage could center on the issue of forbidden sexual relationships or on offerings.

102. YQid. 4:1; Venice 65b. Cf. mYeb. 6:5; bYeb. 61b; Sifra Emor Pereq 1:7, Weiss 94b; Bamberger, *Proselytism in the Talmudic Period*, 83–84.

103. *They* [the priests] *shall not marry a woman defiled by prostitution* . . . . The reference to this verse is first made in mYeb. 6:5.

104. YYeb. 6:5; Venice 7c. This opinion is attributed to sages in mYeb. 6:5.

105. The verse states that the high priest may not marry *a widow, or a divorced woman, or one who is degraded by harlotry. . . . Only a virgin of his own kin may he take to wife;* yBik. 1:5, Venice 64a; yYeb. 8:2, Venice 9c; yQid. 4:6, Venice 66a. In yQid. 4:6 *bwgrt* appears in the printed text, but *gywrt* appears in Venice. In yYeb. 8:2 *gywrt* appears in the Venice edition and in the printed text; however, *bwgrt* appears in parenthesis in the printed edition. The correct reading must be *gywrt.*

106. YQid. 4:1; Venice 65b. Cf. bQid. 74b, 78a, and bYeb. 60b. The Palestinian Talmud contains a passage from Sifré Numbers Maṭot 157; Horovitz 212 in which we learn that a girl who converted while she was younger than three years and one

day may marry into the priestly caste. This ruling, attributed to Simeon, is based on an exegesis of Num. 31:18, *But spare every young woman who has not had carnal relations with a man.* However, the rabbis offer another interpretation of the verse, thus implying a rejection of Simeon's opinion; yBik. 1:5; Venice 64a. The statement is attributed to Simeon b. Yoḥai in Sifré Numbers Maṭot 157; Horovitz, 212. Jacob b. Idi b. Oshiya reports a story about a converted woman in "the South" who was being disqualified from marrying into the priesthood. After investigation, it was discovered that she converted before she was three years and one day old. We are told that Hoshiya, who taught like Simeon, declared her fit; yBik. 1:5, Venice 64a; yYeb. 8:2, Venice 9b. If one is clearly a priest (*khn brwr*), he may not marry a woman who is a convert. The issue is raised in the context of Judah's concern that the converts form a congregation unto themselves, so that they could not marry other groups; yYeb. 8:2; Venice 9b.

107. YBik. 1:5; Venice 64a. Cf. yQid. 4:6, Venice 66a and yYeb. 8:2, Venice 9b. Hoshiyah notes that this is in line with Simeon's statement that a girl under the age of three years and one day upon her conversion is fit to marry into the priestly class. On this passage, see Lee I. Levine, *The Rabbinic Class of Roman Palestine in Late Antiquity* (Jerusalem and New York, 1989), 145. Cf. bYeb. 60b.

108. YKet. 1:4; Venice 25c.

109. YNid. 1:4; Venice yNid. 1:5, 49b. In this case, Yosi rejects the whole concept of clean or unclean blood in this context, because these categories should apply only to Israelites. A similar situation arises in a discussion about a woman who gives birth to a normal fetus and to a sandal-shaped fetus, so that the distinction is made concerning her giving birth to one before she converted and the other after she converted. The *gemara* states that in this case the woman's conversion does not matter, for she does not bring her offering until the sandal-shaped fetus has emerged, no matter the relationship of the two fetuses to their mother's status; yNid. 3:4; Venice 50d. Cf. bNid. 26a.

110. YErub. 9:4, Venice 25d; yḤag. 3:4, Venice 79c; tṬoh. 9:7. The anonymous opinion states that if the proselyte states that he is certain that no libations were taken from the wine, he alone may use it. Aqiba argues that if the wine is permitted to the convert, it should be permitted for all Israelites. Yoḥanan responds that the wine is prohibited to everyone. Bamberger suggests that Aqiba's ruling reflects the rabbis' desire "to protect the convert from financial loss as a result of his conversion"; Bamberger, *Proselytism in the Talmudic Period*, 75.

111. *No Ammonite or Moabite shall be admitted into the congregation of YHWH, none of their descendants, even in the tenth generation, shall ever be admitted into YHWH's congregation. . . . You shall not abhor an Edomite, for he is your kinsman. You shall not abhor an Egyptian, for you were a stranger in his land. Children born to them may be admitted into the congregation of YHWH in the third generation.*

112. On the issue of the rabbis' perception in Mishnah and Tosefta that Israelites formed a distinct descent group, see Porton, *Goyim*, 221–23, 285–307.

The statement that a priest may not marry a converted female is part of a *sugya* which deals with the problem of distinguishing the several causes of one's being unacceptable for intermarrying with Israelites. Some causes are physical, others are genealogical, and the latter are more serious considerations than the former; Neusner, *Qiddushin*, 232.

113. Deut. 23:7–8 state that *the children of the third generation that are born to them* [Egyptian converts] *may enter the congregation of YHWH.*

114. Cf. tQid. 5:4.

115. YQid. 4:3, Venice 65d; yYeb. 8:2, Venice 9b.

116. YSoṭ. 4:5, Venice Soṭ. 4:6, 19d; yYeb. 7:5, Venice 8b. Cf. tYeb. 8:1 (the word "convert" is missing from the text in Tosefta).

117. David Fränkel, *loc. cit.*, prefers Jeremiah in the name of our rabbis and Ba, which appears later in the *sugya*.

118. YYeb. 8:3; Venice 9c.

119. Ibid.

120. YYeb. 1:6, Venice 3b; yQid. 4:1, Venice 65c. Nahman bar Jacob accepts converts from Kardunia and from Palmyra, and Abbahu in the name of Yohanan teaches that the converts from Palmyra are fit. Jacob cites Haninah and Joshua b. Levi to the effect that the one who declares them fit accepts, and the one who accepts does not declare them fit. The point of the passage is that those from Palmyra and Kardunia who claim to be converts are not considered to be non-Israelites or slaves; rather, they are accepted as converts. Finally, Yosi warns against taking special cases as paradigms for actions. He explains that when a person came from Ammon and Moab to convert, they would not accept him. However, in the present, we should not be concerned that all those who wish to convert are disqualified from entrance into the community because they are Moabites or Ammonites; yDem. 2:1; Venice 22c. On the Palmyrenes, see Braude, *Jewish Proselyting*, 65–69.

121. YKil. 8:3, Venice 31c; yShab. 5:1, Venice 7b. Yonah raises Hoshiya's question about the reasons that converts from Libya must wait three generations before they may enter the congregation. Yonah of Bozrah—this is Yonah b. Zaruyah in Venice and the printed edition on yShab. 5:1 and Yonah b. Sirda in the commentary of Moses Margolioth—responds that Libya is the same as Egypt. Yonah refers to a specific bean which is called an Egyptian bean when it is dry, but a Libyan bean when it is wet. Because it is the same bean, these must be the same places.

122. TDem. 6:12–13.

123. YMeg. 1:9; Venice yMeg. 1:11, 71c. In an extended discussion of the languages of the Torah, Jeremiah in the name of Hiyya bar Ba reports that Onqelos the convert translated the Torah in the presence of Eliezer and Joshua and that they praised him as one of the "distinguished among humans" (*ypypt mbny 'dm*). In yQid. 1:1; Venice 59a, Yosi cites Yohanan's statement concerning Onqelos's translation of Lev. 19:20 in the translation of the Torah he did for Aqiba. On Onqelos and Aquila, see Bamberger, *Proselytism in the Talmudic Period*, 238–43. He concludes that Aquila translated the Torah and Onqelos should be associated with Gamaliel. See also Philip S. Alexander, "Jewish Aramaic Translations of Hebrew Scriptures," in Martin J. Mulder, ed., *Mikra: Text, Translation, Reading and Interpretation of the Hebrew Bible in Ancient Judaism and Early Christianity. Compendia Rerum Iudaicarum ad Novum Testatmentum*, II.1 (Assen-Maastricht and Philadelphia, 1988), 217.

124. YḤag. 2:1; Venice 77a. Judah b. Pazzi in the name of Yosi b. Judah reports that Adrianos questioned Onqelos the convert about the Jewish claim that the world is suspended on air. When asked to demonstrate the veracity of the Jews' claim, Onqelos strangled Adrianos' camels and asked him to raise them up. Adrianos responded that he could not raise them after Onqelos had strangled them. Onqelos responded that all the camels lacked was air, so that the Jewish claim about the universe being supported by air was plausible.

125. YDem. 6:7; Venice yDem. 6:11, 25d. Cf. tDem. 6:12–13.

126. YSanh. 10:2; ySanh. 17:2, Venice 28c. Cf. YBer. 4:4; Venice, 8b. Joshua b. Levi explained that the wall to which Hezekiah turned his face, Isa. 38:2, was the wall which Rahab's house touched. Simeon b. Yohai taught about the great merit of Rahab whose deeds saved all of her descendants, and he implies that she and her descendants converted to the worship of YHWH. In yBer. 2:8; Venice 5b–c Jethro and Rahab are described as "cleaving to Israel." In yR.H 1:3, Venice 57a we are told that the nations of the world will be judged according to the worthy ones among them, Jethro and Rahab. On Jethro as a convert see Bamberger, *Proselytism in the Talmudic Period*, 182–91. On Rahab, see Bamberger, 193–95. See also the extended essay of Judith Baskin, "The Rabbinic Transformations of Rahab the Harlot," *Notre Dame English Journal* 11, no. 2 (1978/79): 141–57. Cf. Sifré Numbers Beha'alotekha 78, Horovitz 73.

127. YMeg. 1:11, Venice 1:13, 72b; yMeg. 3:2, Venice 74a; ySanh. 10:5, Venice ySanh. 17:6, 29c. It is reported that some saw Antonius going out with a broken sandal (*mn'wl pḥwt*) on the Day of Atonement. This, however, does not serve for proof that he converted, for even the "fearers of Heaven" go out like this on the Day of Atonement; see Moses Margolioth and David Fränkel, *loc. cit.* The *sugya* contains another debate in which Rabbi told Antonius that he could eat from the Leviathan in the world to come, but he could not eat from the Passover offering because he was not circumcised. Thereupon, Antonius had himself circumcised. The *sugya* ends with Hezekiah and Abbahu in the name of Leazar claiming that Antonius converted and that in the future he will be at the head of the righteous converts. It is further recorded that when Antonius had a menorah made for the synagogue, Rabbi stated, "Blessed is God." Samuel b. Isaac noted that Rabbi did not say, "Blessed is our God," and this is taken as an indication that Antonius had not converted; yMeg. 3:2; Venice 74a. In Leviticus Rabbah 3:2, Margulies, 1, 60, l. 3., Hezekiah and Abbahu in Eleazar's name state that when the righteous come, in the Messianic future, Antonius will be at their head.

128. YA.Z. 2:2, Venice 40d; yShab. 14:4, Venice 14d. The story is told that when Yohanan was ill, Domitian's daughter treated him in Tiberias. So that he would not need to visit her on the Sabbath, she gave him a prescription and told him not to reveal it to anyone. However, while he was in the schoolhouse on the Sabbath, he did reveal the prescription. When she heard about this, some say, she choked on a small bone, while others claim that she converted.

129. IChron. 2:17 reads: *Abigail bore Amasa, and the father of Amasa was Jether the Ishmaelite*, but IISam. 17:25 states: *Amasa was the son of man named Ithra the Israelite*. Samuel b. Nahman explains the apparent inconsistency of calling Amasa's father

an "Ishmaelite" and an "Israelite" by saying that when Amasa's father entered Isaiah's—Isaiah is written in parenthesis in the printed edition, but occurs in the text of the Venice edition—court and found him sitting and expounding Isa. 45:22, *Turn to me and be saved, all the ends of the earth*, he converted and gave him his daughter to marry; yYeb. 8:3; Venice 9c.

130. YSheq. 1:4; Venice 1:5, 46b. Cf. Sifra VaYiqra Nedabah Parashah 2:3, Weiss 4:3; bHul. 5a.

131. YTan. 2:2, Venice 65c; yBer. 4:3, Venice 8c. In yBer. 2:4; Venice 5a the *beraita* is quoted, but it is not part of a dispute between Leazar and Yosi. Cf. tBer. 3:25.

132. YErub. 9:4, Venice 25d; yHag. 3:4, Venice 79c. Yohanan holds the same opinion about *kosht*, a gourd, an alleyway, and the *am ha'ares*.

133. YBer. 2:8; Venice 5b–c; see Braude, *Jewish Proselyting*, 20.

134. YSanh. 2:6; Venice Sanh. 9:6, 20c. See Braude, *Jewish Proselyting*, 33. This disagrees with Simeon b. Yohai who claimed that Solomon married his many wives because of his sexual urges.

135. YSanh. 10:2; Venice 17:2, 29b. The same phrase is attributed to the rabbis in a *beraita* on bSanh. 107b. There it is not attached to the verse from Job and deals with the need to bring one to repentance more than dealing with a convert. The phrase also occurs in Mekhilta Ishmael Amalek 1, Horovitz and Rabin 193, ll. 7–8.

136. YPes. 8:8, Venice 36b and yNaz. 8:1, Venice 57a. Cf. tPis. 7:14. Bamberger claims that "we have here an ancient report that some of the Roman soldiers stationed around the Temple to preserve order during the holiday period . . . themselves converted to the Jewish faith"; Bamberger, *Proselytism in the Talmudic Period*, 232. He claims that the fact that the conversion is mentioned only "incidently" and the fact that Dio Cassius reports "the great impression made on the Roman soldiery by Judaism in general and the Temple in particular" supports the historicity of this report; Bamberger, 232–33. Lieberman holds the same opinion; Saul Lieberman, *Tosefta Ki-fshutah: A Comprehensive Commentary on the Tosefta Part IV Order Mo'ed* (New York, 1962), 614–15. Moore uses this passage, along with Sifré Numbers 71, tPis. 8:4, and bQid. 70a, to argue that "the criterion, which decides whether a man is a proselyte or not is whether he may participate in the Passover meal"; Moore, *Judaism*, 1:330, n. 4. See also Scot McKnight, *A Light among the Gentiles: Jewish Missionary Activity in the Second Temple Period* (Minneapolis, 1991), 83.

Chapter 6

1. David Goodblatt, "The Babylonian Talmud," in Hildegard Temporini and Wolfgang Haase, eds., *Aufstieg und Nidergang der römischen Welt* (Berlin and New York, 1979), II.19.2, 264–65.

2. On the various theories concerning the editing process and date of the Babylonian Talmud, see Jacob Neusner, *The Formation of the Babylonian Talmud: Studies in the Achievements of Late Nineteenth- and Twentieth-Century Historical and*

Literary-Critical Research (Leiden, 1970); Goodblatt, 257–336. The Babylonian Talmud contains a *gemara* to thirty-seven of Mishnah's sixty-three tractates. With the exception of *Berakhot*, there is no Babylonian *germara* to *Zera'im*. The Babylonian Talmud contains all of *Mo'ed* with the exception of *Sheqalim*. There is also no *gemara* to *Eduyyot* or *Abot* in *Neziqin; Middot, Qinnim*, or part of *Tamid* from *Qodashim;* or *Tohorot*, with the exception of *Niddah*. See Goodblatt, 259; Eliezer Berkovits, "Talmud, Babylonian," in Cecil Roth and Geoffrey Wigoder, eds., *Encyclopaedia Judaica* (Jerusalem, 1973), 15, col. 757.

3. Louis Ginzberg, "An Introduction to the Palestinian Talmud," *On Jewish Law and Lore* (New York, 1970), 20–24; Abraham Goldberg, "The Babylonian Talmud," in Shmuel Safrai, ed., *The Literature of the Sages: Part One, Oral Tora, Halakha, Mishna, Tosefta, Talmud, External Tractates. Compendia Rerum Iudaicarum ad Novum Testamentum* (Assen-Maastricht and Philadelphia, 1987), 336.

4. Jacob Neusner, *Judaism, the Classical Statement: The Evidence of the Bavli* (Chicago, 1986), 100.

5. Ibid., 104.

6. BPes. 87b. One *kor* consists of thirty *se'ahs;* see Herbert Danby, *The Mishnah, Translated from the Hebrew with Introduction and Brief Explanatory Notes* (Oxford, reprint 1964), 798. However, the *gemara* and Rashi, *loc. cit.*, disagree on exactly which part of the verse Yohanan derived his teaching from. For similar thoughts in later collections, see Bernard J. Bamberger, *Proselytism in the Talmudic Period* (New York, 1968), 156–58. Bamberger writes, "That the tragedy of exile, which is usually regarded in Jewish tradition as the bitter punishment of sin, should have been interpreted, even by a few teachers, as a method used by Providence for the increase of proselytes, indicates how great was the importance attached by the Rabbis to the missionary movement"; Bamberger, 156–57. See also Ephraim E. Urbach, *The Sages, Their Concepts and Beliefs*, trans. Israel Abrahams (Cambridge and London, 1987), 542–46. On the other hand, this may reflect an attempt by some to find any positive significance at all in the fact that the Israelites no longer resided in the Land of Israel, under their own government, and with their Temple intact.

7. BA.Z. 24a.

8. Papa reported that Ammi and Isaac Nappaha were sitting in the latter's tent reviewing Eliezer's opinion that cattle bought from gentiles could not be offered to YHWH. In refutation of Eliezer's view, his colleagues cited Isa. 60:7: *All the flocks of Kedar shall be assembled for you, the rams of Bebaioth shall serve your needs; they shall be welcome offerings on my altar* . . . . Eliezer replied that these peoples would become *grym grwrym* in the future. Joseph quoted Zeph. 3:9 in support of Eliezer's assertion: *For then I will make the peoples pure of speech, so that they all invoke YHWH by name*. In response to Abayye's objection that this might mean only that they will turn away from their idols, Joseph quoted the end of the verse, *And serve him with one accord*. Zebid offered a slightly different version. He reported that it was Eliezer himself who cited Zeph. 3:9 in support of his claim that they would become *grym grwrym*, that it was Joseph who suggested that this could mean only that they would reject their idols, and that it was Abayye who cited the end of the

verse. On this passage, see Ernst Bammel, "Gerim Gerurim," *Annual of the Swedish Theological Institute* 7 (1968–69): 128–29.

9. BYeb. 63a.

10. IKgs. 14:31.

11. BA.Z. 9a.

12. Cf. William G. Braude, *Jewish Proselyting in the First Five Centuries of the Common Era: The Age of the Tannaim and Amoraim* (Providence, 1940), 28.

13. BBer. 57b.

14. Cf. tBer. 6:2.

15. Cf. yBer. 2:8, Venice 5b–c where we are told that YHWH traverses the earth for righteous people from whom to make converts.

16. BYeb. 47b.

17. BYed. 109b.

18. BNid. 13a. "Those who play with children" is finally interpreted as referring to one who marries a minor who is incapable of bearing children. Braude states that "Isaac's advice is obviously not on the religious but on the practical plane. He does not speak of punishment by God but by men." Exactly what Braude thinks Isaac's statement means is unclear, nor is Braude's explanation comprehensible. Bamberger interprets the passage to mean that "those who direct the reproductive instinct into abnormal channels delay the Messiah. . . . But what converts have to do with all this is exceedingly doubtful"; Bamberger, *Proselytism*, 162. Helbo's comment appears also on bQid. 70b. Hoenig attempts to explain Helbo's statement by stating that he "was writing in the period when the Roman Empire had just adopted Christianity as the official religion of the state and had published an edict making conversion to Judaism a punishable offense for both the converter and the converted"; Sidney B. Hoenig, "Conversion during the Talmudic Period," in David M. Eichhorn, ed., *Conversion to Judaism: A History and Analysis* (New York, 1965), 61. He notes that even Helbo's students rejected his opinion. On Constantius II's laws discouraging conversion to Judaism, see Michael Avi-Yonah, *The Jews of Palestine: A Political History from the Bar Kokhba War to the Arab Conquest* (New York, 1976), 174–76. Amnon Linder, *The Jews in Roman Imperial Legislation* (Detroit, 1987), 138–44 (prohibition against circumcising slaves), 144–51 (laws concerning the purchasing and converting of non-Israelite slaves), 151–53 (law on the confiscation of the property of those who convert to Judaism). Unfortunately, Hoenig does not specify which law(s) he is referring to. Also, there is no way of knowing why Helbo was opposed to converts. All we know is that we have one tradition, repeated three times, which testifies to Helbo's negative attitude toward those who converted to Judaism. Braude attempts to show that the rabbis really did not speak ill of converts or conversion; Braude, *Jewish Proselyting*, 43. Bamberger, *Proselytism*, 163–65, concludes that "Helbo's saying is the opinion of an individual and a most atypical one. He is not the only scholar who was hostile to converts, but such were very few"; Bamberger, *Proselytism*, 164. In Mekhilta Ishmael Mishpatim 18 Eliezer states that the converts have a bad streak in them. In Sifré Numbers Beha'alotekha 85 we read that converts caused the Israelites to sin in

the desert. On the statements of Helbo and Isaac, see Urbach, *The Sages*, 550–52.

19. BQid. 70b. Cf. Rashi, *loc. cit.* Braude claims that this is "not to be taken as animadversions on proselytes." Rather, this "overdrawn contrast" seeks to console the Jews at a time of persecution. In fact, Braude states that Hama b. Hanina and Rabbah bar Huna "very probably welcomed proselytes in the manner of their predecessors and contemporaries." The only negative point that Braude is willing to concede is that this negativity toward converts stems from "disappointment experienced with unstable or dishonest proselytes who caused mischief to their erstwhile hosts"; Braude, *Jewish Proselyting*, 44–45. In fact, this does appear to be a rather ethnocentric statement which is just what one would expect. Exactly why this comment is in response to "unstable or dishonest proselytes" is unclear, for it would be extremely curious if we did not find any rabbinic comments suggesting that native-born Israelites had a special relationship to YHWH which could not be shared by converts. Bamberger states that "this is an expression of national pride, not of positive ill will toward proselytes"; Bamberger, *Proselytism*, 165. This is an attempt to maintain his thesis that rabbinic Judaism was above all positive toward converts.

20. We have several versions of a list that records those who came with Ezra from Babylonia, and the converts appear as a distinct unit within the list; bYeb. 37a, mQid. 4:1, bQid. 70a, mHor. 3:8, bYeb. 85a. The fact that the lists are not exactly the same led Ginzberg and Bamberger to speculate on the relative importance of the various groups which are represented; Bamberger, *Proselytism*, 64–65. The fact that the converts appear in these lists has important ramifications for some of the discussions on whether or not converts could marry into the priestly caste; see Bamberger, 81–84 and chap. 8.

21. BYeb. 48a. This is part of a long passage, which begins on bYeb. 47b, which attempts to find the meaning of "the same law applies to a convert and to an emancipated slave." The *sugya* concludes that because only a slave purchased from a gentile needs to make the declaration concerning the acceptance of the commandments, a slave bought from an Israelite does not need to do this, the only thing that all slaves and the converts have in common is the required ritual immersion. Of course it is impossible to determine for certain whether the comparison came first or the practice of making the declaration came first. It is clear that the conversion of non-Israelite slaves was an accepted practice. Rabin taught in the name of Resh Laqish that it was meritorious to purchase servants from gentiles because the Israelite would bring the servants "under the wings of the *Shekhinah*," which seems to imply that some sages approved of gaining gentile slaves in order to convert them to Judaism; bA.Z. 13b. In yA.Z. 1:4, Venice, 39c Rabin does not appear. We find only Resh Laqish's statement. Cf. Braude, *Jewish Proselyting*, 15. The early Christian emperors assumed that slaves would be converted, and they placed restrictions on the Israelites' owning and converting non-Israelite slaves; Linder, *The Jews in Roman Imperial Legislation*, 144–51.

22. MKer. 1:1 states that "there are thirty-six [transgressions] which are punishable by 'cutting off,'" and the *gemara* discusses why a specific number is mentioned. As part of that discussion the *gemara* refers to Eliezer b. Jacob's comment,

mKer. 2:1, that the convert is regarded as a person who requires the ceremony of atonement until the blood has been sprinkled for him; bKer. 2b. This suggests that the rituals performed upon conversion in some way serve as a means for the converts to atone for their sins. Thus, conversion "purifies" gentiles in some manner. In another discussion of Eliezer b. Jacob's comment in mKer. 2:1, the *gemara* asks why the convert was not mentioned by the anonymous authority behind the mishnah. The text responds that the others mentioned in mKer. 2:1 were people who wished to eat holy things; however, the converts are different, for they are seeking only to enter the congregation; bKer. 8b.

23. YQid. 3:12, Venice 3:14, 64d; yQid. 4:7, Venice 66a.

24. BYeb. 46b. On bBer. 47b the *gemara* claims that mBer. 7:1 excluded a gentile from being counted in the assembly of those required to recite the grace after a meal in order to indicate that a convert who had been circumcised but who had not yet been immersed is still considered a gentile. In support of this view, Zera cites Yohanan's teaching that one does not become a convert until he has been circumcised and immersed, for he is considered to be a gentile until he has undergone the ritual immersion. While at Gabla, Hiyya b. Abba ran across Israelite women who were conceived from converts who were circumcised but who had not performed the ritual ablution. When Hiyya questioned Yohanan, the latter responded that their children would be considered *mamzerim*. The *gemara* states that this corresponds to Yohanan's normal opinion, for Hiyya b. Abba stated in Yohanan's name that a man is not a proper convert unless he has been circumcised and ritually immersed. If he has not performed both rituals, he is considered a gentile. And Rabbah b. Bar Hana had stated in Yohanan's name that the child of a gentile (or a slave) who cohabited with the daughter of an Israelite is a *mamzer;* bYeb. 46a, bA.Z. 59a.

25. BYeb. 46b. According to Rashi, *loc. cit.*, if Yosi did permit the immersion, he also would have required a symbolic circumcision, so that he could be certain that the person was circumcised for the expressed purpose of becoming a convert, but Rashi's interpretation may well result from his belief that all the talmudic rabbis would require both circumcision and immersion for conversion. The *gemara* then concludes that because Judah accepts a convert who has been *either* circumcised *or* immersed, he would allow a person who had been circumcised on the eve of the Sabbath to be immersed on the Sabbath because the immersion would not effect an improvement in the person, which is not allowed on the Sabbath, for the person's circumcision would have effected the conversion. Yosi, however, requires *both* immersion *and* circumcision for conversion; therefore, he would not allow the person who had been circumcised on the eve of the Sabbath to be immersed on the Sabbath because this would complete his conversion and effect an improvement in the man's status on the Sabbath. Cf. yQid. 4:7; Venice 66a, where the same issue of improving a person through ablution on the Sabbath is discussed. On the dispute between Yosi and Judah, see David Halivni, *Sources and Traditions: A Source Critical Commentary on Seder Nashim* (Tel Aviv, 1968), 53–55. Halivni claims that the editor of the *sugya* has combined two separate sources and that only one of them originally mentioned the Sabbath.

26. BYeb. 46b. The tradents for this passage are unclear. The text states: Said Rabbah: "A case came before the court of R. Hiyya b. Rabbi. And Joseph taught: Hoshiya b. Rabbi and Rav Safra taught: R. Hoshiya b. Hiyya."

27. This would mean that one could not convert on a day on which a court did not meet, such as the Sabbath or on festivals; Bamberger, *Proselytism*, 39. Rashi, *loc. cit.*, says that this is based on the fact that Safra considered three sages to have been present: Hiyya b. Rabbi, cited by Rabbah; Oshiya b. Rabbi, cited by Joseph; and Oshiya, cited by Safra. Hiyya b. Abba cites Yohanan's teaching that conversion can take place only in the presence of three, i. e., a rabbinic court. He bases his ruling on the appearance of the word "law," *mšpt*, in Num. 15:16 and on the fact that a law cannot be enacted by fewer than three judges; bYeb. 46b. Hiyya's citation of Yohanan also appears on bQid. 62a–b. There Rashi provides the logic of Yohanan's statement, and he suggests that Num. 15:16, *the same law shall apply to you and to the convert (gr) who resides among you* means that the same court is required for a convert and a native-born Israelite who wishes to change his status. Judah deduced the requirement that a gentile had to appear before a court in order to convert from Deut. 1:16, *[I further charged your magistrates as follows, "Hear out your fellow men,] and decide justly between any man and a fellow Israelite or a convert (grw)*; bYeb. 47a.

28. On bYeb. 47b the rules covering the ablution are discussed. The same laws apply to the ablution for an emancipated slave and for a convert. They must perform their immersion in forty *se'ahs* of water; this is Rashi's interpretation of the statement in the *gemara* that the slave and the convert may immerse only in the same place that the menstruant women may immerse. Any item which prevents the water from touching the menstruant woman, so that her purification is considered invalid, also prevents the water from touching the convert and the emancipated slave, so that the conversion or the emancipation is considered invalid.

29. Although we do not find extended discussions concerning the time of day during which the convert should be immersed, the Babylonian Talmud does make it clear that the circumcision of a convert should normally occur during the day. On bYeb. 72a–b we are told that the symbolic circumcision of a convert who was already circumcised must take place during the day. Eleazar b. Simeon disagrees with this anonymous ruling and states that children who are not circumcised on the eighth day may be circumcised during the day or the night; however, it is unclear whether or not his ruling refers to the convert. I have assumed that it does not; see tShab. 15:9. Perhaps the rule concerning immersion comes from its being paralleled with circumcision. It is also possible that the ritual must be performed during the day because it is a court procedure. YYeb. 8:1; Venice 8d tells us that converted women are immersed during the day. TShab. 15:9 talks about circumcision at night.

30. BYeb. 46a. On bYeb. 46b the *gemara* ignores the plain meaning of the *beraita* and maintains that Eliezer and Joshua did not disagree about one who was immersed but who had not been circumcised, for they would accept that person as a convert. They only disagreed about one who had been circumcised but who

had not undergone the ritual immersion, for Eliezer does not accept this one as a convert, on the basis of the forefathers, while Joshua does accept such a person, by claiming that the forefathers also underwent ritual immersion. One might argue that Joshua based his point on Ex. 19:10, *Go to the people and warn them to stay pure today and tomorrow. Let them wash their clothes.* Joshua could have argued that if they had to wash their clothes, it is logical to assume that they also had to immerse themselves. This is the case because we know that they had to immerse themselves even when they did not need to wash their clothes; e.g., Lev. 15:16: *When a man has an emission of semen, he shall bathe his whole body in water and remain unclean until evening.* The *gemara* responds, however, that the washing in Ex. 19:10 could refer to only cleaning one's clothes, so that there is no logical reason to assume that the men underwent a ritual immersion. However, one can deduce that the males were immersed from Ex. 24:8: *And Moses took the blood and sprinkled it on the people,* for one cannot be sprinkled with blood unless he has undergone a ritual immersion; bKer. 9a. Furthermore, Joshua can logically deduce that the female ancestors had to undergo ritual immersion, for surely they had to perform some ritual before they became worthy to be protected by YHWH, literally, "to come under the wings of the *Shekhinah*."

31. BYeb. 46a.

32. See Braude, *Jewish Proselyting*, 74–76, where he claims that the threefold conversion ritual was practiced throughout the talmudic period.

33. YQid. 3:14; Venice 64d. See Bamberger's discussion of the scholarly views of the issue up to his time; Bamberger, *Proselytism*, 47–52.

34. Bamberger, *Proselytism*, 51. Schiffman, 35–36, accepts Bamberger's conclusions; Lawrence H. Schiffman, *Who Was a Jew? Rabbinic and Halakhic Perspectives on the Jewish-Christian Schism* (Hoboken, 1985), 33–36.

35. Scot McKnight, *A Light among the Gentiles: Jewish Missionary Activity in the Second Temple Period* (Minneapolis, 1991), 81.

36. See ibid., 79–81.

37. Isaac Weil, *Le Prosélytisme chez les Juifs selon la Bible et le Talmud* (Strasbourg, 1880), 60–65.

38. Hoenig, "Conversion during the Talmudic Period," 45.

39. S. Bialoblocki, *Die Bezeihungen des Judentums zu Proselyten und Proselytentum* (Berlin, 1930), 17–19.

40. John Nolland, "Uncircumcised Proselytes?" *Journal for the Study of Judaism in the Persian, Hellenistic and Roman Period* 12, no. 2 (December 1981): 191.

41. Ibid., 192.

42. Ibid.

43. Jacob Neusner, *Eliezer Ben Hyrcanus: The Traditions and the Man* (Leiden, 1973), 1:180. See also David Halivni, *Sources and Traditions*, 55, note 6. While I agree with Neusner that the debate suggests some uncertainty concerning the existence of a set ritual of conversion, I would claim that this was the case even in the amoraic period.

44. H. H. Rowley, "Jewish Proselyte Baptism," *Hebrew Union College Annual* 15 (1940): 318–19.

45. Louis Finkelstein, "The Institution of Baptism for Proselytes," *Journal of Biblical Literature* 52 (1933): 210.

46. Neil J. McEleney, "Conversion, Circumcision, and the Law," *New Testament Studies* 20, no. 3 (April 1974): 331–32.

47. Jonathan Z. Smith, *Imagining Religion: From Babylon to Jonestown* (Chicago and London, 1982), 13.

48. John J. Collins, "A Symbol of Otherness: Circumcision and Salvation in the First Century," in Jacob Neusner and Ernest Frerichs, eds., *"To See Ourselves as Others See Us": Christians, Jews, "Others" in Late Antiquity* (Chico, 1985), 174.

49. Num. 15:15.

50. BKer. 9a. The act of circumcision can be derived from Josh. 5:5—*Now, whereas all the people who came out of Egypt had been circumcised . . .*—or Ezek. 16:6— *When I passed by you and saw you wallowing in your blood, I said to you: "Live in spite of your blood." Yea, I said to you: "Live in spite of your blood."* The sprinkling of the blood from the offerings is based on Ex. 24:4–6: *Early in the morning, he set up an altar at the foot of the mountain. . . . He designated some young men among the Israelites, and they offered burnt offerings and sacrificed bulls as offerings of well-being to YHWH. Moses took one part of blood and put it in basins, and the other part of the blood he dashed against the altar.* Although there is no direct reference to immersion, the *gemara* claims that because there is no sprinkling of blood without immersion, Ex. 24:6 demonstrates that the people immersed themselves. This seems to be a feeble attempt to find justification in the Torah for a ritual which was accepted practice, even though there was no clear biblical basis for it. Cf. Sifré Numbers Shelaḥ 108.

51. BShab. 135a.

52. BShab. 137b.

53. Blessed are you, YHWH, our God, king of the universe, who has sanctified us with your commandments and has commanded us concerning circumcision.

54. Blessed are you, YHWH, our God, king of the universe who has sanctified us with your commandments and has commanded us to lead him into the covenant of our father, Abraham.

55. Jer. 33:25. This seems to be the way in the *gemara* reads the verse.

56. Virtually the same blessing is said upon the circumcision of a slave. This is what we would expect, for the assumption is that the slave was not an Israelite.

57. *Tnw rbnn.*

58. BA.Z. 26a–27a. The *gemara* contains an extended discussion on whether or not an Israelite may heal a gentile without receiving compensation, which then moves into a discussion of whether or not a gentile may circumcise an Israelite. The bridge between these two topics is our *beraita;* bA.Z. 26b. See Tosefot, *loc. cit.*

59. BYeb. 78a–b. Ignoring the matter of "interposing," Rabba's decision seems obvious, for the embryo is not considered an individual, so that when its mother converts before it is born, it is counted as an Israelite upon its birth. One could argue, therefore, that the point may be simply that the child is considered to have been born an Israelite because its mother converted before its birth.

60. BKer. 8b–9a.

61. *Tnw rbnn.*

62. TSheq. 3:21.

63. Sifré Numbers Shelaḥ 108.

64. Tosefta does not contain the requirement that the convert bring the second bird offering.

65. In Sifré Numbers, this verse is used to prove that converts must perform a rite with the blood of their offering, so that the midrash may well serve as the basis of this part of the *sugya*.

66. BKer. 9a.

67. Ibid.

68. Ibid.

69. Ibid. In a parallel *sugya* on bR.H. 31b, a *beraita* states that one of the nine decrees of Yohanan b. Zakkai concerned the requirement that "at the present time," when the Temple is no longer standing, converts should set aside a quarter-*sheqel* or a quarter-*dinar* instead of bringing a bird offering. Simeon b. Eleazar stated that Yohanan took a vote and annulled this rule because it might lead to wrongdoing because the money might be spent for secular purposes. Cf. ySheq. 8:4; Venice ySheq. 8:6, 51b. TSheq. 3:22 states that the bringing of the bird offering applied only while the Temple stood. Jacob Neusner, *A Life of Yohanan Ben Zakkai, Ca. 1–80* C.E., 2d ed., rev. (Leiden, 1970), 210, 212, and *Development of a Legend: Studies on the Traditions concerning Yohanan Ben Zakkai* (Leiden, 1970), 135–36, 154–58, 207–9, 271, 275, 284–85.

70. BKer. 9a. Aha based his decision on an interpretation of Num. 15:14: *And when, throughout your generations, a convert who has taken up residence with you. . . .* The important phrase is *throughout your generations.*

71. YSheq. 8:4; Venice ySheq. 8:6, 51b.

72. BYeb. 47a–b. The passage is introduced by *tnw rbnn.*

73. Hoenig suggests that this procedure was instituted after the Bar Kokhba war because "many Roman spies were disguising themselves as converts to help uncover plots to regain Jewish independence. This is reflected in an increasingly suspicious attitude on the part of the Jews toward those who seek to convert"; Hoenig, "Conversion during the Talmudic Period," 52. Hoenig does not offer any evidence to support his claim. On the date of this passage Schiffman writes: "From the language of our *baraita*', with its stress on the persecution and downtrodden nature of Israel, it is most likely to have been composed in its present form in the aftermath of either the Great Revolt of 66–74 C.E. or the Bar Kokhba Revolt (132–34 C.E.). Regardless of which of these two dates is correct, the *baraita*' reflects the legal rulings prevalent among the Tannaim by the Yavnean period"; Schiffman, *Who Was a Jew?* 20. It is curious that this "tannaitic" practice is not mentioned in any of the earlier texts! Rowley implies that this practice is at least tannaitic, for he argues that converts were immersed before the destruction of the Temple and that the ritual required "spectators" who questioned the convert; Rowley, "Jewish Proselyte Baptism," 324–25.

74. As early as Mishnah and Tosefta these offerings were seen as ethnic obligations which were used to unify the group through mutual support; Gary G. Porton, *Goyim: Gentiles and Israelites in Mishnah Tosefta* (Atlanta, 1988), 182–84.

75. Further on in the text on bYeb. 47b, Eleazar offers an interpretation of Ruth 1:16–18 as proof for the assertion that the gentile is not be excessively encouraged or discouraged from converting. *When she saw how determined she was to go with her, she ceased to argue with her.* In response to Naomi's telling Ruth about the Sabbath boundaries, the latter responded, *Wherever you go, I will go* (Ruth 1:16). When Naomi told her that women are not allowed to be alone with men other than their husbands, Ruth responded, *wherever you lodge, I will lodge.* When Naomi told Ruth about the six hundred and thirteen commandments, the latter said, *Your people shall be my people.* When Naomi told her that idols were forbidden, Ruth responded, *and your God, my God.* Naomi explained that the court had available four means of execution, and Ruth responded, *Where you die, I shall die.* And when she was told that the court had two graveyards under its control, Ruth stated, *and there I will be buried.*

76. *Lkl dbryw.*

77. The agricultural gifts were required only in Israel. See Alan Avery-Peck, *Mishnah's Division of Agriculture: A History and Theology of Seder Zeraim* (Chico, 1985); William D. Davies, *The Gospel and the Land: Early Christianity and Jewish Territorial Doctrine* (Berkeley and Los Angeles, 1974). If the passage is actually tannaitic, the inclusion of the agricultural gifts is less problematic. Cohen argues that the text is tannaitic on the basis of the requirement that two, not three, sages supervise the conversion. Because Yohanan requires a court of three to supervise the conversion ceremony, "if our text was created any time after R. Yohanan, it is hard to imagine that it would not have required a tribunal of three." He also states that "[a] mid-second century c.e. date is also suggested by the text's linguistic parallels with the Mishnah, the Tosephta, and other putative *baraitot*"; Shaye J. D. Cohen, "The Rabbinic Conversion Ceremony," *Journal of Jewish Studies* 41, no. 3 (Autumn 1990): 187. While Cohen's arguments should be taken into consideration, they are not determinative. It is possible that the presence of two sages reflects an alternate tradition to that of Yohanan, for we have no reason to assume that everyone accepted Yohanan's opinion. It is possible that some held that conversion was not necessarily a legal act requiring a rabbinic court. It is also possible that an amora could construct a *beraita* in the style of an actual tannaitic text. Given the fact that scholars have discovered other *beraitot* that were amoraic constructions but written in the style of tannaitic passages, this is not a strong argument. To my mind, the most important difficulty with assigning this text to the tannaitic period is that no text before the Babylonian Talmud mentions anything of this ritual.

78. Porton, *Goyim, passim;* John G. Gager, *Origins of Anti-Semitism: Attitudes Toward Judaism in Pagan and Christian Antiquity* (New York and Oxford, 1985), 57; Robert Goldenberg, "The Jewish Sabbath in the Roman World up to the Time of Constantine the Great," in Hildegard Temporini and Wolfgang Haase, eds., *Aufstieg und Niedergang der römischen Welt* (Berlin and New York, 1979), II.19.1, 414–44; Louis Feldman, *Jew and Gentile in the Ancient World: Attitudes and Interactions from Alexander to Justinian* (Princeton, 1993), 158–70.

79. On bBekh. 30b we find that a convert who is suspected of not observing one Israelite law is suspected of disregarding the whole Torah. However, he is

classified as a nonobservant Israelite because he had converted and become part of the People Israel. The passage also discusses the *am ha'areṣ* who wishes to become a *ḥaber* but who also disregards one of the rules of the Torah. This parallels tDem. 2:4. Cf. Sifra Qedoshim Pereq 8:3; Weiss 91a and tDem. 2:5 which is a similar text. In this latter passage, Yosi b. Judah glosses the anonymous saying. Bamberger believes that this stress on observing the whole of the Torah results from the rise of Christianity; Bamberger, *Proselytism*, 31–32. His only possible link to any historical setting is the reference to Yosi b. Judah, a fourth generation tanna. However, exactly when the earlier versions of this *sugya* were created is unclear. Furthermore, Yosi does not appear in the version in the Babylonian Talmud. On tDem. 2:5, see Richard S. Sarason, *A History of the Mishnaic Law of Agriculture Section Three: A Study of Tractate Demai* (Leiden, 1979), 65–85; Saul Lieberman, *Tosefta Kifshutah: A Comprehensive Commentary on the Tosefta. Order Zera'im, Part I* (New York, 1955), 212.

80. Our passage is part of a larger section which opens with the statement, "a man should always be gentle like Hillel, and not impatient like Shammai."

81. BShab. 31a. David Kraemer suggests that "the subject of both of these exchanges, beyond the superior character of Hillel, is the relationship of Written and Oral Torah"; David Kraemer, "The Formation of Rabbinic Canon: Authority and Boundaries," *Journal of Biblical Literature* 110, no. 4 (Winter 1991): 620.

82. The issue of the priesthood is important, for as we have seen above, and as we shall see below, the question of whether or not converts could marry into the priestly caste occupied the sages a good deal.

83. BShab. 31a. Although Bamberger approves of Lévi's suggestions that these accounts "are not altogether historical," the former does believe that they contain "a kernel of historic fact"; Bamberger, *Proselytism*, 223–25. Bamberger adds that the "theory" that Ben He He and Ben Bag Bag should be identified as a single person who was one of these converts "though not implausible, appears only in medieval sources"; Bamberger, 224. On these passages, see Jacob Neusner, *The Rabbinic Traditions about the Pharisees before 70* (Leiden, 1971), 1:322–24. On the basis of these accounts, Glatzer claimed that "in Hillel's period proselytes were not only welcome; the community was eager to make converts"; Nahum N. Glatzer, *Hillel the Elder: The Emergence of Classical Judaism*, rev. ed. (New York, 1956), 74–78. The quotation is from page 78. Glatzer's reading, even ignoring its assumptions about the historical veracity of the *gemara*, does not take account of Shammai's position, which was not favorable toward to converts. See also Alan F. Segal, *Paul the Convert: The Apostolate and Apostasy of Saul the Pharisee* (New Haven and London, 1990), 97–98. Segal states that "one effect of Hillel's answer is to encourage the convert to enter the stages of training to become a socialized Jew" (p. 98). Segal believes that the rabbis "demanded long training" for the gentile who wished to convert (p. 98). However, at least the conversion ritual mentioned on bYeb. 47b may imply that this was done at the time of the conversion, immediately preceding the ritual. On the other hand, the rabbis are clear that growing up in a Jewish environment socializes the person to the customs of the Israelite community, so that a gentile will have to spend some time learning what to do and

not to do; however, this process may occur after conversion. This seems to be the importance of the dispute between Aqiba and Monobases about the convert who inadvertantly violates the Sabbath; tShab. 8:5 and bShab. 68b. See further McKnight, *A Light among the Gentiles*, 42. McKnight compares Hillel's position in the Talmud to mAbot. 1:2 in which Hillel is described as "loving humankind and bringing them near to the Torah."

84. BYeb. 46b–47a. This is based on an interpretation of Lev. 19:33: *When a convert resides with you in your land.* . . . The *gemara* claims that the phrase *with you*, *'tk*, means that he or she should be well known. From the phrase, *and when a convert resides*, we learn that if one brings witnesses of the conversion, one is believed. Because Lev. 19:33 specifically mentions *in your land*, we could conclude that the above-mentioned discussion applies only to converts who reside within the Land of Israel; however, the phrase *with you* indicates that it applies in any place where Israelites live. According to Judah, the phrase *in your land* means that one who claims to be a convert within the Land of Israel must bring proof of the conversion, while one who makes the claim outside the Land of Israel does not need to produce evidence of the conversion. Sages, however, disagree and rule that the convert must produce support for the claims inside or outside the Land of Israel. Sheshet argues that because we have a biblical verse to support the claim that we believe the proselytes if they bring witnesses, we can argue that we accept their testimony even if they were not eye-witnesses to the actual conversion. Cf. Sifra Qedoshim Pereq 8:1; Weiss 91a.

85. BYeb. 47a. If the man had not been Jewish, his children would have been declared unfit because they were the offspring of the union of a gentile and an Israelite woman.

86. BYeb. 24b. The passage is introduced by *tnw rbnn*.

87. Braude states that "this apparent exclusiveness was motivated by no wish to hoard Messianic bliss unto the Jews but came from unfortunate experiences with disingenuous converts"; Braude, *Jewish Proselyting*, 45. He brings no evidence to support his hypothesis. See Weil who argues that in the Messianic age there will be a universal adoration of God; Weil, *Le Prosélytisme*, 52. On the gentiles' place in the Messianic age, see, for example, bA.Z. 24a–b; yA.Z. 2:1, Venice 40c.

88. BYeb. 24b. See yQid. 4:1; Venice 65b, where those who converted in order to enjoy the material benefits of the reign of Solomon are mentioned and rejected as converts. However, yQid. 4:1; Venice 65c and ySanh. 6:7; Venice 13:9, 23d mention those who converted at the time of David and Solomon. And on ySanh. 2:6, Venice 9:6; 20c we are told that Solomon married many women in order to bring them to the worship of YHWH. Elsewhere on bYeb. 24b we find a comment attributed to Nehemiah which states that those who convert for the sake of a man, for the sake of a woman, for the sake of the king's table, or for the sake of Solomon's slaves are not converts. Nehemiah is also reported to have said that those who converted because of the fear of lions, because an interpreter of dreams told them to convert or those who converted at the time of Mordecai and Esther are not converts unless they converted again "at the present time." However, the *gemara* quotes Isaac b. Samuel b. Marta, who said in the name of Rav that the *halakhah*

follows the one who said that these were all proper converts. See, however, Halivni, who raises questions about the role of Nehemiah's statement in the *gemara;* Halivni, *Sources and Traditions,* 33.

89. Isa. 54:15 is cited in support of these statements, and Rashi, *loc. cit.,* and the *gemara* seem to read the text as follows: *Whoever shall be converted while I am not with you shall be settled among you* which means that only those who convert when things are not going well for Israel will be readily accepted.

90. *L'tyd lb'.*

91. On the meaning of this term, see Bammel, "Gerim Gerurim," 127–31. He rejects the common translation, "self-made proselytes," and argues that the phrase means "proselytes that are dragged about" (p. 128). He sees this as referring to their undergoing an "eschatological test" (p. 130).

92. BA.Z. 3b. Ps. 2:1, 3–4 is cited throughout in support of the claims made by the anonymous *sugya: Why do nations assemble, and peoples plot vain things. . . . Let us break the cords of their yoke, shake off their ropes from us! He who is enthroned in heaven laughs; YHWH mocks at them.*

93. Lev. 19:33.

94. BYeb. 47a. These gifts were given by Israelites to only the poor among the Israelites and were a means of sustaining group solidarity; Porton, *Goyim,* 182–84. Sifré Deuteronomy Re'ah 110 and Ki Taṣa 283–85 teach that the converts may received the agricultural gifts designated for the Israelite poor.

95. BQid. 75a–b. A *beraita, tny',* states that Eleazar ruled that a Cuthean could not marry another Cuthean. Joseph explained that Eleazar treated the Cutheans as being a convert of more than ten generations, for another *beraita, tny',* states that a convert may marry a female *mamzer* only until ten generations have passed; after that time such marriages are prohibited. However, "others" state that the male Cuthean may marry a female *mamzer* until the taint of his gentile nature is no longer evident in him. Abayye states that in the case of an eleventh generation Cuthean's marrying a female *mamzer,* people might say that it is an Israelite who is marrying the female *mamzer.* Dimi suggests that Eleazar agreed with Ishmael that the Cutheans were not real converts, for they converted because they feared the lions, IIKgs. 17:25, and with Aqiba who held that when a gentile has intercourse with a female Israelite the child is a *mamzer.* On the rabbinic opinions of the Samaritans, see the following and the references they contain: R. J. Coggins, *Samaritans and Jews: The Origins of Samaritanism Reconsidered* (Atlanta, 1975). Ferdinand Dexinger, "Limits of Tolerance in Judaism: The Samaritan Example," in E. P. Sanders, ed., *Jewish and Christian Self-Definition,* vol. 2, *Aspects of Judaism in the Graeco-Roman Period* (Philadelphia, 1981), 88–114. James D. Purvis, "The Samaritans and Judaism," in Robert A. Kraft and George W. E. Nickelsburg, eds., *Early Judaism and Its Modern Interpreters* (Atlanta, 1986), 81–98.

96. Rashi, *loc. cit.,* explains that he does not have a parent who can bring him to be immersed.

97. BKet. 11a.

98. Ibid. MKet. 1:2 teaches that the marriage document of a woman who converted at an age of less than three years and one day is the same as that for an

Israelite virgin, 200 *denars*. Abayye argues that if we permit such a woman to change her mind and reject Judaism, the items specified in the marriage contract would be given to a gentile upon the dissolution of the marriage. The *gemara* concludes that when the woman becomes an adult, she has one hour during which she may decide to leave Judaism. If she has not rejected Judaism during that hour, she may never do so again without punishment. Therefore, she does not receive the items mentioned in her marriage contract unless the hour has expired, and she has decided to remain within the Israelite community. Rabba makes the same argument based on the fact that a woman who converted at an age of less than three years and one day is eligible to receive the payment of a fine from a male who had raped her while she was a virgin; see mKet. 3:1 where the fine is derived from Deut. 22:29. The *gemara* reaches the same conclusion in this case; that is, he pays the fine only if the woman has not left Judaism during the first hour of her adulthood.

99. BGiṭ. 85a. In discussing mGiṭ. 9:2—[If a man said in the divorce document], "You are free to marry any man except my father, your father, my brother, your brother, a slave or a gentile," or any one with whom she may not contract a betrothal, [the divorce document] is valid—Rabba asks if the divorce document is valid if in it a man states that the woman he is divorcing may not marry those who are yet to be born. Should we consider the fact that they are not yet born, or the fact that they will be born? Nahman draws attention to the reference in Mishnah to the slave or the gentile, for it is possible that they will convert. Rabba points out that the two cases are different, for while it is natural in the course of things that children will be born, there is no need to assume that the gentiles will convert. For our purposes, the point of the passage is its emphasis on the fact that conversion is freely chosen by a gentile and is totally unpredictable. The point is made in the next *sugya* in the Talmud, which deals with the exclusion in the divorce document of the "husband of her sister," whom she cannot marry unless her sister dies. Again, death is described as being inevitable, while conversion is not.

100. *Tny'*.

101. Some say Hanina.

102. BYeb. 48b. Rashi, *loc. cit.*, states that *you have sought refuge* implies that she did so speedily, and without delay. Therefore, by implication, one who delays does not receive the reward which Boaz asked for Ruth. Cf. Braude, *Jewish Proselyting*, 40; Bamberger, *Proselytism*, 162–63.

103. BYeb. 99a. Cf. yQid. 3:13; Venice yQid. 3:15, 64d and yQid. 3:12 in Qorban Ha'Edah and tQid. 5:11.

104. BYeb. 79b.

105. Deut. 22:2.

106. *Tnw rbnn;* bQid. 72b–73a.

107. BYeb. 77b.

108. MHor. 3:8.

109. Gen. 9:25 states: *Cursed be Canaan; the lowest of slaves shall he be to his brothers;* see Rashi, *loc. cit.*

110. *Tny'*.
111. MHor. 3:8.
112. BHor. 13a. Cf. bYeb. 34b.
113. MQid. 4:6.
114. BQid. 78a. Rashi, *loc. cit.*, distinguishes the *ḥalal* and the convert from the rest of the congregation by reference to sexual matters, which is the topic of this *sugya*. He notes that the convert was produced from an unfit drop of semen, *tph pswlh*.
115. BYeb. 101b–102a; cf. bQid. 14a; Sifré Deuteronomy Ki Taṣa 291; yYeb. 12:1, Venice 12a. On the basis of the phrase *in Israel* in Deut. 25:7, *but if a man does not want to marry his brother's widow, his brother's widow shall appear before the elders in the gate and declare, "My husband's brother refuses to establish a name in Israel for his brother; he will not perform the duty of a levir,"* Samuel b. Judah taught that the *haliṣah* ceremony must be performed before a court composed of Israelites, not converts.
116. BYeb. 101b. Rashi, *loc. cit.*, suggests that both Samuel and his father were converts.
117. BYeb. 102a. Rabba takes Deut. 17:15, *you shall be free to set a king over yourselves, one chosen by YHWH, your God. Be sure to set as king over yourself one from among your brothers . . .*, literally and states that only when he needs to adjudicate one from among his *brothers*, that is, an Israelite, must the judge be an Israelite. When the case involves converts, however, the judge may be a convert. If the judge's mother were an Israelite, he may judge Israelites. In the case of the *haliṣah* ceremony, however, both of the judge's parents must be native-born Israelites. This is derived from the phrase *in Israel his name shall be called*, Deut. 25:10.
118. *I acknowledge this day before YHWH, your God, that I have entered the land that YHWH swore to our fathers to assign us.* Cf. mBik. 1:4.
119. BMak. 19a. Cf. Sifré Deuteronomy Ki Tabo 299; yBik. 1:4, Venice 64a; tBik. 1:2; Mekhilta Ishmael Mishpatim 20.
120. BSanh. 36b, bNid. 49b. Cf. Sifra VaYiqra Parashah 4:3 and Braude, *Jewish Proselyting*, 102.
121. BQid. 76b. Adda b. Ahabah's host was a convert who was challenging Bibi for the right to run the town's government. When they questioned Joseph, he responded that *one from among your brothers shall you set as king over you*, Deut. 17:15, indicates that all rulers should come from among the Israelites. Adda b. Ahabah asked about the instance in which the convert's mother was an Israelite. In that case, Joseph responded, the person is counted as being *from among your brothers*. Therefore, Joseph ruled that Bibi should spend his time with "heavenly matters," and the convert should be the administrator of the town. Zera and Rabbah b. Abbuha approved of the appointment of converts; however, neither in Palestine nor in Nehardea, according to the *sugya*, were converts entrusted with supervisory tasks. In the West, Palestine, they were not appointed as inspectors of measures, and in Nehardea they were not appointed as supervisors of the irrigation system.
122. BB.M. 71a. Cf. Mekhilta Ishmael Neziqin 1, Horovitz and Rabin 248 where we read that a convert may be treated as a Hebrew slave. Braude suggests

that the opinion cited in the *gemara* which prohibits the convert from selling himself as a Hebrew slave is a "manifestation of an effort to protect the interests of the friendless and indigent convert to Judaism"; Braude, *Jewish Proselyting*, 93.

123. MQid. 4:7; mBekh. 1:5; mQid. 4:6; tQid. 5:1–3; tYeb. 11:2; Sifra Emor Pereq 12:11, Weiss 85b; ySoṭ. 4:5, Venice 4:6, 19d; yYeb. 7:5, Venice 8b; yYeb. 8:3, Venice 9c; yBik. 1:5, Venice 64a; yYeb. 8:2, Venice 9c; yQid. 4:6, Venice 66a. See chap. 8.

124. BYeb. 60b; cf. yBik. 1:5; Venice 64a. Simeon b. Yohai stated that a convert under the age of three years and one day may marry a priest, and he based this ruling on Num. 31:18. Also on bYeb. 60b, Joshua b. Levi related that there was a certain town in the Land of Israel the legitimacy of whose inhabitants was disputed. Rabbi sent Romanos to investigate, and the latter conducted an inquiry and found that a convert's daughter who was under the age of three years and one day was married to a priest. When he reported this to Rabbi, he permitted her to remain with her husband. On the other hand, elsehwere on bYeb. 60b we read that a certain priest married a convert who was under the age of three years and one day. When Nahman b. Isaac inquired on whose permission they had contracted the marriage, the priest responded that Jacob b. Idi stated in the name of R. Joshua b. Levi that the *halakhah* is in agreement with Simeon b. Yohai's teaching that a priest may marry a woman who converted when she was under the age of three years and one day. Nahman responded that the priest should divorce his wife or he would place him under a ban. On bYeb. 61b we read that Lev. 21:7's reference to a *zonah* who may not marry a priest refers to a female convert. Cf. mYeb. 6:5; yQid. 4:1, Venice 65b; Sifra Emor Pereq 1:7, Weiss 94b; Bamberger, *Proselytism*, 83–84. Furthermore, on bQid. 21b Samuel states that a priest may not marry a convert; therefore, he may not marry a captive who is a convert. While the *gemara* states that with regard to second intercourse all agree that a priest may not marry a captive who is a convert, with regard to first intercourse, Rav ruled that the priest may marry a convert who is a captive, for the Torah took account of a man's passions.

125. BQid. 73a. Judah said in Rav's name that the priests' daughters were not prohibited from marrying the unfit, so that a priest's daughter is permitted to marry a converted male even though a priest cannot marry a converted female.

126. This is illustrated by the discussions as to whether or not a priest with a physical blemish can marry a convert, bYeb. 76a. Sheshet is asked if a priest whose testicles have been harmed may marry a convert. He concludes that such marriages are permitted, for *the priest loses his sanctity* because of his injury. Thus, the issue clearly concerns the priest's sacred status. Rabba challenges Sheshet's ruling, for he argues that the issue in the case of the Israelite has nothing to do with his holiness, it has to do with the male's ability to procreate. On bQid. 57a Yohanan asked Oshaia if a priest whose testicles were wounded married the daughter of a convert confers upon her the right of eating heave offering? Oshaia offered no response. According to Judah, the woman is not entitled to eat the heave offering. However, according to Yosi, the woman may eat the heave offering whether or not the wounded priest is considered to maintain his holy status. Yohanan's question

must be based on Eliezer b. Jacob's view that a woman who is the daughter of a convert may marry a priest only if her mother was an Israelite; see mBik. 1:5, tQid. 5:3, Sifra Emor Pereq 2:9, Weiss 95a. Cf. yYeb. 8:2, Venice 9b; yQid. 4:6, Venice 66a; mYeb. 8:2; bYeb. 76a–b. On bYeb. 57a Aha b. Hinena taught a *beraita* in which Lev. 22:11, *but a person who is a priest's property by purchase may eat of them . . .* , was cited as a scriptural text from which one could deduce that if a priest whose testicles were injured married the daughter of a convert, she could eat the heave offering. Because Judah would not allow the woman to eat the heave offering, no matter the priest's status, and Yosi would allow her to eat it, no matter the priest's status, the biblical verse must be useful in interpreting Eliezer b. Jacob's opinion. Therefore, because we have a biblical verse, we may assume that the woman whose father was a convert but whose mother was an Israelite may eat the heave offering if she marries a priest whose testicles are injured because her eligibility to marry him is increased by her mother's status; however, her sanctity is not increased.

127. Porton, *Goyim*, 259–68.

128. BQid. 78a–b. Ezek. 44:22 states: *They [the priests] shall not marry widows or divorced women; they may marry only virgins of the stock of the house of Israel, or widows who are widows of priests.* Judah interprets the verse to mean that both of the woman's parents must be Israelites; thus, he would not allow converted women to marry into the priestly families. Eliezer b. Jacob interprets the phrase *from the stock (mzr')* to mean even if a portion of their seed (*mqṣt zr'*) is from an Israelite, they may marry into the priestly class; see Rashi, *loc. cit.* Yosi states that anyone who was conceived by Israelites could marry a priest, and this means that even if both of her parents were converts she could marry a priest if she were conceived after her parents converted. Simeon b. Yohai interprets the verse to refer to one "whose virginity was sown in Israel," that is, a woman who converted before the age of three years and one day; see Rashi, *loc. cit.* In another *sugya*, bQid. 78b, Judah interprets the verse to mean that the priest may marry the widow of those whose daughters may marry into the priesthood, which excludes the widow of a convert; see Rashi, *loc. cit.* The *gemara* interprets Judah's statement in Mishnah in these terms. On bQid. 74a–b Judah disagreed with Simeon b. Yohai and taught that a female convert less than three years and one day may not enter the assembly of the priests.

129. MQid. 4:7.

130. Ibid.

131. BQid. 78b.

132. *A widow, or a divorced woman, or one who is degraded by harlotry—such he may not marry. Only a virgin of his own kin may he take to wife . . . .*

133. *Gywrt mknh;* see Rashi, *loc. cit.*

134. BYeb. 77b.

135. Ibid. On bYeb. 77a Ulla said in Yohanan's name that the daughter who was born to Ammonite parents after they converted may marry a priest. Rabba b. Ulla asked Ulla with whom his view agrees. Judah had stated that the daughter of a male convert is like the daughter of a male *halal*. And Yosi had stated that the daughter of any two converted parents may marry a priest, so that Ulla's comment

is self-evident and unnecessary. If you were to respond that the dispute between Judah and Yosi applied only to those who were fit to enter the congregation, thus excluding the Ammonite, there is no basis in the dispute for the claim that the father's status deprives the daughter of her rights. Therefore, he asks Ulla if he is discussing an Ammonite who married an Israelite woman, for even though the marriage is prohibited, the daughter is still eligible to marry a priest. Ulla responds that this is the case, for Rabin had reported in Yohanan's name that the daughter of an Ammonite convert who had married an Israelite woman and the daughter of an Egyptian convert of the second generation who had married an Israelite woman are eligible to marry a priest, while Resh Laqish declared them ineligible to marry a priest.

136. MB.Q. 4:7; mB.Q. 9:11; tB.Q. 10:16; Sifré Numbers Naśo 2; Sifré Numbers Naśo 4; mB.B. 3:3; tB.B. 2:11; mSheq. 7:6; tKet. 4:16; tB.Q. 9:20; Sifré Numbers Naśo 7; Sifré Numbers Shelaḥ 117; yGiṭ. 4:4, Venice 45d; yQid. 1:5, Venice 60d; yB.B. 3:1, Venice 13d; yB.B. 4:8, Venice 4:11, 14d; yQid. 1:4, Venice 60a; yB.B. 9:1, Venice 16d; yYeb. 4:1, Venice 16d; yPes. 2:2, Venice 29a.

137. For an example of a *sugya* in which the appearance of the convert is secondary to the issues discussed see bErub. 64a. When Abba b. Shumani (or Rabbah b. Shimi; see Munich MS) and Menashya b. Jeremiah of Difti (omitted in Munich MS) were parting company at the Yopati river, they each endeavored to teach the other a new point of law, in accordance with Mari b. Huna's dictum that "a man should not depart from his friend without telling him a point of *halakhah*, so that he will be remembered for it." One of them stated that if an Israelite took possession of the estate of a convert who died without heirs, he should sell a portion of the estate and purchase a Torah scroll with the proceeds, so that he will be worthy of retaining the property he has just acquired.

138. BB.M. 8b. Cf. yQid. 1:4; Venice 60a. This passage seems related to Huna's statement in yQid. 1:4. According to the Venice edition, Huna ruled that in the case of a convert who died without heirs, one could acquire the animal by its being handed over: *'yn mwsyrh qwnh 'l' bnyksy hgr.* The standard commentators to the Palestinian Talmud seem to have ignored the *'l'*, which is in parentheses in the modern standard printed editions of the text, and read the Palestinian *sugya* in terms of the Babylonian version.

139. BYeb. 52b.
140. BErub. 25a. Jeremiah's statement also appears on bB.B. 53b–54a.
141. BB.B. 52b.
142. BB.B. 57a.
143. BB.B. 53a.
144. BB.B. 53b.
145. BB.B. Rashi, *loc. cit.*
146. Rashi, *loc. cit.*
147. BB.B. 54a.
148. BB.B. 53b.
149. YQid. 1:5, Venice 60d; yB.B. 3:1, Venice 13d; yB.B. 4:8, Venice 4:11, 14d.
150. BB.B. 53a–b.

151. BB.B. 55a.
152. BB.B. 56a.
153. Rav Judah said in the name of Rav that this was the plant with which Joshua marked the boundaries of the land of Canaan for the Israelites.
154. *Dtny'*.
155. BQid. 23a.
156. BQid. 22b. This passage is further treated on bGiṭ. 39a: In response to Ulla's statement in the name of Yohanan that if a man declares his slave ownerless property he becomes a free man, but requires a deed of emancipation, Abba referred to the case on bQid. 23a. Ulla did not accept Abba's rejection, and Nahman explained that Ulla believed that a convert's slave comes under the same rule as his wife. Just as his wife is liberated after his death without a divorce document, so his slave is liberated without a deed of emancipation. The *sugya* then ignores the issue of the convert's wife and moves onto a discussion of the slave's acquiring his freedom.
157. BQid. 16a.
158. *Dtny'*; cf. tKet. 4:16.
159. BB.B. 142a. Cf. yB.B. 9:1, Venice 16d.
160. See Rashi, *loc. cit.*
161. Ibid.
162. BB.Q. 49a–b.
163. Whtny'; bB.Q. 42b–43a.
164. BB.Q. 44b. Cf. mB.Q. 4:7 and tB.Q. 4:6.
165. *Tnw rbnn.*
166. *When an ox gores a man or a woman to death, the ox shall be stoned and its flesh shall not be eaten, but the owner of the ox is not to be punished. If, however, the ox has been in the habit of goring, and its owner, though warned, has failed to guard it, and it kills a man or a woman—the ox shall be stoned and its owner, too, shall be put to death. If ransom is laid upon him, he must pay whatever is laid upon him to redeem his life. So, too, if it gores a minor, male or female, [the owner] shall be dealt with according to the same rule. But if the ox gores a slave, male or female, he shall pay thirty sheqels of silver to the master, and the ox shall be stoned.*
167. BB.Q. 49b.
168. BB.Q. 109a–110b.
169. BB.Q. 109a.
170. BB.Q. 109b.
171. *But if a man does not have a kinsman . . . .*
172. Rashi, *loc. cit.*, states that the two cases are derived from the repetition of either *šm* or the root *šwb* in Num. 5:8. If one follows this interpretation, the phrase *a man* means that if the convert died after reaching manhood, one needs to investigate if he had descendants who could inherit from him. However, if he died before he reached manhood, it is not necessary to investigate, for it is likely that he has no heirs who can inherit from him; bB.Q. 109b.
173. *Tnw rbnn.*
174. BB.Q. 110a.

175. BB.Q. 110a.
176. *Tnw rbnn.*
177. BB.Q. 110b.
178. THal. 2:9. Cf. bHul. 133b. See also bZeb. 44b; cf. bMen. 73a, and Sifré Numbers Shelah 117; Horovitz 135. *That they render* (Num. 18:9) refers to the guilt offering which must be brought and given to the priest by one who has robbed a gentile, lied about it, and then confessed. If the convert has died without leaving heirs, the guilt offering, the amount stolen, and the added fifth are given to the priest.
179. BErub. 70b–71a.
180. BMak. 16a–b.
181. BB.Q. 49b.
182. *Tnw rbnn.*
183. The *heqdesh* is any offering dedicated to the Temple. Hiyya b. Joseph explains that *heqdesh* refers to "left overs." Rashi, *loc. cit.*, explains that this refers to a guilt offering which cannot be sacrificed because its owner had died. The animal is left to graze until it develops a blemish at which point it is redeemed, and a burnt offering is purchased with the money paid to redeem it. This offering is then known as an offering "for the altar's summer fruits," so that it is a public sacrifice. Aibu says it refers to a sacrifice dedicated to repairing the Temple.
184. BZeb. 103a. Cf. Sifra Saw Pereq 9:1, Weiss 33d.
185. MKet. 3:4.
186. Lit., in unholiness.
187. Lit., in holiness.
188. BKet. 44b. Cf. yKet. 4:4, Venice 28b; Sifré Deuteronomy Ki Tasa 238.
189. BYeb. 98b. The *gemara* then discusses the need for the text to state that he may marry his brother's wife. This was needed so that we could learn that no special measure was enacted. Similarly, there is a discussion of the difference of opinion concerning his marrying his mother-in-law.
190. MKet. 9:9, tKet. 9:7. We should merely accept the anomaly of the rabbinic *assumption* that gentiles would execute an Israelite marriage contract. It is possible that this relates to the view, held by some sages, that prospective converts would be concerned about following Israelite law even before their conversion.
191. BKet. 90a. Cf. yKet. 9:13; Venice 33c.
192. MYeb. 11:2.
193. BYeb. 97b.
194. MYeb. 11:2.
195. BYeb. 97b.
196. BYeb. 97b–98a. Cf. mYeb. 11:2; yYeb. 11:2, Venice 11d; Sifré Deuteronomy Ki Tasa 289.
197. BSanh. 71b. Rashi, *loc. cit.*, explains that as a gentile only one witness needed to have provided testimony against him, the case could have been heard by one judge, and it was not required that he be warned before hand. On the other hand, the conviction of an Israelite requires that he be warned, that there be two witnesses to his crime, and that he be tried before a court. Rashi further notes that

gentiles were executed by the sword; however, Israelites were executed by stoning. Cf. yQid. 1:1; Venice 58c.
  198. *Hkh.*
  199. BSanh. 71b. However, if he had killed an Israelite while he was a gentile
or had had intercourse with an Israelite's wife, he is still liable for punishment after
he converted. Bamberger writes: "The Gemara finds the second part of this baraita
[the statement concerning the killing of an Israelite] contradictory to the principle
laid down by R. Hanina, and is forced to use pilpulistic methods to settle the
difficulty. . . . The Rabbis, even at the cost of consistency, would not absolve a
convert form the guilt of a serious crime previously committed against a Jew";
Proselytism, 64. Despite the fact that from our point of view this distinction between crimes against gentiles and those against Israelites seems unsatisfactory,
clearly there were rabbis who believed that there was a qualitative difference between the two types of crimes.
  200. The same holds if the betrothal is conditional on the male or female
slave's attaining freedom, on the condition that a relative die, or that the woman
would undergo the *ḥaliṣah* ceremony.
  201. BYeb. 93b, bQid. 63a, bKet. 58b, bB.M. 16b. On bQid. 63a we read that
Judah the Patriarch agreed with Meir, while Yohanan the sandal-maker agreed
with the anonymous opinion. Judah the Patriarch says that she is betrothed, but
the sages do not accept the engagement because it could lead to bad feelings. The
gemara also specifically states that when a gentile woman converts she becomes an
entirely different person. In a discussion of Lev. 18:11, *the nakedness of your father's
wife's daughter, who was born into your father's household—she is your sister; do not uncover
her nakedness,* on bYeb. 23a, the *gemara* again makes it clear that conversion effects
a complete change in a person's status. The discussion centers on the prohibition
against marrying a woman because *she is your sister.* The *gemara* asks if this includes
one's sister from a gentile, with whom betrothal and marriage are not legally valid.
From the phrase *your father's wife's daughter* we deduce that only a woman with
whom one's father can enter into a valid marital relationship is forbidden, even
though the punishment for such a marriage is "cutting off." The text continues
that the gentile should have been included because if she converts, the marriage
would be legally valid. However, the *gemara* concludes that when the gentile
woman converts, she is an entirely different person, *gwp' 'ḥryn' hy'.* Cf. tQid. 4:9
and mQid. 3:5.
  202. MKet. 9:9, tKet. 9:7. We should merely accept the anomaly of the rabbinic *assumption* that gentiles would execute an Israelite marriage contract. It is
possible that this relates to the view, held by some sages, that prospective converts
would be concerned about following Israelite law even before their conversion.
  203. BKet. 90a. Cf. yKet. 9:13; Venice 33c.
  204. *Tnw rbnn.*
  205. BB.M. 72a. Cf. tB.M. 5:21; yB.M. 5:5, Venice 5:7, 10c.
  206. BBekh. 47a. Yohanan bases his decision on the phrase *the first fruit of his
vigor,* Deut. 21:17, which applies to the first-born whether or not the father was an
Israelite at the time of his son's birth. Therefore, mBekh. 8:1 means that if an

Israelite who had never before produced children married a converted woman who had borne young before she converted but who after she converted bore her Israelite husband his first child, the child is considered to be a first-born infant with respect to inheritance but not a first-born to be redeemed from a priest. This case appears so that we do not accept the teaching of Yosi the Galilean in Mishnah who said that the infant is both a first-born with respect to inheritance and also one who must be redeemed from a priest, because it is said in the scriptures: *Opens the womb among the children of Israel* (Ex. 13:2), which implies that the rules apply only if the child comes from the womb of an Israelite woman.

207. BBekh. 47a. Yohanan based this opinion on Isa. 45:18: *[For thus said YHWH, the creator of heaven who alone is God, who formed the earth and made it, who alone established it—.] He did not create it a waste, but formed it for habitation.* Because the verse speaks about the earth in general, it applies to the children born before the male converted.

208. Or Aha b. Rabba.

209. BBekh. 47a. Rabina suggests that the view that the child born after the conversion of a male gentile who had had children before he converted counts as a first-born with respect to inheritance agrees with Yosi the Galilean's view in mBekh. 8:1 who quoted Ex. 13:2, *[Consecrate to me every first-born; man and beast,] the first issue of every womb* . . . . However, because in the case of a female gentile who had children and then converted to Judaism the previous children are ignored, and if her first-born after her conversion is a male, he counts as a first-born for purposes of Israelite law, the same principle is followed with regard to the father. This means that his first-born for reasons of inheritance is the first-born after his conversion. This is part of the discussion of mBekh. 8:1. Cf. bYeb. 62a, where Yohanan cites IIKgs. 20:12, *At that time, King Merodach-baladan, son of Baladan of Babylon* . . . , in support of his opinion.

210. MBekh. 8:1.

211. BBekh. 47b.

212. BKet. 44b. Rabba ruled that one who falsely accuses an orphan of harlotry must bear guilt for his act and be fined. However, one who falsely accuses a convert of harlotry is not guilty. He based his opinion on Ammi's interpretation of Deut. 22:19, *a virgin in Israel,* which excludes the converted woman. And this stands against Yosi b Hanin who, on the basis of the phrase *to the father of the young girl* in Deut. 22:19, ruled that the man who slanders an orphan is exempt because the girl did not have a father; bKet. 44b. Cf. mKet. 4:3, Sifré Deuteronomy Ki Ṭaṣa 238; yKet. 4:4, Venice 28b.

213. BYeb. 22a. Cf. Bamberger, *Proselytism,* 86–91. This is part of a larger *sugya* in which Rabba asked Nahman if he knew that in Palestine they had discussed whether or not the second degrees of incest were applied as a preventative measure to converts. Nahman responded that the rabbis would not have imposed any of the incest laws on the converts except for the fact that they did not want them to think that they had entered a sexually permissive society; therefore, surely they would not have applied the second degrees to them.

214. BB.Q. 88a. On the basis of an analogy with slaves, the *gemara* asks if

Deut. 24:16, *nor children be put to death through parents*, means that one cannot im-
pose capital punishment on the evidence of children who would have no legal
relationship to their fathers, so that converts who have no legal ties with their
parents are disqualified from giving evidence. See, however, bNid. 49b, which
states that converts may give testimony in capital cases involving other converts.
On bB.Q. 88a the text claims that slaves and converts are not comparable because
converts have a legal relationship with their descendants, while slaves do not.

215. BYeb. 97b. The *gemara* states that Aha b. Jacob and Sheshet agree that
converts who are paternal brothers may marry each other's wife, for it is well
known that their father was a gentile, and no one would erroneously deduce from
this that Israelites may marry their brother's wife. They also agreed that maternal
brothers cannot marry each other's wife, for from this one could erroneously conclude that Israelites could marry their brother's wife, because it is clear that they
have a common mother. They differ only with regard to brothers who share the
same mother and the same father. When brothers share both parents, Aha permits
them to marry each other's wife, for children are ascribed only to the father, and
this is why they are identified as the son of such-and-such a father. Sheshet, on
the other hand, prohibits these marriages because he believes that people are spoken of as the child of such-and-such a woman. Aha b. Jacob, according to some,
objected to the illegality of these marriages if they are maternal brothers, for converts are considered as newborn children, so that none of their former relationships matter.

216. Menjamin in the printed edition.

217. BYeb. 78a. Benjamin was a first-generation Egyptian convert who was
married to a woman who was a first-generation Egyptian convert. He sought to
arrange for his son to marry a second-generation Egyptian convert, so that his
grandson would be eligible to enter the congregation because he would be a third-
generation Egyptian convert; Deut. 23:8. Cf. tQid. 5:4; yQid. 4:3, Venice 65d; yYeb.
8:2, Venice 9b; bYeb. 78a; Sifré Deuteronomy Ki Tasa 253, Finkelstein 279–80.

218. BYeb. 78b. Cf. bQid. 67a. Cited on bQid. 67b. The Hebrew term is *pgwm*.
The *gemara* finally interprets this to mean that it refers to the child of an Ammonite
father and Egyptian mother. If the child is a male, he is considered an Ammonite.
If the child is a female, she is considered an Egyptian. Because the male is considered to be an Ammonite, he may never enter the congregation; Deut. 23:4. The
female may not enter the congregation because she is considered to be a second-
generation Egyptian, and only a third-generation Egyptian may enter the congregation; Deut. 23:8.

219. MQid. 3:12.

220. BQid. 66b–67a. Cf. tQid. 5:2 and Saul Lieberman, *Tosefta Ki-fshutah: A
Comprehensive Commentary on the Tosefta. Part VIII Order Nashim* (New York, 1973),
966.

221. BShab. 68a–b. MShab. 7:1 states: "Whoever forgets the principle of the
Sabbath and committed many acts of work on many Sabbaths is liable only for one
sin offering; but if, mindful of the principle of the Sabbath, he forgot it was the
Sabbath and committed many acts of work on many Sabbaths, he is liable for every

Sabbath which he profaned. If he knew it was the Sabbath and yet committed many acts of work on many Sabbaths, he is liable for every main class of work which he performed; if he committed many acts of work of one main class, he is liable only for one sin offering." The *gemara* states that Rav and Samuel both believed that the text referred to one who converted among gentiles, or a child who was taken captive among gentiles, so that he never really knew the laws concering the Sabbath. This teaching is interpreted to mean that even one who converted among gentiles is like one who knew but subsequently forgot the Sabbath laws. Yohanan and Simeon b. Laqish, however, excluded the convert who converted among gentiles, and the child who was taken captive among gentiles, because they did not originally know and then forget. The anonymous text states that if one who was converted among gentiles performs many different acts on the Sabbath, he is liable for only one sin offering for each major class of law he violates. Monobases, however, exempts him from the sin offering. Cf. tShab. 8:5.

222. BPes. 93a. Rabbi taught that if one converted between the normal Passover observed in the first month and the Passover of the second month which was set aside for those unable to observe the first Passover (or if a minor reached puberty during this period), he must observe the second Passover. Nathan held that only those who were required to observe the first Passover may observe the second Passover, so that he would not require the new convert to observe the second holiday. The discussion of the second Passover occurs in Num. 9:1–14. The dispute between Rabbi and Nathan appears in tPis. 8:4. Cf. Mekhilta Ishmael Bo, 15; Horovitz and Rabin 56, ll. 9–11.

223. BYeb. 71a. The phrase *a sojourner and a hired servant*, Lev. 22:10, is the basis of this ruling. According to Shemaia, Aqiba used the verse to include a circumcised Arab and a circumcised Gibeonite. The *gemara* claims that the biblical text excludes a converted male who had been circumcised but had not been immersed, for he is not considered to be a full convert. This stands against Eliezer who regarded a male as a convert if he had been circumcised, even if he had not undergone a ritual immersion. On bPes. 92a, Rabbah b. Bar Hanah quotes Yohanan to the effect that the dispute between the Hillelites and the Shammaites in mPes. 8:8 concerns an uncircumcised gentile. The Hillelite position is a preventive measure, so that the convert will not argue after he has become defiled by a corpse that last year he ate the Passover sacrifice after he was immersed; therefore, this year he will again immerse and then eat the Pascal lamb, without realizing that the previous year he was a gentile, while now he is an Israelite. Bamberger, following Büchler, argues that the Shammaites were resisting the Hillelites' attempt to apply the categories of Israelite uncleanness to the gentiles. Bamberger sees this dispute "dating as it does from the time when the Temple still stood," as a "practical matter." "No doubt," he writes, "the semi-converts, the 'fearers of the Lord,' who were in Jerusalem at Passover time were powerfully affected by the sight of the vast multitudes assembling there, and desired to take part in the feast. Thus, Passover might well be the critical point at which half-way converts made their final decision. It was natural for the question to arise whether such last moment converts could participate at once in the celebration"; Bamberger, *Proselytism*, 71. This

is, of course, mere conjecture. On this passage, see McEleney, "Conversion, Circumcision, and the Law," 330, and Nolland, "Uncircumcised Proselytes?" 182–83.

224. BPes. 91b. Cf. yPes. 8:7; Venice 36a, where we find a similar discussion attributed to different sages. Bamberger, *Proselytism*, 71.

225. BSuk. 28b. This ruling is based on interpreting the definite article in the phrase *the native-born* in Lev. 23:42, *you shall live in booths seven days; all the native-born in Israel shall live in booths*, as a reference to converts. Cf. Sifra Emor Pereq 17:9; Weiss 103a.

226. Or a minor who reached puberty during the week.

227. BSuk. 27b. Eliezer bases his ruling on the phrase *all citizens* in Lev. 23:42, *You shall live in booths seven days; all citizens in Israel shall live in booths*. The rabbis, on the other hand, permit any Israelite to construct a booth during the festival week, so that while they agree with Eliezer's ruling, they do not base it on an interpretation of Lev. 23:42.

228. *Tnw rbnn*.

229. BR.H. 29a. Cf. tR.H. 2:5 and Sifra Emor Parashah 11:1, Weiss 101c.

230. BMen. 51b; cf. mSheq. 7:6.

231. Hisda "said," *'mr*, while Hiyya "taught," *tny*.

232. BHul. 134a–b.

233. The uncertainty concerns whether she gave birth to his child before or after she converted. If she gave birth after she converted, she is required to bring a sacrifice before she may eat the holy things. If she ate the holy things without bringing the sacrifice, she is subject to the penalty of "cutting off"; see Rashi, *loc.cit.*

234. The case of doubt is that described in mHal. 3:6, for it is uncertain whether the dough was in a state requiring the removal of the dough offering at the time of the conversion. If the dough offering had not been properly removed and given to the priest, the dough is considered *tebel*, and anyone who uses it for food is subject to death at the hands of heaven.

235. This refers to the first-born of an ass. The doubt is whether the ass gave birth to the firstling before or after her owner converted. If it were after the conversion the firstling cannot be used until it has been redeemed by giving a lamb to the priest, Ex. 13:13. However, one need not give the lamb to the priest if it is a case of uncertainty; see Rashi, *loc.cit.*

236. The issue is whether or not the firstling were born after the person converted. If it were after, and the person slaughtered it outside of the Temple precincts, the person may be liable for the punishment of "cutting off."

237. That is, the lamb used for the redemption of the first-born of an ass. Cf. Bamberger, *Proselytism*, 72–73.

238. BMen. 61b. Cf. Sifra Ṣaw Parashah 11:3; Weiss 39b. A *beraita* states that *by him who offers*, Lev. 7:29, teaches that converts and freed slaves are included among those who may make a wave offering before YHWH.

239. BMen. 43a. A *beraita, tnw rbnn*, teaches that converts, along with priests, Levites, Israelites, women, and freed slaves must wear fringes. Simeon excludes women because it is a time-bound positive commandment.

240. BSoṭ. 26a. A convert's wife suspected of adultery must drink the bitter waters or she does not receive her marriage settlement upon divorce, tSoṭ. 5:4. The *gemara* states that this is self-evident, for this is a legally recognized marriage. However, because one could interpret the clause *speak to the children of Israel*, Num. 5:12, to mean that converts do not perform the *soṭah* ritual, the specific statement that they do perform the ritual was needed. One could also argue that the clause *and say* (Num. 5:12) includes the convert's wife. However, see bBer. 19a which quotes the dispute in Mishnah between Aqabyyah b. Mahaleel who used to say that the *soṭah* ritual is not administered to a convert and sages who said that it is. Cf. mEd. 5:6; Sifré Numbers Naśo 7; ySoṭ. 2:5, Venice 18b.

241. BSoṭ. 38a. A *beraita* states that on the basis of *thus shall you bless the children of Israel* (Num. 6:23), one could argue that the priestly benediction is recited only upon Israelites. However, *say to them* (Num. 6:23) indicates that it is recited for converts, women, and freed slaves. Cf. Sifré Numbers Naśo 39; Horovitz, 43; Sifré Numbers Naśo 43; Horovitz, 49, where the women, converts, and freed slaves are included on the basis of *I will bless them* in Num. 6:27.

242. BKet. 37a. Cf. yYeb. 4:11, Venice 6a; yNid. 1:4, Venice 1:5, 49b. Papa b. Samuel cited the following *beraita* to Joseph: If a woman convert discovered menstrual blood on the day of her conversion, Judah ruled that she begins counting the days of her uncleanness from the time she discovered it. Yosi, however, held that she is subject to the same laws as all other Israelite woman, so that she transmits uncleanness for the previous twenty-four hours or during the time between her last examinations. With regard to marriage, Judah ruled that a convert must wait three months after her conversion to contract a marriage with an Israelite, while Yosi ruled that she could get married at once. Cf. bYeb. 35a which contains a long discussion on this issue.

243. BBekh. 3b. A gentile named Achii gave an animal to a female convert to fatten. The woman asked Rabba if the laws of the firstlings applied. Rabba responded that no one accepts Judah's ruling that the laws of firstlings apply to the case of a partnership between an Israelite and a gentile. In this case, the converted woman is treated like a full Israelite with regard to the laws of firstlings, and she is clearly distinguished from the gentile.

244. BYeb. 74b. Shisha b. Idi argued that Lev. 12:2, *speak to the children of Israel*, indicates that the laws relating to the periods of uncleanness after childbirth are applicable to Israelite women. From Lev. 12:2's reference to *women*, we learn that the laws also apply to converts and freed slaves; on bKer. 7b this appears anonymously as a *beraita, tnw rbnn*. Therefore, these verses refer to only the offerings a woman brings after childbirth and not to other things, such as her being permitted to eat the heave offering, for converts and freed slaves do not eat heave offering. This stands against Rabba who had claimed that Lev. 12 does refer to the heave offering.

245. BBekh. 46b. Cf. Bamberger, *Proselytism*, 74–75, where he calls this a "bit of far-fetched casuistry." Exactly why *this* discussion *alone* is "far-fetched casuistry" is unclear.

246. BNid. 26a. YNid. 3:4; Venice 50b discusses the number of offerings a

woman must bring if she gives birth to a normal fetus and to a sandal-shaped fetus. If she gave birth to one before she converted and to the other after she converted, or to both of them after she converted, Huna stated that it was established before Jeremiah that she should bring two offerings. Here, bNid. 26a, Jeremiah holds that she is liable for only one offering, that required for an Israelite woman who gave birth to a child.

247. BSanh. 56a. Miyasha said that according to sages, a gentile who blasphemed YHWH by employing substitutes of the ineffable Name is punishable by death. This is derived from Lev. 24:15–16—*Anyone who blasphemes his God shall bear his guilt; if he also pronounces the name YHWH, he shall be put to death. The whole community shall stone him; convert or native-born, if he has thus pronounced the Name, he shall be put to death.* The native-born Israelite and the convert are punished only if they pronounce the actual Name; however, the gentiles are executed even if they use a substitute for the name. This view, or one very similar to it, is also attributed by the *gemara* to Isaac the smith. Meir deduces that the convert and the Israelite are stoned, while the gentile is decapitated.

248. BSanh. 85b. A *beraita, tny'*, states that Deut. 24:7—*if a man is found to have kidnapped one from among his brothers*—teaches that one is liable whether he kidnapped a man, a woman, a convert, a freed slave, or a minor.

249. BShab. 146a. Deut. 29:14—*[I made this covenant, with its sanctions, not with you alone] but both with those who are standing here with us this day before YHWH, our God and with those who are not with us here this day*—is quoted in support of this claim. See Bamberger, *Proselytism*, 153.

250. BShebu. 39a; cf. tSot. 7:5. The *gemara* argues that the opening phrase of Deut. 29:14, *but with him who stands here with us [this day]*, indicates that those who stood at the base of Mount Sinai accepted the revelation. The second part of the verse, *and with those who are not with us here this day*, indicates that the future generations of native-born Israelites and those who would convert to Judaism in the future are also obligated to accept the revelation given at Mount Sinai. In fact, the *gemara* realizes that one could argue that they were obligated to observe only those commandments given at Sinai. However, Esther 9:27, *[the Jews] undertook and irrevocably obligated [themselves and their descendants, and all who might join them, to observe these two days in the manner prescribed and at the proper time each year]*, means that they *undertook and irrevocably obligated themselves* to those things they had accepted long ago, including those laws which came after Sinai, such as the reading of the *megillah*. The *sugya* states that they could *undertake* only what they had *obligated themselves* to earlier. The verb *qbl* appears in both Deut. 29:14 and Esther 9:27, and this probably serves as the link between the two verses.

251. BB.Q. 88a. In a discussion of whether or not a slave can be considered an Israelite's brother in terms of Deut. 19:19, *you shall do to him as he schemed to do to his brother*, and Deut. 17:15, *you shall be free to set a king over yourself, one chosen by YHWH, your God. From among your brothers, you shall set a king over you . . .* , we learn that everyone considers a convert to be an Israelite's brother. However, both the slave and the convert are excluded from the kingship because Deut. 17:15 is interpreted to mean "among the choicest of your brothers," *mmwbḥr šb'hyk*. Rashi, *loc.*

cit., notes that the convert under discussion is one who was conceived and born after his parents had converted. However, to be king, one must have a native-born Israelite mother.

252. BB.M. 71a. Cf. bQid. 20a, bArakh. 40b, bYeb. 46a. In a *beraita, tny'* on bB.M. 71a, Rabbi discusses to whom an Israelite may sell himself as a slave. Lev. 25:39 refers to an Israelite's selling himself to another Israelite in order to pay a debt, *if your kinsman under you continues in straits and must give himself over to you . . .*, and Lev. 25:47 mentions an Israelite's selling himself to a convert, *and if a convert (gr) and a resident (wtwšb) among you has prospered, and your kinsman being in straits, comes under his authority and gives himself over to the resident convert (gr twšb) among you, or to an offshoot of a convert's family (mšpht gr). . . .* Rabbi concludes that an Israelite may sell himself to a righteous convert, *gr ṣdq*, a resident alien, and even to one who worships an idol, the convert's former family.

253. Cf. mDem. 6:10; tDem. 6:12–13; yA.Z. 3:6, Venice 3:8, 43b.

254. BQid. 17b–18a.

255. BA.Z. 64a. Some would-be converts came before Rabbah b. Abbahu who told them to sell their possessions before they converted, for they could not benefit from the sale of their idols after they converted. In support of Nahman's view that the price of the idol in the possesion of a gentile is permitted to an Israelite, the *gemara* cites tA.Z. 7:16. Sheshet says that the problem is that the Israelite will wish that the idol be preserved, so that it will bring a good price. The *sugya* then reverts to the discussion of a convert's dividing his gentile father's estate with his gentile brother before the former takes possession of it. Papa finally concludes that the convert is treated leniently, so that he will not believe that he would inherit more if he were a gentile.

256. BB.Q. 80a. According to mB.Q. 7:7, no one may raise pigs anywhere, and one may raise a dog only if it is chained. A gentile who was not required to follow Israelite law could raise these animals, so that they would be available as bequests to the gentile's children. However, the convert, who must follow Israelite law, could not raise these animals; therefore, he would have to dispose of them. Interestingly, Israelites could not sell village dogs to gentiles; Porton, *Goyim*, 93–94.

257. Based on a version of tKet. 3:3.

258. BKet. 28b.

259. BYeb. 35a. On bKet. 37a, a *beraita, tny'*, states that Judah held that converts must wait three months before they contract a marriage after their conversion. Yosi, however, permits immediate betrothal and marriage. Rabbah explained that Yosi believed that a woman who engages in unlawful intercourse employs a contraceptive, so that she will not become pregnant. The *gemara* states that this is acceptable in the case of a convert. Because she intends to join the Israelite community, she is careful not to become pregnant before she converts. Therefore, she would always have a contraceptive ready. On the need for a convert to wait for three months after her conversion before she can marry, see bYeb. 34b; yYeb. 4:11, Venice 6a; yNid. 1:4, Venice 1:5, 49b. See, *infra*, Eleazar b. Zadoq's comment on bHor. 13a.

260. Weil draws parallels between Israelite and Roman law with regard to

the distinction between a person's status at birth and at conception; Weil, *Le Prosélytisme*, 80–82. Some sages implied that there was an inherent difference between children conceived while their parents were gentiles and those who were conceived after they converted. On bYeb. 42a Rabba stated that a male convert and a female convert must wait three months after their conversion before resuming sexual relations because there is a distinction between a child conceived before they converted and one conceived after they converted, "seed that was sown in holiness and seed that was not sown in holiness."

261. BSanh. 57b–58a. Cf. bYeb. 98b. The *gemara* cites a *beraita* which states that a convert born after his mother's conversion but conceived before her conversion possesses relatives only on his mother's side of the family. Therefore, if a converted male married his maternal sister who was born before their mother converted, but who converted with her mother, he must divorce her. He may, however, remain married to a paternal sister. He must divorce his father's maternal sister (see Rashi, *loc. cit.*, who explains that the reference to forsaking one's father in Gen. 2:24 includes his father's maternal sister), but he may remain married to his father's paternal sister. While he must divorce his mother's maternal sister, Meir and sages disagree concerning his mother's paternal sister. Meir holds that he must divorce her, for he may not marry any of the women in his mother's family, while sages hold that he may remain married to her. In addition, the convert may marry his maternal brother's wife, his paternal uncle's wife, or any other relations by marriage, including his father's wife. If he had married a woman and her daughter, he must divorce one of them. If his wife died, some held that he could marry his mother-in-law, while others forbid it. Freedman writes: "The guiding principal in all this is: 'a proselyte is as a new born babe,' who stands absolutely in no relationship to any preconversion relation. Consequently, his brothers and sisters, father, mother, etc. from before his conversion lose his relationship on his conversion. Should they too subsequently become converted, they are regarded as strangers to him, and he might marry, e.g., his mother or sister. This is the Biblical law. But since heathens themselves recognised the law of incest in respect of maternal relations, the Rabbis decreed that this should hold good for a proselyte too, i. e., that he is forbidden to marry his maternal relations who were forbidden to him before his conversion, so that it should not be said that he abandoned a faith with a higher degree of sanctity than the one he has embraced (since he cannot be expected to understand the principle of complete annulment of relationships). In this case, since he was born in sanctity, he is really not a proselyte at all. He is so styled because he too is legally a stranger to all his father's and mother's preconversion relations. As for his mother's paternal sister, R. Meir held that since she is partly maternally related, she is forbidden, as otherwise it would be thought that a proselyte is permitted to marry his maternal relations. But the Rabbis held that there was no fear of this, and since the relationship is in its source paternal, it is not forbidden." Jacob Shachter and H. Freedman, *Sanhedrin: Translated into English with Notes, Glossary, and Indices* (London, 1935), 394, note 1.

262. BYeb. 98a. Upon hearing of the marriage, sages declared that the law of matrimony does not apply to converts. The *gemara* then asks, if the convert be-

troths a woman, would it not be invalid? The *sugya* then suggests that only the prohibition against marrying one's brother's wife does not apply to converts. But that opinion should not be valid here, for his brother had married her after he converted, so that it is as if they were Israelites. And, if he had married her before he converted, there would be no need to state the law, for such a marriage would not be valid according to Israelite law. However, one could assume that in the case of a brother's betrothal before he converted, we should enact a preventive measure so that one would not reach the incorrect conclusion concerning the events after he converted; therefore, we learn from Yosi's report that such a special measure was not enacted.

263. Munich MS reads Yosi b. Yasin.

264. BYeb. 98a. The *sugya* ends in the same words as the previous one, note 262. Also, the *sugya* reports Aqiba's exegesis of Jonah 3:1 which the *sugya* accepts as valid, so that further on, in an analysis of this *sugya*, the *gemara* also accepts as accurate the report on Aqiba's legal ruling.

265. MYeb. 2:8.

266. BYeb. 24b. Cf. yQid. 4:1; Venice 65b. The *gemara* states that Mishnah implies that she may become a proper convert. However, this seems to disagree with Nehemiah's statement that a man may not be accepted as a convert because he wishes to marry an Israelite woman, nor may a woman be accepted as a convert because she wishes to marry an Israelite man.

267. MQid. 3:5; cf. tQid. 4:9.

268. BQid. 62a–b; cf. mQid. 3:5; tQid. 4:9. Weil suggests that the prohibition against accepting converts because they wish to marry Israelites is a counter against the "conversions *in extremis* si fréquemment pratiquées dans l'autres cultes"; Weil, *Le Prosélytisme*, 53. Further, Weil notes that conversion is a difficult decision with regard to one's family and one's social relationships, so that the rabbis' reticence to accept converts is an admirable trait; Weil, 53–54. He also draws attention to the dangers that insincere converts can cause; Weil, 53–54.

269. BBer. 8b. Cf. bPes. 112b. Braude states that "the advice not to marry a proselytess may have been a witticism evoked in the course of discussing an obscurely worded ancient Baraita"; Braude, *Jewish Proselyting*, 46–47. There is no convincing reason not to believe that some rabbis would have opposed marriages between native-born Israelites and converts, given the ethnic solidarity of the Israelite people.

270. BYeb. 34b–35a. Cf. tYeb. 6:6; yYeb. 4:11, Venice 6a; yNid. 4:5, Venice 49b; bKet. 37a.

271. Deut. 23:4–9.

272. TQid. 5:4. Cf. Sifré Deuteronomy Ki Taṣa 253; Finkelstein 279–80.

273. BYeb. 78a. Deut. 23:9 states: *Sons born to them [Egyptians and Edomites] may be admitted into YHWH's congregation in the third generation.* The *gemara* offers two detailed analyses of the verse; one which explains the need for both *sons* and *generation*, and one which demonstrates the need for both *born* and *to them*. On bYeb. 69a and bQid. 74b–75a we find that an Egyptian convert of the second generation cannot marry into the congregation of Israel, but his son, who is a convert

of the third generation, may marry into the congregation. This principle is used by Yohanan as an explanation of a difference of opinion between Yosi and an anonymous tanna. On bYeb. 77b we find a long discussion on whether or not an Egyptian convert of the second generation can marry a priest and whether or not an Ammonite woman and her children "are eligible." On bYeb. 84b we find that converts can marry second-generation Egyptian converts.

274. BBer. 28a. Cf. mYad. 4:4, tYad. 2:17.

275. BYeb. 76a–b. In response to the argument that only marriages between converts and Israelites are acceptable, Joseph brings up the case of Solomon and suggests that IIKgs. 3:1, *Solomon allied himself by marriage with Pharaoh king of Egypt. He married Pharaoh's daughter,* implies that they engaged in a legally acceptable marriage. The *gemara* responds that Solomon first had the woman converted. To this the text responds that no converts were accepted into the community during the reigns of David and Solomon, bYeb. 24b. Because the prohibition against accepting converts was a means of preventing them from converting merely to enjoy the benefits of the prosperity brought on by the administrations of David and Solomon, this prohibition would not apply to Pharaoh's daughter who had both wealth and power. Therefore, the text implies that she would have been accepted as a convert. The text then suggests that in fact the marriage was not valid because she was a first-generation Egyptian woman, and only the third-generation Egyptian converts can marry Israelites, Deut. 23:9. To those who might suggest that the laws in the Torah do not apply now, for surely one cannot find Egyptians like those mentioned in the Torah, the *gemara* cites the story of Benjamin the Egyptian convert who arranged marriages so that his grandson would be a third-generation Egyptian convert and thus able to enter the community. On Benjamin the Egyptian convert, see bYeb. 78a; tQid. 5:4; y.Qid. 4:3, Venice 65d; yYeb. 8:2, Venice 9b; Sifré Deuteronomy Ki Taṣa, 253. It is interesting that at this point the *gemara* does not cite the end of the *sugya* in which the sages disagree over whether or not one can still find Egyptians, Moabites, Ammonites, and the like, for some held that the tribes had intermarried to such an extent that the laws of Deut. 23 no longer applied. The *sugya* concludes that Solomon's marriage was not a legally acceptable marriage, even though the biblical text implies that it was. In fact, the technical terminology is used only out of respect for Solomon and the great love he felt for Pharaoh's daughter. Cf. ySanh. 2:6, Venice 9:6, 20c, where Yosi explains that Solomon married non-Israelite women in order to bring them to the Torah and under the wings of the *Shekhinah.*

276. BYeb. 77a. Cf. tQid. 5:3; yQid. 4:3, Venice 65d; yYeb. 8:2, Venice 9b; ySoṭ. 4:5, Venice 4:6, 19d; yYeb. 7:5, Venice 8b; yYeb. 8:3, Venice 9c.

277. *Wkdtny'.*

278. Along with a Cuthean, a *natin,* a *ḥalal,* or a *mamzer.*

279. BYeb. 68a and bQid. 74b. However, on bQid. 78a and bYeb. 60b, Simeon b. Yohai rules that a female who converted at an age of less then three years and one day may marry a priest. He supports his decision with Num. 31:18: *Spare every young woman who has not had carnal relations with a man.* The rabbis, on the other hand, interpreted this to mean that the captives should be made into slaves. This

appears as a comment on Eliezer b. Jacob's statement in mQid. 4:7. Simeon b. Yohai's interpretation is based on the fact that Pinhas the priest was present at the events recorded in Numbers, so that we can assume that these young women were allowed to marry into the priestly caste.

280. MQid. 4:3.

281. BQid. 74a–b.

282. BYeb. 69a and bQid. 75a.

283. Yosi taught that those whose children are unfit for the priesthood disqualify the women whom they marry, but those whose children are not unfit do not disqualify the women whom they marry.

284. The text reads "Dosa or the son of Harkinas."

285. On the Cordenians, see Bamberger, *Proselytism*, 35–36.

286. BYeb. 16a–b. Cf. bNid. 56b which contains the discussion of Yohanan's statements. The text on bYeb. 16b attempts to explain why Yohanan and Sabya would not accept converts from Tarmod. One held that it was because they were slaves who married Israelite women, so that the children were *mamzerim*. The other held that the reason was "because of the daughters of Jerusalem," which is taken to mean that the men from Tarmod raped the women when Jerusalem was conquered, while the other soldiers sought to steal the gold and silver. On the Palmyrenes, see Braude, *Jewish Proselyting*, 65–69, and on the Karduyim, 69–72; cf. Bamberger, *Proselytism*, 34–35. He claims that the Palmyrenes were disliked because they took part in the destruction of both Temples; however, the problem with their converting to Judaism was that they were considered to be *mamzerim*. Exactly who these people were and where they originated is still open to question. Cf. yYeb. 1:6, Venice 3b; yQid. 4:1, Venice 65c; yDem. 2:1, Venice 22c; yKil. 8:3, Venice 31c; yShab. 5:1, Venice 7b, where they are loosely connected with Egypt.

287. BBekh. 30a.

288. BSanh. 94a. See Bamberger, *Proselytism*, 160–61 for sources with a similar message. Bamberger claims that this passage "seems to be expedient rather than religious in spirit"; Bamberger, 160. Exactly what this means is unclear.

289. BPes. 113b. As part of a series of parallel *sugyot* which enumerate various types of things, we learn that three love each other: converts, slaves, and ravens. Braude suggests that "this may have been spoken tongue in cheek," so that it is not to be taken as a negative statement about converts; Braude, *Jewish Proselyting*, 47. On the other hand, it may point to the perceived clannishness of converts.

290. *Tnw rbnn.*

291. BB.M. 59b. With reference to one who wounds the feelings of a convert, *hm'nh*, the following three verses are cited: Ex. 22:20: *You shall not wrong (twnh) a convert;* Lev. 19:33: *When a convert resides with you in your land, you shall not wrong him (twnw);* and Lev. 25:17: *A person should not wrong (twnw) his fellow country man ('mytw).* And the *gemara* states that the convert is included among *his fellow country man.* Concerning one who oppresses, *hlwhsw*, a convert, the following three passages are listed: Ex. 22:20: *[You shall not wrong a convert] or oppress him (tlhsnw);* Ex. 23:9: *You shall not oppress a convert (tlhs);* and Ex. 22:24: *If you lend money to my people,*

to the poor among you, do not act toward him as a creditor, and the *gemara* states that this includes the convert.

292. *Tny'.*

293. BB.M. 59b. See Marcus Jastrow, *A Dictionary of the Targumin, the Talmud Babli, and Yerushalmi, and the Midrashic Literature* (New York, reprint, 1971), 967. Bamberger writes that "Eliezer *did not want* converts to relapse. What he means is that because the convert is probably weak in his loyalty to Judaism, and may be driven back to heathenism if we treat him unkindly, Scripture takes particular pains to warn us against injuring him. While the passage reflects a poor opinion of proselytes, it is far from indicating a disapproval of proselytization"; Bamberger, *Proselytism,* 166. This latter distinction may be too subtle.

294. *Tny'* or *tmyn'.*

295. *You shall not wrong a convert (gr) or oppress him, for you were strangers (grym) in the land of Egypt.*

296. BB.M. 59b. Rashi, *loc. cit.,* interprets Nathan's statement as follows: Because you were strangers, *grym,* it is totally improper (*gn'y*) to mention one's being a convert (*grym*). Cf. mB.M. 4:10, tB.M. 3:25, bB.M. 58b, Sifra BeHar Pereq 4:2, Weiss, 107d and parallels. Cf. Bamberger, *Proselytism,* 158–59.

297. Cf. bB.M. 111b. A *beraita, tny',* offers an interpretation of Deut. 24:14, *You shall not abuse a needy and destitute laborer, whether from among your brothers or from among your converts who are in your land and in your gates,* in which we are told that the phrase *from among your converts* refers to the righteous convert, and the phrase *who are in your gates* refers to the *gr twšb.* Another passage, bYeb. 48b, takes Deut. 5:14, *or the stranger in your gates,* to refer to the righteous convert. Therefore, *the stranger* mentioned in Ex. 23:12 refers to the *gr twšb.*

298. BB.M. 58b. Cf. mB.M. 4:10, tB.M. 3:25; Sifra BeHar Pereq 4:2, Weiss, 107d and parallels.

299. BHag. 5a. Resh Laqish said that one who perverts the judgment, *mty dynw,* due to a convert is considered as if he acted unjustly toward YHWH. In support of his claim, Resh Laqish quotes Mal. 3:5, *[And I will act as a relentless accuser against those who have no fear of Me:] . . . who subvert [the cause of] . . . the convert (wmy gr),* and suggests that it could be read "who subverts Me." The consonants in Mal. 3:5 are vocalized in the Massoretic text as *umate.* Resh Laqish suggests that the word could be read *umati.* Cf. Bamberger, *Proselytism,* 158–59. See also mB.M. 4:10; tB.M. 3:25; Sifra BeHar Pereq 4:2, Weiss, 107d; and parallels. In the *Amidah* the righteous converts are also mentioned along with the righteous on the basis of Lev. 19:32–33: *You shall rise before the aged and show deference to the old; you shall fear your God . . . . And when a convert resides with you;* bMeg. 17b.

300. BGit. 45b. Cf. yA.Z. 2:2; Venice 41a. Rabbah b. Samuel explained that the reason that Simeon b. Gamaliel permitted Israelites to use the Torahs produced by the gentile in Sidon was that the gentile was a convert who eventually left the Israelite community and returned to his gentile way of life.

301. BQid. 73a.

302. BZeb. 116a. Joshua claims that Jethro converted when he heard about

the battle with the Amalekites, while Eleazar of Modim states that Jethro, like the other gentile nobles, was awestruck upon experiencing the world-disrupting events which accompanied the revelation on Mount Sinai. The discussion is based on Ex. 18:1, *Jethro [priest of Midian, Moses' father-in-law,] heard [all that God had done for Moses and for Israel His people . . .].* Joshua relies on Ex. 17:13, *And Joshua overwhelmed the people of Amalek with the sword,* which ends the story of the battle between the Israelites and Amalek, Ex. 17:8–13. Eleazar of Modim refers to Ps. 29:9, *While in his temple all say "Glory!"* With regard to the dividing of the Sea of Reeds, Eleazar cites Josh. 5:1, *When all the kings of the Amorites [on the western side of the Jordan, and all the kings of the Canaanites near the Sea,] heard [how YHWH had dried up the waters of the Jordan for the sake of the Israelites until they crossed over, they lost heart, and no spirit was left in them because of the Israelites.]* This verse does not really apply, for it refers to the Jordan, not to the Sea of Reeds. It does, however, move us into the book of Joshua, so that it serves as a transition to the discussion of Rahab which follows. Freedman suggests that the verb "heard" in Josh. 5:1 and in Ex. 18:1 links the two verses, so that its connotation in the former verse applies also to the latter. See H. Freedman, *Zebahim* (London, 1948), 575, n. 1. Rav, bSanh. 94a, assumes that Jethro converted on the basis of Ex. 18:9—*And Jethro rejoiced (wyḥd)*—which he claims refers to Jethro's passing a sharp, *ḥd,* knife over his flesh; that is, it refers to his circumcision upon his converting. Samuel, bSanh. 94a, claims that this verse teaches that Jethro's flesh prickled, *ḥd,* when he heard of the destruction of the Egyptians. On Jethro as a convert, see Bamberger, *Proselytism,* 182–91 and Louis Ginzberg, *The Legends of the Jews,* trans. Paul Radin and Henrietta Szold (Philadelphia, 1911), 3:63–67, 72–77.

303. BZeb. 116a–b mentions that Rahab was worthy of conversion because of the cord, window, and flax. Rashi, *loc. cit.,* refers to the passage in Mekhilta Ishmael and states that she was worthy of redemption because of the cord she threw out the window so that the spies could enter her house and be hidden among the flax. Cf. Mekhilta Ishmael Amalek/Yitro 1, Horovitz and Rabin, 189, ll. 2–6 on Ex. 18:1 and notes. On Rahab see Bamberger, *Proselytism,* 193–95 and Ginzberg, *Legends of the Jews,* 4:5; 3:25. See also the extensive essay by Judith Baskin, "The Rabbinic Transformations of Rahab the Harlot," *Notre Dame English Journal* 11, no. 2 (1978/79): 141–57.

304. BMeg. 14b.

305. Judah adds that Huldah the prophetess was also one of Rahab's descendants. His claim is based on a pun. IIKgs 22:14 identifies Huldah as *the wife of Shallum son of Tikvah (tqwh) son of Harhas.* Judah notes that in Josh. 2:18 we read *you tie this length (tqwt) of crimson cord* in the story of Rahab and the spies. Therefore, we can connect Huldah to Rahab.

306. BMeg. 14b.

307. BSanh. 39b. See Bamberger, *Proselytism,* 204.

308. BSoṭ. 10a. According to Samuel b. Nahmani, at the gate of Enaim, Gen. 38:14, Tamar informed Judah that she was a convert.

309. Ruth 3:18–22. On bYeb. 63a Eleazar interprets Gen. 12:3, *and all the families of the earth will be blessed through you,* to mean that YHWH told Abraham that he

intended for Ruth and Naamah to convert to Judaism. Cf. Braude, *Jewish Proselyting*, 27, and Ginzberg, *Legends of the Jews*, 1:257.

310. BSuk. 49b; cf. bHag. 3a. Ps. 47:10 states: *The great of the peoples are gathered together, the retinue of Abraham's God.* Rabba reads this as a reference to the converts who will join Abraham's God. The deity is designated as the God of Abraham, and not the God of Isaac or Jacob, because Abraham was the convert. He left his family and rejected the worship of their divinities in order to follow YHWH. See Bamberger, *Proselytism*, 175–79, and Ginzberg, *Legends of the Jews*, 1:195–217 for discussions of Abraham's conversion. Elsewhere, bNed. 32a, Yohanan teaches that the Israelites went into Egyptian bondage because Abraham allowed the king of Sodom to take the persons he had captured. Abraham should have attempted to convert these people to the service of YHWH. Similarly, because Abraham, Isaac, and Jacob refused to accept Timna, Lotan's sister, as a convert, she became Eliphaz's concubine and her descendant, Amalek, was allowed to afflict Israel, bSanh. 99b. Bamberger, 179, notes that in Sifré Deuteronomy He'ezenu, 336, Timna's desire for conversion is not mentioned. Yohanan, bMeg. 13a, implies that Pharaoh's daughter converted before she pulled Moses out of the river, for she had gone to purify herself from the idols of her father's house. This is based on the fact that in IChron. 4:18, Bithya, Pharaoh's daughter, is called a Jew. Cf. bSot. 12b, where the statement is attributed to Yohanan in the name of Simeon b. Yohai without a reference to IChron. 4:18. On Bityah, see Bamberger, 181–82. Ginzberg, 2:266 gives her name as Thermutis and writes that "God sent scorching heat to plague the Egyptians, and they all suffered with leprosy and smarting boils. Thermutis, the daughter of Pharaoh, sought relief from the burning pain in a bath in the waters of the Nile. But physical discomfort was not her only reason for leaving her father's palace. She was determined to cleanse herself as well of the impurity of the idol worship that prevailed there."

311. BA.Z. 10b. The *gemara* records that the fictitious official of the Roman government, Keti'ah b. Shalom, achieved eternal life by circumcision; this may suggest that immediately before he died he converted to Judaism; Braude, *Jewish Proselyting*, 75. Bamberger states that "the name given here to this martyr-convert is fictitious"; Bamberger, *Proselytism*, 236. However, after connecting this account with a story in Deuteronomy Rabbah, Bamberger concludes that "there is a recollection, correct in essence even though confused in detail, of the conversion and martyrdom of a great Roman figure"; Bamberger, 238; and see pp. 235–38. Thus, according to Bamberger, the story of this "fictitious" Roman official is somehow historically reliable!

312. BGit. 56b.

313. BA.Z. 11a. The emperor sent a contingent of Roman soldiers after him, but Onqelos convinced them to convert by quoting biblical verses to them. The emperor sent another cohort after him and told them not to talk with Onqelos. However, Onqelos told them a parable which demonstrated that unlike a human governor, YHWH served his people, Israel. Onqelos stated that in a procession the torchlighter carries the light in front of the torchbearer, the torchbearer in front of the leader, the leader in front of the governor, the governor in front of the chief

officer. "But," Onqelos asked, "does the chief officer carry the light in front of the people?" The Roman soldiers replied, "No!" Onqelos continued: "Yet the Holy One, blessed be he, does carry the light before Israel, for it is written: *YHWH went before them daily [in a pillar of cloud, to guide them along the way, and in a pillar of fire by night, to give them light, that they might travel day and night.]* (Ex. 13:21)." Upon hearing about YHWH's concern for the common people, they too converted. Following these events, the emperor sent another cohort with instructions that they should not enter into a conversation with Onqelos. The soldiers arrived and seized him. While he was walking with them he saw a *mezuzah* on a door. He placed his hand upon the *mezuzah*, whereupon the soldiers asked him about it. He responded with the following parable which again demonstrated YHWH's concern for his people: According to universal custom, a human king dwells within, and his servants keep guard on the outside. However, with regard to the Holy One, blessed be he, his servants dwell inside, while he keeps watch outside, for it is said, *YHWH shall guard your going out and your coming in from this time forward and for ever* (Ps. 121:8). Upon hearing the parable, this last group of soldiers also converted. The emperor did not send any more soldiers. On Onqelos and Aquila, see Bamberger, *Proselytism,* 238–43. He concludes that Aquila translated the Torah and Onqelos should be associated with Gamaliel. Weil just accepts everything the rabbinic and medieval sources claim; Weil, *Le Prosélytisme,* 40.

314. The rabbis believed that the concern that YHWH had for the People Israel would impress any number of gentiles at any time; see bYeb. 79a and yQid. 4:1; Venice 65c. The relevant part of the *sugya* also appears in ySanh. 6:7; Venice ySanh. 13:9, 23d. See Bamberger, *Proselytism,* 201–3, and Bammel, "Gerim Gerurim," 129–30.

315. *Pws'y yśr'l.*

316. BGiṭ. 56b–57a.

317. In a *sugya* on bB.B. 99a which discusses the *cherubim* on the ark, Onqelos the convert interpreted IIChron. 3:10 to mean that the *cherubim's* faces were turned sideways in the manner of a student taking leave of his teacher. On bA.Z. 11a the *gemara* states that it is permitted to burn articles at an Israelite king's funeral, and it discusses those items which may be burnt. In the course of the discussion we are told that in the instance of the death of Gamaliel the elder, Onqelos the convert burnt for him seventy Tyrian *manehs,* defined as items which Gamaliel had used which were worth seventy Tyrian *manehs.* The point of the story seems to be the equating of Gamaliel with Israelite royalty. For our purposes, it underscores Onqelos's devotion to Gamaliel. On Onqelos and Gamaliel in earlier collections, see Shamai Kanter, *Rabban Gamaliel II: The Legal Traditions* (Chico: 1980), 177–78, 125–26.

318. BGiṭ. 56a. In a section devoted to the destruction of Jerusalem and the Second Temple, we are told that the emperor sent Nero to the Land of Israel. No matter in which direction he shot his arrows, they all fell in Jerusalem. Nero then turned to a small schoolboy and asked him to recite the last biblical verse he had learned. The boy responded with Ezek. 25:14—*I will wreak my vengeance on Edom through my people Israel [and they shall take action against Edom in accordance with my*

blazing anger; and they shall know my vengeance—declares YHWH, God]—and Nero
concluded that YHWH wanted to destroy the Temple and to place the blame on
him. Therefore, he ran away and converted. The story ends by stating that Meir
descended from him. The story demonstrates the belief that even the Roman
nobility would accept the Hebrew Bible, notably from the mouth of an Israelite
child who had studied the text, as well as explaining why Nero did not move
against Jerusalem. Also, even the gentiles accepted the validity of the Torah as a
guide for their actions. Furthermore, even great sages could be descended from
converts because converts were worthy ancestors. Cohen writes that Meir was
linked to Nero "because according to rabbinic tradition, R. Meir's family resided
in the general area where, according to folk legend, Nero hid himself at the end
of his life." Naomi G. Cohen, "Rabbi Meir, A Descendant of Anatolian Proselytes.
New Light on his Name and the Historic Kernel of the Nero Legend in Gittin
56a," *Journal of Jewish Studies* 23, no. 1 (Spring 1972): 55–56. Cohen argues that the
rabbinic legend accords with those Romans who viewed Nero in a positive light
which stands against the Christian tradition which saw Nero, who persecuted the
Christians, as the anti-Christ. She writes, "the Nero legend in *Gittin* 56a is to be
taken as part of the Judaeo-Christian polemic. We find here an implicit, but none
the less emphatic rejection of the Christian version of the legend by means of the
development of the earlier stratum, the one which located the earthly and rather
popular Nero, as a fugitive in Asia Minor"; Cohen, 59. Cohen concludes that given
the fact that Meir is never associated with his father and that the name seems close
to Phrygian, that is, Anatolian, names (Cohen, 53–54), he probably was of Anatolian origin; Cohen, 59. Bastomsky argues that rabbinic Judaism has merged two
pictures of Nero, one negative and one positive. The former is related to his send-
ing of Vespasian to destroy the Temple, and the latter is reflected in his being
pictured as Meir's ancestor. "But these two pictures can be reconciled in his evil
deeds foreshadowing the appearance of the Messiah, when all men shall become
Jews. Out of the war and the destruction of the Temple, the Jews with their capac-
ity for survival had wrought a legend of good working through evil." S. J. Bastomsky, "The Emperor Nero in Talmudic Legend," *Jewish Quarterly Review*, n. s. 54,
no. 4 (April 1969): 324. Compare the stories about Antoninus the emperor in yMeg.
1:11, Venice 1:13, 72b; yMeg. 3:2, Venice 74a; ySanh. 10:5, Venice 17:6, 29c. Note,
however, that in the stories about Antoninus on bA.Z. 10a–b we do not find any
reference to the emperor's conversion.

319. BSanh. 96b. Nebuzaradan encountered the seething blood of the priest
Zechariah b. Jehoiada who had been stoned to death in the Temple court by order
of King Joash, IIChron. 24:17–22. Nebuzaradan sought to appease Zechariah's
blood by slaughtering a total of 94,000 scholars, schoolchildren, and priests. When
this did not stop the blood from boiling, he cried out "Zechariah, Zechariah, I have
destroyed the flower of them, do you wish me to destroy all of them?" At that
point the blood stopped seething. Nebuzaradan then realized that if the Israelites
had been severely punished because they killed just one man, surely he, Nebuzaradan, would be even more severely punished for his slaughter of the Israelites. At
that point, he converted.

320. BGiṭ. 57b. See Bamberger, *Proselytism*, 207–8.

321. BGiṭ. 57b, bSanh. 96b. Bamberger, *Proselytism*, 222–23. On bYoma 71b, a certain high priest refers to Shemaia and Abtalion as children of gentiles. Cohen writes that they are pictured as descendants of Sennacherib "no doubt . . . [because] they were believed to have originated from the Eastern Diaspora"; Cohen, "Rabbi Meir," 55.

322. IIKgs. 5.

323. BGiṭ. 57b, bSanh. 96b. According to Bamberger, there are some versions of this passage which suggest that Aqiba was a convert; Bamberger, *Proselytism*, 238. Cf. Aaron Hyman, *Toldoth Tannaim Ve'Amorim* (Jerusalem, reprint, 1964), 3:988. However, neither Finkelstein nor Margalioth refer to Aqiba as a convert. Louis Finkelstein, *Aqiba: Scholar, Saint, and Martyr* (New York, 1975); Mordecai Margalioth, *Encyclopedia of Talmudic and Geonic Literature* (Tel Aviv, 1962), 2:725–34. Cohen writes that "Akiba's portrayal as the descendant of Sisera (king of Canaan), must be ascribed to his belonging to the simplest of Palestinian stock"; Cohen, "Rabbi Meir," 55.

324. On Tineius Rufus, see Emil Schürer, *The History of the Jewish People in the Age of Jesus Christ (175 B.C.–A.D. 135)*, ed. Geza Vermes and Fergus Millar (Edinburgh, 1979), 1:518, 547–51; E. Mary Smallwood, *The Jews under Roman Rule: From Pompey to Diocletian* (Leiden, 1976), 436, 438, 445–46, 449, 457, 459, 463, 550–51.

325. BA.Z. 20a. Given the fact that Bamberger scoured the rabbinic texts to find "converts," it is curious that he does not include this story. Perhaps it was too fanciful even for him.

326. BMen 44a. The point of the story is that even the commandment of wearing fringes is important. Cf. Sifré Numbers Shelaḥ 115; Horovitz 128, l. 16–129, l. 11.

327. BR.H. 17b–18a. Valeria, or Bluria, the convert asked Gamaliel to explain the contradiction between *who shows no favor*, Deut. 10:17, and *YHWH bestow his favor upon you*, Num. 6:26. Graetz raises the possibility that Valeria might be the same as Veturia Paulla (Paulina) who took the name Sarah upon her conversion, and who is known as "Mater Synagogarum" from her tombstone in Rome; Heinrich Graetz, *Die jüdischen Proselyten im Römerreiche unter den Kaisern Domitian, Nerva, Trajan, und Hadrian* (Breslau, 1884), 24–25. Bamberger states that "there is a good deal to commend" Graetz's suggestion; however, he does not fully accept this identification because that would lead to the rejection of the present passage as "unhistorical," for there is no evidence that Yosi the Priest was ever in Rome; Bamberger, *Proselytism*, 234. Cf. Weil, *Le Prosélytisme*, 39. On the other hand, all attempts to demonstrate the historical veracity of these Babylonian *beraitot* are based on assumptions which are hardly verifiable.

328. BYeb. 46a. Hisda discusses the slaves of the convert Valeria who performed a ritual ablution before her in order to convert and in the process achieved their emancipation. However, the text concludes that they must have done this before she converted, for in that case the gentile has no right to freed Israelite slaves, so that their conversion also effected their emancipation.

329. BA.Z. 70a. This occurs in a long section in which Rabba responds to

gentiles. Rabba said that Issur the convert had told him that when he was a gentile they used to joke that the Israelites did not observe the Sabbath, for if they had, the streets would have been filled with the discarded purses that they could not carry after the onset of the Sabbath. Rabba responds that the absence of purses can be explained by reference to Isaac's ruling that one may carry a purse he finds on the street on the Sabbath for a distance of less than four cubits.

330. BB.B. 149a. Issur the convert had deposited 12,000 *zuz* with Rabba. Although his son Mari was conceived before Issur's conversion, he was born after he converted. The question arose concerning Mari's claim to his dead father's money. Rabba noted that he was not entitled to it as an heir, bQid. 18a. He was not entitled to it as a gift, for the rabbis had applied the same rules to a dying man's gift as they did to his normal bequests, so that only those entitled to inherit from the person could receive a gift from him. The *gemara* lists and dismisses other standard forms of acquiring movable property. Thus, according to Rabba he himself could claim the money because it became ownerless property on the death of the convert who had died without legal heirs. In Rabba's view Mari was not an heir because he had been conceived before his father converted. Ika b. Ammi stated that the only way for Mari to acquire the money was for Issur to issue an acknowledgment that the money belonged to Mari, and in fact, this occurred. Bamberger, *Proselytism*, 256–57.

331. BQid. 22b–23a.

332. BBer. 17b. Rav Judah interprets the *stubborn of heart* in Isa. 46:12 as referring to the Gubaeans, and Joseph says that the fact that none of them ever converted to Judaism supports Judah's interpretation. Ashi claims that this refers to the people of Mata Mehasia who, even though they witnessed the gathering of the scholars twice a year, still never converted to Judaism.

CHAPTER 7

1. Sifré Numbers Shelaḥ 108; Horovitz 112, ll. 6–11. Cf. bKer. 8b–9a.

2. Bernard J. Bamberger, *Proselytism in the Talmud Period* (New York, 1968), 42.

3. Ibid., 50.

4. William G. Braude, *Jewish Proselyting in the First Five Centuries of the Common Era: The Age of the Tannaim and Amoraim* (Providence, 1940), 74.

5. George F. Moore, *Judaism in the First Centuries of the Christian Era: The Age of the Tannaim* (reprint; Cambridge, 1966), 1:331.

6. Lawrence H. Schiffman, *Who Was a Jew? Rabbinic and Halakhic Perspectives on the Jewish-Christian Schism* (Hoboken, 1985), 19.

7. S. Bialoblocki, *Die Bezeihungen des Jundentums zu Proselyten und Proselytentum* (Berlin, 1930), 19.

8. H. H. Rowley, "Jewish Proselyte Baptism," *Hebrew Union College Annual* 15 (1940): 321.

9. John J. Collins, "A Symbol of Otherness: Circumcision and Salvation in the First Century," in Jacob Neusner and Ernest Frerichs, eds., *"To See Ourselves as*

Others See Us": Christians, Jews, "Others" in Late Antiquity (Chico, 1985), 171. Collins is more cautious than some of the other scholars. He notes that "we may assume that synagogues would normally have insisted on circumcision, but in a place like Alexandria there may have been exceptions." Collins further notes that Aseneth "is a representative or model proselyte," and "the fact that the main literary portrayal of the proselyte experience from the Hellenistic Diaspora concerns a woman should perhaps warn us not to attach too much importance to circumcision." He further notes that there is no ritual connected with Aseneth's conversion; Collins, 176. Basing himself on the story of Izates' conversion, Collins writes that "circumcision is not an entry requirement but an obligation consequent to admission"; Collins, 179. On the fact that there were "uncircumcised Jews" in the ancient world, see Jonathan Z. Smith, "Fences and Neighbors: Some Contours of Early Judaism," in Jonathan Z. Smith, *Imagining Religion: From Babylon to Jonestown* (Chicago and London, 1982), 8–14. Smith writes, "It was possible for a group of Jews to define themselves as Jews without circumcision"; Smith, 13.

10. Joachim Jeremias, *Jerusalem in the Time of Jesus: An Investigation into Economic and Social Conditions during the New Testament Period*, trans. F. H. and C. H. Cave (Philadelphia, 1969), 320.

11. Emil Schürer, *A History of the Jewish People in the Age of Jesus Christ (175 B.C.–A.D. 135)*, rev. and ed. Geza Vermes, Fergus Millar, Martin Goodman (Edinburg, 1986), 3:173.

12. McKnight, after noting the diversity of Judaism, writes: "The 'officials' of 'Judaism' never met to discuss the matter of requirements [for conversion], come to a decision, and send out the decision through official 'apostles.' In fact, the evidence suggests that different Jews had different requirements at different periods in history, and it further seems that individual Jews may have shown an amazing diversity themselves"; Scot McKnight, *A Light among the Gentiles: Jewish Missionary Activity in the Second Temple Period* (Minneapolis, 1991), 78.

13. McKnight argues that offering of sacrifices would have been a normal activity of anyone within the Israelite community; however, it was not "a rite of entry"; McKnight, *A Light among the Gentiles*, 86. He concludes, "we simply do not have the evidence to conclude confidently that Jews generally saw sacrifice as a requirement [for conversion]. I can conclude only that sacrifice was probably required by a least some Jewish leaders"; McKnight, 87. McKnight's view is similar to that of Rowley, who states that the bringing of the sacrifices had "less of an initiatory character about that than about the baptism. For sacrifices were a part of the normal life into which the proselyte entered, if he lived in Palestine, prior to the destruction of the Temple"; Rowley, 327. Schiffman dates the practice of bringing sacrifices as part of the conversion ritual to "as early as c. 30 C.E."; Schiffman, *Who Was a Jew?* 31.

14. MKer. 2:1.

15. Ibid. A priest who "lacks atonement" cannot receive the blood of the sacrificial animals and place it on the altar; mZeb. 2:1. Nor may such a priest accept a meal offering; mMen. 1:2.

16. MKel. 1:8.

17. MHag. 3:3.

18. MKel. 1:5.

19. MZeb. 12:1. Normally such a priest must wait until evening before he is declared "clean." Such a priest is considered to be in a state of "second-grade" uncleanness. He renders heave offering invalid, he may not touch holy things, and he may not enter the Temple beyond the Court of the Gentiles. See Herbert Danby, *The Mishnah: Translated from the Hebrew with Introduction and Brief Explanatory Notes* (reprint, Oxford, 1964), 773, n. 6.

20. MMeʻ. 2:1–2:9.

21. On the phrase "lacks atonement," see Schiffman, 30–31. Schiffman writes: "'Lacking in atonement' is a technical term for those who have completed the prescribed purification ritual, including immersion, but are still not permitted to partake of sacrifices until they have brought an offering and its blood has been sprinkled on the altar"; Schiffman, 30. Schiffman argues that the anonymous part of the mishnah considers the sacrifice to be "a part of the initiatory conversion rites," while for Eliezer b. Jacob it is a purification rite; Schiffman, 30.

22. Given the parallels with the others "who lack atonement," it seems likely that the convert would have had to undergo a ritual immersion as well as offer a sacrifice.

23. TKer. 1:11.

24. TSheq. 3:20.

25. Lev. 11:32 states: *And anything on which one of them [the swarming things] falls when dead shall be unclean; be it any article of wood, or a cloth, or a skin, or a sack—any such article that can be put to use shall be dipped in water, and it shall remain unclean until evening; then it shall be clean.* Lev. 22:4–7 read: *If one touches anything made unclean by a corpse, or if a man has an emission of semen, or if a man touches any swarming thing by which he is made unclean or any human being by whom he is made unclean—whatever his uncleanness—the person who touches such shall be unclean until evening and shall not eat of the sacred donations unless he has washed his body in water. As soon as the sun sets, he shall be clean; and afterward he may eat of the sacred donations, for they are his food.* The tannaitic discussions of these issues appear in tractate *ṭebul yom* in both Mishnah and Tosefta.

26. TSheq. 3:21–22. TSheq. 3:21 also appears in tKer. 1:12. There it immediately follows Eliezer b. Jacob's comment. The conjunction of these two *sugyot* suggests that the editor(s) of the latter passage believed that Eliezer was discussing the bird offering of the converts, so that they included the discussion of that offering at this point.

27. On the sin offering see Jacob Milgrom, *Studies in Cultic Theology and Terminology* (Leiden, 1983), 67–95 and Baruch A. Levine, *In the Presence of the Lord: A Study of Cult and Some Cultic Terms in Ancient Israel* (Leiden, 1974), 101–14. On the whole offering, see Levine, 22–26. Lev. 4 and Num. 5 deal with the sin offering. Lev. 1 treats the whole offering.

28. Schürer, *A History of the Jewish People in the Age of Jesus Christ (175 B.C.–A.D. 135)*, 2:260–62; Anson Rainey, "Sacrifice," in Cecil Roth and Geoffrey Wigoder, eds., *Encyclopedia Judaica* (Jerusalem, 1972), 14: 600–602.

29. TSheq. 3:21 also states that if the convert brings an offering for his skin disease or one for his period as a Nazirite, he must bring another offering "for his atonement." It seems unlikely that a gentile would have been a Nazirite, and the rules concerning skin diseases do not apply to gentiles. In fact, if a gentile converted with a skin disease he or she had to be examined again after becoming a convert. These offerings were probably mentioned only because they were a type of sin offering; that is, they were taken from the same animals and birds and offered in the same manner as the converts' offering. Therefore, the only reason for their being mentioned is to underscore the point that the offering which the proselyte brings must be for the sole purpose of effecting conversion.

30. Sifré Numbers Shelaḥ 108, Horovitz 112, ll. 1–14. Num. 15:14–16 state: *And when, throughout the ages, a convert (gr) who has taken up residence (ygwr) with you, or one who lives among you, would present an offering by fire of pleasing odor to YHWH— as you do, so shall it be done by the rest of the congregation. There shall be one law for you and for the resident convert (gr); it shall be a law for all time throughout the ages. You and the convert shall be alike before YHWH; the same ritual and the same rule shall apply to you and to the convert who resides among you (wlgr hgr).*

31. Technically speaking the entire whole-offering was not consumed on the altar because the priest received its skin. Also, the priest received the breast and the right shoulder of the peace-offering, so that it was not completely burnt on the altar; Schürer, 2:261. On the peace-offering, see Levine, 27–54.

32. YSheq. 8:4; Venice 8:6, 51b.

33. Yohanan's role in this passage is problematic. Simeon, not Yohanan, appeared in Tosefta, although Simeon is not pictured as having "annulled," *bṭylh*, the practice. This may have been connected with Yohanan because he was known for having changed a number of the rituals connected with the Temple. See Jacob Neusner, *Development of a Legend: Studies on the Traditions concerning Yohanan Ben Zakkai* (Leiden, 1970), 135–36. Jacob Neusner, *A Life of Yohanan Ben Zakkai Ca. 1–80 C.E.*, 2d ed., rev. (Leiden, 1970), 203–10.

34. BKer. 8b–9a.

35. On bKer. 9a we find a *beraita* which demonstrates that one bird is sufficient even though we might think that the converts needed to bring two birds.

36. In a parallel passage on bR.H. 31b, this is identified as Simeon b. Eleazar.

37. Neusner, *Development*, deals with the various versions on 135–36, 154–58, 207–9, 271, 275, 284–85.

38. Hyman states that Idi appears only here; Aaron Hyman, *Toldoth Tannaim Ve'Amoraim: Comprising the Biographies of All the Rabbis and Other Persons Mentioned in Rabbinic Literature, Compiled from Talmudic and Midrashic Sources and Arranged Alphabetically* (Jerusalem, 1964), 1:142. He reports a tradition attributed to Adda bar Ahaba. There were three sages by this name; Hyman, 1:100–103. Cf. Mordecai Margolioth, *Encyclopedia of Talmudic and Geonic Literature, Being a Biographical Dictionary of the Tanaim, Amoraim, and Geonim with the Collaboration of Prominent Scholars* (Jerusalem, 1962), 1:47–50. Margolioth lists two sages by this name.

39. On the complex ideas which the early rabbis held concerning the gentiles'

uncleanness, see Gary G. Porton, *Goyim: Gentiles and Israelites in Mishnah-Tosefta* (Atlanta, 1988), 267–83.

40. Collins, 171–74.

41. Smith, 13.

42. TShab. 15:9.

43. Sifra Tazriʿa Pereq 1:6; Weiss 58c.

44. YShab. 19:4; Venice 17a and yYeb. 8:1; Venice 9a.

45. BShab. 135a.

46. The passage also appears in Genesis Rabbah 46:12; however, there it is rather garbled, for it seems to have combined the discussion of the need to circumcise one on the Sabbath with the need to symbolically circumcise a convert.

47. TShab. 15:9.

48. BYeb. 72a.

49. Mekhilta Ishmael Mishpatim 18 on Ex. 22:20; Horovitz and Rabin 311–12, ll. 11–18.

50. Collins notes that circumcision "was virtually synonymous with Judaism in the Roman period" and that "there is no doubt that circumcision was widely perceived by gentiles as a symbol of Judaism's otherness"; Collins, 163. Collins points to a good deal of extra-Jewish evidence for the practice of circumcision among the Jews; however, he does write that "we may infer from Philo that there were some Jews in Alexandria who dispensed with the practice of circumcision"; Collins, 171. Although Philo defends the need for circumcision, he does not simply dismiss the allegorists as non-Jews or as totally incorrect. Collins further notes that Philo was ambiguous concerning the necessity of converts to undergo circumcision; Collins, 171–74.

51. YShab. 19:5; Venice 17b. Cf. bYeb. 72a–b.

52. YYeb. 8:1; Venice 8d.

53. YMeg. 2:3; Venice 73b.

54. BShab. 137b.

55. Blessed are you, YHWH, our God, king of the universe, who has sanctified us with your commandments and has commanded us concerning circumcision.

56. Blessed are you, YHWH, our God, king of the universe, who has sanctified us with your commandments and has commanded us to lead him into the covenant of our father, Abraham.

57. The gentile father would of course not participate in this ritual. In fact, upon conversion, the proselyte severs all ties with his gentile relatives.

58. Jer. 33:25. This seems to be the way the *gemara* reads the verse.

59. Virtually the same blessing is said upon the circumcision of a slave. This is what we would expect, for the assumption is that the slave was not an Israelite.

60. BA.Z. 26b.

61. MPes. 8:8. In mEd. 5:2, Yosi reports this dispute along with five other disputes. See J. N. Epstein, *Prolegomena ad Litteras Tannaiticas: Mishna, Tosephta et Interpretationes Halachicas*, defuncti auctoris opus edendum curavit E. Z. Melamed (Jerusalem, 1957), 147.

62. Jacob Neusner, *The Traditions about the Pharisees before 70* (Leiden, 1971), 2:141–42.

63. Ex. 12:48: *If a convert who dwells with you (wky ygwr 'tk gr) would offer the passover to YHWH, all his males must be circumcised; then he shall be admitted to offer it; he shall then be as a citizen of the country (k'zrh h'rs). But no uncircumcised person may eat of it.*

64. Num. 19:14–21 deal with those persons and items which become unclean by contact with a person who has died. The relevant verses state: *A person who is clean shall take hyssop, dip it in the water, and sprinkle on the tent and on all the vessels and people who were there, or on him who touched the bones or the person who was killed or died naturally or the grave. The clean person shall sprinkle it upon the unclean person on the third day and on the seventh day, thus cleansing him by the seven day. [The person being cleansed] shall then wash his clothes and bathe in water, and at nightfall he shall be clean.*

65. One could claim that the conversion was completed, but that the person still needed to be purified before he could participate in the Passover sacrifice like other Israelites. However, this begs the question concerning what one means by conversion. See the discussion of Beasley-Murray on this passage; G. R. Beasley-Murray, *Baptism in the New Testament* (Grand Rapids, 1962), 28–29. He concludes as follows: "The proselyte's bath enabled the freshly made Jew to enter upon his privileges of worship; it did not make the heathen a Jew"; Beasley-Murray, 29. Taylor argues that this is not a "special proselyte baptism" but an "immersion bath necessary for anyone who was unclean from any cause whatsoever before he would be eligible to eat the Passover meal (Hallowed Things)"; 195. Taylor argues that the "immersion bath" was originally associated with the sacrifice which the converts brought and that the bath served "solely as a bath of purification"; 195. When the sacrificial cult ended, the bath was kept as part of the conversion ritual; 196. T. M. Taylor, "The Beginnings of Jewish Proselyte Baptism," *New Testament Studies* 2, no. 3 (February 1956): 195. Rowley believes that "the fact that there is testimony to the immersion would suggest that it was witnessed," so that this probably refers to a "baptism" and not a mere "bath"; Rowley, 317. Torrance refers to this passage as the oldest "discussion of the necessity of Proselyte Baptism," T. F. Torrance, "Proselyte Baptism." *New Testament Studies* 1, no. 2 (November 1954): 154.

66. TPis. 7:14.

67. Lieberman notes that in some versions of Tosefta, Yosi or Yosi b. Judah appears in place of Eleazar b. Sadok. On bPes. 92a the tradent is Simeon b. Eleazar. Also, some versions replace *zkr* with *zr* with reference to the person about whom the Houses agree. Lieberman concludes that the Hillelites assumed that all gentiles suffered from corpse uncleanness, so that they were not cleansed immediately upon their conversion. Saul Lieberman, *Tosefta Ki-fshutah: A Comprehensive Commentary on the Tosefta. Part IV Order Mo'ed* (New York, 1962), 613–14.

68. YPes. 8:8; Venice 36b.

69. *You shall then stay outside the camp seven days; every one among you or among your captives who has slain a person or touched a corpse shall cleanse himself on the third and seventh day.*

70. BPes. 92a.

71. The rest of the *sugya* in the Babylonian Talmud relies on tPis. 8:12, which it eventually quotes.

72. For a discussion of the Shammaite-Hillelite passages, see Schiffman, 27–30. Schiffman concludes that this is evidence that the immersion was a conversion ritual. On the basis of these passages and the discussions of John the Baptist in the New Testament, Schiffman concludes that "immersion was already a necessary requirement for conversion in late Second Temple times. Nonetheless, we cannot prove that immersion was a *sine qua non* for conversion before the early first century c.e."; Schiffman, 30.

73. Lieberman, 614–15.

74. TPis. 7:14; yPes. 8:8, Venice 36b; and yNaz. 8:1, Venice 57a.

75. McKnight, 83.

76. Beasley-Murray, 24–25.

77. YYeb. 8:1; Venice 8d.

78. For example, bYeb. 78a–b discuss the problem of a female convert's body "interposing" between the water and the embryo in her womb.

79. BYeb. 46a.

80. Schiffman notes the importance of immersion as a conversion rite for women, and he claims that "for women, from the Yavnean period on, the only requirement besides acceptance of the Torah was immersion"; Schiffman, 26.

81. YYeb. 3:12; Venice 3:14, 64d.

82. Rowley holds that this is "an initiation ceremony equal with the circumcision of the male proselyte, and for the female proselyte the only initiation ceremony after the destruction of the Temple. Prior to that destruction both male and female proselytes were required to offer a sacrifice, but there was less of an initiatory character about that than about the baptism"; Rowley, 327.

83. YQid. 4:7; Venice 66a.

84. YErub. 4:5; Venice 22a.

85. MBer. 7:1.

86. BBer. 47b.

87. BYeb. 46a and bYeb. 46b. In the parallel on bA.Z. 59a, Hiyya b. Abbah does not actually attribute these statements to Yohanan; it is merely cited as Yohanan's opinion by the anonymous *gemara.*

88. BYeb. 46b. The *gemara* also deduces that conversion must occur before a court of three rabbis and that the ritual immersion must take place during the day.

89. BYeb. 46a–b.

90. *YHWH said to Moses: "Go to the people and warn them to stay pure today and tomorrow. Let them wash their clothes."*

91. *When a man has an emission of semen, he shall bathe his whole body in water.*

92. BKer. 9a.

93. McKnight holds that "in light of the sociological nature of a Jewish community and in light of needed rituals for women, it is more than likely (in my opinion) that baptism became a requirement for most of Judaism during the Second Temple Period"; McKnight, 84. Rowley agrees and states: "while it cannot be definitely established by specific evidence, it is probable that a baptismal rite was

practised in the case of proselytes to Judaism in the period preceding the destruction of the Temple"; Rowley, 320.

94. In the Palestinian Talmud, Joshua holds that the male must be both immersed and circumcised.

95. Cf. bYeb. 71a.

96. Cohen, "Rabbinic Conversion Ceremony," 193.

97. Smith, 13.

98. Collins, 176.

99. Collins, 179, states that "circumcision is not an entry requirement but an obligation consequent to admission."

100. BYeb. 47a–b. The passage is introduced by *tnw rbnn*. Cohen's "Rabbinic Conversion Ceremony" is a detailed discussion of this passage.

101. Hoenig suggests that this procedure was instituted after the Bar Kokhba war because "many Roman spies were disguising themselves as converts to help uncover plots to regain Jewish independence. This is reflected in an increasingly suspicious attitude on the part of the Jews toward those who seek to convert." Hoenig does not offer any evidence to support his claim. Sidney B. Hoenig, "Conversion during the Talmudic Period," in David M. Eichhorn, ed., *Conversion to Judaism: A History and Analysis* (New York, 1965), 52. While noting that this pericope reflects late amoraic practice (87), McKnight writes, "Jewish literature, in general, places high value on repentance and obedience . . . . These moral virtues were undoubtedly expected of converts, and some form of 'pledges' (or a pre-understanding) of obedience to the Torah was undeniably an integral aspect of conversion to Judaism"; McKnight, 87. However, the evidence drawn from Philo, Qumran, and the Apocrypha and Pseudepigrapha most likely reflect the various biases of these authors; it is doubtful that they are relevant to the rabbis or even to actual practice within the Israelite community. Schiffman claims that this *beraita* reflects tannaitic practice and should be dated from immediately after the Great Revolt or the Bar Kokhba War; Schiffman, 20. If the ritual recorded here was common tannaitic practice, it is difficult to understand why it is not mentioned in any earlier document.

102. YQid. 4:1; Venice 65b.

103. As early as Mishnah and Tosefta these offerings were seen as ethnic obligations which were used to unify the group through mutual support; Porton, 182–84.

104. For the meaning of this phrase, see Cohen, "Rabbinic Conversion," 179 and 182, n. 10. Elsewhere on bYeb. 47b Eleazar offers an interpretation of Ruth 1:16–18 as scriptural proof for the assertion that the gentile is not be excessively encouraged or discouraged from converting. See Cohen, "Rabbinic Conversion," 197 for a discussion of this midrash on Ruth.

105. *Lkl dbryw*.

106. The agricultural gifts were required only in Israel. See Alan Avery-Peck, *Mishnah's Division of Agriculture: A History and Theology of Seder Zeraim* (Chico, 1985), and William D. Davies, *The Gospel and the Land: Early Christianity and Jewish Territorial Doctrine* (Berkeley and Los Angeles, 1974).

107. John G. Gager, *The Origins of Anti-Semitism: Attitudes Toward Judaism in Pagan and Christian Antiquity* (New York and Oxford, 1985), 57; Robert Goldenberg, "The Jewish Sabbath in the Roman World up to the Time of Constantine the Great," in Hildegard Temporini and Wolfgang Haase, eds., *Aufstieg und Niedergang der römischen Welt* (Berlin and New York, 1979), II.19.1, 414–44; Louis Feldman, *Jew and Gentile in the Ancient World* (Princeton, 1993), 158–70.

108. YQid. 4:1; Venice 65b.

109. Cohen, "Rabbinic Conversion Ceremony," 187.

110. Ibid., 186.

111. Rowley argues the "spiritual state of the proselyte was therefore essential to the valid performance of the baptismal rite"; Rowley, 328.

112. YQid. 4:1; Venice 65b.

113. Ibid.

114. The passage also mentions those who converted at the time of Solomon in order to enjoy the benefits of serving the Israelite king, following the interpretation of David Fränkel, *loc. cit.*, those who were converted because of the fear of lions, that is, the Samaritans, IIKgs. 17:25, and those who converted at the time of Mordecai and Esther.

115. YQid. 4:1; Venice 65b.

116. Ibid.

117. IIKgs. 17:25.

118. Lit., "not for the sake of Heaven."

119. David Fränkel, *loc. cit.*, notes that IIKgs. 17:32 reads *they feared YHWH*.

120. YGiṭ. 1:4. 1:4 is missing in the Venice edition, so that this is improperly marked as Venice yGiṭ. 1:5, 43c.

121. YB.M. 5:5; Venice 5:7, 10c.

122. YQid. 4:1; Venice 65c. The relevant part of the *sugya* appears in ySanh. 6:7; Venice 13:9, 23d.

123. YQid. 4:1, Venice 65b; bYeb. 24b; bA.Z. 3b; bYeb. 76a–b.

124. We saw above that most scholars have claimed that Eliezer and Joshua do not really disagree concerning the requirement of circumcision; however, only by harmonizing the texts in the Palestinian *gemara* with those in the Babylonian Talmud and by ignoring the simple reading of the passages in both Talmuds can one come to that conclusion.

125. Cohen, "Rabbinic Conversion," suggests that the ceremony recorded in bYeb. 47a–b had three purposes: (1) To regulate conversion, 195–96, (2) to ensure that the convert knows what awaits him or her, 196–99, (3) to administer the rituals properly, 199–201. Cohen also argues that the ritual recorded in bYeb. was not an initiation ritual; 201–3.

126. On conversion and purification, see Cohen,"Rabbinic Conversion," 194.

127. On the problem of the Levitical impurity of gentiles, see Adolph Büchler, "The Levitical Impurity of the Gentiles in Palestine before the Year 70," *Jewish Quarterly Review*, n. s., 17 (1926–27): 1–81 and Gedalyahu Alon, "The Levitical Uncleanness of the Gentiles," reprinted in Gedalyahu Alon, *Jews, Judaism, and the Classical World*, trans. Israel Abrahams (Jerusalem, 1977), 146–89. Werblowsky

argues that proselyte immersion was originally designed to purify the converts from their gentile impurity; it was not an initiatory ritual." R. J. Zwi Werblowsky, "A Note on Purification and Proselyte Baptism," in Jacob Neusner, ed., *Christianity, Judaism and Other Greco-Roman Cults: Studies for Morton Smith at Sixty* (Leiden, 1975), 3:200–205.

128. Porton, 269–83.

129. McKnight holds the view that "the origins of Jewish proselyte baptism . . . may have been in the entrance requirements of Jewish Christianity"; McKnight, 85. Schiffman claims that the immersion of converts "should be seen as an initiatory rite in which the convert is cleansed of his transgressions and impurities and emerges from the bath as a new person, starting a new life"; Schiffman, 26.

130. McKnight notes that "as early as ca. 160 B.C. we find a convert being circumcised at conversion (Jth. 14:10) to demonstrate a complete break from an idolatrous and immoral past in order to join Judaism—with its nation, God, land, and Torah. . . . We do not know from this text that the rite was demanded from him by others for conversion to be 'authentic' or whether he decided on his own to do this as a demonstration of his zeal. What we do know is that in the middle of the second century B.C. we have clear evidence . . . that converts were circumcised. What is surprising is that there is no further unambiguous evidence of circumcision for converts until the writings of Josephus"; McKnight, 79.

131. Gen. 17:10ff.

132. McKnight writes that "circumcision, Judaism, and national identity were intertwined. Such a connection could be utilized for proselytizing since, if being a male Jew meant being circumcised, then becoming a Jew would probably involve being circumcised"; McKnight 80.

133. McKnight notes that two passages in Josephus indicate that some required circumcision for converts, while others did not. The references are to the story of two nobles from Trachonitis who were residing in Palestine (*Vita* 112–13) and to the story of Izates *(Antiquities* 20.35–49); McKnight, 80. McKnight concludes: "The rabbinic tradition shows that circumcision would have been seen at least as an act of the obedient convert. Further, I do not doubt that by and large it was seen as a requirement and that it was practiced. However, in light of the debates over the matter, it is probable that circumcision as a requirement had not yet become established custom or tradition prior to the first century A.D. . . . . I hesitate to conclude that circumcision was a requirement throughout Second Temple Judaism, because the evidence is not completely unambiguous and there may well have been some diversity on the matter. Circumcision was probably required for male converts most of the time and in most local expressions of Judaism. It was *the* ritual that separated the Jew from the Gentile (at least in Jewish perception), and therefore it would have been *the act* that permitted the would-be convert to cross the boundary and enter the community"; McKnight, 81–82. I would add the evidence is no less ambiguous for later periods of Judaism in late antiquity.

134. See the comparatively recent attempt by John Nolland to prove that all converts had to be circumcised and the article by N. J. McEleney in which he

seeks to demonstrate that circumcision was unnecessary: John Nolland, "Uncircumcised Proselytes?" *Journal for the Study of Judaism* 12, no. 2 (December 1981): 173–94; N. J. McEleney, "Conversion, Circumcision, and the Law," *New Testament Studies* 20, no. 2 (1974): 328–33. Both of these articles merely demonstrate the impossibility of determining anything for certain about the conversion ritual. McEleney argues that in the first century there were those who held that not all Jews or converts had to be circumcised. McEleney gives three reasons for circumcision: "(1) Obedience to the precept . . . because the Law commanded it." (2) It was, from the period of the Maccabees onward "a sign of fidelity to the covenant." (3) "Circumcision was . . . a sign of one's identification with the Jewish people, particularly in times of crisis"; 333. He also argues that the shedding of blood upon the circumcision gave it "a sacrificial aspect" and that it "has a redemptive aspect too"; 334. Nolland takes up McEleney's interpretations of the various texts he analyzes point by point and concludes McEleney is incorrect in his claims that there were Jews who would not have required converts to be circumcised. The most Nolland is willing to concede is that "even if he [Joshua on bYeb. 46b] did consider that circumcision could be dispensed with, the idea certainly never got any further than pure theory"; Nolland, 192.

135. Cohen claims that by the early or mid-second century C.E. circumcision and immersion were "equally obligatory" for men; Cohen, "Rabbinic Conversion," 195. Schiffman holds that "it is most likely that circumcision was required from the earliest beginnings of the conversion procedure in Second Temple times. However, before the Maccabean Revolt such a requirement cannot be documented, since the Second Temple sources are so very scanty." Schiffman also believes that the rite of circumcision "served as a test of sincerity and dedication" to the Jewish people; Schiffman, 25.

136. McKnight uses the ambiguity concerning a conversion ritual as an indicator of the fact that Judaism was not a missionary religion; McKnight, 88. Basing himself on *Joseph and Aseneth* and the lack of clear indications that there was a uniform conversion ritual, McKnight concludes that "the real requirement . . . [for conversion] is repentance from sin and communion with Israel. In other words, perhaps the most determinative factor for converts to Judaism was sociological (transfer to Israel) rather than rituals and theology"; McKnight, 89. Feldman, however, believes that many non-Jews were attracted to Judaism and that it actively sought converts; Feldman, 293–415.

137. E. P. Sanders, *Paul, the Law, and the Jewish People* (Philadelphia, 1983), esp. 17–64.

CHAPTER 8

1. Shaye J. D. Cohen, "From the Bible to the Talmud: The Prohibition of Intermarriage," *Hebrew Annual Review* 7 (1983): 23. Cohen devotes his article to demonstrating that "The prohibition against intermarriage was not biblical," although "the process which yielded [this view] . . . was well under way by the time

of the Maccabees, and was substantially complete by the time of the Talmud," 23. Cohen's article covers pages 23–39.

2. If we can take the frequent rabbinic admonitions against Israelites' participating in gentile religious festivals and the like as evidence that some Israelites did in fact take part in these events, then there is some evidence that Israelites also shared in the gentile's religious life.

3. Gary G. Porton, *Goyim: Gentiles and Israelites in Mishnah and Tosefta* (Atlanta: 1988), esp. 221–39. Although Mishnah and Tosefta strongly and virtually consistently strive to keep the Israelite from participating in the gentile's "idolatrous" cults, the former can take the latter's word that an item which he has purchased from Israelites will not be used in the worship of a foreign deity, 246, n. 9. On the other hand, under no circumstances is the marriage between an Israelite and a gentile acceptable or legally valid.

4. Cohen, 27–28.

5. This, of course, has been seen as a positive stance by some and as a negative and particularistic trait of Judaism by others; see the works cited by Cohen, 23–24, n. 1.

6. Porton, 285–307, esp. 291–92.

7. Lev. 21:7 states, *They [priests] shall not marry a woman defiled by harlotry, nor shall they marry one divorced from her husband.* Lev. 21:13–15 read: *He [the high priest] may marry only a woman who is a virgin. A widow, or a divorced woman, or one who is degraded by harlotry—such he may not marry. Only a virgin of his own kin may he take to wife—that he may not profane his offspring among his kin, for I, YHWH, have sanctified him.* A priest can also be defiled by his daughter's actions: *When the daughter of a priest defiles herself through harlotry, it is her father whom she defiles;* Lev. 21:9.

8. Lev. 21:16–23: *No man of your [Aaron's] offspring throughout the ages who has a defect shall be qualified to offer the food of his God. No one at all who has a defect shall be qualified: no man who is blind, or lame, or has a limb too short or too long; no man who has a broken leg or a broken arm; or who is a hunchback, or a dwarf, or who has a growth in his eye, or who has a boil-scar, or scurvy, or crushed testes. No man among the offspring of Aaron the priest who has a defect shall be qualified to offer the food of his God. He may eat of the food of his God, of the most holy as well as of the holy; but he shall not enter behind the curtain or come near the altar.*

9. On the *mamzer*, see Lawrence H. Schiffman, *Who Was a Jew? Rabbinic and Halakhic Perspectives on the Jewish-Christian Schism* (Hoboken: 1985), 10–11 and *passim*.

10. Josh. 9:27.

11. MQid. 4:2.

12. MQid. 4:1.

13. TQid. 4:15. If the female cannot marry into the priestly class, this would agree with Judah's statement in mQid. 4:6; see Saul Lieberman, *The Tosefta According to Codex Vienna, with Variants from Codices Erfurt, Genizah Mss. and Editio Princeps (Venice 1521) Together with References to Parallel Passages in Talmudic Literature and a Brief Commentary. The Order of Nashim: Sotah, Gittin, Kiddushin* (New York,

1973), 292, note to lines 45–46 and Saul Lieberman, *Tosefta Ki-fshutah: A Comprehensive Commentary on the Tosefta Part VIII Order Nashim* (New York, 1973), 962.

14. TQid. 5:2. This is the reading which Lieberman prefers; Lieberman, *The Tosefta Order Nashim: Sotah Gittin Kiddushin*, 293, note on line 2 and Lieberman, *Tosefta Ki-fshutah Part VIII Nashim*, 966. Cf. bQid. 72b.

15. TQid. 5:2. This is the reading which Lieberman prefers; Lieberman, *The Tosefta Order Nashim: Sotah, Gittin, Kiddushin*, 293, note on line 2 and Lieberman, *Tosefta Ki-fshutah Part VIII Nashim*, 966. Cf. bQid. 72b; Sifré Deuteronomy Ki Taṣa 247, Horovitz 276. The difference of opinion between Yosah and Judah is set in a narrative context in the Palestinian Talmud; yQid. 3:12; Venice 3:14, 64c. Yosah's and Judah's opinions also appear in the Babylonian *gemara*, and their opinions are the same as those attributed to them in Mishnah; bYeb. 78b. Cf. bQid. 67a. Cited on bQid. 67b; cf. bQid. 66b–67a.

16. Menahem Haran, *Temples and Temple-Service in Ancient Israel: An Inquiry into the Character of Cult Phenomena and the Historical Setting of the Priestly School* (Oxford, 1978). Roland deVaux, *Ancient Israel*, vol. 2: *Religious Institutions*, with bibliography, indexes, and a map (New York and Toronto, 1965), 345–405.

17. Baruch A. Levine, *The JPS Torah Commentary: Leviticus* (Philadelphia, 1989), 144.

18. Levine, 145.

19. As we saw above, Lev. 21:7 prohibits a priest from marrying a prostitute or a divorced woman *because he is holy (qdš) to his God*. The high priest is allowed to marry only a virgin because YHWH *sanctified him, (mqdšw)*.

20. On the rules concerning marriages with priests, see Emil Schürer, *The History of the Jewish People in the Age of Jesus Christ (175 B.C.–A.D. 135)*, ed. Geza Vermes, Fergus Millar, Matthew Black, rev. ed. (Edinburgh, 1973–87), 2:240–43. On the priestly concern for proper descent lines in the Bible, see Howard Eilberg-Schwartz, *The Savage in Judaism: An Anthropology of Israelite Religion and Ancient Judaism* (Bloomington and Indianapolis, 1990), 163–73.

21. MQid. 4:6–7.

22. The full text states: "The daughter of a male impaired priest is unfit for the priestly class forever. The daughter of an Israelite who married a woman of impaired priestly lineage is fit for the priestly class. The daughter of an impaired priest who was married to an Israelite is unfit for the priestly class. R. Judah says: 'The daughter of a male convert is like the daughter of a male impaired priest.'" TQid. 5:3 contains a more complete version of Judah's comment: "The daughter of a male convert is like the daughter of an impaired male priest, for she is unfit for [marrying into] the priestly caste."

23. MQid. 4:7. The text also states that the male convert and the freed male slave are the same, "even until the tenth generation, unless his mother is an Israelite." Exactly what this means is open to some question, for the antecedent of "his" is unclear. Albeck states it refers either to the mother of the convert's son or to the fact that the child's father was a native-born Israelite. Albeck brings the variant from mBik. 1:5 which reads *'mn* for *'mw* and states that this refers to the

daughter's mother. See Hanokh Albeck, *The Six Orders of the Mishnah: Seder Nashim* (Tel Aviv, 1959), 327. Cf. Jacob Neusner, *A History of the Mishnaic Law of Women. Part Four Sotah, Gittin, Qiddushin: Translation and Explanation* (Leiden, 1980), 255–56. The same opinion, only in different words, is attributed to Eliezer in mBik. 1:5: "A woman [who is] the daughter of converts may not marry into the priestly class, unless her mother is an Israelite." This of course does not make sense, for it is unclear how the woman's mother can be both a convert and an Israelite, unless it means that the child was born after its mother converted. But, given the fact that the terms "convert" and "Israelite" most often indicate different classes of the People Israel, this does not seem likely.

24. The fact that converts' family lineage was not the same as that of native-born members of the People Israel is used to justify their being excluded from serving as judges in capital cases. While anyone may serve as a judge in a civil case, only Israelites, Levites, and priests may judge capital cases. Therefore, converts cannot serve as judges in capital cases; mSanh. 4:2. Similarly, neither a *mamzer* nor a *natin* could serve as a judge in all cases; mHor. 1:4. Cf. Sifra VaYiqra (Hobah) Parashah 4:3, Weiss 19a where those listed in mHor. 1:4 are exempted from the requirement of making a public offering under the terms of Lev. 4:14 because they are not suitable to serve as judges.

25. MB.M. 4:10, tB.M. 3:25, bB.M. 58b, Sifra BeHar Pereq 4:2, Weiss 107d, Sifra Qedoshim Pereq 8:2; Weiss 91a, Mekhilta Ishmael Mishpatim 18 on Ex. 22:20; Horovitz and Rabin 311, l. 11–312, l. 18. Mekhilta Ishmael Mishpatim 18 on Ex. 22:20; Horovitz and Rabin 311, ll. 3–5.

26. TQid. 5:2.

27. TQid. 5:3.

28. TQid. See Lieberman, *Tosefta Ki-fshutah. Part VIII*, note to line 19 for the manuscript support for this reading.

29. TQid. 4:15. This ruling should be contrasted with tQid. 4:16, which states that if any of these women marry a gentile, their children are *mamzerim*.

30. Sifra Emor Pereq 2:9, Weiss 95a. Sifra presents these views as an exegesis of Lev. 21:15. *[Only a virgin of his own kin may he [the priest] take to wife]—that he may not profane his offspring among his kin* is the basis of the ruling that a priest may not marry the daughter of an impaired male priest. Judah's statement is connected to the end of the verse, *For I, YHWH, have sanctified him.*

31. Sifra Emor Pereq 1:7, Weiss 94b.

32. Porton, 236, n. 64.

33. Sifré Numbers Matot 157, Horovitz, 212.

34. This is an interpretation of Num. 31:18, *but spare every young woman who has not had carnal relations with a man.*

35. YQid. 4:1; Venice 65b. However, the text does raise some questions about the correctness of this view. The anonymous conclusion of the *sugya* does accept the position. In yYeb. 8:2; Venice 9b, Hoshiah the Elder accepts the view that converts are considered to be prostitutes with regard to marriage into the priestly class. The text also accepts Judah's statement that the daughter of a convert is like the daughter of an impaired priest.

36. YQid. 4:1; Venice 65b.

37. YQid. 3:12; Venice 3:14, 64c. See also yYeb. 9:1; Venice 10a.

38. The issue is usually phrased in terms of the women's ability to eat the heave offering, and this is derived from Num. 18:8–13. Num. 18:11 states: *This, too, shall be yours [Aaron's]: the gift of offerings of their contributions (trwmt mtnm), all the elevation offerings of the Israelites, I give to you, to your sons, and to the daughters that are with you, as a due for all time; everyone of your household who is clean may eat it.* The clean members of the priestly households may also eat the first fruits, Num. 18:12. The priests' wives and daughters could also eat the peace offerings, Lev. 7:30–34 and Lev. 10:14–15. On exactly who among the priestly caste could eat from which offerings, see Schürer, 2:260–67.

39. YBik. 1:5; Venice 64a.

40. *They [the priests] may marry only virgins of the stock of the house of Israel.*

41. This is the *gemara's* understanding of Yosi's statement in mQid. 4:7. This interpretation also appears on bQid. 78a–b.

42. According to the *gemara* "all of these views" are derived from Lev. 21:15, *only a virgin of his own kin may he take to wife.*

43. It is attributed to Simeon in the *gemara,* but to Simeon b. Yohai in Sifré Numbers.

44. The text states that the priests normally protected their dignity by marrying only women who had at least one native-born Israelite parent.

45. YBik. 1:5; Venice 64a.

46. *Šhyw qwryn 'lyh 'r'r.*

47. YBik. 1:5; Venice 64a. Cf. yQid. 4:6; Venice 66a.

48. The verse states that the high priest may not marry *a widow, or a divorced woman, or one who is degraded by harlotry. . . . Only a virgin of his own kin may he take to wife;* yBik. 1:5, Venice 64a; yYeb. 8:2, Venice 9c; yQid. 4:6, Venice 66a. In yQid. 4:6 *bwgrt* appears in the printed text, but *gywrt* appears in Venice. In yYeb. 8:2 *gywrt* appears in the Venice edition and in the printed text; however, *bwgrt* appears in parentheses in the printed edition. The correct reading must be *gywrt.*

49. Deut. 23:4–9: *No Ammonite or Moabite shall be admitted into the congregation of YHWH; none of their descendants, even in the tenth generation, shall ever be admitted into the congregation of YHWH. . . . You shall not abhor an Edomite, for he is your kinsman. You shall not abhor an Egyptian, for you were a stranger (gr) in his land. Children born to them may be admitted into the congregation of YHWH in the third generation.*

50. Also a gentile, a slave, a Samaritan, an impaired priest, a *mamzer,* or a *natin.*

51. YSoṭ. 4:5, Venice 4:6, 19d; yYeb. 7:5, Venice 8b. Cf. tYeb. 8:1 where the word "convert" is missing.

52. David Fränkel, *loc. cit.,* prefers Jeremiah in the name of our rabbis and Ba because this attribution appears later in the *sugya.*

53. The point seems to be that unless the offsprings, both males and females, are permitted, the marriages cannot take place. According to Yosi, because the high priest cannot marry a widow, the convert's children are also prohibited. This opinion is repeated later in the *sugya* when Zakkai and Alexandria pose a question to Yosa who then quotes Jeremiah in the name of our rabbis along with Ba.

54. This view is connected to the phrase *among his kin* in Lev. 21:15. If the widow comes from two nations, which means in this context that her parents are an Ammonite and an Israelite, the high priest may marry her, for in this case the males are prohibited, but the females are permitted.

55. YYeb. 8:3; Venice 9c.

56. BYeb. 60b.

57. Ibid.

58. Ibid.

59. BYeb. 61b. It is possible that Nahman held that all female gentiles, even very young women, engaged in sexual activity, but this would be unique. Given the ways in which the Talmud was constructed, there is no need to assume that Nahman agreed with the equation of the harlot with the converted woman merely because it appears close to his opinion.

60. BQid. 21b.

61. BQid. 78a–b. This seems to be related to the passage on yBik. 1:5; Venice 64a.

62. *They [the priests] shall not marry widows or divorced women; they may marry only virgins of the stock of the house of Israel, or widows who are widows of priests.*

63. BQid. 78b.

64. BQid. 74a–b.

65. BYeb. 76a.

66. BQid. 57a.

67. BYeb. 57a.

68. *But a person who is a priest's property by purchase may eat of them.*

CHAPTER 9

1. See the discussions in Bernard J. Bamberger, *Proselytism in the Talmudic Period* (New York, 1968), 63, and William G. Braude, *Jewish Proselyting in the First Five Centuries of the Common Era: The Age of the Tannaim and Amoraim* (Providence, 1940), 122ff. The actual expression *qtn šnwld* does not appear in Mishnah, Tosefta, or the early midrashim.

2. We shall see below, however, that the principle of a convert's becoming like "a newborn child" is not consistently applied.

3. Sifra BeHar Parashah 5:1, Weiss 109b specifically states that the forbidden relationships mentioned in Lev. 18 apply to Israelites and to converts. The problem involves which familial relationships exist for a convert. See also yYeb. 11:2; Venice 12a. There we discover that if a gentile who converted was married to a woman and her daughter or to a woman and her sister, he must send one of his wives away after he joins the Israelite community because now he is engaged in a relationship forbidden in Lev. 18. On bYeb. 97b Aha b. Jacob and Sheshet discuss whether converts who are paternal brothers may marry their brother's wife in light of Lev. 18:16.

4. BB.Q. 88a. This is based on interpreting Deut. 24:16 to mean that parents are not put to death by the testimony of their children.

5. See BB.Q. 49b, for example.

6. This stylized list appears in several places. MGiṭ. 2:6 continues mGiṭ. 2:5's discussion of those who may or may not deliver a divorce document from a man to his wife. The former text states the general rule that the person who delivers the document must know what he is doing when he accepts it from the husband and when he delivers it to the woman, so that if the agent changed status between the time he accepted the document and he delivered it, a divorce has not occurred. The implication is that upon conversion, the gentile has become one who can serve as a knowledgeable agent for other Israelites. TSanh. 5:4 builds on mSanh. 3:3's list of those who may not give testimony. Tosefta adds those mentioned in our list to those mentioned in Mishnah, and adds a general rule—"Anyone who is fit (*kšr*) at the end and the beginning is fit. [If] he is fit at the beginning but unfit (*pswl*) at the end or [if] he is unfit at the beginning but fit at the end, he is unfit"—which is reminiscent of the general rule in mGiṭ. 2:6. Cf. Gary G. Porton, *Goyim: Gentiles and Israelites in Mishnah-Tosefta* (Atlanta, 1988), 141–42.

7. YNid. 1:4, Venice 1:5, 49b; yYeb. 4:11, Venice 6a.

8. BKet. 28b, bKet. 37a, bYeb. 35a.

9. The Palestinian Talmud also compares the change in status from gentile to convert to one who achieved puberty; yShebu. 2:1, Venice 33d; yHor. 3:2, Venice 3:3, 47b.

10. This has been fully worked out in Porton, *Goyim*, esp. 173–307.

11. Porton, *Goyim*, 173–203.

12. MHal. 3:6, tHal. 1:12.

13. MPe. 4:6. Cf. Sifré Deuteronomy Ki Taṣa 282, Finkelstein 298; Sifra Qedoshim Pereq 1:6, Weiss 87b.

14. TDem. 6:2. The situation with the tithes is complicated, for the gentiles could bring tithes if they wished; however, they do not seem to have been required to do so. See Porton, *Goyim, passim*.

15. Sifra Qedoshim Pereq 3:4, Weiss 88b; Sifré Deuteronomy Ki Taṣa 284, Finkelstein 301; Sifré Deuteronomy Ki Taṣa 285, Finkelstein 302 .

16. Sifré Deuteronomy Re'ah 110, Finkelstein 171.

17. BYeb. 47a–b.

18. BYeb. 47a.

19. BHul. 134a–b.

20. On the agricultural rules and the importance of the Land of Israel, see the following: Porton, *Goyim*, 173–203; Lawrence A. Hoffman, *The Land of Israel: Jewish Perspectives* (Notre Dame, 1986); William D. Davies, *The Gospel and the Land: Early Christianity and Jewish Territorial Doctrine* (Berkeley and Los Angeles, 1974); Alan Avery-Peck, *Mishnah's Division of Agriculture: A History and Theology of Seder Zeraim* (Chico, 1985); Daniel Sperber, *Roman Palestine: 200–400 The Land* (Ramat Gan, 1978); "Aretz-Israel" in Shlomo J. Zevin, ed., *Encyclopedia Talmudica: A Digest of Halachic Literature and Jewish Law from the Tannaitic Period to the Present Time Alpha-*

betically Arranged, trans. David B. Klein, ed. Harry Freedman (Jerusalem, 1978), 3:1–68.

21. Most relevant in this connection are Jacob Neusner, *The Idea of Purity in Ancient Judaism: The Haskell Lectures, 1972–1973* (Leiden, 1973) and Morton Smith, "The Dead Sea Sect in Relation to Ancient Judaism," *New Testament Studies* 7 (1960): 347–60. See also Shaye J. D. Cohen, *From the Maccabees to the Mishnah* (Philadelphia, 1987), 128–131. For a differing view concerning the importance of purity, see E. P. Sanders, *Jewish Law from Jesus to the Mishnah* (Philadelphia, 1990), 184–236.

22. Porton, *Goyim*, 269–83.

23. MZab. 2:1; tZab. 2:1; mZab. 2:3; mNeg. 7:1; tNeg. 2:14–15; Sifra Negaim Pereq 1:1, Weiss 59d–60; tNid. 1:3; Sifra Zabim Parashah 1:1, Weiss 74d; Sifra Maṣorah Parashah 5:1, Weiss 78d; Sifra Tazriʻa Parashah 1:1, Weiss 57c; Sifra Aḥarei Mot Pereq 12:1, Weiss 84d.

24. YBik. 3:3; Venice 65c.

25. BSanh. 71b.

26. YQid. 1:1; Venice 58c.

27. BYeb. 48b.

28. BSanh. 71b.

29. BYeb. 92b, bYeb. 93b, bQid. 63a, bKet 58b, bB.M. 16b. In the *gemara* the issue is whether or not one can vow to take possession of, or sanctify, something which does not already exist. Thus, the woman as an acceptable marriage partner does not exist at the time of betrothal. She may legally be married to an Israelite only after she has converted.

30. MB.B. 8:1–2.

31. MB.B. 4:7; tB.Q. 4:6; yB.Q. 4:8, Venice 4c; bB.Q. 44b.

32. Those converts who died with legally acceptable heirs would be covered by the verses in Exodus.

33. The Palestinian *gemara* focuses on to whom the anonymous text in mB.Q. 9:11 should be attributed; yB.Q. 9:9; Venice 9:15, 7a. The Babylonian Talmud, bB.Q. 109a–b, expands on the discussion in tB.Q. 10:17 and draws out some implications of Aqiba's and Yosi's views in Tosefta.

34. *When a man or woman commits any wrong toward a fellow man, thus breaking faith with YHWH, and that person realizes his guilt, he shall confess the wrong that he has done. He shall make restitution in the principal amount and add one-fifth to it, giving it to him whom he has wronged. If the man has no kinsman (g'l) to whom restitution can be made, the amount repaid shall go to YHWH for the priest . . . .*

35. MB.Q. 9:11.

36. Sifré Numbers Naśo 4, Horovitz 7.

37. If it is a loan, the thief does not have to bring a guilt offering to the Temple or make restitution to the priests upon the convert's death. Aqiba focuses solely on the guilt offering mentioned in Num. 5:8; tB.Q. 10:17. The guilt offering of one who stole from a convert who died without heirs appears in the list of items given to the priests in tHal. 2:9; Sifré Numbers Qorah 119, Horovitz 142; yHal. 4:11, Venice 60b; bB.Q. 110a–b; bHul. 133b.

38. MB.B. 3:1–8.
39. MB.B. 3:3.
40. MB.B. 4:1–5:5.
41. MB.B. 4:9.
42. Tosefa contains one long passage which ignores the property given as a gift or that which brothers jointly inherited, but which discusses the dead convert's fields, his slaves, and his utensils; tB.B. 2:11. TSheq. 3:11 deals with property which the convert dedicated to the Temple before his death.
43. TKet. 4:16.
44. TKet. 4:14–16.
45. YGiṭ. 4:4; Venice 45d.
46. YB.B. 4:8; Venice 4:11, 14d.
47. YQid. 1:4; Venice 60a. MQid. 1:4 requires that large domesticated animals be delivered to the purchaser.
48. YB.B. 3:1, Venice 13d; yQid. 1:5, Venice 60d.
49. BB.M. 8b.
50. BB.M. 55a.
51. BQid. 23a.
52. BB.B. 52b, bB.B. 57a, bB.B. 53a, bB.B. 53b, bB.B. 54a.
53. *When brothers dwell together and one of them dies and leaves no son, the wife of the deceased shall not be married to a stranger (l'yš zr), outside the family. Her husband's brother shall unite with her, take her as his wife and perform the levir's duty. The first son that she bears shall be accounted to the dead brother, that his name may not be blotted out in Israel. But if a man does not want to marry his brother's widow, his brother's widow shall appear before the elders in the gate and declare "My husband's brother refuses to establish a name in Israel for his brother; he will not perform the duty of the levir." The elders of his town shall then summon him and talk to him. If he insists, saying, "I do not want to marry her," his brother's widow shall go up to him in the presence of the elders, pull the sandal off his foot, spit in his face, and make this declaration: Thus shall be done to the man who will not build up his brother's house! And he shall go in Israel by the name of "the family of the unsandaled one."*
54. Roland deVaux, *Ancient Israel*, vol. 1: *Social Institutions* (New York and Toronto, 1965), 38. DeVaux also notes that "Discussion about the purpose of the levirate seems to be endless."
55. TYeb. 2:6 and tYeb. 11:2.
56. BYeb. 17b.
57. MYeb. 11:2.
58. TYeb. 2:5. TYeb. 2:6 contains the same ruling only in a different form. TYeb. 2:5 includes the "wife of a convert" among those who do not participate in the rite of *halisah* or in the levirate marriage, *l' mtyybmwt wl' hwlṣwt*. TYeb. 2:6 refers to the convert as one of those who does not engage in the rite *halisah* or in the levirate marriage, *l' mybmyn wl' hwlsym*. The two texts are complementary, with the first referring to the females, and the latter discussing the males. Lieberman connects the statement in 2:5 with mYeb. 11:2; however, the two need not be related, for Tosefta's matched statements could be meant to underscore the fact that the

convert has severed all ties with his gentile brother(s). Mishnah deals with a highly specific case—two brothers who convert along with their mother—which could raise some real questions. Tosefta's two matched lists are devoid of any specifics. Saul Lieberman, *Tosefta Ki-fshutah: A Comprehensive Commentary on the Tosefta Part VI Order Nashim* (New York, 1967), 18. The language of tYeb. 2:6 is repeated in tYeb. 11:2. The latter text adds that if one of those mentioned in the text who are not obligated to enter into the levirate relationship with their sisters-in-law does marry them, they invalidate the women from marrying into the priesthood. Furthermore, if the brothers claim their sisters-in-law and then perform the rite of *halisah*, they have accomplished nothing.

59. Mishnah states: "[Concerning] the converted woman whose sons convert with her—they do not perform the rite of *halisah*, and they do not enter into levirate marriages. Even if she conceived the first one not in a state of sanctity and bore him in a state of sanctity and the second one she conceived him and bore him in a state of sanctity." Tosefta states: "[Concerning] the converted woman whose sons convert with her—they do not perform the rite of *halisah* and they do not enter into levirate marriages, and they are not obligated [to follow the prohibition against marrying] a brother's wife (Lev. 18:16). [If] she conceived while not in a state of sanctity but bore in a state of sanctity, they neither perform the rite of *halisah* nor engage in levirate marriages, but they are obligated [to follow the prohibition against marrying] a brother's wife. If she conceived and bore in a state of sanctity, lo, she is like an Israelite in all matters."

60. Lev. 18:16.

61. *Mykn 'th 'wmr.*

62. Sifré Deuteronomy Ki Tasa 289; Finkelstein, 204.

63. YYeb. 11:2; Venice 11d–12a.

64. The *gemara* first attempts to establish whether the convert has a different relationship with his mother than with his father by citing a dispute between Yosi the Galilean and Aqiba. Yosi taught that a convert was culpable for cursing his mother, but he was not culpable for cursing his father. Aqiba interpreted Lev. 20:9, *if anyone insults his father or his mother,* to mean that one who is culpable for cursing his mother is also culpable for cursing his father, but one who is not culpable for cursing his mother is not culpable for cursing his father. However, Aqiba concedes that in the case of one who knows who his mother is but not his father, a *shetuqi,* the convert is culpable for cursing his mother but not his father. This appears in Sifra Qedoshim Pereq 9:9, Weiss 92a. Jacob b. Aha and Yosa in Yohanan's name state that Yosi and Aqiba disagreed only concerning a convert whose mother conceived him while she was not in a state of sanctity but bore him while she was in a state of sanctity. If the convert were conceived and born after his mother converted, Yosi would concede Aqiba's point; that is, he would be culpable if he cursed either parent.

65. This is the way Moses Margolioth, *loc. cit.*, and David Fränkel, *loc. cit.*, read the passage. Neusner speaks of an anonymous "they"; Jacob Neusner, *The Talmud of the Land of Israel: A Preliminary Translation and Explanation,* vol. 21: *Yebamot* (Chicago and London, 1987), 354.

66. *'mr kwn kn 'mr rby ywḥnn 'swr.*

67. Moses Margolioth, *loc. cit.*, identifies these people as the members of the yeshiva, and Neusner identifies them as "the disciples"; Neusner, *Yebamot*, 354.

68. This is David Fränkel's, *loc. cit.*, explanation of *ḥwwn b'yyn mymr.* Neusner translates as "proposed to state"; Neusner, 354.

69. If the converted dead brother had had intercourse with the woman before he converted, he would not have established a marital relationship with her because Israelites could not contract legal marriages with non-Israelites. According to the *gemara*, one convert cannot marry his brother's wife because it is possible that others will not realize that the brothers are converts, and they will mistakenly conclude that Israelite brothers may marry each other's wives.

70. BYeb. 97b.

71. Ibid.

72. Cf. Bamberger, *Proselytism*, 86–91 and Braude, *Jewish Proselyting*, 122–26.

73. Porton, *Goyim*, 241–58.

74. MDem. 6:10, tDem. 6:12. Sarason notes that unlike the Israelites, who inherit from their Israelite parents, a convert has no "automatic inheritance rights"; Richard S. Sarason, *A History of the Mishnaic Law of Agriculture Section Three: A Study of Tractate Demai* (Leiden, 1979), 229.

75. In discussing how an Israelite who has sold himself into slavery may be redeemed, Lev. 25:50 states: *He shall compute with his purchaser . . . .* Rabbah claims that the verse means that the slave should deal with the one who bought him and not with his master's heirs, which implies that the slave's gentile master has heirs.

76. For our purposes, we do not need to ascertain the exact meaning of "the words of the scribes." For discussions of the phrase, see Shmuel Safrai, "Halakha," *The Literature of the Sages First Part: Oral Tora, Halakha, Mishna, Tosefta, Talmud, External Tractates. Compendia Rerum Iudaicarum ad Novum Testamentum Section Two: The Literature of the Jewish People in the Period of the Second Temple and the Talmud,* ed. Shmuel Safrai (Assen/Maastricht and Philadelphia, 1987), 151–53.

77. *Mdrbnn gzyrh hw'.*

78. *Yḥzwr lšwrw.*

79. Ex. 13:13.

80. Deut. 21:17.

81. MBekh. 8:1. Yosi bases his opinion on Ex. 13:2: *The first issue of every woman among the Israelites.* Because the firstborn of an Israelite woman must be redeemed, the children which the woman produced as a gentile are totally ignored. On Yosi's ruling, see Jack N. Lightstone, *Yose the Galilean I. Traditions in Mishnah-Tosefta* (Leiden, 1979), 120–24.

82. MBekh. 8:1.

83. The matter does appear in Mekhilta deRabbi Simeon b. Yohai, Bo 13:2, Epstein, 38.

84. BBekh. 47a–b.

85. Deut. 21:17.

86. Gen. 1:28.

87. TB.Q. 9:20.

88. Ex. 21:22.

89. BB.Q. 49a. The discussion continues on bB.Q. 49b; however, the continuation merely attempts to show that the tannaim also differed on this issue.

90. The Talmudic phrase is *gr wntgyyr kqṭn šnwld dmy;* see bYeb. 22a, bYeb. 48b, bYeb. 62a, bYeb. 97b, bBekh. 47a.

91. McKnight writes: "the rabbinic dictum that a proselyte is equal to a Jew in every respect is both late and most probably not a reflection of the phenomena of life—or else many of the laws would be nonsensical. . . . Second, the very existence of separate halakot for proselytes is a revelation in itself, which demonstrates that they were not seen as Jews in every respect"; Scot McKnight, *A Light among the Gentiles: Jewish Missionary Activity in the Second Temple Period* (Minneapolis, 1991), 45.

Chapter 10

1. Gary G. Porton, *Goyim: Gentiles and Israelites in Mishnah-Tosefta* (Atlanta, 1988).

2. Sifra Qedoshim Pereq 8:3, Weiss 91a. Sifra attaches Tosefta's passage to the equating of the *'zrḥ* and the *gr* in Lev. 19:34.

3. BBekh. 30b.

4. TDem. 2:5.

5. TDem. 2:4. Cf. BBekh. 30b. TDem. 2:3–7 are stylistically similar. Each opens with the phrase *x wqbl 'lyw* . . . Interestingly, the same thing is said about the *am ha'areṣ* as is said about the convert; neither is accepted unless he or she is willing to accept the obligation to follow the whole Torah. For a discussion of this section of Tosefta, see Richard S. Sarason, *A History of the Mishnaic Law of Agriculture Section Three: A Study of Tractate Demai Part One* (Leiden, 1979), 80–84. This pericope should be compared to Abun's statement recorded in the Palestinian Talmud that the community should seek the readmittance of an apostate Israelite before it seeks to admit a convert; yHor. 3:5; Venice 3:7, 39d. The context suggests that native-born Israelite apostates are more important than converts. Compare yA.Z. 2:2; Venice 41a which implies that converts who leave the Israelite community and return to their previous way of life still have some value to Israelites. Specifically, Israelites are permitted to buy ritual objects from them.

6. BShebu. 39a.

7. TSoṭ. 7:5. The *sugya* does not appear in the Erfurt MS. The reference to the converts is based on an interpretation of *and not with you alone. . . . but with those who are not with us here this day* in Deut. 29:13–14: *I make this covenant, with its sanctions, not with you alone, but both with those who are standing here with us this day before YHWH, our God, and with those who are not with us here this day.*

8. BShab. 146a.

9. This is most clearly spelled out in numerous passages in the early midrashic collections; see chap. 4.

10. YShab. 6:1; Venice 8d.

11. Porton, *Goyim*, 182–84.

12. Ibid., 185–86.

13. The gentiles' relationship to these laws are complex, for the non-Israelites' responsibilities differed depending on whether their activity related to the status of the farmer or to the holiness of the Land of Israel; ibid., 184–86.

14. Ibid., 186–88.

15. Others assumed either that gentiles could not separate these gifts because they could not own real estate within the Land of Israel or that in fact gentiles did not generally separate these gifts to YHWH, even though they were permitted to do so; ibid., 189–98.

16. Sarason, 210. This is a discussion of tDem. 6:2.

17. MPe. 4:6.

18. Sifra Qedoshim Pereq 1:6 on Lev. 19:9, Weiss 87b.

19. Sifré Deuteronomy Ki Taṣa 283 on Deut. 24:19, Finkelstein 298.

20. YPe. 4:7, Venice 4:8, 18c. The discussion here focuses on the *lqṭ*, gleaning. See also yDem. 6:1, Venice 6:2, 25b which contains a discussion of the Israelite's need to remove the tithe before he pays rent on a field which he had rented from a gentile who converted.

21. MḤal. 3:6.

22. TḤal. 1:12.

23. BḤul. 134a–b. The dough offering is mentioned among Hisda's and Hiyya's four paradigmatic causes of doubt in which the converts must assume that they are required to fulfill the obligation just like native-born Israelites.

24. Sifra Qedoshim Pereq 3:4, Weiss 88b and Sifra Qedoshim Pereq 3:5, Weiss 88b.

25. Sifré Deuteronomy Re'ah 110, Finkelstein 297–98; Sifré Deuteronomy Ki Taṣa 284, Finkelstein 301; Sifré Deuteronomy Ki Taṣa 285, Finkelstein 302; Sifré Deuteronomy Ki Tabo 303, Finkelstein 321.

26. Sifré Deuteronomy Re'ah 138, Finkelstein, 193.

27. Porton, *Goyim*, 173–203.

28. TPe. 3:1 states that the Hillelites and the Shammaites agreed that produce could not be declared ownerless for the benefit of gentiles.

29. TGiṭ. 3:13.

30. BYeb. 47a.

31. Ibid.

32. Ex. 23:19: *The choice first fruits of your soil you shall bring to the house of YHWH, your God.* See mBik. 1:2.

33. Deut. 26:1–3.

34. MBik. 1:4.

35. TBik. 1:2. Judah says that all of the converts bring the offering but do not recite the Avowal.

36. Mekhilta Ishmael Mishpatim 20, Horovitz and Rabin 335. Mekhilta states: "*Which YHWH, your God* (Ex. 23:19) [was said] to exclude converts and slaves [from the requirement of bringing the first fruits]. *Gives to you* (Ex. 23:19) [was said] to exclude women, those of doubtful gender, and androgynous beings. One might think that this means (*mšm'*) it excludes them from reciting [the Avowal], and it

excludes them from bringing [the first fruits; however] Scripture says, *you shall bring,* in every case. And what is the difference between these and those? These bring and recite the Avowal, and those bring but do not recite the Avowal." The problem is determining the antecedents of "these" and "those." According to mBik. 1:4–5, converts, slaves, women, those of doubtful gender, and androgynous beings may bring the offering, but they may not recite the Avowal. If we accept Mishnah, it seems likely that the "these" refers to native-born Israelite males, and "those" refers to the other groups mentioned in the text. If this passage is totally independent of Mishnah's rulings, it is impossible to guess the antecedents. In fact, it is possible that Mekhilta's last sentence was meant to counter the possibility that those mentioned in the *sugya* did not need to bring the first fruits, a point which seems to follow from the passage's opening sentences.

37. YBik. 1:4; Venice 64a.

38. Gen. 17:5.

39. MM.S. 5:14.

40. Sifré Deuteronomy Ki Tabo 301, Finkelstein 320. Although this is an exegesis of Deut. 26:11, there is virtual agreement that it refers to the Avowal connected with the second tithe and not with the Avowal recited upon bringing the first fruits, as an exegesis on this biblical passage would suggest. This interpretation is derived from the fact that Sifré Deuteronomy quotes mM.S. 5:14.

41. On the second tithe, see Peter J. Haas, *A History of the Mishnaic Law of Agriculture: Tractate Maaser Sheni* (Chico, 1980) and Alan J. Avery-Peck, *Mishnah's Division of Agriculture: A History and Theology of Seder Zeraim* (Chico, 1985), 259–303.

42. The rabbis identified the unnamed offering in Deut. 14:22–26 as the second tithe; *You shall set aside every year a tenth part of all the yield of your sowing that is brought from the field. You shall consume the tithes of your new grain and wine and oil, and the Firstlings of your herds and flocks in the presence of YHWH, your God, in the place where he will choose to established his name, so that you may learn to revere YHWH, your God, forever. Should the distance be too great for you, should you be unable to transport them, because the place where YHWH, your God, has chosen to establish his name is far from you and because YHWH, your God, has blessed you, you may convert them into money. Wrap up the money and take it with you to the place that YHWH, your God, has chosen, and spend the money on anything you want—cattle, sheep, wine, or other intoxicant, or anything you may desire. And you shall feast there, in the presence of YHWH, your God, and rejoice with your household.* MM.S. 5:10 indicates that the clause *I have cleared out the consecrated portion from my house,* Deut. 26:13, specifically refers to this offering. According to Mishnah, an Avowal, Deut. 26:13–26, *When you have set aside in full the tenth part of your yield—in the third year, the year of the tithe—and have given it to the Levite, the stranger (gr), the fatherless, and the widow, that they may eat their fill in your settlements, you shall declare before YHWH, your God: "I have cleared out the consecrated portion from the house; and I have given it to the Levite, the stranger, the fatherless and the widow, just as you commanded me; I have neither transgressed nor neglected any of your commandments: I have not eaten of it while in mourning; I have not cleared out any of it while I was unclean, and I have not deposited any of it with the dead. I have obeyed, YHWH, my God; I have done just as you commanded me. Look down from your holy abode, from heaven, and bless*

your people Israel and the soil you have given us, a land flowing with milk and honey, as you swore to our fathers, was recited upon presentation of the second tithe to the priest.

43. Sperber does not list mM.S. 5:14 in his index, nor does he have an entry for convert or proselyte; Daniel Sperber, *Roman Palestine, 200–400: The Land— Crisis and Change in Agrarian Society as Reflected in Rabbinic Sources* (Ramat-Gan, 1978).

44. *[Moses said to Hobab son of Reuel the Midianite, Moses' father-in-law, "We are setting out] for the place of which YHWH has said, 'I will give it to you.' [Come with us and we will be generous with you; for YHWH has promised to be generous to Israel]."*

45. Sifré Numbers Beha'aloteka 78, Horovitz, 75. Elsewhere, on the basis of Num. 26:55, *According to the names of the tribes of their father shall they inherit,* we learn that converts were not assigned a portion of the Land of Israel; Sifré Numbers Qorah 119, Horovitz, 142. This idea is also expressed in Sifré Numbers Pinhas 132, Horovitz, 174.

46. It is true that according to Meir, priests and Levites may not make the Avowal which accompanied the second tithe because they did not receive portions of the Land at the time of the Conquest. However, Yosi maintains that because they had cities on the outskirts of the land, Num. 35:2ff, they could recite the Avowal; mM.S. 1:14. See Haas, *A History of the Mishnaic Law of Agriculture,* 186–87.

47. Porton, *Goyim,* 205–20.

48. Gen. 2:1–4.

49. Ex. 20:8–11.

50. Deut. 5:12–15.

51. Porton, *Goyim,* 206–11.

52. This would be a logical conclusion from the mention of *the converts within your settlements,* Ex. 20:10 and Deut. 5:14.

53. TDem. 6:13.

54. YErub. 4:5; Venice 22a.

55. TShab. 8:5.

56. BShab. 68b.

57. MShab. 7:1.

58. See Baruch M. Bokser, *The Origins of the Seder: The Passover Rite and Early Rabbinic Judaism* (Berkeley and Los Angeles, 1984).

59. This is most strongly asserted in Mekhilta Ishmael. In several comments on Ex. 12:49, Mekhilta repeats the point that the convert and the native-born Israelite are equal; cf. Mekhilta Ishmael Bo 15 on Ex. 12:49; Horovitz and Rabin 57, ll. 6–9 which is paralleled in Sifré Numbers Beha'aloteka 71, Horovitz, 67, ll. 10–12. The midrash asks why Ex. 12:49 states that there should be one law for the native and the convert, given that Ex. 12:48 noted that the convert *shall be like the native-born.* The conclusion is that Ex. 12:48 equates the convert and the native with regard to Passover, while Ex. 12:49 equates the two with reference to all of the laws in the Torah. Despite this fact, the midrash also notes that in Ex. 12:19 the convert is specifically mentioned with regard to the prohibition against possessing leaven during Passover, and there the text states that the Torah specifically mentions the convert whenever it discusses something which is obligatory for Isra-

elites; Mekhilta Ishmael Bo 10 on Ex. 12:19; Horovitz and Rabin, 35, ll. 3–4. Cf. Sifré Numbers Shelaḥ 111 on Num. 15:29, Horovitz, 118, ll. 5–7. This seeming contradiction is a result of the language of the Hebrew Bible. The midrashists had to deal with the biblical text they had before them, so that they had to explain why the convert is specifically mentioned in Ex. 12:19.

60. YPes. 8:2; Venice 35d. The issue involves changes of status, for Yohanan also mentions that a slave who separated the Passover offering before he was free must separate a new one after he is freed and that a minor who separated the Passover sacrifice must separate a new one after he has sprouted two pubic hairs.

61. MPes. 8:8, mEd. 5:2. In tPis. 7:14 Leazar b. Sadoq states that the Hillelites and the Shammaites agreed concerning an uncircumcised male who is sprinkled and then permitted to eat the Passover sacrifice. He suggests that they disagreed concerning a circumcised gentile, and it is to this case that he attaches the dispute found in Mishnah. Cf. yPes. 8:8, Venice 36b; bPes. 92a, Jacob Neusner, *The Rabbinic Traditions about the Pharisees before 70* (Leiden, 1971), 2:141–42, and Bamberger, *Proselytism*, 69–71. On bPes. 92a, Rabbah b. Bar Hanah in Yohanan's name suggests that the Houses disagreed concerning an uncircumcised gentile.

62. TPis. 7:14; yPes 8:8, Venice 36b; yNaz. 8:1, Venice 57a.

63. BYeb. 71a. Cf. bPes. 92a. The phrase *a sojourner and a hired servant*, Lev. 22:10, is the basis of this ruling. Bamberger, following Büchler, argues that the Shammaites were resisting the Hillelites' attempt to apply the categories of Israelite uncleanness to the gentiles. Bamberger sees this dispute, "dating as it does from the time when the Temple still stood," as a "practical matter." "No doubt," he writes, "the semi-converts, the 'fearers of the Lord,' who were in Jerusalem at Passover time were powerfully affected by the sight of the vast multitudes assembling there, and desired to take part in the feast. Thus, Passover might well be the critical point at which halfway converts made their final decision. It was natural for the question to arise whether such last moment converts could participate at once in the celebration"; Bamberger, *Proselytism*, 71. This is, of course, mere conjecture.

64. Num. 9:1–14.

65. TPis. 8:4. Moore uses this passage along with Sifré Numbers Beha'aloteka 71, bQid. 70a, bPes. 93a, and yPes. 8:8, Venice 36b to argue that "the criterion" which defined a convert was his or her ability to celebrate Passover; George F. Moore, *Judaism in the First Centuries of the Christian Era: The Age of the Tannaim* (reprint; Cambridge, 1966), 1:330, n. 4. Lieberman discusses the text in Tosefta in light of the later versions in the Babylonian and Palestinian Talmuds and comes to the conclusion that the issue is whether the second Passover is secondary or a completion of the first; that is, both are of equal importance; Saul Lieberman, *Tosefta Ki-fshutah: A Comprehensive Commentary on the Tosefta Part IV Mo'ed* (New York, 1962), 620–21. For the importance of Passover, see Bokser. For the importance of Passover as a means of distinguishing between Israelites and non-Israelites, see Porton, *Goyim*, 211–13, 219–20. Cf. Mekhilta Ishmael Bo, 15; Horovitz and Rabin 56, ll. 9–11 and Sifré Numbers Beha'aloteka 71, Horovitz, 67, ll. 7–9.

66. YHag. 1:1; Venice 76a.

67. YPes. 8:7; Venice 36a. Jacob bar Aha in the name of Assi rules that a group of converts may not join together to offer the Passover sacrifice because they will defile it. On bPes. 91b this opinion is attributed to Jacob in the name of Yohanan. Cf. Bamberger, *Proselytism*, 71.

68. TR.H. 2:5. Sifra Emor Parashah 11:1, Weiss 101c; bR.H. 29a.

69. TMeg. 2:7. In yMeg. 2:3; Venice 73b we find that a gentile who was circumcised after sunlight on Purim still must hear the reading of the *megillah*.

70. Sifra Emor Pereq 17:9, Weiss 103a. On bSuk. 27b we read that if gentiles converted during the week of Sukkot, they are required to live in the booths for the remainder of the week. In yHag. 1:1; Venice 76a we find a dispute concerning whether or not a gentile who converts during the week of Passover or the week of Sukkot needs to observe the last day of the holiday.

71. Sifra Aharei Mot Pereq 7:9, Weiss 83a.

72. Sifré Numbers Naśo 39, Horovitz, 42 and 43, Horovitz, 49. Cf. bSot. 38a. We are also told that the pure gold frontlet worn by the high priest makes the converts as acceptable to YHWH as the native-born Israelites; Sifré Numbers Shelah 109, Horovitz, 112–13.

73. MEd. 5:6; Sifré Numbers Naśo 7, Horovitz, 11; ySot. 2:5, Venice 18b; bSot. 26a.

74. TBer. 5:14.

75. Ex. 12:3–4 note that each household is required to select a lamb for the Passover sacrifice: *But if the household is too small for a lamb, let him share one with a neighbor who dwells nearby, in proportion to the number of persons: you shall contribute for the lamb according to what each household will eat.*

76. MB.M. 4:10.

77. TB.M. 3:25.

78. Sifra BeHar Pereq 4:2, Weiss 107d.

79. Sifra Qedoshim Pereq 8:4, Weiss 91a. The midrash juxtaposes Lev. 19:34, *love the convert (gr) as yourself*, with Lev. 19:18, *you shall love your neighbor as yourself.*

80. Mekhilta Ishmael Mishpatim 18, Horovitz and Rabin 311.

81. *You shall not wrong a convert (gr) or oppress him, [for you were strangers (grym) in the land of Egypt].*

82. Mekhilta Ishmael Mishpatim 18 on Ex. 22:20, Horovitz and Rabin, 311–12.

83. BB.M. 58b, bB.M. 59b.

84. BHag. 5a; cf. bMeg. 17b.

85. MQid. 4:1. MHor. 3:8 contains a similar division of the People Israel.

86. THor. 2:10.

87. BYeb. 37a, bYeb. 85a, bQid. 75a.

88. MYeb. 8:2; yYeb. 8:3, Venice 9b; yQid. 4:6, Venice 66a; yHor. 3:5, Venice Hor. 3:7, 48b. See Meir's characterization of converts as a "nation," *'wmwt* in tQid. 5:11; yQid. 3:15, Venice 64d; and bYeb. 99a.

89. See above, chap. 8.

90. MYeb. 11:2; tYeb. 2:5; tYeb. 2:6; tYeb. 11:2; tYeb. 12:2; Sifré Deuteronomy Ki Taşa 289, Finkelstein, 308; yYeb. 11:2, Venice 11d; bYeb. 97b.

91. MKet. 9:9; tKet. 9:7; yKet. 9:13, Venice 33c; bKet. 90a.
92. TKet. 10:4.
93. Sifra Aharei Mot Pereq 13:18, Weiss 86c; bYeb. 23a; yYeb. 11:2; Venice 12a.
94. Sifra Aharei Mot Pereq 13:18, Weiss 86c.
95. BYeb. 97b.
96. YYeb. 11:2, Venice 12a.
97. MKet. 4:3.
98. Sifré Deuteronomy Ki Taṣa 238, Finkelstein, 270. Cf. yKet. 4:4; Venice 28b and bKet. 44b.
99. MDem. 6:10, tDem. 6:12, bQid. 17b, bA.Z. 64a, bB.Q. 80a.
100. MB.B. 8:1–2.
101. MB.Q. 4:7.
102. TB.Q. 4:6.
103. YB.Q. 4:8; Venice 4c.
104. TB.Q. 9:20.
105. MB.Q. 5:4.
106. TB.Q. 4:6.
107. Mekhilta Ishmael Mishpatim 11; Horovitz and Rabin, 287.
108. Sifré Numbers Masei 160; Horovitz, 216–17.
109. Ibid.
110. MB.B. 3:3 and mB.B. 4:9.
111. TSheq. 3:11.
112. TB.B. 2:11. Cf. yQid. 1:3; Venice 59d.
113. TB.B. 2:11. Cf. bB.Q. 12a.
114. TKet. 4:16.
115. YB.B. 9:1; Venice 16d. Cf. yYeb. 4:1; Venice 5a.
116. YGiṭ. 4:4; Venice 45d.
117. YQid. 1:5; Venice 60d. Cf. yB.B. 3:1; Venice 13d and yB.B. 4:8; Venice 4:11, 14d. Venice incorrectly marks this as page 18.
118. YQid. 1:4; Venice 60a. Huna states that one may not acquire the animal of a convert who has died without heirs by accepting delivery of the animal's reins. This is the reading of the text on bB.M. 8b where Helbo quotes Huna. This reading is accepted by David Fränkel, *loc. cit.*, and Moses Margolioth, *loc. cit.* Venice reads that it is an acceptable way to acquire the dead convert's property. Neusner also accepts this reading; Jacob Neusner, *The Talmud of the Land of Israel: A Preliminary Translation and Explanation*, vol. 26: *Qiddushin* (Chicago and London, 1984), 67.
119. The reliability of a claim made by adults that a child found in the market is their son is also refined through reference to a convert who died without heirs; yB.B. 3:1, Venice 13d. Also, the problem of using leaven after Passover is discussed in terms of a proselyte who died without heirs; yPes. 2:2, Venice 29a.
120. BB.M. 8b. Cf. yQid. 1:4; Venice 60.
121. BYeb. 52b.
122. BErub. 25a. Cf. bB.B. 53b–54a.
123. BB.B. 53a–b. Cf. bB.B. 55a, bB.B. 56a, yQid 1:5, Venice 60d; yB.B. 3:1, Venice 13d; yB.B. 4:8, Venice 4:11, 14d.

124. BQid. 23a. Cf. bQid. 22b, bGiṭ. 39a.

125. BQid. 16a.

126. *Dtny';* cf. tKet. 4:16.

127. BB.B. 142a.

128. This is clearly brought out in the several discussions from Mishnah onward concerning the improbability of Israelites lacking relatives who might receive compensation from one who stole from them, lied about the theft, and then admitted it; mB.Q. 9:11; tB.Q. 10:16; bB.Q. 109a; yB.Q. 9:15, Venice 7a; Sifré Numbers Naśo 2, 4; Sifré Numbers Shelaḥ 117. In all instances Num. 5:8, *If the man has no kinsman to whom restitution can be made,* is taken to refer to a convert, for they are the only members of the People Israel who would not have a relative to whom restitution could be made.

129. Sperber notes that "the use of the term *hefker* for ownerless land suggests that the land was consciously made ownerless and not merely that it became ownerless through the cease of its owners who had no kin or the like. In the latter case the term used is . . . (*nichese ha-ger*) property of the convert"; Sperber, 106, n. 17. Sperber's comment indicates that "the property of the convert" has become a technical term which refers to a specific type of ownerless property.

130. MKet. 4:3.

131. BB.Q. 49a.

132. BMak. 16a–b.

133. On the ability of the converts to enter the Temple precincts, see Joseph H. Baumgarten, "Exclusions from the Temple: Proselytes and Agripp I," *Journal of Jewish Studies: Essays in Honour of Yigael Yadin,* 33, nos. 1–2 (Spring–Autumn 1982): 215–25. Although Baumgarten focuses most of his attention on Josephus and the evidence from Qumran, he does deal in passing with the rabbinic materials. He concludes: "none of the sources we have considered provides decisive evidence that proselytes were actually excluded from the Jerusalem Temple. Rabbinic texts preserve *halakhoth* which presuppose the entrance of *gerim* into the Temple courtyard"; Baumgarten, 225.

134. Porton, *Goyim,* 259–68.

135. Sifra VaYiqra Parashah 2:3, Weiss 4c. Cf. ySheq. 1:5; Venice 46b.

136. MSheq. 7:6. Cf. bMen. 51b. Similarly, if a gentile sent an offering to the Temple from outside the Land of Israel but did not include the drink offering, the community paid for the latter; mSheq. 7:6.

137. MHal. 3:6.

138. Sifré Deuteronomy Shoftim 175; Finkelstein 221.

139. YHal. 3:4; Venice 3:5, 59b.

140. TMen. 10:13 and tMen. 10:17.

141. Sifra VaYiqra Pereq 17:3, Weiss 13c.

142. BMen. 61b.

143. Sifra Aḥarei Mot Pereq 10:1, Weiss 84a. The text also prohibits the blood of animals killed during a hunt.

144. Sifra Ṣaw Parashah 11:3, Weiss 39b.

145. Sifra Emor Parashah 7:1, Weiss 98a.

146. Sifra Ṣaw Parashah 4:3, Weiss 33c.

147. Sifra Ḥobah Parashah 1:1, Weiss 15b.
148. Sifré Numbers Shelaḥ 109; Horovitz, 113.
149. Sifré Numbers Shelaḥ 108; Horovitz, 112.
150. Sifré Numbers Shelaḥ 111; Horovitz, 118.
151. Sifra Ṣaw Pereq 9:1, Weiss 33d; bZeb. 103a.
152. Sifra VaYiqra Nedabah Pereq 11:2, Weiss 10c.
153. TZeb. 13:11.
154. Sifra Aḥarei Mot Pereq 9:7, Weiss 84a.
155. TZab. 2:1.
156. Porton, *Goyim*, 269–83. On purity as a cultural demarcator, see Mary Douglas, *Purity and Danger* (New York, 1966) and *Natural Symbols* (New York, 1973). See also Jacob Neusner, *The Idea of Purity in Ancient Judaism: The Haskell Lectures, 1972–1973* (Leiden, 1973).
157. MZab. 2:1. TZab. 2:1 presents a problem, for it states that gentiles, converts, and the *twšb* do not convey uncleanness. It is possible that the *w* between *gr* and *twšb* is an error, so that the text should read that the *gr twšb* does not convey uncleanness through genital emissions. In this reading, the convert is not mentioned.
158. MNeg. 7:1. Cf. tNeg. 2:14–15 and Sifra Negaim Pereq 1:1, Weiss 59d–60a.
159. TNid. 1:3.
160. Sifra Zabim Parashah 1:1; Weiss 74d. Cf. bShab. 83a, bNid. 24b, mZab. 2:1, and tZab. 2:1.
161. Sifra Maṣorah Parashah 5:1; Weiss 78d.
162. Sifra Tazriʿa Parashah 1:1; Weiss 57c.
163. Lev. 13:24.
164. The passage is curious because it notes that the rules concerning burnt skin apply to gentiles before they convert. This is problematic because Israelite purity rules normally do not apply to gentiles. In fact, the inclusion of the gentile before he converts may be a result of the style of the *sugya*, which deals with the application of the rules of the biblical passages to opposing cases: Before and after revelation, before and after conversion, and a child before and after it is born; Sifra Tazriʿa Pereq 7:4, Weiss 65a. MNeg. 9:1 parallels the part of the text which discusses a burn caused by any type of fire; cf. bPes. 75a–b and bḤul. 8a. The latter does not exegete Lev. 13:24, and neither specifically mentions the convert.
165. Sifra Tazriʿa Negaʿim Pereq 1:1, Weiss 59d–60a. Cf. mNeg. 7:1 and tNeg. 2:14–15. The ruling is based on juxtaposing Lev. 13:1–2 with Lev. 13:38.
166. Sifra Tazriʿa Pereq 6:6, Weiss 64c; cf. mNeg. 9:1.
167. Sifra Aḥarei Mot Pereq 12:1; Weiss 84d on Lev. 17:15. Here the midrash differentiates between the full convert, *gr*, and the resident alien, the *gr twšb*. On the *gr twšb*, see Moore, *Judaism*, 1:338–41; S. Bialoblocki, *Die Beziehungen des Judentums zu Proselyten und Proselytentum* (Berlin, 1930), 4–11; Emil Schürer, *The History of the Jewish People in the Age of Jesus Christ (175 B.C.–A.D. 135)*, rev., ed. Geza Vermes, Fergus Millar, Martin Goodman (Edinburgh, 1973–87), 3:171–72.
168. BYeb. 74b, bKer. 7b, bNid. 26a; cf. yNid. 3:4; Venice 50b.

CHAPTER 11

1. For a discussion of diversity within early Judaism, see J. Andrew Overman and William Scott Green, "Judaism in the Greco-Roman Period," in David Noel Freedman, ed., *The Anchor Bible Dictionary* (New York, 1992), 3:1037–54.

2. Alan F. Segal, *Paul the Convert: The Apostolate and Apostasy of Saul the Pharisee* (New Haven and London, 1990), 79.

3. Scot McKnight, *A Light among the Gentiles: Jewish Missionary Activity in the Second Temple Period* (Minneapolis, 1991), 7.

4. For a convenient summary of the ways in which the rabbis pictured themselves as differing from the rest of the Israelite population, see Jacob Neusner, *There We Sat Down: Talmudic Judaism in the Making* (Nashville and New York, 1972), 44–128. See also Lee I. Levine, *The Rabbinic Class of Roman Palestine in Late Antiquity* (Jerusalem and New York, 1989) and Stuart A. Cohen, *The Three Crowns: Structures of Communal Politics in Early Rabbinic Judaism* (Cambridge, 1990).

5. Levine, *The Rabbinic Class*, 83–97.

6. Ibid., 127–33.

7. See William S. Green, "What's in a Name?—The Problematic of Rabbinic 'Biography,'" in William S. Green, ed., *Approaches to Ancient Judaism: Theory and Practice* (Missoula, 1978), 77–96.

8. One need only review the titles in Rambo's biography to see that this has been the major source of information concerning converts and conversion. Even when scholars turn to the past, they focus on the testimony of "converts" from whom we have "first-person" evidence, such as Paul, Augustine, or Luther. Lewis R. Rambo, "Current Research on Religious Conversion," *Religious Studies Review* 8, no. 2 (April 1982): 146–59.

9. The only other account we have of a convert to Judaism in Late Antiquity is Josephus's story of the conversion of the royal family of Adiabene. See *Antiquities* 20.17–53; *Jewish War* 2.520, 5.474–75, 6.356–57; Jacob Neusner, "The Conversion of Adiabene to Judaism: A New Perspective," *Journal of Biblical Literature* 83 (1964): 60–66; Lawrence H. Schiffman, "The Conversion of the Royal House of Adiabene in Josephus and Rabbinic Sources," in Louis H. Feldman and Gohei Hata, eds., *Josephus, Judaism, and Christianity* (Detroit, 1987), 293–312; McKnight, *A Light among the Gentiles, passim.*

10. A. Bopegamage, "Status Seekers in India: A Sociological Study of the Neo-Buddhist Movement," *Archives Européennes de Sociologie* 20, no. 1 (1979): 19.

11. It is significant that the line of descent goes back to Jacob, for he is the only Patriarch who produced no non-Israelites. Abraham fathered Ishmael, as well as Isaac, and Isaac sired Esau, as well as Jacob.

12. On the ways in which individuals develop commitment, see Rosabeth Kanter, *Commitment and Community* (Cambridge, Mass., 1972). Cf. Segal, *Paul the Convert*, 75–79.

13. See, however, the story of the astrologer in yShab. 6:1; Venice 8d.

14. TDem. 2:4–5. Cf. Sifra Qedoshim Pereq 8:3 and b.Bekh. 30b.

15. In fact, see Abun's statement in yHor. 3:5; Venice 3:7, 48b, in which he

claims that apostate Israelites should be admitted into the community before converts.

16. BGiṭ. 45b; cf. yA.Z. 2:2; Venice 41a.

17. George F. Moore, *Judaism in the First Centuries of the Christian Era: The Age of the Tannaim* (Cambridge, reprint 1966), 1:324–25.

18. William G. Braude, *Jewish Proselyting in the First Five Centuries of the Common Era: The Age of the Tannaim and Amoraim* (Providence, 1940), 79–99.

19. Bernard J. Bamberger, *Proselytism in the Talmudic Period* (New York, reprint 1968), 31. Cf. Isaac Weil, *Le Prosélytisme chez les juifs selon la bible et le talmud* (Strasbourg, 1880), 59, where he quotes the passage from bBekh. 30b. See also Marcel Simon, "Sur les débuts du prosélytisme juif" in A. Coquot and M. Philonenko, eds., *Hommages a André Dupont-Sommer* (Paris, 1971), 509.

20. Arthur D. Nock, *Conversion: The Old and the New in Religion from Alexander the Great to Augustine of Hippo* (London, 1961), 14.

21. Lawrence H. Schiffman, *Who Was a Jew? Rabbinic and Halakhic Perspectives on the Jewish-Christian Schism* (Hoboken, 1985), 21.

22. TSoṭ. 7:5. Cf. bShebu. 39a. On bShab. 146a we read that the converts' "guiding star" witnessed the revelation on Mount Sinai.

23. Mekhilta Ishmael Mishpatim 18 on Ex. 22:20.

24. BSuk. 49b; cf. bHag. 3a.

25. David A. Snow and Richard Machalek, "The Sociology of Conversion," *Annual Review of Sociology* 10 (1984): 170; David A. Snow and Richard Machalek, "The Convert as Social Type," in Randall Collins, ed., *Sociological Theory 1983* (San Francisco, Washington, London, 1983), 265.

26. Segal, *Paul the Convert*, 75.

27. C. L. Staples and Armand L. Mauss, "Conversion or Commitment? A Reassessment of the Snow and Machalek Approach to the Study of Conversion," *Journal for the Scientific Study of Religion* 26 (1987): 146.

28. YQid. 4:1; Venice 65b.

29. McKnight, *A Light among the Gentiles*, 7.

30. Segal, *Paul the Convert*, 75.

31. Snow and Machalek discuss this process in terms of the converts' reconstructing their biographies. However, their words seem appropriate in this case also, for clearly the Talmud's astrologer has had to rethink his formerly held beliefs. Snow and Machalek state: "Some aspects of the [convert's] past are jettisoned, others are redefined, and some are put together in ways previously inconceivable"; Snow and Machalek, "Convert," 266.

32. William James, *The Varieties of Religious Experience* (New York, 1902), 160.

33. Segal, *Paul the Convert*, 76.

34. Cf. Segal, *Paul the Convert*, 80: "Gradual conversion was the typical and expected pattern for virtually every sectarian group in Judaism, although sudden and emotional conversion may have occurred occasionally."

35. BZeb. 116a–b.

36. YQid. 4:1, Venice 65c; ySanh. 6:7, Venice 13:9, 23d; bYeb. 79a.

37. BGiṭ. 56a.

38. BShab. 31a.

39. YPes. 8:7; Venice 36a and bPes. 91b. The implications of this story are unclear. It is possible that this ruling relates to the ethnic nature of Passover and that it is meant to indicate that converts need the assistance of a native-born Israelite in order to receive fully the benefits due to those who celebrate the creation of the People Israel. It is also possible that converts are totally outside of the system within which Passover must be observed. They can "tag along" to no ill effect. But they cannot do it on their own because it really doesn't pertain to them. Avery-Peck suggested this latter interpretation in a private communication.

40. Mekhilta Ishmael Amalek/Yitro 1:1 on Exodus 18:7.

41. YQid. 4:1; Venice 65b.

42. YGiṭ. 1:4; Venice 1:5, 43c.

43. MQid. 3:5.

44. TQid. 4:9.

45. YQid. 4:1; Venice 65b.

46. Sifré Numbers Beha'alotekha 80.

47. BYeb. 47a.

48. BYeb. 24b and yQid. 4:1; Venice 65b. These comments are attributed to a variety of sages.

49. YMeg. 1:11, Venice 1:13, 72b; yMeg. 3:2, Venice 74a; ySanh. 10:5, Venice 17:6, 29c.

50. BA.Z. 10b.

51. YQid. 4:1, Venice 65c; ySanh. 6:7, Venice 13:9, 23d; bYeb. 79a.

52. BGiṭ. 56a.

53. BSanh. 96b.

54. BGiṭ. 56b–57a.

55. BA.Z. 11a.

56. Sifré Numbers Shelaḥ 115 and bMen. 44a.

57. Sifré Deuteronomy VeZot 354.

58. BR.H. 17b–18a.

59. YMeg. 1:11, Venice 1:13, 72b; yMeg. 3:2, Venice 72a; ySanh. 10:5, Venice 17:6, 29c.

60. YḤag. 2:1; Venice 77a.

61. John Lofland and Rodney Stark, "Becoming a World-Saver: A Theory of Conversion to a Deviant Perspective," *American Sociological Review* 30 (1965): 862–74; John Lofland, *Doomsday Cult: A Study of Conversion, Proselytization, and Maintenance of Faith,* 2d ed. (New York, 1977); John Lofland, "'Becoming a World-Saver' Revisited," in James T. Richardson, *Conversion Careers: In and Out of the New Religions* (Beverly Hills and London, 1978), 10–24. For discussions of these theories, see Beverly R. Gaventa, *From Darkness to Light: Aspects of Conversion in the New Testament* (Philadelphia, 1986), 5, and Segal, *Paul the Convert,* 289. It should be noted that this model was derived from the study of a specific contemporary religious movement, the Unification Church of the Reverend Sun Myung Moon.

62. Arthur L. Greil, "Previous Dispositions and Conversion to Perspectives of Social and Religious Movements," *Sociological Analysis* 38, no. 2 (1977): 117.

63. Ibid., 118.

64. Ibid., 118–19.

65. Ibid., 119–21.

66. Ibid., 122–23.

67. Max Heirich, "Change of Heart: A Test of Some Widely Held Theories about Religious Conversion," *American Journal of Sociology* 83, no. 3 (November 1977): 673.

68. Ibid., 674–75.

69. Ibid., 675.

70. Ibid., 675–77.

71. Peter Brown opens *The World of Late Antiquity: From Marcus Aurelius to Muhammad* (London, 1971), 7, with the following words: "This book is a study of social and cultural change."

72. Jacob Neusner, *A History of the Jews of Babylonia*, 5 vols. (Leiden, 1965–70).

73. Sifré Deuteronomy VeZot 344.

74. On the importance of stress as a reason for conversion, see Heirich, "Change of Heart," 656, 662–63, 665–66; Segal, *Paul the Convert*, 291–92.

75. TṬoh. 9:7 and yErub. 9:4; Venice 25d assume that a gentile would guard his wine from contamination, so that it might be used by himself and other Israelites after he converted. THor. 2:11 assumes that women who plan to convert guard their chastity, so that they are valued more than slaves who have no control over their bodies, a view repeated on bHor. 13a and bYeb. 34b. The *sugya* on bKet. 28b has reworked the story in tKet. 3:3 and claimed that one can accept the testimony of a gentile who converted, because he would have taken care to observe accurately the situation in case he was called to testify in an Israelite court after he converted.

76. Segal, *Paul the Convert*, 74.

77. McKnight, *A Light among the Gentiles*, 7.

78. Ibid., 47.

79. Ibid., 90.

80. Nock, *Conversion*, 13.

81. John J. Collins, "A Symbol of Otherness: Circumcisions and Salvation in the First Century," in Jacob Neusner and Ernest S. Frerichs, eds., *"To See Ourselves as Others see Us": Christians, Jews, "Others" in Late Antiquity* (Chico, 1985), 175.

82. Gaventa, *From Darkness to Light*, 45.

83. Ibid., 46.

84. Segal reminds us that those who joined Christianity were warned that they may have to give up their obligations to parents or spouses, Mark 3:31–35; 10:28–31; Luke 9:54–60; Segal, *Paul the Convert*, 111.

85. MB.B. 8:1–2.

86. See the articles in James T. Richardson, *Conversion Careers: In and Out of the New Religions* (Beverly Hills and London, 1978).

87. Cf. Martin Goodman, "Proselytising in Rabbinic Judaism," *Journal of Jewish Studies* 40, no. 2 (Autumn 1989): 175–85.

88. For a detailed discussion of encapsulation, see J. Lofland and L. H. Lofland, *Deviance and Identity* (Englewood Cliffs, 1969).

89. See note 86, above.

90. Sifré Numbers Beha'alotekha 78.

91. MDem. 6:10, tDem. 6:12–13.

92. MGiṭ. 2:6.

93. YNid. 1:4, Venice 1:5, 49b; yYeb. 4:11, Venice 6a; bKet. 37a; bYeb. 37a.

94. MḤul. 10:4, mḤal. 3:6, mPe. 4:6, mPe. 5:8.

95. For a complete discussion of those things for which a convert was held responsible, see chap. 9, above.

96. See, for example, yQid. 4:7; Venice 66a.

97. YQid. 1:1, Venice 58c; bSanh. 56a; bSanh. 71b.

98. BSanh. 71b.

99. YBik. 3:3; Venice 65c.

100. BYeb. 48b.

101. On the ethnicity of rabbinic Judaism, see Gary G. Porton, *Goyim: Gentiles and Israelites in Mishnah-Tosefta* (Atlanta, 1988).

102. MEd. 5:6; Sifré Numbers Naśo 7; ySoṭ. 2:5, Venice 18b; bBer. 19a.

103. MBik. 1:4.

104. MM.S. 5:14.

105. TBik. 1:2; Mekhilta Ishmael Mishpatim 20; Sifré Deuteronomy Ki Tabo 318; bMak. 19a.

106. YBik. 1:4; Venice 64a.

107. Sifra Ṣaw Pereq 9:1; Weiss 33d.

108. BZeb. 103a.

109. Sifra VaYiqra Nedabah Pereq 11:1; Weiss 10c.

110. Sifra Aḥarei Mot Pereq 9:7; Weiss 84a; Sifra Aḥarei Mot Parashah 6:1; Weiss 83c. Cf. mZeb. 14:4–10, tZeb. 13:1–19, esp., tZeb. 13:11.

111. Sifré Numbers Shelaḥ 109.

112. YPes. 8:7, Venice 36a; bPes. 91b.

113. Sifré Numbers Beha'alotekha 78.

114. Sifré Numbers Masei 160.

115. YSanh. 10:6; Venice 17:7, 29c.

116. MQid. 4:1.

117. MHor. 3:8, tHor. 2:10, bYeb. 37a, bYeb. 85a, bQid. 75a.

118. TQid. 5:1.

119. TQid. 5:1; bYeb. 99a; yQid. 3:13, Venice 3:15, 64d.

120. Chap. 8, above.

121. See, for example, mYeb. 11:2; tYeb. 12:2; bYeb. 97b–98a; Sifré Deuteronomy Ki Taṣa 289; yYeb. 11:2, Venice 11d.

122. YYeb. 12:1; Venice 12b–c.

123. Sifré Numbers Beha'alotekha 78.

124. MHor. 1:4

125. Sifra VaYiqra Parashah 4:2–3.

126. YHor. 1:4; Venice 46a.

127. BSanh. 36b, bNid. 49b.

128. BB.M. 71a.

129. This is not the first study to recognize the fact that the converts were not fully assimilated into the People Israel. For example, Moore wrote the following: "Equality in law and religion does not necessarily carry with it complete social equality, and the Jews would have been singularly unlike the rest of mankind if they had felt no superiority to their heathen converts"; Moore, *Judaism*, 1:335. It seems to me, however, that the issue is not so much a feeling of superiority as the belief that Israelites were fundamentally different from gentiles, and even if they entered the People Israel that difference was not totally erased.

130. Arnold van Gennep was the first to identify the state of marginality in his discussion of *rites de passage*; Arnold van Gennep, *The Rites of Passage*, trans. Monika B. Vizedom and Gabrielle L. Caffee (London and Chicago, 1960).

131. Suzanne Miers and Igor Kopytoff, *Slavery in Africa: Historical and Anthropological Perspectives* (Madison, 1977), 15.

132. For a discussion of the pervasiveness of this phenomenon among humans and other animals, as well as the sociobiological reasons for this method of classification, see Vernon Reynolds, Vincent Falger, and Ian Vine, eds., *The Sociobiology of Ethnocentrism: Evolutionary Dimensions of Xenophobia, Discrimination, Racism and Nationalism* (Athens, 1986).

133. Rodney Needham, *Primordial Characters* (Charlottesville, 1978), 5.

134. Barbara A. Babcock, *The Reversible World: Symbolic Inversion in Art and Society* (Ithaca, 1978).

135. Kurt H. Wolff, *The Sociology of Georg Simmel* (New York, 1950), 407.

136. Porton, *Goyim*, 298.

137. W. D. Davies, *The Territorial Dimension of Judaism* (Berkeley, Los Angeles, London, 1982), 7.

138. Ibid., 9.

139. Daniel Sperber, *Roman Palestine, 200–400: The Land* (Ramat-Gan, 1978), 160–86.

140. YBer. 2:8; Venice 5b–c.

141. Mekhilta Ishmael Mishpatim 18.

142. Mekhilta Ishmael Bahodesh/Yitro 1.

143. Mekhilta Ishmael Mishpatim 18.

144. BPes. 87b.

145. BBer. 57b.

146. BGiṭ. 56a.

147. BGiṭ. 57a, b.Sanh. 96b. Cf. bYoma 71b.

148. YHag. 1:1; Venice 66a.

149. BQid. 70b.

150. Mekhilta Ishmael Mishpatim 18.

151. Ibid., 20.

152. Sifré Numbers Beha'alotekha 85.

153. Sifré Numbers Maṭot 157. Cf. bQid. 74b, 78a, bYeb. 60b.

154. YSanh. 10:2; Venice 17:2, 29b. This is attributed to rabbis on bSanh. 107b.

155. BYeb. 47b, 109b, bQid. 70b.

156. BYeb. 109b.

157. BNid. 13a.

158. MB.M. 4:10, tB.M. 3:25, Sifra Behar Pereq 4:2, Sifra Qedoshim Pereq 8:4, Mekhilta Ishmael Mishpatim 18, Sifré Numbers Beha'alotekha 80, bB.M. 59b.

159. BBekh. 30a.

160. Miers and Kopytoff, *Slavery in Africa*, 19.

161. Ibid., 19.

BIBLIOGRAPHY

Anonymous. "Apostasy in Jewish Law." *Encyclopaedia Judaica*, 3:211–12. Edited by Cecil Roth and Geoffrey Wigoder. Jerusalem, 1972.

———. "Aretz-Israel." *Encyclopedia Talmudica: A Digest of Halachic Literature and Jewish Law from the Tannaitic Period to the Present Time Alphabetically Arranged*, 3:1–68. Edited by Shlomo J. Zevin. Translated by David B. Klein. Jerusalem, 1978.

Albeck, Hanokh. *The Six Orders of the Mishnah: Order Nashim*. Tel Aviv, 1959.

———. *The Six Orders of the Mishnah: Order Qodashim*. Tel Aviv, 1958.

———. *The Six Orders of the Mishnah: Order Tohorot*. Tel Aviv, 1957.

———. *The Six Orders of the Mishnah: Order Zera'im*. Tel Aviv, 1959.

———. *Untersuchungen über die halakhischen Midraschim*. Berlin, 1927.

Alexander, Philip S. "Jewish Aramaic Translations of Hebrew Scriptures." *Mikra: Text, Translation, Reading and Interpretation of the Hebrew Bible in Ancient Judaism and Early Christianity. Compendia Rerum Iudaicarum ad Novum Testatmentum*, 217–54. Edited by Martin J. Mulder. Assen/Maastricht and Philadelphia, 1988.

Alon, Gedalyahu. *Jews, Judaism and the Classical World: Studies in Jewish History in the Times of the Second Temple and Talmud*. Translated by Israel Abrahams. Jerusalem, 1977.

Avery-Peck, Alan J. *Mishnah's Division of Agriculture: A History and Theology of Seder Zeraim*. Chico, 1985.

———. *The Talmud of the Land of Israel A Preliminary Translation and Explanation*. Vol. 6: *Terumot*. Chicago and London, 1988.

Avi-Yonah, Michael. *The Jews of Palestine: A Political History from the Bar Kokhba War to the Arab Conquest*. New York, 1976.

Babcock, Barbara A. *The Reversible World: Symbolic Inversion in Art and Society*. Ithaca, 1978.

Bamberger, Bernard J. *Proselytism in the Talmudic Period*. New York, 1968.

Bammel, Ernst. "Gerim Gerurim." *Annual of the Swedish Theological Institute* 7 (1968–69): 127–31.

Barth, Fredrik. *Ethnic Groups and Boundaries: The Social Organization of Cultural Difference*. Bergen-Oslo, 1969.

Baskin, Judith. "The Rabbinic Transformations of Rahab the Harlot." *Notre Dame English Journal* 11, 2 (1978/79): 141–57.

Bastomsky, S. J. "The Emperor Nero in Talmudic Legend." *Jewish Quarterly Review*, n. s., 54, 4 (April, 1969): 321–25.

Baumgarten, Joseph H. "Exclusions from the Temple: Proselytes and Agripp I." *Journal of Jewish Studies: Essays in Honour of Yigael Yadin* 33, 1–2 (Spring–Autumn, 1982): 215–25.

Beasley-Murray, G. R. *Baptism in the New Testament*. Grand Rapids, 1962.
Berkovits, Eliezer. "Talmud, Babylonian." *Encyclopaedia Judaica*, 15:755–68.
Berreman, Gerald D. "Race, Caste, and Other Invidious Distinctions in Social Stratification." *Majority and Minority: The Dynamics of Race and Ethnicity in American Life*, 21–39. Edited by Norman R. Yetman. 4th ed. Boston, Sydney, London, Toronto, 1985.
Bertholet, Alfred. *Die Stellung der Israeliten und der Juden zu dem Fremden*. Freiburg i. B./Leipzig, 1896.
Bessac, Frank D. "Comments." *Current Anthropology* 5, 4 (October, 1964): 293–94.
Bialoblocki, S. *Die Beziehungen des Judentums zu Proselyten und Proselytentum*. Berlin, 1930.
Bokser, Baruch M. "An Annotated Bibliographical Guide to the Study of the Palestinian Talmud." *Aufstieg und Niedergang der römischen Welt*, II.19.2. 192–99. Edited by Hildegard Temporini and Wolfgang Haase. Berlin and New York, 1979.
———. *The Origins of the Seder: The Passover Rite and Early Rabbinic Judaism*. Berkeley and Los Angeles, 1984.
Bopegamage, A. "Status Seekers in India: A Sociological Study of the Neo-Buddhist Movement." *Archives Eruopéennes de Sociologie* 20, 1 (1979): 19–39.
Boyarin, Daniel. *Intertexuality and the Reading of Midrash*. Bloomington and Indianapolis, 1990.
Braude, William G. *Jewish Proselyting in the First Five Centuries of the Common Era: The Age of the Tannaim and Amoraim*. Providence, 1940.
Brown, Peter. *The World of Late Antiquity: From Marcus Aurelius to Muhammad*. London, 1971.
Büchler, Adolph. "The Levitical Impurity of the Gentiles in Palestine Before the Year 70." *Jewish Quarterly Review*, n. s., 17 (1926–27): 1–81
Charlesworth, James H. "Jewish Astrology in the Talmud, Pseudepigrapha, the Dead Sea Scrolls and the Early Palestinian Synagogue." *Harvard Theological Review* 70 (1970): 183–200.
C.M.H. "Sifra." *Jewish Encyclopedia*, 2:30. Edited by Isidore Singer. New York, reprint, n.d.
Coggins, R. J. *Samaritans and Jews: The Origins of Samaritanism Reconsidered*. Atlanta, 1975.
Cohen, Naomi G. "Rabbi Meir, A Descendant of Anatolian Proselytes. New Light on His Name and the Historic Kernel of the Nero Legend in Gittin 56a." *Journal of Jewish Studies* 23, 1 (Spring, 1972): 51–59.
Cohen, Shaye J. D. "Conversion to Judaism in Historical Perspective: From Biblical Israel to Post-biblical Judaism." *Conservative Judaism* 36, 4 (Summer, 1983): 31–45.
———. "From the Bible to the Talmud: The Prohibition of Intermarriage." *Hebrew Annual Review Biblical and Other Studies in Honor of Robert Gordis* 7 (1983): 23–39. Edited by Reuben Ahroni.
———. *From the Maccabees to the Mishnah*. Philadelphia, 1987.
———. "The Rabbinic Conversion Ceremony." *Journal of Jewish Studies* 41, 3 (Autumn, 1990): 177–203.

Cohen, Stuart A. *The Three Crowns: Structures of Communal Politics in Early Rabbinic Judaism.* Cambridge, 1990.

Collins, John J. "A Symbol of Otherness: Circumcision and Salvation in the First Century." *"To See Ourselves as Others See Us": Christians, Jews, "Others" in Late Antiquity,* 163–86. Edited by Jacob Neusner and Ernest Frerichs. Chico, 1985.

Danby, Herbert. *The Mishnah, Translated from the Hebrew with Introduction and Brief Explanatory Notes.* Oxford, reprint, 1964.

Davies, William D. *The Gospel and the Land: Early Christianity and Jewish Territorial Doctrine.* Berkeley and Los Angeles, 1974.

———. *The Territorial Dimension of Judaism.* Berkeley, Los Angeles, London, 1982.

deVaux, Roland. *Ancient Israel.* Vol. 2: *Religious Institutions.* New York and Toronto, 1965.

Dexinger, Ferdinand. "Limits of Tolerance in Judaism: The Samaritan Example." *Jewish and Christian Self-Definition.* Vol. 2: *Aspects of Judaism in the Graeco-Roman Period,* 88–114. Edited by E. P. Sanders with A. I. Baumgarten and Alan Mendelson. Philadelphia, 1981.

Donin, Hayim H. *To Be A Jew: A Guide to Jewish Observance in Contemporary Life.* New York, 1972.

Douglas, Mary. *Natural Symbols.* New York, 1973.

———. *Purity and Danger.* New York, 1966.

Eilberg-Schwartz, Howard. *The Savage in Judaism: An Anthropology of Israelite Religion and Ancient Judaism.* Bloomington and Indianapolis, 1990.

Enloe, Cynthia H. *Ethnic Conflict and Political Development.* Boston, 1973.

Epstein, J. N. *Prolegomena ad Litteras Tannaiticas.* Edited by E. Z. Melamed. Jerusalem, 1958.

Feldman, Louis. *Jew and Gentile in the Ancient World: Attitudes and Interactions from Alexander to Justinian.* Princeton, 1993.

Finkelstein, Louis. *Aqiba: Scholar, Saint, and Martyr.* New York, 1975.

———. *Siphre ad Deuteronomium.* New York, reprint, 1969.

———. "The Institution of Baptism for Proselytes." *Journal of Biblical Literature* 52 (1933): 203–11.

———. "The Mekhilta and Its Text." *Proceedings of the American Academy of Jewish Research* 5 (1933–34): 3–54.

Finn, Thomas M. "The God-Fearers Reconsidered." *Catholic Biblical Quarterly* 47 (1985): 75–84.

Fraade, Steven D. *From Tradition to Commentary: Torah and Its Interpretation in the Midrash Sifre To Deuteronomy.* Albany, 1991.

Freedman, H. *Kiddushin. Translated into English with Notes, Glossary, and Indices.* London, 1936.

———. *Zebahim. Translated into English with Notes, Glossary, and Indices.* London, 1948.

Friedman, M. *Mekhilta deRabbi Ishmael.* New York, reprint, 1948.

———. *Sifré deBe Rav.* New York, reprint, 1947.

Gager, John G. *The Origins of Anti-Semitism: Attitudes Toward Judaism in Pagan and Christian Antiquity.* New York and Oxford, 1985.

Gaventa, Beverly R. *From Darkness to Light: Aspects of Conversion in the New Testament*. Philadelphia, 1986.

Gereboff, Joel D. *Rabbi Tarfon: The Tradition, the Man, and Early Rabbinic Judaism*. Missoula, 1979.

Ginzberg, Louis. "An Introduction to the Palestinian Talmud." *On Jewish Law and Lore*, 3–60. New York, 1970.

———. *The Legends of the Jews*. Translated by Paul Radin and Henrietta Szold. Philadelphia, 1911.

Glatzer, Nahum N. *Hillel the Elder: The Emergence of Classical Judaism*. Rev. ed. New York, 1956.

Goldberg, Abraham. "The Babylonian Talmud." *The Literature of the Sages Part One: Oral Tora, Halakha, Mishna, Tosefta, Talmud, External Tractates. Compendia Rerum Iudaicarum ad Novum Testamentum*, 323–45. Edited by Shmuel Safrai. Assen/Maastricht and Philadelphia, 1987.

———. "The Palestinian Talmud." *The Literature of the Sages, Part One: Oral Tora, Halakha, Mishna, Tosefta, Talmud, External Tractates. Compendia Rerum Iudaicarum ad Novum Testamentum*, 303–22. Edited by Shmuel Safrai. Assen/Maastricht and Philadelphia, 1987.

Goldenberg, Robert. "The Jewish Sabbath in the Roman World up to the Time of Constantine the Great." *Aufstieg und Niedergang der römischen Welt*, II.19.1, 414–44. Edited by Hildegard Temporini and Wolfgang Haase. Berlin and New York, 1979.

———. *The Sabbath Law of Rabbi Meir*. Missoula, 1979.

Goodblatt, David. "The Babylonian Talmud." *Aufstieg und Niegergang der römischen Welt*, 2.19.2. 285–88. Edited by Hildegard Temporini and Wolfgang Haase. Berlin and New York, 1979.

Goodman, Martin. "Proselytising in Rabbinic Judaism." *Journal of Jewish Studies* 40, 3 (Autumn 1989): 175–85.

Graetz, Heinrich. *Die jüdischen Proselyten im Römerreiche unter den Kaisern Domitian, Nerva, Trajan, und Hadrian*. Breslau, 1884.

Green, William S. "Otherness Within: Toward a Theory of Difference in Rabbinic Judaism." *"To See Ourselves as Others See Us" Christians, Jews, "Others" in Late Antiquity*, 49–70. Edited by Jacob Neusner and Ernest S. Frerichs. Chico, 1985.

———. *The Traditions of Joshua Ben Hananiah. Part I: The Early Traditions*. Leiden, 1981.

———. "What's in a Name?—The Problematic of Rabbinic 'Biography.'" *Approaches to Ancient Judaism: Theory and Practice*, 77–96. Edited by William S. Green. Missoula, 1978.

Greil, Arthur L. "Previous Dispositions and Conversion to Perspectives of Social and Religious Movements." *Sociological Analysis* 38, 2 (1977): 115–25.

Haas, Peter J. *A History of the Mishnaic Law of Agriculture: Tractate Maaser Sheni*. Chico, 1980.

Halevy, Elimelech Epstein. "Amalekites in the Aggadah." *Encyclopaedia Judaica*, 2:791.

Halivni, David. *Sources and Traditions: A Source Critical Commentary on Seder Nashim.* Tel Aviv, 1968.

Hammer, Reuven. *Sifre: A Tannaitic Commentary on the Book of Deuteronomy.* New Haven and London, 1986.

Haran, Menahem. *Temples and Temple-Service in Ancient Israel: An Inquiry into the Character of Cult Phenomena and the Historical Setting of the Priestly School.* Oxford, 1978.

Heirich, Max. "Change of Heart: A Test of Some Widely Held Theories about Religious Conversion." *American Journal of Sociology* 83, 3 (November, 1977): 653–80.

Herr, Moshe D. "Sifra." *Encyclopaedia Judaica,* 14: 1518–19.

——. "Sifrei." *Encyclopaedia Judaica,* 14: 605–8.

Hoenig, Sidney B. "Conversion during the Talmudic Period." *Conversion to Judaism: A History and Analysis.* Edited by David M. Eichhorn. New York, 1965.

Hoffman, Lawrence A. *The Land of Israel: Jewish Perspectives.* Notre Dame, 1986.

Hoffmann, David. *Zur Einleitung in die halachischen Midraschim.* Berlin, 1886–87.

Horovitz, H. S. *Siphre D'Be Rab.* Jerusalem, 1966.

Horovitz, H. S., and I. A. Rabin. *Mechilta D'Rabbi Ismael.* Jerusalem, 1960.

Hunt, Chester L., and Lewis Walker. *Ethnic Dynamics: Patterns of Intergroup Relations in Various Societies.* Homewood, 1974.

Hyman, Aaron. *Toldoth Tannaim Ve'Amorim.* Jerusalem, reprint, 1964.

James, William. *The Varieties of Religious Experience.* New York, 1902.

Jastrow, Marcus. *A Dictionary of the Targumim, the Talmud Babli and Yerushalmi, and the Midrashic Literature.* New York, reprint, 1971.

Jeremias, Joachim. *Jerusalem in the Time of Jesus: An Investigation into Economic and Social Conditions during the New Testament Period.* Translated by F. H. Cave and C. H. Cave. Philadelphia, 1977.

Kanter, Rosabeth. *Commitment and Community.* Cambridge, 1972.

Kanter, Shamai. *Rabban Gamaliel II: The Legal Traditions.* Chico, 1980.

Keyes, Charles F. *Ethnic Change.* Seattle and London, 1981.

Kirzner, E. W. *Baba Kamma: Translated into English with Notes, Glossary, and Indices.* London, 1935.

Klein, Isaac. *A Guide to Jewish Religious Practice.* New York, 1979.

Kraabel, A. Thomas. "The Disappearance of the God-fearers." *Numen* 28 (1981): 113–26.

Kraemer, David. "The Formation of Rabbinic Canon: Authority and Boundaries." *Journal of Biblical Literature* 110, 4 (Winter, 1991): 613–30.

Kraft, Robert A., and George W. E. Nickelsburg. *Early Judaism and Its Modern Interpreters.* Atlanta, 1986.

Lauterbach, Jacob Z. *Mekhilta deRabbi Ishmael.* Philadelphia, reprint 1976.

——. "The Two Mekhiltas." *Proceedings of the American Academy of Jewish Research* 4 (1932–33): 113–29.

Lehrman, S. M. *Zabim: Translated into English with Notes.* London, 1948.

Levine, Baruch A. *In the Presence of the Lord: A Study of Cult and Some Cultic Terms in Ancient Israel.* Leiden, 1974.

————. *The JPS Torah Commentary: Leviticus.* Philadelphia, 1989.

Levine, Lee I. *The Rabbinic Class of Roman Palestine in Late Antiquity.* Jerusalem and New York, 1989.

Lieberman, Saul. *Tosefeth Rishonim: A Commentary Based on Manuscripts of the Tosefta and Works of the Rishonim and Midrashim in Manuscripts and Rare Editions, Part IV: Mikwaoth—Uktzin.* Jerusalem, 1939.

————. *Tosefeth Rishonim: A Commentary Based on Manuscripts of the Tosefta and Works of the Rishonim and Midrashim in Manuscripts and Rare Editions, Part II: Seder Nashim Nezikin Kadashim.* Jerusalem, 1939.

————. *The Tosefta According to Codex Vienna, with Variants from Codices Erfurt, Genizah Mss. and Editio Princeps (Venice 1521), Order Nashim: Sotah, Gittin, Kiddushin.* New York, 1973.

————. *The Tosefta According to Codex Vienna, with Variants from Codices Erfurt, Genizah Mss. and Editio Princeps (Venice 1521), Together with References to Parallel Passages in Talmudic Literature and a Brief Commentary. The Order of Nashim Yebamoth, Kethuboth, Nedarim, Nazir.* New York, 1967.

————. *Tosefta Ki-fshutah: A Comprehensive Commentary on the Tosefta, Part III: Order Mo'ed.* New York, 1962.

————. *Tosefta Ki-fshutah: A Comprehensive Commentary on the Tosefta, Part IV: Order Mo'ed.* New York, 1962.

————. *Tosefta Ki-fshutah: A Comprehensive Commentary on the Tosefta, Part VI: Order Nashim.* New York, 1967.

————. *Tosefta Ki-fshutah: A Comprehensive Commentary on the Tosefta, Part VIII: Order Nashim.* New York, 1973.

————. *Tosefta Ki-fshutah: A Comprehensive Commentary on the Tosefta, Part IX: Nezikin.* New York, 1988.

————. *Tosefta Ki-fshutah: A Comprehensive Commentary on the Tosefta, Part X: Order Nezikin.* New York, 1988.

————. *Tosefta Ki-Fshutah: A Comprehensive Commentary on the Tosefta, Part I: Order Zera'im.* New York, 1955.

————. *Yerusalmi Ki-fshuto: A Commentary Based on the Manuscripts of the Yerushalmi and the Books of Our Rabbis, the Rishonim, and Midrashim in Manuscripts and Ancient Manuscripts, Part I: Shabbat, Erubim, Peshim.* Jerusalem, 1934.

Lightstone, Jack N. "R. Sadoq." *Persons and Institutions in Early Rabbinic Judaism,* 49–148. Edited by William S. Green. Missoula, 1977.

————. "Yose the Galilean in Mishnah-Tosefta and the History of Early Rabbinic Judaism." *Journal of Jewish Studies* 30, 1 (Spring, 1980): 37–45.

————. *Yose the Galilean I: Traditions in Mishnah-Tosefta.* Leiden, 1979.

Linder, Amnon. *The Jews in Roman Imperial Legislation.* Detroit, 1987.

Loeb, M. *Sifra debe Rav.* Bucharest, 1860.

Lofland, John. "'Becoming a World-Saver' Revisited." *Conversion Careers: In and Out of the New Religions,* 10–24. Edited by James T. Richardson. Beverly Hills and London, 1978.

————. *Doomsday Cult: A Study of Conversion, Proselytization, and Maintenance of Faith.* 2d ed. New York, 1977.

Lofland, John, and L. H. Lofland. *Deviance and Identity.* Englewood Cliffs, N.J.: 1969.

Lofland, John, and Rodney Stark. "Becoming a World-Saver: A Theory of Conversion to a Deviant Perspective." *American Sociological Review* 30 (1965): 862–74.

MacLennan, R. S., and A. T. Kraabel. "The God-Fearers: A Literary and Theological Invention," *Biblical Archaeologist Review* 1∠ (1986): 46–53.

Margalioth, Mordecai. *Encyclopedia of Talmudic and Geonic Literature.* Tel Aviv, 1962.

McEleney, Neil J. "Conversion, Circumcision, and the Law." *New Testament Studies* 20, 3 (April 1974): 319–41.

McKnight, Scot. *A Light among the Gentiles: Jewish Missionary Activity in the Second Temple Period.* Minneapolis, 1991.

Meyers, Carol. *Discovering Eve: Ancient Israelite Women in Context.* New York and Oxford, 1988.

Miers, Suzanne, and Igor Kopytoff. *Slavery in Africa: Historical and Anthropological Perspectives.* Madison, 1977.

Milgrom, Jacob. *Studies in Cultic Theology and Terminology.* Leiden, 1983.

Moore, George F. *Judaism in the First Centuries of the Christian Era: The Age of the Tannaim.* Cambridge, reprint 1966.

Morgan, John H. *Understanding Religion and Culture: Anthropological and Theological Perspectives.* Washington, 1979.

Needham, Rodney. *Primordial Characters.* Charlottesville, 1978.

Neusner, Jacob. *A History of the Jews in Babylonia.* Leiden, 1965–70. 5 vols.

———. *A History of the Mishnaic Law of Appointed Times.* Leiden, 1981–82. 5 vols.

———. *A History of the Mishnaic Law of Damages.* Leiden, 1982. 5 vols.

———. *A History of the Mishnaic Law of Holy Things.* Leiden, 1978–79. 6 vols.

———. *A History of the Mishnaic Law of Purities.* Leiden, 1974–77. 20 vols.

———. *A History of the Mishnaic Law of Women.* Leiden, 1979–80. 5 vols.

———. *A Life of Yohanan Ben Zakkai, Ca. 1–80 C.E.* 2d ed., rev. Leiden, 1970.

———. *Development of a Legend: Studies in the Traditions Concerning Yohanan ben Zakkai.* Leiden, 1970.

———. *Eliezer ben Hyrcanus: The Traditions and the Man.* Leiden, 1973. 2 vols.

———. *Judaism and Its Social Metaphors: Israel in the History of Jewish Thought.* Cambridge, New York, New Rochelle, Melbourne, Sydney, 1989.

———. *Judaism, the Classical Statement: The Evidence of the Bavli.* Chicago, 1986.

———. *Judaism: The Evidence of the Mishnah.* Chicago and London, 1981.

———. *Midrash in Context: Exegesis in Formative Judaism.* Philadelphia, 1983.

———. *Sifra in Perspective: The Documentary Comparison of the Midrashim of Ancient Judaism.* Atlanta, 1988.

———. *Sifré to Deuteronomy: An Introduction to the Rhetorical, Logical, and Topical Program.* Atlanta, 1987.

———. "The Conversion of Adiabene to Judaism: A New Perspective." *Journal of Biblical Literature* 83 (1964): 60–66.

———. *The Formation of the Babylonian Talmud: Studies in the Achievements of Late Nineteenth- and Twentieth-Century Historical and Literary-Critical Research.* Leiden, 1970.

————. *The Idea of Purity in Ancient Judaism. The Haskell Lectures, 1972–1973.* Leiden, 1973.

————. *The Mishnah: A New Translation.* New Haven and London, 1988.

————. *The Modern Study of the Mishnah.* Leiden, 1973.

————. *The Rabbinic Traditions about the Pharisees before 70.* Leiden, 1973. 3 vols.

————. *The Talmud of the Land of Israel: A Preliminary Translation and Explanation.* Vol. 26: *Qiddushin.* Chicago and London, 1984.

————. *The Talmud of the Land of Israel: A Preliminary Translation and Explanation.* Vol. 21: *Yebamot.* Chicago and London, 1987

————. *The Tosefta, Its Structure and Its Sources.* Atlanta, 1986.

————. *The Tosefta, Translated from the Hebrew. Fourth Division Neziqin (The Order of Damages).* New York, 1981.

————. *There We Sat Down: Talmudic Judaism in the Making.* Nashville and New York, 1972.

Newman, Louis E. *The Sanctity of the Seventh Year: A Study of Mishnah Tractate Shebiit.* Chico, 1983.

Nock, Arthur D. *Conversion: The Old and the New in Religion from Alexander the Great to Augustine of Hippo.* London, 1933.

Nolland, John. "Uncircumcised Proselytes?" *Journal for the Study of Judaism* 12, 2 (December, 1981): 173–94.

Novak, David. *The Image of the Non-Jew in Judaism: An Historical and Constructive Study of the Noachide Laws.* New York, 1983.

Overman, J. A. "The God-Fearers: Some Neglected Features." *Journal for the Study of the New Testament* 32 (1988): 17–26.

Overman, J. Andrew, and William Scott Green. "Judaism in the Greco-Roman Period." *The Anchor Bible Dictionary,* 3: 1037–54. Edited by David Noel Freedman. New York, 1992.

Porton, Gary G. "Defining Midrash." *The Study of Ancient Judaism I: Mishnah, Midrash, Siddur,* 55–92. Edited by Jacob Neusner. New York, 1981.

————. *Goyim: Gentiles and Israelites in Mishnah-Tosefta.* Atlanta, 1988.

————. "The Artificial Dispute: Ishmael and Aqiba." *Christianity, Judaism, and Other Greco-Roman Cults: Studies for Morton Smith at Sixty,* 4:18–29. Edited by Jacob Neusner. Leiden, 1975.

————. *The Traditions of Rabbi Ishmael.* Leiden, 1976–82. 4 vols.

————. "Midrash: Palestinian Jews and the Hebrew Bible in the Greco-Roman Period." *Aufstieg und Niedergang der römischen Welt,* 2.19.2. 103–38. Edited by Hildegard Temporini and Wolfgang Haase. Berlin and New York, 1979.

————. *Understanding Rabbinic Midrash: Texts and Commentary.* Hoboken, 1985.

Primus, Charles. *Aqiva's Contribution to the Law of Zera'im.* Leiden, 1977.

Purvis, James D. "The Samaritans and Judaism." *Early Judaism and Its Modern Interpreters,* 81–98. Edited by Robert A. Kraft and George W. E. Nickelsburg. Atlanta, 1986.

Rabinowitz, L. I. "Talmud, Jerusalem." *Encyclopaedia Judaica,* 15:772.

Rainey, Anson. "Sacrifice." *Encyclopaedia Judaica,* 14: 599–607.

Rambo, Lewis R. "Current Research on Religious Conversion." *Religious Study Review* 8 (April, 1982): 146–59.

Reynolds, J., and R. F. Tannenbaum. *Jews and Godfearers at Aphrodisias: Greek Inscriptions with Commentary*. Cambridge, 1987.

Reynolds, Vernon, Vincent Falger, and Ian Vine. *The Sociobiology of Ethnocentrism: Evolutionary Dimensions of Xenophobia, Discrimination, Racism and Nationalism*. Athens, 1986.

Richardson, James T. *Conversion Careers: In and Out of the New Religions*. Beverly Hills and London, 1978.

Rowley, H. H. "Jewish Proselyte Baptism." *Hebrew Union College Annual* 15 (1940): 313–34.

Safrai, Shmuel. "Halakha." *The Literature of the Sages First Part: Oral Tora, Halakha, Mishna, Tosefta, Talmud, External Tractates. Compendia Rerum Iudaicarum ad Novum Testamentum Section Two: The Literature of the Jewish People in the Period of the Second Temple and the Talmud*, 121–210. Edited by Shmuel Safrai. Assen/Maastricht and Philadelphia, 1987.

Sanders, E. P. *Jewish Law from Jesus to the Mishnah*. Philadelphia, 1990.

———. *Paul and Palestinian Judaism: A Comparison of Patterns of Religion*. Philadelphia, 1977.

Sarason, Richard S. *A History of the Mishnaic Law of Agriculture, Section Three: A Study of Tractate Demai*. Leiden, 1979.

Schiffman, Lawrence H. "The Conversion of the Royal House of Adiabene in Josephus and Rabbinic Sources." *Josephus, Judaism, and Christianity*, 293–312. Edited by Louis H. Feldman and Gohei Hata. Detroit, 1987.

———. *Who Was a Jew? Rabbinic and Halakhic Perspectives on the Jewish-Christian Schism*. Hoboken, 1985.

Schürer, Emil. *A History of the Jewish People in the Time of Jesus Christ*. Translated by Sophia Taylor and Peter Christie. New York, 1891.

———. *The History of the Jewish People in the Age of Jesus Christ (175 B.C.–A.D. 135)*. Edited by Geza Vermes, Fergus Millar, and Matthew Black. Edinburgh, 1979–87. 4 vols.

Schwab, Moise. *Le Talmud de Jerusalem: Traduit pour la Premiere Fois. Tome Septeieme: Traites Yebamoth et Sota*. Paris, 1885.

Segal, Alan F. *Paul the Convert: The Apostolate and Apostasy of Saul the Pharisee*. New Haven and London, 1990.

Shachter, Jacob, and H. Freedman. *Sanhedrin: Translated into English with Notes, Glossary, and Indices*. London, 1935.

Simon, M. *Gittin: Translated into English with Notes, Glossary, and Indices*. London, 1936.

Simon, Marcel. "Sur les débuts du prosélytisme juif." *Hommages a André Dupont-Summer*, 509–20. Edited by A. Caquot and M. Philonenko. Paris, 1971.

Smallwood, E. Mary. *The Jews Under Roman Rule: From Pompey to Diocletian*. Leiden, 1976.

Smith, Jonathan Z. *Imagining Religion*. Chicago and London, 1982.

———. *Map Is Not Territory.* Leiden, 1978.

Smith, Morton. *Palestinian Parties and Politics That Shaped the Old Testament.* Philadelphia, 1971.

———. "The Dead Sea Sect in Relation to Ancient Judaism." *New Testament Studies* 7: 347–60.

Snow, David A., and Richard Machalek. "The Convert as Social Type." *Sociological Theory 1983,* 259–89. Edited by Randall Collins. San Francisco, Washington, London, 1983.

———. "The Sociology of Conversion." *Annual Review of Sociology* 10 (1984): 167–90.

Sperber, Daniel. *Roman Palestine, 200–400: The Land.* Ramat-Gan, 1978.

Spiro, Melford E. "Religion: Problems of Definition and Explanation." *Cultural and Human Nature: Theoretical Papers of Melford E. Spiro,* 187–222. Edited by Benjamin Kilborne and L. L. Langness. Chicago, 1987.

Staples, C. L., and Armand L. Mauss. "Conversion or Commitment? A Reassessment of the Snow and Machalek Approach to the Study of Conversion." *Journal for the Scientific Study of Religion* 26 (1987): 133–47.

Strack, Herman L. *Introduction to the Talmud and Midrash.* New York, reprint 1965.

Strack, H. L., and G. Stemberger. *Introduction to the Talmud and Midrash.* Translated by Markus Bockmuehl. Edinburgh, 1991.

Tannenbaum, Robert F. "Jews and God-Fearers in the Holy City of Aphrodite." *Biblical Archaeologist Review* 12 (1986): 54–57.

Taylor, T. M. "The Beginnings of Jewish Proselyte Baptism." *New Testament Studies* 2, 3 (February 1956): 193–98.

Theodor, J., and Ch. Albeck. *Midrash Bereshit Rabba: Critical Edition with Notes and Commentary.* Jerusalem, 1965.

Torrance, T. F. "Proselyte Baptism." *New Testament Studies* 1, 2 (November, 1954): 150–54.

Urbach, Ephraim E. "The Laws Regarding Slavery as a Source for Social History of the Period of the Second Temple, the Mishnah and Talmud." *Papers of the Institute of Jewish Studies London,* 1. 1–94. Edited by J. G. Weiss. Jerusalem, 1964.

———. *The Sages: Their Concepts and Beliefs.* Translated by Israel Abrahams. Cambridge and London, 1987.

van den Berghe, Pierre L. "Race and Ethnicity: A Sociological Perspective." *Majority and Minority: The Dynamics of Race and Ethnicity in American Life,* 54–61. Edited by Norman R. Yetman. 4th ed. Boston, Sydney, London, Toronto, 1985.

van Gennep, Arnold. *The Rites of Passage.* Translated by Monika B. Vizedom and Gabrielle L. Caffee. London and Chicago, 1960.

Wacholder, Ben Zion. "The Date of the Mekilta de-Rabbi Ishmael." *Hebrew Union College Annual* 39 (1968): 117–44.

Wegner, Judith Romney. *Chattel or Person? The Status of Women in the Mishnah.* New York and Oxford, 1988.

Weil, Isaac. *Le Prosélytisme chez les juifs solon la bible et le talmud.* Strasbourg, 1880.

Weiss, I. H. *Sifra deBe Rav.* New York, reprint 1946.

Werblowsky, R. J. Zwi. "A Note on Purification and Proselyte Baptism." *Christian-*

ity, Judaism and Other Greco-Roman Cults: Studies for Morton Smith at Sixty, 3: 200–205. Edited by Jacob Neusner. Leiden, 1975.

Wolff, Kurt H. *The Sociology of Georg Simmel*. New York, 1950.

Zahavy, Tzvee *The Traditions of Eleazar ben Azariah*. Missoula, 1978.

Zeitlin, Solomon. "A Note on Baptism for Proselytes." *Journal of Biblical Literature* 52 (1933): 78–79.

———. "The Halaka in the Gospels and Its Relation to the Jewish Law in the Time of Jesus." *Hebrew Union College Annual* 1 (1924): 357–63.

▨ INDEX OF BIBLICAL CITATIONS ▨

35:9, 63
35:10, 63
35:15, 53
35:22–24, 63
35:24, 214

Psalms
2:1, 297n. 92
2:3–4, 297n. 92
29:9, 318n. 302
39:13, 256n. 84
47:10, 319n. 310
119:19, 256n. 84
121:4, 256n. 82
121:8, 320n. 313
135:19–20, 44
146:9, 256n. 82

Ruth
1:16–18, 294n. 75, 330n. 104
2:12, 102
3:18–22, 318n. 309

I Samuel
10:12, 244n. 96

II Samuel
1:13, 257n. 90
1:16, 257n. 91
17:25, 284n. 129
21:7–11, 269n. 31

Zephaniah
3:9, 91, 386n. 8

INDEX OF RABBINIC
▓ LITERATURE CITATIONS ▓

GENESIS RABBAH

LEVITICUS RABBAH

MEKHILTA DERABBI ISHMAEL

Sifra

SIFRÉ DEUTERONOMY

SIFRÉ NUMBERS

Masei
160, 250n. 122, 261n. 124, 350nn.
108–9, 357n. 114

Maṭot
262n. 141, 281n. 106, 282n. 106,
336n. 33, 358n. 153

Naśo
2, 232n. 37, 261nn. 128–29, 277n.
72, 302n. 136, 351n. 128
4, 232n. 37, 240n. 41, 261n. 128,
277n. 72, 302n. 136, 340n. 36,
351n. 128
7, 231n. 27, 242n. 65, 261n. 52,
302n. 136, 310n. 240, 349n. 73,
357n. 102
39, 260nn. 112–13, 310n. 241,
349n. 73
43, 260n. 112, 310n. 241

Pinḥas
132, 260n. 112, 347n. 45

Qoraḥ
119, 240n. 41, 260n. 121, 340n. 37,
347n. 45

Shelaḥ
107, 237n. 6
108, 258n. 102, 259nn. 105, 108,
116, 266n. 14, 292n. 50, 293n.
63, 323n. 1, 326n. 30, 352n. 149
109, 259nn. 107, 110, 260n. 113,
349n. 72, 352n. 148, 357n. 111
111, 255n. 68, 259n. 109, 348n. 59,
352n. 150
115, 259n. 106, 322n. 326,
355n. 56
117, 261n. 130, 302n. 136, 304n.
178, 351n. 128
124, 259n. 111

TOSEFTA

'Abodah Zara
7:16, 312n. 255

Baba Batra
2:11, 232nn. 39, 40, 239nn. 24, 26–
28, 302n. 136, 341n. 42, 350nn.
112–13
7:1, 239n. 23

Baba Meṣa'a'
3:25, 235n. 76, 244n. 96, 252n. 47,
255n. 73, 317nn. 296, 298–99,
336n. 25, 349n. 77, 359n. 158
5:21, 245n. 107, 269n. 30, 305n.
205

Baba Qama
4:6, 232n. 36, 239n. 30, 241n. 59,
303n. 164, 340n. 31, 350nn.
102, 106

8:1, 244n. 87
9:20, 239n. 33, 302n. 136, 343n.
87, 350n. 104
10:16, 39, 112, 232n. 37, 239nn.
35, 38, 261n. 128, 278n. 79,
277n. 72, 302n. 136, 351n. 128
10:17, 240n. 42, 340nn. 33, 37
10:18, 240n. 41

Berakhot
3:25, 242n. 72
5:14, 242n. 66, 349n. 74
6:2, 287n. 14

Bikurim
1:2, 224n. 47, 231n. 28, 243n. 76,
264n. 158, 299n. 119, 345n. 35,
357n. 105

INDEX OF RABBIS

▓ INDEX OF SCHOLARS ▓

INDEX OF TOPICS